PROFESSIONAL
TEAM FOUNDATION SERVER 2010

Continues

PROFESSIONAL

Team Foundation Server 2010

PROFESSIONAL

Team Foundation Server 2010

Ed Blankenship
Martin Woodward
Grant Holliday
Brian Keller

WILEY

Wiley Publishing, Inc.

Professional Team Foundation Server 2010

Published by
Wiley Publishing, Inc.
10475 Crosspoint Boulevard
Indianapolis, IN 46256
www.wiley.com

ISBN: 978-0-470-94332-8
ISBN: 978-1-118-08577-6 (ebk)
ISBN: 978-1-118-08575-2 (ebk)
ISBN: 978-1-118-08576-9 (ebk)

Manufactured in the United States of America

10 9 8 7 6 5 4 3 2 1

For general information on our other products and services please contact our Customer Care Department within the United States at (877) 762-2974, outside the United States at (317) 572-3993 or fax (317) 572-4002.

Wiley also publishes its books in a variety of electronic formats. Some content that appears in print may not be available in electronic books.

Library of Congress Control Number: 2011921772

To Mom, Dad, Nathan, Tiffany, Zach, Daniel, Mike, and Grandma.

—ED BLANKENSHIP

To Margaret Elizabeth Woodward.

—MARTIN WOODWARD

I would like to dedicate this book to my wife, Emma, and my family for giving me strength, encouragement, and support in all my endeavors.

—GRANT HOLLIDAY

Elisa, this book is for you. I can't thank you enough for your love, support, and encouragement. You are the foundation in our team. (Sorry, I couldn't resist! But it's true.)

—BRIAN KELLER

ABOUT THE AUTHORS

ED BLANKENSHIP is currently an Application Lifecycle Management (ALM) and Team Foundation Server Consultant with Notion Solutions. He is also a Microsoft Most Valuable Professional (MVP) in Visual Studio ALM and Team Foundation Server, and has been awarded as an MVP for four years. He was voted in 2010 as the Microsoft MVP of the Year (Visual Studio ALM and Team Foundation Server) by his peers. Blankenship has been working with Team Foundation Server and Visual Studio Team System for nearly five years since the beginning of those products in 2005. He previously was the Release Engineering Manager at Infragistics, where he led a multi-year Team Foundation Server and Visual Studio Team System (VSTS) implementation globally to improve the development process lifecycle. He has authored and served as technical editor for several Wrox books. He has also authored numerous articles, and spoken at various user groups, events, radio shows, and conferences. You can find him sharing his experiences at his technical blog at www.edsquared.com/.

MARTIN WOODWARD is the Senior Program Manager for Visual Studio Team Explorer Everywhere and part of the Team Foundation Server group at Microsoft. Previously, Woodward was also Team System Most Valuable Professional (MVP) of the year. Not only does he bring a unique insight into the inner workings of Team Foundation Server, he has experience from more than a half decade of real-world use at companies big and small, which he is always happy to share through his writings, on his blog at woodwardweb.com, or when speaking at events internationally.

GRANT HOLLIDAY is a Program Manager at Microsoft in Redmond, Washington. He is a member of the Visual Studio Team Foundation Server product group, and is responsible for the internal server deployments at Microsoft. Before joining Microsoft in 2008, he was a Microsoft Most Valuable Professional (MVP) and worked as a consultant for Team Foundation Server customers in Australia.

BRIAN KELLER is a Senior Technical Evangelist for Microsoft, specializing in Visual Studio and Application Lifecycle Management (ALM). Keller has been with Microsoft since 2002, and has presented at conferences all over the world, including TechEd, the Professional Developers Conference (PDC), and MIX. Keller is also a regular personality on MSDN's Channel 9 website, and is co-host of the popular show, "This Week on Channel 9." Outside of work, he can usually be found enjoying the great outdoors while either rock climbing, backpacking, skiing, or surfing.

ABOUT THE TECHNICAL EDITORS

MICKEY GOUSSET is a Senior Technical Developer for Infront Consulting Group, a consulting company focused on the Microsoft System Center family of products. He is a Microsoft Application Lifecycle Management (ALM) Most Valuable Professional (MVP), a certified professional in Team Foundation Server and SCOM 2007, and author of the books *Professional Team Foundation Server* (Indianapolis: Wiley, 2007) and *Professional Application Lifecycle Management with Visual Studio 2010* (Indianapolis: Wiley, 2010). He runs Team System Rocks! (www.teamsystemrocks.com), a community site devoted to Visual Studio, Team Foundation Server, and ALM, where he also blogs regularly. He speaks on ALM and System Center topics at various user groups, code camps, and conferences.

STEVEN ST. JEAN is a Development/ALM Consultant with 20 years of industry experience. He is currently working with Notion Solutions, an Imaginet company, where he assists clients of all sizes in maturing their development processes throughout the entire application lifecycle with a focus on the Microsoft tools stack.

CREDITS

EXECUTIVE EDITOR
Robert Elliott

PROJECT EDITOR
Kevin Shafer

TECHNICAL EDITORS
Mickey Gousset
Steven St. Jean

PRODUCTION EDITOR
Rebecca Anderson

COPY EDITOR
Mildred Sanchez

EDITORIAL DIRECTOR
Robyn B. Siesky

EDITORIAL MANAGER
Mary Beth Wakefield

FREELANCER EDITORIAL MANAGER
Rosemarie Graham

MARKETING MANAGER
Ashley Zurcher

PRODUCTION MANAGER
Tim Tate

**VICE PRESIDENT AND EXECUTIVE
GROUP PUBLISHER**
Richard Swadley

VICE PRESIDENT AND EXECUTIVE PUBLISHER
Barry Pruett

ASSOCIATE PUBLISHER
Jim Minatel

PROJECT COORDINATOR, COVER
Katie Crocker

PROOFREADER
Sheilah Ledwldge, Word One New York

INDEXER
Robert Swanson

COVER DESIGNER
Ryan Sneed

COVER IMAGE
© Fuse / Getty Images

ACKNOWLEDGMENTS

I REALLY WANT TO THANK EVERYONE involved with putting this book together, including the author team, editors, reviewers, and everyone who was able to give us great feedback! Thanks to Martin, Grant, and Brian for the great teamwork and contributions that have made this book awesome. I have really appreciated their guidance along the way — I truly enjoyed working with y'all.

The help from the entire product team to put together such a product and help us along the way can't be discounted as well! Thanks to Brian Harry, Matt Mitrik, Mario Rodriguez, Anu and the Lab Management team, Gregg Boer, Jim Lamb, and Jason Pricket on the product teams at Microsoft. I appreciate all of their contributions, and primarily their in-depth insight into the product over the years to help with a better understanding of all the moving wheels of Team Foundation Server. I also want to think all of my Microsoft MVP and Notion/Imaginet colleagues. Specifically, I want to thank Mike Fourie, Tiago Pascoal, Anthony Borton, Steve Godbold, Mickey Gousset, Steve St. Jean, Chris Menegay, Dave McKinstry, Joel Semeniuk, Adam Cogan, and Neno Loje for all their help.

Thank you to everyone who has helped me throughout my career over the years! Thanks for pushing me to get better in my craft and fueling my enthusiasm. Thanks to my family and friends for their guidance along the way and constantly supporting me. Couldn't have done this without each of you.

—ED BLANKENSHIP

I WOULD LIKE TO THANK my co-authors for letting me join them in putting together the book about Team Foundation Server that I have always wanted to be a part of. I have learned so much from Brian, Grant, and Ed over the years, but it has been a great privilege to work with them more closely. I would also like to acknowledge the help and support from Mickey Gousset and Jean-Luc David in encouraging me into the book-writing process, and to thank Jamie Cool, Lori Lamkin, and Brian Harry for their support of this project.

The whole of the Team Foundation Server group (past and present) have obviously been essential in the making of this book. But special appreciation must go to Aaron Hallberg, Buck Hodges, Phillip Kelley, Jim Lamb, James Manning, Matthew Mitrik, John Nierenberg, and Jason Prickett for their contributions, along with all the ALM Rangers and ALM MVPs that make the Team Foundation Server community such a vibrant one to be in. Thanks also to my great friend and mentor Corey Steffen for his support of my involvement in the Team Foundation Server community, which is what led me to be able to work with such a great team here at Microsoft.

Finally, I would also like to thank William and Jamie for letting Daddy spend even more time in his office, and, of course, my wife, Catherine, who's encouragement, support, and patience are not only the reason this book got finished, but are the driving force of so much in our lives.

—Martin Woodward

FIRST OF ALL, I'D LIKE TO THANK my co-authors, Ed, Martin, and especially Brian. Together, we form a dream team of Team Foundation Server knowledge and experience. It's exciting to finally be sharing this with the world.

I'd also like to thank Joe Schwetz, Brian Harry, and Charles Sterling for giving me the wonderful opportunity to work at Microsoft. It's a big decision to pack up and move 8,000 miles across the ocean away from friends and family, but the last few years have been a great adventure, and I'm glad that I made the move.

A special thank you to those who I have worked with closely over the last few years and have learned much from (in alphabetical order): Andrew Gillaspie, Bill Essary, Buck Hodges, Craig Harry, Chandru Ramakrishnan, Diana Kumar, Doug Mortensen, Erin Geaney, Kia Sedighi, Mark Friedman, Philip Kelley, Sam Heald, Shuaib Sharief, Tom Moore, and William Bartholomew. Without the many thousands of questions and discussions that we've had, this book would not have been possible.

Finally, I'd like to thank the rest of the Team Foundation Server product group, the MVP community, and all the Australians in Seattle for their friendship and support.

—Grant Holliday

I NEED TO ONCE AGAIN ACKNOWLEDGE the people in the developer division at Microsoft who build the sets of technologies that make a book like this a reality. It's an honor to work with people like Brian Harry, Doug Neumann, Aaron Bjork, Siddharth Bhatia, Charles Sterling, Jeff Beehler, Sam Guckenheimer, Anu Bharadwaj, Vinod Malhotra, and countless others who wake up every day with a burning desire to build great software. I've never worked with a team of engineers that is more customer-focused on solving problems and driving innovation. And, of course, I want to thank the team of people behind this book—Ed, Martin, Grant, Kevin, Bob, Mickey, and Steve. There's a certain bond that seems to develop among people who go through an arduous journey together. Surely writing a book must be right up there with the likes of fighting in a war or surviving a shipwreck. Thanks for bringing me along for the ride, guys. Let's do it again . . . just not right away.

—Brian Keller

CONTENTS

PART IV: TEAM FOUNDATION BUILD

CHAPTER 14: OVERVIEW OF BUILD AUTOMATION

CHAPTER 15: USING TEAM FOUNDATION BUILD

FOREWORD

IT'S HARD TO IMAGINE A BETTER GROUP OF PEOPLE to write a book about Team Foundation Server than Martin, Grant, Ed, and Brian. Between the four of them, you have an expert in just about every aspect of Team Foundation Server.

Twenty years ago (I can't believe it's been 20 years) when we started building SourceSafe, it was a different world. There was no Internet as we know and love it today. Local area networks (LANs) were gaining adoption and e-mail was becoming mainstream. Windows/NT was just being developed. Client-server computing was in its infancy. Software development process was equally immature. Testing was ad hoc. Requirements were informal. Design was strictly done by developers. SourceSafe was a great tool for the time.

Over the past 20 years, software has come to play a critical role in nearly everyone's life — from your cell phone, to your banking system. Part of that change has been a significant evolution in the way we build software. Now, more than half of what you need to know about software development comes after you learn to program — collaboration, unit testing, project management, requirements, load testing, functional testing, build automation, release management, architecture, and more. As software becomes more critical, so do the tools and processes we use to build it.

Software projects are now bigger. The requirements change faster. Their success is more critical to the business, and a lot more people (with diverse responsibilities) are involved. Team Foundation Server was designed from the ground up to address this much more demanding world of software development. It is a tool that enables diverse teams of people to collaborate to build great software. It is also a platform upon which third parties and end users innovate with new capabilities and development process support. At the same time, it's designed to scale from small teams up to very large teams, and to grow with you as your needs evolve.

Being an expert in everything about Team Foundation Server is a daunting task. It's a big product. This book is an excellent starting point to getting a solid understanding of Team Foundation Server. It provides a good overview of why you would use it, how to plan for deployment, how to use it, and how to customize and extend it. I highly recommend it for anyone new to Team Foundation Server, or anyone wanting to learn to grow their use beyond basic source code control and bug tracking.

Brian Harry
Technical Fellow
Team Foundation Server, Microsoft

INTRODUCTION

OVER THE PAST DECADE, Microsoft has been creating development tools that have been designed for the ever-growing engineering teams of software developers, testers, architects, project managers, designers, and database administrators. In the Visual Studio 2010 line of products, there are tools for each team member to use to contribute to a software release. However, it's not enough to allow for awesome individual contributions. You must also organize the collaboration of those contributions across the larger team.

Beginning in the Visual Studio 2005 release, Microsoft introduced a new server product named Team Foundation Server to complement its development products. Now in its third release, Team Foundation Server 2010 has grown with all of the investment from the past decade, and fits nicely in the Visual Studio *application lifecycle management* (ALM) family of products. Before the Visual Studio 2010 release, the Visual Studio ALM family of products was given the brand of Visual Studio Team System, which is no longer used in the latest release.

As you will find out, Team Foundation Server 2010 is a very large product with lots of features for managing the software development lifecycle of software projects and releases. The authors of this book collectively gathered from their past experience since the first release of Team Foundation Server to document some of the tips and tricks that they have learned along the way. The backgrounds of the authors are quite diverse — managing one of the largest Team Foundation Server environments, designing the collaboration pieces for non-.NET development teams, evangelizing the Visual Studio and Team Foundation Server products, managing releases at a software development company, and a consulting background where customers are helped each week to solve real-world challenges by taking advantage of Team Foundation Server.

WHO THIS BOOK IS FOR

If you have been looking to Team Foundation Server to meet some of your software development team's challenges for collaboration, then this book is for you. You may have seen the Team Foundation Server product in your MSDN subscription and decided to set up a new environment internally. You may now be wondering how to administer and configure the product.

This book is for everyone ranging from the developer using Team Foundation Server for day-to-day development, to the administrator who is ensuring that the environment is tuned to run well and build extensions to the product to meet the needs of their software development team. You may also be preparing for the 70-512 Microsoft certification exam for administering Team Foundation Server 2010, and you will find many of the exam topics covered in this book.

This book does not require any knowledge of Team Foundation Server to be useful, but is not meant for developers or testers who are just starting out their craft. Team Foundation Server can be used for teams as small as one to five team members to teams consisting of tens of thousands. Code samples in the book are presented in C#, but could also be implemented in other .NET languages (such as Visual Basic.NET).

You can find a road map for the book based on your team role later in this "Introduction" under the section named "How This Book Is Structured."

WHAT THIS BOOK COVERS

This book covers a complete overview of the Team Foundation Server 2010 product, and provides hands-on examples for using the product throughout many of the chapters. This book only covers the latest version of Team Foundation Server 2010 (including Service Pack 1 in some areas), and does not expose the reader to how to use earlier versions of Team Foundation Server.

The book is divided into five main parts, with detailed chapters that will dive into each of the feature areas of Team Foundation Server 2010.

- ➤ *Part I* — Getting Started
- ➤ *Part II* — Version Control
- ➤ *Part III* — Project Management
- ➤ *Part IV* — Team Foundation Build
- ➤ *Part V* — Administration

HOW THIS BOOK IS STRUCTURED

You may have picked up this book and are wondering where to get started. This book has been written so that you start reading in a particular chapter without needing to understand concepts introduced in previous chapters. Feel free to read the book from cover to cover, or, if you are in a hurry or need to reference a specific topic, jump to that particular chapter. The next sections describe where you might get started in the book based on your role, and the topics that might be most relevant for you.

Developers

There are plenty of features that are available for developers who are using Team Foundation Server 2010. You might begin by reading Chapter 4, "Connecting to Team Foundation Server," to get started with exploring the different options available for connecting to your server.

After that, you can begin your review of the version control features available in Part II of the book:

- ➤ *Chapter 5* — "Overview of Version Control"
- ➤ *Chapter 6* — "Using Team Foundation Version Control"

➤ *Chapter 7* — "Ensuring Code Quality"

➤ *Chapter 9* — "Branching and Merging"

➤ *Chapter 10* — "Common Version Control Scenarios"

Once you have a good grasp of the version control features, you may want to familiarize yourself with the work item tracking and reporting features in Part III of the book:

➤ *Chapter 11* — "Introducing Work Item Tracking"

➤ *Chapter 13* — "Reporting and SharePoint Dashboards"

Finally, if you want to automate your build process, you can take advantage of reviewing those features in Part IV of the book:

➤ *Chapter 14* — "Overview of Build Automation"

➤ *Chapter 15* — "Using Team Foundation Build"

➤ *Chapter 16* — "Customizing the Build Process"

Testers

Team Foundation Server 2010 and Visual Studio 2010 include a host of new features for testing. You might begin by reading Chapter 4, "Connecting to Team Foundation Server," to get started with exploring the different options available for connecting to your server.

After that, you will want to increase your understanding of the work item tracking features (which help track test cases, bugs, tasks, requirements, and so on), as well as the project reporting features in Part III of the book:

➤ *Chapter 11* — "Introducing Work Item Tracking"

➤ *Chapter 13* — "Reporting and SharePoint Dashboards"

If you are a technical tester, and will be automating test cases using the numerous automated test capabilities, then you will want to familiarize yourself with the version control features (which is where you will store the source code for your automated tests) in Part II of the book:

➤ *Chapter 5* — "Overview of Version Control"

➤ *Chapter 6* — "Using Team Foundation Version Control"

➤ *Chapter 9* — "Branching and Merging"

➤ *Chapter 10* — "Common Version Control Scenarios"

Finally, if you are interested in the new testing and virtual lab management features available in Team Foundation Server 2010, you can consult Part V of the book:

➤ *Chapter 22* — "Testing and Lab Management"

MICROSOFT TEST MANAGER

If you are using Microsoft Test Manager (available if you have acquired either Visual Studio 2010 Ultimate or Visual Studio 2010 Test Professional), you may want to consult the companion to this book, *Professional Application Lifecycle Management with Visual Studio 2010* (Indianapolis: Wiley, 2010). Several chapters in that book discuss the features available in Microsoft Test Manager for test case management, executing manual tests, filing rich actionable bugs, and automating user interface tests. For more information about this book, visit `http://bit.ly/VS2010ALMBook`.

Project Managers and Business Analysts

As a project manager or business analyst, you will want to ensure that you have insight into the software release or project, and be able to interact. You may also be interested in what customizations are possible with the process that Team Foundation Server uses for your teams. Project managers might also be interested in the capability to synchronize project data in Team Foundation Server with a Microsoft Office Project Server 2010 instance. Business analysts may want to create and track requirements, including the traceability options from inception to implementation.

You might begin by reading Chapter 4, "Connecting to Team Foundation Server," to get started with exploring the different options available for connecting to your server. All of the features that would be relevant for project managers and business analysts are discussed in Part III of the book:

➤   *Chapter 11* — "Introducing Work Item Tracking"

➤   *Chapter 12* — "Customizing Process Templates"

➤   *Chapter 13* — "Reporting and SharePoint Dashboards"

Executive Stakeholders

Executive stakeholders find plenty of use for Team Foundation Server by gathering insight into how software releases and projects are progressing, and often want easily accessible dashboards with the information. The executive that leads the engineering organization may also be interested in planning a Team Foundation Server deployment, including who should administer the server.

You might begin with the chapters in Part I of the book:

➤   *Chapter 2* — "Planning a Deployment"

➤   *Chapter 4* — "Connecting to Team Foundation Server"

After you have a good understanding of the concepts in those chapters, you can then explore the necessary work item tracking and reporting features available in Part III of the book:

➤   *Chapter 11* — "Introducing Work Item Tracking"

➤   *Chapter 13* — "Reporting and SharePoint Dashboards"

Team Foundation Server Administrators

If you find yourself in the position of administering a Team Foundation Server 2010 instance, this book provides plenty of great information for performing that role. In Part I of the book, you might begin by reading Chapter 2, "Planning a Deployment," to understand what is required for setting up a Team Foundation Server environment. You can then install a new server by going through Chapter 3, "Installation and Configuration." If you are upgrading from a previous version of Team Foundation Server, then you may want to begin by reading through Chapter 23, "Upgrading from Earlier Versions," before you get started with the upgrade process.

It is recommended that, as a Team Foundation Server administrator, you understand all of the aspects that end users will take advantage of, including version control, work item tracking, and automated builds. You can read all of the chapters in Parts I through IV for information about those aspects of Team Foundation Server 2010.

Additionally, Part V is dedicated to administrative topics that will be of interest to administrators:

- ➤ *Chapter 17* — "Introduction to Team Foundation Server Administration"
- ➤ *Chapter 18* — "Scalability and High Availability"
- ➤ *Chapter 19* — "Disaster Recovery"
- ➤ *Chapter 20* — "Security and Privileges"
- ➤ *Chapter 21* — "Monitoring Server Health and Performance"
- ➤ *Chapter 22* — "Testing and Lab Management"
- ➤ *Chapter 23* — "Upgrading from Earlier Versions"
- ➤ *Chapter 24* — "Working with Geographically Distributed Teams"
- ➤ *Chapter 25* — "Extending Team Foundation Server"

Extensibility Partner

If you are interested in extending the capabilities of Team Foundation Server 2010, you will find many opportunities and extensibility points throughout this book. You may want to begin by reading through Chapter 25, "Extending Team Foundation Server." You will also find extensibility options covered in several other chapters of the book:

- ➤ *Chapter 7* — "Ensuring Code Quality"
- ➤ *Chapter 12* — "Customizing Process Templates"
- ➤ *Chapter 13* — "Reporting and SharePoint Dashboards"
- ➤ *Chapter 16* — "Customizing the Build Process"

WHAT YOU NEED TO USE THIS BOOK

To perform many of the hands-on examples in the book, it will be helpful to have a Team Foundation Server 2010 environment that you can use to test out the different features in the product. You do not necessarily need separate hardware, since you can now install Team Foundation Server 2010 on client operating systems such as Windows 7 and Windows Vista. Don't worry about setting up and configuring a new Team Foundation Server 2010 environment yet, since you will learn about that in Chapters 2 and 3.

Chapter 1 discusses a few options on how to acquire Team Foundation Server 2010, including an entire virtual machine image for demonstration purposes. Chapter 4 also discusses the different tools that you can use to connect to your Team Foundation Server environment that will be needed throughout the book.

FURTHER LEARNING

Each of the authors will write technical articles about Team Foundation Server and other Visual Studio products from time to time that you may benefit from for further learning. Feel free to check out the author's blog sites and subscribe to them in your favorite RSS reader.

- ➤ *Ed Blankenship* — www.edsquared.com

- ➤ *Martin Woodward* — www.woodwardweb.com

- ➤ *Grant Holliday* — http://blogs.msdn.com/b/granth

- ➤ *Brian Keller* — http://blogs.msdn.com/b/briankel

CONVENTIONS

To help you get the most from the text and keep track of what's happening, we've used a number of conventions throughout the book.

> Boxes like this one hold important, not-to-be forgotten information that is directly relevant to the surrounding text.

> *Notes, tips, hints, tricks, and asides to the current discussion are offset and placed in italics like this.*

> **SIDEBAR**
>
> Asides to the current discussion are offset like this.

As for styles in the text:

➤ We *highlight* new terms and important words when we introduce them.

➤ We show keyboard strokes like this: Ctrl+A.

➤ We show filenames, URLs, and code within the text like so: `persistence.properties`.

We present code in two different ways:

```
We use a monofont type for most code examples.
We use boldface to emphasize code that is of particular importance
        in the present context.
```

SOURCE CODE

As you work through the examples in this book, you may choose either to type in all the code manually, or to use the source code files that accompany the book. All of the source code used in this book is available for download at `www.wrox.com`. Once at the site, simply locate the book's title (either by using the Search box or by using one of the title lists) and click the Download Code link on the book's detail page to obtain all the source code for the book.

> *Because many books have similar titles, you may find it easiest to search by ISBN; this book's ISBN is 978-0-470-94332-8.*

Once you download the code, just decompress it with your favorite compression tool. Alternatively, you can go to the main Wrox code download page at `www.wrox.com/dynamic/books/download.aspx` to see the code available for this book and all other Wrox books.

ERRATA

We make every effort to ensure that there are no errors in the text or in the code. However, no one is perfect, and mistakes do occur. If you find an error in one of our books (like a spelling mistake or faulty piece of code), we would be very grateful for your feedback. By sending in errata, you may save another reader hours of frustration and, at the same time, you will be helping us to provide even higher quality information.

To find the errata page for this book, go to www.wrox.com and locate the title using the Search box or one of the title lists. Then, on the book details page, click the Book Errata link. On this page you can view all errata that has been submitted for this book and posted by Wrox editors. A complete book list (including links to each book's errata) is also available at www.wrox.com/misc-pages/booklist.shtml.

If you don't spot "your" error on the Book Errata page, go to www.wrox.com/contact/techsupport.shtml and complete the form there to send us the error you have found. We'll check the information and, if appropriate, post a message to the book's errata page and fix the problem in subsequent editions of the book.

P2P.WROX.COM

For author and peer discussion, join the P2P forums at p2p.wrox.com. The forums are a Web-based system for you to post messages relating to Wrox books and related technologies, and to interact with other readers and technology users. The forums offer a subscription feature to e-mail you topics of interest of your choosing when new posts are made to the forums. Wrox authors, editors, other industry experts, and your fellow readers are present on these forums.

At p2p.wrox.com, you will find a number of different forums that will help you not only as you read this book, but also as you develop your own applications. To join the forums, just follow these steps:

1. Go to p2p.wrox.com and click the Register link.

2. Read the terms of use and click Agree.

3. Complete the required information to join, as well as any optional information you wish to provide, and click Submit.

4. You will receive an e-mail with information describing how to verify your account and complete the joining process.

> *You can read messages in the forums without joining P2P. However, in order to post your own messages, you must join.*

Once you join, you can post new messages and respond to messages other users post. You can read messages at any time on the Web. If you would like to have new messages from a particular forum e-mailed to you, click the Subscribe to this Forum icon by the forum name in the forum listing.

For more information about how to use the Wrox P2P, be sure to read the P2P FAQs for answers to questions about how the forum software works, as well as many common questions specific to P2P and Wrox books. To read the FAQs, click the FAQ link on any P2P page.

PART I
Getting Started

1

Introducing Team Foundation Server 2010

WHAT'S IN THIS CHAPTER?

➤ Getting to know Team Foundation Server 2010

➤ Understanding what's new in Team Foundation Server 2010

➤ Acquiring Team Foundation Server 2010

This chapter introduces you to Microsoft Visual Studio Team Foundation Server 2010. Here you will learn what it is for, the key concepts needed when using it, and how to acquire Team Foundation Server.

For those who are already familiar with Team Foundation Server from previous versions, the discussion in this chapter highlights areas that are new or have changed substantially. However, because understanding the legacy of a technology is always helpful, this chapter also includes some of the history of the Team Foundation Server product, which will help explain how it became what it is today.

Later chapters in this book will go into more depth with an examination of the architecture of the Team Foundation Server product.

WHAT IS TEAM FOUNDATION SERVER?

Developing software is difficult — a fact that is repeatedly proven by how many projects fail. An essential factor in the success of any software development team is how well the members of the team communicate with each other, as well as with the people who wanted the software developed in the first place.

Microsoft Visual Studio 2010 Team Foundation Server provides the core collaboration functionality for your software development teams in a very tightly integrated product. The functionality provided by Team Foundation Server includes the following:

- ➤ Project management
- ➤ Work item tracking (WIT)
- ➤ Version control
- ➤ Test case management
- ➤ Build automation
- ➤ Reporting
- ➤ Virtual lab management

Each of these topics is explored extensively in the upcoming chapters of this book.

Team Foundation Server is a separate server product designed specifically for engineering teams with developers, testers, architects, project managers, business analysts, and anyone else contributing to software development releases and projects. Logically, Team Foundation Server is made up of the following two tiers, which can be physically deployed across one or many machines:

- ➤ *Application Tier* — The *application tier* primarily consists of a set of web services with which the client machines communicate by using a highly optimized web service-based protocol.

- ➤ *Data Tier* — The *data tier* is made up of a SQL Server database containing the database logic of the Team Foundation Server application, along with the data for your Team Foundation Server instance. The data stored in the database is used by Team Foundation Server's reporting functionality. All the data stored in Team Foundation Server is stored in this SQL Server database, thus making it easy to back up.

Team Foundation Server was designed with extensibility in mind. There is a comprehensive .NET Application Programming Interface (API) for integrating with Team Foundation Server. There is also a set of events that allow outside tools to integrate with Team Foundation Server as first-class citizens. The same .NET programming model and event system is used by Microsoft itself in the construction of Team Foundation Server, as well as the client integrations into Visual Studio.

Team Foundation Server 2010 has plenty of competitors, including other enterprise Application Lifecycle Management (ALM) systems and purpose-specific products (such as source control systems). The main benefit for having all of the different systems available in one product is that the product team at Microsoft is able to fully integrate the different systems. This allows for true innovation in the development tools space, as you will notice with several of the new tools that are available in this latest release. Instead of having to worry about integrating the separate systems yourself, you can take advantage of the work that Microsoft has done for you.

> *Jason Zander, General Manager for Visual Studio, makes this particular point well in a blog post about Team Foundation Server 2010. You can find the blog post at* http://blogs.msdn.com/b/jasonz/archive/2009/10/21/tutorial-getting-started-with-tfs-in-vs2010.aspx.

When you compare enterprise ALM products currently on the market, you will discover that Team Foundation Server 2010 was designed to be easily customizable and extensible. Team Foundation Server ensures that developers using any development platform can participate and easily use Team Foundation Server.

WHAT'S NEW IN TEAM FOUNDATION SERVER 2010

If you have used legacy versions of Team Foundation Server, you may be curious about what is new in the latest release. Team Foundation Server 2010 is the most significant release of Team Foundation Server since the launch of the product with Team Foundation Server 2005. As this book demonstrates, it is a big release with considerable new functionality and improvements across the board. While many of these features are explained throughout this book, if you have used a previous version of Team Foundation Server, then the features described in the following sections will be new to you.

Project Management

The biggest change in the project management area is that work items are now hierarchical — you can have child and parent links between work items. You can also customize work item links. In addition, you can have hierarchical queries so that a tree of work item results can be displayed. Queries can be organized into subfolders, and permissions can be assigned as to who can view and modify team queries.

There are several new work item controls both to enhance functionality in regular work items, and to support the new test functionality. The Microsoft Office Excel and Project integrations have both also seen significant improvements, especially in the capability to modify the formatting and layout of data, while providing the capability to round-trip data changes.

There are several new Agile Development Process planning workbooks available by default, along with significant usability improvements to the default reports. SharePoint Web parts have been added to enable access to work item information directly from the project portal. Dashboards have been introduced that can make use of additional functionality available when running the project portal on a full Microsoft Office SharePoint Server (MOSS) over and above the features available using a standard Windows SharePoint Services site.

Version Control

The most visual addition pertaining to version control is that branches are now treated as first-class objects. A significant new user interface (UI) has been added to assist management and visualization of branches, including tracking changes as they have occurred across branches and time. History and labeling have undergone huge changes, including the capability to view labels from the history view, and the capability to view history of a merged file.

Rollback support is provided, along with the capability to share a workspace between users on the same machine.

> *There have been significant changes in the underlying version control model employed by Team Foundation Server 2010 that are particularly noticeable when renames and merges are performed. For more information on the changes, the reasons behind the changes, and how the changes present themselves in the UI, take a look at the blog post at* `http://blogs.msdn.com/mitrik/archive/2009/05/28/changing-to-slot-mode-in-tfs-2010-version-control.aspx`.

Build

The build automation system has undergone huge revisions in Team Foundation Server 2010. The first change you will notice is the new and improved build report. However, probably the most significant change is that the build is now based around Windows Workflow Foundation 4.0, instead of relying on MSBuild to drive the non-compilation portions of an automated build. You now have the capability to use build agent pooling, gated and buddy builds, and integration with Source and Symbol servers.

Administration

The installation and general administration experience of Team Foundation Server is now drastically improved and simplified. The SharePoint and reporting components are now optional, and can be added at any time. Team Foundation Server supports the use of network local balancing in front of Team Foundation Server application tier machines. The new team project collection concept allows for collection move, archive, backup, and restore, independent of other collections running on the server instance.

There is a dedicated Administration Console in Team Foundation Server to assist with common administrative functions for the server instance. Team Foundation Server 2010 can also now be installed on 64-bit server operating systems, and the clients all work on 64-bit client systems (including an `AnyCPU`-compatible .NET object model so that custom applications do not have to be compiled specifically for x86 processors).

ACQUISITION OPTIONS

Microsoft has also greatly improved how you may acquire Team Foundation Server 2010, and reduced the costs associated with purchasing Team Foundation Server 2010. There are several options available to you, as discussed in the following sections.

Licensing can be somewhat confusing, but Team Foundation Server licensing follows the licensing pattern of other Microsoft server products. There is a server license. Additionally, with some notable exceptions, each user that connects to the server should have a Client Access License (CAL) in Team Foundation Server 2010.

> *For more information about those exceptions, or questions about what you will need to purchase, you can seek help from a Microsoft Partner with the ALM Competency, your local Microsoft Developer Tools Specialist, or reference the End-User License Agreement (EULA).*

Trial

One of the easiest ways to acquire Team Foundation Server is on a 90-day trial basis. You can download the full version of Team Foundation Server and try out all of the features without having to purchase a full copy. The DVD ISO image for the trial edition is available at `http://tinyurl.com/TFS2010Trial`.

If you install the trial edition of Team Foundation Server 2010, you can easily apply a product key to activate the trial edition. You could even move the team project collection from the trial server to a different server instance once your team has decided to fully adopt Team Foundation Server.

Alternatively, if you need a 30-day extension, you can perform one extension using the Team Foundation Server Administration Console once the time gets near the end of the trial period. Any extensions after the first extension can be requested from a Microsoft representative, which may be very helpful if you are in the middle of the acquisition process.

If you would rather have a virtual machine that is ready to use (including all of the software necessary to demo and evaluate Visual Studio 2010 and Team Foundation Server 2010), you can download the all-up Visual Studio 2010 virtual machine images. The virtual machines have expiration dates, but new virtual machine images are made available as the expiration date draws near.

> *You can find the latest version of the virtual machines at any time at* `http://go.microsoft.com/fwlink/?LinkId=208083`.

Volume Licensing

Microsoft has plenty of options for volume licensing, including Enterprise, Select, Open Value, and Open License Agreements that will help your company significantly reduce the overall cost of acquiring Team Foundation Server 2010. There are different options available based on your company size and engineering team size. This option is by far the most popular choice for companies looking to acquire Team Foundation Server, MSDN subscriptions, and Visual Studio licenses.

If your company acquired an earlier version of Team Foundation Server through a volume licensing program, and also purchased Software Assurance (SA), you may be entitled to a license of Team Foundation Server 2010 without additional cost, if the SA was still active on the date that Team Foundation Server 2010 was released.

> *For more information about volume licensing, discuss your options with your Microsoft internal volume licensing administrator, your local Microsoft Developer Tools Specialist, or a Microsoft Partner with the ALM Competency.*

MSDN Subscription

One of the biggest changes that Microsoft has introduced in the Visual Studio 2010 release is the inclusion of a full production-use license of Team Foundation Server 2010 with each Visual Studio

MSDN subscription license and a Team Foundation Server 2010 CAL. This now enables developers, testers, architects, and others with an active MSDN subscription to take advantage of Team Foundation Server.

> *For more information about MSDN subscriptions and for links to download Team Foundation Server 2010, visit the MSDN Subscriber Downloads website at* `http://msdn.microsoft.com/subscriptions`.

Microsoft Partner Network

Companies that are members of the Microsoft Partner Network and have achieved certain competencies can be entitled to development and test use licenses of several of the products included with an MSDN subscription, including Team Foundation Server 2010.

> *For more information about the requirements and benefits available for Microsoft Partners, you can visit* `http://partner.microsoft.com`.

Retail

If you are not able to use any of the other acquisition methods, you can always acquire Team Foundation Server 2010 through retail channels, including the online Microsoft Store. You can purchase the product directly from Microsoft online at `http://store.microsoft.com/microsoft/Visual-Studio-Team-Foundation-Server-2010/product/4D531C01` or `http://tinyurl.com/TFS2010Retail`. It is also available from many other popular retail sites.

One of the nice benefits of purchasing a server license using the retail channel is that you also receive a CAL-exclusion for up to five named users. This benefit is only available from licenses purchased through the retail channel, and is not included with other acquisition avenues discussed in this chapter.

> **TEAM FOUNDATION SERVER WORKGROUP EDITION**
>
> Earlier versions of Team Foundation Server included the option of a workgroup edition, which was an edition of Team Foundation Server that was limited to five users. In Team Foundation Server 2010, there is only one edition of Team Foundation Server available, and the workgroup edition has been removed from the product lineup.
>
> The CAL-exclusion available for Team Foundation Server 2010 licenses purchased through the retail channel is the replacement concept for small teams. This allows the team to grow easily without having any technical limitations in place for growth.

Hosted Team Foundation Server Instances

One of the new options for using Team Foundation Server 2010 is the capability to have a hosted instance available for your company. This is similar to hosted websites in that, for a fee, an external company provides a Team Foundation Server instance for your team's use. This frees your team from the management and administration burdens of Team Foundation Server. It also enables your company to have a new server instance available quickly.

As of this writing, the following are a few of the options that you have available:

➤ *CodePlex* — If you have an Open Source project, you can freely use the Team Foundation Server instance available at www.codeplex.com.

➤ *DiscountASP.net* — Private hosting is available for a monthly fee. For more information, see www.discountasp.net/tfs/go/go.aspx?i=14875.

➤ *SAAS Made Easy* — Private hosting is available for a monthly fee. For more information, see www.saasmadeeasy.com/.

➤ *Phase2* — Private hosting is available for a monthly fee. For more information, see www.phase2.com/hosted_team_foundation_server_overview2.aspx.

➤ *TeamDevCentral* — Private hosting is available for a monthly fee. For more information, see www.teamdevcentral.com/.

➤ *Windows Azure* — Microsoft has announced that it is currently working on private hosting available using the Windows Azure platform. This service is not currently available as of this writing. However, you should continue to monitor future news from Microsoft for availability.

SUMMARY

As you learned in this chapter, Team Foundation Server 2010 is a product with lots of features and functionality. This chapter introduced the types of features that are available, including those that are new to the latest release. Additionally, you learned about the different acquisition methods for getting the software for Team Foundation Server 2010.

The next few chapters will familiarize you with planning a Team Foundation Server deployment, installing a brand-new server, and then the different methods available for connecting to your new server. Chapter 2 begins that discussion with an examination of Team Foundation Server deployment.

2

Planning a Deployment

WHAT'S IN THIS CHAPTER?

➤ Organizing a plan for adoption

➤ Setting up timelines for adoption

➤ Structuring team projects and team project collections

➤ Hardware and software requirements

Before installing or configuring Team Foundation Server, it is helpful to lay out a plan and to identify the areas that need some preparation work to ensure a successful adoption.

This chapter discusses methods for gaining consensus in your organization for the adoption. You will learn about some potential adoption timelines and strategies to ensure a smooth transition for your teams from legacy systems to Team Foundation Server. Finally, the discussion walks you through some of the immediate preparation steps for gathering what you will need before you start the installation and configuration of your new Team Foundation Server environment.

In Chapter 1, you read about the high-level features that are available in Team Foundation Server 2010, including what is new for this release. Now it's time to convince your boss and team that it would be worthwhile to adopt Team Foundation Server.

The following sections examine some of the ways that you can prepare for your proposal to your team.

IDENTIFYING AND ADDRESSING SOFTWARE ENGINEERING PAIN

One key to selling the idea of an Application Lifecycle Management (ALM) solution is to identify the pain points that your organization and teams are experiencing, and to address those pain points with possible solutions. Your organization may have a completely different set of pain points that should be addressed than what is covered in this section, but you may find that some of the common problems people are seeking solutions for are the same problems that plague your organization.

This section identifies some common problems that plague many development organizations, and provides some helpful discussion about how Team Foundation Server and the ALM family of Visual Studio 2010 products attempt to address those pain points. You may have additional pain points that you would like to solve, and it is always good to flesh those out to ensure that you are identifying and solving them as part of your adoption of Team Foundation Server.

Transparency into the Release or Project

Does your team have difficulty understanding any of the following questions during the release cycle?

- ➤ Are we on track to release at the end of the month?
- ➤ How much implementation has been accomplished on the requirements in this release?
- ➤ How are our testers doing in authoring and executing their test cases?
- ➤ What changed in last night's build?
- ➤ Why did this set of files change in this recent check-in? Was it used to implement a requirement or fix a bug?
- ➤ Which requirements are getting good test coverage versus requirements that are largely untested?

Teams that have a problem getting visibility into their release process often want to start by finding a tool that will gather all of the data necessary to easily answer some of these questions. Team Foundation Server 2010 is one of the best products available for transparency, since it allows you to store all of the different artifacts from the beginning to the end of the software development lifecycle. Not only does it provide a way to capture that information, but there are rich links between those artifacts and systems that allow you to make informed decisions. Team Foundation Server 2010 provides rich information by exposing the end-to-end relationships that exist across artifacts.

Collaboration Across Different Teams and Roles

Some teams have difficulty providing information and communicating across different teams. Testers may not feel that they have enough information about bugs that are returned to them as rejected, and developers may feel that they don't have enough information about the requirements they are supposed to implement or the bugs that they are supposed to fix.

If your team is experiencing some of these problems, you may benefit from being able to easily see information and notes about the different artifacts in the software process that are stored in Team Foundation Server 2010.

Automated Compilation, Testing, Packaging, and Deployment

Teams may end up spending a lot of time at the end of release cycles completing manual steps to compile, package, and deploy their applications. They may be performing these actions on a developer machine, and manually copying to staging and production environments.

These manual steps are often error-prone, and can result in unforeseen issues and failed deployments. By taking advantage of the automated build system in Team Foundation Sever 2010, your team can reduce the complexity of this process, and turn it into a repeatable end-to-end solution that occurs at regular intervals, or is triggered by changes introduced by your developers.

Additionally, you can leverage the automated build system to introduce a "gauntlet" of checks that each check-in may go through to verify the quality of those changes by using the gated check-in feature in the Team Foundation Build system. This can help your team reduce entropy by preventing defects from ever being introduced to the version control repository.

Managing Test Plans

The testing or quality assurance departments may be organizing their test cases using Word or Excel documents, which often results in not being able to effectively organize your catalog of test cases. Additionally, tracking the execution progress of each individual test case may be extremely difficult, and, thus, it becomes difficult to gauge the progress of testing in your release.

Team Foundation Server allows you to manage your collection of test cases, both manual and physical, and also allows you to manage the progress of test execution during the release cycle. This includes the capability to track tests across multiple configurations that your product or application needs to support.

Parallel Development

Development teams have notoriously experienced difficulty in managing changes across multiple lines of development that can occur concurrently. By supporting the previous release, while stabilizing the next release, and then also performing early work on a feature release, you can end up having trouble keeping each of those parallel lines of development organized. Integrating changes made between those releases is especially time-consuming and error-prone, especially if developers are manually applying fixes to each of those code lines.

Testers are often curious about how bug fixes and changes have been included in a particular release. And they might often need to figure out if fixes have been applied to other releases of the application.

The version control system in Team Foundation Server provides excellent branching and merging tools for easily managing parallel development, including the capability to track changes across branches. This helps you easily see which branches have changes integrated into them, as well as how and when those changes got there.

HOW TO ADOPT TEAM FOUNDATION SERVER

The value from Team Foundation Server is realized when it is utilized in a team. Therefore, ensuring a successful Team Foundation Server adoption requires alignment with many people in your organization. The following sections should help you avoid some common pitfalls, and provide you with some suggestions on where to start with what may seem like a large and daunting product.

Adoption Timeline

In general, splitting up the adoption by team/application has been proven to be a successful approach. Some of the effort may end up being the same for most teams, and lessons you learn from earlier transitions will help you become more successful in the following transitions.

Following is a sample of a typical adoption timeline. Your particular deployment may be different from what is listed here, based on your organization's requirements for the server.

- ➤ Planning for Team Foundation Server Deployment: 1 week
- ➤ Identifying the process for adoption and process template customizations: 2 to 4 days
- ➤ Designing the branching and merging strategy: 1 day
- ➤ Customizing the process template: 1 to 4 weeks (depending on the level of customization of the process identified)

Following is a timeline for each team or application:

- ➤ Developing custom migration tool: 2-4 weeks (only needed if not using one commercially or freely available.)
- ➤ Testing the migration: 1 to 2 weeks
- ➤ Initial training sessions for teams: Occurs 1 week before transition (about half a day per team member)
- ➤ Migrating source code: 1 to 2 days
- ➤ Migrating work items: 1 to 2 days
- ➤ Follow-up training sessions for teams: Occurs 1 week after transition (about half a day per team member)

Phased Approach

Another approach that works well is adopting each piece of Team Foundation Server separately in different phases of a larger deployment project. This allows you to plan each phase, execute that adoption, and then train the teams on the new features and processes available in that particular phase.

Some find that teams are better able to absorb training for the new features when they are exposed to them incrementally. You may have a higher success rate by splitting up the project, and then focusing your time and attention on making each part succeed. However, you'll eventually find some teams very eager to adopt future phases, so be sure you don't keep them waiting too long!

When introducing any new tooling into a large organization, it is important that you address the key pain points first. Many companies will identify traceability of work through the development lifecycle, and this is often an area that is poorly addressed by existing tooling. For others, the version control system being used may be out-of-date and performing poorly. It is, therefore, usually the version control or work item tracking components that people begin using when adopting Team Foundation Server.

Luckily, Team Foundation Server is flexible enough that you can still get value from the product when only using one or two components of the system. Once you have adopted both version control and work item tracking, the next area to tackle to gain the most benefit is likely to be Team Foundation Build. By automating your build system and increasing the frequency of integration, you reduce the amount of unknown pain that always occurs when integrating components together to form a product.

The key is to gradually remove the unknown and unpredictable elements from the software delivery process, and to always look for wasted effort that can be cut out.

Automating the builds not only means that the build and packaging process becomes less error-prone, it also means that the feedback loop of requirements traceability is completed. You are now able to track work from the time that it is captured, all the way through to a change to the source code of the product, and into the build that contains those changes.

At this point, you may identify the need to document your test cases and track their execution throughout the release. With the traceability between test cases and requirements, you'll be able to better identify the requirements in your product that are covered appropriately by your testers.

After a period of time, you will have built up a repository of historical data in your Team Foundation Server data warehouse, and you can start to make use of the reporting features to predict if you will be finished when you expect (for example, is the amount of remaining work being completed at the required rate?). You will also be able to drill into the areas that you might want to improve — for example, which parts of the code are causing the most bugs.

To put all of this together, you'll more than likely end up with the following adoption phases:

- ➤ Phase I: Version Control
- ➤ Phase II: Work Item Tracking
- ➤ Phase III: Automated Builds
- ➤ Phase IV: Test Case Management
- ➤ Phase V: Reporting
- ➤ Phase VI: Virtual Lab Management

You'll notice that the book has generally been laid out in this order to help you address each area in order of typical adoption.

After getting used to the tooling, you should look at your overall process and adopted process templates to ensure that all of the necessary data is being captured — and that all the work item types and transitions are required. If there are unnecessary steps, then consider removing them. If you notice problems because of a particular issue, consider modifying the process to add a safety net. It is important to adjust the process not only to fit the team and organization, but also to ensure that you only adjust your processes when you need to, and not just because you can. See Chapter 11 for more information about process templates, work items, and other topics related to tracking work.

Hosting Team Foundation Server

For the team to have trust in Team Foundation Server, you must ensure that it is there when they need it, and that it performs as well as possible. For organizations that depend on creating software, your version control and work item tracking repositories are critical to getting your work done. Therefore, those features should be treated on the same level as other mission-critical applications in the organization.

The Team Foundation Server infrastructure is a production environment for your company. Ideally, it should be hosted on a server with adequate resources (both physical memory and disk space). If hosted in a virtual environment, then you should ensure that the host machine has sufficient resources to handle the load of all guest machines.

When planning upgrades, configuration changes, or when performing training, you should use a test Team Foundation Server environment. For some organizations, the test requirements justify the purchase of a hardware platform equivalent to the production environment.

However, for many scenarios, simply using a virtual Team Foundation environment will provide a suitable environment for testing. These virtual environments are especially useful when developing a new process template, or testing work item process modifications. Microsoft provides an evaluation version of Team Foundation Server pre-configured as a virtual hard disk (VHD) file. This is frequently used as a test bed for work item modifications and new process templates.

Identifying Affected Teams

One essential activity is to identify all of the different teams in your company that would be affected by deploying Team Foundation Server. Following are some examples of those types of affected teams:

- ➤ Developers
- ➤ Testers/Quality Assurance
- ➤ Product/Program Managers
- ➤ Project Managers
- ➤ Business Analysts

➤ Designers

➤ User Experience

➤ Change Management

➤ Release Management

➤ Technical Documentation/User Education

➤ Technical Support

➤ Information Technology

➤ Executives or other stakeholders

➤ Remote Teams

Generating Consensus

If anything, you should over-communicate any plans for rolling out Team Foundation Server and/or a new process. Change is difficult for some people, and this has been one technique that seems to ease those concerns.

Once you have identified all of the affected teams, it's helpful to generate consensus by suggesting that each team nominate a team member to represent them as decisions are made about the deployment. This is generally a good way to ensure that everyone is involved, and that information ends up getting disseminated throughout the organization. You can have this "advisory" group help determine how to configure the server and the process that ends up being adopted. Going through this process allows those who are involved to have some buy-in to the deployment and, ultimately, champion the success of the change within their teams.

One word of caution, however, is that you should be sure to have an executive stakeholder in this group who is available to make final decisions when there are disagreements. It's important to ensure that decisions made by the group end up benefiting the business, so having this "final-authority" representative is helpful. The others in the group will feel better about giving their input and hearing out why a particular decision is made, even if it's not the decision they were behind.

Team Foundation Server Administrator

You will likely need to identify a resource who is responsible for managing the configuration and health of the Team Foundation Server environment. Your organization may not necessarily need a full-time resource for this task, but this will generally take a good amount of regular effort to ensure that this mission-critical environment is running smoothly for your company. This role might fill several of the following example hats:

➤ Champion and lead the adoption in the organization.

➤ Implement process changes.

➤ Identify and write new reports.

➤ Manage permissions and administer the environment.

> ➤ Identify and implement maintenance windows.

> ➤ Design and implement branching and merging strategies.

> ➤ Architect build resources and build processes for use in the organization.

> ➤ Administer the virtual lab management assets.

Some larger organizations have even identified a team to manage each of the areas that Team Foundation Server may touch in the software development lifecycle. This can be considered a *shared engineering* team that works with its "customers" in the organization to implement the needs of the company. Those customers are the teams using the Team Foundation Server environment internally. This team's work for managing the Team Foundation Server environment can even be prioritized by the advisory group mentioned previously, and should be represented in the group (if not even serving as the chair person).

A common question comes up about whether an IT or engineering organization should own the management of the Team Foundation Server environment. There are pros and cons to either sole-ownership. IT organizations have had experience in managing corporate applications, but might not fully understand the needs of software development teams and departments. However, engineering departments might not have the expertise to manage hardware and disaster-recovery concerns that keep the servers running in optimal health.

A shared responsibility approach has proven to be successful. For example, the IT department may own ensuring that the actual hardware is being maintained, backups are being run regularly, and that networking, power, and cooling needs are taken care of. The engineering organization can own the application (Team Foundation Server) itself, which would include installing service packs or patches, configuring the team projects, and managing security. That shared management responsibility requires close collaboration across each department, which is essential for running a smoothly operating environment.

Pilot Projects

One of the key ways that your organization can learn what you might need to customize in Team Foundation Server 2010 is to identify a team, small project, or release that is willing to be the "guinea pig" to test out Team Foundation Server 2010. By setting up a pilot project, you can learn lots of information that might be helpful before rolling out to a larger audience in your organization.

Following is some of the information you will possibly discover:

> ➤ Custom reports that you might need to provide that your business has been used to receiving from legacy applications.

> ➤ Common pitfalls that your pilot team has experienced that can be addressed when training other teams

> ➤ New features that might be more valuable to adopt ahead of other features in the products

Don't underestimate the amount of information you will learn from this pilot team and project. It can certainly bring your organization more comfort in proving that the system will help you solve your organization's pain points.

MIGRATION STRATEGIES

Oftentimes, software development teams will have been using several different systems to track their source code, bugs, project management tasks, requirements, and even test cases. You might be in a situation where you want to migrate from those legacy systems to Team Foundation Server.

There are several different approaches and, thankfully, there are plenty of tools that are available to assist you with your migration.

> *If you are upgrading from a previous version of Team Foundation Server, be sure to see Chapter 23 for information on planning the upgrade, instead of following the migration techniques mentioned in this section.*

Version Control

Migrating from a legacy version control systems to Team Foundation Server version control is one of the most common starting places for software development teams.

Visual SourceSafe (VSS)

Your team may be using Visual SourceSafe (VSS) and looking to migrate from it before the end of that product's support lifecycle at Microsoft. Team Foundation Server 2010 actually ships with a VSS Converter tool that allows you to migrate source code from your VSS repositories and include the history during that migration.

Other Version Control Systems

If you aren't currently using VSS, then you have options as well. The Team Foundation Server product team at Microsoft has been working on a platform for migration and synchronization scenarios. This platform is freely available on CodePlex, and is updated on a regular basis. As of this writing, it currently contains adapters for migrating from a file-based system and from IBM Rational ClearCase.

The Team Foundation Server Integration Platform has been built on an extensible platform that allows for different adapters to be created to migrate source code from other systems. The CodePlex project has received numerous and regular contributions from the product team, and you can expect more adapters will come out in the future.

If you are feeling up to the challenge, you can also create a custom adapter for your version control system using the Team Foundation Server Integration Platform's extensibility hooks. You might consider contributing to the CodePlex project for others to take advantage of the custom adapter if they run into the same migration scenario that you faced!

> *You can find out more information about the Team Foundation Server Integration Platform by visiting the CodePlex project's site at* http:// tfsintegration.codeplex.com/.

There is also a family of third-party migration solutions that will allow you to migrate your source code from popular legacy source control systems.

 Chapter 8 discusses more about migrating from legacy version control systems, including VSS.

Work Item Tracking

In addition to migrating source code, most teams will want to think about migrating *work items* from their legacy systems. These may be bugs, requirements, test cases, tasks, and so on.

Thankfully, the Team Foundation Server Integration Platform mentioned previously was also designed to move work items in addition to source code. Currently, there is an adapter that allows you to move your legacy artifacts over from IBM Rational ClearQuest into Team Foundation Server 2010. Again, custom adapters can be built using the extensible architecture of the Team Foundation Server Integration Platform to migrate work items from other tracking systems.

There are several other methods that you could use to import your work item tracking data. You may use Microsoft Office Excel and the integration that Team Explorer adds to allow you to import spreadsheets of information. There are also commercial tools available for importing artifacts from HP Quality Center into Team Foundation Server. If you are interested in migrating test cases from Excel documents that are exported from other applications, you can also use the Test Case Import tool available on CodePlex (http://tcmimport.codeplex.com).

Chapter 11 has more in-depth information and an introduction to Team Foundation Server work item tracking.

STRUCTURING TEAM PROJECT COLLECTIONS AND TEAM PROJECTS

A common question that ultimately will come up after setting up Team Foundation Server is how you should go about structuring your team project collections and team projects. It's helpful to plan your strategy before ever installing and setting up the environment so that you make the right choices from the beginning. Changing the strategy can lead to a lot of effort in reorganizing, and you'll even find that some changes are downright impossible. Team Foundation Server supports creating a strategy that will be effective, flexible, and scalable to your organizations.

Ultimately, the strategy will be formed based on the isolation needs for your organization. Software development teams have traditionally described three constant concepts for how they managed their applications:

➤ *Projects* — These are the units of work centered around a given effort with a start and end date. You can easily map these to product releases, contracts, or initiatives. The projects and team within it usually followed a process like Scrum, Capability Maturity Model Integration (CMMI), and so on.

➤ *Products/codebases* — This is described as the "source code" that makes up an application product, or group of products (suite/family). It is what the developers, designers, and other specialties work on, and its byproduct (files such as `.exe`, `.dll`, and so on) is consumed by a *customer*.

➤ *Organizations* — These are the divisions, business units, departments, or teams that work on projects that deliver products to end customers.

Team project collections provide the capability to group a set of tightly related team projects. When you are thinking about them, it helps to focus on correlating them with products/codebases or application suites. For example, if your company makes four unique products that have almost no code-sharing between them, it would be practical to create four team project collections. If, on the other hand, your company has several products that compose a solution or product suite with high code reuse, framework sharing, or even simultaneous release, then you will have only one team project collection.

Some organizations have multiple business units or departments that traditionally manage their own software configuration management servers/repositories. These organizations will find that team project collections also benefit them by isolating each business unit, but still being able to consolidate the management and maintenance of a single Team Foundation Server environment. This type of functionality would be described as *multi-tenancy*.

Ultimately, you will end up wanting to decide the isolation needs of the departments in your organization, and how you might segregate certain resources like build and virtual lab resources based along those lines.

> *Chapters 17 and 18 provide a more in-depth look at team project collections and scalability features.*

SCOPE OF A TEAM PROJECT

At its very core, a *team project* contains all of the artifacts such as source code, work items, builds, reports, and an associated SharePoint team portal site.

In general, a team project is "bigger than you think." A good way of thinking about what must be grouped into a single team project is to think about the impact of a typical requirement for your software development project. If the requirement would affect the ASP.NET front end, Java middleware, and SQL database repository, then all these projects and teams of developers probably want to be working on the same team project.

Following are three general areas that are used when scoping a team project. But every organization is different, and yours might need to combine these aspects when deciding on your approach.

➤ Application

➤ Release

➤ Team

continues

(continued)

For some organizations, it makes sense to only have a single team project in a single project collection. Others may have more than a hundred.

Team Project Per Application

In general, *team project per application* is the most common approach when scoping team projects, and probably the position you should first consider. Generally, requirements are addressed by the entire application, and a group of people are assigned to work on it. The applications typically have a long lifecycle, going from inception, active development into the support, and then finally to end-of-life phases.

Team Project Per Release

The *team project per release* methodology is useful for very large teams working on long-running projects. After every major release, you create a new team project. At this point in time, you can carry out changes that might have come about from your post-release review. You might take the opportunity to reorganize your version control tree, improve process templates, and copy over work items from the previous release that didn't make it.

This methodology tends to be suited to large independent software vendors (ISVs) working with products with a very long lifetime. In fact, Microsoft themselves use this approach for many of their products. In these cases, it is generally safer to start as a team project per application, and then move to a team project per release (if required) to make reporting easier. This is traditionally the case if the releases tend to span a long timeframe (such as a multi-year project or release cycle).

Team Project Per Team

For smaller teams (less than 50) where the number of people working on the team tends to stay fairly static, but the applications they work on are in a constant state of flux, the *team project per team* approach may be most suitable. This is most often seen in consulting-style organizations, where the same group of people may be responsible for delivering applications for clients with rapid turnaround. If your team members are often working on more than one project at a time, the same team or subset of the team works together on those projects over time, or if the project lifecycle is measured in months rather than years, then you may want to consider this approach.

Alternately, a single team project collection per customer could be used for the consulting-style organizations that must provide all of the artifacts (source code, work item history, and so on) to the client at the end of the project, since the team project collection contains the entire work. If you do not have to deliver all of the artifacts of the project to the customer as a requirement, however, you should not necessarily use the individual team project collections approach.

Considering Limitations in Team Foundation Server

When deciding the appropriate team project collection and team project structure for your organization, it is helpful to understand the limitations of the feature set in Team Foundation Server that may affect your desired strategy based on your team's goals with using the product.

Ultimately, you can use the knowledge of these limitations to arrive at the most appropriate scoping of team project collections and team projects for your organization. You will want to ensure that you think about possible changes to the products, application families, teams, and organizational structure, and how these feature limitations may impact those changes in the future.

Renaming a Team Project

Unfortunately, you are not able to rename a team project once you have created it. There is no workaround for this limitation. You will want to ensure that you have fully reviewed and arrived to your team project structuring strategy before creating any team projects.

Additionally, you will want to consider the names you give to team projects that represent products or product families whose names have not been determined. Once you pick a name for the team project (especially if it uses a code name or some other early project name), that name will be used for the entire lifetime of the team project.

One key difference for a team project collection is that you can change the name of a team project collection at a later time. The limitation does not apply to team project collections.

Moving Work Items Across Team Projects or Team Project Collections

Since you can choose to use completely different process templates for team projects, you are unable to move work items across the team project boundary. Ensure that you pick the appropriate scoping level for a team project. For example, if you want to create a bug in one application, and later find out that it is really for another application that is in another team project, then you will find out that you cannot move the bug to the other team project. In this case, you will have to create a copy (since the "bug" artifact may not even be named the same in the other team project's process template) of the work item in the next team project.

Instead, you may consider scoping the team project larger to include multiple applications in the same application family. You can then split the applications within the team projects by using the Area Path hierarchy. To move a bug between two applications that are stored in the same team project, you would then just change the Area Path to the one that represents the other application. However, all applications or teams that use a team project must use the same process template. Chapter 11 provides more information about Area Paths.

Managing Work Items from Multiple Team Projects in Office Excel or Project

Similarly to the previous limitation, since team projects can have different process templates, the Microsoft Office Excel and Project add-ins for managing work items do not work with work items from multiple team projects. As mentioned, you will want to ensure that you scope the team project to be larger, and use the Area Path hierarchy to distinguish between applications or teams. Then use the Iteration Path hierarchy to distinguish between releases and iterations/sprints.

Tracking Merged Changes Across Branches in Multiple Team Projects

You are unable to use the branch visualization and track merged changes visualization features for branches that span across the team project boundary. In general, you should avoid the need for creating branches across team projects in your branching and merging strategy if you will want to use the visualization features that are introduced in Team Foundation Server 2010.

Reports and Dashboards Scoped to Team Project

If you have larger team projects that encompass multiple applications in an application family, teams, and so on, you will notice that the standard reports and dashboards will be scoped to use the data inside of the entire team project. Each of the reports enables you to filter the data, including some by Area Path and Iteration Path fields for the work item data.

Additionally, the SharePoint dashboard features allow you to create multiple custom dashboards. Each custom dashboard can then include web parts that are scoped to a specific Area Path and Iteration Path as well.

Moving Team Projects Between Team Project Collections

Once a team project is created in one team project collection, you are unable to move the team project to another existing team project collection. This is because there may be a conflict between the IDs that are used for the different artifacts (like changeset, work item, and build unique identifiers).

One option you do have is the capability to split a team project collection, which allows you to create a clone of the team project collection, and then remove all of the unwanted team projects from each copy. This allows you to essentially move a team project to a *new* team project collection. There is no workaround available for moving a team project to an *existing* team project collection.

Artifacts Scoped to a Team Project Collection

One of the important concepts for team project collections is that all of the artifacts that are contained within a team project collection are isolated from other team project collections. For example, all of the different link types between version control files and changesets, work items, builds, test cases, test results, and so on, can only be contained within the team project collection.

Another example would be that you won't be able to add a link between a test case that exists in one team project collection and a requirement that exists in another team project collection. If you need this type of traceability, you will want to include team projects that need to link between artifacts within the same team project collection.

Additionally, you are able unable to branch and merge across team project collections, even though you are able to branch across multiple team projects within the same team project collection. There is no workaround available for this feature, so ensure that you scope the team project collection appropriately to account for this feature limitation.

Finally, you are unable to create work item queries that need to pull work items from team projects across multiple team project collections. However, you can create a work item query to pull work items from multiple team projects inside of the same team project collection. Also, the reporting warehouse contains information about artifacts stored in all team project collections and team projects, so you can create custom reports that pull that information together.

Server Limitations

Team Foundation Server is an extremely scalable product. However, you should be aware of and understand its limitations so that you optimize the performance of the environment. It is also helpful to know that most of the limits are not enforced by the product, and are general best practices and recommendations from the product group in order to maintain a certain level of performance.

Team Foundation Server can support thousands of team project collections mainly because of the new scale-out capabilities. The limits are more tied to the SQL Server hardware utilized in your deployment. A SQL Server instance can support 30 to 100 *active* team project collections. This range is related to the physical memory available to SQL. *Active* team project collections are those being accessed daily by the team.

Given this, if your deployment structure requires hundreds of team project collections, you have essentially two choices:

➤ You may buy additional hardware and make available more SQL Server instances for use by the Team Foundation Server environment.

➤ You could consider grouping team projects more aggressively within existing team project collections.

In order to maintain high performance, you should limit the number of a team projects stored within a team project collection. The actual number of team projects to include in a team project collection is limited by the complexity of the work item types defined within the process templates being used by each of those team projects. The work item types included in the standard process templates (for example the Microsoft Solutions Framework for Agile Software Development v5.0 process template) have been shown to support more than 500 team projects on a server on adequate hardware.

PREPARATION FOR A TEAM FOUNDATION SERVER ENVIRONMENT

The following sections examine some of the preparation steps that are beneficial to take care of before you start to install a new Team Foundation Server.

> *If you are upgrading from earlier versions of Team Foundation Server, then you will find the upcoming sections beneficial in understanding the necessary preparation steps. You can also consult Chapter 23, which is dedicated solely to upgrading.*

Understanding the Architecture and Scale-Out Options

You have multiple options when configuring your Team Foundation Server deployments. You can deploy all the components (Team Foundation Server application, SQL Server, Reporting Services, and Windows SharePoint Services) onto one machine. This is called a *single-server installation,* and should work fine for a total of 450 users or less. In general, single-server installations are the easiest installations, as shown in Figure 2-1.

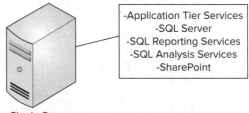

FIGURE 2-1: Single-server installation

For more than 450 users, a *multi-server installation* should be considered. There are several flavors of multi-server installations. At its most basic, there are two servers. One server is the data tier, running SQL Server, and the other is the application tier, running Team Foundation Server, Reporting Services, and Windows SharePoint Services (WSS), as shown in Figure 2-2.

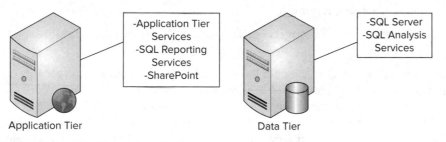

FIGURE 2-2: Multi-server installation

Your organization may have an existing SharePoint Portal Server, and/or SQL Server Reporting Services Server that it wants to use in conjunction with Team Foundation Server. For that scenario, you would then have a server for running the Team Foundation Server application tier, a server for running the SQL Server databases, and separate servers for running SharePoint Portal Server and/or Reporting Services. Figure 2-3 shows a sample topology using this particular scenario.

For high-availability scenarios, clustering of machines is available at each point in the architecture. As previously discussed, the Team Foundation Server application-tier machines can be located behind a network load-balancing device. The SQL Server instances referred to by the Team Foundation Server application and project collections can also be clustered. Figure 2-4 shows an example of a larger topography that includes high-availability scaling.

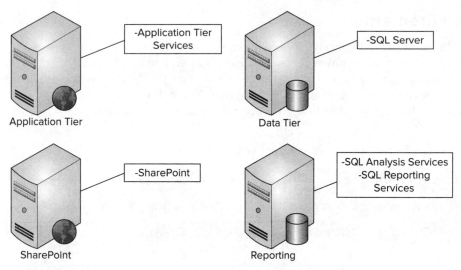

FIGURE 2-3: Existing server used with Team Foundation Server

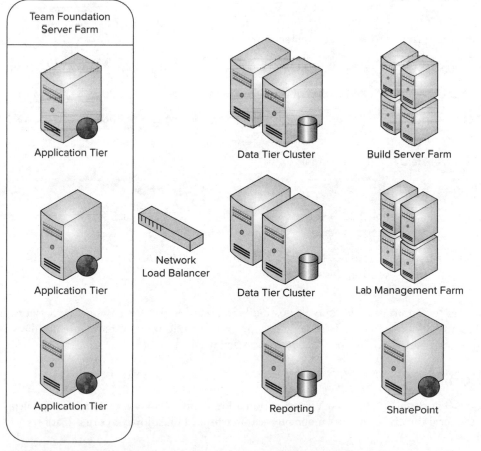

FIGURE 2-4: Larger topography that includes high-availability scaling

Hardware Requirements

Table 2-1 shows the hardware requirements for a single-server installation, where the application tier and data tier reside on the same physical machine. However, keep in mind that these numbers are minimum recommendations, and, obviously, the more hardware you can throw at a problem, the better, especially if you use the environment more heavily. You will want to continue to monitor the environment for performance and utilization to scale the resources as necessary.

TABLE 2-1: Hardware Requirements for Single-Server Installation

NUMBER OF USERS	CPU	HARD DISK	MEMORY
Fewer than 250 users	One 2.13 GHz processor	125GB	2GB
250 to 500 users	One 2.3 GHz dual-core processor	300GB	4GB

For a multi-server installation (where you have distinct physical servers for the application tier and the data tier), Table 2-2 lists the application tier hardware requirements, and Table 2-3 lists the data tier hardware requirements.

TABLE 2-2: Application Tier Hardware Requirements

NUMBER OF USERS	CPU	HARD DISK	MEMORY
500 to 2,200 users	One 2.13 GHz dual-core Intel Xeon processor	500GB	4GB
2,200 to 3,600 users	One 2.13 GHz quad-core Intel Xeon processor	500GB	8GB

TABLE 2-3: Data Tier Hardware Requirements

NUMBER OF USERS	CPU	HARD DISK	MEMORY
450 to 2,200 users	One 2.33 GHz quad-core Intel Xeon processor	2TB SAS Disk Array	8GB
2,200 to 3,600 users	Two 2.33 GHz quad-core Intel Xeon processors	3TB SAS Disk Array	16GB

Keep in mind that the application tier may be hosting WSS and/or SQL Server Reporting Services, in addition to Team Foundation Server. This might require you to bump up your hardware numbers in some form or fashion to account for the extra processing needed.

Virtualization

Virtualization is a hot topic these days. Virtualization allows you to buy a large server, and then virtually host several different servers on one physical machine. This allows an organization to make the most of a physical machine's resources. There are some pieces of the Team Foundation Server environment that can be safely hosted in a virtual environment, and some that require careful consideration and performance tuning before being virtualized.

Ideally, the following pieces should be installed on physical servers or properly tuned virtual machines:

➤   SQL Server Database Engine

➤   SQL Server Reporting Services

➤   SQL Server Analysis Services

SQL Server is the foundation for holding all the information regarding Team Foundation Server. Should it become corrupted, the entire Team Foundation Server system will go down. To minimize the chances of database corruption, you should carefully consider the possible drawbacks before hosting SQL Server 2008 or SQL Server 2008 R2 in a virtualized environment. In earlier editions of SQL Server, virtualization was not supported. However, this is no longer the case, since there were quite a few improvements included in the latest versions.

Specifically, for Team Foundation Server, you will want to monitor the disk I/O metrics to ensure that the virtualized database servers are able to keep up with the amount of I/O that is generated for database transactions that come from Team Foundation Server. No matter which virtualization technology you use, you will want to ensure that you set up the virtual environment for peak performance. The key is to continually monitor the performance indicators for the environment, and make appropriate modifications. Any degradation of performance should be reviewed, especially if you choose to virtualize your data tier server.

> *For some tips on properly setting up a virtual environment that will include SQL Server, see to the recommendations in Chapter 18.*

The following can be safely installed in a virtualized environment with minimum to no impact on the Team Foundation Server system:

➤   Team Foundation Server application tier

➤   Windows SharePoint Services (WSS)

➤   Team Foundation Build servers

➤   Team Foundation Proxy servers

Planning for Software Prerequisites

In addition to the hardware requirements for Team Foundation Server, you will want to prepare for a new installation by ensuring certain software prerequisites are met.

Operating Systems

Team Foundation Server 2010 has introduced support for some 64-bit operating systems for the application tier server in addition to 32-bit operating systems. Table 2-4 lists the supported operating systems for the application tier server.

TABLE 2-4: Supported Operating Systems for Application Tier

OPERATING SYSTEM	NOTES
Windows Server 2003 with Service Pack 2	32-bit only
Windows Server 2003 R2	32-bit only
Windows Server 2003 R2 with Service Pack 2	32-bit only
Windows Server 2008 with Service Pack 2	
Windows Server 2008 R2	Recommended
Windows Vista with Service Pack 2	
Windows 7	

> *Team Foundation Server 2010 now supports the capability to install on a server that is running a client operating system such as Windows 7 or Windows Vista. However, you will not be able to take advantage of reporting features or integration with SharePoint products if you install using a client operating system.*

SQL Server

Team Foundation Server 2010 uses SQL Server to store its data, SQL Server Analysis Services to store an Online Analytical Processing (OLAP) cube for the data warehouse, and SQL Reporting Services as a presentation layer for rich reports. You can use the default instance or a named SQL instance for any of the components. Table 2-5 lists the supported versions of SQL Server.

TABLE 2-5: Supported SQL Server Versions

SQL SERVER VERSION	NOTES
SQL Server 2008 Express	Used when installing Team Foundation Server using the "Basic" configuration wizard.
SQL Server 2008	
SQL Server 2008 R2	Recommended. Available separately to license.

You can use an existing instance of SQL Server, as long as it meets certain requirements. See the latest version of the Team Foundation Server Installation Guide *available on the Microsoft Downloads site at* http://tinyurl.com/ TFS2010InstallGuide.

Included Edition

When purchasing Team Foundation Server 2010, you are able to install SQL Server 2008 Standard for limited use if you are installing on a single server. This "limited use" privilege only permits you to use that SQL instance for Team Foundation Server 2010 databases. This means that you would not be able to use the instance for any custom databases or other applications that you have installed within your organization.

Enterprise Editions of SQL Server

If you are using an Enterprise edition of SQL Server that you have licensed separately, Team Foundation Server 2010 will take advantage of features that are only made available in the Enterprise edition. Following are some of the features that Team Foundation Server can take advantage of:

➤ *Online re-indexing* — This is particularly useful for the periodic maintenance jobs that Team Foundation Server runs to keep the SQL instance healthy, because it is capable of keeping the database online while it performs those steps. This can lead to better performance and reduced blocking calls.

➤ *Perspectives in Analysis Services* — The schema for the OLAP cube for the data warehouse will take advantage of a feature called *perspectives*. Perspectives in SQL Analysis Services allow a more focused view of the dimensions, measures, and data that are included in the OLAP cube.

➤ *Index compression* — Team Foundation Server will take advantage of index compression, which will help increase performance by reducing I/O and memory utilization. (This feature may require more CPU utilization, however, but shouldn't be a problem, since I/O is typically the bottleneck for the data tier.)

➤ *Clustering data tiers for high availability and redundancy* — If you are looking to have a clustered data tier, then you will want to take advantage of the Enterprise edition, because it allows you to have as many failover clusters as the underlying operating system supports.

➤ *Query optimizations* — Team Foundation Server can benefit from certain query optimizations that are only available in the Enterprise edition of SQL Server.

➤ *Data-driven subscriptions in Reporting Services* — This feature allows you to subscribe to a report and set up recurring e-mails, and so on, that use data to drive what parameters are set in each report that gets sent.

➤ *Scale-out deployment for Reporting Services* — This feature is particularly necessary if you decide to have multiple application tiers together as a Team Foundation Server farm, and want to have SQL Reporting Services installed on each of those front-end servers.

SharePoint Products

Team Foundation Server 2010 has the capability to integrate with a new or existing SharePoint environment. Starting with Team Foundation Server 2010, this integration is optional and not required for installation. You can choose to integrate with SharePoint at the time of installation or add it later.

Table 2-6 lists the supported version of SharePoint products that can be used for integration.

TABLE 2-6: Supported Versions of SharePoint Products

SHAREPOINT PRODUCT	NOTES
Windows SharePoint Services (WSS) 3.0	
Microsoft Office SharePoint Server (MOSS) 2007	Available separately to license
SharePoint Foundation 2010	
SharePoint Server 2010	Recommended. Available separately to license

If you are using a full version of SharePoint Server such as Microsoft Office SharePoint Server (MOSS) 2007 or SharePoint Server (SPS) 2010, Team Foundation Server 2010 will take advantage of features only available in the full version (such as Excel Services). It does so by providing a set of "rich" dashboards that display charts contained in Microsoft Office Excel workbooks. The "rich" dashboards would not be available for your team portal sites when using the free versions of SharePoint products (WSS 3.0 or SharePoint Foundation 2010), but you would instead get a "lite" version of two dashboards, instead of the full range of dashboards available in the out-of-the-box process templates.

If you will be using a full version of SharePoint Server, you should consider installing the front-end components on different hardware than the hardware that will be used for running Team Foundation Server. This allows you to manage SharePoint independently of Team Foundation Server, which, in turn, allows you to lower your maintenance burden and prevent performance bottlenecks that may occur when both are running on the same server.

> *Chapter 13 provides a more in-depth look at integrating with SharePoint.*

Service Accounts

You will need several accounts. Table 2-7 lists the recommended service accounts that you will likely use when setting your Team Foundation Server environment. The table assumes using Team Foundation Server in an environment that uses Active Directory Domain Services.

TABLE 2-7: Recommended Service Accounts

SERVICE ACCOUNT	SAMPLE ACCOUNT NAME	NOTES
Team Foundation Server	yourdomain\ TFSSERVICE	Should have the "Account is sensitive and cannot be delegated" option enabled.
Team Foundation Server Reporting	yourdomain\ TFSREPORTS	Must be a user account (not Network Service). Should be given the "Allow log on locally" permission.
Team Foundation Server Build	yourdomain\TFSBUILD	
Team Foundation Server Proxy	yourdomain\TFSPROXY	
Lab Management	yourdomain\TFSLAB	Must be a user account (not Network Service), and can be used with "physical" environments, even when not using virtual lab management features.

The following is a list of best practices for Team Foundation Server service accounts:

➤ Built-in service accounts such as Network Service are supported, except as noted in Table 2-7.

➤ The service account user should be an Active Directory account if the Team Foundation Server environment consists of more than one server.

➤ Service accounts should be given the "Log on as a service" permission, except the Team Foundation Server Reporting service account.

File Share Folders

As you are using certain features in Team Foundation Server 2010, you will end up needing several shared folder locations. Table 2-8 lists the recommended folder share locations and their purposes. The suggested permissions for each of these shares is for full control for the TFSSERVICE and TFSBUILD service accounts, and read-only permissions for all team members, with the exception of libraries for Visual Studio Lab Management (which should include full control permissions for the TFSLAB service account).

TABLE 2-8: Suggested Folder Share Locations

DESCRIPTION	SUGGESTED NAME	PURPOSE
Build drops	\\fileserver\Builds	Used by the automated build system to copy outputs of the build process.
Symbol Server	\\fileserver\Symbols	Used by the automated build system for publishing debugging symbols.
Lab Management Library	\\fileserver\LabLibrary	Used by the lab management system for storing virtual machine and environment templates.

SMTP Server

One of the nice features in Team Foundation Server 2010 is the capability to set up custom alerts with different events that occur on the system. This allows users to self-subscribe to receiving e-mails for a multitude of different scenarios that may occur — for example, when a work item is assigned to a user, a triggered build has failed, or a check-in occurs to a particular folder in version control.

To ensure that your team members will be able to take advantage of this functionality, you must have a Simple Mail Transfer Protocol (SMTP) server internally that will accept anonymous e-mail traffic from the Team Foundation Server application tier server(s).

Firewall Concerns and Ports Used

To ensure the best connections between the servers in the Team Foundation Server 2010 environment and also client connectivity, you will want to ensure that certain ports are opened at each firewall that network traffic may flow through. Table 2-9 lists the default ports that Team Foundation Server 2010 uses for network traffic.

TABLE 2-9: Required Ports

PORT	DESCRIPTION
8080	Team Foundation Server Application Tier
8081	Team Foundation Server Proxy
9191	Team Foundation Server Build Service
80	SharePoint Default Web Site
17012	SharePoint Central Administration
1433	SQL Server
1434	SQL Browser Service

PORT	DESCRIPTION
2382	SQL Server Analysis Services Redirector
2383	SQL Server Analysis Services
80	SQL Server Reporting Services

Source: Team Foundation Server 2010 Installation Guide

Friendly DNS Names

To ease future scenarios where you may want to move to new hardware, upgrade to new versions of Team Foundation Server, or scale out components, you may want to create friendly DNS entries that point to the individual components for Team Foundation Server. Additionally, it is helpful to have something "friendly" to provide to end users as a connection address instead of server names that can be cryptic.

Table 2-10 lists the suggested friendly DNS entries that you should create for your Team Foundation Server environment (even if it is only a single server). Each of these entries can either be DNS A or CNAME records and assume an internal DNS suffix of domain.local below.

TABLE 2-10: Friendly DNS Records

DNS RECORD ENTRY	POINTS TO
tfs.domain.local	Application Tier server *or* Network Load Balancer IP for Team Foundation Server Application Tier server farm Used for Team Foundation Server application tier, Team Web Access, SQL Reporting Services, and SharePoint (if hosted on application tier server)
data.tfs.domain.local	Data Tier server *or* SQL Server Cluster IP Used for Location of the configuration database, team project collection databases, and the relational warehouse database
warehouse.tfs.domain.local	SQL Server Analysis Services instance
india.proxy.tfs.domain.local	One friendly DNS entry for each remote location with a proxy server (Optional)
sharepoint.tfs.domain.local	Separate friendly DNS entry for the SharePoint server if it is separated out from the application tier server (Optional)
lab.tfs.domain.local	System Center Virtual Machine Manager server used for Team Foundation Server Lab Management (Optional)

> *For more information about how to configure all of the components of Team Foundation Server 2010 to use friendly DNS names instead of the default server names, as well as the scenarios where this is helpful, visit the blog post by Ed Blankenship at* www.edsquared.com/2011/01/03/Using+Friendly+DNS+Names+I n+Your+TFS+Environment.aspx.

Legacy Visual Studio Versions

If team members are using older versions of Visual Studio, you will want to ensure that they are able to connect to Team Foundation Server 2010. Visual Studio 2005 and Visual Studio 2008 versions of Team Explorer have a *Forward Compatibility Update* available to allow connecting to a Team Foundation Server 2010 environment. Existing essential functionality that was available in each of those versions of the IDE is maintained after installing the update. No new features that are available in the Visual Studio 2010 release are made available with the update. Those users can install Visual Studio 2010 or Team Explorer 2010 to use side by side with the older version of the IDE.

If you have team members who will be using older versions of Visual Studio (such as Visual Studio 2003, Visual Studio 6, and so on) or other development environments that support the Microsoft Source Code Control Interface (MSSCCI), then you can install the latest version of the Team Foundation Server 2010 MSSCCI Provider currently available on the Visual Studio Gallery. The MSSCCI Provider enables team members to perform essential version control operations in the legacy development environments. As with the Forward Compatibility Update, those team members should have Visual Studio 2010 or Team Explorer 2010 installed and running side by side to ensure they have access to the rest of the features of Team Foundation Server 2010.

SUMMARY

This chapter reviewed possible ways that you can approach gaining support for adopting Team Foundation Server, and examined potential timelines for adoption. You learned how to identify the key players on your teams who will be instrumental in the success for the adoption.

There are many different ways for structuring your team project collections and team projects, and this chapter discussed the different possibilities and limitations that should help you formalize the most appropriate strategy for your teams.

You learned about the different hardware recommendations and software prerequisites that will be required for certain functionality. Additionally, being prepared also means ensuring that the environment and accounts are ready before installation, so a list of suggested items to check off was presented.

In Chapter 3, you will learn how to actually install and set up your new Team Foundation Server environment. You will learn how to set up the prerequisites, and identify where each component of the Team Foundation Server environment should be installed. Finally, you will learn about the process of configuring Team Foundation Server and creating the first team project.

3

Installation and Configuration

WHAT'S IN THIS CHAPTER?

➤ Preparing to install Team Foundation Server 2010

➤ Installing and configuring Team Foundation Server 2010

➤ Creating your first team project with Team Foundation Server 2010

Prior to the 2010 release, installing and configuring Team Foundation Server could have easily consumed an entire weekend or more. Installation errors were difficult to diagnose, configuration was done entirely via the command line, and configuration options were largely inflexible. Thankfully, Team Foundation Server 2010 is a monumental leap forward when it comes to installation, configuration, and administration.

Team Foundation Server 2010 now provides a GUI-based configuration and administration console, a flexible architecture with options for choosing which components you want to use, robust validation logic prior to each configuration step, and many more fit-and-finish features, all of which will make your job as an administrator much easier than with past releases.

In this chapter, you will learn how to install and configure Team Foundation Server 2010. Along the way, you will learn more about the improvements Microsoft has made to installation and configuration in this release. Some advanced configuration areas will be reserved for later chapters, but after reading this chapter, you will be able to install and configure a simple Team Foundation Server deployment in a matter of minutes.

WHAT YOU'LL NEED

Prior to starting your installation, you should acquire the installation media for all of the components you will need. It is also a good idea to think about which updates you may need (such as service packs), and which clients and optional components you want to use with Team Foundation Server 2010. You should also download and review the latest Team Foundation Server 2010 Installation Guide.

Team Foundation Server 2010

There are several ways to obtain Team Foundation Server 2010. By far, the most common is via an MSDN subscription. When purchased with an MSDN subscription, all editions of Visual Studio 2010 include one server license and one client access license (CAL) for Team Foundation Server 2010. MSDN subscribers can log in to `http://msdn.microsoft.com/subscriptions` to download software. Team Foundation Server 2010 can be found as part of the Visual Studio 2010 category.

Another common way for organizations to obtain Team Foundation Server is via volume licensing. You may need to contact the volume licensing administrator at your organization to get access software from Microsoft's Volume Licensing Service Center (VLSC). Usually, only a handful of administrators at an organization have access to download software from the VLSC.

> *Most of the download packages available to MSDN subscribers and volume licensing customers are provided as* `.iso` *files. An* `.iso` *file is essentially a container of multiple files and directories packaged together as a single file.* `.iso` *files can be mounted as virtual CD/DVD drives, or can be burned to physical CD/DVD media. For more details on working with* `.iso` *files, see* `http://msdn .microsoft.com/en-us/subscriptions/aa948864.aspx`.

Team Foundation Server 2010 is also available via traditional retail channels. If you purchased Team Foundation Server 2010 via retail, you will receive physical DVD media in the software box.

Finally, Microsoft makes a 90-day, fully functional trial edition of Team Foundation Server 2010 available for download. Team Foundation Server 2010 trial edition can be downloaded at `www .microsoft.com/visualstudio/en-us/download`, along with other trial editions of Visual Studio 2010 (such as Visual Studio 2010 Ultimate).

USING A TRIAL EDITION

The trial edition of Team Foundation Server 2010 is a great way to evaluate the product prior to making a purchasing decision. But you should set a reminder for yourself at least 45 days before the end of the trial so that you can decide whether to make a purchasing decision, or if you decide not to purchase, whether any important data must be migrated off of your Team Foundation Server trial deployment.

Depending on the reseller you choose, and the purchasing process used by your organization, it can sometimes take a few weeks to fulfill your purchase. You don't want to find yourself locked out of your development project while you're waiting for an order to be processed.

Upgrading from a trial edition to a paid edition is a simple process outlined at `http://msdn.microsoft.com/en-us/library/ms404852.aspx`. That article also provides instructions for how to locate the product key you will need to perform the upgrade.

Team Foundation Server 2010 Installation Guide

You should download the latest version of the Team Foundation Server 2010 Installation Guide. This guidance is updated on a regular basis by Microsoft, and contains detailed system requirements, checklists, step-by-step instructions, and other important information required to install and configure Team Foundation Server 2010. This chapter provides additional context and walkthroughs to supplement the Installation Guide, but it is not a replacement for the guide itself.

You can download the Team Foundation Server 2010 Installation Guide at `http://go.microsoft .com/fwlink/?LinkId=127730`.

> *The Installation Guide is provided as a* `.chm` *file. Prior to viewing this guide, you may have to save it locally, then right-click the file, and select Unblock. Next, click OK. You can now double-click the file to open it.*

SQL Server 2008

In Chapter 2, you learned about how Team Foundation Server 2010 makes use of SQL Server 2008 to store your data. If you are using an existing deployment of SQL Server, then you won't need to download installation media. However, if you are planning to use a dedicated SQL Server deployment for your Team Foundation Server 2010 instance, you may need to obtain the appropriate SQL Server media.

SQL Server 2008 Express edition can be used with Team Foundation Server 2010. But you will not be able to take advantage of reporting capabilities with Team Foundation Server 2010 unless you use SQL Server 2008 Standard edition (or higher). If you want to use the Express edition, this will be installed for you automatically by Team Foundation Server 2010 (if it isn't already installed).

If you plan to set up a new instance of SQL Server 2008 Standard edition (or higher), you can obtain this installation media by using the same channels described earlier (MSDN, VLSC, retail, or trial). A limited-use license of SQL Server 2008 Standard edition is included with your license of Team Foundation Server 2010.

> *See the Visual Studio 2010 and MSDN Licensing whitepaper at* `http://go .microsoft.com/?linkid=9721784` *to help you understand the licensing implications for each edition of SQL Server 2008. For example, even though you can download SQL Server 2008 R2 (any edition) or SQL Server 2008 Enterprise edition via your MSDN subscription, you must license this software separately. Using it with Team Foundation Server 2010 is not included in your MSDN subscriber product use rights.*

Operating System

In Chapter 2, you learned about the operating systems supported by Team Foundation Server 2010. Installing and configuring your operating system is out of the scope of this chapter, but is an important step for you to undertake before you can set up Team Foundation Server 2010.

Note that you will need to enable Internet Information Services (IIS) before you can configure Team Foundation Server 2010. Detailed instructions for doing this depend on the operating system you are using, and can be found in the Team Foundation Server 2010 Installation Guide.

As you learned in Chapter 2, Team Foundation Server 2010 can now be installed on a client operating system (Windows Vista or Windows 7). Installing on a client operating system will provide you with most of the capabilities of Team Foundation Server 2010, including source control, work item tracking, test case management, build automation, and Lab Management. If you wish to use reporting and/or SharePoint integration, or your Team Foundation Server deployment will be used by more than a few users, then you should install Team Foundation Server 2010 on Windows Server.

SharePoint

In Chapter 2, you learned about how SharePoint can be used as a supplemental workspace for your development project. If you wish to use Windows SharePoint Services 3.0 with Team Foundation Server 2010, this can be automatically installed and configured during your Team Foundation Server 2010 configuration. If you want to use another edition of SharePoint, you should install and configure this separately. (Consult the documentation for the edition of SharePoint you choose for more information.)

Client Software

You should also consider which client software you want to use with Team Foundation Server 2010. Chapter 4 covers several types of software clients, such as Visual Studio, Eclipse, Project, and Excel. At a minimum, to complete the exercises in this chapter, you should install Team Explorer 2010.

> *Team Explorer 2010 can be downloaded at* `http://tinyurl.com/`
> `TeamExplorer2010`*. Team Explorer 2010 is also included with Visual Studio 2010 Professional, Premium, and Ultimate editions. So, if you have any of these products installed, you won't need to download and install Team Explorer separately.*

Service Packs and Other Updates

Microsoft periodically releases service packs and other updates for the Visual Studio line of products, including Team Foundation Server. Prior to making Team Foundation Server available to your development team, you may want to think about which updates you need to apply after you have installed and configured the server. By installing updates prior to bringing the server online, you can minimize potential downtime in the future when the service has active users.

There are several types of updates provided by Microsoft. The most common include the following:

➤ *Service Packs* — Service packs are by far the most well-tested and supported updates provided by Microsoft. It is highly recommended that you install service packs, because they usually fix several bugs, improve stability and performance, and occasionally add or improve features. As of this writing, Service Pack 1 is available for both Visual Studio 2010 and Team Foundation Server 2010. You can apply Service Pack 1 to Team Foundation Server 2010 without installing Service Pack 1 to your Visual Studio clients (and vice versa) if you would like to perform a staged rollout.

➤ *Hotfixes* — Hotfixes (also called QFEs, which means Quick Fix Engineering) are provided by Microsoft to address specific issues. Since hotfixes don't receive as much testing as a service pack does, they can sometimes introduce new issues. For this reason, you should only consider installing a hotfix if it addresses a specific issue you have observed in your environment. Occasionally, multiple hotfixes are packaged together for convenience, known as a *hotfix rollup*.

> *Microsoft Support can help you determine if you need a specific hotfix. Hotfixes are usually described by a Microsoft Knowledgebase (KB) article. You can search the Microsoft Knowledgebase at* http://support.microsoft.com/search/. *Some hotfixes are available for download, and others require that you contact Microsoft Support to obtain access.*

➤ *General Distribution Release* — A General Distribution Release (GDR) falls somewhere between a hotfix and a service pack. GDRs are also well-tested and supported, but generally address a narrower set of issues than a service pack does. As of this writing, there has been one significant GDR for Team Foundation Server 2010, which is related to Lab Management functionality. If you are installing Service Pack 1 of Team Foundation Server, it already contains this GDR.

➤ *Feature Packs* — Feature packs are updates that Microsoft provides, which add or enhance new features to existing products. As of this writing, one feature pack is available for Team Foundation Server 2010. The Team Foundation Server 2010 and Project Server Integration Feature Pack provide a more connected experience between software development teams and an organization's project management office.

A final update to be aware of is that Microsoft re-released Team Foundation Server 2010 in August of 2010 to address a rare (but critical) issue impacting a small number of customers who were upgrading from previous releases of Team Foundation Server. You should ensure that you are installing Team Foundation Server 2010 from media that was acquired on or after August 5, 2010. You can read more about this update at http://support.microsoft.com/kb/2135068.

Once you have the installation media, and have configured your operating system and necessary prerequisites, you can begin to install Team Foundation Server 2010.

INSTALLING TEAM FOUNDATION SERVER

Setting up Team Foundation Server 2010 can be divided into two distinct phases: installation and configuration. During the *installation phase*, you can decide which components you want to copy onto your machine. During the *configuration phase*, you decide which optional components to enable, which accounts to use for permissions, which SQL Server instance to use, and other such settings.

> *A common practice within many organizations is to make use of a tool called sysprep in order to prepare an operating system and additional installed software to be more easily deployed to multiple machines. However, not all software is compatible with the sysprepping process. One advantage of the new dual-phase setup approach employed by Team Foundation Server 2010 is that you can now install it as part of a sysprepped image. Team Foundation Server 2010 configuration can then be deferred until after you have generalized your sysprepped image onto specific machines. Sysprepping Team Foundation Server 2010 after the configuration phase is not supported.*

To begin the installation phase, insert your Team Foundation Server 2010 installation media. If you are using an .iso file, this may mean virtually mounting your .iso file as a DVD, as explained earlier.

Open the media and browse to the appropriate folder depending on your target hardware, either \TFS-x86 (32-bit) or \TFS-x64 (64-bit). Run setup.exe. After accepting the licensing terms, you will be presented with a list of components you can install, and a chance to change the installation path, as shown in Figure 3-1.

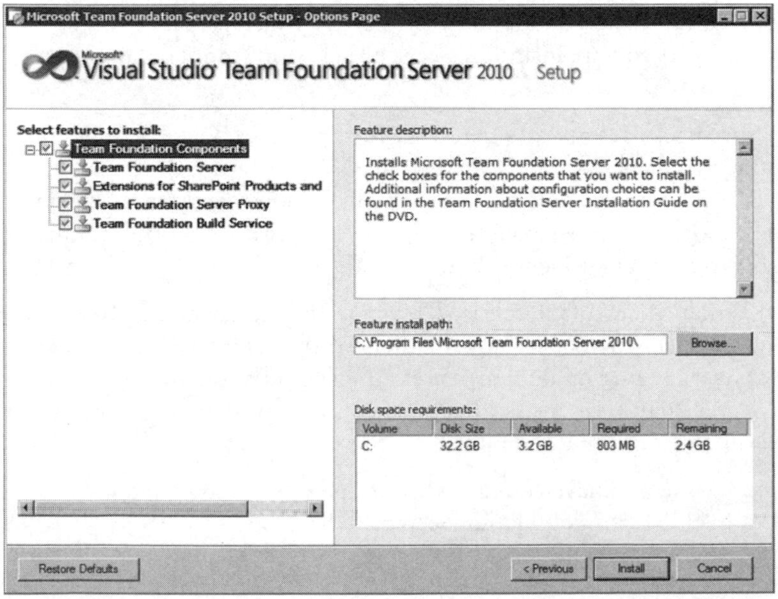

FIGURE 3-1: Installation options

The components available for installation are as follows:

➤ *Team Foundation Server* — This includes the components required to set up a new Team Foundation Server 2010 instance, or to add a new application tier to an existing Team Foundation Server 2010 instance.

➤ *Extensions for SharePoint Products and Technologies* — If you intend to use a remote SharePoint server (or farm) with Team Foundation Server 2010, you must install and configure this component on your SharePoint server (or, if using a farm, each SharePoint server within that farm). If you are using SharePoint locally (on the same machine as your Team Foundation Server 2010 instance), you do not need to install this component.

➤ *Team Foundation Server Proxy* — If you want to configure this machine as a Team Foundation Server 2010 proxy server, you should install this component.

➤ *Team Foundation Build Service* — If you want to configure this machine to host a Team Foundation Build controller and/or one or more Team Foundation Build agents, you should install this component.

If you forget to install a component, you can always re-run setup.exe to add missing components later on. There is also no harm (other than using up some disk space) in installing components here that you end up not using later on.

> *If you are installing Team Foundation Server 2010 on a client operating system (that is, Windows Vista or Windows 7), your installation options will be slightly different from those shown in Figure 3-1. The Extensions for SharePoint Products and Team Foundation Server Proxy components are not available for installation on a client operating system.*

If you don't already have the .NET Framework 4 installed, the installation process will prompt you to restart your computer. The installation process will continue automatically after your computer has restarted. After the installation phase is complete, you will have the option of starting the configuration phase by launching the Team Foundation Server Configuration Tool. If you choose not to configure Team Foundation Server now, you can always launch the Configuration Tool by clicking Start ➪ Programs ➪ Microsoft Team Foundation Server 2010 ➪ Team Foundation Administration Console. Then, click the component you want to configure (such as Application Tier or Build Configuration), and click Configure Installed Features.

Next, you will learn about the variety of installation types available to you via the Team Foundation Server Configuration Tool.

INSTALLATION TYPES

Team Foundation Server 2010 introduces several wizards for configuring your server. This provides you with a guided (yet flexible) way of picking the best configuration experience for your desired usage of Team Foundation Server. The individual wizards can be accessed along the left-hand side of the Configuration Tool, as shown in Figure 3-2.

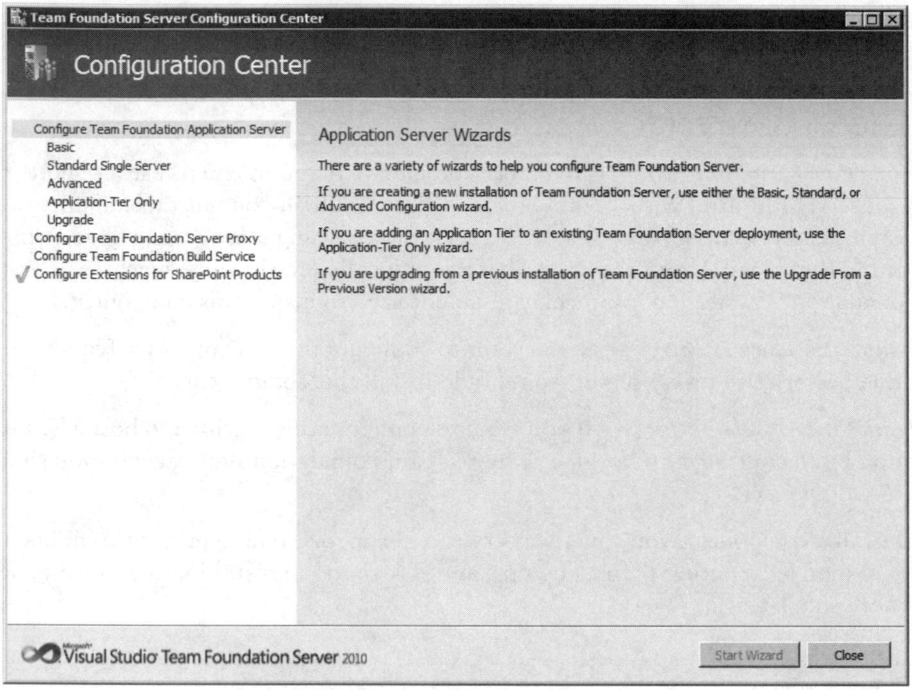

FIGURE 3-2: Team Foundation Server Configuration Tool

The exact wizards that are available to you will depend on your operating system, which components you installed during the installation phase, and which components (if any) have already been configured (as indicated by a green checkmark).

Table 3-1 describes the individual wizards.

TABLE 3-1: Available Wizards

WIZARD	DESCRIPTION
Basic	The Basic wizard is the quickest and easiest way to get up and running with Team Foundation Server for small teams. The Basic wizard enables you to use source control, work item tracking, test case management, and Lab Management. However, Reporting Services and SharePoint integration will not be available using the Basic wizard. These two components can be added later if you are installing Team Foundation Server on a Windows Server operating system. With the Basic wizard, you can utilize an existing SQL Server 2008 instance, or let Team Foundation Server install and configure SQL Server 2008 Express edition for you.

WIZARD	DESCRIPTION
Standard	The Standard wizard assumes that you are installing Team Foundation Server 2010 on a single server. The Standard wizard enables you to use source control, work item tracking, test case management, Lab Management, reporting, and SharePoint integration. You should not use this wizard if you want to install using remote SharePoint or SQL Server deployments, or if you want to use a version of SharePoint other than Windows SharePoint Services 3.0.
Advanced	The Advanced wizard provides maximum flexibility for your configuration. It also provides the same capabilities of Team Foundation Server 2010 as the Standard wizard does. But the Advanced wizard allows you to define remote systems for SharePoint, SQL Server, and SQL Server Reporting Services. This wizard also allows you to configure Kerberos authentication, to use a non-default instance of SQL Server, and to use editions of SharePoint Services other than Windows SharePoint Services 3.0. Finally, the Advanced wizard gives you the option of disabling Reporting Services and/or SharePoint integration altogether, though you can always add these components later.
Application-Tier Only	The Application-Tier Only wizard can be used to configure Team Foundation Server 2010 in a high-availability environment, as described in Chapter 18. You can employ multiple application tier nodes to provide load balancing and fault tolerance for your deployment. This wizard can also be used if you are moving your Team Foundation Server application tier from one server to another, or in a disaster-recovery scenario as described in Chapter 19.
Upgrade	The Upgrade wizard is used if you are upgrading from Team Foundation Server 2005 or Team Foundation Server 2008. Upgrading is described in Chapter 23.
Configure Team Foundation Server Proxy	This wizard can be used to configure this machine as a Team Foundation Server proxy server. More information on configuring proxy servers can be found in Chapter 24.
Configure Team Foundation Build Service	This wizard can be used if you want to configure this machine as a build controller and/or one or more build agents. Team Foundation Build is detailed in Part 4.
Configure Extensions for SharePoint Products	This wizard should be used if you are planning on configuring Team Foundation Server to integrate with SharePoint running on a remote machine, or in a remote SharePoint farm. If you are using a farm, you will need to run this wizard on every machine in that farm.

The rest of this chapter uses the Basic wizard as an example. If you are new to Team Foundation Server 2010, you may want to consider using the Basic wizard to set up your first Team Foundation Server 2010 deployment on a testing server. When you are ready to configure your actual Team Foundation Server deployment, you should spend some time reading the Team Foundation Server 2010 Installation Guide and Part V of this book to familiarize yourself with the various configuration types that are available, and map these to the needs of your development team.

For example, if you have a very large team, you may want to consider configuring Team Foundation Server in a dual-tier environment. If you have a geographically distributed team, you may want to set up Team Foundation Server proxy instances at remote sites. You may want to configure a dedicated build farm with multiple machines running build agents, and so on.

Next you will begin a simple configuration using the Basic wizard.

CONFIGURING TEAM FOUNDATION SERVER

From the Team Foundation Configuration Tool, select the Basic wizard and click Start Wizard. Click Next to advance past the Welcome page. You will be prompted to indicate which instance of SQL Server you want to use, as shown in Figure 3-3.

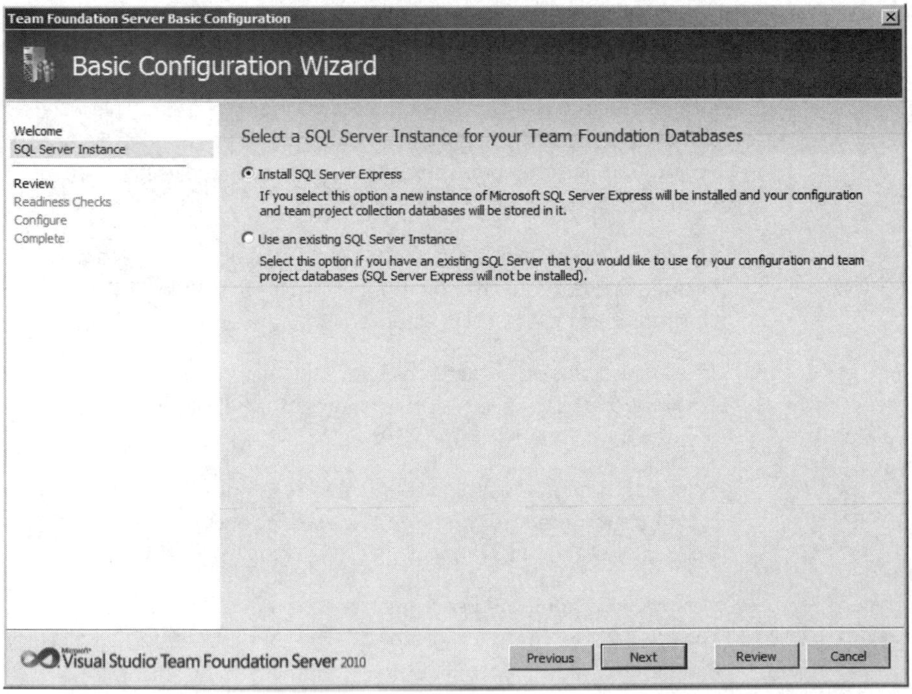

FIGURE 3-3: SQL Server instance selection page

You can choose an existing instance of SQL Server, or let the Basic wizard install and configure SQL Server 2008 Express edition for you.

> *Letting Team Foundation Server install and configure SQL Server 2008 Express edition is a quick way to get up and running, and should work well for a test server. But for a production server, you should consider taking the time to install and configure SQL Server 2008 Standard edition (or higher). This will make it easier to take advantage of capabilities like Reporting Services later on, and will avoid the 4GB database size limitation imposed by SQL Server 2008 Express edition. The Team Foundation Server 2010 Installation Guide includes step-by-step instructions for installing SQL Server 2008 Standard edition for use with Team Foundation Server 2010.*

After selecting your SQL Server instance, click Next. You will be shown a list of the configuration settings you chose, such as those shown in Figure 3-4, and will be given a chance to go back and make changes. The Basic wizard only has a few pages, but other wizards have more.

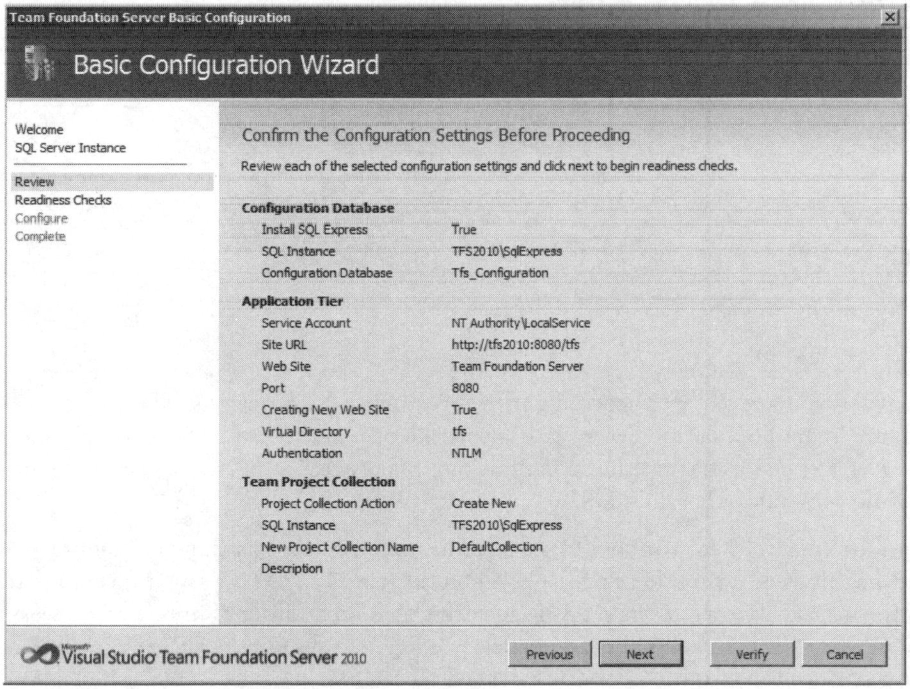

FIGURE 3-4: Configuration settings confirmation page

When you are satisfied with your options, click Next. (Clicking Verify will also have the same effect.) The wizard will attempt to verify that the changes you are proposing will be successful if you proceed.

It is worth noting that no changes are being made to your server at this time. This process can be valuable in helping you discover that you may be missing a prerequisite, or it can warn you that certain configuration changes are going to be made for you.

When this step has finished, you will see a screen similar to Figure 3-5. If there are potential problems with your configuration, you will be shown any errors or warnings, usually with information on how to address them.

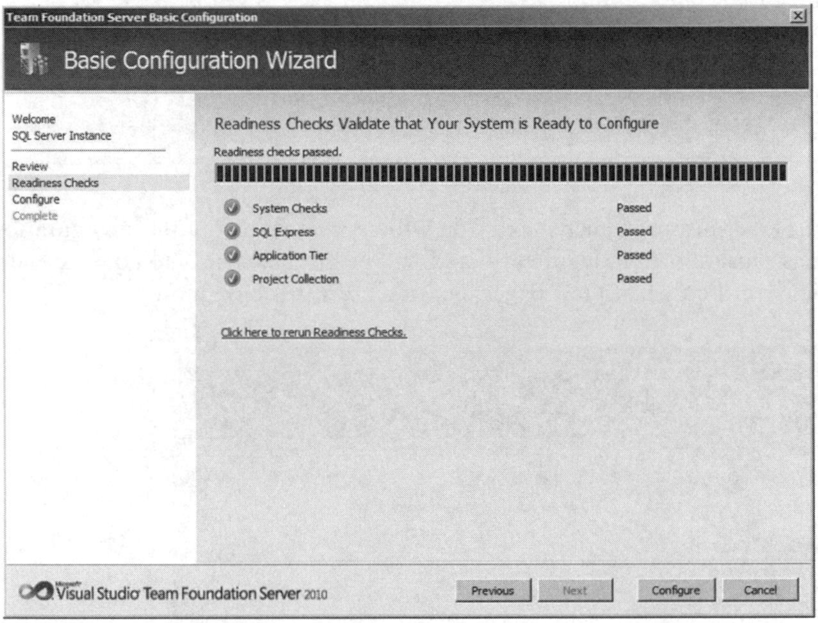

FIGURE 3-5: Readiness Checks page

Click Configure when you are ready to proceed with your configuration options. The wizard will attempt to configure Team Foundation Server 2010 using the options you selected. If you opted to install SQL Server Express as part of the configuration, this process may take several minutes. Otherwise, it should only take a few minutes.

When the configuration is finished, you should see a confirmation screen, as shown in Figure 3-6. Take note of any warnings or errors that are displayed on this page, as well as any informational notices (such as the message shown in Figure 3-6 indicating that an additional firewall port was opened during configuration). You can also access detailed log information by clicking the link at the bottom of this page of the wizard. Click Close when you are finished.

At the conclusion of this step, you will have successfully configured an instance of Team Foundation Server 2010 on your machine. This instance is now running as a service, and you can begin to interact with it, or further configure it. You can even launch subsequent wizards from the Team Foundation Configuration Tool, such as to configure a build controller and agent.

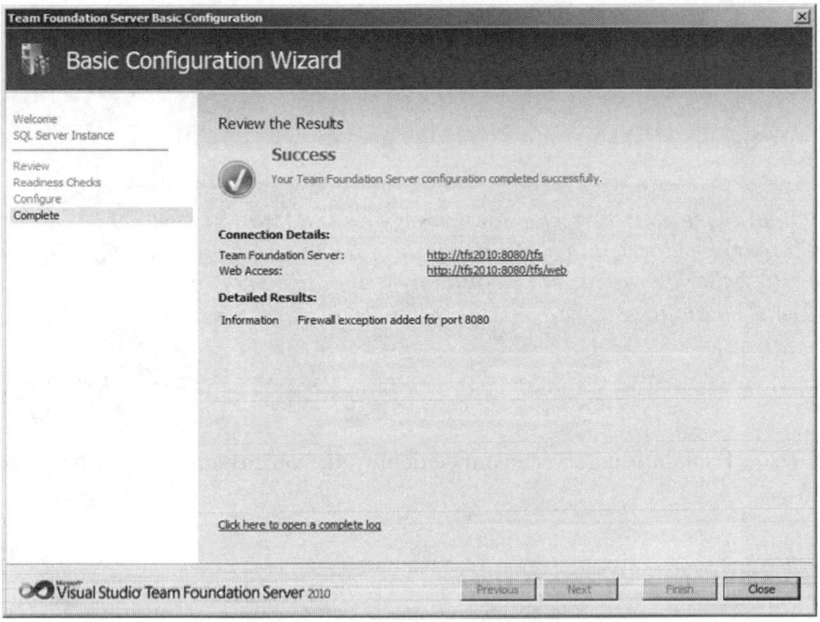

FIGURE 3-6: Configuration results page

The Team Foundation Server Administration Console (shown in Figure 3-7) can now be used to monitor your server, to stop or start services, and to make additional configuration changes. Some common configuration changes include configuring a Simple Mail Transfer Protocol (SMTP) server (for e-mail alerts), enabling Kerberos authentication, assigning friendly names to the URLs used by clients to connect to Team Foundation Server, or adding a System Center Virtual Machine Manager (SCVMM) server to provide functionality for Lab Management.

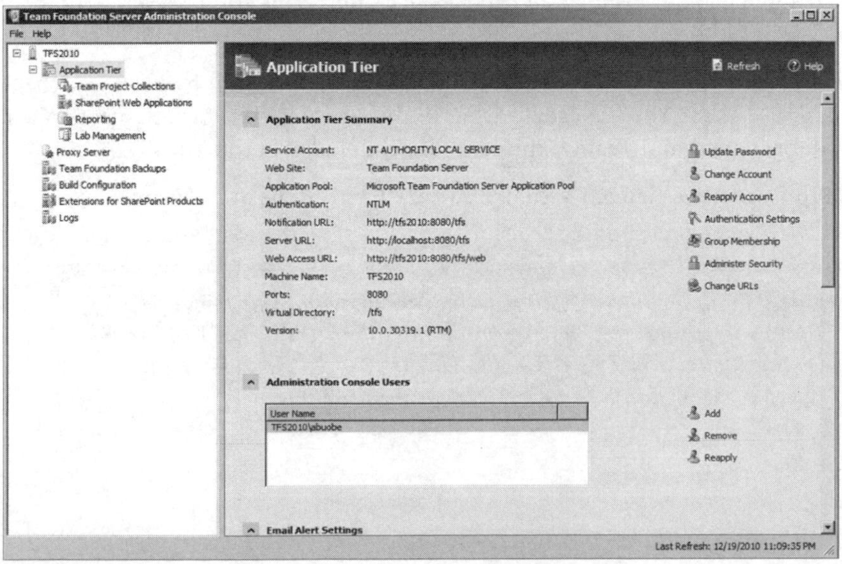

FIGURE 3-7: Team Foundation Server Administration Console

You may also want to add components that you skipped during the initial configuration, such as Reporting Services or SharePoint integration. The MSDN Library provides detailed instructions on how to perform all of these tasks, and more, at `http://msdn.microsoft.com/en-us/library/dd273719.aspx`.

> *In some cases, you may see an incorrect error message on the Lab Management tab, indicating that you need to contact Microsoft in order to purchase Lab Management functionality before it can be configured. If you see this message, you can install Team Foundation Server 2010 Service Pack 1 and the error message will disappear.*

Now that you have your Team Foundation Server instance deployed, you can create your first team project.

CREATING YOUR FIRST TEAM PROJECT

A *team project* is the basic container of work that is used by Team Foundation Server 2010. You will learn much more about team projects throughout the rest of this book. For now, you just need to know that you'll need to create a team project before you can store any source control, work items, or other artifacts in Team Foundation Server.

To create a team project with Team Foundation Server 2010, you must use Team Explorer 2010. Team Explorer 2010 is an add-on for Visual Studio 2010 that allows you to work with source control, work items, build definitions, and more, without ever leaving Visual Studio. Team Explorer also installs the necessary add-ins to work with Team Foundation Server 2010 from within Excel and Project. You will learn much about clients that can access Team Foundation Server 2010 in Chapter 4.

If you don't already have Team Explorer 2010 installed, you can either install it by itself (see the download link in the section, "What You'll Need," earlier in this chapter), or you can install Visual Studio 2010 Professional (or higher) and Team Explorer will be included automatically.

After Team Explorer 2010 is installed, launch Visual Studio 2010 from the Start menu.

> *Even if you installed Team Explorer 2010 standalone, instead of as part of Visual Studio 2010 Professional (or higher), you will still access Team Explorer 2010 from within the Visual Studio 2010 shell. This is why you access Team Explorer 2010 by opening Visual Studio 2010 from the Start menu.*

If the Team Explorer window is not already visible within Visual Studio, you can enable it by clicking View ⇨ Team Explorer. Team Explorer is shown in Figure 3-8.

If you installed Team Explorer on the same machine as your Team Foundation Server 2010 deployment, your server name may already be populated for you (indicated by *localhost* as shown in Figure 3-8).

If you installed Team Explorer on a different machine, you should add your Team Foundation Server host manually by clicking the Connect to Team Project button (the rightmost button near the top of the Team Explorer window). From the Connect to Team Project dialog, click Servers to add a new server. Click Add and supply the address of your Team Foundation Server. You can find this in the Team Foundation Server Administration Console under Application Tier ⇨ Server URL (such as `http://tfs2010:8080/tfs`).

After you have added your server, click OK, then Close, then select the server you want to connect to in the drop-down box for "Select a Team Foundation Server." If you used the Basic configuration, you will have a single team project collection called `DefaultCollection`. Select this collection and click Connect.

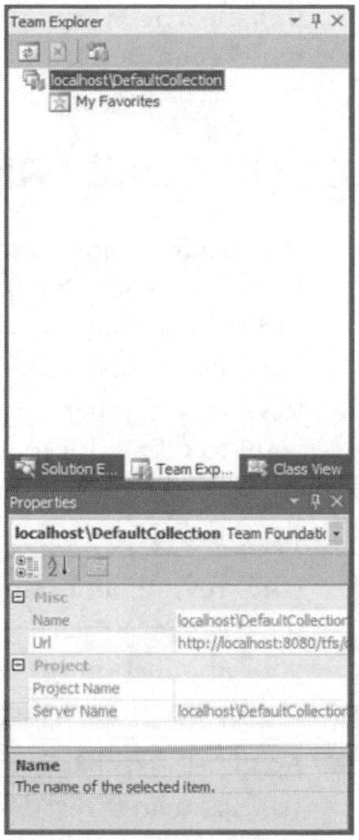

FIGURE 3-8: Team Explorer 2010

A team project collection provides a way of grouping together one or more team projects. You will learn more about team project collections later in this book.

Click File ⇨ New ⇨ Team Project to launch the New Team Project wizard shown in Figure 3-9. Provide a name for your team project and, optionally, a description. Click Next when finished.

You will then be prompted to select the process template that you want to use for this new team project, and afterward, you will be asked how you want to configure source control for your project. For now, you can accept the default options and click Finish. The wizard will spend a few minutes creating your team project.

When you are finished, the Team Explorer window will display your team project as shown

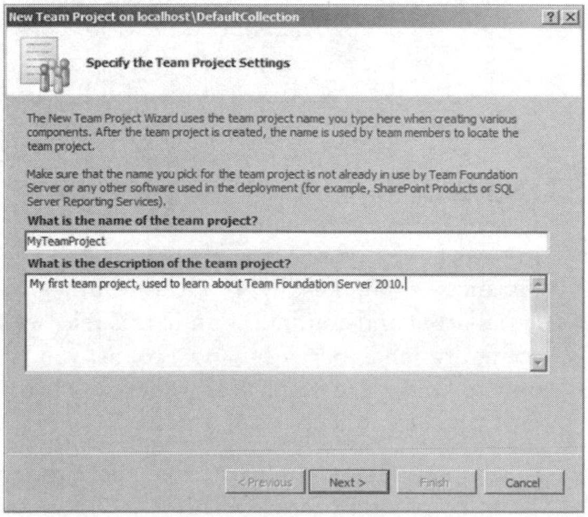

FIGURE 3-9: New Team Project wizard

in Figure 3-10. You can now begin creating work items, source control, build definitions, and so on, for this team project.

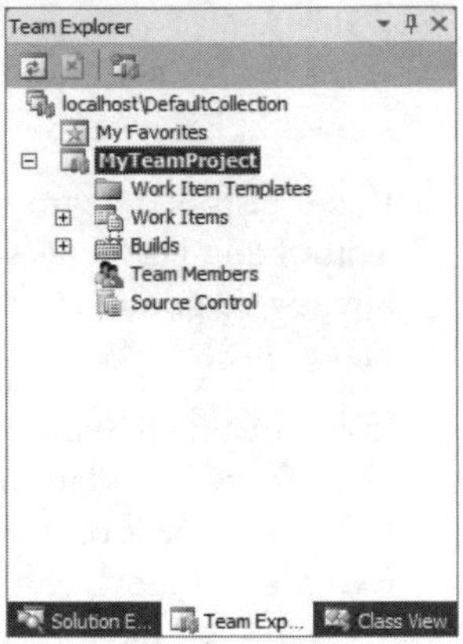

CONFIGURE FRIENDLY DNS NAMES

If you have followed the previous steps, then you now have a Team Foundation Server deployment that you can share with your team. You can start adding users to security groups (as explained in Chapter 20), and these users can begin connecting to your server. However, as mentioned in Chapter 2, there's one additional configuration step that you may want to take prior to advertising the address of your server, and that is to consider assigning friendly DNS names to the endpoints.

Friendly DNS names allow you to assign easy-to-remember names to your Team Foundation Server endpoints, which redirect (behind the scenes) to your actual server. You can assign friendly DNS names to your application tier (for example, `tfs.contoso.com`), your data tier (for example, `data.contoso.com`), and other components such as your Analysis Services instance or proxy servers.

FIGURE 3-10: New team project

In addition to being easier to remember for your users, these friendly DNS names can also protect you as an administrator as well. For example, if you need to move your Team Foundation Server instance from one machine to another (such as during a backup/restore, or migration to new hardware), you can simply redirect the friendly DNS names instead of needing to advertise new server names to the clients who connect to your Team Foundation Server instance.

You can perform this step at any time in the future, but doing so now (before your server is being used) will avoid the effort required to switch clients to the new names.

> *Ed Blankenship authored a detailed blog post that describes how to use friendly DNS names with Team Foundation Server 2010. See* `http://tinyurl.com/FriendlyDNSforTFS`.

SUMMARY

In this chapter, you learned how to install and configure a simple Team Foundation Server 2010 instance. Along the way, you learned about the various improvements Microsoft has made to installation and configuration in this release, such as a more flexible architecture, a graphical configuration experience, and a robust validation and error reporting system. You also learned how to create a team project, which will become the basic container of work for your software development project.

In Chapter 4, you will learn more about the various client applications you can use to work with Team Foundation Server 2010.

4

Connecting to Team Foundation Server

WHAT'S IN THIS CHAPTER?

➤ Understanding the basic Team Foundation Server architecture

➤ Understanding Team Foundation Server URLs

➤ Getting to know Team Foundation Server roles and security

➤ Connecting to Team Foundation Server from various development tools

➤ Understanding Team Explorer concepts, tools, and windows

At this point, you should now have a working Team Foundation Server project collection to work with — either one that you have installed yourself using the instructions in Chapter 3, or one that has been provided for you. This chapter teaches you how to connect to an instance from the various products that can talk to Team Foundation Server, and you also learn about some common troubleshooting techniques if you are unable to connect.

But first, some more information on the Team Foundation Server architecture would be useful.

TEAM FOUNDATION SERVER ARCHITECTURE

Figure 4-1 shows the major logical servers available in a Team Foundation Server installation. The main Team Foundation Server application is hosted on the application tier. The initial contact from the client machine on your desktop is made to this Application Tier (AT) machine. From this, the client machine obtains all the other connection information to allow it to talk to the other components involved in a typical Team Foundation Server installation (the SharePoint portal, Analysis Services for reports, and so on).

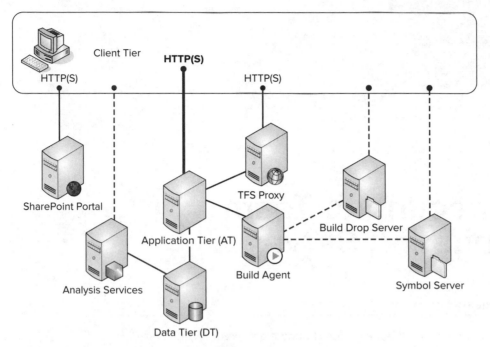

FIGURE 4-1: Logical architecture of a Team Foundation Server installation

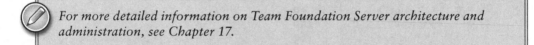

For more detailed information on Team Foundation Server architecture and administration, see Chapter 17.

Communication between the client and the application tier is performed using the Team Foundation Server Web Service Protocol. This is made up of a set of web services to which the client connects using the HTTP or HTTPS protocol, depending on how the application tier was configured. Authentication of the client connection is performed using either Windows Integrated Authentication (also known as NTLM), Kerberos, or, if over an SSL/TLS encrypted connection then Basic Authentication may be used.

Windows Integrated Authentication is the typical form of authentication, unless the server has been explicitly configured otherwise. On a Windows-based client machine, the client's default credentials for that server are used — usually the same credentials that were used to log in to the Windows machine in a domain environment. This provides for a seamless, single sign-on (SSO) capability.

You use the same credentials to talk to Team Foundation Server that you use to log in to your Windows workstation, and all the actions you perform against Team Foundation Server are audited against these credentials. On non-Windows machines, the credentials (that is, domain, username, and password) can be provided to allow authentication, or Kerberos can be configured if you require SSO infrastructure in your heterogeneous environments.

The majority of client/server communication in a Team Foundation Server instance is over HTTP or HTTPS. This is true for all the version control, work item tracking, SharePoint, and Reporting Services data. The exceptions to this are for connecting directly to the data warehouse running in Analysis Services from an analytics client (such as Microsoft Excel), or when communicating with the build drop location or Symbol server.

> *See Chapter 15 for more information on builds and Symbol servers.*

In addition to the application tier machine address, clients may also need to be configured with the address of a Team Foundation Server Proxy if used for remote development.

A Team Foundation Server Proxy provides a way to cache requests for files from version control. If two developers in a remote site request the same version of the same file, then the proxy server allows for the second developer to be served the file from the local proxy, rather than having to download the files over the wide area network (WAN) a second time.

> *For more information on the Team Foundation Server Proxy and working with geographically distributed teams, see Chapter 24.*

ADDRESSING TEAM FOUNDATION SERVER

A Team Foundation Server instance is referred to by the URL at which the actual application hosting Team Foundation Server is located. Figure 4-2 shows the basic makeup when connecting to Team Foundation Server.

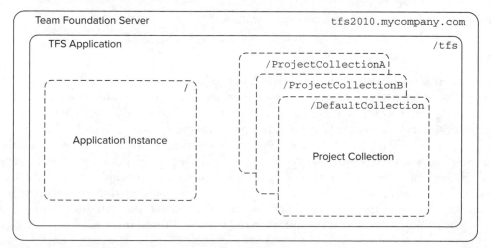

FIGURE 4-2: Team Foundation Server URL scheme

The URL is in the following format:

```
<protocol>://<serverName>:<port>/<virtualDirectory>/<collectionName>
```

Following is an explanation of the individual parts of the URL:

➤ `protocol` — This is the means used to connect to Team Foundation Server (that is, HTTP or HTTPS).

➤ `serverName` — This is the Domain Name Server (DNS) name pointing to your Team Foundation Server application tier instance (or the network load balancer in front of it, if you are using a high-availability architecture). Note that the DNS name can be a friendly name that has been created in your organization to help locate the server. It doesn't have to be the actual machine name of your application tier. Also, if you ever plan on accessing the connection from outside of your company network (that is, over the Internet), ensure that you use the fully qualified domain name such as `tfs2010.mycompany.com`.

➤ `port` — This is the port used to connect to the application tier. In a default installation, this is port 8080. The port can be omitted if it is the standard port for the protocol (that is, port 80 for HTTP or port 443 for HTTPS).

➤ `virtualDirectory` — This is the path in which the Team Foundation Server application was installed. By default, this is `tfs`. The `virtualDirectory` is new in Team Foundation Server 2010. In previous versions, the application was always installed at the root of the website that was hosting the application. However, in the 2010 release, this was moved down into the `tfs` folder to make it easier to host Team Foundation Server on the same default website as other applications on the server (such as SharePoint and the Reporting Services sites). This makes it significantly easier to have Team Foundation Server running on the standard port 80 or port 443, which, in turn, makes it much easier to make accessible over the Internet.

See Chapter 3 for more information on installation.

➤ `collectionName` — This is the name of the project collection to which you are connecting. By default, Team Foundation Server has at least one project collection created — usually called `DefaultCollection`. However, as discussed in Chapter 3 and covered in depth in Chapter 17, multiple project collections can be created. In a graphical client such as Visual Studio or Eclipse, providing the URL of the Team Foundation Server instance is sufficient, and the user interface will then present the available project collections on that instance that are available for you to connect to. However, for many command-line tools, the full URL to your project collection is required. If the `collectionName` is missing, the server will assume that the collection marked as default is the desired one and will direct requests to it. If no collection is marked as default, then the URL will result in an error.

Following are some example URLs to connect to Team Foundation Server:

- ➤ `http://tfs2010:8080/tfs`

- ➤ `http://tfs2010:8080/tfs/DefaultCollection`

- ➤ `http://tfs2010:8080/tfs/AdventureWorks`

- ➤ `https://tfs.codeplex.com/tfs/TFS01`

- ➤ `https://mywhs.homeserver.com/tfs`

- ➤ `https://tfs.mycompany.com/tfs`

Note that none of these URLs are valid directly in a web browser. They are used as the root of the URL that the Team Foundation Server client uses to locate and communicate with the web services of that server instance. However, after the `virtualDirectory` part of the URL, if the special name of `web` is used, this will redirect you to a web-based client for Team Foundation Server called Team Web Access (for example `http://tfs2010:8080/tfs/web`, or `https://tfs.codeplex.com/tfs/web/`).

> *See the section, "Accessing Team Foundation Server Through a Web Browser," later in this chapter for more information on Team Web Access.*

INTRODUCING TEAM FOUNDATION SERVER SECURITY AND ROLES

The significant functionality that Team Foundation Server has in relation to security, groups, and permissions can be very daunting at first. However, at its core, there are a few simple concepts to initially be aware of with Team Foundation Server security:

- ➤ Users
- ➤ Groups
- ➤ Permissions

> *For detailed information about Team Foundation Server security, see Chapter 20.*

Users

Team Foundation Server makes use of Windows users. There is no separate concept of a Team Foundation Server user — just a Windows user who has permission to use Team Foundation Server resources. If Team Foundation Server is in an Active Directory environment (the preferred configuration), domain users can be granted permission to use Team Foundation Server. Local users may also be used (that is, users defined locally to that machine in what is considered as "Workgroup mode").

When you install Team Foundation Server, the user who installs and configures the product is required to have administrative permissions on the server. By default, that user is also granted the permissions of a Team Foundation Server administrator within the product.

The user details (that is, username, display name, e-mail address, and so on) are all taken from the Windows user details. Authentication of the users is performed using Windows authentication. This means that there is no separate infrastructure required to create or administer users specifically for Team Foundation Server. Existing user creation systems inside the company can be used, along with handling of password policies, password resets, and so on.

Groups

In Team Foundation Server, there are two types of groups that you must be concerned with:

➤ Windows security groups (that is, domain, distribution, or local groups)

➤ Team Foundation Server groups

As you will learn in Chapter 20, the Windows security groups are basically a collection of users maintained by the Windows security systems. For example, to complete the installation of Team Foundation Server as described in Chapter 3, the user must be in the local Administrators group on the server.

Team Foundation Server has its own group structure maintained in the server. Within the system, there are three levels of groups:

➤ Server groups

➤ Team project collection groups

➤ Team project groups

Server groups impact the Team Foundation Server instance, and are one of the few things in Team Foundation Server that cross the boundary between project collections. The default groups (detailed in Chapter 20) have hard-coded names that cannot be changed or removed from the server (for example, Team Foundation Administrators or Team Foundation Valid Users).

When a user is a member of the server group, the user has permissions at the Team Foundation instance level. For example, users in the Team Foundation Administrators group can create new project collections. Users in the Team Foundation Valid Users group can connect to the Team Foundation Server instance and view which project collections are available (but they might not have permission to actually connect to a particular project collection). Modifications of the server groups must be performed using the Team Foundation Server Administration Console, as introduced in Chapter 3.

Team project collection groups are created as part of the collection creation process. The default groups and their members are detailed in Chapter 20. However, they control who is an administrator for the project collection, who can connect and use it, and so on.

Finally, *team project groups* control who can do what inside a particular team project. The main groups are as follows:

➤ *Administrators* — Members can perform all operations in the team project, including assignment of security permissions to other users.

➤ *Contributors* — Members can add, modify, and delete items within the team project. You typically want your main development group for a team project to be a contributor.

➤ *Readers* — Members have read-only access to data in the team project.

A Team Foundation Server group membership is made up of Windows users and groups, or other Team Foundation Server groups. At each level, custom groups can be created and allocated certain permissions.

Permissions

Each user or group in Team Foundation Server can be allocated one or more of more than 80 separate permissions available on the server controlling each aspect of the product. Each permission has an explicit Allow or Deny state.

Typically, when getting started with Team Foundation Server, you should stick with controlling access to the server by simply placing a user in one of the team project groups. Members of those groups then inherit a default set of permissions from, and get assigned into, other groups (such as the Team Foundation Valid Users group), allowing them to connect to the Team Foundation Server instance.

> *For more information about fine-grained control of users' permissions over the default Team Project Administrator, Contributor, or Reader, see Chapter 20.*

TEAM EXPLORER

Visual Studio Team Explorer is the client interface to Team Foundation Server. It provides the functionality necessary to be able to connect to and work with the Team Foundation Server. In Visual Studio 2010, all versions (apart from the free Express editions) now include the Team Explorer client as part of the default installation. However, in the previous version of Visual Studio, it required a separate installation. Team Explorer Everywhere is also available to provide the client-side interface in the Eclipse IDE and cross-platform (that is, on Mac, UNIX, or Linux machines).

Visual Studio Team Explorer is also available as a separate installation on the Team Foundation Server installation media, on the Team Explorer Everywhere media, or as a separate download. If installed on a machine without Visual Studio 2010 installed, it will install a cut-down version of Visual Studio 2010, and, inside that, provide all the rich client-side functionality to work with Team Foundation Server.

Use of Team Explorer is covered by the Client Access License (CAL) required for a specific user to connect to Team Foundation Server, regardless of the number of machines from which the user connects. The use of Team Explorer Everywhere requires an additional purchase of the client software for each user on top of the Team Foundation Server CAL.

Understanding Team Explorer in Visual Studio 2010

By now, you should have provisioned a Team Foundation Server instance with a project collection and team project created, either by installing one yourself (following the instructions in Chapter 3), by downloading a trial virtual machine (VM) from Microsoft, or by leasing a hosted Team Foundation Server solution from a hosting provider. You must now connect to your Team Foundation Server instance from the machine that you want to use for development.

Connecting to Team Foundation Server 2010 from Visual Studio 2010

The most common initial route is attempting to connect to Team Foundation Server 2010 from Visual Studio 2010. Luckily, there are many ways to get connected.

You can click Team ⇨ Connect to Team Foundation Server, or, from the Start page in Visual Studio 2010, click the Connect to Team Foundation Server link in the top left-hand side. An alternate way from Team Explorer is to click View ⇨ Team Explorer, and click the button with a plus sign on it.

Whatever way you use to connect, you are then presented with a rather dauntingly empty Connect to Team Project dialog, as shown in Figure 4-3.

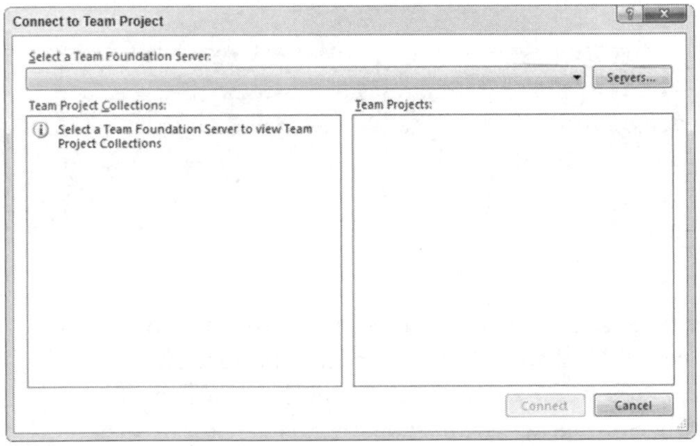

FIGURE 4-3: Connect to Team Project dialog

Normally, at this point, the drop-down to select a Team Foundation Server will also be empty. To add your server to the list, click the Servers button. This presents yet another empty dialog — the Add/Remove Team Foundation Server dialog. Click the Add button.

Finally, you can enter the details of the Team Foundation Server instance to which you wish to connect. Enter the name of your Team Foundation Server instance (that is, `tfs2010` or `tfs .mycompany.com`). At the bottom of the dialog shown in Figure 4-4, you will be given a preview of the URL that will be used to connect to the Team Foundation Server.

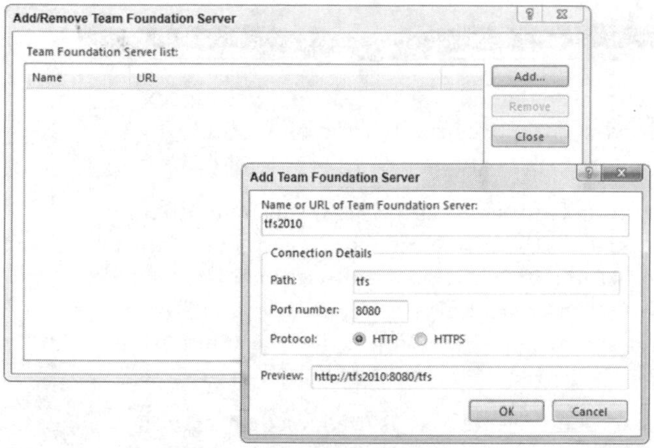

FIGURE 4-4: Add Team Foundation Server dialog

For a default install of Team Foundation Server, this URL will be correct, as long as you have typed in the correct name for the server. However, if the URL is not correct (for example, you need to use HTTPS instead of HTTP, or perhaps you need to connect on a different port), you must alter the settings accordingly. Alternatively, if you have the URL that you should use to connect to your server, simply type it into the Name box at the top of the dialog, and all the appropriate settings will be picked up.

Click OK to add the server to the list, and then click Close to get back to the Connect to Team Project dialog. The dialog should now be populated and a bit more welcoming. The example shown in Figure 4-5 is a more typical view of the dialog once a few team projects and an additional team project collection have been created.

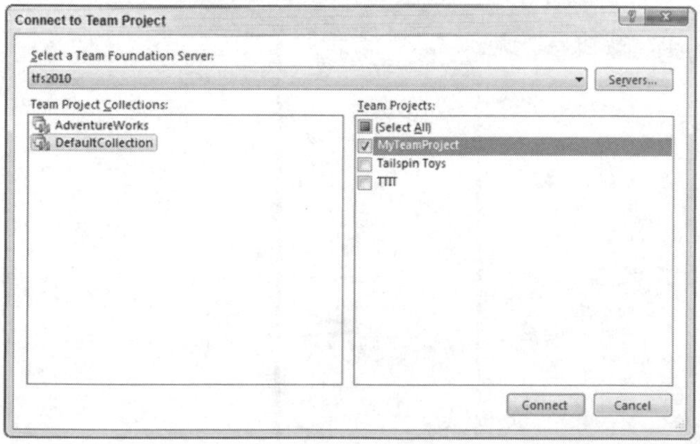

FIGURE 4-5: Populated version of Connect to Team Project dialog

Selecting a project collection on the left-hand side of the Connect to Team Project dialog shown in Figure 4-5 gets Visual Studio to request the team projects available on that project collection. If you check the team project (or projects) checkbox and then click Connect, you control which team projects are displayed in Team Explorer. Note that, while you are selecting the team projects at this point, it is actually the project collection that you are connecting to.

STORING YOUR TEAM FOUNDATION SERVER PASSWORD ON WINDOWS

On Windows-based systems, the default credentials for that site are used when connecting to Team Foundation Server. These are usually your Windows login credentials, which provide for a seamless SSO experience inside a domain.

However, sometimes you must log in to Team Foundation Server using a different set of credentials. This is especially true in the case where your Team Foundation Sever is being hosted over the Internet in a different domain from the one you are logged in to. In the case where the default credentials are not appropriate, Team Explorer will prompt you for your username and password using the standard Windows authentication prompt.

You can also store these credentials so that they are always used for that server by Windows. On Windows 7, click Start, then type `Credential Manager`. On Windows Vista, click Control Panel ⇨ User Accounts ⇨ Manage Your Network Password. On Windows XP, go to Start ⇨ Control Panel ⇨ User Accounts ⇨ Manage Passwords. Once there, add the Team Foundation Server instance that contains your project with the domain, username, and password that you should use.

Team Explorer

Once connected, you should now see Team Explorer inside Visual Studio 2010, as shown in Figure 4-6. If you do not see Team Explorer, go to View ⇨ Team Explorer.

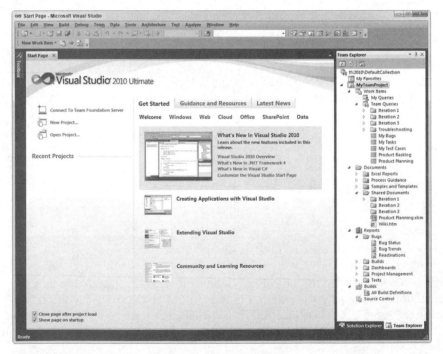

FIGURE 4-6: Team Explorer inside Visual Studio 2010

The Team Explorer View has three buttons along the top (discussed here as shown in Figure 4-6 from left to right):

➤ *Refresh* — Clicking this button re-requests the data in the Team Explorer view from Team Foundation Server. The data can take a while to populate.

➤ *Stop Refresh* — During the population of data during a refresh, the Stop Refresh button is enabled to allow you to cancel that action.

➤ *Connect to Team Project* — This button is used to get back to the dialog shown in Figure 4-5, as well as to adjust which team projects are visible in Team Explorer, or to connect to a different server.

At the root of the Team Explorer View, you see the project collection to which you are connected. You can only be connected to one project collection at a time from Visual Studio, and you must use the Connect to Team Project dialog to swap connections.

Directly underneath the project collection is the My Favorites node. Other items and folders in the Team Explorer tree may be added to the My Favorites node and used as a quick way of storing shortcuts to common areas that are deep down in the tree. The favorites are stored on the individual client machine, and are not stored or synchronized with the server or other team members.

After My Favorites is a node for each of your team projects that you have selected that you wish to see. You can expand the team project to see the various Team Explorer contributions for that project.

A typical project has five nodes under each Team Project:

➤ Work Items

➤ Documents

➤ Reports

➤ Builds

➤ Source Control

However, some nodes such as Documents or Reports may not appear if those items have not been configured for the team project. Also, some extensions such as the Team Foundation Server Power Tools add additional child nodes to the team project in Team Explorer if the tools are installed on the client machine (such as Work Item Templates and Team Members).

> *The Team Foundation Server Power Tools are a set of enhancements, tools, and command-line utilities that can be installed in addition to Team Explorer. They provide a great deal of additional functionality, and are frequently updated. Many of the individual power tools are called out in other chapters of this book, but for the current list of the latest power tools, see* http://msdn.microsoft .com/en-us/vstudio/bb980963.aspx.

Work Items

The `Work Items` node in Team Explorer has two child nodes, `Team Queries` (stored work item queries that are visible to people in the team project) and `My Queries` (queries that are only visible to the user). Under those nodes are a set of folders containing various work item queries. The actual queries and work item types available will differ depending on the process template selected during team project creation.

> *For more information on work items, see Part III of this book.*

To create a work item, right-click the `Work Items` node and select the work item type (that is, a Bug, Issue, Task, User Story, and so on). Alternatively, you could go to Team ➪ New Work Item and select the work item type (for example, Bug). This will then display a New Bug in the work item editor, as shown in Figure 4-7. Fill out the mandatory fields, and set the Assigned To user to be yourself.

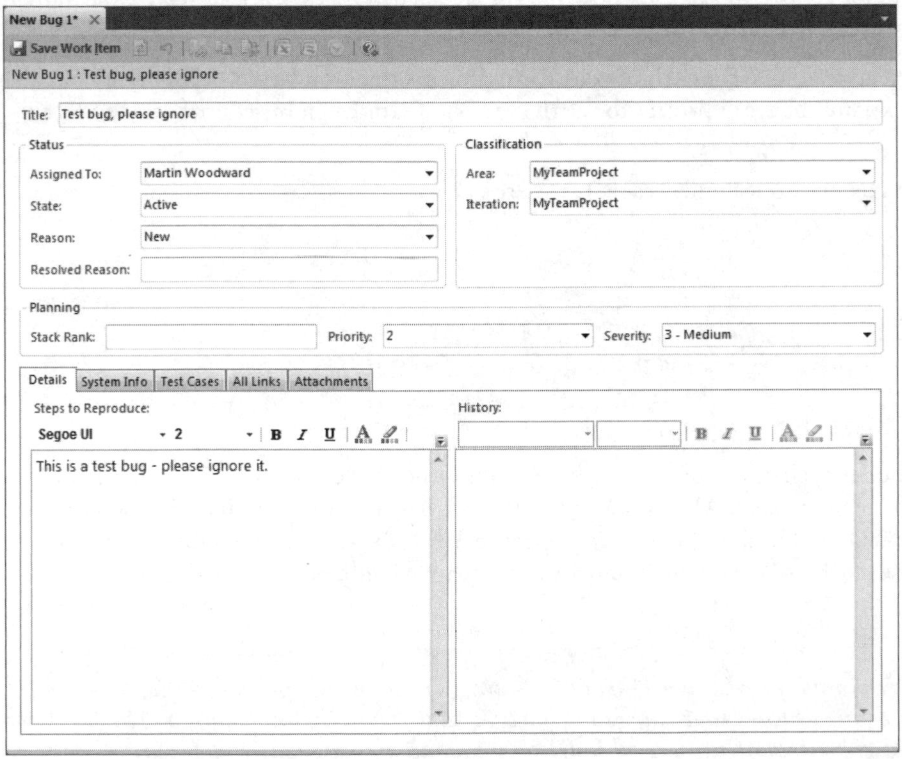

FIGURE 4-7: New Bug in the work item editor

Save the work item by clicking File ➪ Save, by pressing *Ctrl+S*, or by clicking the usual Save button in Visual Studio. Your work item will now be updated and have a work item number. Also, the history field will populate, showing you the changes that have occurred during the life of the work item.

Now that you have a work item, you can run a query to find it. A *query* is simply a set of search criteria coded into a SQL-like querying language called Work Item Query Language (WIQL, often pronounced "wickle"). Double-click a query in Team Explorer under the `Work Items` node to run it, or right-click the query to edit it or perform other actions. When you run a query, the results are displayed in the query results list, as shown in Figure 4-8.

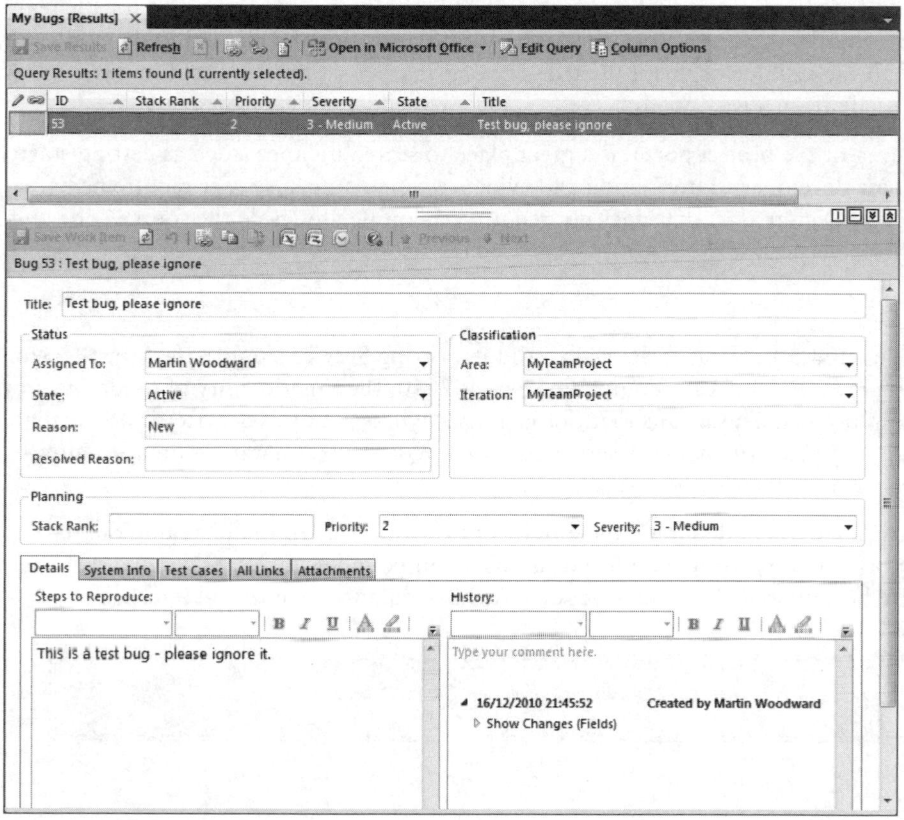

FIGURE 4-8: Query results list

The query results are displayed in a tabular form at the top of the results, and the details of the selected work item are displayed below. Note that you can edit several work items in this view, and they will be highlighted in bold in the query results list.

Clicking Save All will save all the edits made to all work items in a single transaction. This view is sometimes referred to as the "triage view," because it allows you to quickly view many work items, and, at the same time, make many edits. Double-clicking a work item in the table of results will open the work item in a work item editor by itself.

As mentioned, the actual data that is displayed for a work item, its states and transition, and even the types of work items in the system are all completely customizable with Team Foundation Server.

> *For more information about working with work items, see Part III of this book.*

Documents

The Documents node will only appear if you have a valid SharePoint portal specified for the team project. In Team Foundation Server 2010, the project portal is optional. Expanding the node will give you a list of all the visible document libraries in your SharePoint portal, and allow you to view the file contents easily from Visual Studio.

The Documents area of the project portal is a great place to store guidance (such as getting started information for new developers, information and evidence supporting customer requirements, and so on), or any project artifact that does not require versioning alongside the source code and deliverables of the project.

Reports

The Reports node will only appear if there is a valid Reporting Service site specified for the team project. As with Documents, in Team Foundation Server 2010, the functionality of reports is now optional for a team project. This means that, for instances where Analysis Services is not available (such as when running Team Foundation Server against a SQL Express database on a Windows 7 laptop), the Reports node will not be displayed.

If present, then the Reports node shows a hierarchy of the available reports in Team Foundation Server. These reports are displaying data live from the Team Foundation Server data warehouse. However, they are best viewed once you have some real live data to analyze and interpret.

> *Reporting is covered in more detail in Chapter 13.*

Builds

The Builds node displays any build definitions created for the team project. As of Team Foundation Server 2010 Service Pack 1, it is the only node in Team Explorer with children that is not capable of organizing those children into a hierarchy of folders — they are simply displayed in a flat alphabetical list. A *build definition* is a description of an automated build that is performed using Team Foundation Server.

> *Build automation capabilities are described in detail in Part IV of this book.*

Source Control

Last but not least, you have the Source Control node, which is home to version control or source code management. Double-clicking the Source Control node displays the Source Control Explorer with a folder containing the data for that team project highlighted, as shown in Figure 4-9.

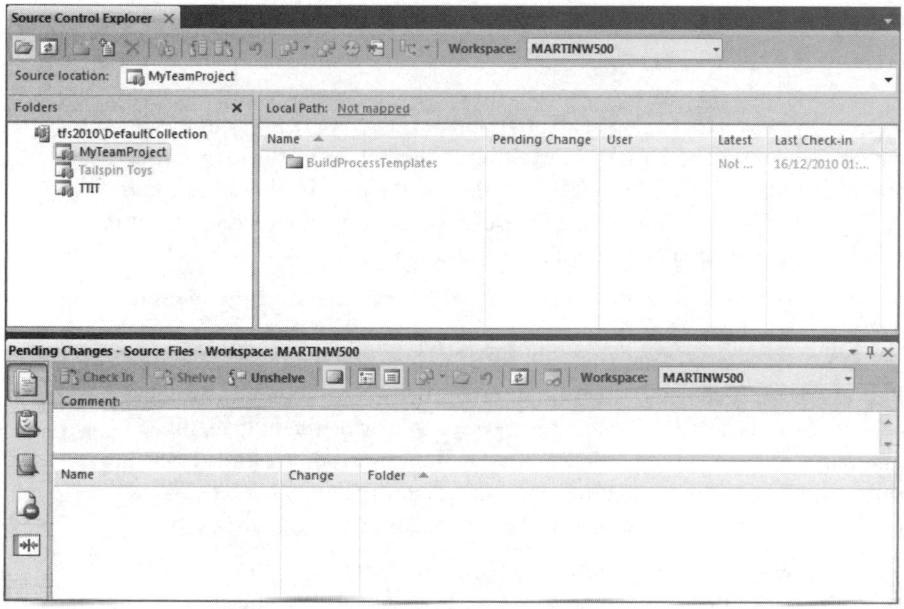

FIGURE 4-9: Source Control Explorer

For a brand-new team project, the folder will be fairly empty, likely just containing a folder called `BuildProcessTemplates`. However, even the creation of this folder is governed by the Team Foundation Server Process Template, as discussed in Part III of this book.

RED X IN TEAM EXPLORER

If a node under the team project in Team Explorer is showing a red X on the icon as shown on the `Reports` node in the following figure, and the node contains no children, this indicates a problem in communicating with the web services that provides the data for the relevant node.

Red X issues are most common on the `Documents` and `Reports` nodes, and are usually an indication of one of the following two problems:

➤ *Authorization* — This is the most common cause. The user has been given permission to access Team Foundation Server by adding the Windows user into a team project group. However, that user has not been granted permissions in

continues

(continued)

> SharePoint or Reporting Services, which have separate authorization controls. (Chapter 20 provides more information on this.) A common way to prevent this is to use Active Directory groups to control access to Team Foundation Server resources, and have that group listed as a member of the team project group. You should also configure the correct permissions in SharePoint and Reporting Services. In this way, once the user is added to the Domain Group, the user inherits the correct permissions in all the various systems.

> ➤ *Connectivity* — This cause is more common when accessing over the Internet or from a different domain. Often, the application tier machine can be addressed using a fully qualified domain name (such as `tfs.mycompany.com`). However, the Reports server and SharePoint portal have only been configured with a locally resolvable name such as `sharepoint` or `reports`. Provide the fully qualified domain name in the Team Foundation Server Administration Console to ensure that all clients connecting to that instance of Team Foundation Server can resolve all machines in all networks from which they are going to access the server.

> If you see red X issues in Team Explorer for work items, builds, or source control, then that is a sign of a more unusual error. In those cases, see the event logs on the Team Foundation Server to determine if there are any server-side errors causing the problem. If you have users with Team Explorer Everywhere installed, then that client gives the reason for the error as a child node to the node that is having trouble. This can sometimes be a helpful way to understand what the problem is for all users.

> In the instance shown in the previous figure, the issue was caused because the user did not have permission to access the Reports site. Add the user as a Team Foundation Content Manager role in the SQL Server Reporting Services site (accessible from `http://tfs2010/Reports` in this instance, and then Properties ➪ New Role Assignment).

Connecting to Older Versions of Team Foundation Server

Visual Studio 2010 is capable of connecting to Team Foundation Server 2005 and Team Foundation Server 2008. Newer functionality is not available with the older servers, but all the fundamentals (such as work item tracking, version control, and so on) all function correctly.

When providing the connection details of a 2005 or 2008 instance of Team Foundation Server, be sure to remove the `virtualPath` portion of the URL, because this was only introduced in the 2010 release (that is, `http://tfs2008:8080/`). Figure 4-10 shows the connection details as configured for a 2008 server with the path section empty, and the correct URL in the preview.

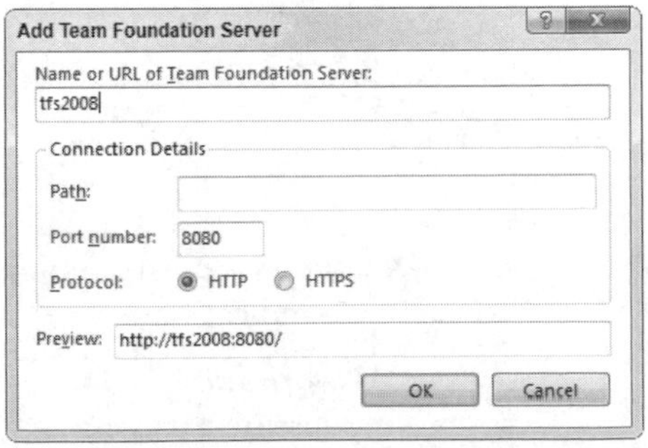

FIGURE 4-10: Connection details as configured for a 2008 server

Connecting to Team Foundation Server 2010 from Older Versions of Visual Studio

There are two main routes to take when connecting older versions of Visual Studio to Team Foundation Server 2010. For versions of Visual Studio prior to 2005, the Microsoft Source Code Control Interface (MSSCCI) provider is the approach to take. Visual Studio 2005 and Visual Studio 2008 are capable of connecting directly, once a forward-compatibility patch has been applied.

> For a detailed explanation of the matrix of compatibility between versions of the client and server, along with what was addressed in each version, see the blog post from the Team Foundation Server team at `http://tinyurl .com/tfsCompatMatrix`.

Visual Studio 2008 and Visual Studio 2005

Both the 2005 and 2008 versions of Visual Studio were aware of Team Foundation Server. The corresponding versions of Team Explorer should be installed from the corresponding version of Team Foundation Server installation media. In other words, Visual Studio 2005 requires Team Explorer 2005 from the Team Foundation Server 2005 installation media, and Visual Studio 2008 requires Team Explorer 2008 from the Team Foundation Server 2008 media.

Then the latest Visual Studio service packs should be applied. See `http://msdn.microsoft.com/ en-us/vstudio/aa718359.aspx` for links to download the latest service packs for the respective versions of Visual Studio. Bear in mind that you require the full Visual Studio service pack, not the Team Foundation Server service pack.

Once up to the latest service pack, Visual Studio 2005 and 2008 must have the Team Explorer Forward Compatibility Update GDR applied. The term GDR here is a reference to a type of patch issued by Microsoft. The GDR for Visual Studio 2008 clients can be found at `http:// go.microsoft.com/fwlink/?LinkId=166481`, and the GDR for Visual Studio 2005 can be downloaded from `http://go.microsoft.com/fwlink/?LinkID=166482`.

> For more information on the 2005 GDR, see `http://tinyurl.com/2005GDR`, and for the 2008 GDR (along with detailed information about the compatibility matrix between different versions of the client and server), see `http://tinyurl .com/tfsCompatMatrix`.

In addition to a raft of fixes to ensure compatibility with the latest version of the server, the forward-compatibility GDRs allow for a full project collection URL to be specified in the Add Team Foundation Server dialog shown in Figure 4-11. This enables connectivity to the 2010 server, despite the introduction of the virtual path for the Team Foundation Server application, and the notion of a project collection being new to the 2010 release.

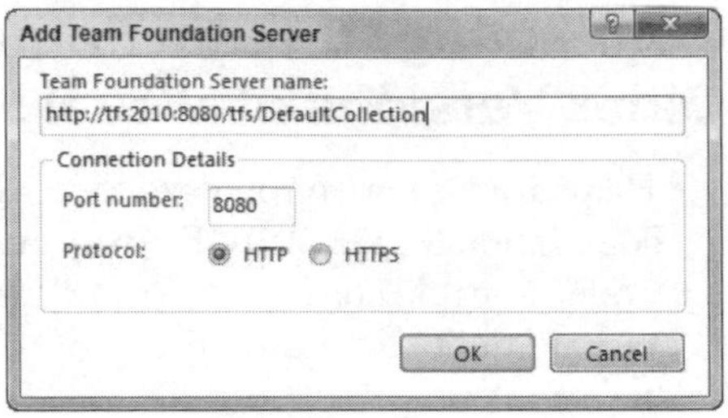

FIGURE 4-11: Add Team Foundation Server dialog in Visual Studio 2008

OLDER CLIENTS NOT ABLE TO CONNECT ERROR

Because unpatched older versions of clients can cause problems when talking to Team Foundation Server 2010, the server contains code that checks that the client is not one of the known older releases. It does this by looking at the User-Agent in the HTTP header as the client connects to the web services on the server. If the client is a known incompatible version, the following error is displayed to the user:

```
TF253022: You must update your client with the Forward Compatibility
Update in order to connect to the Team Foundation Server that you
selected To obtain this update, go to the Microsoft Web site:
http://go.microsoft.com/fwlink/?LinkId=16648
```

If this error in encountered, the client version should be patched or upgraded. For more information on how the client version detection is performed, see http://tinyurl.com/TF253022.

Prior Visual Studio Versions

Prior to Visual Studio 2005, the interface popularized by Visual Studio was MSSCCI (often pronounced *Miskey*). The MSSCCI spec was originally designed for the Visual Studio integration with Visual SourceSafe (VSS), but was implemented by other development tools manufacturers, and implemented by other version control tool vendors.

The Team Foundation Server team also makes a MSSCCI provider available as part of the Team Foundation Server Power Tools available at http://tinyurl.com/Msscci2010. The MSSCCI provider requires that the 2010 version of Team Explorer be installed on the machine. For more information on the MSSCCI provider, see Chapter 6.

Connecting to Team Foundation Server from Eclipse and Cross-Platform

As part of the Team Foundation Server 2010 release, Microsoft also released Team Explorer Everywhere 2010. Team Explorer Everywhere 2010 contains two major components:

➤   Team Foundation Server plug-in for Eclipse

➤   Team Foundation Server cross-platform command-line client

The Team Explorer Everywhere 2010 release was based on technology developed and released for all previous versions of Team Foundation Server by a partner company called Teamprise. In 2009, Microsoft acquired the technology and the development team, who now work as part of the core Team Foundation Server team in Microsoft.

While the Eclipse and cross-platform capabilities for Team Foundation Server have been available as long as the server has, the decision to sell and support the product from within the core Team Foundation Server team has led to increasing numbers of organizations deciding to standardize on Team Foundation Server for management of their entire application development portfolio.

Service Pack 1 for Team Explorer Everywhere 2010 was also made available to support the rollout of Team Foundation Server 2010 Service Pack 1. But that latest version can work against the 2010, 2008, and 2005 versions of the server.

Unusually for a team in the Microsoft Visual Studio organization, Team Explorer Everywhere is written in Java, and is supported across the major platforms, including Windows, Mac OS X, and forms of UNIX (such as Linux, HP-UX, Solaris, and AIX).

Team Foundation Server Plug-in for Eclipse

The plug-in for Eclipse provided as part of Team Explorer Everywhere installs as a standard Repository Provider plug-in inside development environments based on Eclipse 3.2 and above. This not only includes the latest versions of the standalone Eclipse IDE, but also tools such as Rational Application Developer, Adobe FlexBuilder, MyEclipse, and so on, as well as tooling to support embedded development. By providing the functionality as a standard plug-in to Eclipse written using 100 percent Java technologies like the rest of the Eclipse IDE, it is very easy to install and use for developers used to other version control providers in Eclipse.

As shown in Figure 4-12, Team Explorer Everywhere provides more than just version control capabilities to Eclipse. The entire Team Explorer 2010 experience as described earlier in this chapter is provided to Eclipse developers, meaning that all parts of a development organization can be peers when using Team Foundation Server to manage the development lifecycle. Team Foundation Server treats source code or any other file as just a file. From a version control point of view, all code is created equal as far as Team Foundation Server is concerned.

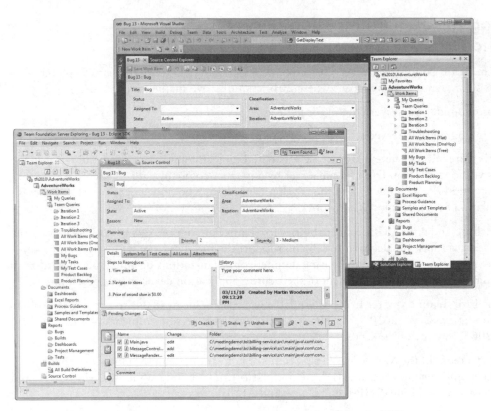

FIGURE 4-12: Team Explorer within Eclipse compared with Visual Studio 2010

The plug-in for Eclipse is installed from the Team Explorer Everywhere media, or via a download of the plug-in update site archive. The Service Pack 1 version of the media contains a full release of the plug-in at that version, so it can be installed directly from it.

> *For further information on getting started with version control using the Eclipse integration, see Chapter 6. Building Java applications using Team Foundation Server is also covered in Chapter 15.*

Cross-Platform Command-Line Client for Team Foundation Server

Team Explorer Everywhere also provides you with the capability to perform version control operations with many UNIX and Linux style operating systems using the cross-platform command-line client for Team Foundation Server (tf), as shown in Figure 4-13.

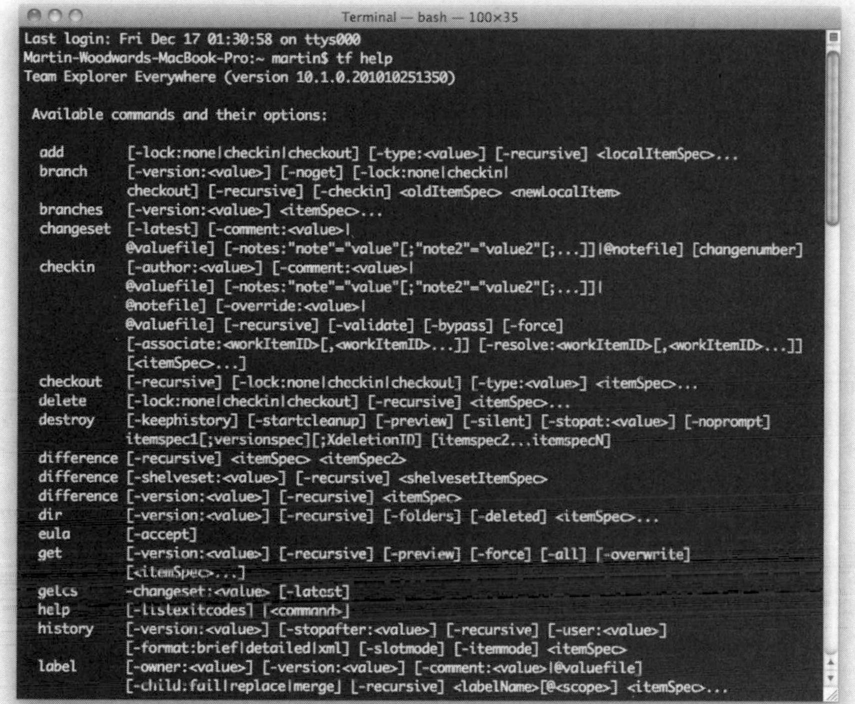

FIGURE 4-13: Cross-platform Command-line client on Mac OS X

The command syntax is very similar to the version control command-line tool (tf.exe) that is installed on Windows as part of the Team Explorer installation. This allows for tools and scripts to be written against both flavors of the tool.

USE HYPHENS FOR MAXIMUM PORTABILITY

The Team Foundation version control command line accepts a number of parameters for each command. In most of the documentation and examples, parameters are prefixed by a forward slash character (that is, /collection:TeamProjectCollectionUrl). However, in many UNIX shells, the forward slash character is an escape character. This means that, to actually pass a forward slash through to the tf command, you would need to escape it (usually with another forward slash).

To avoid this confusion, all versions of the command-line client are capable of accepting both a hyphen or a forward slash to prefix a parameter. For example, -collection:TeamProjectCollectionUrl is a valid way to pass in the collection URL on both Windows and in all UNIX shells.

Therefore, if you are writing a script or a tool that makes use of the command line, use hyphens to ensure that the tool can run more easily on all platforms.

ALTERNATE WAYS TO CONNECT TO TEAM FOUNDATION SERVER

As well as installing Team Explorer or Team Explorer Everywhere, there are many other ways of connecting to Team Foundation Server. On the server itself, there is the Team Foundation Server Administration Console. But, from the client, there are many different connectivity options, depending on what you want to do.

Accessing Team Foundation Server Through a Web Browser

In Team Foundation Server 2010, a web-based client called Team Web Access (TWA) is installed by default on the application tier machines, and is available under a special `web` directory under the `virtualPath` (that is, `http://tfs2010:8080/tfs/web`). As shown in Figure 4-14, TWA is ideal for users who do not wish to install a dedicated Team Foundation Server client. It requires no additional software to be installed on the client machine, other than a modern web browser (the site works in Firefox, Safari, and Chrome, as well as Internet Explorer). It is also used in many places to provide a link that can be used to point to data in Team Foundation Server — for example, when passing around a link to a work item or shelveset.

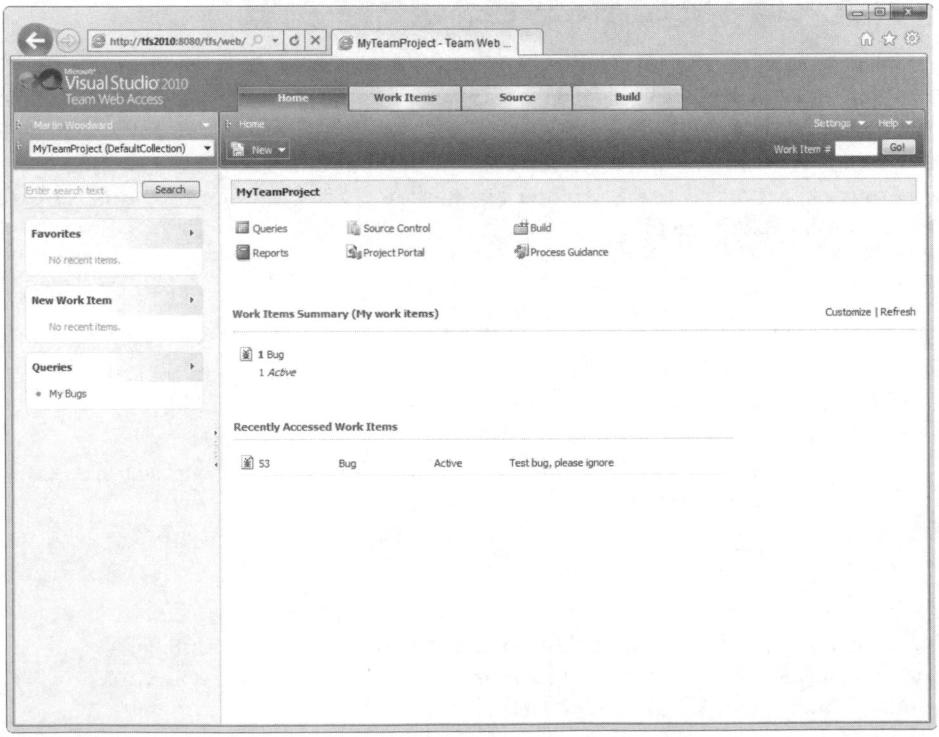

FIGURE 4-14: Team Web Access

At a high level, the following functionality is provided by TWA:

➤ Creating and editing work items and work item queries

➤ Managing areas and iterations

➤ Read-only access to version control (including Source Control Explorer), as well as shelvesets, and the capability to compare versions of files in version control

➤ Queuing and managing build definitions

When you initially browse to TWA, you are prompted to select to which team project collection and team projects you wish to connect. After you make the selection, it is remembered for subsequent visits. However, you can change the project collection by clicking the Team Project drop-down in the top left-hand corner and selecting <Connect to a different project>.

Using Team Foundation Server in Microsoft Excel

As part of the Team Explorer installation process, team support is added to Microsoft Excel. This allows for the capability to add and edit work items directly from Excel spreadsheets, as shown in Figure 4-15.

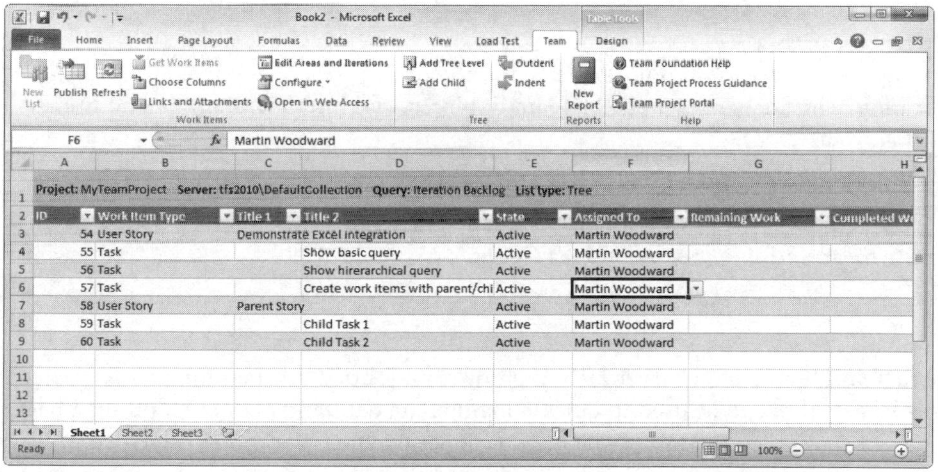

FIGURE 4-15: Adding and editing work items directly from Excel spreadsheets

To connect to Team Foundation Server from Excel, go to the Team ribbon and click New List. Select the query that you would like to use as the basis of data to load into Excel. Or, if you would like to simply create a bunch of new work items, select Input List.

Usually, starting with a query is the easiest way, because you can still add and edit work items from it. If you pick the My Bugs query, you should be presented with the bug created earlier in this chapter or other bugs that may be assigned to you. You may add additional fields from the work item into the spreadsheet by clicking the Choose Columns button and adding additional columns into the list.

Note that if you select a hierarchical query — for example, a query that shows parent/child relationships such as an Iteration Backlog query in the standard Iteration folders created as part of an Agile process template — then you will have multiple Title columns for each level in the hierarchy, as shown in Figure 4-15. Adding a work item as a child of another is as simple as creating a new row and placing the title for that work item in the Title 2 column. If you need an additional column, or wish to quickly insert a new line to create the child node, simply click on the Add Child button in the Team ribbon.

To open an existing query as an Excel spreadsheet, you can right-click any work item query in Visual Studio 2010 and select Open in Microsoft Excel.

You can also easily generate several reports in an Excel workbook that analyze current status and historical trends based on the criteria specified in a flat (that is, not hierarchical) query. Simply right-click the query and select Create Report in Microsoft Excel. This will then connect Excel directly to Analysis Services to show the data directly from the Team Foundation Server data warehouse.

> *For more information, see the MSDN documentation at* http://tinyurl
> .com/xlreports.

There are also pre-built Excel-based reports created in the Agile process template in the Excel Reports folder under the Documents node in Team Explorer, making the building of additional reports in Excel very easy.

> *For more information on reporting, see Chapter 13.*

A new feature in Team Foundation Server 2010 is a powerful set of Agile planning tools created as a series of spreadsheets that can be used to quickly manipulate data and plan out a product backlog or sprint. As part of the Agile process template, the Product Backlog workbook is created in the Shared Documents folder under the Documents node, and then inside the Iteration 1 folder is an example of an Iteration Backlog workbook.

Using Team Foundation Server in Microsoft Project

In addition to providing Excel integration, the installation of Team Explorer also installs a Team ribbon into Microsoft Project, as shown in Figure 4-16. This provides the capability to add and edit work items directly in Microsoft Project, and to view data about the progress of the work items.

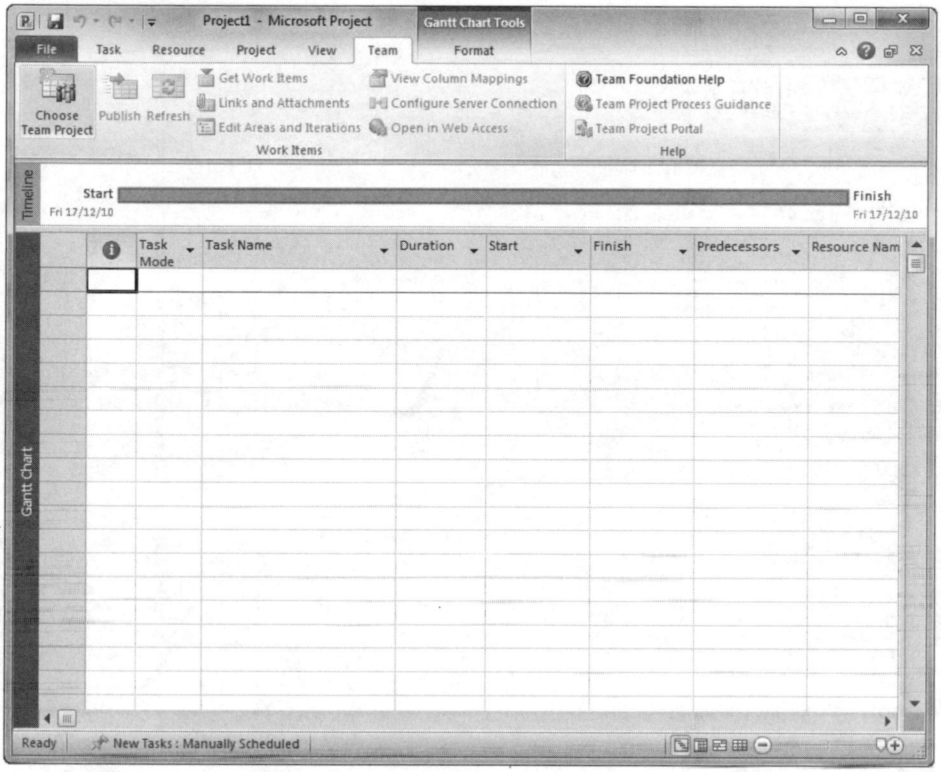

FIGURE 4-16: Team ribbon in Microsoft Project

Because of the enhanced linking capabilities in Team Foundation Server 2010, predecessors and successors can be created easily using Microsoft Project linked to work items, allowing you to control which work items depend on each other.

MSDN Subscribers with the Ultimate level can also access a Project Server Feature Pack. This feature pack allows for the synchronization of work items between a Team Foundation Server and Project Server, and allows for fine-grained control of which data is automatically kept in sync between the two systems. The Project Server integration feature pack requires Service Pack 1 of Team Foundation Server to be installed, and clients should also be using Service Pack 1 for Visual Studio, as well as Team Explorer Everywhere 2010 Service Pack 1.

Windows Explorer Integration with Team Foundation Server

As part of the Team Foundation Server Power Tools (http://msdn.microsoft.com/en-us/vstudio/bb980963.aspx), Windows Shell integration can optionally be installed. Once it is installed, when you browse a folder that is mapped in a Team Foundation Server workspace, files and folders are decorated depending on the status (that is, whether or not the files are checked out).

Right-clicking the file or folder provides access to some basic version control operations under the Team Foundation Server menu (Figure 4-17) that can be very useful when working with Team Foundation Server outside of Visual Studio or Eclipse.

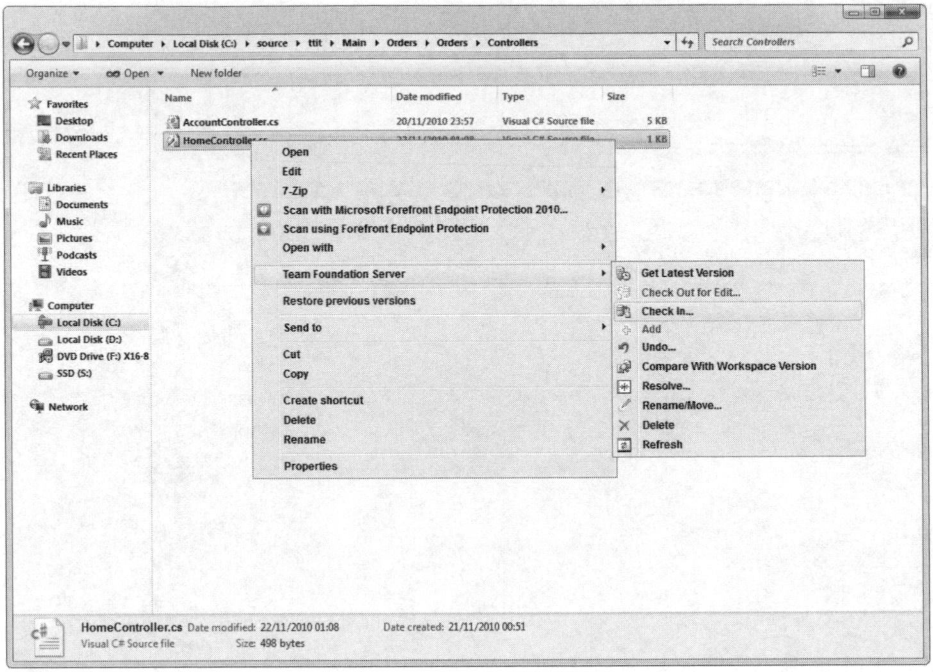

FIGURE 4-17: Windows shell integration

Expression Blend Integration with Team Foundation Server

Within Expression Blend 4, users accessing solutions that have already been bound to Team Foundation Server for version control using Visual Studio 2010 can access version control functionality directly within the Expression Blend tool. In addition, feedback collected from a SketchFlow application can be converted into a Team Foundation Server work item if the project is bound to Team Foundation Server.

Simply right-click the feedback item and select Convert Feedback into TFS Work Item.

Connecting Microsoft Test Manager to Team Foundation Server

Microsoft Test Manager 2010 is the new dedicated interface for testers working with Team Foundation Server. It is installed as part of Visual Studio Test Professional 2010, or with Visual Studio 2010 Ultimate.

The first time you start the application, you will be prompted to provide details about your Team Foundation Server instance. You are then able to select the project collection, team project, and Test Plan to which you wish to connect.

After the initial connection, your preference will be remembered, and you will automatically be connected to that Test Plan. To change Test Plan, or to connect to a different project or project collection, simply click the name of the Test Plan in the top right-hand corner of the screen, as shown in Figure 4-18.

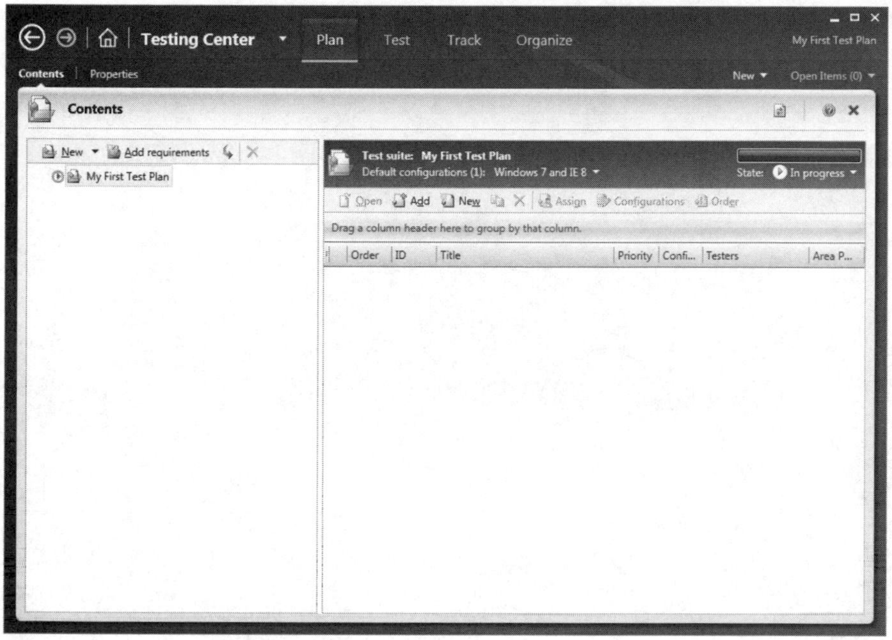

FIGURE 4-18: Microsoft Test Manager

Access to Team Foundation Server via Third-Party Integrations

Team Foundation Server supports a rich and vibrant third-party ecosystem through its powerful extensibility mechanisms, as outlined in Chapter 25. The same .NET object model that is installed as part of the Team Explorer integration is available for use by other third-party applications installed on your machine.

Integrations are available into other parts of Microsoft Office (such as Word and Outlook) from partners using these APIs. Also, many development tools and projects now integrate with Team Foundation Server using the extensibility hooks provided by Microsoft, or by wrapping calls to the version control command-line client.

SUMMARY

In this chapter, you learned how to get connected to Team Foundation Server from your desktop machine. You learned about the architecture of a typical Team Foundation Server installation, and how the Team Foundation Server URL is used to provide the connection information to the server. The discussion also highlighted the basic access control and permissions system used by Team Foundation Server.

The client software for Team Foundation Server (Team Explorer) was introduced. You learned about how to begin using this interface to access the functionality provided by the server.

The rest of this book examines that functionality in detail. Chapter 5 begins that examination with a general discussion about version control, and how to share your source code with the rest of the team.

PART II
Version Control

5

Overview of Version Control

WHAT'S IN THIS CHAPTER?

> ➤ Understanding the purpose, core concepts, and benefits of version control

> ➤ Analyzing the strengths and weaknesses of common version control products

Version control is the single most important tool you can use when developing software, regardless of the particular provider you use to give you version control functionality. Most software developers use version control tools in their day-to-day jobs, and yet, the fundamental concepts and reasoning behind version control is rarely discussed.

This chapter starts by explaining the fundamental concepts of version control and what functionality you typically find from a tool-independent viewpoint. Then various important version control tools are examined, and their strengths and weaknesses are analyzed. The chapter concludes with a high-level look at the version control capabilities of Team Foundation Server, and looks at when Team Foundation Server is or is not the correct tool for your team.

WHAT IS VERSION CONTROL?

Version control is known by many names. *Source control* is frequently used, but the term *revision control* and even *software/source configuration management (SCM)* can be used to refer to the same broad set of functionality. Because a modern software project consists of much more than merely a set of source code, the term version control is used throughout this book, although the terms can be used interchangeably (and often are — even in the Team Foundation Server product).

Broadly speaking, version control provides the following capabilities:

> ➤ A place to store the source code, images, build scripts, and so on, that are needed to build your software project.

➤ The capability to track the history of changes to those files, and to view the state of the file at various points in the software lifecycle.

➤ Mechanisms and tooling to make it easy to work in parallel with a team of software developers on the same project.

If you make a mistake when editing your code, a version control system lets you roll back time and get back to the state before you just accidentally deleted the past weeks' worth of work. A version control system allows you to know what the code is that is running on someone's machine. Version control allows multiple teams of developers to work on the same files at the same time, and not get in each other's way.

While version control is so important that its correct use is required for regulatory compliance in some industries, it also has clear benefits for all software development. Yet, a remarkable number of organizations still do not use a version control system. Copying the folder containing your source code to another location is not a version control system — it is a backup. In the past, version control systems could be expensive, complex, and difficult to use. Today, version control is such a fundamental aspect of software development that, in its basic form, is a commodity item, and is increasingly easy to use. But even if you are a developer working on your own for a project, you intimately know the safety net provided by a version control tool is worth the investment.

However, not all version control systems are the same. Even more confusing, some tools use the same words for very different activities. To thoroughly understand the nature of a version control system, you must be familiar with some core concepts.

Repository

In general, code is stored on a machine somewhere in a *repository* of some kind. The repository is usually represented as a tree of files, similar to the regular directory structures that everyone is familiar with in modern hierarchical filesystems. However, the repository differs from a filesystem in one very important aspect. Whereas a filesystem is a collection of folders and files, a version control repository tracks the changes to those files, thus allowing you to know the state of the files at any given point in time.

Additionally, a version control system must provide a number of features to make it useful. You need a way to share that version control repository with others on your team, make changes to the code, and share those changes with each other.

> *In this chapter, to keep things simple, the discussion refers to the repository as if there is a single master repository on a central server somewhere allowing your team to work. This is the traditional centralized version control system that most developers are familiar with. However, not all version control systems work that way. In a distributed version control system (DVCS) such as Git or Mercurial, the machines work in a peer-to-peer manner. In other words, each machine is a full repository in its own right. This has some advantages and disadvantages that will be examined later in this chapter.*

Obviously, storing every version of every file can take up a lot of disk space. Version control systems frequently employ various tricks to ensure that the repository is efficient with storage. For example, Team Foundation Server will store the initial version of the file, and then store the changes between each version (known as *deltas*) for subsequent changes.

The "delta-fication" process in Team Foundation Server is actually much more complex than this. Optimizations are in place to ensure that this is only done for certain file types, and also that recently accessed versions of files are cached in a ready-to-download state to avoid the computationally expensive task of rebuilding the file every time a developer requests a copy.

Working Copy

The files in the repository must be in a local area on the developer's machine. This allows the developer to work with the files, make changes to them, and debug before he or she decides to *check-in* or *commit* those changes to the repository. This local version is known as the *workspace* with Team Foundation Server, but in some version control systems, it can also be called a *sandbox* or *working copy*.

> *In Team Foundation Server, a* workspace *is actually more than just a working copy of the filesystem. Check out Chapter 6 for more information about workspaces.*

Using a local working copy of the repository, a developer can work in parallel with others on the team, and know that the working copy of the code will not change until the developer performs a specific action — either making a change to the code, or updating the code from the repository by getting all the files that have changed since the last time he or she got a copy.

Working Folder Mappings

A *working folder mapping* is the link between the place in the repository where the files are stored, and the place in your local filesystem where you have a working copy of that part of the repository. The term *working directory*, *workspace mapping* or *sandbox* can also be used to mean the working folder mapping.

> *Note that the terms "workspace," "working folder," and "sandbox" have been used in different version control systems to mean slightly different, but similar, things, which can be confusing when you are trying to understand a new version control system. This is one of the reasons it is important to understand the core concepts now so that this discussion can utilize a set of agreed-upon terms throughout the rest of the book. Each version control system you use is slightly different, and once you think about the problem in the way the tool allows you to work, it is often difficult to think about version control in other ways. This change in context is a problem that people encounter when moving from one version control system to another and, therefore, one that is addressed in Chapter 6 when discussing Team Foundation Server in more detail.*

Get

Once you have set up a working folder mapping, you must download the files from the repository to your local machine. In Team Foundation Server (as well as with some other version control tools) this process is known as *Get*. In Concurrent Version Systems (CVS) and Subversion (SVN), the same process is known as *check-out* — a word that means something slightly different in some version control systems like Team Foundation Server, as will be described shortly.

Add

What if you do not have any files in your repository yet? When you first start using a version control system, it is empty. In this case, you need to *add* some files. You select which files and folders to take from your local machine and add to the repository, so that you can share them with the rest of your team. When you do this, you seldom want to add all of the local files.

For example, you might have some compiled binaries derived from your source or files that are generated by your tools in the source directory each time a build is done. You typically do not need or, indeed, want to share these files. Therefore, Team Foundation Server provides tooling to help you select which files from a folder you are actually interested in adding, and to filter out those which you want to exclude.

Check-out

If you want to work on a file, then some version control systems (such as Team Foundation Server) require you to inform the server that you are working on them so that others on the team can know (and so that the server can check that you still have permission to edit the file). This operation is known as a *check-out* with Team Foundation Server.

In Visual SourceSafe (VSS), a single file can only be edited by one user at a time. Therefore, when a file is checked out, it is *locked* for editing for other users. In Team Foundation Server, the default behavior is that multiple people can edit the same file simultaneously (which is generally a best practice to allow in a version control system to maximize productivity). However, you do have the option of locking the file as you check it out if you wish to prevent edits for some reason.

Note that the use of the term "check-out" is slightly different in this context as opposed to the use of the term in the context of CVS and SVN. In those systems, "check-out" means to download the files to your working copy locally. Also, in those systems, there is no notion of requiring you to explicitly check out a file before working on it.

In SVN, for example, you can edit any file that you can download. All files in your working copy are writable when you download them from version control, and you just edit away. You can also explicitly lock a file if you wish, but this is unusual in a typical SVN workflow. This has advantages, because it means that there is much less friction when editing files locally, and involves less communication with the server. However, it comes with the loss of the capability to know exactly who on your team is currently working on which files.

Changeset

As you check out and edit files, you are building up a set of changes that will need to be applied to the repository when you wish to commit those changes. This set of changes to be done is called a *changeset* or *changelist*. The changeset consists of all the changes you want to do with the files (for example, editing, adding, or renaming a file).

Check-in

At some point, you have a set of changes that you want to commit to the repository so that you can share them with your team, or simply so that you are able to draw a line in the sand as being at a point that you want to save your state with the repository. You want to commit your set of changes with the server. This action is called a *check-in* in Team Foundation Server, but can be called by other names (such as *commit*) by other tools.

In more modern version control systems such as Team Foundation Server or Subversion (SVN), the check-in is performed on the repository as a single atomic transaction. That is, if, for some reason, your changes could not be applied to the repository (for example, if someone else has edited a particular file with a conflicting change while you were working on it), then none of the changes in your changeset are checked in until you resolve any issues preventing the check-in. In addition, if someone were to get a copy of the repository while you were doing your check-in, he or she would not get your changes. Only after your check-in has completed successfully are your changes visible to the rest of the team.

When you check in, you can also provide some additional data. In most version control tools, you can provide a comment describing the reason why you made the changes (and it is best practice to leave a meaningful comment). Team Foundation Server also provides the capability to provide additional metadata about each check-in, which will be described in more detail in Chapter 6.

History

As mentioned previously, a version control repository is like a filesystem that stores all the changes made to it. This extra dimension on the filesystem is known as the *history*. For a particular file or folder, the version control system can tell you everything that has happened to that file or folder over time. The history is one of the features that makes a version control system useful by allowing you to know what code you actually shipped to a customer who received a release at a given point in time. But it is also useful for many other things — for example, being able to go back in time and understand why the code is as it is now, to understand who has worked on a particular area in the past, or to figure out what has changed between two particular versions when suddenly something stops working that used to work great before.

The majority of version control systems provide the capability to *label* or *tag* files with a text description. This is a way of marking the repository to leave a meaningful name to a set of files in a particular version (for example, when you have done a build that you want to deploy). The label makes it easy to find that snapshot at a later time, and to see what the repository contained at that instance.

Team Foundation Server provides for all of this history functionality, but, in addition, makes it very easy to see what changes occurred to a file before it had been renamed. Similarly, changes that occurred before a file was branched or merged can be easily viewed from the files history.

Branching and Merging

A *branch* is a copy of a set of files in a different part of the repository. This allows two or more teams of people to work on the same project at the same time, checking in changes as they go, but without interfering with the other teams. At some point in the future, you may want some or all of the code to join up again. This is when you need to *merge* the changes from one branch into the other branch. When merging changes from two files in separate branches, if the same bit of code has been edited differently in both places, then this is called a *conflict*, and the version control system will require someone to decide what the code should be in the merged version.

In many version control systems (including versions of Team Foundation Server prior to the 2010 release), a branch is simply another folder containing a copy of data from elsewhere in the repository. In Team Foundation Server 2010, a branch folder is decorated differently, and branches are now a first-class object with additional metadata and behavior to a regular folder.

There are many ways to approach branching, and you should carefully consider what branching strategy you may want to adopt. Chapter 9 provides more information on this.

If all you want to do is save your work in progress so that you can store a copy of it on the server, or possibly share it with others in your team without checking in the code, then you may also want to consider the *shelving* features of Team Foundation Server. Chapter 6 provides more information on shelving and unshelving.

COMMON VERSION CONTROL PRODUCTS

There are many version control products that have been created over time, and many that are in use today. The most common tools used as of this writing are Visual SourceSafe (VSS), Subversion (SVN), and Team Foundation Server. This section takes a look at these various products, as well as a discussion of distributed version control systems (DVCS), which, while not greatly used in the enterprise at this time, are becoming an increasingly important player in the Open Source community.

Microsoft Visual SourceSafe

Visual SourceSafe (VSS) was originally created by One Tree Software and acquired by Microsoft in 1994. Microsoft Visual SourceSafe 2005 was the final release of the product, and has been scheduled for retirement from mainstream support in 2012. Despite its age, VSS is still a well-used version control product, and was pioneering for its day. It was very easy to install and set up, largely because it uses a filesystem-based repository, and does not require a dedicated server. The early design did present some issues, however. Check-ins into the repository were not atomic, and thus caused problems in team environments. Additionally, the filesystem-based approach could lead to instabilities in the repository, which gave VSS a reputation for sometimes corrupting the repository.

Table 5-1 shows a contrast between the strengths and weaknesses of VSS.

TABLE 5-1: Strengths and Weaknesses of VSS

STRENGTHS	WEAKNESSES
VSS is easy to install and use.	This is an aging product; no longer actively developed.
VSS has broad support in developer tools.	It does not perform well over wide area networks (WANs).
VSS has wide adoption in the industry.	There are no atomic check-in transactions.
	It has very limited branch support (through sharing features).

Team Foundation Server is seen as Microsoft's replacement product for VSS. But Team Foundation Server also addresses far more scenarios (for example, work item tracking, reporting, team builds) than VSS was ever intended for.

Apache Subversion

Subversion (SVN) is an Open Source version control project founded by CollabNet in 2000. SVN became a top-level project in the Apache Foundation in 2010. The system was originally designed to be a successor to the older Open Source CVS version control project. Since that time, it has surpassed the CVS market share, and expanded beyond the original goal of replacing CVS. However, SVN is still heavily influenced by that design, and should be familiar to CVS users.

While SVN has a large market share today, it is being challenged by distributed version control systems such as Git and Mercurial in the Open Source space. But development of SVN is still continuing, and features continue to be added.

Table 5-2 shows a contrast between the strengths and weaknesses of SVN.

TABLE 5-2: Strengths and Weaknesses of SVN

STRENGTHS	WEAKNESSES
SVN works under an Open Source licensing model (free to use).	Like CVS, SVN makes use of .svn directories inside the source folders to store state of the local working copy, and to allow synchronization with the server. However, it can have the affect of polluting the local source tree, and can cause performance issues with very large projects or files.
SVN is in wide use by Open Source projects.	A lack of check-out can mean a reduced capability of identifying when code is being worked on by others. However, this can often be mitigated by good team communication.

continues

TABLE 1-2 *(continued)*

STRENGTHS	WEAKNESSES
The server works on a variety of operating systems.	Renames are handled as a copy-and-delete operation in the repository, which can cause problems when merging branches.
SVN provides broad support with developer tools on all platforms.	Configuring authentication and performing certain administration functionality can be challenging in a Windows environment.
SVN provides good support for offline and occasionally connected development teams.	There is no shelving functionality.

Team Foundation Server

First publicly released in 2006, Microsoft Visual Studio Team Foundation Server is the reason you are reading this book, and so, by the end of this book, you will be very familiar with its functionality. Chapter 6 provides more information on the version control capabilities. However, it is worth highlighting the strengths and weaknesses of Team Foundation Server in this context, as shown in Table 5-3.

TABLE 5-3: Strengths and Weaknesses of Team Foundation Server

STRENGTHS	WEAKNESSES
It is more than just version control, and provides tight integration with the work item tracking, build, and reporting capabilities of the product.	Offline support and support for occasionally connected developers is not as good as SVN or DVCS.
It has first-class Visual Studio and Eclipse integration.	The differences in the version control model (such as read-only files in the local filesystem until you check out a file) can confuse SVN users, and can cause issues when attempting to edit files outside of a development environment with Team Foundation Server integration.
It has many features appealing to enterprise-class customers, such as centralized security administration, integration with Active Directory for authentication, and single-sign-on (SSO), as well as SharePoint integration.	The server product only runs on Windows platforms, but a client is available cross-platform.

STRENGTHS	WEAKNESSES
It is highly scalable.	
Shelveset support allows you to store changes on the server without committing to the main code repository.	
Check-in policies govern rules that the code should pass before you are able to commit it to the repository.	
Gated check-in support allows a build automation run to pass before the code is committed to the main repository.	
All data is stored in a SQL Server database for security and ease of backup.	

Distributed Version Control Systems

Distributed version control systems (DVCS) have been around for more than a decade, but only in recent years have they gained widespread adoption with the creation of systems such as BitKeeper, Git, Mercurial, and Bazaar. Git and Mercurial are probably the most well known of these types of tools, and have seen the widest adoption of DVCS to date.

There are some common (but fundamental) differences between the way a DVCS tool operates versus the more traditional centralized version control systems tools discussed previously. The key difference is that the local developer machines have the capability of acting as a DVCS repository themselves, and being peers to each other. Changes are not serialized as a set of versions in a centralized repository. Rather, they are stored as changes in the local repository, which can then be pushed or pulled into other users' repositories. While a centralized repository is not required, in many environments, it is common for a repository to act as the central hub that contains the master copy of the code on which the team performs automated builds, and that is considered by the team to be the definitive version.

Although the DVCS community has seen fast development in recent times, with a number of interesting projects in the space, it is too early to say which projects will dominate in the future. However the use of Git for the Linux kernel and its inclusion in the latest versions of tools from Eclipse and Apple suggest that, in the non-Windows space at least, it will continue to be popular. Mercurial is considered by some to be more Windows-friendly and easier to learn.

Table 5-4 shows a contrast between the strengths and weaknesses of a DVCS.

TABLE 5-4: Strengths and Weaknesses of a DVCS

STRENGTHS	WEAKNESSES
It has full repository support when offline from others. It also has fast local repository access.	Using developer repositories can reduce the frequency with which changes are synced with the rest of the team, leading to a loss of visibility as to the progress of teams overall.
You can easily have multiple repositories, and highly flexible topologies. You can use repositories in circumstances where branches might be used in a centralized server approach, which can, therefore, help with scalability.	There is no centralized backup of progress for developers until changes are pushed to a central repository.
It encourages frequent check-ins to a local repository, thus providing the capability to track those changes and see the evolution of the code.	Current DVCS solutions lack some security, auditing, and reporting capabilities common to enterprise requirements.
It is well-suited to many Open Source project workflows. It allows participation in the project without any centralized server granting permission. It works well for large projects with many partly independent developers responsible for certain areas.	Most centralized systems (such as SVN and Team Foundation Server) allow for optional locking of files to prevent later merge conflicts. The nature of DVCS tools makes this impossible.
Because of the way DVCS systems typically track changes, and because the nature of having distributed repositories means that merges happen more frequently, DVCS merges are usually less likely to produce conflicts, compared with similar changes merged from separate branches in a centralized version control system. However, merges still can obviously conflict, and the more the code has changed between merges, the more likely it is to require effort in performing the merge.	

SUMMARY

This chapter introduced the basic concepts of version control and why it is needed. You learned about some of the common version control tools in the market today, and about their strengths and weaknesses.

Team Foundation Server is one of the leading tools in the market today. While it has some unique version control capabilities, and scales very well from very small to very large teams, broadly speaking, when looking at the version control capabilities alone, it is comparable to most modern centralized version control systems in terms of feature sets.

The key factor that makes many organizations choose to standardize on Team Foundation Server is the tight integration between work item tracking, version control, build, and reporting features, all the way through the product. By closely binding your version control with your work item tracking, you get greater traceability. The intimate knowledge of the version control system by the build system gives rise to powerful build features, with no additional work by the administrators. The close link between builds and work items means that testers know which builds fix which bugs, and what files in version control were affected, so which tests need to be re-run. It's the sum of the whole that really makes Team Foundation Server stand out from the competition.

As discussed, every version control system is different, and a developer's understanding of a version control system is key to effectively working with it. Chapter 6 delves deeper into the version control features offered by Team Foundation Server, and how to work with them. The core concepts and tools will be discussed, along with some help and advice in transitioning to Team Foundation Server from other version control systems.

6

Using Team Foundation Version Control

WHAT'S IN THIS CHAPTER?

➤   Understanding version control

➤   Using the Source Control Explorer

➤   Viewing the history of files and folders

➤   Using the version control command line

➤   Using Team Foundation version control in Eclipse and on non-Windows platforms

➤   Understanding version control security and permissions

➤   Understanding source control settings and configuration

➤   A guide to Team Foundation Server for Visual SourceSafe users

➤   A guide to Team Foundation Server for Subversion users

Version control is one of the primary reasons that people adopt Team Foundation Server. Most professional developers have had some prior experience with a version control system. The first thing you must come to terms with is that every version control system is different. While change can be unsettling at first, there are clear benefits in moving to Team Foundation Server.

Team Foundation Server provides a robust, powerful, and scalable version control infrastructure that you can rely on to support the needs of your software development efforts. From teams of 1 to teams of 5,000 or more, Team Foundation Server is a mission-critical system supporting many organizations today. It was built from scratch by Microsoft, and is not based on its previous version control offering, Visual SourceSafe (VSS).

Team Foundation Server stores all its version control data in a SQL Server database alongside the work item and build information. Team Foundation Server's version control system is designed to work using Internet-based protocols. It works great over high-latency network connections, such as those found in the typical enterprise wide area network (WAN), or over the public Internet. It provides highly flexible security and permission capabilities tied into an integrated authentication model.

This chapter first examines the fundamental concepts that you must understand to come to grips with the version control model used by Team Foundation Server. Then, the common version control tool windows are explained, along with how to access common version control operations and get started using Team Foundation Server version control on your first project.

In this chapter, you will look at the use of the version control command line, and special considerations to take into account when using Team Foundation version control cross platform. You will learn how to configure version control security and permissions in Team Foundation Server, and how to configure common settings for source control. Finally, you will see a short guide to Team Foundation Server for developers familiar with Microsoft VSS or Apache Subversion (SVN).

> *As noted in Chapter 5, version control goes by many names, including "source control," "revision control," and so on. This book mostly uses the term "version control" to indicate that Team Foundation Server can handle much more than source code, including everything that you use to create your product (such as build scripts, website images, and original artwork) that you wish to version alongside your source. However, the terms "version control" and "source control" can be used interchangeably. Even in Team Foundation Server, you will see references to both terms.*

GETTING STARTED WITH TEAM FOUNDATION SERVER VERSION CONTROL

Before diving into the details of Team Foundation Server version control, let's first add a Visual Studio 2010 solution to version control.

First, create a simple solution that you want to share with your team. For this example, let's use a simple `HelloWorld` console application (but you could use any of your own applications).

You must ensure that you are connected to Team Foundation Server. For more information on this, see Chapter 4, but, basically, in Visual Studio, go to Team ➪ Connect to Team Foundation Server. Enter details of the project collection and team projects that you wish to connect to. Then click Connect.

Now, let's add the solution to version control. Simply right-click the solution in Solution Explorer and select Add Solution to Source Control. You should see the screen shown in Figure 6-1.

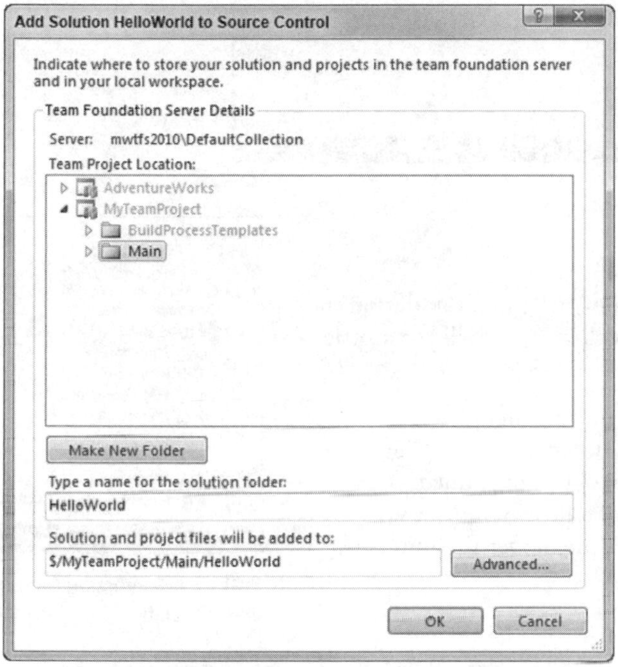

FIGURE 6-1: Add Solution dialog

> If this is the first source code being added to your team project, then a good tip is not to accept the default of placing your solution directly under the team project in version control. Instead, make a new folder called `Main` and place your solution in it — that is, `$/MyTeamProject/Main/HelloWorld`. This will put you in a good position should you want to adopt a branching strategy later on in your project development. Create the `Main` folder even if you have no idea what a branch is yet. Chapter 9 of this book explains all about branching, and this folder will come in handy then.

You are nearly there. To commit your changes so that other people on the team can see your project, you need to *check in* the files. To do this, open the Pending Changes view (View ⇨ Other Windows ⇨ Pending Changes) and click the Check In button. You can provide a comment for your changes if you wish, as shown in Figure 6-2.

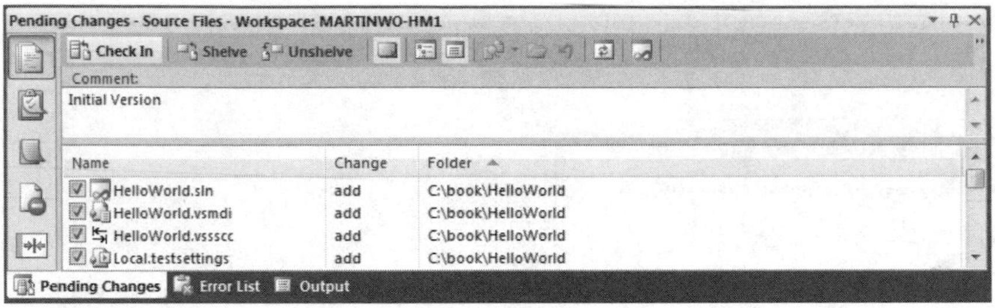

FIGURE 6-2: Pending Changes view

And there you have it. Your changes are now in Team Foundation version control. If you look in Solution Explorer, you will see a little padlock next to your files, as shown in Figure 6-3.

If you right-click on the files, you will see new menu options are available, such as Get Latest, Check Out for Edit, and View History. All of these commands and more will be explained later in this chapter, but first let's step back a little and discuss some concepts at the core of Team Foundation Server version control.

FIGURE 6-3: Version controlled files in Solution Explorer

> *In Visual Studio, you can have a number of different version control providers. While Team Foundation Server is installed by default in Visual Studio 2010, if you have been using a different version control tool previously, you may not see the Team Foundation Server functionality. To switch to Team Foundation Server for version control, go to Tools ➪ Options ➪ Source Control, and ensure that your current source control plug-in is set as Visual Studio Team Foundation Server.*

TEAM FOUNDATION SERVER VERSION CONTROL CONCEPTS

You can just dive in and start using Team Foundation Server version control with very little effort or training. However, at some point, you might bump into a couple of areas that might prove confusing unless you understand the basics of how Team Foundation Server sees the world when it comes to version control. The first fundamental concept you must understand is the notion of the *workspace*.

Workspace

One of the first problems with the term "workspace" is that it can be a somewhat overloaded term. For example, to Eclipse developers, the term "workspace" can mean the Eclipse workspace, which is entirely different from the Team Foundation notion of workspace, even though they both conceptually contain source code. To others familiar with version control systems such as Polytron Version Control System (PVCS) or ClearCase, the term "workspace" also means something similar, but again quite different from Team Foundation Server. For SVN developers, the concept of a "workspace" is completely foreign, and they might assume that this is just the working copy (it is, but also more than just that).

A workspace can be thought of as the container that bridges the gap between your local computer and the Team Foundation Server repository. As shown in Figure 6-4, the workspace contains several important pieces of information.

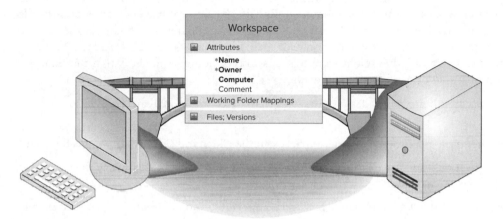

FIGURE 6-4: Workspace in Team Foundation Server

Workspaces are identified by a name and the hostname of the computer the workspace is for. The name can be up to 64 characters in length, and you can also provide a comment that may be a useful reminder if you have multiple workspaces on the same computer. The workspace also contains the working folder mappings that indicate which folders on your local machine map to which folders on the server.

CHANGING THE COMPUTER NAME OR OWNER FOR A WORKSPACE

The owner and computer name of the workspace are not editable in Visual Studio or Eclipse. However, you may occasionally need to edit these. To do this, use the `tf workspaces /updateComputerName:OldComputerName` or `tf workspaces / updateUserName:OldUserName` commands.

Note that the `updateCompterName` option does not move the workspace from one machine to another. You are telling Team Foundation Server that the hostname of the machine that this workspace is on has changed for some reason (that is, it was renamed or restored from a backup). Similarly, the `updateUserName` option doesn't change the owner of the workspace. It tells Team Foundation Server that your name has changed from, say, `DOMAIN\mwoodward` to `DOMAIN\martinwo`.

Under the hood, Team Foundation Server actually stored the Windows security identifier (SID) of the account. The update call simply tells the server to update its cache with the current username for that same SID.

There is also information about the state of your workspace stored on the server. The server remembers which versions of which files you have downloaded to your local computer, and also stores which of those files you are in the process of changing, and any files that you have decided to lock so that others cannot edit those files at the same time as you do.

Using the workspace to remember the files and versions downloaded is one of the ways that Team Foundation Server is optimizing the network traffic between your computer and the server. When you ask the server to Get Latest, it already knows what versions you have of all the files, so it can simply send you the ones that have been modified. Equally, because your workspace stores the files you are currently working on, Team Foundation Server has the capability to highlight this fact to others in your team so that they know that someone else is currently editing a file that they were about to modify. Therefore, they might want to speak to the teammate to check that the changes they are both planning on performing will make sense.

The workspace embodies two key design principles that are common in Team Foundation Server:

➤ Only send the maximum information between the client and server that you need to send

➤ Only do something (such as download the latest version of a file, or modify the contents of a file) when you explicitly tell it to

However, this comes at a trade-off. This one is very important, and is the single thing that people find most confusing when they are new to Team Foundation version control:

➤ Always tell the server when you do something to a file or folder that is in your workspace (such as editing the file, renaming it, or adding a file into a folder).

But this trade-off allows Team Foundation Server to offer some niceties that people used to other version control systems might appreciate. For example, if a file has been renamed on the server, then the next time you perform a Get Latest, your local file will be renamed (meaning that the file with the old name automatically goes away, but if you had changes you were working on for that file, then they will automatically stay with the file under the new name).

Also, if a file is deleted on the server, then when you perform a Get Latest, that file will automatically be deleted in your local filesystem. This way, you are never left with old stale files in your local filesystem like you might have been used to when using some other version control systems.

Working Folder Mappings

As mentioned previously, part of the information contained in the workspace is the working folder mappings. At the simplest level, a *working folder mapping* says which folders on your local machine map to which folders in the repository. For example, if you were to map `C:\Local\MyTeamProject` to `$/MyTeamProject` and then download the files to your local machine by performing a Get Latest, then you would have a copy of the latest versions of all the files from the server in your local directory.

> *.NET (and, therefore, Team Foundation Server) imposes a 260-character limit for the full file path, which stems from a limitation of certain APIs in Windows around file handling. Conventions for source code can result in long folder and file names. This is especially true for Java projects, but can be true with many large Visual Studio solutions. Therefore, a useful tip is to store source code in a folder off from the root of a hard drive (such as* `C:\source`) *on Windows, or at a suitable mount point in UNIX file systems. This way, you will have more characters available for the files in your local path.*

With Team Foundation Server, working folder mappings are stored in your Team Foundation Server workspace. They are not shared between other people using the repository (unlike PVCS, for example). Viewing the current set of working folder mappings is very easy:

➤ With Visual Studio, go to File ➪ Source Control ➪ Workspaces. Select your workspace and click Edit.

➤ With Eclipse, right-click on the project in Package Explorer and go to Team ➪ Manage Workspaces. Select your workspace and click Edit.

Alternatively, you can use the `tf workfold` command or the Team Foundation Server Sidekicks, which you will learn about later in this chapter.

Figure 6-5 shows the working folder mappings from Visual Studio. The example shows a fairly complex working folder mapping layout — it is much more usual to see an example with only one or two Active working folder mappings. However, the figure shows some additional working folder mapping features available in Team Foundation Server. Let's take a closer look.

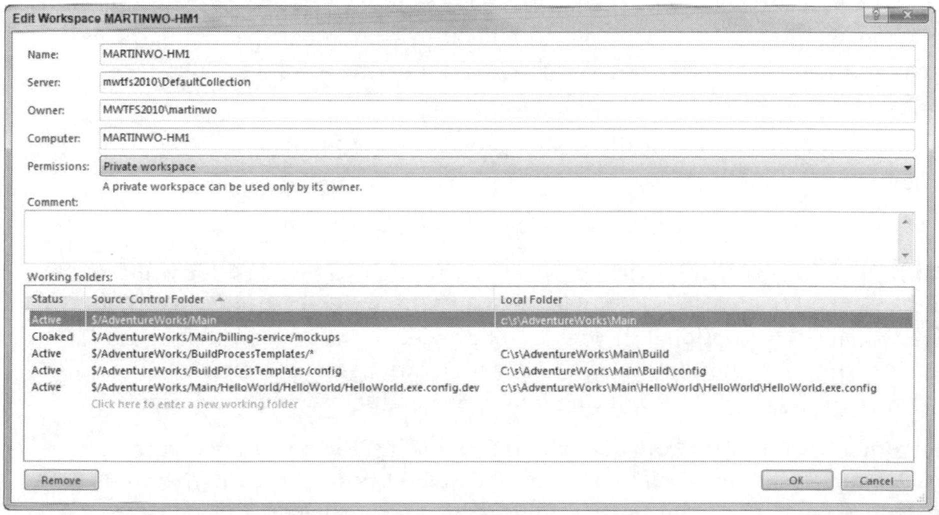

FIGURE 6-5: Working folder mappings in Visual Studio

Active Working Folder Mappings

The first working folder mapping is straightforward. This maps the contents of `$/AdventureWorks/Main` to `C:\s\AdventureWorks\Main` recursively. If you create this working folder mapping and then perform a Get from `$/AdventureWorks/Main/HelloWorld`, the contents of that folder would be downloaded to `C:\s\AdventureWorks\Main\HelloWorld`.

Cloaked Working Folder Mappings

The second mapping in Figure 6-5 is not an Active mapping, but is cloaked. A *cloaked working folder mapping* tells the server that you do not wish to download the contents that are cloaked. In other words, you do not want them to appear in your local filesystem, nor do you want to get any files in that folder if the contents of that folder are changed on the server.

In Figure 6-5, you see a cloaked working folder mapping that is a child of the previous Active recursive mapping for `$/AdventureWorks/Main`. This means that the large graphic files contained in the `$/AdventureWorks/Main/billing-service/mockups` folder are not downloaded to the local machine, saving bandwidth and disk space.

COPYING COMPLEX WORKING FOLDER MAPPING CONFIGURATIONS

A typical working folder mapping configuration can be quite simple. However, some version control trees require a more complex folder mapping to be used, which you may want to share with the team or copy to another workspace on a different machine. To copy the working folder mappings from another workspace, you have several options.

From the Edit Workspace dialog shown in Figure 6-5, you can simply copy and paste working folder mappings between different instances of the dialog. You can even copy the mappings, paste them into a text editor, such as Notepad, to perform a mass edit of them, and then copy/paste those back into the working folder mappings section.

From the command line, you can create a new workspace using the following command:

```
tf workspace /new /template:workspacename[;workspaceowner]
```

In this way, you can specify an existing workspace to use as a template for your new workspace, taking the working folder mappings from that existing workspace. The workspaceowner is optional. If you do not provide it, the server will look for a workspace with that name belonging to your user. However, you can use the workspaceowner field to copy a working folder mapping set used by a colleague.

Finally, if you have the Team Foundation Power Tools installed, you can create workspace templates to share with your team by right-clicking the Team Members node in Team Explorer ➪ Team Settings ➪ General, and create/edit a workspace template to share with your team.

Recursive Working Folder Mappings

By default, a standard working folder mapping, as detailed previously, is applied recursively. When you map a folder to a location in the version control repository, a mapping is implicitly created for all subfolders. However, you can override the implicit mapping, as was done in the second and fourth line in Figure 6-5.

If you do not want a working folder mapping to be recursive, then you can use an asterisk as a wildcard to say that you wish to map only the server folder and its immediate files to your local workspace, as seen in the third line of Figure 6-5.

Mapping Individual Files

Despite the name, working folder mappings do not only apply to folders. They can actually apply to any path in version control, including individual files. For example, in Figure 6-5, the file called `HelloWorld.exe.config.dev` is being called `HelloWorld.exe.config` in the local workspace.

WORKSPACE PERMISSIONS

With Team Foundation Server 2005 and 2008, the owner of the workspace was set at the time the workspace was created, and could only be used by the owner of the workspace. With Team Foundation Server 2010, both of these restrictions have been removed. Changing the owner is simply a case of editing the owner field in the Edit Workspace dialog (see Figure 6-5). To control who can use the workspace, the owner can select from one of three *permission profiles* for his or her workspace: Private workspace, Public workspace (limited), or Public workspace.

Under the hood, a workspace actually has four permissions that a user can have on the workspace:

`Read` — The `Read` permission exists, but was not enforced in the shipping product. In theory, it would control who would have the capability to see that the workspace exists, see what mappings it had, and what pending changes exist in the workspace. However, when Team Foundation Server 2010 was released, any valid users are now able to view these properties just as they could do in the 2008 and 2005 releases.

`Use` — The `Use` permission is more interesting. It dictates who is allowed to change the state of the workspace — to get files, check out files, and so on.

`CheckIn` — The `CheckIn` permission is separated out so that, in certain cases, other people can use the workspace, but only the owner can check in those changes.

`Administer` — The `Administer` permission controls who can change the mappings, name, owner, comment, computer, and so on, as well as who can delete the workspace and change the workspace permissions.

With Visual Studio, these permissions are set by choosing one of the three permission profiles mentioned previously. A *private workspace* is the default, and the behavior is similar to that familiar to users of Team Foundation Server before

continues

(continued)

the 2010 release. Only the owner can use the workspace. The permissions for that workspace are simply `owner: Read`, `Use`, `CheckIn`, and `Administer`.

A *public workspace (limited)* means that any valid user may use the workspace, but only the owner is allowed to perform check-ins or change the properties of the workspace. In this case, the permissions for the valid users would be `valid-user: Read`, `Use`. If the owner sets a workspace to be a public workspace, then all valid users essentially have the same rights as the owner (that is, `valid-user: Read`, `Use`, `CheckIn`, and `Administer`). It also means that any valid user would also be allowed to change the owner of the workspace, and then set the workspace permissions back to Private, so this should be used with caution.

Public workspaces can be useful when sharing the same machine to make changes in parallel, but you wish to maintain a proper audit history about which users actually checked in the changes from that particular machine. The limited public workspaces can also be used when you have requested that someone help you make some changes on a machine in your workspace, but you want them to do it under their own logon credentials and have a guarantee that they will not be able to check in those changes for you.

The Edit Workspace dialog only allows you to pick from one of the three permission sets. If you have more complex workspace permission requirements (such as sharing a workspace between a few specified users, rather than with all valid users), then you can actually have full control using the .NET object model.

For more details on workspace permissions in Team Foundation Server 2010, see the blog post by Phillip Kelley (a developer on the Team Foundation Server version control team) at `http://blogs.msdn.com/b/phkelley/archive/2010/02/04/improvements-to-workspaces-in-tfs-2010.aspx`.

Get

Thus far in this chapter, you have seen the term Get Latest a few times already without explicitly knowing what it means. To download the files from the Team Foundation Server repository to your local filesystem, you perform what Team Foundation calls a *Get*. Note that this is a different term from the one used by SVN or CVS to perform this action (referred to in those systems as *checkout*). The term "checkout" means something else in Team Foundation Server, which you will learn about shortly.

When you get files from version control you can do one of two things:

➤ *Get Latest* — This downloads the latest versions of all the files as of the time you asked to start getting them.

➤ *Get Specific Version* — This downloads a version that you have specified by date, label, changeset number, or simply the latest version. This specification of the version is called a *versionspec* in Team Foundation Server.

In Team Foundation Server, the only time that you get files is when you specifically tell the server that you want to. This means that you can ensure that you know the state of your files, but, again, this can be a little different from what a VSS user expects who is used to getting the latest file as they perform a check-out.

VERSIONSPECS

In the Get dialog shown in the following figure, there is a section for Version. Here, you are specifying what Team Foundation Server understands as a version specification, or *versionspec*. A versionspec specifies the version that you want to work with, and can be specified using one of the following types: changeset, label, date, workspace, or latest.

You'll learn more about changesets later in this chapter, but changesets are the fundamental unit of versioning in Team Foundation Server. Changesets have a numeric ID associated with them. A changeset versionspec is denoted by C123456 to Team Foundation Server, where 123456 is the ID of the changeset.

A *label versionspec* says you want a version that belongs to a particular named label. They are denoted by LmyLabel where *myLabel* is the label name.

Date versionspecs are denoted with a D, and then, in the command line, you can pass any date format supported by the .NET Framework on any of the date formats for the local computer (for example, D2008-04-22T22:15).

A *workspace versionspec* means the version most recently downloaded into the workspace. This is denoted by a W, meaning the current workspace (or Wworkspace Name;workspaceOwner) when specifying a workspace written as a string.

Finally, the *latest* version is a versionspec in its own right denoted by L when written as a string. When you use the Get Latest command in Visual Studio or Eclipse, you are actually telling the client to perform a *Get* of versionspec *L*.

Certain commands (for example when viewing the history of a file) can accept ranges of versionspecs denoted by the tilde character (~). Different types of versionspecs can be mixed in those instances. For example, D2004-04-11T18:37~L would say you wanted a range of versions beginning with 11th April 2004 at 6:37 p.m. up until the latest version.

Check-out

With Team Foundation Server, when you initially get the files into your workspace, they are marked as read-only in your local filesystem. Before you start editing the file, you must *check out* the file from Team Foundation Server to let the server (and others on your team) know that you are editing that file. This happens automatically for you if you are editing a file from within Visual Studio as soon as you start typing in the file. But you must do it explicitly if you want to edit the file outside Visual Studio. When you have finished with the file and want to commit it back to the repository, you perform a *check-in*.

> *One of the many benefits of Team Foundation Server integration in the IDE (such as Visual Studio or Eclipse) is that you do not have to manually check out the file. When you start to type inside the code editor, the file is checked out for you by the Team Foundation Server integration. You can control this automatic behavior if you do not like the defaults by setting a preference on your local machine, which you will learn about later in this chapter.*

As mentioned previously, the term "checkout" is used by many version control systems, but means different things, depending on the system. In VSS, "checkout" means "give me the latest version of the file and lock it so that no one else can edit it." In SVN (and also CVS), "checkout" means "get the latest version."

With Team Foundation Server "check out" means "tell the server I want to edit the file and mark the file as writable in my local filesystem." As shown in Figure 6-6, when you check out the file, you also get the option to lock the file using a lock type (which you will learn more about later in this chapter). The default is to not lock the file at all as you edit it.

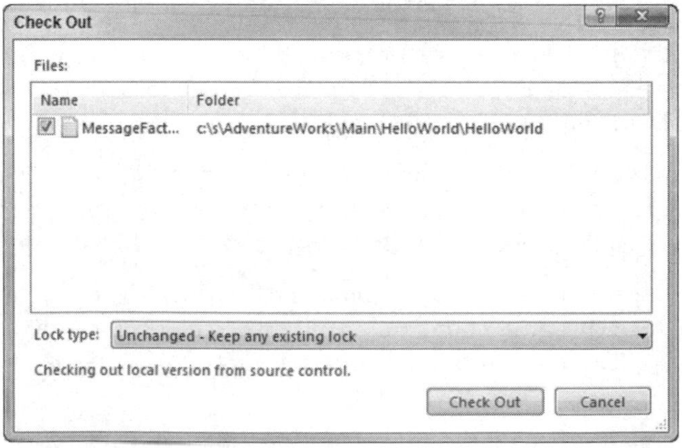

FIGURE 6-6: Check Out dialog

To understand more about the check-out process, let's examine the lifecycle of a modification to a file in Team Foundation version control, as shown in Figure 6-7.

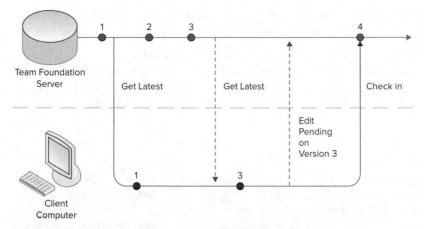

FIGURE 6-7: The normal edit process

In Figure 6-7, the line at the top represents the state of a file on the server, with the line at the bottom the state of the file in the workspace. The file is created and checked in at version 1 by someone on your team. You perform a Get Latest and download the file to your local filesystem. At this point, the file is marked as read-only locally. People on your team make some edits to the file (versions 2 and 3). You then perform a Get Latest, check out the file to say that you have an edit pending on version 3, and then check in.

Now, let's examine what happens if you did not perform a Get Latest before you did the check-out.

In Figure 6-8, you can see that you perform a Get Latest of the file after version 1. Versions 2 and 3 are created on the server just as before, but then you check out the file for edit without getting the latest. You therefore still have version 1 in your workspace when you go to check out the file, and so the server registers that you have and edit pending on version 1. When you attempt to check the file in, you will be warned that you have conflicting changes on the file (in other words, it has been edited by someone else while you were editing it), and you are prompted to merge those changes before you are able to check in the file.

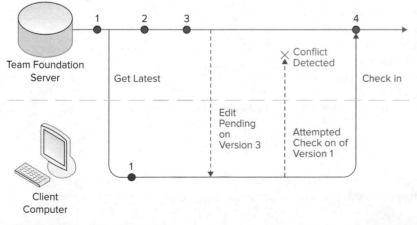

FIGURE 6-8: A conflicting edit

At this point, a VSS user can get very annoyed with Team Foundation Server. Why on earth did it not just get the latest version of the file when you asked to check it out?

The reason is because getting the new version of the file might first introduce dependencies from elsewhere that you have not downloaded yet. If, between versions 1 and 3, a dependency was introduced on another file that did not appear until version 2, then you wouldn't have it, and your source code wouldn't compile. Team Foundation Server plays it safe, and only gets files when you tell it to.

> *The behavior described here of not getting the latest version on check-out is the safest way for Team Foundation Server to behave. However, there is a preference you can set in your IDE so that everyone in the team project can force the client machine to get the latest when it performs a check-out. The preference is detailed, along with many other useful version-control configuration settings, later in this chapter.*

Locks

By default, Team Foundation Server does not automatically lock a file on check-out. That is, more than one person can edit a file at the same time. The first person to check in a file does so as normal — subsequent people will be prompted to merge their changes with the other modifications that have been made since checking out their version of the file if it was no longer the latest. This behavior is extremely useful in ensuring that teams can develop on the same code base in parallel (especially with files such as a Visual Studio `.vbproj` or `.csproj` that must be edited every time someone on the team adds or renames a file in the project).

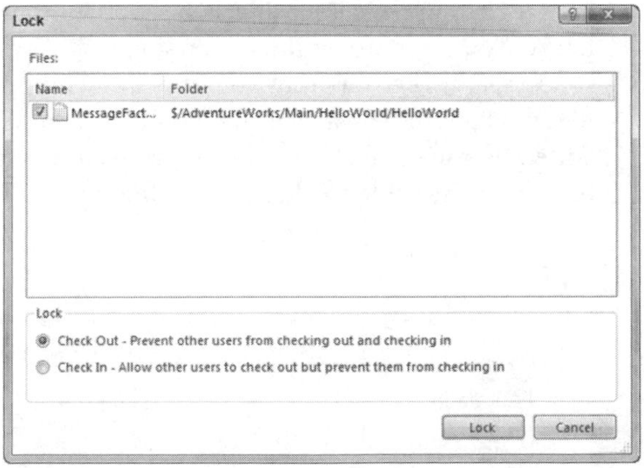

However, there are times when you wish to temporarily prevent someone from making changes to a particular file or folder in source control. For this reason, as shown in Figure 6-9, Team Foundation Server provides two types of locks that you can place on a file in your workspace: a *check-out lock* or a *check-in lock*.

FIGURE 6-9: Two types of locks

Check-out Lock

A check-out lock will be familiar to users of older version control systems such as VSS or PVCS. It prevents other users from checking out the locked file while you hold the check-out lock.

A check-out lock may not be placed on a file if other users already have that file checked out in their workspaces.

As an example, you might use a check-out lock when you are making some major or complex revisions to a file, and you want to ensure that no one else makes any changes to that file until you are done, because you do not want the additional complexity of having to merge their changes into yours before you check in.

The disadvantage of a check-out lock is that no one can easily make that file editable in their local workspace, or work on it while you have the lock held. Therefore, you are reducing the capability for your team to work in parallel on the same codebase. They are blocked from doing any work on that file until you have released the lock (usually by checking in the file).

Check-in Lock

With a check-in lock, other users can still check out the file on which you have placed the lock, but will be unable to check in until you have released the lock. Check-in locks can be placed on files that others have checked out, but, by placing the check-in lock on the file, you are guaranteeing that you will have the right of first check-in (provided no one else has a lock of any type on that file).

As an example, you might use a check-in lock when you will be making some major changes to a file, but you notice that a team member who is currently not available (possible because they are in a different time zone) has that file checked out. You send that person an e-mail or leave a message asking that they contact you before checking in their changes, because you are in the middle of doing a major refactoring. However, you want to ensure they have seen your message, so you place a check-in lock to ensure that they cannot check in until you have released the lock.

Using Locks Effectively

With any locks, you must ensure that your team communication is effective to explain why you need to lock the file. Locking should only be used where necessary because it reduces the capability for your team to work in parallel, and so can reduce productivity if overused.

In Source Control Explorer, you can see any pending changes against a particular file from other users, and who has a lock. If there are multiple changes, you might need to right-click the item, select Properties, and then look at the Status tab. However, it does not tell you what type of lock they have. To determine this information, you can make use of the `tf status /format:detailed` command.

Note that locking should only be used to temporarily lock a particular file or folder. The lock is held as part of the locking user's workspace. If you wish to restrict the capability of developers to edit a file or folder for a longer term (for example, if you want to restrict access to a branch in your codebase that represents the state of the code in production), then you should consider making use of version control permissions as detailed later in this chapter.

You can unlock a file at any time using the unlock command, but locks are also automatically released when you check in any changes related to that item in version control.

UNLOCKING FILES OF OTHER USERS

Occasionally, you will need to remove the lock placed on a file by another user in your system — for example, if the person has left the company, or is unavailable for a long period of time. To perform this operation, you need the `UnlockOther` permission in version control, which is granted to team project administrators by default.

If you have permission, you can easily unlock individual files using the command-line `tf lock /lock:none` command, from the Team Foundation Server Sidekicks tool, or from the Team Members Team Foundation Server Power Tool in Visual Studio.

If you need to remove locks because the users have left the company and they will no longer be working on the codebase, then the easiest way is to delete their workspaces. This will not only remove the locks contained in the workspaces, it will also free up the server resources associated with keeping track of that user's workspace. To do this, use the command-line `tf workspace /owner:FormerUserName` to find the workspaces belonging to that user and then the `tf workspace /delete WorkspaceName;FormerUserName` command, or the Team Foundation Server Sidekicks utility discussed later in the chapter.

Check-in of Pending Changes

As you make changes to the files in your workspace, you are building up a list of *pending changes*. Any changes you make (edits, adds, deletes, undeletes, renames, moves, branches, merges, and so on) are stored as pending changes in your workspace.

In Team Foundation Server, when you wish to commit your list of changes to the server, you perform a *check-in*, as shown in Figure 6-10.

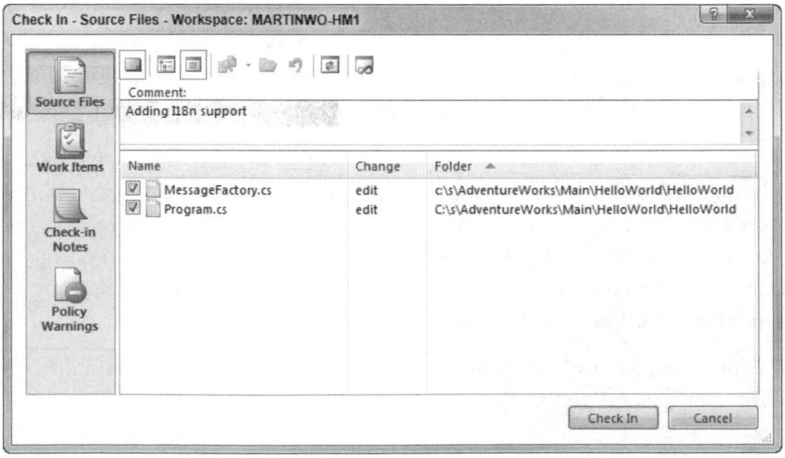

FIGURE 6-10: Check-in window

A check-in is performed as a single atomic transaction. During the check-in operation, the server first checks to see if you are able to perform the check-in for these files (that is, you have the "Check in" permission for the files set to Allow), that there are no check-in locks on the files, and that you are attempting to check in a change of the latest version of the file. If, for some reason, the check-in cannot occur (for example, because someone else has edited a file while you had it checked out and has committed their changes), then the entire check-in operation will fail. You will be informed of the reason, along with instructions on how to take corrective action. This is a different behavior from systems such as VSS that do not have the notion of an atomic check-in.

Assuming you are able to check in the files, the modified files are uploaded to the server and committed to the version control repository, along with any comment that you may have provided with the change. If any of the files you have checked out were not changed (for example, you checked out a file, but ended up not editing it), then those files will be automatically removed from the list of changes that you are committing. Once a set of changes has been committed, it is known as a *changeset*. (Changesets will be examined in more detail shortly.)

COMMENTING YOUR CHECK-INS

As is common with version control systems, when performing a check-in to Team Foundation Server, you can provide a comment to summarize your change. It is a best practice to add a comment, and with Team Foundation Server, you can actually enforce this by using a check-in policy as part of the Team Foundation Server Power Tools. Adding comments means that when you look at the history later, it is easy to quickly see why changes were made.

When providing comments, you should concentrate on *why* you were making the change, not *what*. For example "edited HelloWorld.cs" or "Fixed bug 1234" are not particularly useful comments because you could easily get that information from looking at the details of the changeset. Instead, a comment of "Refactored code into more discrete methods to make it easier to test and maintain" would be a much more useful comment.

While performing a check-in, it is best practice to also associate the change with a *work item* (such as a bug, task, feature, requirement, user story, and so on). In this way, you can easily get end-to-end traceability of requirements on through to changes of code, and into builds, which is a key feature of Team Foundation Server.

> *For more information on work items see Part III (Chapters 11 through 13) of this book.*

Check-in Notes

While checking in files, it is often useful to capture metadata about the change from the person committing the check-in. For example, who performed a code review of the changes or a reference to a third-party ticking system. In other version control systems, this is often implemented by the developers adopting a convention when providing check-in comments. However, Team Foundation Server provides a mechanism for capturing structured data about a check-in — the *check-in notes*.

In the Pending Changes view or the Check-in dialog, you have access to the check-in notes channel to capture data about the check-in, as shown in Figure 6-11. Check-in notes are all text-based responses and no validation is available, other than to optionally check that a value has been provided. A check-in note could be many lines (in fact up to 2GB of data). However, typically it is just a single name or value.

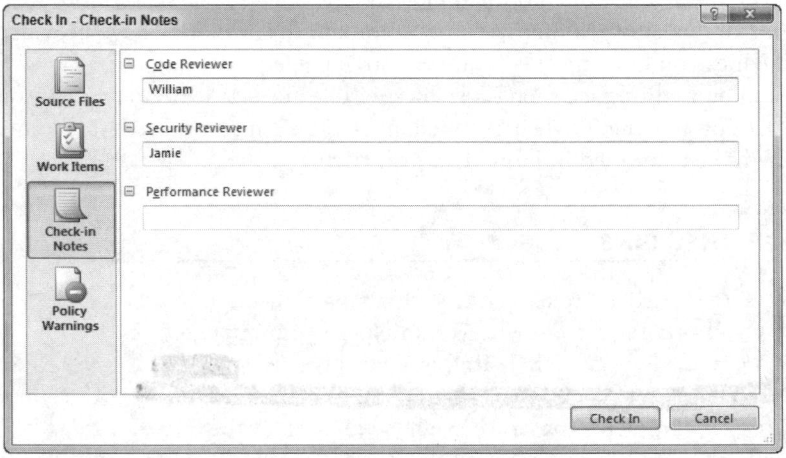

FIGURE 6-11: "Check-in Notes" window

To configure the check-in notes for a team project, you must have the "Manipulate security settings" permission set to Allow (which is the default for administrators). In Visual Studio, go to Team ➪ Team Project Settings ➪ Source Control. Click the Check-in Notes tab, as shown in Figure 6-12.

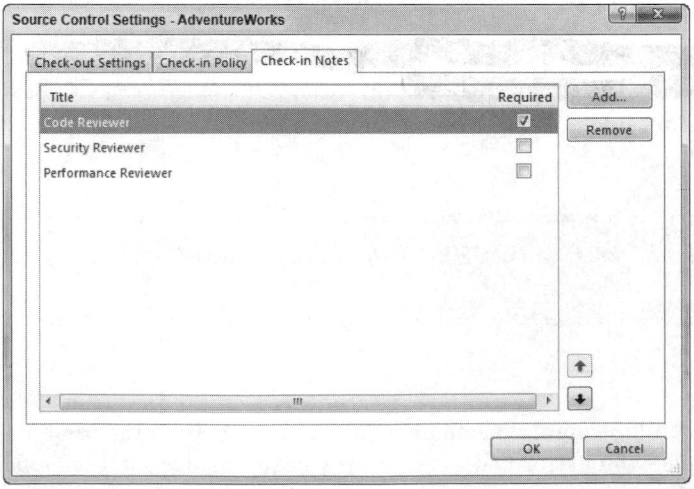

FIGURE 6-12: Check-in Notes tab

From the Check-in Notes tab, you can add, edit, remove, and reorder check-in note titles, as well as make any check-in note field mandatory. If a check-in note is required, then, when a user attempts to perform a check-in without providing a value for that field, the user will be prompted for a value before being allowed to check in.

Check-in Policies

For more complex validation of a check-in before submission, check-in policies may be configured by users who have the "Manipulate security settings" permission set to Allow (typically a team project administrator).

A check-in policy is a piece of code that runs in the client performing the check-in, which validates if the check-in is allowed to occur. For Visual Studio, this code is written in .NET. In Eclipse or the cross-platform command-line client, the check-in policy is written in Java. Figure 6-13 shows the check-in policies available in Visual Studio 2010.

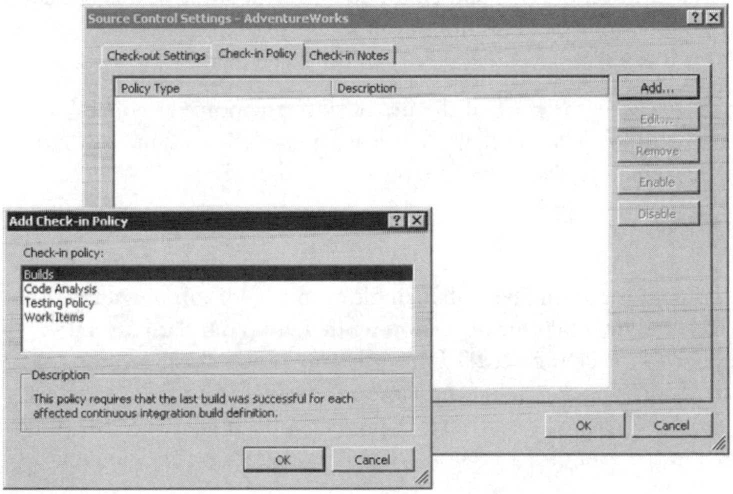

FIGURE 6-13: Check-in policies for Visual Studio 2010

Additional check-in policies are available as part of the Team Foundation Server 2010 Power Tools. Also note that the check-in policies enforced by Team Explorer Everywhere in Eclipse and the cross-platform command-line client must be configured from a Team Explorer Everywhere client by a user with appropriate permission. This is because those clients use a separate (Java-based) implementation for check-in policies. Once configured by the administrator in Visual Studio and in Eclipse, the check-in policies will be in effect for all users checking in affected files to that team project.

If a user attempts to perform a check-in that fails validation of the check-in policy, the user will be warned about the policy failure, as shown in Figure 6-14.

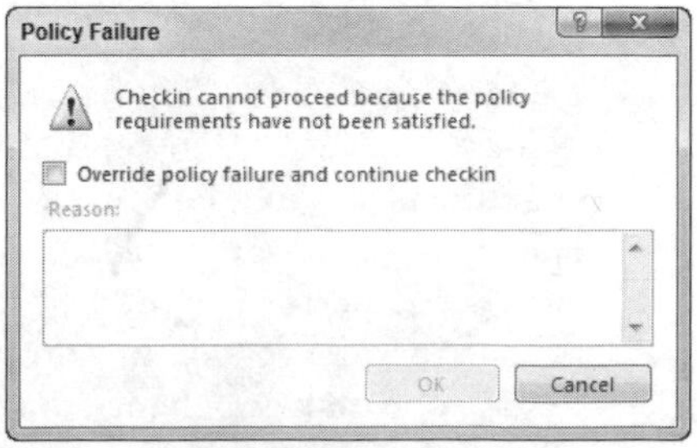

FIGURE 6-14: Policy Failure warning

If necessary, it is possible to override the policy.

> 🖉 *For more information on check-in policies and other mechanisms to ensure code quality, see Chapter 7.*

Undo Pending Changes

Sometimes, even the best developers make mistakes and wish that they could simply revert their changes, instead of checking them in. In Team Foundation Server, this is accomplished by performing an Undo Pending Changes. This will allow you to select which changes you wish to undo, and those files will be rolled back to the previous version that you downloaded into your workspace (not the latest version on the server, because that could be different).

If the change you are undoing is the addition of a file (called an *add*), the pending add is removed from your list of pending changes. However, the file is not automatically deleted from the disk, allowing you to go back to add that file if you have mistakenly undone the change.

Note that undoing a pending change reverts the state of the file back to the point at which you last checked it in. If you want to actually undo a change that you have already checked in, you should look at the `tf rollback` command, which is also covered later in this chapter.

Changeset

When you perform a check-in, all the information about that single atomic check-in operation is stored as a *changeset*. The changeset is the fundamental unit of versioning in Team Foundation version control. It is represented by a number — the changeset ID. The only way that a change to the contents of a version control repository can occur is by creating a changeset. In fact, this is true even when creating the version control repository. When you create a team project collection, one of the things that the setup process does is check in the root of the version control repository `$/` as changeset 1.

> **REMOVING SOURCE CONTROL FILES FROM YOUR LOCAL FILESYSTEM**
>
> A great demonstration of the fact that changeset numbers are the unique unit of versioning in Team Foundation Server can be seen by noting how to get Team Foundation Server to remove a file from your local filesystem without deleting it from version control.
>
> Occasionally, you will have a file in your workspace that you do not want locally for some reason, but you want to leave it in version control. The obvious course of action is just to go out to the filesystem and delete it from the disk. The problem is that you have not told Team Foundation Server that you have deleted it locally, so if you perform a Get Latest on the folder, because the server thinks you already have that file version in your workspace, it doesn't send the file to you again until someone makes a change to that file.

However, if you perform a Get Specific Version on the file or folder and set the changeset to 1, the file will be deleted locally and will show in Source Control Explorer as Not Downloaded. Performing a Get Latest on the file will download it again.

Why does this work? Because changeset 1 is the changeset that was created when the team project collection was created, and the root of the version control repository ($/) was checked in. By saying that you want to get the version of the file at changeset 1, you are telling the server you want to get that file as it was at a point in time, which is represented by changeset 1. The file didn't exist at changeset 1, and so it is deleted from your local filesystem.

The changeset contains all the information about the change — what adds, edits, renames, deletes, branches, merges, and so on, occurred at that instant — along with the additional information of what work items were associated with the change, any check-in notes, and check-in policy compliance. The date of the changeset, and who checked it in, are also tracked by the server for auditing purposes. Note that this is different from VSS, where the date on the client machines actually could affect the date of that file in the version control repository.

Changeset IDs increment across the whole project collection. For example, a check-in to $/TeamProjectA/FileX.txt could be changeset 25, and the next check-in might affect $/TeamProjectB/FileY.txt, making that changeset 26. Therefore, if you view the history of a single file, you will see the IDs of the changesets in which changes occurred to that file. Files are not individually versioned as they are in VSS, but their version is the ID of the changeset in which they were altered, as shown in Figure 6-15.

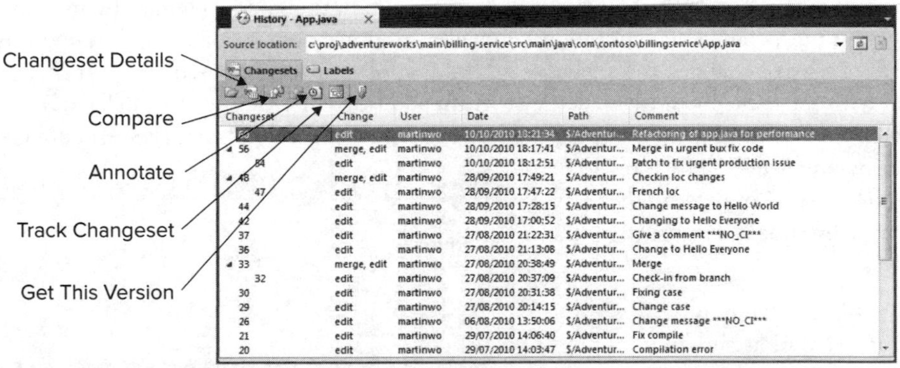

FIGURE 6-15: History view in Visual Studio 2010

The changes that occurred in a changeset are immutable — you cannot go back in time and rewrite history. However, the owner of a changeset (or an administrator) is able to edit the changeset comment and check-in notes after the event. In addition, a work item may be linked to a particular changeset at any point after the changeset is created, and that work item would show up in the associated work items channel when viewing the changeset details.

> ### ROLLING BACK A CHANGESET
>
> Occasionally, a change will be committed to the repository that needs to be reverted. In versions of Team Foundation Server prior to the 2010 release, this was performed by checking in a copy of the previous version, and could be done manually or via the `rollback` command available in the Team Foundation Power Tool command-line `tfpt`.
>
> In Team Foundation Server 2010, rollback was introduced as a full change type. However, access to the functionality still requires use of the command line — but this time, the `tf rollback` command.
>
> For more information on how to use rollback, see `http://msdn.microsoft.com/en-us/library/dd380776.aspx`.

Shelvesets

Sometimes, when you work on a set of files, it is useful to store the changes on the server without committing those changes to the main code line that the rest of the team is working on. Perhaps because you want to save progress on a particularly large change, you might want to share a set of changes with a colleague on a different machine, or possibly because you must stop work on what you are currently doing and go work on a more urgent task before resuming where you left off.

Team Foundation Server provides a simple mechanism to help in those instances — the *shelveset*.

A set of pending changes can be saved to the server in a shelveset — a process called *shelving*. A shelveset is uniquely identified by the owner and a name given to the shelveset.

Shelvesets share much in common with changesets. They can contain the same metadata (work item associations, check-in notes, comments, and so on). However, they are not versioned in the same way. If the same person saves a set of changes to a shelveset with the same name, the contents of that shelveset will be overridden with the contents of the new shelveset. In addition, shelvesets can be deleted. Unlike when a file is deleted in version control, if you delete a shelveset, the contents of that shelveset are gone. A shelveset cannot be undeleted. Therefore, a shelveset is a temporary store of data on the server, but one whose lifetime is controlled by the owner of the shelveset.

To get the contents of a shelveset into a workspace, you *unshelve* it, as shown in Figure 6-16. You can unshelve into different workspaces, on different computers. You can e-mail the name of a shelveset to a team member, and that person can find it by your user ID, look at the details, compare the files in it with other versions, and even unshelve the contents into their workspace, provided they have suitable working folder mappings for the shelved files.

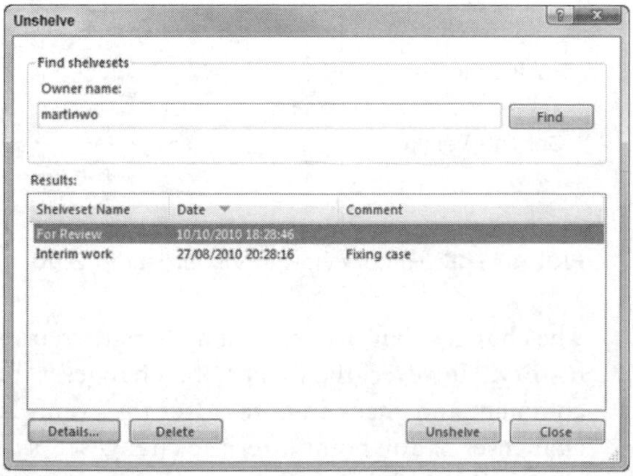

FIGURE 6-16: Unshelving a shelveset

For many instances, judicious use of shelvesets can be a quick and easy way of passing around and storing version control data with your team, and can reduce the need for temporary private branches of code. However, shelvesets do take up some resources on the server, and so you should delete old shelvesets when no longer needed.

Branches

Generally speaking, a *branch* in Team Foundation Server can be thought of as a folder that contains a copy of the source tree from another area in the tree taken at a point in time. A branch is useful when parallel areas of development are required.

> *For more information about branching concepts see Chapter 5. For more detail and best practices on how to branch and merge with Team Foundation Server, see Chapter 9.*

In Team Foundation Server 2005 and 2008, a branch was exactly that — a folder. However, in Team Foundation Server 2010, branches are now a first-class citizen. As shown in Figure 6-17, a branch has a unique icon in source control to distinguish it from regular folders. It also can contain additional metadata (such as the owner), and description, as well as the relationships between it and other branches.

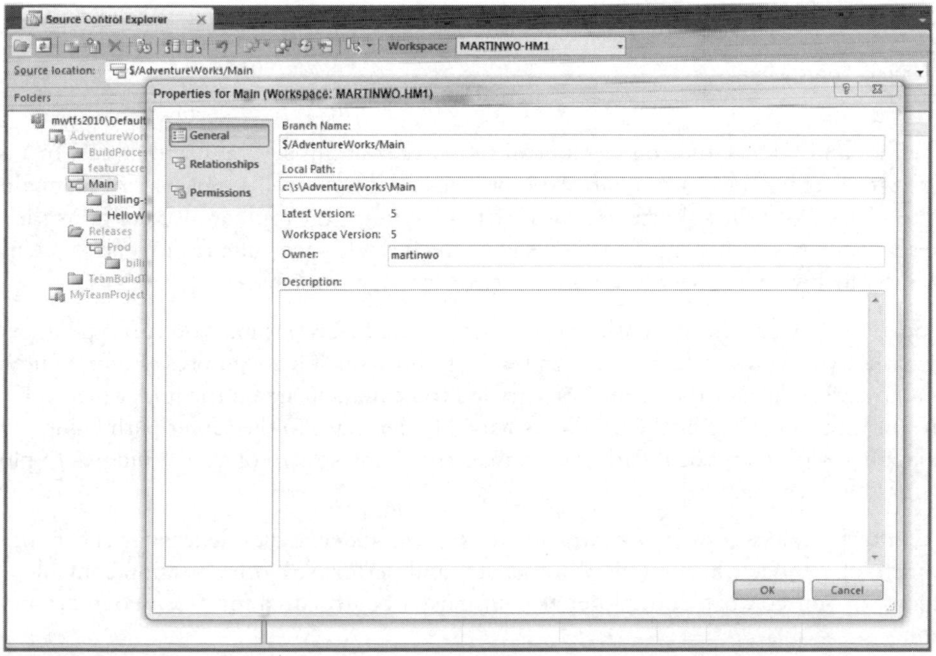

FIGURE 6-17: Information displayed for a branch

You can convert an existing folder to a full branch object very easily by right-clicking the folder in Source Control Explorer and selecting Branching and Merging ⇨ Convert to Branch. If you created a `Main` folder when adding your solution to version control at the beginning of this chapter, then convert this to a full branch now.

USING SOURCE CONTROL EXPLORER

The *Source Control Explorer* (Figure 6-18) provides a view of your current Team Foundation version control workspace. You can show the Source Control Explorer by double-clicking the Source Control node in Team Explorer for a particular team project, or, in Visual Studio, you can go to View ⇨ Other Windows ⇨ Source Control Explorer.

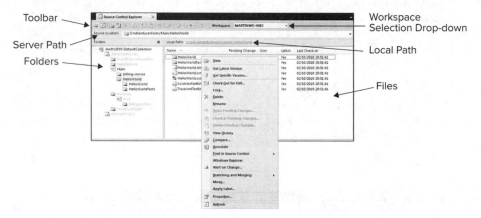

FIGURE 6-18: Source Control Explorer

Apart from the files and folders, the Source Control Explorer contains several useful areas. In Visual Studio 2010, the toolbar for the source control editor is inside the control — not part of the main Visual Studio toolbars. As well as shortcuts to a variety of actions, the toolbar also contains the Workspace selection drop-down menu that shows you which workspace you are currently viewing, and allows you to quickly switch between workspaces or manage workspaces.

The Source Location shows the server path that you are currently navigating. You can type in or paste a server path if you know exactly where you want to browse. When you press Enter, you will navigate to that area. If you click the drop-down arrow, you can navigate up the folder hierarchy from your current location. The Local Path shows which folder maps to the server path being viewed. If a mapping is present, Local Path is clickable, and doing so will open a Windows Explorer window showing that local path.

From Source Control Explorer, you can view, add, delete, and undelete files, as well as check in, check out, branch, merge, view history, view properties, and perform all other version control operations. Think of Source Control Explorer as your master control area for Team Foundation version control.

Pending Changes View

Another vitally important view in Team Foundation version control is the *Pending Changes view* shown in Figure 6-19. In Visual Studio, if you do not have the Pending Changes view available, go to View ➪ Other Windows ➪ Pending Changes.

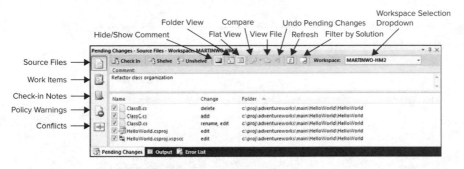

FIGURE 6-19: Pending Changes view

The Pending Changes view consists of a number of *channels*, with each channel having a set of toolbar buttons that appear in the top of the view. The main channel is the Source Files channel. This shows the files that you have checked out in the selected workspace.

Note that the workspace selected is shown in the Workspace selection drop-down, which behaves in the same way as the drop-down in the Source Control Explorer. However, in Visual Studio, there is no link between these drop-downs. If you are checking out files, but cannot see your changes, it is probably because you have the wrong workspace selected in the Workspace selection drop-down in the Pending Changes view.

The standard view for pending changes is the Flat view. However, you may also view by folder, and also filter the changes so that only those related to the currently open solution are displayed.

The Work Items channel shown in Figure 6-20 allows you to select which work item the changes should be associated with. You can select the work item query that should be used to find your work items from the toolbar when the work item channel is selected. If supported by the process template, then a check-in action might be available when associating with a work item in a particular state (such as Active) to *Resolve* it and move the work item to the next state. The Check-in Notes channel

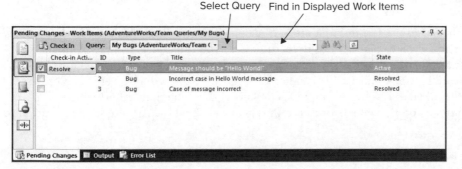

FIGURE 6-20: Work Items channel

shown in Figure 6-21 displays all the check-in notes that apply to the changes in your source files. If you have files from multiple team projects in your pending change list, you will see the combined list of check-in notes for both the team projects. Mandatory check-in notes will be highlighted. While a single line is provided for each note, multiple lines can be entered simply by pressing Enter inside the check-in note.

FIGURE 6-21: Check-in Notes channel

The Policy Warnings channel shown in Figure 6-22 displays details of any existing check-in policy validation errors. The policies will be evaluated when you first view the Policy Warnings channel, or at check-in. If you wish to re-evaluate the check-in policies at any point (for example, if you had a policy validation warning that you think you have now fixed), right-click in the Description area and select Evaluate from the context menu.

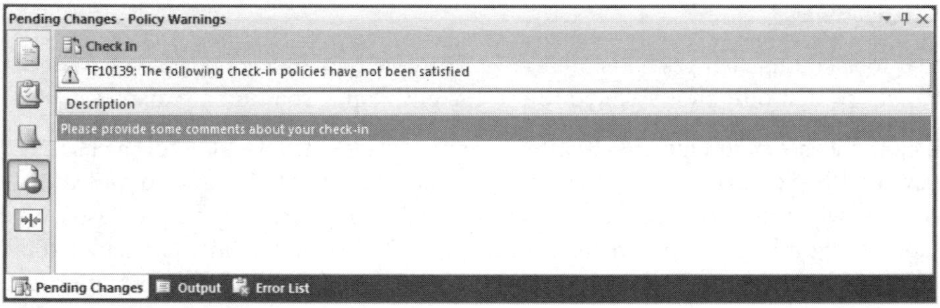

FIGURE 6-22: Policy Warnings channel

Finally, the Conflicts channel shown in Figure 6-23 displays any conflicts that exist in the current workspace, and allows you to take actions to rectify them. You can select multiple conflicts by holding down Shift while clicking to select a range. If you hold down Ctrl while clicking, you can select a nonsequential set of conflicts. With either key sequence, you will be given a common set of actions that can be taken to resolve the multiple conflicts at the same time. Alternatively, you can automerge all conflicts, or all conflicts of a certain type, by clicking the AutoResolve All button in the toolbar.

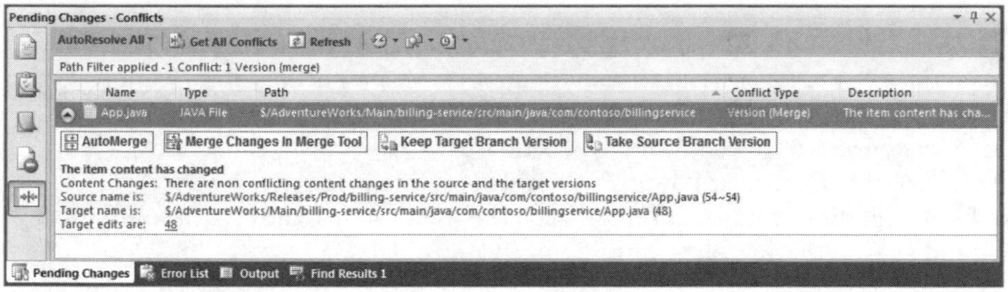

FIGURE 6-23: Conflicts channel

> For more information on conflict resolution and the AutoResolve options, see
> http://msdn.microsoft.com/en-us/library/ms181432.aspx.

Note that, as well as accessing version control operations from the Source Control Explorer and the Pending Changes view, many common version control operations are available directly from the context menu inside Solution Explorer, or from the context menu inside the editor of the file.

MANAGING SOLUTION SOURCE CONTROL BINDINGS

The mapping between a solution in Visual Studio and the version control settings is stored in the .sln file. If you wish to customize the bindings, or remove them entirely, then go to File ➪ Source Control ➪ Change Source Control while editing a file in the solution. You will see the Change Source Control dialog shown in the following figure, where you can customize or remove the bindings.

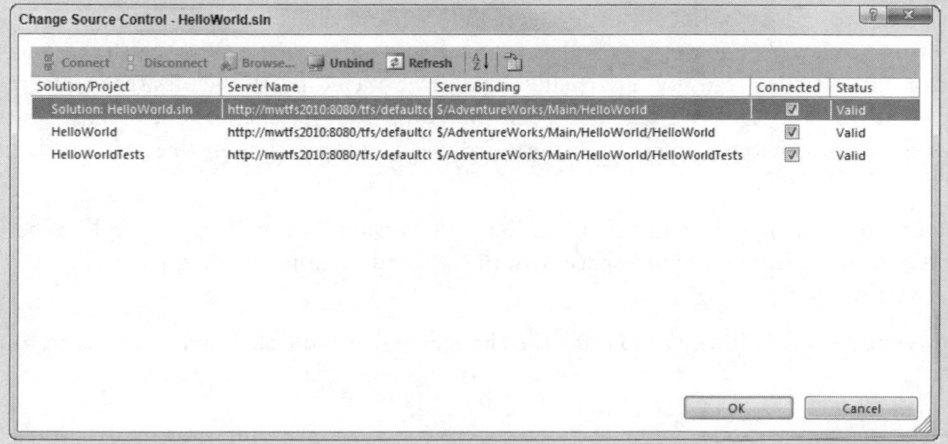

continues

(continued)

If you used the `VSS2TeamFoundation` tool to import a VSS repository into Team Foundation Server, you should find that your bindings for the solution have been automatically converted for you. If not, you can use the `tfpt bind` command in the Team Foundation Server Power Tools to do this in an automated way. Or you can fix the bindings the first time you open the solution by removing the old bindings and adding the new ones in the Source Control Dialog.

However, if you moved your source over from the latest version from VSS or any other version control system, you might have to modify the bindings the first time you open the solution. Equally, if you have been provided with a copy of some source code that was previously checked into a Team Foundation Server repository that you do not have access to, then you can use this dialog to remove the bindings.

Chapter 8 provides more information on migrating from legacy version control systems.

Viewing History

The means by which you can view the history of files, folders, and changesets has been updated and enhanced in Team Foundation Server 2010. To view the history of a file or folder, in Source Control Explorer, right-click the file or folder, and select View History from the context menu. This opens a new document tab in Visual Studio, as shown earlier in Figure 6-15.

The new History window is now a tabbed document window in Visual Studio. This allows you to open multiple History windows for research, something that was not possible in previous versions. The History window also provides a view of both the changesets associated with the file or folder, as well as any labels.

You have several options when you click the Changeset tab. You can select a changeset and click the View button to view the file version for that particular changeset. You can click the Changeset Details button to view the details for a particular changeset, including all the files that make up the changeset and any associated work items. You can compare two different versions of a file or folder to see the differences. Clicking the Annotate button allows you to see, line by line, who made what changes to a particular file.

Finally, you can select a changeset and click the Get This Version button. This will replace the current version of this file in your workspace with the selected version, enabling you to easily return to an earlier version of a file.

The History window also allows you to track the changes across multiple branches, merges, and renames.

Chapter 9 provides more information on branching and merging.

Labeling Files

A *label* is a marker that can be attached to files and folders. This marker allows all the files and folders labeled together to be retrieved as one collective unit. Labeling was available in previous versions of Visual Studio, but it had some issues. Labeling an item could sometimes be a tedious and complex process, and labeling a large number of files could be very slow.

With Visual Studio 2010, labeling has been updated to make it easier to use and manage. To create a new label, in Source Control Explorer, right-click the file or folder you want to label, and from the context menu, select Apply Label. This opens the New Label window, as shown in Figure 6-24.

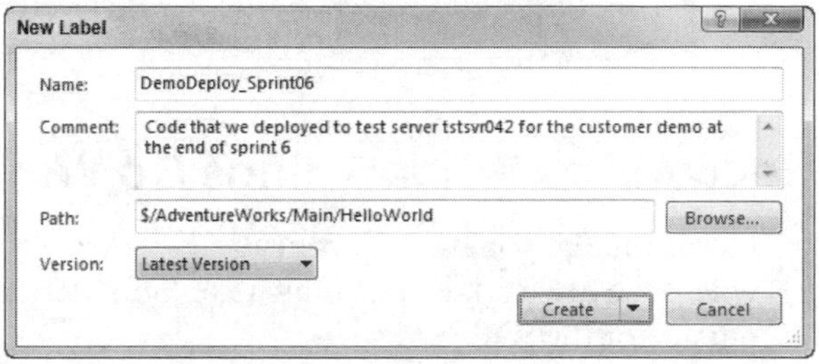

FIGURE 6-24: New Label window

In this window, you can enter the label name and a comment. You can also select the version that you want to label. You can choose to label by Changeset, Date, Label, Latest Version, or Workspace Version. Click the Create button to create the label.

Notice that the Create button is a drop-down arrow. Clicking the arrow provides you with two options. You can create the label as is, or you can create the label and then edit it. If you select Create and Edit, the label will be created, and you will be presented a new tab, as shown in Figure 6-25.

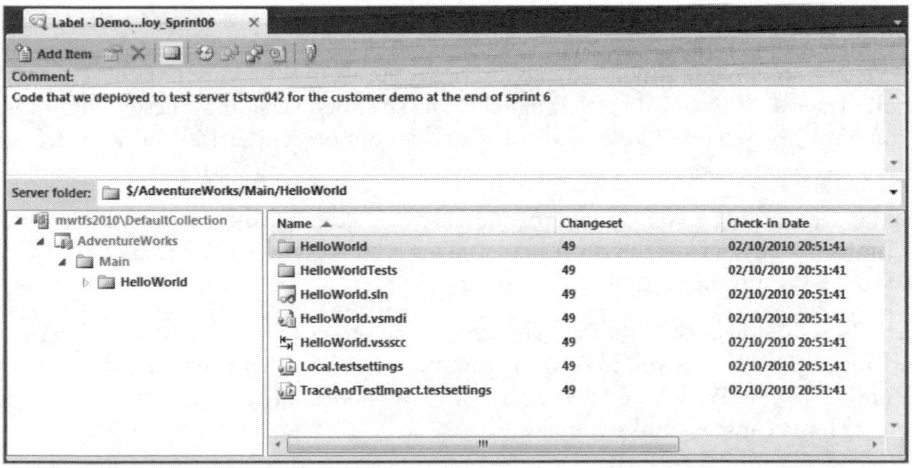

FIGURE 6-25: Selecting "Create and Edit" when creating a label

This tab allows you to make multiple changes to the label. You can add new files to the label. You can change the version of an individual file that the label is currently applied to. And you can remove files from the label. All of this is made easily accessible by using a tree-view control. Managing labels in Visual Studio 2010 is now a much easier process.

> *In Team Foundation Server, labels are editable at any point after they are created by any user with the "Administer shelved changes" permission set to Allow. This is very different from VSS, where labels are fixed once created, and more like the tagging behavior in SVN. Because of this reason, labels in Team Foundation Server should not be used for strict auditing purposes.*

Recovering When Things Go Wrong

Occasionally, you can get your local workspace into a confusing state — this is most common when you are initially learning Team Foundation Server, or if you are doing a lot of changes outside of the IDE.

If you have been editing files outside of Visual Studio, manually overriding the read-only attribute to do so (and possibly deleting files from your local filesystem while trying to work on a problem) is a common and quick way to get your workspace into a confusing state.

Once you understand Team Foundation Server, you will find that this never happens to you. However, until you understand how the server thinks about version control, the following tips can help you get your workspace back into a state that is more understandable. If you find that you have a development workflow that requires you to take any of the following steps as part of a normal day, then you are doing something wrong, and you should look again at how you are using Team Foundation Server version control.

Get Specific, Force Overwrite, Force Get

The Get Specific Version dialog has options to "Overwrite writable files that are not checked out" and "Overwrite all files even if the local version matches the specified version." These two options can help you if you have been editing files outside of Visual Studio or Eclipse and you want to replace them with the server version.

The default behavior when doing a Get is to warn you when you attempt to download a new version of a file that is writable locally, and not to download it. This is to prevent overwriting of changes that you may have made locally and wanted to keep.

If you force a Get, you will download all files again, even if the server thinks you already have a copy in your workspace. This allows you to recover from the situation where you have deleted a file locally, but have not told Team Foundation Server, and so it will normally not send the file to you when you perform a Get because it thinks you have it.

Detect Local Changes in Eclipse

In the Team Foundation Server plug-in for Eclipse available as part of Team Explorer Everywhere, if you right-click a project in Package Explorer and select Detect Local Changes, your local workspace will be compared with the server version, and the plug-in will attempt to check out files that you have changed. Any adds or deletes will be marked as pending as required. Note that renames cannot be detected in this way. They would appear as a delete for the old name, and an add for the new name, meaning that you would lose the ability to easily track the history prior to the rename.

Return Online Power Tool

In the Team Foundation Server 2010 Power Tools, the command-line `tfpt online` command is available. This command is designed to help sync changes in your workspace while you were disconnected from the server. It will compare the server versions with your local versions, and attempt to check out modified files, perform adds and deletes, and so on, in a similar manner to the Detect Local Changes option in Eclipse.

> *Once you have installed the Power Tools, you can use the* `tfpt help online` *command to view more options.*

Re-create the Workspace

If all else fails, then the nuclear option is to go to the Manage Workspaces dialog (File ➪ Source Control ➪ Workspaces in Visual Studio), delete your workspace, and create it again. Move any files that were in your local working folders to a temporary directory, and start all over again.

This is the Team Foundation Server equivalent of rebooting your version control state. When you delete a workspace, all information about what files you have downloaded, what locks you might have invoked, and what files you had checked out is removed from the server. Therefore, this option should not be taken lightly, but is guaranteed to get you back into a known good state.

TEAM FOUNDATION SERVER VERSION CONTROL IN ECLIPSE

So far, this chapter has mostly focused on the experience when performing version control operations inside Visual Studio 2010. However, Team Foundation Server 2010 is available inside a number of environments, not just older versions of Visual Studio (such as Visual Studio 2008 or Visual Studio 2005, which had Team Foundation Server integration), but also even older versions or IDEs that support the Microsoft Source Code Control Interface (MSSCCI) API for version control.

With the 2010 release of Team Foundation Server, Microsoft released its first version of an integration to the product from the popular Open Source IDE Eclipse, and Eclipse-based IDEs such as Rational Application Developer or MyEclipse. This integration is included in the Microsoft Visual Studio Team Explorer Everywhere product, and is also available to developers with a Visual Studio Ultimate MSDN subscription.

Previously, the Eclipse integration was available from a partner company called Teamprise. Microsoft acquired the technology assets of Teamprise in November 2009, and also hired the core development team — setting them to work on the Team Explorer Everywhere product, which is built on the Teamprise technology.

Team Explorer Everywhere is an implementation of the Team Foundation Server protocol written entirely in Java, utilizing the same web services that the .NET implementation uses. Therefore, the Team Explorer Everywhere clients run anywhere that Eclipse and Java run, not just on Windows, but on Mac, Linux, and many common UNIX platforms. Microsoft is fully committed to keeping Team Explorer Everywhere and Eclipse up-to-date so that developers in Eclipse can be full contributors to a software development team using Team Foundation Server.

While many of the experiences in working with Team Foundation Server in Eclipse are similar to working inside Visual Studio 2010 (especially the Source Control editor, work item tracking, and build automation functionality, as shown in Figure 6-26), there are a few differences because of the way that version control tools typically integrate with an Eclipse environment.

FIGURE 6-26: Working in Eclipse

ECLIPSE WORKSPACES VERSUS TEAM FOUNDATION SERVER WORKSPACES

Unfortunately, the word "workspace" in the Eclipse and Team Foundation Server worlds mean different, yet slightly overlapping, things. A Team Foundation Server workspace was defined earlier in this chapter. The Eclipse workspace contains a set of Eclipse projects, along with the set of user preferences for that instance and other configuration data.

However, the set of projects in an Eclipse workspace maps well into the concept of working folder mappings in a Team Foundation Server workspace. To reduce the complexity of dealing with multiple concepts called "workspace," the Team Foundation Server plug-in for Eclipse only allows for one active Team Foundation Server workspace per Eclipse workspace. In Team Explorer Everywhere 2010 Service Pack 1, you can easily switch which Team Foundation Server workspace is the active one from the pending changes view.

Installing the Team Foundation Server Plug-in for Eclipse

The Team Foundation Server plug-in for Eclipse is available on the media for Team Explorer Everywhere when purchased at a retailer or downloaded from MSDN. A fully-functional trial version of the plug-in is available from the Microsoft Download Center. The plug-in ships as an Eclipse Update Site Archive, which not only allows for easy installation, but also allows an organization to host the update site on an internal server should it want a particular approved version to be used by the entire Eclipse community in the organization.

To install the Team Foundation Server plug-in from the media (or the download), go to Help ⇨ Install New Software in Eclipse. This displays the Available Software wizard. Click the Add button to add an Eclipse update repository, and then click Archive and select the `UpdateSiteArchive` zip file, as shown in Figure 6-27. Then click OK.

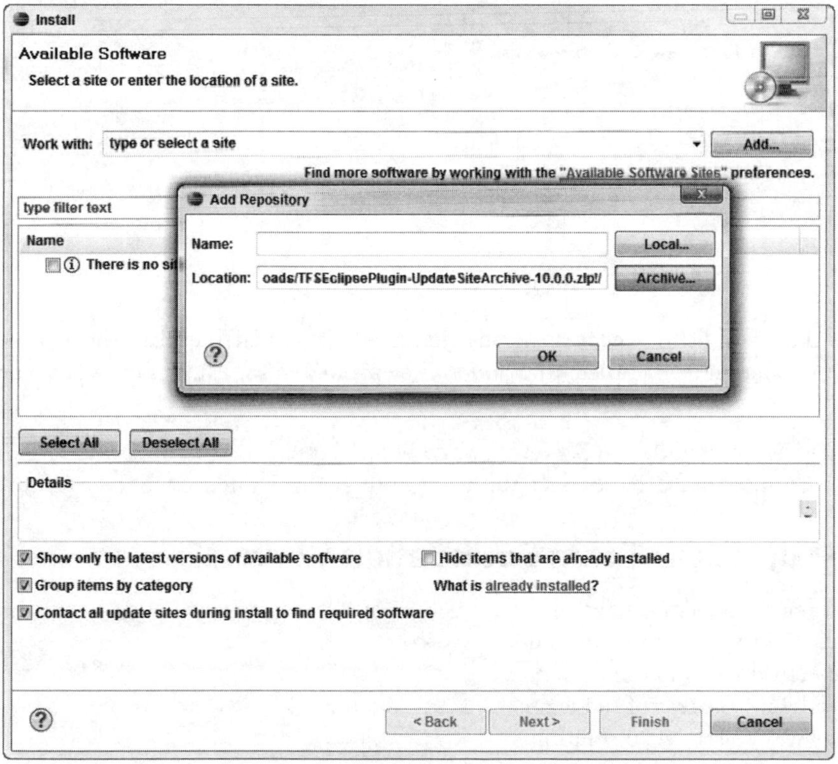

FIGURE 6-27: Adding the update archive to Eclipse

Select the check box for Visual Studio Team Explorer Everywhere 2010. Optionally, you can uncheck the setting for "Contact all update sites during install to find required software," as shown in Figure 6-28. This works because a typical Eclipse-based product contains the requirements for Team Explorer Everywhere, and not checking external update sites will reduce the installation time.

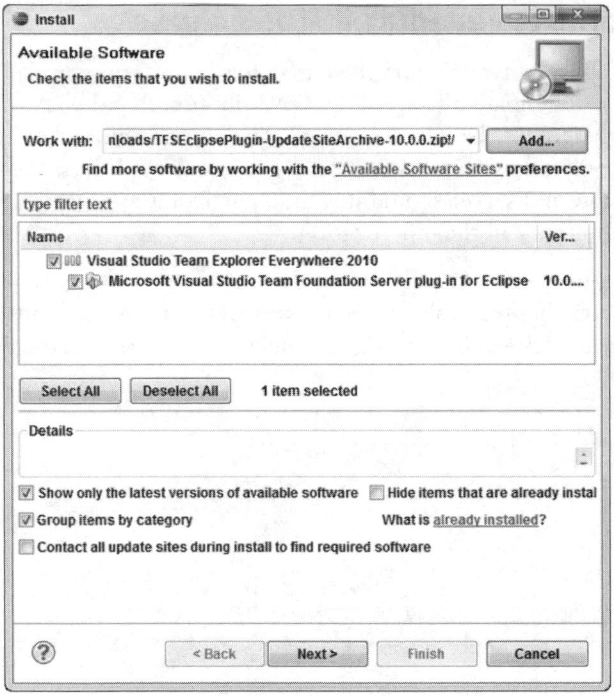

FIGURE 6-28: Selecting not to contact all update sites

Go through the rest of the wizard and accept the license terms. Once you click Finish, the Team Foundation Server plug-in should be installed, and you will be prompted to restart Eclipse (which you should do).

This will add several new Team Foundation Server views to Eclipse, and a Team Foundation Exploring perspective that you can use to connect and work with Team Foundation Server resources.

Sharing Eclipse Projects in Team Foundation Server

Now that you have the Team Foundation Server integration installed, the next thing you want to do is add your Eclipse project into Team Foundation Server so that it is shared with the rest of the team. This is done in a similar way to the "Add solution to source control" functionality in Visual Studio.

However, in Eclipse, version control providers make this functionality available by right-clicking the project in Eclipse and selecting Team ➪ Share Project. This displays a list of version control repository types. As shown in Figure 6-29, Team Foundation Server will now be available in that list.

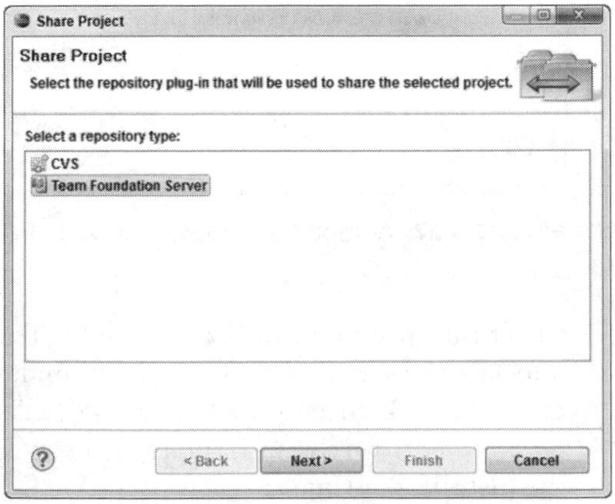

FIGURE 6-29: Team Foundation Server displayed as a repository type

Select Team Foundation Server. On the next screen shown in Figure 6-30, you will be prompted to provide details about your Team Foundation Server. Enter the name or fully qualified URL for your Team Foundation Server instance. At this point, you can click the Advance tab to change the default server, path, port, and protocol from the defaults. However, for most instances, the defaults work fine.

Note that, if your Team Foundation Server instance is not installed at `http://server_name:8080/tfs`, then you will want to ensure that you share your Team Foundation Server address with the development team using the fully qualified URL (that is, `https://mytfs.mycompany.com/tfs`) instead of the hostname to ensure that the right connection settings are used. At this initial connection, you can also provide your HTTP proxy settings to use when talking to Team Foundation Server if they differ from the proxy settings used by Eclipse. You can also specify any Team Foundation Server proxy that you may be using.

FIGURE 6-30: Details about Team Foundation Server

On the next page in the wizard (Figure 6-31), you will be asked to pick the project collection and team project in which you wish to share your Eclipse project.

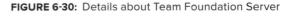

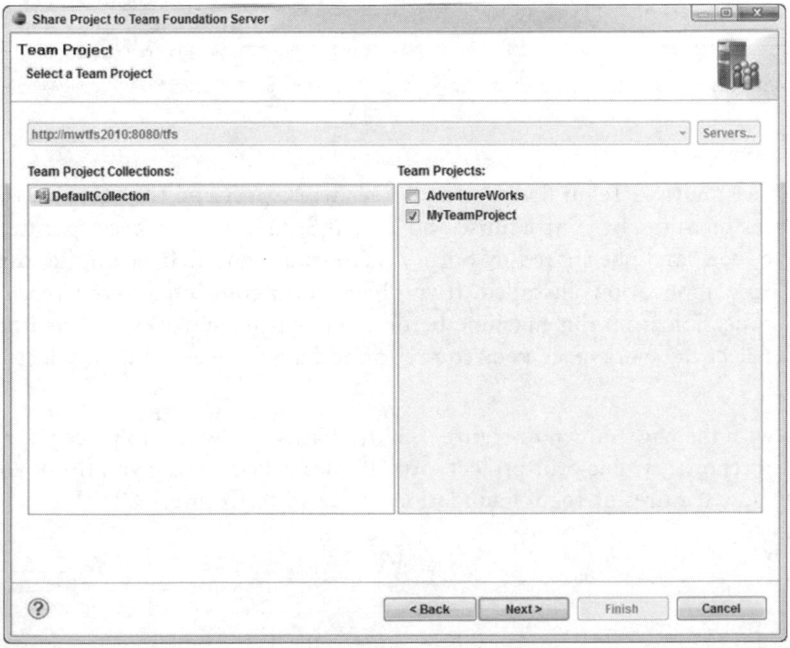

FIGURE 6-31: Picking the project collection and team project

On the next page in the wizard (Figure 6-32), you will be prompted to select which Team Foundation Server workspace to use to share your project.

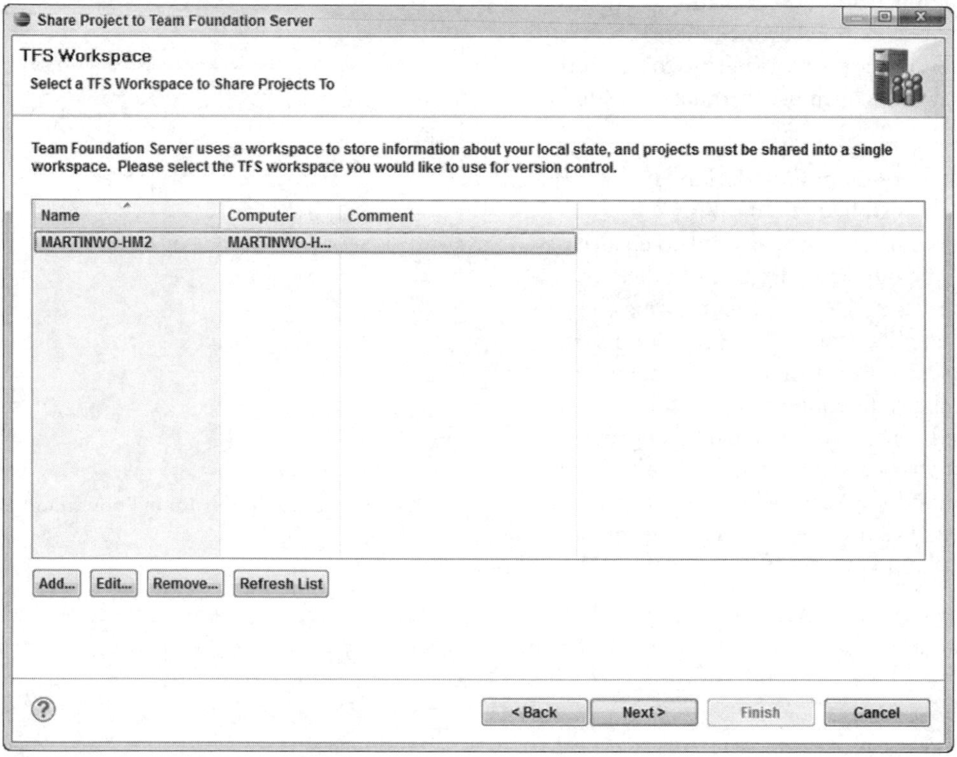

FIGURE 6-32: Choosing a Team Foundation Server workspace

Note that you may wish to use multiple Team Foundation Server workspaces on the machine to keep your Eclipse workspaces separate, or your Eclipse and Visual Studio workspaces separate. However, a single workspace can safely be shared by both Visual Studio and Eclipse on the same machine, should you have both applications installed. If you have never connected to the Team Foundation Server project collection from this machine before, a new private workspace will be created for you by default. Select the workspace you require (or add a new one and then select it) and click Next.

You will then be presented with the page shown in Figure 6-33 that asks you where to place your project in the version control repository. Put your project into a folder called Main if you think you might want to use the branching features of Team Foundation Server in the future.

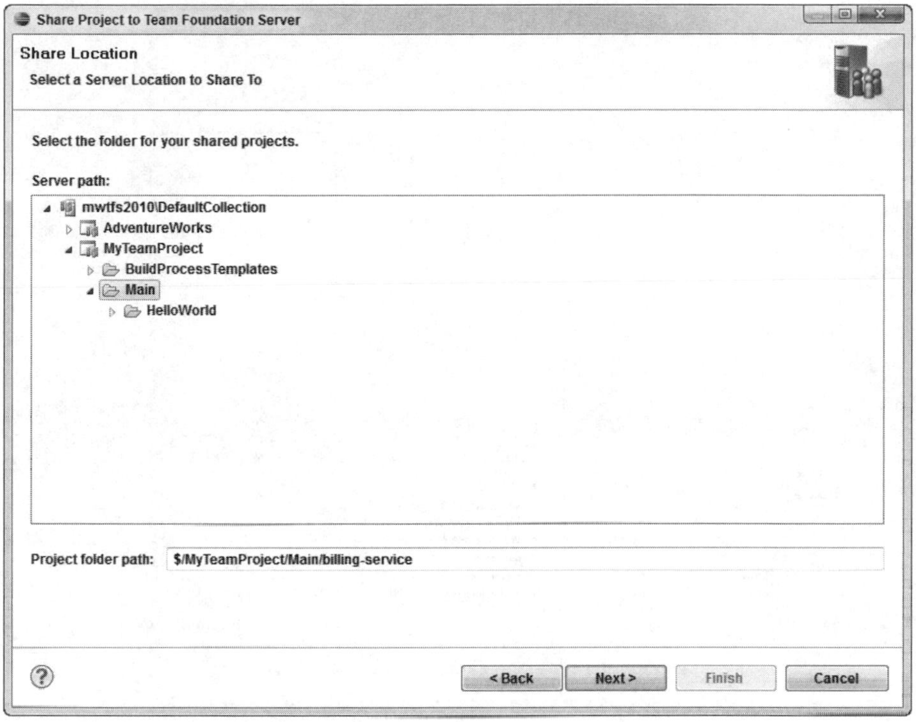

FIGURE 6-33: Choosing where to share a project in version control

The final page in the Share Project wizard will confirm the details of the sharing, allowing you to review the details before you click Finish. Note that the plug-in will automatically create any required working folder mappings.

The Pending Changes view is now opened by default, allowing you to check in your project into Team Foundation Server by clicking the Check In button, as shown in Figure 6-34. Note that the project resources in Package Explorer are decorated, indicating that they are under Team Foundation version control.

Once you have checked in your files, you can work with the rest of your team using Team Foundation Server just as the .NET developers would in Visual Studio. In Eclipse, the version control functionality is available by right-clicking a file and selecting Team from the context menu.

At this point, you might also want to add the Team Explorer view to your perspective to make it easier to work with work items and builds, or to provide access to Source Control Explorer. To do this, go to Windows ➪ Show View ➪ Other ➪ Team Foundation Server ➪ Team Explorer. Position the view where you find it most suitable — such as the bottom left-hand corner, under the Package Explorer.

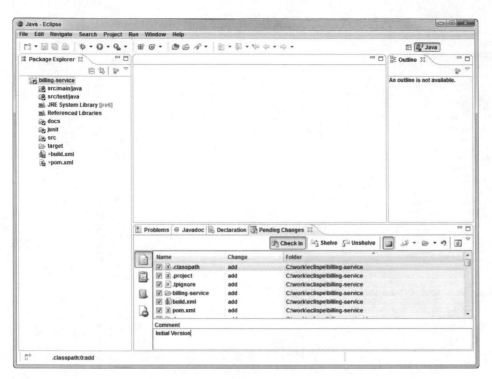

FIGURE 6-34: Check In button in Pending Changes view

Importing Projects from Team Foundation Server

If someone else on your team has already added the Eclipse project to Team Foundation Server, you will want to download the project locally to work on it. In Eclipse, this is accomplished by importing the project into your Eclipse workspace. You can run the Import wizard by connecting to Team Foundation Server through the Team Foundation Server Exploring Perspective, performing a Get on the files using Source Control Explorer, and then right-clicking the project folder and selecting Import from the context menu.

A simpler way to run the Import wizard is to simply go to File ➪ Import in Eclipse. As shown in Figure 6-35, under the Team node, you will find Team Foundation Server if you have the plug-in correctly installed.

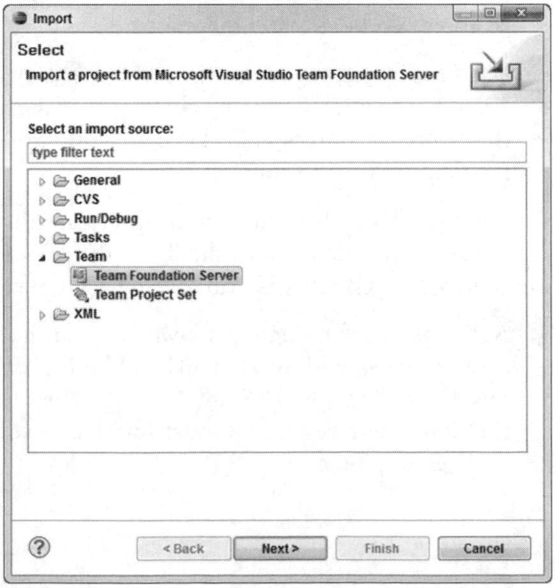

FIGURE 6-35: Selecting Team Foundation Server as the repository type to import from

Connect to the Team Foundation Server project collection and select your workspace in the same way as detailed previously. Then you need to select which project to import, as shown in Figure 6-36.

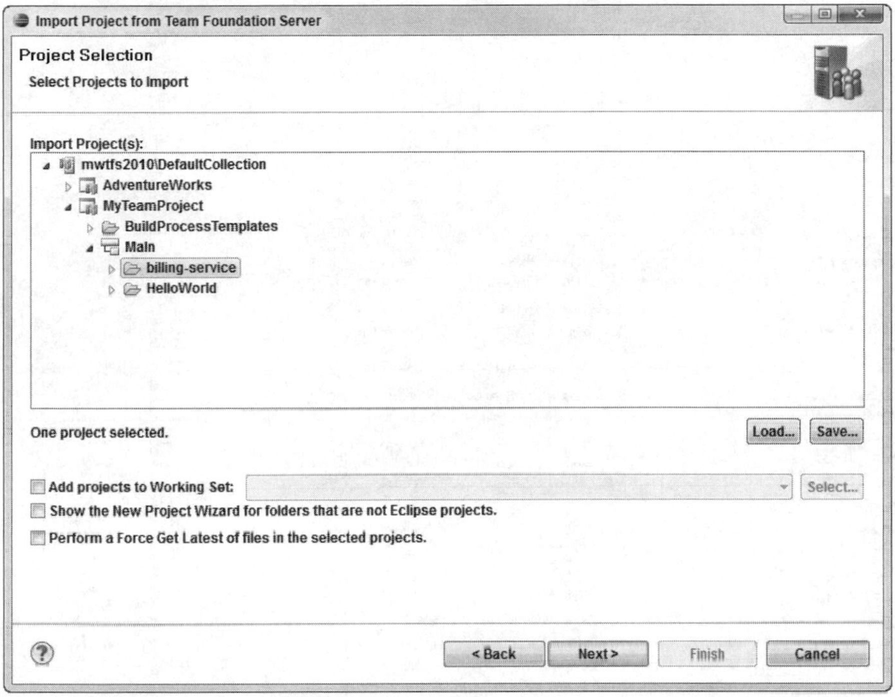

FIGURE 6-36: Selecting projects to import

Note that if you have multiple projects to import, you can Shift-click to select a range, or Ctrl-click on the individual folders (Command-click on the Mac). With Team Explorer Everywhere, it is recommended that you share your Eclipse .project files with Team Foundation Server. However, if you do not, you will want to check the "Show the New Project Wizard for folders that are not Eclipse projects" option on this dialog so that you can define your project settings.

Finally, you will be given a confirmation page explaining which projects you will be importing before you click Finish to download the files to your local machine.

The Import wizard will automatically open the Pending Changes view for you in your current perspective. However, you might also want to add the Team Explorer view into the perspective to make accessing Team Foundation Server easier. To do this, go to Windows ➪ Show View ➪ Other ➪ Team Foundation Server ➪ Team Explorer, and position the view appropriately.

Now that you have a project in the workspace, right-clicking a file managed by Team Foundation Server and selecting the Team menu will show the available version control functions, as shown in Figure 6-37.

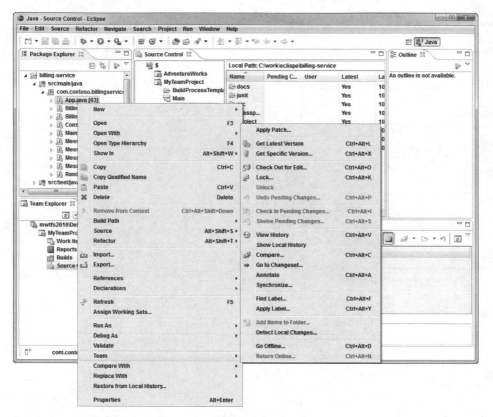

FIGURE 6-37: Available version control functions

Differences Between the Eclipse and Visual Studio Clients

While Microsoft is fully committed to supporting Eclipse developers using Team Foundation Server, there are some differences between the functionality available in one client over the other. For example, Eclipse developers are often familiar with the notion of *synchronize* (a perspective allowing you to easily see the differences between your local workspace and the server repository), and so the Team Foundation Server plug-in for Eclipse provides this capability. The closest alternative in Visual Studio would be a folder compare.

The Eclipse integration is designed to provide full support for development tasks, and so Team Foundation Server administration activities (such as managing security permissions or creating new team projects) are not supported outside of Visual Studio. Table 6-1 provides more details.

TABLE 6-1: Comparison of Team Foundation Server Functionality Available in Eclipse and Visual Studio

FEATURE	ECLIPSE + TEAM EXPLORER EVERYWHERE 2010	VISUAL STUDIO TEAM EXPLORER 2010
Agile, Scrum, CMMI, and custom process templates	X	X
Iteration planning	X	X
Project reporting	X	X
Atomic check-in	X	X
Check-in policies	X	X
Work item linking	X	X
Work item hierarchy	X	X
Synchronize perspective	X	
Visual branch hierarchy		X
Shelve/unshelve	X	X
Team Foundation Build	X (Ant/Maven builds)	X
Continuous Integration	X	X
Gated check-in	X	X
Server administration		X

TEAM FOUNDATION SERVER VERSION CONTROL FROM THE COMMAND LINE

You can manipulate the version control repository from the command line by using the `tf` command (which is short for "Team Foundation"). In fact, the command-line tool offers much more flexibility and functionality.

On Windows platforms, the command line ships as part of Visual Studio Team Explorer, which is installed as part of Visual Studio 2010. From a Visual Studio command prompt (Start ➪ All Programs ➪ Microsoft Visual Studio 2010 ➪ Visual Studio Tools ➪ Visual Studio Command Prompt (2010)), you can use the `tf help` command to see the available functionality. On non-Windows platforms, the command-line client is available as part of Team Explorer Everywhere. Unzip the command-line client and put the `tf` command in your path. You can then use the `tf help` command to get a list of the commands available.

> *The majority of the documentation for the command-line client describes arguments prefixed by a forward-slash character (/). However, certain UNIX shells use the / character as an escape character, meaning that if you wanted to use it on the command line, you would have to escape it (that is, use //). Therefore, both the Windows and cross-platform versions of the tf command support the hyphen character (-) as a prefix to arguments. For example, the following commands are identical on Windows:*
>
> ```
> tf checkin /comment:"This is a test"
> tf checkin -comment:"This is a test"
> ```

The cross-platform and Windows clients are broadly compatible with mostly the same commands and arguments supported across versions, allowing for reuse of scripts and integrations using the command-line interface. However, they do come from two different implementations of the command-line interface. The Windows version is written in .NET, and the cross-platform implementation is in Java. Therefore, there are some small differences. However, the majority of functionality is the same with both clients.

Getting Help

As mentioned previously, you can use the tf help command to see a list of commands available. To see the syntax for a single command, type **tf help** *command*, where *command* is the name of the command you want to see more about.

> *Consult the MSDN documentation online at* http://msdn.microsoft.com/ en-us/library/cc31bk2e.aspx *for more information regarding use of the* tf *command line.*

Using the Command Line

Following is an example that shows a very basic way of working with the command line to demonstrate how it works.

Assuming you have never connected to Team Foundation Server before, the first thing you must do is create a workspace on your local computer.

```
tf workspace -new -collection:http://servername:8080/tfs/
    defaultCollection -login:user@DOMAIN,Passw0rd MyWorkspace
```

In this example, MyWorkspace is the name of your workspace and http://servername:8080/tfs/ defaultCollection is the URL to your team project collection. You are passing in your credentials with the command. Note that if you do not provide any credentials when you are working on Windows or you are using Kerberos on non-Windows platforms, you will connect with the credentials of the currently authenticated user. Once you have created the workspace, the credentials used are cached in the current user's profile, unless told otherwise.

Next, you create a working folder mapping:

```
tf workfold -map -workspace:MyWorkspace $/TeamProject/Main/Path .
```

Here you are creating a working folder mapping in `MyWorkspace` between the server path `$/TeamProject/Main/Path` and the current directory (.).

Now, you want to download the code:

```
tf get
```

Then you check out the file that you want to edit:

```
tf checkout myfile.txt
```

You edit the changes locally (using the text editor of your choice — in this case, `vi`, but you might choose Notepad on Windows):

```
vi myfile.txt
```

Next, you check in the pending changes in `MyWorkspace`:

```
tf checkin -comment:"Making changes from the command line"
```

Your changes have now been checked in and a changeset has been created. You can look at those changes from any of the other version control clients by performing a Get to download the changes you just committed using the command line.

TEAM FOUNDATION VERSION CONTROL POWER TOOLS AND THIRD-PARTY UTILITIES

The functionality provided by Team Foundation Server is so rich, and the extensibility through the Team Foundation Server .NET API so straightforward, that a number of Power Tools and third-party utilities have been created to expose that functionality in easier-to-use ways. While there are too many to mention them all here, the following sections detail some of the more invaluable ones that should be in every Team Foundation Server power user's arsenal.

Microsoft Visual Studio Team Foundation Server Power Tools

The Team Foundation Server Power Tools are created by the Team Foundation Server team itself at Microsoft, and provide a number of great features that might not have been ready to put into the final release at the time it was published, or were not considered necessary for the majority of users. Many of the features originally delivered in Power Tools (such as Annotate, folder diff, rollback, and so on) appeared first in the Power Tools before arriving in the full product in a later release.

The Power Tools are available free from http://msdn.microsoft.com/en-us/ vstudio/bb980963.aspx.

The main Power Tools install some extensions into Visual Studio, as well as a new command-line client on Windows called tfpt. The Power Tools include the following that are of particular interest in the version control area:

➤ *Windows Shell Extensions* — This is a TortoiseSVN-like extension to Windows Explorer and the common file dialogs that allow many basic source control operations from Windows without having to run Visual Studio or the command-line tool.

➤ *Custom Check-in Policy Pack* — This is a set of common check-in policies to supplement the ones that come out-of-the-box with Visual Studio. The most commonly used is the "Check for comments" policy that enforces that a comment must be provided with each check-in.

➤ *Team Explorer Enhancements* — This provides some additional menu options in Visual Studio (such as opening a folder in Windows Explorer from the context menu in Source Control Explorer), and supports the finding of files in version control by status or wildcard.

➤ *Team Members* — This adds a Team Members node to Team Explorer, allowing you to organize users into sub-teams and access collaborative tools such as IM and e-mail, as well as the downloading and installation of custom Team Foundation components. From the Team Members node, you can also search for a user's shelvesets, look at pending changes, and see a check-in history.

➤ *Command-line* (tfpt) *tool* — tfpt help shows a list of the commands available, including tf online, which will compare your local working folder with what the server thinks you have in your workspace. It will also help you pend adds, edits, deletes, and so on, for files that you might have changed outside of Visual Studio or while offline. Another useful command is tfpt scorch, which will ensure that your local working folders match exactly what the server thinks you should have — any additional files are deleted, while any modified files are re-downloaded and replaced.

Team Foundation Server MSSCCI Provider

The MSSCCI provider enables integration of Team Foundation Server version control with products that support the older MSSCCI API originally created for VSS, but adopted by many IDE developers. The MSSCCI provider is developed by the team at Microsoft responsible for Team Foundation Server.

The MSSCCI provider is available as a free download from http://msdn .microsoft.com/en-us/vstudio/bb980963.aspx.

Because this provider was created long after the original developers probably created the tool using the API, and because it is for a version control system very different from the ones that the developers of the IDE would have tested against, your mileage may vary — many people use this in lots of different development environments. However, the download page for the MSSCCI provider states that it is tested against the following products:

➤ Visual Studio .NET 2003

➤ Visual C++ 6 SP6

➤ Visual Basic 6 SP6

➤ Visual FoxPro 9 SP2

➤ Microsoft Access 2007

➤ SQL Server Management Studio

➤ Enterprise Architect 7.5

➤ PowerBuilder 11.5

➤ Microsoft eMbedded VC++ 4.0

Team Foundation Sidekicks

The Team Foundation Sidekicks from Attrice Corporation have been an indispensible, free, third-party utility for many versions of Team Foundation Server, and the 2010 release still has plenty to offer, despite some of the original features now being available as part of Visual Studio.

The Sidekicks install some functionality inside of Visual Studio, and also a set of very useful standalone tools that include the following:

➤ *Permission Sidekick* — This provides you with the capability to view and control a user's permissions in various parts of Team Foundation Server, as well as preview what a user's effective permissions are and why.

➤ *Shelveset Sidekick* — This provides powerful shelveset search and administration capabilities.

➤ *Labels Sidekick* — This provides powerful label search and edit capabilities, as well as the capability to do side-by-side comparisons between two labels, detailing the differences in version control and the work items associated with those changes.

➤ *History Sidekick* — This provides powerful search and compare functionality relating to history and changesets.

➤ *Status Sidekick* — This allows you to search and view pending changes for other users in the system, as well as unlock, undo, or report on those changes if you have the appropriate permissions.

➤ *Workspace Sidekick* — This provides powerful search and administrative functionality around all workspaces on the project collection.

Some of the functionality available in the Team Foundation Sidekicks from Attrice can also be replicated by use of the `tf` command line. However, the Sidekicks are much more user-friendly and easier to discover. But the tools can be quite complex, so power users of Team Foundation Server might discover that many of the features will only be available if you have the appropriate permissions on the server.

> *The Team Foundation Sidekicks are available as a free download from* `www.attrice.info/cm/tfs/`.

CONFIGURING VERSION CONTROL

Team Foundation Server is highly configurable, and contains a very fine-grained and flexible security model. This is especially true for version control.

Security and Permissions

Before you start using the version control features widely in your team, you should determine which individuals will take on the responsibility of being an administrator. The majority of the developers on the team would typically be classified as contributors. The way you organize your roles should be determined by a matter of convenience and organizational requirements.

For each team project in Team Foundation Server, there are typically four groups created by default, each with a set of permissions that are defined for them and control what members of that group can do. The following roles and responsibilities are common for a large organization:

- ➤ *Project Administrators* — The team project administrators are responsible for setting up version control permissions for each contributor (either directly, or through the IT staff). They also set the security and policies for your code check-in and coordinate with the build team. Project Administrators typically have full rights to version control in a team project.

- ➤ *Contributors* — Contributors have write access to the source code to check in and check out code, shelve, and create changesets. Typically, you would assign this role to the majority of your developers. Contributors can perform all version control operations on files from workspaces that they own, but they are typically not able to control other users' changes.

- ➤ *Readers* — Readers can view the code, but are unable to make changes to the version control repository. This could be assigned to other developers in your organization who may need to refer to the code in your team project, but do not need to be able to check in changes to it without going through a contributor.

- ➤ *Builders* — These are members of the build team who have full permissions to the build components, but also typically require contributor level access to version control to be able to edit and check in changes to files used in the build.

> *For more information on security and privileges, see Chapter 20.*

Version control has a very flexible permissioning model that can control exactly what is permissible at the folder and even file level. You can view the security settings for a file or folder by right-clicking it in Source Control Explorer from Visual Studio, and selecting Properties ⇨ Security.

Figure 6-38 shows the Security tab, and the inherited security settings. To alter the settings for the folder or branch, deselect the Inherit Security Settings check box.

FIGURE 6-38: Settings in Security tab

Be careful when removing the checkmark for Inherit Security Settings in Visual Studio 2008 or Visual Studio 2005. In those versions, when you deselect the check box, all the permissions are cleared, including Read permission for the administrators. If you click OK without realizing this, then you would no longer be able to see the file or folder in version control to be able to edit the permissions on it again. The workaround for this is to use Team Explorer on the Team Foundation Server application tier while logged in as an administrator, and then add permissions back from there. This issue was fixed in Visual Studio 2010. In that release, when you remove the checkmark, the inherited permissions are copied over so that you can edit them.

For each permission, there are two options, along with an Unset state for either:

➤ *Allow* — This option is fairly straightforward, and simply grants authorization for the user or group to perform the action.

➤ *Deny* — This option explicitly denies authorization for that user or group to perform the action. If a user belongs to a group that triggers Deny, the user is not allowed to perform that action, even if he or she is in another group that explicitly allows the permission.

➤ *Unset* — If a permission is unset (that is, not set to either Allow or Deny), the user is not allowed to perform that action. However, if the user is also in a group that has an Allow set for the permission, and the user has no explicit Deny set in any of his or her groups, the user will be allowed to perform the action.

The following security permissions are available through the Security tab in Visual Studio. You can also set these permissions from the `tf` command-line tool on Windows.

➤ *Read* — Users can read the contents of the file and view its properties. For a folder, once they have read permission, users can see the folder and what files are in it.

➤ *Check out* — Users can check out and make pending changes to the item.

➤ *Check in* — Users can check in the item and edit any comments to changesets that they created.

➤ *Label* — Users can create a label including that item, as well as edit and delete labels belonging to them.

➤ *Lock* — Users can lock and remove their own locks for folders and files.

➤ *Revise other users' changes* — Users can edit the comments on changesets committed by another user.

➤ *Unlock other users' changes* — Users can remove the locks placed on files by another user.

➤ *Undo other users' changes* — Users can undo a pending change in a workspace owned by another user.

➤ *Administer labels* — Users can edit or delete the labels created by another user.

➤ *Manage permissions* — Users can edit the version control permissions using the dialog shown in Figure 6-38, and they can grant themselves additional access.

➤ *Check in other users' changes* — Users can check in changes on behalf of another user.

➤ *Merge* — Users can merge changes into this folder.

➤ *Manage branch* — Users can convert any folder under that path to a branch, and edit branch properties. Users can branch this branch only if they also have the Merge permission for the target path.

Team Project Source Control Settings

Most settings in source control are stored at the team project level, and are initially set as part of your process template during project creation. However, an administrator can edit these settings from Visual Studio after the project has been created. You can access the settings from Team ⇨ Team Project Settings ⇨ Source Control.

Check-out Settings

The behavior of check-outs can be configured at the team project level from the Source Control Settings dialog shown in Figure 6-39. By default, in many process templates, multiple check-out is enabled. If you disable this, when a user does a check-out on a file, a check-out lock will be automatically added (a behavior more familiar to VSS users). This will reduce the degree to which developers can work on files in parallel, and so it can impact productivity.

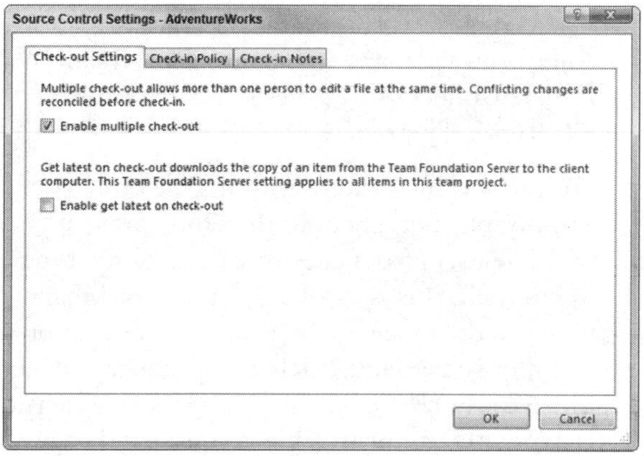

In the case of files like common Visual Studio project files (such as .vbproj and .csproj files, or even the .sln file), not being able to edit them in parallel can give rise to many productivity issues. Those files may need to be edited when a file in the project is added or renamed. Also, the ability to force clients to Get Latest as they do a check-out can be enabled (which is, again, a more familiar behavior to VSS users).

FIGURE 6-39: Source Control Settings dialog

Check-in Policy Settings

As described earlier in this chapter, check-in policies for Visual Studio clients may also be configured at the team project level from the Source Control Settings dialog.

For users of Team Explorer Everywhere, an administrator must separately configure the check-in policy settings for those clients (including the cross-platform command-line client) by right-clicking the team project in the Team Explorer view in Eclipse, and selecting Check-in Policies. The Team Explorer Everywhere check-in policies also slightly differ in the policies that are available, and all policies have a configurable scope — that is, the files under the team project that should be subjected to the check-in policy.

Once check-in policy settings have been configured by the administrator, they are applied to all users of version control for the team project.

Check-in Notes

The check-in notes for the team project are also configurable from the Source Control Settings dialog in Visual Studio. New notes can be added, the order of the notes configured, and any notes can be made mandatory. Once check-in notes have been configured in Visual Studio, they apply to all users of version control for the team project, regardless of which client they use.

File Types

In addition to the team project-scoped settings, you may also configure the way Team Foundation Server handles files with specific extensions. This configuration is project collection-wide, and is accessed from Team ⇨ Project Collection Settings ⇨ Source Control File Types (Figure 6-40).

For the specified extensions in a file type, you can disable merging and, therefore, prevent multiple users from checking out that file type in parallel. This is especially useful for binary files and documents where a merge tool is not commonly available (such as a graphical image file or an Excel spreadsheet). Unless an extension is explicitly disabled, a file is considered to be text-file capable of being merged.

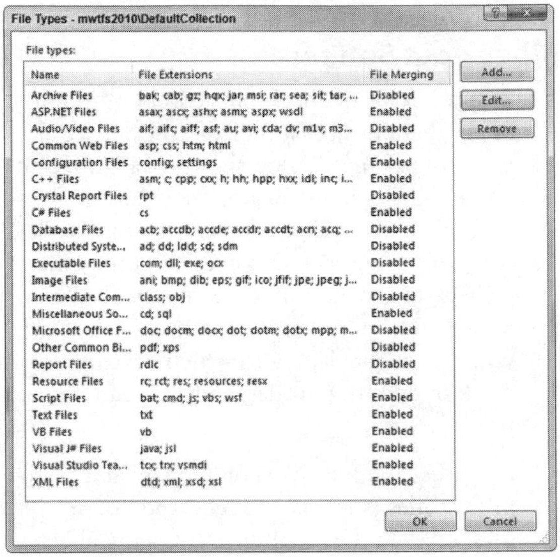

FIGURE 6-40: File Types dialog

Local User Settings

In Visual Studio, you can access a number of settings that control the individual user source control behavior from Tools ⇨ Options ⇨ Source Control. If you have been unable to find any Team Foundation Server functionality or menus available in Visual Studio, then the first thing to check is that your current source control plug-in is set as Visual Studio Team Foundation Server, as shown in Figure 6-41.

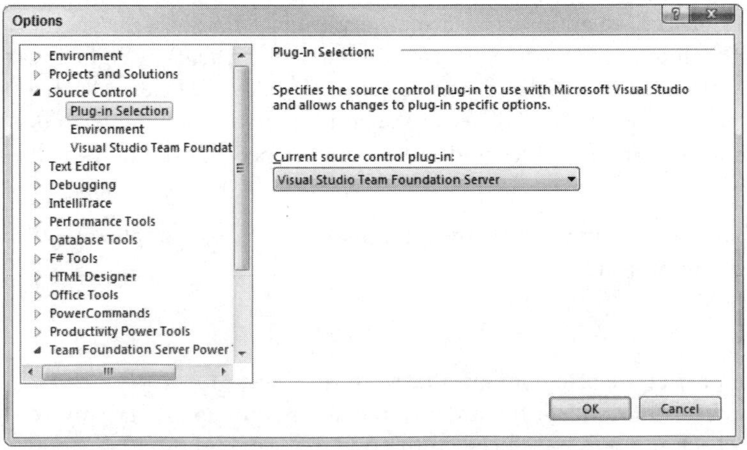

FIGURE 6-41: Source control plug-in set to Visual Studio Team Foundation Server

In the Environment settings window shown in Figure 6-42, you can configure default behaviors that happen when you open or close a solution, and also what should happen when you save or edit a file in Visual Studio that is currently checked in.

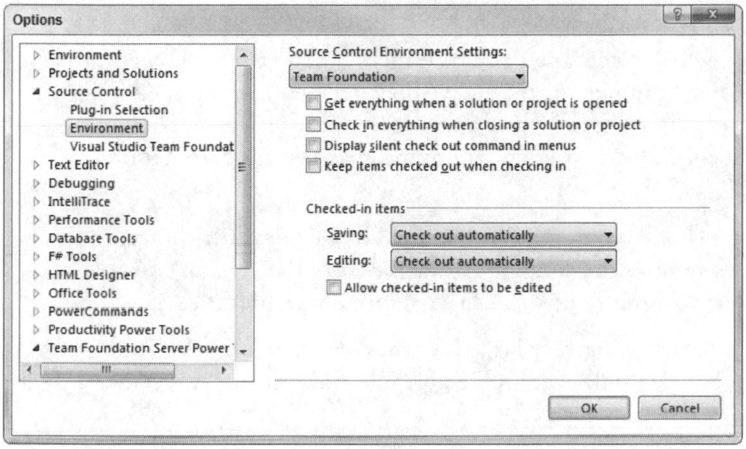

FIGURE 6-42: Environment settings window

The Visual Studio Team Foundation Server settings dialog shown in Figure 6-43 is where users can define their Team Foundation proxy server. (See Chapter 24 for more information on the proxy.) Users can also opt to get latest on check-out as a personal preference, rather than it being enforced at the team level. They can configure Source Control Explorer to show deleted items so that they can easily be viewed and potentially undeleted. Users can also control other default behaviors for Source Control Explorer and the Pending Changes window. Also in this section, users can configure their own external compare and merge tool settings by clicking the Configure User Tools button.

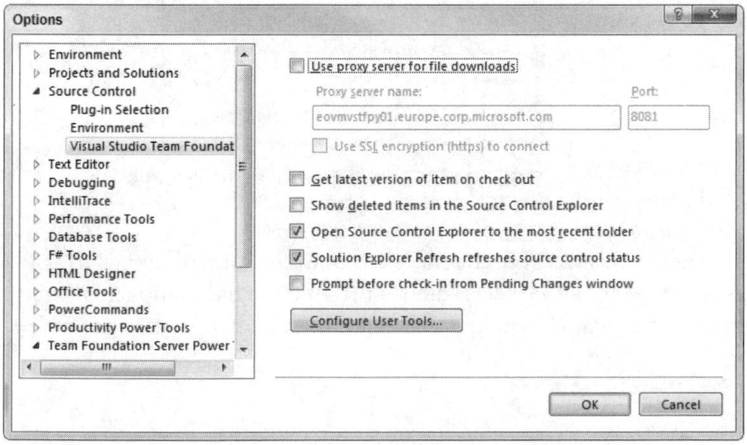

FIGURE 6-43: Visual Studio Team Foundation Server settings window

DELETE VERSUS DESTROY

When you delete files from version control in Team Foundation Server, you are simply marking that version as deleted. The file still exists, which allows for it to be viewed in Source Control Explorer as the preference is enabled and to be undeleted.

There are times, however, when exceptional circumstances dictate that you need the file to really be gone. For example, maybe a developer accidentally checked in a file containing his or her password in breach of company policy, or worse, checked in a file with personally identifiable customer data in it, or real credit card details, and so on.

In those instances, the `tf destroy` command can be used by an administrator with appropriate permissions to remove the contents of the file from the version control database. This can be done without removing the existence of the file from history.

This is also useful if you are removing very large files that have been checked in to Team Foundation Server, but you only want to be able to obtain the most recent versions of them.

When you execute the `destroy` command normally, the data is actually not deleted from the Team Foundation Server database immediately, but is purged from the database by a periodic administration job. To request that the administration job is executed as soon as possible, use the `/startcleanup` option when calling `destroy`.

The Configure User Tools dialog shown in Figure 6-44 allows users to specify per-file extensions, which external process is used by Visual Studio to perform the compare or merge operation, and the command-line arguments to pass to it. Otherwise, the standard compare and merge tools that ship with Visual Studio will be used.

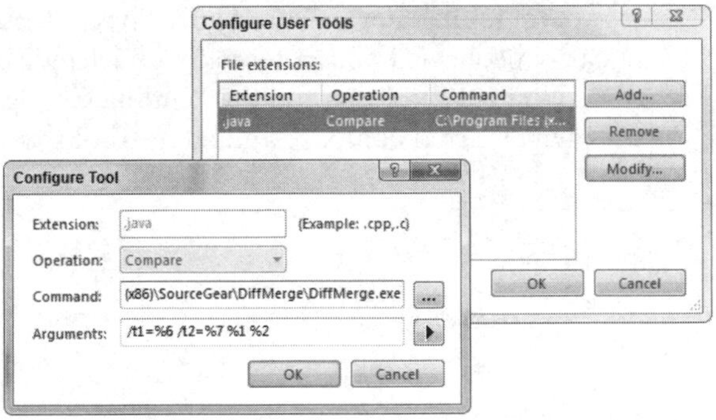

FIGURE 6-44: Configure User Tools dialog

Eclipse Preferences

In Eclipse, user version control preferences are accessed from the standard Eclipse Preferences dialog (Team ➪ Team Foundation Server). As shown in Figure 6-45, there are several preferences for Source Control, external compare and merge tools, and other preferences that can be set. Note that if an external compare or merge tool is not configured for a particular extension in Eclipse, the standard Eclipse compare or merge editor will be used.

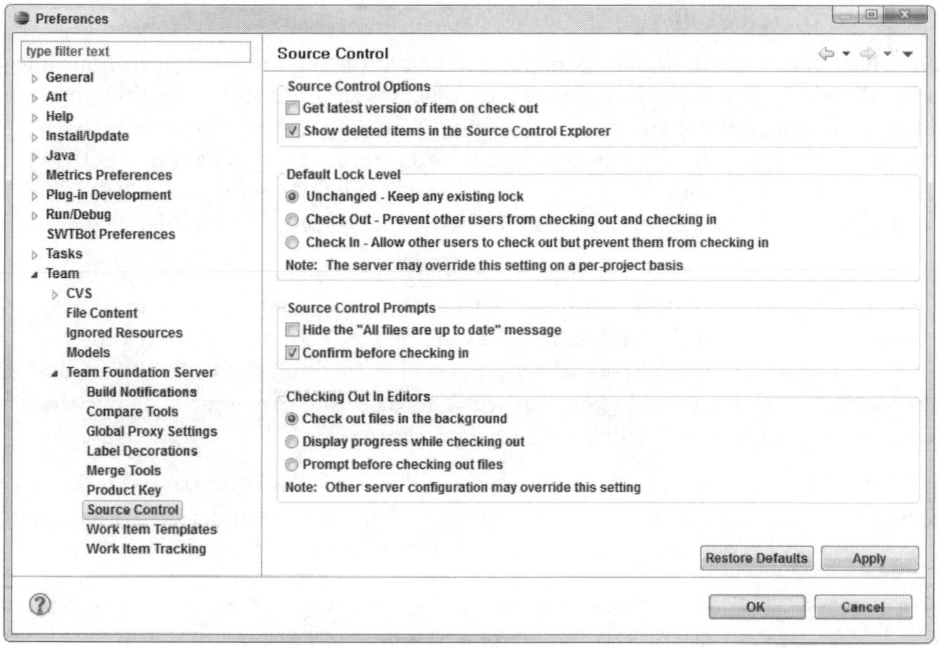

FIGURE 6-45: Eclipse Preferences dialog

SWITCHING VERSION CONTROL TO TEAM FOUNDATION SERVER

Chapter 8 details your options for moving the code from your old version control system into Team Foundation Server. However, in addition to bringing your code over, you must also ensure that your developers are comfortable with Team Foundation Server's version control capabilities. Regardless of the version control system you used in the past, Team Foundation Server is going to behave differently from what you are used to.

The first thing to understand is that Team Foundation Server is much more than just version control. The true value of Team Foundation Server comes from the tight integration between version control, work item tracking, build, and test data, all stored in the same SQL Server database, allowing you to track the progress of your entire application development lifecycle.

In terms of the version control capabilities, however, there are differences that usually trip up unsuspecting developers who have previously used the most common version control systems outside of Team Foundation Server (in particular, VSS and SVN).

Team Foundation Server for Visual SourceSafe Users

Team Foundation Server was designed to feel familiar to VSS users. Similar terms and concepts such as Get, check-out, check-in, and so on, are used to describe similar actions. However, despite these similarities there are some fundamental differences between VSS and Team Foundation Server.

Speed, Reliability, and Scalability

One of the first things that you will notice about Team Foundation Server is that operations like check-out, get latest, or even just navigating down into folders is significantly faster than in other version control systems, especially if you have been using VSS over a WAN. Team Foundation Server was designed for modern, Internet-style protocols, and stores all of its data in a SQL Server database. By contrast, a VSS repository is a collection of files stored in a network folder accessed by using standard Windows file-sharing protocols, which do not scale well over high-latency networks.

Because Team Foundation Server uses a real SQL Server database for storage, the reliability of that store is very high. With VSS, there is no atomic check-in process, and the transfer of data to the repository is non-transactional. Therefore, if there were a loss of connectivity between the VSS client and the network share during a version control operation, the integrity of the affected files (and, thus, the repository as a whole) could be affected. This data integrity issue does not affect Team Foundation Server because of the difference in architectures.

VSS was recommended for teams of 20 or less developers, whereas Team Foundation Server can scale to thousands of active users. By using flexible architectures, Team Foundation Server can scale well when server resources become the limiting factor, or when you want to ensure server up-time.

> *Chapter 18 provides more information about scalability and high availability with Team Foundation Server.*

Versions

As was discussed earlier in this chapter, Team Foundation Server versions file by the changeset in which they were modified. Therefore, file versions do not increment individually. The first time VSS users look at the history of a file and see a nonsequential series of numbers in the history is often the first time that they realize they are talking to a fundamentally different version control tool. With Team Foundation Server, the date and time of the change is recorded by the server, not the client, so issues around dates and times caused by an incorrect clock on a VSS client disappear.

Pinning and Sharing

Team Foundation Server does not have an exact equivalent to the pinning and sharing features of VSS. Frequently, these were used as basic branch support, whereas Team Foundation Server now has full branch and merge capabilities, encouraging more robust software engineering practices.

> *Chapter 9 provides information on branching and merging.*

Labels and History

In VSS, labels could be thought of as a point in time in the repository, and labels appear in the history view. All changes before that point in time were included in the label. The closest equivalent to this in Team Foundation Server is the changeset, which is the fundamental unit of versioning in the repository. If you record the changeset at which a build is performed, you know exactly which versions of files it contains.

In Team Foundation Server, labels are more flexible. Now you can pick and choose which version of a file is included in that label — and you can edit that later on. You can think of a label in Team Foundation Server as tagging which file versions make up that label. Because labels are so different in Team Foundation Server, they do not show up as points in time in the standard view of a file's history, but are instead shown on a separate tab in the history view.

Team Foundation Server stores and displays history in some other different ways from VSS. In VSS, when you create a new file inside a folder, it creates a new version of the parents in addition to the new child. The same is true for renames, deletes, and updates.

In Team Foundation Server, this is just recorded on the child item, and no new version is created for the parents. The most noticeable effect of this is that the "Last Check-in" time of a parent folder does not change when a change is made inside the folder, or to one of its children. To determine when the last changes were made to a folder in Team Foundation Server, you simply right-click the folder and select View History, which is a significantly faster operation than its VSS counterpart.

Keyword Expansion

VSS has a feature called *keyword expansion* where source code could include certain keywords such as `$Author: $`, `$Revision: $`, or `$Date: $` and the appropriate data would be inserted into the tag on every check-in to version control. This was especially useful when no integration into VSS was available inside the IDE, and so finding out any of this information was often a fairly slow task in the separate VSS client application, or when viewing a printout of code.

However, keyword expansion did present many issues when comparing the differences between file versions, or when performing merges. Team Foundation Server takes a fundamentally different approach, and does not alter the contents of your files as you check them in. Therefore, keyword expansion is no longer supported. VSS users are often surprised by this, but the powerful IDE integration combined with the speed and performance of Team Foundation Server means that this is rarely an issue, once you get over the fact that it is not there.

File Timestamps

In VSS, the last modified date and created date of a file are maintained from the machine on which the file was originally edited. Team Foundation Server does not store this metadata about the files, and so the dates on the files will be the date and time that they were downloaded to the filesystem by performing a Get operation.

This can cause some issues for organizations that have constructed a build and deployment infrastructure around that file metadata. However, because Team Foundation Server manages the local files in your workspace much better, it is usually safe to use incremental Gets from Team Foundation Server into a workspace to be able to detect which files have changed based on the metadata, and only build and deploy those files.

Team Foundation Server will remove files from the workspace if they are deleted on the server, and will also perform move/rename operations to ensure that your local workspace stays accurate and doesn't contain old orphaned files, as could happen in VSS.

Concurrent Editing of Files

Team Foundation Server is capable of supporting multiple developers editing the same file at the same time, and has powerful merge functionality to facilitate and resolve conflicts that might occur as a result. The feature is usually enabled in most team project process templates, and is a boon to developer productivity.

In VSS, check-outs and check-ins only occur when making an edit to a file. In Team Foundation Server, a check-out is required for all modifications, including renames, moves, and deletes. The check-in operation will also commit all those changes in a single atomic transaction, including any adds, edits, moves, renames, and deletes. Because of this, it is much easier to maintain a repository that is always consistent.

Get Latest on Check-out

As discussed earlier in this chapter, by default, a check-out operation in Team Foundation Server will enable the editing of the file version that you already have in your workspace. It will not automatically get the latest version of that file for you by default. You should explicitly perform a Get Latest when it is a good time for you to update your local code to match the repository version — typically at the start of each day, as well as before and after each check-in.

New Features in Team Foundation Server

VSS developers should familiarize themselves with the many new features offered by Team Foundation Server, as described in this chapter and the rest of this book. Shelving is one such feature that is often overlooked by new developers because equivalent functionality is not available in VSS.

Team Foundation Server for Subversion Users

The jump to Team Foundation Server from SVN is much greater than from VSS because of differences in the version control model, and also because of the terminology used. Despite these differences, the broad capabilities of the two tools are similar, and the ways that Team Foundation Server handles labels, as well as branching and merging, will be much more familiar to SVN users.

Again, the key difference to understand is that Team Foundation Server is much more than just a version control tool, and comes with very tight integration to work item tracking, build, and test management.

Differences in Terminology

SVN (and CVS) users are used to a different set of terms than those used by Team Foundation Server, as outlined in Table 6-2.

TABLE 6-2: Terminology Differences between SVN and Team Foundation Server

SVN	TEAM FOUNDATION SERVER
Check-out	Get Latest (and also Map Working Folder)
Update	Get Latest (or Get Specific Version)
(not required)	Check-out
Commit	Check-in
Revision	Changeset (see also versionspec)
Add	Add
Delete	Delete
Copy	Branch
Move	Move, rename
Revert	Rollback
Status	Status, pending changes list
Diff	Compare
Blame	Annotate
Log	History

Differences in Version Control Model

For version control, Team Foundation Server uses a fundamentally different model than SVN. At the heart of this difference is the *workspace*. You learned about workspaces earlier in this chapter, but the main differences are that, in the case of Team Foundation Server, the following is true:

➤ Files are initially read-only locally.

➤ You must explicitly check out a file to say that you want to edit it, at which point it becomes writable.

➤ No .svn directories appear in your workspace. Team Foundation Server keeps track of your local changes at the server. This provides better performance and scalability for large source trees.

➤ You should tell Team Foundation Server about changes you are making to files in your local workspace.

In practice, many of these differences are pretty transparent if you are using the IDE integration with Visual Studio or Eclipse. However, they are much more apparent in the command line, or if you want to edit files outside of the IDE.

Shell Extension Functionality

A popular method of accessing SVN from Windows platforms is via the TortoiseSVN windows shell extensions. Equivalent shell extension functionality is available as part of the Team Foundation Server 2010 Power Tools, which, as mentioned earlier, is a separate free download from Microsoft.

Differences in History

Team Foundation Server tracks renames as a specific change type, meaning that renames can easily be tracked in history, rather than appearing as a delete and add. Viewing the history for a specific file allows you to view the history before a rename occurred, and also changes that occurred in a previous branch before the file was merged into the current location. In Visual Studio, a full graphical visibility of merge history is available alongside the branch hierarchy, allowing you to easily see in which branches a particular change has been merged.

Offline Support

SVN was designed around an infrequently connected and offline model from the repository, as is common when working on Open Source software collaboration projects. By contrast, the Team Foundation Server model is much more online-driven. While this has advantages in typical enterprise development scenarios where being online with the server is more usually the norm, it does mean that offline working support requires some manual effort with Team Foundation Server.

Administration and Setup

Setup of SVN is initially driven by a typical installer on Windows, or a package management system on most UNIX-style operating systems. However, the initial configuration of the server for use by the team requires extensive use of the command line and editing of configuration files. Security configuration is more complex, and configuring SVN to delegate to Windows user accounts for authentication requires work. The SVN server does run on many platforms, but as a result, can feel a little alien to an administrator used to Windows-based systems.

Setup and administration of Team Foundation Server is performed via a set of wizards and graphical tools on Windows. Initial setup of a basic Team Foundation Server installation providing version control, build, and work item tracking functionality is very straightforward, and will install any pre-requisites (such as IIS or SQL Server Express) if not present, or no existing full SQL Server installation is available. Team Foundation Server can be installed on client versions of Windows such as Windows Vista or Windows 7, but for a large team, it is recommended that it be installed on a full server version of Windows. Team Foundation Server can even be installed on editions of Windows Server that include a domain controller such as Small Business Server.

> *Chapter 8 provides more detail about the tools and techniques available to help migrate your source code from another version control system into Team Foundation Server. Chapter 9 provides a more detailed explanation and guidance relating to branching and merging. Chapter 10 provides more detailed walkthroughs of using version control in specific scenarios.*

SUMMARY

This chapter introduced you to all the core concepts in Team Foundation Server version control, and provided some insights on how to get started and use the tooling in day-to-day development. You also learned about where to find settings and configuration for the server, and how to manage security permissions. You learned about the common difficulties people have when switching version control from VSS or SVN.

Chapter 7 goes more in-depth with an examination of using some of the features of version control, such as check-in policies, along with some best practices, all to ensure code quality.

7

Ensuring Code Quality

One of the nice things about having an integrated version control system is the ability to track traceability with other artifacts in Team Foundation Server that will enable the team to develop higher quality code. Team Foundation Server 2010 integrates the version control system with the work item tracking, automated builds, and test case management systems to enable your team to do just that.

This chapter examines the different methods that you can use to ensure code quality, such as gated check-ins, check-in policies, and tips for managing code reviews in Team Foundation Server.

WHAT IS QUALITY?

The "cost" of fixing a bug has often been studied, and there is now a general consensus that the cost increases exponentially from the time the bug was introduced. In his March 2007 Equity keynote address, Barry Boehm indicated that the relative cost increases can be as high as 150 times the cost if the problem would have been found at the very beginning of the software development lifecycle. Ensuring quality on your development team starts before the Quality Assurance (QA) or Testing departments ever get their hands on the software.

Team Foundation Server 2010 supports ensuring different types of quality. Most often, people associate quality with testers or a QA department. Testing is absolutely one way of ensuring quality, but this chapter focuses more on increasing the quality of code while it is being developed before it ever gets promoted into a test environment.

> *For more information about testing, see the book titled* Professional Application Lifecycle Management with Visual Studio 2010 *(Indianapolis: Wiley, 2010). Part III of that book describes the types of testing that can be achieved by using the Visual Studio 2010 family of products, including Microsoft Test Manager (primarily for manual testing), Visual Studio, and Team Foundation Server 2010.*

The IEEE standard definition of *software quality* has two particular parts:

➤ The degree to which a system, component, or process meets specified requirements

➤ The degree to which a system, component, or process meets customer/user needs or expectations

Additionally, software developers may also want to consider other aspects that contribute to the end user's perception of the quality of software, as well as being viable to maintain once it is released. For example, you might consider some of these aspects:

➤ Elegance of design

➤ User experience

➤ Reusability

➤ Maintainability

➤ Performance

CHECK-IN POLICIES

Check-in policies define a set of conditions that must be met, or processes that must be run, before a developer is able to check in source code to the version control repository. To configure your check-in policies, right-click on your Team Foundation project and select Team Project Settings ⇨ Source Control. Figure 7-1 shows the Check-In Policy tab where you will find several options for modifying the check-in policies.

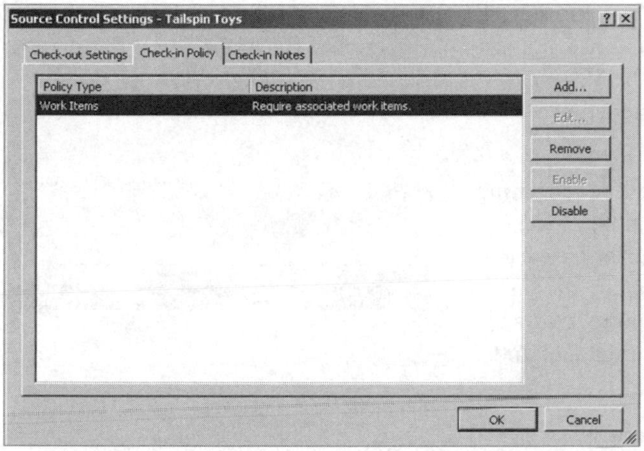

FIGURE 7-1: Check-In Policy tab in the Source Control Settings dialog

If you click the Add button in the Source Control Settings dialog shown in Figure 7-1, you will be prompted to select a check-in policy type, as shown in Figure 7-2. Select one of the four options shown in Figure 7-2 and click the OK button.

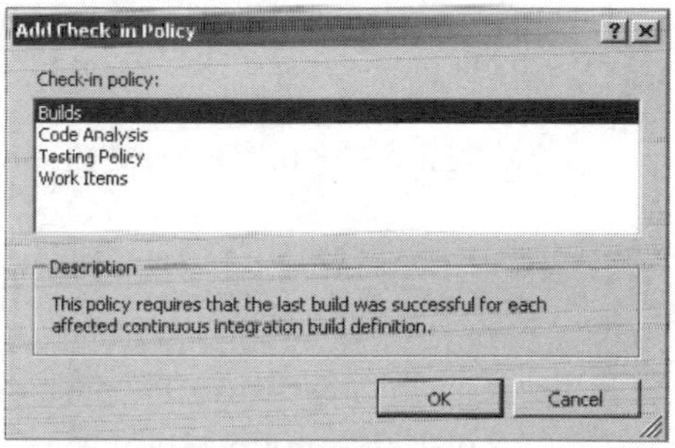

The following list describes the default policy types included in Team Foundation Server 2010 version control:

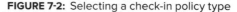

FIGURE 7-2: Selecting a check-in policy type

➤ *Builds* — This option requires that the last build of the project was successful. If it was not, then new changes cannot be checked in until the offending code has been fixed. It is to prevent developers from piling-on a build that is currently failing.

➤ *Code Analysis* — This option adds a check to ensure that a specific static code analysis rule set has been run, and is passing without errors before source code can be committed to the version control repository. You are able to configure using a standard Microsoft defined rule set, or you can store a custom rule set in the version control repository, and then choose it to use for the check-in policy.

➤ *Testing Policy* — This policy ensures that developers have run a set of automated tests before checking in their source code changes. These tests can be unit tests, web performance tests, Coded UI tests, or any other test that is available to the MSTest framework.

➤ *Work Items* — Team leaders may want to require that a work item be associated with every check-in. That way, changes can be documented, which will make it easier to track any problems. Associating work items to changesets also begins the traceability process. By indicating that a particular set of source code changes are the implementation of a feature task or the fix for a bug, you can ensure that links will exist between the work items, changesets, and even the specific changes in the files included in the changeset. This also helps deter developers from implementing undocumented features or changes by requiring that a work item actually exists.

Once the check-in policy has been selected, try checking in code without complying with the new policy. You can add additional policies as well so that they are each evaluated prior to check-in. The Policy Failure dialog shown in Figure 7-3 will appear. At this point, you will have the option to override the policy requirement and must provide a comment about the failure.

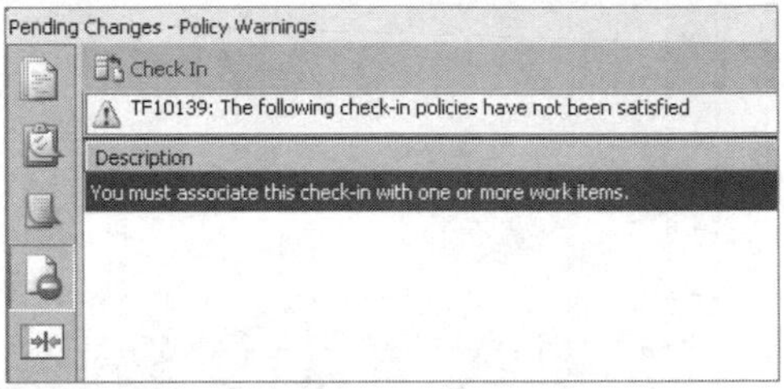

One thing to note is that anyone can override a check-in policy at any time. There are currently no security privileges or permissions to prevent overriding

FIGURE 7-3: Policy Failure dialog

check-in policies. Overriding the check-in policy should only be done when absolutely necessary. Otherwise, it will start to negate the reason for introducing the policy in the first place.

One possible solution to ensuring that check-in policies are honored (and not overridden) is by setting up a gated check-in build, and customizing it to evaluate the check-in policies of the shelveset. This will produce exceptions during evaluation if any of the check-in policies fail, thus producing a failed build where the check-in will be rejected.

Monitoring Check-In Policy Overrides

Since all users are able to override check-in policies, there are two different options for monitoring when team members override policies. Creating e-mail alerts and exploring the data warehouse are the two methods administrators can use to research check-in policy overrides.

If it is found that a particular check-in policy is frequently overridden, then the administrators may want to question why it is enabled in the first place. If a particular individual or group of individuals is found to be frequently overriding a check-in policy, then you may want to consult with them to help them understand the reason that the policy is in place.

Additionally, for further enforcement, you can customize a gated check-in to also evaluate the check-in policies as part of the verification build process, as mentioned previously.

E-Mail Alerts

Using the Alerts Explorer that is available in the latest version of the Team Foundation Server 2010 Power Tools, you can create an e-mail alert that will send a notification whenever a check-in policy is overridden.

> *The latest version of the Team Foundation Server 2010 Power Tools can be found on the MSDN Visual Studio Power Tools site at* `http://msdn.microsoft.com/en-us/vstudio/bb980963`*.*

To use the Alerts Explorer, navigate the Team menu in Visual Studio 2010, and then click on the Alerts Explorer menu option. Figure 7-4 shows the check-in alert templates that are available after clicking the "New Alert" toolbar button.

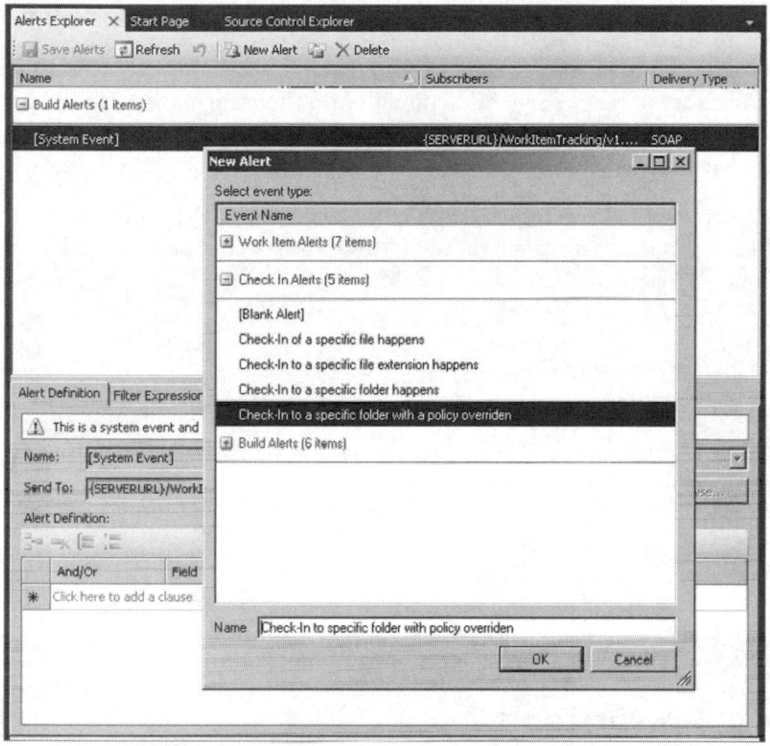

FIGURE 7-4: Available check-in alert templates

There is a template specifically designed for creating an e-mail alert when a check-in policy is overridden. The only customizations that still must be made are what folder or team project should be monitored, and what e-mail address should be used when the event occurs. Figure 7-5 shows the alert template using a team project named "Tailspin Toys."

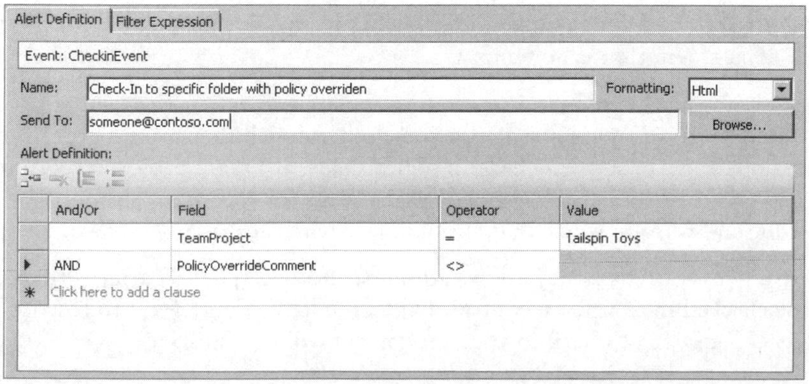

FIGURE 7-5: Alert template using a team project named "Tailspin Toys."

After receiving an e-mail alert, you can easily respond to the person who is overriding the check-in policies by replying to the alert e-mail. The person's e-mail address will be used by default as the reply-to address.

Data Warehouse

Check-in policy override information is also stored in the relational data warehouse. The relational data warehouse is normally named Tfs_Warehouse, and you will find the information for the policy overrides in the table named DimChangeset. The column name is PolicyOverrideComment and it is set to NULL for changesets that have successful evaluations of check-in policies.

Since all changesets that have overridden check-in policies require a comment, then filtering the changesets by those with values is simple. Listing 7-1 shows a T-SQL query that can be used to find the details about the check-in policy overrides.

LISTING 7-1: Querying for Changesets with Check-In Policy Overrides

```
SELECT [ChangesetSK]
     , [ChangesetID]
     , [ChangesetTitle]
     , [PolicyOverrideComment]
     , [LastUpdatedDateTime]
     , [TeamProjectCollectionSK]
     , [CheckedInBySK]
FROM [Tfs_Warehouse].[dbo].[DimChangeset]
WHERE [PolicyOverrideComment] IS NOT NULL
```

Check-In Policy Pack in Power Tools

After installing the latest version of the Team Foundation Server 2010 Power Tools, you will find several new check-in policies available in the additional Check-In Policy pack. Whenever you use any of these check-in policies, it is important to ensure that all team members have the Power Tools installed, because check-ins for policies that a team member does not have will fail with a message indicating that Visual Studio Team Explorer was unable to find the check-in policy.

Following are the check-in policies available in the Power Tools:

➤   *Changeset Comments Policy* — This policy simply checks to ensure that the developer has specified a changeset comment that is not empty.

➤   *Custom Path Policy* — Using this policy allows you to specify a different check-in policy to only be applied to a folder in the team project, or some other match that can be expressed as a regular expression. You can scope a check-in policy below the team project level (for example, you might have a custom check-in policy that checks for specifying property values in a project file and want to scope that check-in policy to only *.*proj files).

➤   *Forbidden Patterns Policy* — This policy allows administrators to specify patterns that are not permitted to be checked in to version control. For example, you may want to restrict developers from checking in .dll files into your version control repository.

➤ *Work Item Query Policy* — Enabling this policy allows administrators to specify that developers can only associate their check-ins with work items that are included in a specified work item query. For example, an administrator can create a team work item query that only includes non-closed work items, which would effectively allow developers to only associate with an open work item.

Creating Custom Check-In Policies

In addition to using the out-of-the-box check-in policies covered until this point, you can also create your own check-in policies to help improve quality and implement governance across your development projects. Thankfully, the check-in policy system is one of the many extensibility points in Team Foundation Server. Custom check-in policies can be created and deployed by creating a simple .NET class library of any language.

Simply follow these steps for creating a check-in policy implemented in C#:

1. To begin, start Microsoft Visual Studio 2010 by choosing Start ➪ All Programs ➪ Microsoft Visual Studio 2010 ➪ Microsoft Visual Studio 2010.

2. Create a new C# class library project by choosing File ➪ New Project, and then choose Class Library, as shown in Figure 7-6.

FIGURE 7-6: Creating a new class library project

3. Choose a location and a name for the project, and then click OK.

4. You can delete the default class file that gets created, which is always named `Class1.cs`.

5. Add the following two references to the project. Both assemblies should be available from the .NET tab of the Add Reference dialog. If you don't see these assemblies, ensure that you have Visual Studio Team Explorer 2010 installed. Figure 7-7 shows the Add Reference dialog.

➤ `Microsoft.TeamFoundation.VersionControl.Client.dll`

➤ `System.Windows.Forms.dll`

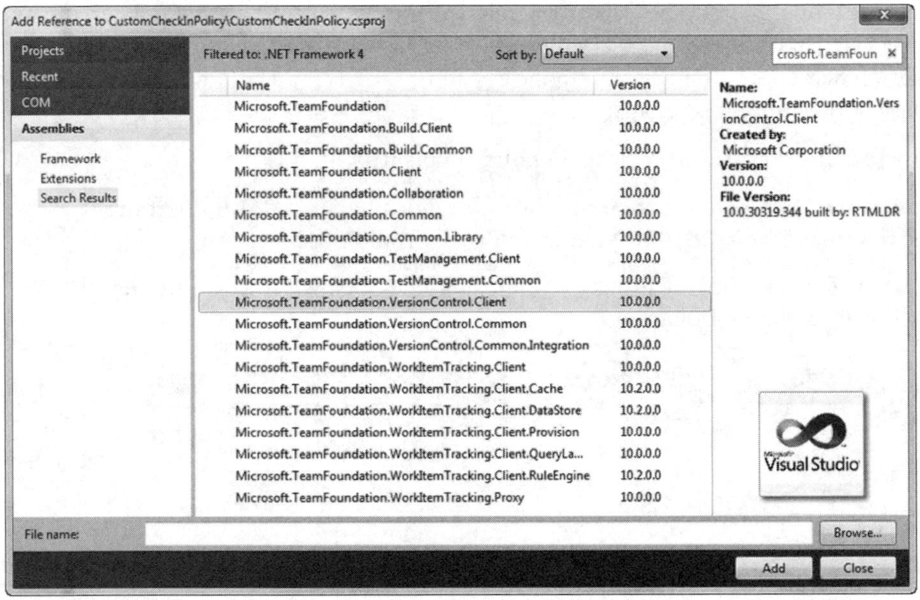

FIGURE 7-7: Add Reference dialog

6. Create a new class by choosing the Add ➪ Class command from the context menu for the project.

7. Choose a name for the class that represents the functionality for the new check-in policy, and click OK.

At this point, you will want to add `using` statements for the two namespaces that match the assemblies that were referenced. The class should also be marked as serializable by adding the `Serializable` attribute to the class. The class also must derive from `PolicyBase`, which is the base class for all check-in policies.

After deriving from the base class, Visual Studio can help to implement all of necessary interface members of the base class — specifically, `IPolicyDefinition` and `IPolicyEvaluation` interfaces.

Listing 7-2 shows the full source code for an example check-in policy.

LISTING 7-2: CustomCheckInPolicy.cs

```csharp
using System;
using System.Windows.Forms;
using Microsoft.TeamFoundation.VersionControl.Client;

namespace CustomCheckInPolicy
{
    [Serializable]
    class CheckForCommentsPolicy : PolicyBase
    {
        /// <summary>
        /// Contains the description for this check-in policy.
        /// </summary>
        public override string Description
        {
            get { return "Users should provide a meaningful comment
                for the check-in."; }
        }

        /// <summary>
        /// This method is invoked whenever a user adds this policy as a new
        /// check-in policy or when editing the configuration for the check-in
        /// policy.  You can display a custom UI to edit any configuration data
        /// for the different options that may be available by the policy.
        /// </summary>
        /// <param name="policyEditArgs">Arguments for the configuration dialog
        /// box.</param>
        /// <returns>Should return true if the dialog box is opened.</returns>
        public override bool Edit(IPolicyEditArgs policyEditArgs)
        {
            return true;
        }

        /// <summary>
        /// This method is invoked whenever the policy is being evaluated.  The
        /// method can be invoked by the policy framework at several points in
        /// the check-in lifecycle.</summary>
        /// <returns>An array of PolicyFailures that results from the
        /// evaluation.</returns>
        public override PolicyFailure[] Evaluate()
        {
            string comment = PendingCheckin.PendingChanges.Comment.Trim();

            if (String.IsNullOrEmpty(comment))
                return new PolicyFailure[] {
                    new PolicyFailure("A meaningful comment is required
                        for check-ins.", this)};
            else
                return new PolicyFailure[0];
        }

        /// <summary>
```

continues

LISTING 7-2 *(continued)*

```
        /// A string that describes the policy's name.  This is most notably
        /// used in the check-in policies dialog for a team project.
        /// </summary>
        public override string Type
        {
            get { return "Check for Comments Policy"; }
        }

        /// <summary>
        /// A string that describes the check-in policy and is displayed in the
        /// add new check-in policy dialog.
        /// </summary>
        public override string TypeDescription
        {
            get { return "This policy will ensure that users enter a
                meaningful comment for their check-in."; }
        }

        /// <summary>
        /// This property can contain the instructions for installing the
        /// check-in policy.
        /// </summary>
        public override string InstallationInstructions
        {
            get { return "To install this custom check-in policy,
                contact your administrator."; }
        }

        /// <summary>
        /// This method is activated whenever the user double-clicks on the
        /// policy failure.
        /// </summary>
        public override void Activate(PolicyFailure failure)
        {
            MessageBox.Show("Please provide a meaningful comment
                for your check-in.", "Resolving the Policy Failure");
        }

        /// <summary>
        /// This method is invoked whenever the user activates help for a
        /// check-in policy.  Most often this is done by pressing F1.
        /// </summary>
        public override void DisplayHelp(PolicyFailure failure)
        {
            MessageBox.Show("This policy checks for a meaningful,
                non-empty comment for the check-in.", "Policy Help");
        }
    }
}
```

Following are the members to note in this code:

➤ `Evaluate` *method* — This method is the primary functionality for the check-in policy. This is where the pending check-in can be checked. It will return any violations to the user in the form of an array of `PolicyFailure` objects. The base class has a protected property named `PendingCheckin` that contains all of the necessary details about the check-in that could be helpful for a check-in policy.

➤ `Type` *property* — This property simply determines how the check-in policy will look to administrators configuring version control settings for a team project.

➤ `Edit` *method* — Check-in policies can store configuration data in the form of serialized information on the server. The `Edit` method provides a mechanism for showing a user interface to the end user who wants to configure those options.

Deploying Check-In Policies

Check-in policies are not evaluated by the server, but rather on the machine from where the check-in is occurring. After you compile the assembly that contains the custom check-in policy, the assembly must then be deployed to all development machines, as well as registered in the Windows registry.

Follow these steps:

1. Open the Windows Registry Editor by starting `regedit.exe`.

2. Navigate to the `HKEY_CURRENT_USER\Software\Microsoft\VisualStudio\10.0\TeamFoundation\SourceControl\Checkin Policies` key. You will notice the other registered check-in policies are listed in this key.

3. Choose New ➪ String Value from the context menu for the registry key (by right-clicking the registry key) to create a new string value entry.

4. Enter the filename of the compiled `DLL` assembly without the file extension for the name of the new string value. In the previous example, this would be `CustomCheckInPolicy`.

5. Open the new string value by double-clicking the entry and specify for the value the fully qualified path and filename to the `DLL` assembly containing the custom policy.

6. Finally, add the new check-in policy after restarting Visual Studio 2010 using the method presented earlier in this chapter and shown in Figure 7-1.

Additionally, if you would like to simplify the deployment of custom check-in policy assemblies, the Team Foundation Server 2010 Power Tools includes a formalized mechanism for distributing both custom work item controls and custom check-in policies. This process works by storing the assembly files in a specific version control repository folder, and then indicating for the Power Tools to load them automatically. For more information about how this process works, you can consult the section, "Working with Custom Components," in the Team Members help file located in the installation directory for the Power Tools.

GATED CHECK-IN

Gated check-in is a new feature in Team Foundation Server 2010 that further integrates the build system with version control. Essentially, the gated check-in system will validate all check-ins through the build system before allowing the check-in to be committed by the build process. It is an evolution of a build concept called *Continuous Integration* in that a build does occur for every check-in, however, the major difference is that the check-in is actually only committed after the build has successfully completed.

Check-in policies and Continuous Integration can surely help improve quality, but falls short with one main problem. It still allows poor quality code to be committed to the version control system. For example, source code that doesn't even compile can be committed using Continuous Integration, which can then block the team if they get the latest version that includes the code that does not compile successfully.

Gated check-in solves this problem by ensuring that only code that meets the automated verification steps included in a build process ends up committed, and all other submitted changes are rejected.

Figure 7-8 shows the traditional workflow of check-ins with Continuous Integration builds.

Figure 7-9 shows the workflow of check-ins with gated check-in builds. Notice that if the build fails, then the pending changes will remain as a shelveset instead of being committed to the version control repository.

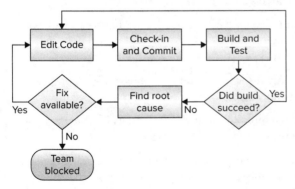

FIGURE 7-8: Traditional workflow of check-ins with Continuous Integration builds

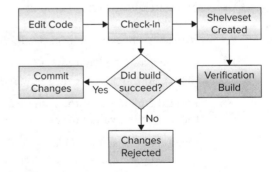

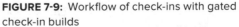

FIGURE 7-9: Workflow of check-ins with gated check-in builds

Why Gated Check-In?

One of the main reasons gated check-in is valuable is because it ensures that the rest of the team is not blocked by a bad check-in. Imagine a situation with a team of 100 developers, and then one of the developers checks in source code at the end of the day that causes projects not to compile or tests to fail.

Normally, in the scenario where the team is using Continuous Integration, a failed build will occur, and each build after it will fail as well, until the compilation error or test failure is resolved. If the developer has already left for the day, then it's possible that other team members would now be blocked after getting the latest version that now includes the bad check-in.

With gated check-in, the bad check-in will not have been committed, and the failed build will leave the changes around as a shelveset for that developer to resubmit after fixing the compilation problem. For builds after the failed build, other team members getting the latest version will not have to resolve the issue, and the team will not be impeded when they begin their day.

When Not to Use Gated Check-In

One of the downsides of using gated check-in builds is the amount of time it takes for changes to be integrated into the branch after the changes are submitted. Each check-in will trigger a build that must complete before the changes are committed if successful. At a minimum, other team members would not be able to get the submitted changes until the build has completed. If the team has a build that takes a while (for example, more than an hour), then the team must wait for at least an hour for it to be integrated in the branch. As an alternative, team members can unshelve the changes if they are needed before the build completes.

Another point to consider with gated check-in builds is the sheer number of builds that are triggered. The build queue can get rather large, unless you have plenty of build agents in your build lab.

You might additionally attempt to further speed up the build by configuring the build process to only run a subset of all of the automated tests. Some teams will call this subset the *build verification tests (BVT)*. You can use the category and priority attributes for tests, and then customize the build process to only run certain priorities or tests with certain categories.

> *The topics of build controllers and agents, as well as the hardware requirements for team builds, are explored in more detail in Chapter 15.*

Setting Up a Gated Check-In Build

Configuring a build definition to be a gated check-in build is extremely simple. After creating the build definition, the Trigger options tab allows for specifying that this build should be triggered for gated check-in.

Follow these steps:

1. Open Visual Studio 2010 and navigate to the Team Explorer window. Expand the Builds node for your team project.

2. Choose the Edit Build Definition command from the context menu for the build definition that has been created (by right-clicking the build definition node in the Team Explorer window). Switch to the Trigger options tab, as shown in Figure 7-10.

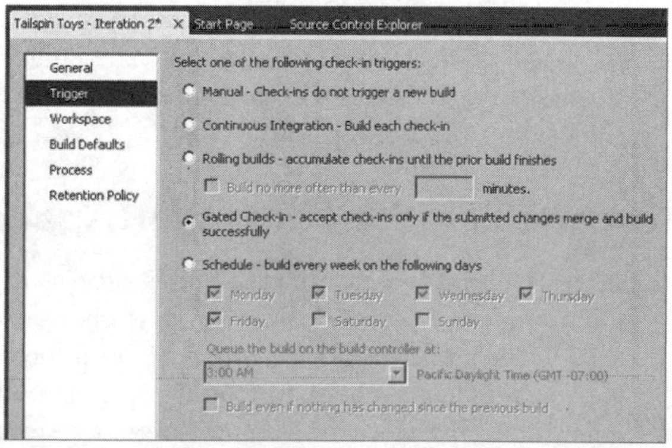

FIGURE 7-10: Switching to the Trigger options tab

3. Choose the Gated Check-In trigger option and save the build definition before closing the build definition editor window.

> *Other build definition configuration options are explored in more detail in Chapter 15.*

Developers commonly ask how the system knows which version control folders will trigger a gated check-in build. This actually depends on the workspace defined for the build definition. For example, if your build definition only included a mapping for $\TeamProject\DEV, then only changes in that particular folder or subfolders would cause the gated check-in build to be triggered.

Checking In for Validation

After checking in to a version control folder that affects a gated check-in build, the developer is presented with the dialog shown in Figure 7-11.

This dialog shows the developer which build definition is affected by the check-in, and subsequently will be triggered for validation of the check-in. If there are multiple build definitions that would be affected, then the developer would be able to choose the build definition to use for validation.

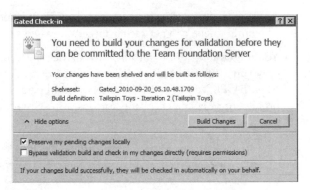

FIGURE 7-11: "Gated Check-In" dialog

The "Gated Check-in" dialog also displays the name of the shelveset that will be created with the pending changes once the Build Changes button is clicked. The developer can edit the name of the shelveset as well.

The other options that are available are to bypass the check-in build completely (if the user has the "Override check-in validation by build" permission), and to preserve the pending changes in the local workspace. This last option is particularly useful if the developer is going to continue editing source code where the pending changes are needed before the build completes and is committed to the version control repository.

Reconciling the Local Workspace

After the build has completed and is successful, one last task remains, and that is reconciling the local workspace, especially if pending changes were preserved. By preserving the pending changes during the gated check-in process, a developer is able to continue making edits to the source code, assuming that the check-in would succeed and be committed. However, this leaves pending changes existing on the workspace after the changeset has been committed by the build server.

Reconciling the workspace is the method for undoing any unneeded pending changes in the workspace that are successfully committed by the gated check-in build. This can be accomplished in three different ways:

> *Build Report* — The build report (accessible by double-clicking a build in the Build Explorer window) has an option at the top of the report that allows you to reconcile the workspace easily. Figure 7-12 shows this option at the top of the Build Report.

FIGURE 7-12: Option to reconcile the workspace

> *Build Explorer* — Selecting the Reconcile Workspace command on the context menu for a build in the Build Explorer window is another method for reconciling the workspace. Figure 7-13 demonstrates this method.

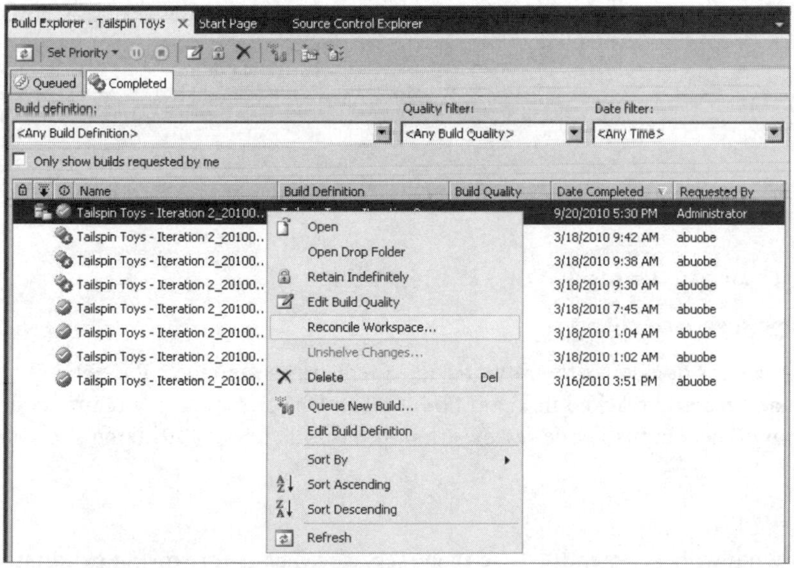

FIGURE 7-13: The Reconcile Workspace command

> *Build Notifications Tray Application* — The final method is available if the Build Notifications Tray application is running. The first time a gated check-in build is triggered by a developer, the tray application starts and is configured to monitor that build definition.

Alternatively, it can be launched from the Microsoft Visual Studio 2010 ⇨ Team Foundation Server Tools ⇨ Build Notifications command on the Start Menu. This application can run even when Visual Studio is not open. After the build has successfully completed, a dialog like Figure 7-14 is shown to the developer who checked in the changes. This dialog allows the developer to reconcile the workspace as well.

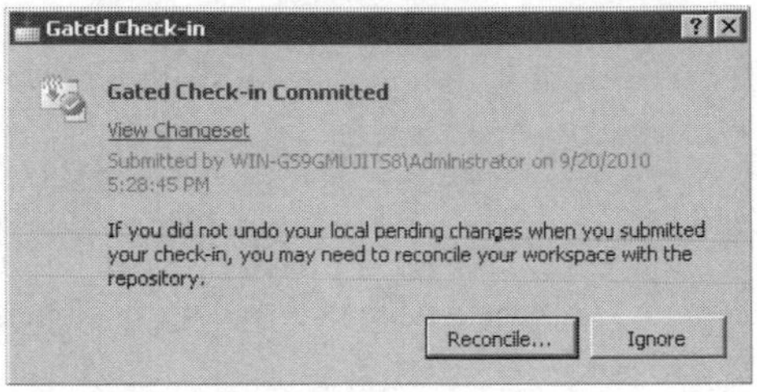

FIGURE 7-14 Dialog to reconcile the workspace

> *If the build has failed, the option in each of the methods mentioned here will be to unshelve the submitted changes, instead of reconciling the workspace, so that the developer can fix the issue and resubmit the changes for another gated check-in validation build.*

MANAGING CODE REVIEWS

Code reviews are formal or informal reviews of code by a lead or peer developer before a developer checks in his or her source code changes. The following are some examples of what the code reviewer is looking for when they review the code:

➤ Best practices

➤ Potential bugs

➤ Performance

➤ Security threats

➤ Following internal coding standards

➤ Previous code review suggested changes

Although Team Foundation Server does not officially provide a feature to manage code reviews, the reviews can easily be managed and tracked in Team Foundation Server to match a team's code review process. The first way to accomplish code reviews that you'll look at is by utilizing shelvesets.

Shelvesets

Most often, any code-reviewing workflow tends to use shelvesets as a means for storing pending changes for others to view.

Some teams even withhold check-in security privileges from the junior developers on a team in controlled branches, but provide the team with check-out privileges. This essentially allows developers to shelve their changes so that a lead developer (who has check-in privileges) can check in the code on behalf of the original developer.

As mentioned in the previous paragraph, controlled branches can help your team with quality by isolating changes to separate branches, and then allowing promotion of source code changes by merging them as they are promoted. Chapter 9 provides more information about branches. Figure 7-15 shows the Pending Changes window, which has an option to unshelve changes. In the dialog shown in Figure 7-16, a developer can specify the username of another user who has shelvesets to unshelve changes to the local workspace.

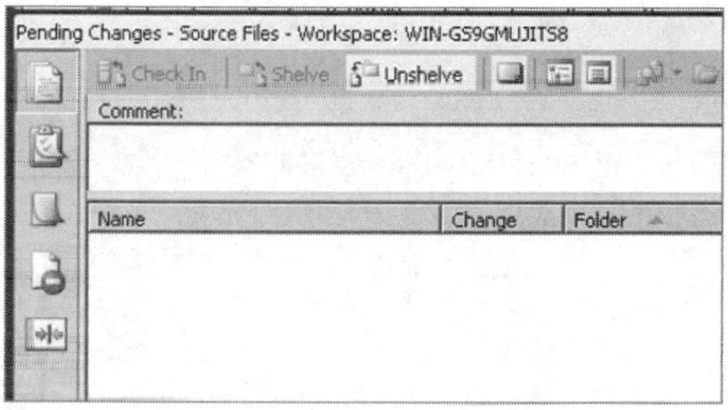

FIGURE 7-15: Pending Changes window

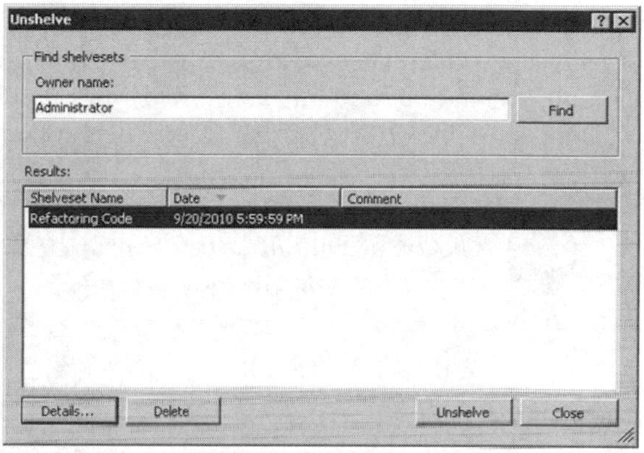

FIGURE 7-16: Specifying another user to unshelve changes to local workspace

Code reviewers can then review any of those pending changes in isolation in their local workspace. They can send e-mails with the findings, or even create a work item to document any recommended changes.

Check-In Note for Code Reviewer

After the developer has made any appropriate changes to the submitted changes, the code reviewer's name can then be documented in the check-in notes that are available. By switching to the check-in notes channel in the Pending Changes dialog shown in Figure 7-17, the developer can enter the name for the code reviewer.

This information can then be used for research when opening existing changesets. Additionally, the information is available in the data warehouse so that it can be reported on at a later date.

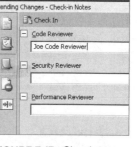

FIGURE 7-17: Check-in notes channel in the Pending Changes dialog

Third-Party Tools

There are also several community-created tools for managing code reviews with Team Foundation Server. The goal of the community providing these tools has been to formalize the code review process so that the workflow becomes simple for developers and code reviewers. The community tools additionally use Team Foundation Server to store all of the details and artifacts for the code review process.

Team Foundation Server Sidekicks

The Attrice Corporation (`www.attrice.info`) provides a free set of tools named the Team Foundation Server Sidekicks. This toolset is a collection of Team Foundation Server utilities that help utilize the information stored in Team Foundation Server to perform common research actions.

The sidekicks are available to be run as a separate application, or optionally installed as an add-in to Visual Studio. There is a Code Review Sidekick that helps with reviewing changesets (after they have been committed) or work items (and their associated changesets). It allows for each of them to be reviewed, and provides details about what files are included, whether there was a policy violation, and any associated work items. Comparing the file with the previous version of the file is possible after selecting the changeset details from the tool.

 The Team Foundation Server 2010 Sidekicks from the Attrice Corporation are freely available at `www.attrice.info/cm/tfs/`.

TeamReview

Another freely available tool for managing code reviews is available at CodePlex. The CodePlex project is called TeamReview, and it contains a related set of artifacts and tools to manage the code review process.

This particular set of tools uses a dedicated work item type that is imported called "Code Review Response," and a Visual Studio add-in that facilitates the creation of those work items. Creating the work item using the add-in allows the tool to store metadata in the work item about what file and line numbers the response is tied to, so the developer can easily get to the exact spot in the code when the review is to be acted on.

TeamReview is freely available at the CodePlex project dedicated to it. Check it out at `http://teamreview.codeplex.com/`.

SUMMARY

This chapter reviewed the different methods that are available in Team Foundation Server for managing quality before testing even begins.

Check-in policies were explored, including those policies available out-of-the-box, and those in the Policy Pack included in the latest version of the Team Foundation Server Power Tools. Creating custom check-in policies was also reviewed, including how to deploy the custom check-in policy to development machines.

You also learned about the gated check-in build feature, which ensures that changes submitted to Team Foundation Server compile and pass a series of build verification tests prior to being committed to the version control repository and shared with the rest of the development team.

Finally, the management of code reviews was examined, including the capability to review shelvesets from other team members, and using a check-in note to store the code reviewer's name.

In Chapter 8, you will learn about migrating source code from legacy systems, including Visual SourceSafe to the Team Foundation Server version control repository.

8

Migration from Legacy Version Control Systems

WHAT'S IN THIS CHAPTER?

> ➤ Understanding the difference between upgrade and migration

> ➤ Comparing tip versus history migration techniques

> ➤ Migrating from Visual SourceSafe using VSS Converter

> ➤ Understanding the Team Foundation Server Integration platform

> ➤ Getting to know third-party tools for other legacy systems

Most teams adopting Team Foundation Server don't have the blessing of starting from the very beginning with their applications. More than likely, there is an existing repository of source code that teams will want to move in some capacity into Team Foundation Server, and continue software development from there.

That team may be using the latest version of Microsoft Visual SourceSafe (VSS), only to discover being in an unsupported scenario in April 2011, which is the month that Microsoft discontinues mainstream support for Visual SourceSafe 2005. Their goal may be to move to a new version control system such as Team Foundation Server so that they can receive support if they are in a situation where they might need it in the future. The team may also be using one of the available version control systems — either commercial or Open Source.

One thing is certain: The process of moving to a new version control system gives you the rare opportunity to reorganize and clean up parts of the source code organization that has needed attention. This chapter explores the different options that are available for migrating existing source code into Team Foundation Server.

MIGRATION VERSUS UPGRADE

There are Team Foundation Server administrators who may say that they want to *migrate* from Team Foundation Server 2005/2008 to Team Foundation Server 2010. More than likely, they may mean that they want to *upgrade* to the newer version. If the Team Foundation Server administrator chooses the incorrect approach, the team will experience a loss of data and more work through the transition to Team Foundation Server 2010.

Upgrade

The term *upgrade* refers to the process of using the Team Foundation Server Upgrade configuration wizard to move data from a previous version of Team Foundation Server to the latest version. This scenario is different from setting up a new Team Foundation Server 2010 server and then attempting to "move" source code and work items into that new server. Upgrades are always fully supported, and are tested in many configurations before being released. In an upgrade, data on the server is transformed at the database level, and all data and metadata are preserved.

By using the appropriate configuration wizard, the process is capable of using a full-fidelity upgrade to keep all of the data and history with the least amount of effort for the administrator and the team members using the server.

There are also different types of upgrades:

➤   *In-place upgrade* — An *in-place upgrade* is defined as an upgrade that, when complete, will use the same set of hardware that is running the current Team Foundation Server version.

➤   *Migration-based upgrade* — A *migration-based upgrade* is defined as an upgrade involving a second, duplicate set of hardware that will host the new version of Team Foundation Server when the process is complete. Note that, despite having a similar name, a migration-based upgrade is *not* a migration.

> *Chapter 23 examines topics related to the process of upgrading Team Foundation Server from previous versions.*

Migration

A *migration* refers to the process of replaying actions from one system into another system. One of the key differences as compared to an upgrade is that a migration is a *lower fidelity data transfer*. In Team Foundation Server, only version control and work item tracking data can be migrated between servers — build data, reports, and numerous other pieces of metadata cannot be migrated. In general, available migration tools have significantly less testing than the upgrade process, and most available tools have limited support (because they are released out-of-band for the normal release).

In the case of a migration, the data transformations are done using only the public APIs, which are limited in providing only certain pieces of information while moving data. The result of these limitations is that some data is lost or distorted in the process of migration. Examples of this are artifact IDs (changeset numbers, work item IDs), date-timestamps, area paths, and iteration paths.

> *Matthew Mitrik, a Program Manager on the Team Foundation Server Version Control team, has written several blog posts about this particular concept, and discusses each of the different scenarios. For more information, visit* `http://blogs.msdn.com/b/mitrik/archive/2010/01/25/upgrade-vs-migration-definitions.aspx`.

MIGRATING HISTORY OR LATEST VERSION

One of the first determinations your team must make is whether you want to migrate all of the source code history from your legacy version control system, or just take the latest version (which is sometimes referred to as the *tip* version) at a particular milestone. Most teams will immediately answer, "We want the history. We cannot move without all of the history." However, that may not always be the wisest choice for your team.

The clear advantage of migrating history is the capability to immediately benefit from all of the history your team has been putting into the version control system over the months (if not years). Source code history can be extremely valuable when needing to determine how long a change has been included in the product, or how it was first introduced.

Another advantage of moving the history in Team Foundation Server is the capability to take the legacy servers that housed the existing source code out of commission. Not having to support two separate systems can definitely be a strong benefit for some teams.

However, there are possible downsides to migrating the source code history into a new system such as Team Foundation Server. Following are some of those downsides:

➤ *Testing* — Migrations should be treated like any type of software development project. Time and effort should be dedicated to testing the migration numerous times in a test environment to ensure that the migration occurs exactly as planned.

➤ *Third-party purchase* — It is possible that the team may want to leverage a third-party migration tool that is commercially available. This involves purchasing a license and a potential support contract for help from the vendor when using the migration tool.

➤ *Custom software development* — It is also possible that a custom tool or Team Foundation Server Integration Platform adapter will need to be developed and tested. This is particularly the case whenever a tool is not available commercially.

➤ *Playback execution time* — In addition to planning, development, and testing time as part of a migration effort, you must also consider the amount of time that it will take to actually play back all of the history into Team Foundation Server. Essentially, each action that has ever occurred in the legacy version control system must be committed in sequence into Team Foundation Server. Conservatively, the team should estimate 24 hours of playback execution time for the migration for every one to two gigabytes of source code history.

Ultimately, the return on investment for moving the source code history should be determined and weighed against the downsides. If the team does end up only moving over the tip version, they can always leave around the legacy version control system in a read-only state to allow team members to research history in the archive if needed.

> *For more information about this particular topic, the hosts of the Developer Smackdown podcast and their guest, Ed Blankenship, discuss Team Foundation Server Migrations in an episode that is available at* `http://developersmackdown.com/Archives/SingleShow/32.`

MIGRATING FROM VISUAL SOURCESAFE

If a team is currently using Microsoft Visual SourceSafe (VSS), then they are certainly in luck. Team Foundation Server 2010 includes a migration tool that can migrate the full history from a VSS database. This tool includes several features that will assist an administrator in migrating source code easily from the VSS database. Following are some of those features:

➤ Move entire repository or only specified folders.

➤ Map locations from the legacy repository to new locations in the Team Foundation Server version control repository.

➤ Analyze the VSS repository for corruption and other migration issues before migration begins.

➤ Map VSS users to Active Directory (AD) domain user accounts.

➤ Update source control bindings during migration from VSS bindings to the appropriate Team Foundation Server bindings in the Visual Studio solutions and projects.

> *As with most tools included with Team Foundation Server 2010, you should make sure that the latest service pack and hotfixes are installed, especially for the VSS migration utility. The product team is constantly improving the utility, and new features or bug fixes may be included in the latest release.*

As mentioned earlier in this chapter, a team may find itself looking at a situation where they will likely be unable to receive support from Microsoft if there were ever a catastrophic problem that causes data loss from their VSS repository. Based on the experiences and lessons learned from several disaster-recovery scenarios for version control systems, you should never leave yourself in a situation where you aren't able to receive support.

> *As of this writing, Microsoft Visual SourceSafe 2005 Standard Edition is scheduled to end mainstream support on April 12, 2011. When Microsoft ends mainstream support for a product, it ceases to release non-security hotfixes, provide telephone support, and supply other mainstream support options. Certain extended support options may be available to some companies for some of the benefits, but such companies must act quickly within 90 days from the end of mainstream support to take advantage of them. The most up-to-date information about the support lifecycle for Visual SourceSafe 2005 is available at* `http://support.microsoft.com/lifecycle/?p1=10433`. *A company can also contact its Microsoft representative to inquire further about support options after mainstream support has ended.*

The VSS Converter utility plays back each of the check-ins into Team Foundation Server during the migration. It does so by creating changesets of files that were checked in at relatively the same time by the same user and with the same comment. Also, the changes must not conflict with one another to be included in the same changeset. For example, if a user added a specific file and then deleted it in the relatively same time period, then those two actions will not be committed in the same changeset during migration.

One of the outcomes that will be noticed is the fact that the date and timestamp for the new changesets will be set to the time that the migration action actually occurred, instead of the original time. The original check-in date and timestamp will be stored in the changeset's comment for reference purposes. Additionally, the original user will not be stored in the comment if that user is not mapped appropriately (as described later in this section). If the user is mapped appropriately, the username will be in the changeset's username field.

This section examines the different options that teams have available if they want to migrate the full history from VSS into the Team Foundation Server version control repository.

Preparing to Use the VSS Converter Tool

The very first step before attempting to begin a migration effort is to ensure that the VSS repository has been fully backed up. This provides the capability to restore it to its original state if there are any errors that occur during the migration. Be sure to always run the migration utility against a copy of the database, instead of against the actual database.

One key step is to ensure that, if the VSS database version is older than the latest version (Visual SourceSafe 2005), then the database should be upgraded before the migration occurs. The DDUPD utility can be used for upgrading to the latest version after installing Visual SourceSafe 2005. During the analyze phase, the VSS Converter tool will check whether the database has been upgraded correctly before it proceeds to the migration execution phase.

The development team may choose to not migrate all of the history that is stored in the VSS repository, and instead choose to migrate only a subset of that history. The VSS Converter utility provides a mechanism for specifying a start timestamp or label, and will begin migrating from the oldest available check-in to the latest in sequence. A team might decide that they only need the last year's worth of history to reduce the amount of migration execution time that is needed. If that is the case, then the administrator should use the archive functionality that is available in VSS to archive all content before the selected date.

> *Using the archive functionality in VSS will permanently remove the source code and history specified. Be sure to back up the VSS database before taking this step if you need to keep that data.*

For those instances where migration execution time needs to be minimized as much as possible, ensure that all of the servers and computers needed in the migration exist on the same local network, or even on the same network switch. The servers and computers that will be used in the migration effort are the migration computer that will be executing the VSS Converter utility, the server hosting the file share that contains the VSS database, and the Team Foundation Server 2010 server.

Finally, prepare the team for the migration by informing them of the time frame of when the migration will occur. For example, some teams will start a migration at the close of business on Friday so that the migration can be executed during the weekend, and the new location will be available by the beginning of the business day on Monday. Ideally, the team will have checked in all files, removed any check-outs, and not used the VSS database while the migration is occurring. To ensure that only the migration utility has access to the repository, permissions can be removed from the file share for all users except the account that will be executing the migration.

Analyzing the Visual SourceSafe Repository

After the preparation steps have been taken for a VSS migration, the next step is to use the `Analyze` function in the VSS Converter utility to discover any potential issues that should be addressed before the migration phase can continue.

Analyze Settings File

To begin the analyze phase, a file is created with the proper settings to give the VSS Converter utility enough information about the intended migration to check for potential issues. Listing 8-1 shows an example of an `Analyze` settings file.

LISTING 8-1: Analyze Settings File for VSS Converter Utility

```xml
<?xml version="1.0" encoding="utf-8"?>
<SourceControlConverter>
<ConverterSpecificSetting>
    <Source name="VSS">
        <VSSDatabase name="\\VSSSERVER\VSSDatabase" />
        <UserMap name="C:\VSSMigration\UserMap.xml" />
    </Source>
```

```
      <ProjectMap>
          <Project Source="$/Main" />
          <Project Source="$/SharedLibrary" />
          <Project Source="$/ProducttA" />
          <Project Source="$/ProductB" />
      </ProjectMap>
  </ConverterSpecificSetting>
  <Settings>
      <Output file="C:\VSSMigration\Logs\ContosoVSSAnalyze.xml" />
  </Settings>
  </SourceControlConverter>
```

The main information that is specified in the Analyze settings file is the location of the VSS database that should be migrated. The VSSDatabase node is used to specify the folder location (whether local or available on a network path) that contains the srcsafe.ini file. However, do not specify srcsafe.ini in the value that is specified.

The UserMap node is what is used for specifying where to store the user mapping file that will be generated by the Analyze function. More information about how this user mapping file is used will be presented later in this section. If no user mapping file is specified, then the VSS Converter utility will create one in the working directory with the name of UserMap.xml.

The ProjectMap section describes the location of each folder in the VSS repository that will be used as the source locations during the migration phase. Be sure to include each of the locations you intend to use during the migration phase; otherwise, they will not be included during the analyze phase.

Finally, the Ouput node is used to specify the name and location of the output file that should be created from the Analyze file. Be sure to name this differently from what will be used during the migration phase so that you can have a copy of both after the migration has completed.

Executing the Analyze Phase

The Analyze function for the VSS Converter utility can be kicked off by executing the following command from a Visual Studio 2010 command prompt, where *AnalyzeSettings.xml* is the name of the Analyze settings file that was created earlier:

```
VSSConverter.exe Analyze AnalyzeSettings.xml
```

The analyze phase can take a good amount of time, and should be monitored in case any errors occur. This allows the administrator to resolve those issues and begin the analyze phase again to start from the point where it left off.

User Mapping

One of the benefits of using the Analyze function in the VSS Converter utility is the capability to automatically create a user mapping file that will assist in mapping VSS users to the AD domain users. If any users are no longer with the company (and, therefore, unavailable in AD and/or Team Foundation Server), the administrator can use the user mapping file to specify which account to use for those actions.

Listing 8-2 shows an example of a user mapping file that is created during the analyze phase.

LISTING 8-2: Example User Mapping File from VSS Converter Analyze Function

```xml
<?xml version="1.0" encoding="utf-8"?>
<UserMappings>
    <UserMap From="Admin" To=""></UserMap>
    <UserMap From="Guest" To=""></UserMap>
    <UserMap From="Ed" To=""></UserMap>
    <UserMap From="Martin" To=""></UserMap>
    <UserMap From="Grant" To=""></UserMap>
    <UserMap From="JeanLuc" To=""></UserMap>
</UserMappings>
```

The file that is created does not specify the `To` attribute for each of user mapping entries. If an AD user account does not exist with the same name of the VSS user that is listed, then the proper account name should be provided. Listing 8-3 shows an example user mapping file that has explicitly listed the full AD account information for some users.

LISTING 8-3: Example User Mapping File for VSS Converter with Full Mapping

```xml
<?xml version="1.0" encoding="utf-8"?>
<UserMappings>
    <UserMap From="Admin" To="CONTOSO\VSSUser"></UserMap>
    <UserMap From="Guest" To="CONTOSO\VSSUser"></UserMap>
    <UserMap From="Ed" To="CONTOSO\edb"></UserMap>
    <UserMap From="Martin" To="CONTOSO\martinw"></UserMap>
    <UserMap From="Grant" To="CONTOSO\granth"></UserMap>
    <UserMap From="JeanLuc" To=""></UserMap>
</UserMappings>
```

VSS users can be mapped to the same AD account. Additionally, the `To` attribute doesn't have to be specified for each of the VSS users. That is, it doesn't have to be specified if the exact username appears in the AD domain, and is the intended user to be used for mapping. However, it never hurts to be explicit!

Reviewing and Resolving Issues

Once the analyze phase has completed, the output file will list all of the potential issues that were discovered. Each of these issues should be reviewed individually and should either be resolved or specifically ignored to continue with the migration. Following are the most common issues that are discovered during the analyze phase:

➤ *Checked out files* — Any files that were checked out during the analyze phase will be listed in the issues output report.

➤ *Data integrity issues* — Any files that are determined to have data integrity issues are listed. The VSS ANALYZE utility may be able to address some of these issues. For more information about this situation, see the Microsoft Knowledge Base article at http://support.microsoft.com/kb/133054.

➤ *History not included in mapped projects* — This type of issue indicates that one of the mapped projects listed in the Analyze settings file contains history in a folder that is not listed in the project mapping section. This commonly occurs when folders and files are moved around in the VSS repository. For example, using the previous example Analyze settings file, if the $/Main folder contains a folder named Product1 that was moved into it from the $/ProductC/Product1 location, then you will see this particular issue show up in the report, since the $/ProductC location is not specified as folder to be migrated. This can be ignored if the history contained in the non-mapped original folder before the move operation ($/ProductC/Product1) is not necessary to be migrated.

➤ *Sharing and pinning* — Since Team Foundation Server does not contain a feature comparable to the sharing and pinning feature of VSS, a listing will be included for anywhere this may occur. The migration utility will essentially create individual copies of these shared files that will not have any links between them.

Migration

At this point, you are ready to begin the migration execution phase with the VSS Converter utility. Be sure that you have addressed all issues from the output file of the Analyze function created previously before continuing.

Migration Settings File

First, a migration settings file must be created with the appropriate information needed by the VSS Converter utility. It is very similar to the Analyze settings file, with some notable additions. Listing 8-4 shows an example migration settings file, with the key additions marked in bold.

LISTING 8-4: Migration Settings File for VSS Converter Utility

```xml
<?xml version="1.0" encoding="utf-8"?>
<SourceControlConverter>
<ConverterSpecificSetting>
    <Source name="VSS">
        <VSSDatabase name="\\VSSSERVER\VSSDatabase" />
        <UserMap name="C:\VSSMigration\UserMap.xml" />
    </Source>
    <ProjectMap>
        <Project Source="$/Main" Destination="$/TeamProject/Main" />
        <Project Source="$/SharedLibrary"
            Destination="$/TeamProject/SharedLibrary" />
        <Project Source="$/ProducttA"
            Destination="$/TeamProject/Products/ProductA" />
        <Project Source="$/ProductB"
            Destination="$/TeamProject/Products/ProductA" />
    </ProjectMap>
</ConverterSpecificSetting>
<Settings>
    <TeamFoundationServer name="tfs.contoso.local" port="8080" protocol="http"
        collection="tfs/DefaultCollection" />
    <Output file="C:\VSSMigration\Logs\ContosoVSSMigrate.xml" />
</Settings>
</SourceControlConverter>
```

The `Destination` attribute for the `Project` node is the first thing that should be added for each of the project mapping entries. This tells the VSS Converter utility where in Team Foundation Server it should migrate from the source locations. Each of the team projects that are specified must be created before the migration utility runs, so be sure to create which team projects are specified. If any of the specified folders already exist in the team project, they must be empty. Also be sure to not overlap any of the destination mappings with one another. Each of these will be checked when the migration utility is executed.

The Team Foundation Server instance to be used should also be specified using the `TeamFoundationServer` node. Since Team Foundation Server 2010 introduced the concept of team project collections, the collection to be used must be specified, in addition to the server's name.

Executing the Migration

The `Migrate` function for the VSS Converter utility can be kicked off by executing the following command from a Visual Studio 2010 command prompt, where *MigrateSettings.xml* is the name of the migration settings file that was created earlier:

```
VSSConverter.exe Migrate MigrateSettings.xml
```

Again, the migration execution phase can take a considerable amount of time, depending on the amount of source code, number of migration actions, and network conditions. It should be monitored for potential issues that may pop up. If an error does occur during the migration phase, the VSS Converter utility can be started again at any point, and can begin again in what is called an *incremental migration*. Simply specify that you want it to continue as an incremental migration when prompted, and the tool will proceed from where it left off.

After the migration tool has finished, the Team Foundation Server version control repository is ready to be used by the team after all permissions are given.

TEAM FOUNDATION SERVER INTEGRATION PLATFORM

The Team Foundation Server product team at Microsoft has dedicated resources for creating a platform called the Team Foundation Server Integration Platform, which enables customers to build migration and synchronization tools. It is essentially an entire framework that includes a user interface (UI) for configuring the migration/synchronization run, a service for executing the actions, and even a conflict resolution experience for detecting when the tool is unable to handle migration/synchronization actions.

Microsoft has provided the free utility and source code on a dedicated CodePlex project site at http://tfsintegration.codeplex.com/. Frequent updates are uploaded on a regular basis to the CodePlex project site, and the Visual Studio ALM Rangers have created quite a bit of documentation that is available to get you started. Figure 8-1 shows a screenshot of the Team Foundation Server Integration Platform configuration utility.

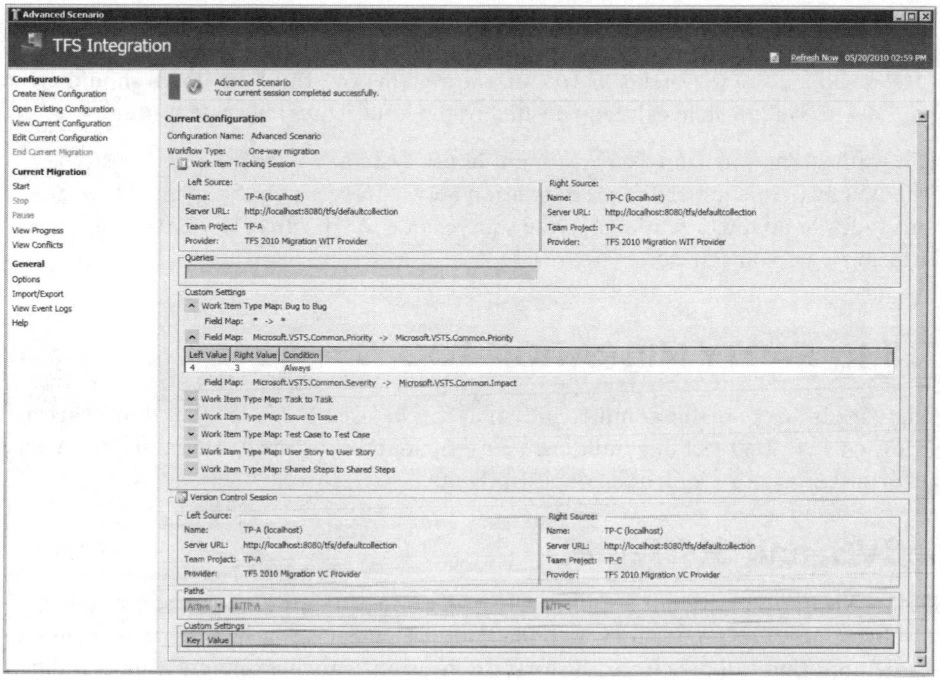

FIGURE 8-1: Team Foundation Server Integration Platform configuration utility

The Team Foundation Server Integration Platform can assist with migrating both version control artifacts and work items from legacy systems to Team Foundation Server 2010 using an adapter system. The Team Foundation Server adapters have been created, and all that you need to do is create a version control or work item tracking adapter for the legacy system.

Examples for creating custom adapters, as well as other adapters, are available out of the box. Following are some of the adapters that were available as of this writing:

➤ Team Foundation Server 2008 Version Control

➤ Team Foundation Server 2010 Version Control

➤ Team Foundation Server 2008 Work Item Tracking

➤ Team Foundation Server 2010 Work Item Tracking

➤ ClearCase

➤ ClearQuest

➤ SharePoint List

➤ SharePoint Document Library

➤ File System

The framework was intended to be used to create custom adapters for legacy systems. The CodePlex site lists the team's backlog for creating adapters for popular version control and work item tracking products. Feel free to suggest new systems or vote on the systems you think the team should create adapters for that have CodePlex items already created in the Issue Tracking system.

If the system you want to migrate from is a custom in-house system, you can create a custom adapter using the API available in the Team Foundation Server Integration Platform. There are examples of both types of adapters available in the source code for the Team Foundation Server Integration Platform to get you started.

POPULAR THIRD-PARTY MIGRATION TOOLS

Several third-party tools are available commercially that can be used by teams that don't have a tool available for them, or don't feel like building a custom adapter for the Team Foundation Server Integration Platform. Let's take a look at a couple of them.

Subversion, CVS, and StarTeam

The team at Timely Migration has built a tool that is very successful at migrating source code history from a Subversion (SVN) repository to Team Foundation Server. It handles many common situations, such as migrating full or selected history, discovering branches and creating them in Team Foundation Server, and converting tags into Team Foundation Server version control labels.

In addition to SVN, the Timely Migration tool supports migrating from a CVS or StarTeam repository with similar features as the SVN migration tool.

> *For more information about the Timely Migration tool, visit their website at* www.timelymigration.com/features.aspx. *There is a charge for the tool, as well as any support hours that are needed during the test and actual migration execution runs. You can download a trial version of the tool, which is a fully-featured evaluation edition that allows you to test migrations before purchasing the product.*

ClearCase

Thankfully, the Team Foundation Server Integration Platform includes an adapter that will allow teams to migrate from an IBM Rational ClearCase source control repository to Team Foundation Server. You can choose to either migrate full history or selected history with the available adapters.

More information about the Team Foundation Server Integration Platform was presented earlier in this chapter.

> *You can also use Team Foundation Server Integration Tools, which has a compiled copy of the platform and is the minimally necessary tool for migrating from ClearQuest. The Integration Tools release can be located on the Visual Studio Gallery at* `http://visualstudiogallery.msdn.microsoft.com/en-us/5a8d1703-7987-4081-ba2f-9d0b68b0ed3e.`

SUMMARY

Migrating source code from a legacy system can be a tough endeavor for administrators and teams. This chapter reviewed the different techniques and tools necessary for migrating from a legacy system, whether that be using the VSS Coverter that ships with Team Foundation Server 2010, the Team Foundation Server Integration Platform on CodePlex, or one of the popular third-party commercial tools. You also learned about some suggestions for ensuring a smooth migration no matter which legacy source control system your team has been using.

In Chapter 9, you will learn about the branching and merging features available in Team Foundation Server Version Control. You will learn about the new branching and track changes visualization tools, as well as some common best practices for branching and merging strategies.

9

Branching and Merging

WHAT'S IN THIS CHAPTER?

➤ Understanding branching terminology and concepts

➤ Getting to know common branching strategies

➤ Using the branching and merging tools

The use of branching in version control can open up a whole world of possibilities for improving development productivity through parallelization. Yet, for many developers, branching and merging is slightly scary and full of uncertainty. Because of a lack of good tooling in the past, many developers still shy away from making use of branching and merging, despite Team Foundation Server having good support. At the other extreme, some people, who see all the great branch and merge functionality now available, can go a little crazy with their newly found power. Overuse of branches can impact developer productivity and reduce the maintainability of their repository as a result.

No matter which side of the spectrum you find yourself on, this chapter explains the fundamental principles behind the important branching and merging strategies, and provides some key guiding principles to help you apply them to your organization's needs. This chapter highlights the branching and merging tooling available with Team Foundation Server 2010, and then concludes by walking you through the application of this tooling with some example scenarios.

BRANCHING DEMYSTIFIED

There are lots of terms and concepts peculiar to the world of branching and merging. The following sections provide some definitions and context for those basic terms and concepts.

Branch

As stated in Chapter 5, a *branch* is a copy of a set of files in a different part of the repository that allows two or more teams of people to work on the same part of a project in parallel. In

Team Foundation Server 2010, when you perform the branch, it doesn't actually create new copies of all those files on the server. It just creates a record pointing to them — one of the reasons why creating a new branch containing thousands or even millions of files can be done quickly.

Merge

A *merge* is the process of taking code in two branches and combining it back into one codebase. For example, if you had two teams of developers working on two branches, and you wanted to bring the changes together, then you would merge them. If the changes consisted simply of edits to different files in the branches, then the merge would be simple — but it can get more complicated, depending on what was edited in both branches.

For example, if the same line of the same file was edited in both branches, the person performing the merge must make a decision as to which change should win. In some circumstances, this will result in a *hybrid merge*, where the combination of the *intent* behind the two changes requires a different result than simply the *text* in those versions being combined. When you branch, Team Foundation Server keeps track of the relationship between branches, as shown in Figure 9-1.

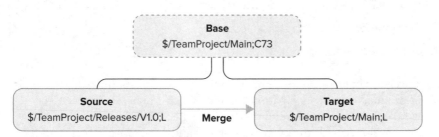

FIGURE 9-1: The relationship between the source and target branches

The branch containing your changes that you want to merge is called the *source* branch. The branch that you want to merge the changes into is the *target* branch. The common ancestor between them is called the *base version*. When you merge, you can select a range of changes in the source branch to merge into the target branch.

Conflict

If the same file has been edited in both the source and target branches, Team Foundation Server will flag this as a *conflict*. (Interestingly, the notion of which file is the same changed significantly in Team Foundation Server 2010 to improve the merging experience. See the sidebar, "Slot Mode Versus Item Mode," later in this chapter.) Regardless of the changes made in the 2010 release to simplify the merge experience, if the same file has been edited in both places, then it will always be flagged as a conflict, even if the changes are to completely different sections of the file.

For certain changes (such as a file that was edited in two different places), Team Foundation Server can make a good guess about what should happen (that is, you want to see a file containing the changes from both places). This is called an *automerge*. A best practice is to let the tool perform an automerge, but you should then validate the merge results afterward to ensure the correct intent of the two changes has occurred. For example if two different bugs were fixed, you probably want both changes. However, if the two changes were just fixing the same bug in two different ways, perhaps a different solution is in order. In most cases, where the development team has good communication, the changes are a result of different changes being made to the file. Automerge usually does a great job of merging them together, making it easy for the developer to simply validate the changes.

There can also be many cases where the actual outcome is unclear, and so automerging is not available. For example, if you deleted the file in one branch and edited it in another, do you wish to keep the file with the changes or have it removed? The person performing the merge is responsible for deciding the correct *conflict resolution* based on an understanding of the code, and communicating with the team members who made the conflicting changes to understand their intent.

As with life in general, conflict is never good in version control. Making the decision about the correct conflict resolution in version control can be a complex and time-consuming process. Therefore, it is best to adopt a branching strategy that minimizes the likelihood of conflicts occurring. However, conflicts will occur, and Team Foundation Server provides the tooling to deal with them, so conflicts should not be feared.

Branch Relationships

When you branch a folder, the relationships between those branches form a standard hierarchical relationship. The source of the branch is the *parent*, and the target of the branch is the *child*, as shown in Figure 9-2. Children who have the same parent are called *sibling* branches.

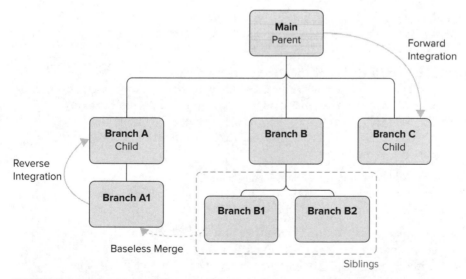

FIGURE 9-2: Hierarchical relationship in branches

Baseless Merge

A *baseless merge* is a merging of two arbitrary branches in version control without reference to a base version. This is sometimes necessary if the source code was originally imported in a flat structure without the branch relationship being in place, or if you wish to merge between a branch and another branch that is not a direct parent or child (for example, `Branch A1` and `Branch B1` in Figure 9-2).

Because no base version is being used to compare against, the probability of the server detecting conflicts occurring between the two branches is much higher. For example, if a file were renamed in one branch and edited in the other, it will show up as a file delete conflicting with the file edit, and then a file add that gives no hint as to which file it was related to, or that there was an edit intended for this file in the other branch. For this reason, baseless merges are discouraged with Team Foundation Server 2010, and the functionality is only available via the command line. Standard merging (that is, one with a base version) through the Visual Studio or Eclipse clients are the encouraged method — and only one branch up or down (that is, a parent to a child or vice versa) is allowed. Therefore, your branching model should attempt to constrain most merges between parent and child branches to minimize the amount of baseless merging required.

Forward/Reverse Integration

Forward integration (FI) occurs when you merge code from a parent branch to the child branch. *Reverse integration (RI)* occurs when you merge code from a child branch up to the parent branch. The terms FI and RI can often shoot around quite freely during a branching debate, so it is important to understand what they mean. If you are doing feature development in branches, it is common to use FI at various points during the feature development cycle, and then to use RI at the end. See the section, "Feature Branching," later in this chapter for more information.

SLOT MODE VERSUS ITEM MODE

In Team Foundation Server 2010, one of the biggest changes to occur was fairly invisible to users, but actually represents a fundamental shift in how Team Foundation Server works under the hood.

In the initial versions of Team Foundation Server, everything in version control was an item, identified by an `itemID`. Each time a new file was added to the system, it was given a new ID. Because of this, files could easily be tracked during a rename operation. The item stayed the same; just its full path changed. For example, `$/tpa/foo.txt` would get renamed to `$/tpa/bar.txt`, but the ID would remain the same to signify it was that item.

While `itemID`s worked well and gave Team Foundation Server some great functionality to track changes between moves, renames, and so on, it did make for some very complex cases, especially when those items were branched and merged.

In Team Foundation Server 2010, the `itemID`s are now synonymous with the full path — that is, a particular `itemID` is unique to that full path. When a file is renamed, it essentially becomes a different item because its ID has changed. The net effect of this is that, in Team Foundation Server 2010, merges are simpler, and performance of the version control server is much better.

For more detailed information on the changes, see the blog post from Matt Mitrik of the Version Control team for Team Foundation Server at `http://blogs.msdn.com/b/mitrik/archive/2009/05/28/changing-to-slot-mode-in-tfs-2010-version-control.aspx`.

COMMON BRANCHING STRATEGIES

Depending on the organization of your team, and the software that you need to develop, there are numerous branching strategies that you can adopt, all with various pros and cons. However, just as every strategy in chess is made up of simple moves, every branching strategy uses one or more combinations of some basic techniques. This section details some of the basics techniques, how they are used, and why.

When developing your own branching strategy, you should take into account the needs of your organization. In all likelihood, you may adopt a strategy that combines one or many of the basic techniques described here.

When looking at any strategy for branching and merging, you should keep in mind the following important rules:

➤ Prefer simplicity over control.

➤ Only branch when you really need to. (You can branch after the fact if you find you need to.)

➤ If you ever want to merge two branches together, keep the time between merges to a minimum.

➤ Ensure that your branch hierarchy matches the path you intend your merges to follow.

> *For additional guidance on branching and merging with Team Foundation Server 2010, see the "Visual Studio TFS Branching Guide 2010" project on CodePlex at* `http://tfsbranchingguideiii.codeplex.com`*. This guidance is created by a community of Visual Studio ALM Rangers, and combines the knowledge of Microsoft people with Microsoft Most Valued Professionals (MVPs) and other technical specialists in the community. The guidance also includes hands-on labs, along with a set of diagrams that can be a useful starting point when creating your own branching plan.*

No Branching

It may be counterintuitive, but the simplest branching technique is to not branch at all. This should always be your default position. Do not branch unless you know you need to. Remember that you are using a version control tool that tracks changes over time. You can branch at any point in the future from any point in the past. This gives you the luxury of not having to create a branch "just in case" — only create branches when you know you need them.

However, there are things you can do to prepare yourself to make branching easier in the future if you decide you need a branch.

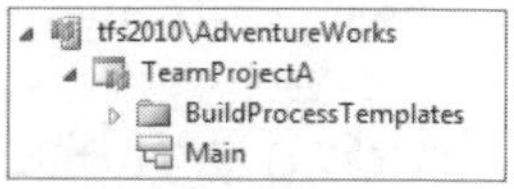

Figure 9-3 illustrates the most important thing that you should do if you think you might possibly need to branch in the future. When you first create your team project in Team Foundation Server, create a folder called Main

FIGURE 9-3: A branch called Main

and check it in. Then, right-click on the folder in Source Control Explorer and select Branching and Merging ➪ Convert to Branch to get to the screen shown in Figure 9-4.

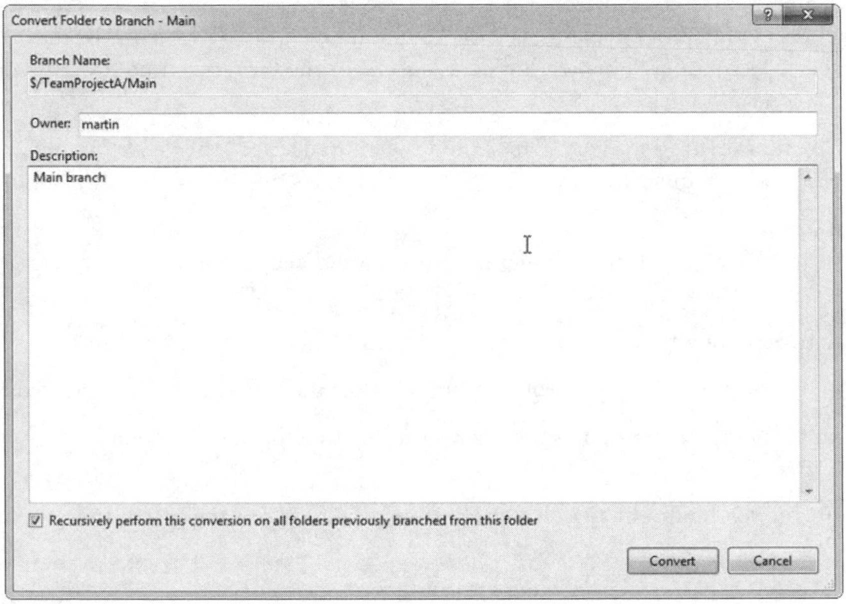

FIGURE 9-4: Convert Folder to Branch screen

With no branching, you only have one branch of code to work in for all teams. This technique works great when you have small teams working on the same codebase, developing features for the same version of the application, and only supporting one version of the application at a time. At some point, no matter how complex your branching strategy evolves to support your business needs, you need at least one stable area that is your *main* (or *mainline*) code. This is a stable version of the code that will be used for the build that you will create, test, and deploy.

However, during stabilization and test periods, while you are getting ready to release, it may be necessary for the team to not check in any new code into the codebase (that is, undergo a *code freeze*). With smaller teams working on a single version, this does not impact productivity, because the people who would be checking in code are busy testing to ensure that the application works, as well as getting ready for deployment.

With this technique there is no way to start work on something new before the final build of the current version has been performed. The code freeze period can, therefore, be very disruptive because there is no way to start work on the next version until the current one has shipped. It's these times when other strategies become useful for teams of any size, even a team of one.

Branch per Release

After no branching, the second most common branching technique is *branch per release*. With this technique, the branches contain the code for a particular release version, as shown in Figure 9-5.

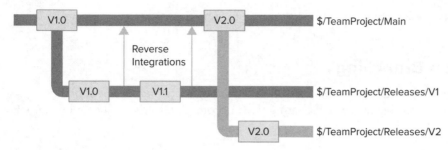

FIGURE 9-5: Branch per release

Development starts in the `Main` branch. After a period of time, when the software is considered ready, a branch is made to the `V1` branch, and the final builds are performed from it. It is then released into production (with the code in the final production build getting a label to indicate which versions of which files were in that version). Meanwhile, development of new features for version 2 (`V2`) continues on the `Main` branch.

Let's say that some bugs are discovered in production that must be addressed, and a small change is necessary to reflect how the business needs something to work. However, the development group does not want to include all the work for `V2` that has been going on in the `Main` branch. Therefore, these changes are made in the `V1` branch, and builds are taken from it. Any bug fixes or changes that must also be included in the next version (to ensure the bug is still fixed in that next release) are merged back (that is, reverse-integrated) into the `Main` branch. If a bug fix was already in the `Main` branch, but needed to go into `V1`, then it might simply be merged (that is, forward-integrated) into it. At a certain point, the build is determined to be good, and a new `V1.1` build is performed from the `V1` branch, and deployed to production.

During this time, development on the next version can continue uninterrupted without the risk of features being added into the code accidentally and making their way into the `V1.x` set of releases. At a certain point, let's say that it is decided that `V2.0` is ready to go out the door, the mainline of code is branched again to the `V2` branch, and the `V2.0` build is created from it. Work can continue on the next release on the `Main` branch, but it is now easy to support and release new builds to customers running on any version that you wish to keep supporting.

Branch per release is very easy to understand and allows many versions to be supported at a time. It can be extended to multiple supported releases very easily, and makes it trivial to view and compare the code that was included in a particular version of the application. Branch per release is well-suited to organizations that must support multiple versions of the code in parallel — such as a typical software vendor.

However, for a particular release, there is still no more parallelism of development than in a standard "no branching" strategy. Also, if the organization must only support two or three versions at a time (that is, the latest version, the previous version, and, perhaps, the version currently being tested by the business), this model can lead to a number of stale branches. While having lots of old, stale branches doesn't impact the performance of Team Foundation Server, or even cause any significant additional storage requirements, it can clutter the repository and make it difficult to find the versions you are interested in — especially if the organization releases new versions frequently. If this is the case, you may wish to move old branches into an "Archive" folder, and only have the active branches (that is, the versions that the development team are currently supporting) in the "Releases" folder.

Code-Promotion Branching

An alternative to branch per release is *code-promotion branching* (or *promotion-level branching*). This technique involves splitting the branches into different promotion levels, as shown in Figure 9-6.

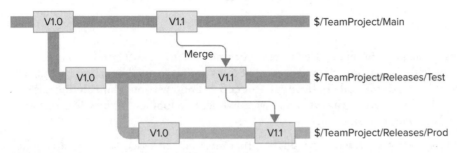

FIGURE 9-6: Code promotion branching

As before, development starts with just the Main branch. When the development team is ready to test the application with the business, it pushes the code to the Test branch (also often called the QA branch). While the code is being tested, work on the next development version is carried out in the Main branch. If any fixes are required during testing, they can be developed on the Test branch and merged back into the Main branch for inclusion in the next release. Once the code is ready to release, it is branched again from Test to Prod. When the next release cycle comes along, the same is done again. Changes are merged from Main to Test, then Test to Prod.

Code-promotion branching works well in environments that have a single version running in production, but have long test-validation cycles that do not involve all of the development team. This allows development to continue on the next version in Main while test and stabilization of the build occurs in the Test branch. It also makes it trivial for the development team to look at the code currently on each system. Finally, the branch structure makes it easy to create an automated build and deployment system using Team Foundation Build that can automatically update the QA/Test environment as code is pushed to the QA branch.

> For more information on the build capabilities of Team Foundation Server 2010, see Part IV of this book.

Feature Branching

The previous branching strategies all involve a single team working on the system in its entirety as they work toward a release. All features for that release are developed in parallel, and the build can only be deployed once all features in flight have been completed and tested. However, in large systems, or systems that require very frequent deployment (such as a large commercial website), *feature branching* (or *branch per feature*), as shown in Figure 9-7, can be useful.

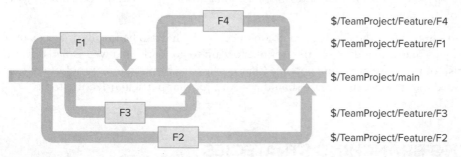

FIGURE 9-7: Feature branching

Feature branching is used when a project requires multiple teams to be working on the same codebase in parallel. In Figure 9-7, you see four feature teams working in separate branches (F1, F2, F3, and F4). Note that in a real branching structure, the feature branches themselves would likely have meaningful names such as FlightSelling, InsuranceExcess, or whatever shorthand is used by the project to refer to the feature under development. The Main branch is considered "gold code," which means that no active development goes on directly in this branch. However, a feature must be reverse-integrated into this branch for it to appear in the final release build and for other teams to pick it up.

Initially, F1 is started with a branch from Main. But, while it is being developed, a second and third team start F2 and F3, respectively. At the end of development of the feature, F1 is merged back into the Main branch, and the F1 branch is deleted. Then that team starts on feature F4. The next feature to finish is F3, followed by F2. At each point, once the feature is merged into the Main branch, a new version of the software is released to the public website. But only one version is ever supported at any time.

Feature branching allows for a large amount of parallel development. However, this comes at the cost of delaying the pain of integrating each team's changes together until the feature is complete, and you are merging the feature branch back into Main branch. For example, in Figure 9-7, when merging the F2 branch, all changes and inevitable conflicts introduced by features F1, F2, F3, and F4 must be analyzed and resolved.

The longer a period of time that code is separated into branches, the more independent changes occur, and, therefore, the greater the likelihood of merge conflicts. To minimize conflicts, and to reduce the amount of *integration debt* building up, you should do the following:

➤ *Keep the life of a feature short.* Features should be as short as possible, and should be merged back into the Main branch as soon as possible.

➤ *Take integrations from the* Main *branch regularly.* In the example shown in Figure 9-7, when F1 is merged back into Main, the feature teams still working on their features should merge those changes into their feature branches at the earliest possible convenient point.

➤ *Organize features into discrete areas in the codebase.* Having the code related to a particular feature in one area will reduce the amount of common code that is being edited in multiple branches, and, therefore, reduce the risk of making conflicting changes during feature development. Often, the number of teams that can be working in parallel is defined by the number of discrete areas of code in the repository.

When using feature branching, the whole team doesn't necessarily have to be involved. For example, one or two developers might split off from the rest of the team to go work on a well-isolated feature when there is a risk of the move not being possible (that is, they are working on a proof of concept), or when it is decided that the current release should not wait for that particular feature to be implemented.

IMPLEMENTING BRANCHING STRATEGIES

So far, this chapter has covered a lot of the theory behind branching. This section puts that theory into action as it walks you through implementing a branching strategy using the branch tools available with Team Foundation Server 2010.

The Scenario

For this example, let's look at a fictional organization called Tailspin Toys that has installed Team Foundation Server and is using the version control functionality. Let's say that you are a member of the internal IT team, which supports an order-fulfillment intranet site critical to the operation of the business. The team has only one version of the site in production at any one time. However, because of the criticality of the software, the IT team has lengthy test cycles involving a series of expert (but non-technical) users who come in from the business to ensure that the software is working as required.

The IT team has a single team project called `TTIT` and a single ASP.NET web application checked into the team project root folder at `$/TTIT/Orders`. They also have an automated build set up in Team Foundation Server.

The team has some issues when it comes to managing source. The development process is plagued by problems and inefficiencies. There are significant periods when developers are forbidden from checking in to the repository while getting ready for a release. The delays cause the developers to end up creating large shelvesets filled with changes that become unmanageable.

Occasionally, urgent bugs are required to be fixed in the production codebase. This is done by the developer getting the label that represents the production codebase, adding the fix, building it on a local machine, and manually pushing the modified files out to production. Ensuring that the correct files are pushed to production and that the source code fix is added back into version control is a manual process that has caused some problems. There have been instances where fixes to production were missing when the next version rolled out, and had to be repeated again.

But, luckily, there are some people in the development organization who recognize the problems and want to come up with a branching plan to alleviate some of them. You have been selected to roll out this plan.

The Plan

After some careful consideration, the team decides that a code-promotion strategy fits their organization quite well. Figure 9-8 shows the plan that the organization has decided to adopt.

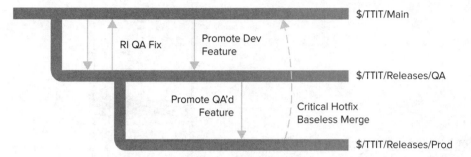

$/TTIT/Main

RI QA Fix

Promote Dev Feature

$/TTIT/Releases/QA

Promote QA'd Feature

Critical Hotfix Baseless Merge

$/TTIT/Releases/Prod

FIGURE 9-8: Example branch strategy

The code will consist of the following three branches, as suggested by the code-promotion branching strategy:

➤ `Main` — This is where the main development effort is conducted. This is the branch from which the regular continuous integration build is performed, and where new features are developed.

➤ `QA` — This is where the code will live while it is being tested by the business. Because these test periods can be very lengthy, new code development will carry on in the `Main` branch. Any fixes or modifications to the version under test will be performed directly on the `QA` branch, and reverse-integrated back into `Main`. An automated build will be created that will run early in the morning during the week. The results of that build will be pushed to the `QA` web server daily for testing by the business the following day.

➤ `Prod` — This represents the code that is currently running in production. Code normally goes from `Main` to `QA` into `Prod`. A build is also created for this branch so that urgent hotfixes can be checked in and repeatedly built. Urgent hotfixes like this are very much the exception, though. If an urgent hotfix is performed, a baseless merge is performed to push that fix back into `Main`. Note that the results of the `Prod` build are first deployed to a test environment to ensure that they work as expected before manually running a script that pushes the code to production.

Implementation

Figure 9-9 shows the current codebase.

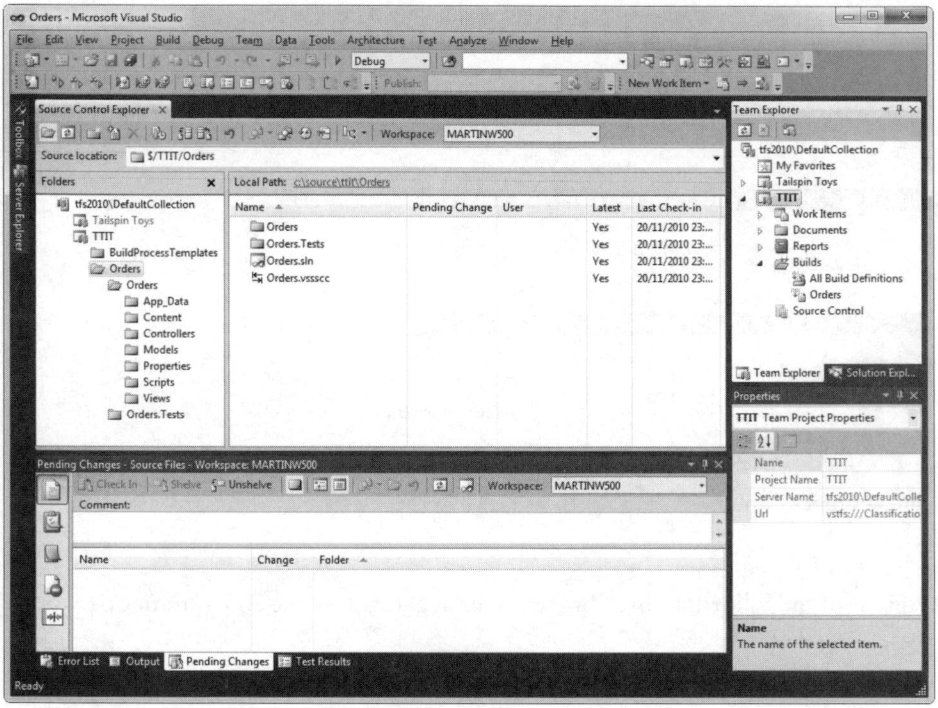

FIGURE 9-9: Current codebase in Source Control Explorer

The first thing you want to do is to move the code currently at the root of the team project in version control into a `Main` branch. This will be the most disruptive of the changes, because it will require the build to be reconfigured, and team members to re-sync their workspaces. So, you decide to do this late one night, a few weeks before the IT team is due to push a release to the test team.

To move the code into a branch, you right-click on the `Orders` folder containing the solution and select Move. Then you manually enter a path of **$/TTIT/Main/Orders** in the Move dialog shown in Figure 9-10. Note that the `Main` folder does not have to exist at this point. Moving the files to that location will cause Team Foundation Server to create the parent folder.

FIGURE 9-10: Entering a path in the Move dialog

As soon as this is done, you edit the build definition's workspace so that it only looks at the `Orders` Source Control Explorer folder under the `Main` folder, as shown in Figure 9-11.

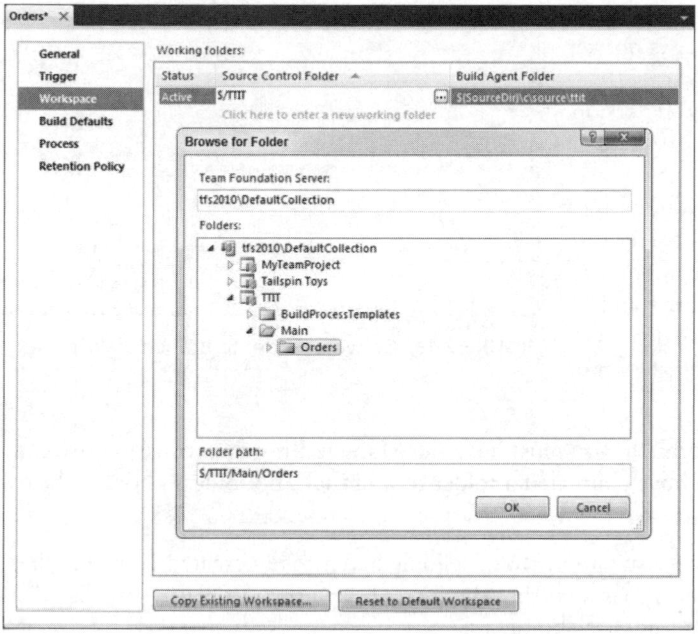

FIGURE 9-11: Editing the build definition's working folders

You also modify the Process for the build to remove the solution file from the old location, and add it in again at the new location, as shown in Figure 9-12. You then manually queue a new build to ensure that everything is working well. Everything works, so you send an e-mail notifying the team of the change to version control, and you go home for the evening.

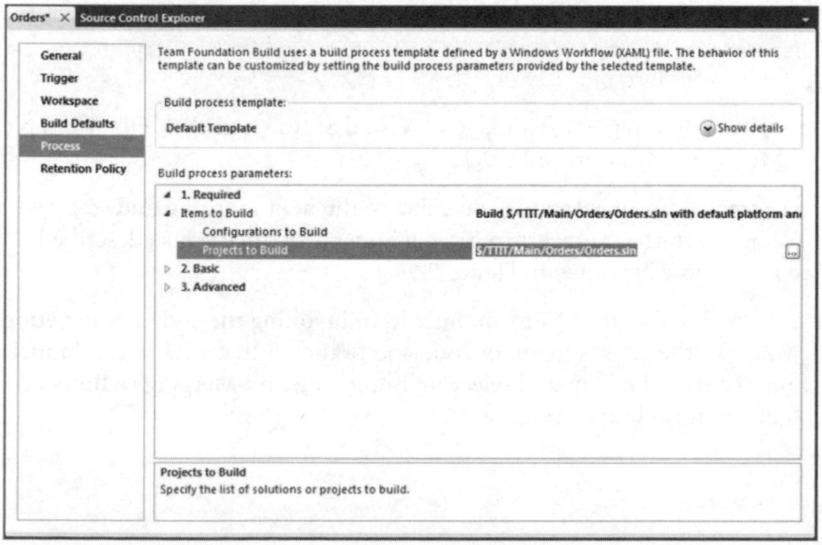

FIGURE 9-12: Modifying the Process for the build

Now, as an aside, note that the source is in the correct path, but the `Main` folder is not yet a branch. In Team Foundation Server 2010, branches became a first-class entity in version control. They are represented by a different icon than a folder, and have additional metadata such as Owner, Description, and Branch Relationships. To convert a folder to a branch, you right-click the folder in Source Control Explorer and select Branching and Merging ⇨ Convert to Branch. This displays the Convert Folder to Branch dialog shown in Figure 9-13.

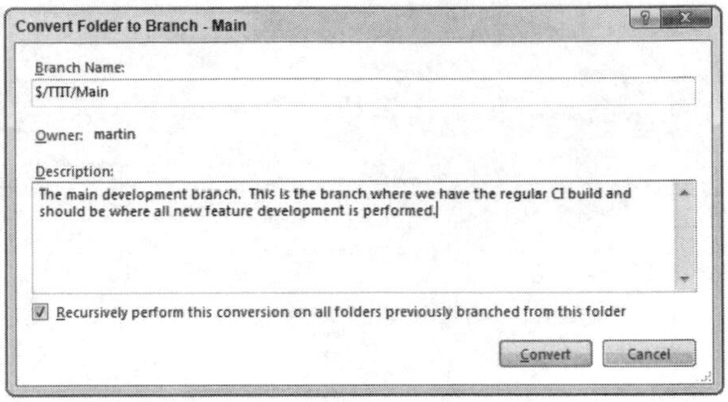

FIGURE 9-13: Convert Folder to Branch dialog

Note that to convert a folder to a branch, you must have the Manage Branch permission in Team Foundation Server. Also, once you have converted a folder to a branch, no folders above or below it may be a branch.

In this Tailspin Toys example, this doesn't apply. But if people had already created new branches from the `Main` folder, you would want to ensure that the check box shown in Figure 9-13 is selected because this will also convert those folders to branches.

> *When an upgrade is performed from an existing Team Foundation Server 2008 instance to a new Team Foundation Server 2010 repository, all existing branch folders are imported as folders. This is because before Team Foundation Server 2010, branches did not exist as first-class citizens. Therefore, after upgrading from Team Foundation Server 2008, you may wish to also manually convert those folders into branches using this method.*

If you must convert a branch back to a regular folder, go to Visual Studio and click File ⇨ Source Control ⇨ Branching and Merging ⇨ Convert to Folder.

Now, let's get back to the example implementation. You come in the next morning and start to get the branches set up. You perform the "Convert to Branch" operation on `Main` as described previously, and the source tree is now as shown in Figure 9-14.

When the build is ready to be released to the QA team, instead of invoking the code freeze period that used to be enforced, you take the latest version of code and branch it to create the `QA` branch. You do this by right-clicking the `Main` branch, and selecting Branching and Merging ⇨ Branch, which displays the Branch dialog for a branch (Figure 9-15).

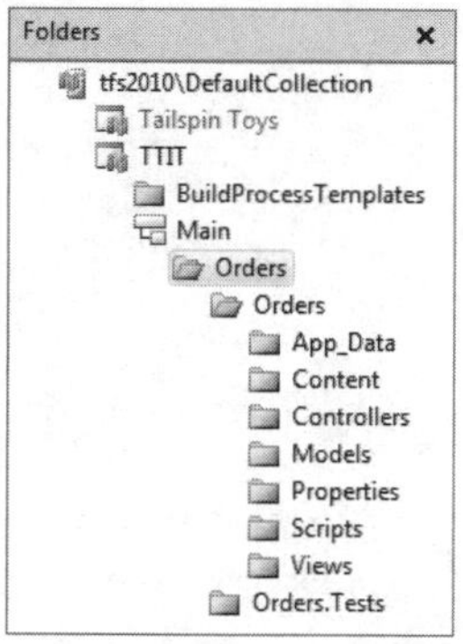

FIGURE 9-14: Main as a branch folder

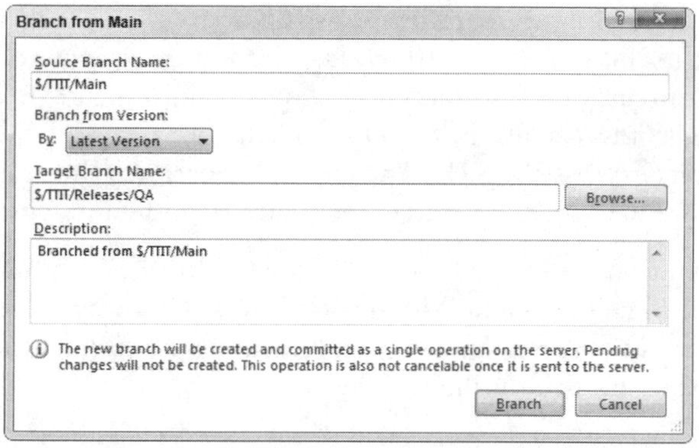

FIGURE 9-15: Branch dialog for a branch

In this dialog, you enter the full path that you would like to create, which, in this example scenario, is $/TTIT/Releases/QA. If the Releases folder does not already exist, it will be created automatically as part of this operation. As shown in Figure 9-15, there is a warning that this will be committed to the repository as part of a single transaction.

This behavior is slightly different from that experienced when branching a folder or file. When you branch a folder or file in the Visual Studio or Eclipse clients, it is assumed that you are making a copy of the file in your local workspace as well. Figure 9-16 shows an example of the branch dialog when a folder is selected.

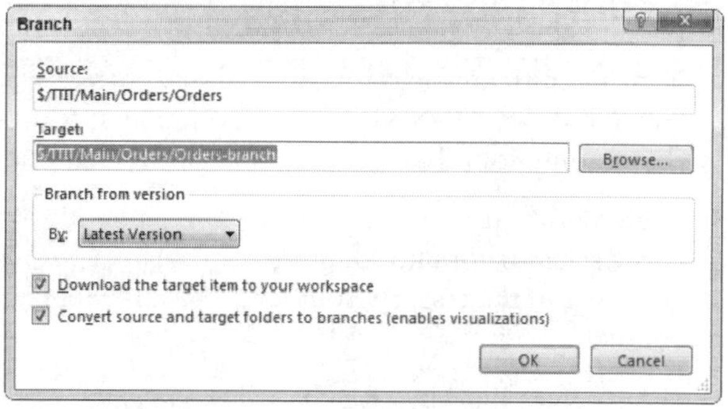

FIGURE 9-16: Branch dialog when a folder is selected

You also get the option to convert the folders to a full branch in Team Foundation Server — but you do not have to. This is a subtle point. While branches are first-class objects in Team Foundation Server, you can branch any folder or file to another place in the repository just like you could do in Team Foundation Server before the 2010 release. This is a great way to copy areas of the repository to a different part of the repository, but make the history of changes that occurred in the old location easily accessible in the new one. In Team Foundation Server 2010, a rename is actually implemented under the covers as a simultaneous branch, and a delete of the source location.

In the instance of branching a file or folder, this is done as a two-phase operation. The branch changes are made in your workspace, and then you check these in.

However, in the vast majority of instances, you want to branch an entire branch in version control. Usually, you will not be making changes to the files or performing validation before check-in.

So, performing these in a single atomic transaction represents both an improvement on usability in the 2010 release, and is a much more efficient use of server resources. (This is functionally equivalent to the `tf branch` command line with the `/checkin` option supplied, which was introduced in Team Foundation Server 2008 SP1.) Therefore, you perform the branch as indicated in Figure 9-15 and the source tree is now as shown in Figure 9-17.

A new build definition (called `Orders QA`) is created for the `QA` branch, with a scheduled trigger of 6 a.m. Monday to Friday. That way, a fresh build is ready and waiting for the test team each morning if changes have been made to the `QA` branch during the day.

FIGURE 9-17: QA branch created

> *Chapter 15 provides more information on creating build definitions.*

Dealing with Changesets

During initial testing, it is noticed that there is a small bug with the stylesheet on Internet Explorer 6 on Windows XP. None of the development team was running this configuration, but it is still commonly found in real-world business environments, so the team decides to create a fix for it.

The modification is made to the `Site.css` file in the `QA` branch and checked in as changeset `102`. The next scheduled build (`Orders QA_20101121.4`) picks up this change and adds it to the code running in the test environment. Once the fix has been verified, the fix must be merged into the `Main` branch.

For merges like this, it is best if the merge is performed as soon as possible, and by the developer that made the change. That way, it is fresh in his or her mind, and isn't forgotten about, or the fix misunderstood. The testing team has set a policy that the related bug cannot move to the Closed state until an urgent fix has been merged into the `Main` branch — which is a sensible policy.

To merge that code, the developer right-clicks on the source branch (in this case, the `QA` branch) and selects Branching and Merging ⇨ Merge. This displays the Merge Wizard dialog, as shown in Figure 9-18.

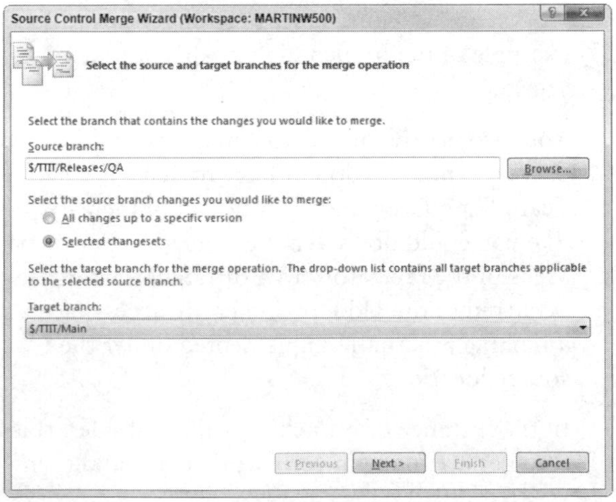

FIGURE 9-18: Source Control Merge Wizard

The developer opts to merge selected changesets to ensure that only the change the developer is aware of is picked up. The developer checks that the target branch has been identified as Main, and then clicks Next. This displays the changesets selection page.

On this page, you can select a single changeset or a continuous range of changesets that you wish to merge. In the case of the example testing team, they just have the one changeset that they are interested in (102), so the developer selects that and clicks Next. This provides a final confirmation page (Figure 9-19) and, when the developer clicks Finish, the merge is performed. The source repository now looks like Figure 9-20.

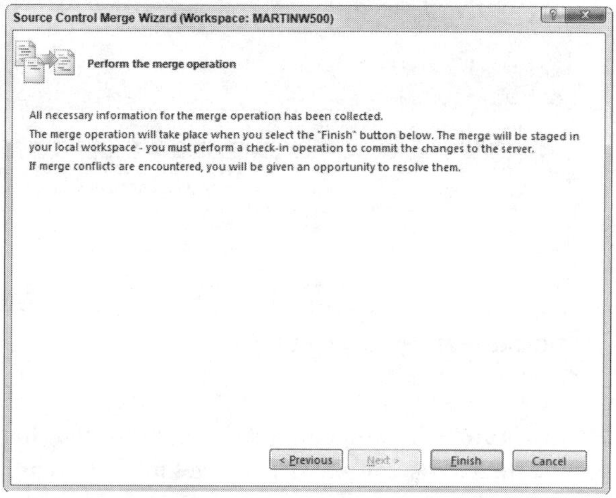

FIGURE 9-19: Final confirmation page

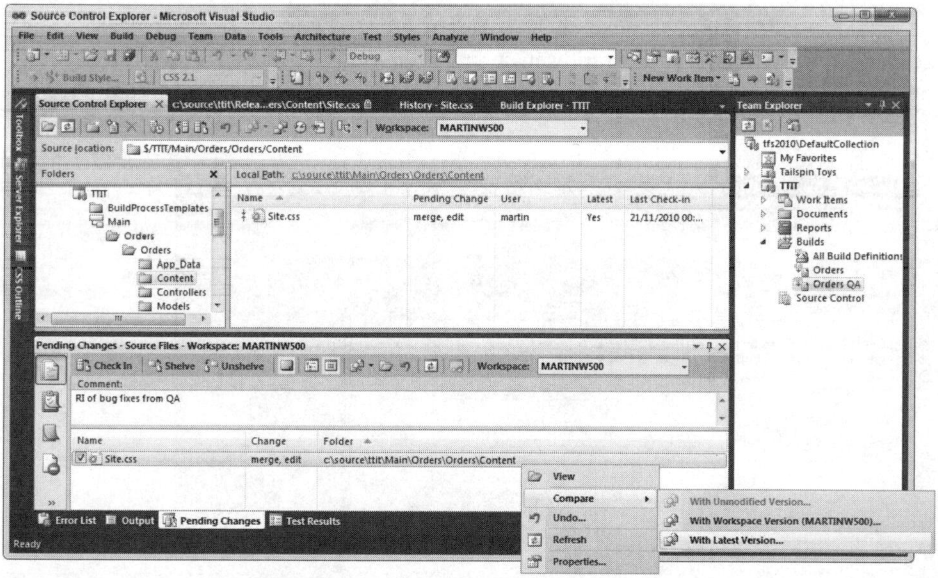

FIGURE 9-20: Displaying the results of a merge

The stylesheet file currently has a pending merge on it. At this point, it is good practice to compare the current version of the file with the latest version to ensure that the change you are making is still the correct one. In this case, it is, so the developer associates the changeset with the original bug, checks in the merge, and then marks the bug as Closed.

At this point, if you right-click on the file in Source Control Explorer and select View History, you would see the History for the file, as shown in Figure 9-21 (once the tree nodes have been expanded).

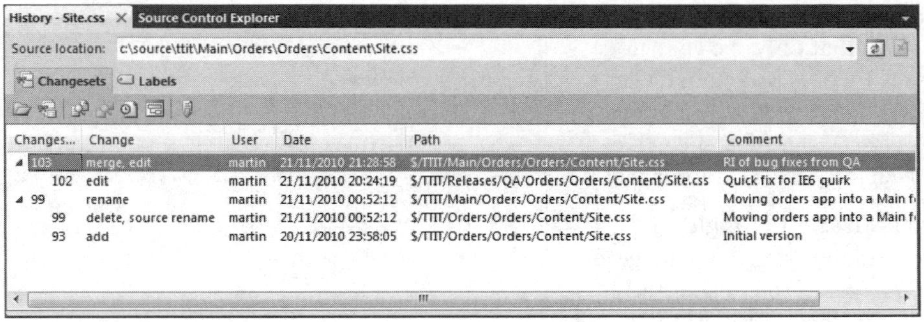

FIGURE 9-21: History for the file

In Figure 9-21, you can see the merge of the changes back into `Main` at changeset `103`. By expanding the node, you can see the changes made to that file in the source branch (in this case, the edit of the file in the `QA` branch in changeset `102`). Then, further back in history, you can see the rename (move) of the file when the code was moved under the `Main` folder. Finally, if you expand that rename node, you can see all the history of the file before it was in the current branch structure.

Another way to visualize this change and see that it made it into the correct branches is to right-click on changeset `102` in the History view and select Track Changeset. This displays the Select Branches dialog (Figure 9-22) that allows you to select which branches you would like to view.

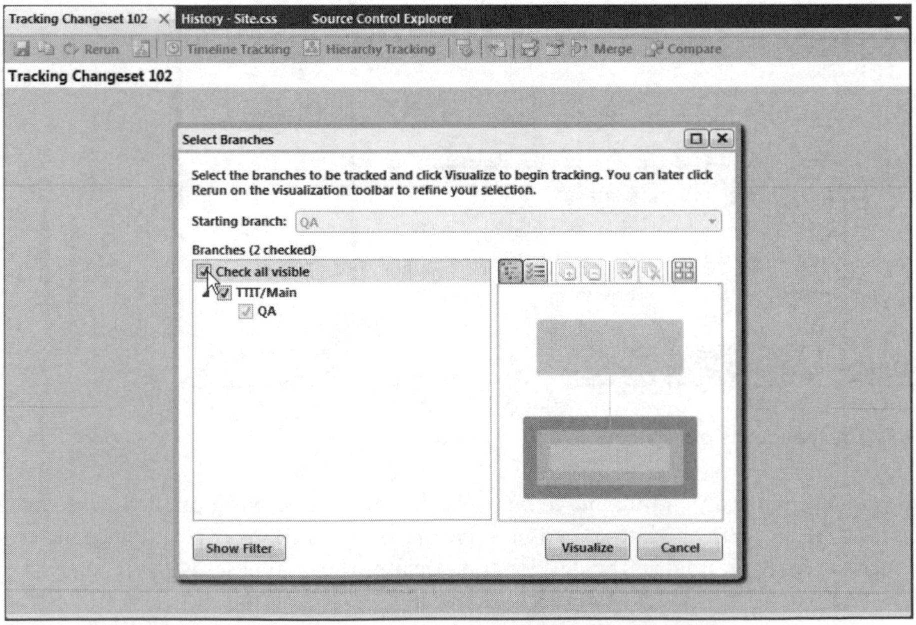

FIGURE 9-22: Select Branches dialog inside the Track Changeset view

For the example scenario, the developer selected the Check All Visible check box and clicked the Visualize button. Initially, this sequence will show a hierarchical view of branches, which are colored according to which branches the changes in changeset 102 made it into. If you were to look at Figure 9-23 in color, you would see the result for this scenario was that everything showed up colored green to indicate that everything was good.

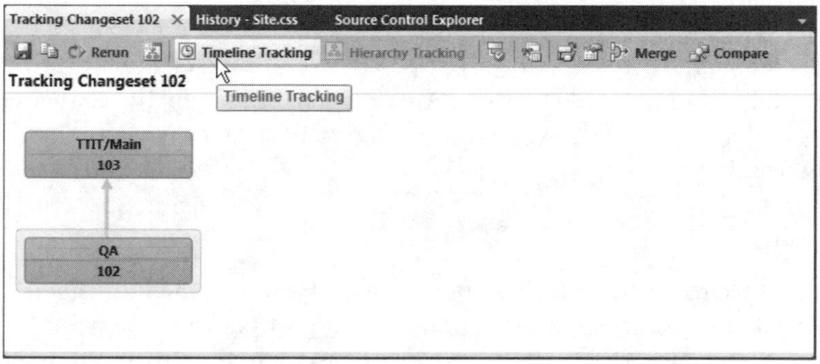

FIGURE 9-23: Branches shown in hierarchical view

An alternative visualization is available by clicking the Timeline Tracking button, as highlighted in Figure 9-23. This displays the changes in a familiar timeline style view, as shown in Figure 9-24. Again, if this were in color, you would see that all the branches are green, which means that the code made it to where it should be.

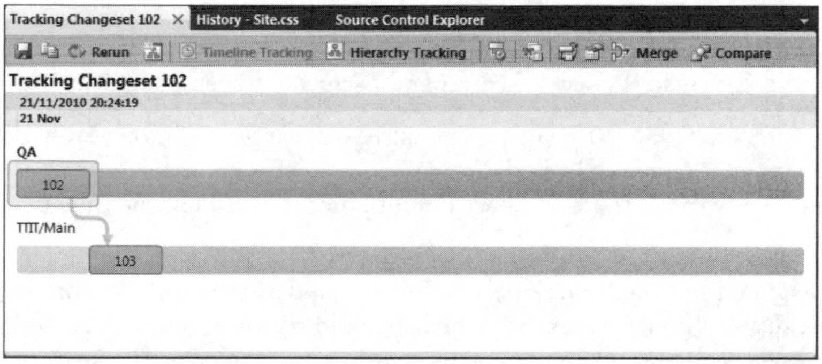

FIGURE 9-24: Timeline Tracking view

Back at Tailspin Toys, the TTIT product has undergone a bunch more testing on the QA branch, and development continues in the Main branch. At the end of the testing period, it is decided that the application is good, and so the build that was created with the stylesheet fix in changeset 102 (build Orders QA_20101121.4) is deployed to production.

However, all is not well. Once deployed to production, the Chief Information Officer (CIO) of the company notices an incorrect footer file at the bottom of the main page. The page still contains text that reads, "To learn more about ASP.NET MVC visit `http://asp.net/mvc`." While this doesn't affect functionality in anyway, the CIO would like the issue fixed ASAP because she is about to demo the application to the board of directors.

It's a small, low-risk fix. In days gone by, this would be exactly the sort of thing for which one of the IT team would jump into the production environment and just fix it. However, it's exactly the sort of change that can be forgotten about back in the development branch. So, to ensure that the change is not overlooked, the team decides to do it in version control using the new branch plan.

First, they must create the `Prod` branch. There are two ways to do this. One is to create the branch from the label that was applied as part of the build process. Another is to branch by the changeset that included the required fix. Let's take a brief look at both methods and see which is more appropriate for this example scenario.

Branch from Label

As previously discussed, it is possible to create branches after the fact. However, the branch with check-in used by Visual Studio and Eclipse when creating branches only works when branching by the latest version, a changeset, or a date. In the initial version of Visual Studio 2010, it did not work when branching from a label. This was fixed initially in a hotfix (KB983504) and then in Service Pack 1. However, it was still possible to perform the branch using the command line before Service Pack 1.

To do this, the developer opens up a Visual Studio 2010 command prompt window and enters the following commands:

```
tf branch $/TTIT/Releases/QA $/TTIT/Releases/Prod /version:L"Orders QA_20101121.4"
tf checkin /recursive /noprompt $/TTIT/Releases/Prod
```

The first command creates the branch from the specified label created by the build process. At this point, the changes are in the workspace, so the second command performs a check-in on the branch.

Whichever way you perform a branch by label, the advantage of this is that it will branch only the files that were included in the specified label, and that label was created automatically by the build process to only include the files that were in the workspace definition of the build at the time the build was performed.

The major downside is that, as stated in Chapter 6, labels in Team Foundation Server are editable. Someone with appropriate permissions could have edited the label, and removed or included certain key files after the label was created by the build process. This is unlikely in the example Tailspin Toys environment, but it is possible.

Branch from Changeset

From the build report shown in Figure 9-25, you can see the build associated with changeset `102` was successful. As discussed in Chapter 6, the changeset represents a unique (immutable) point in time in the version control repository. Therefore, if you were to branch from changeset `102`, this would include the files at the exact state that they were in when the build was performed.

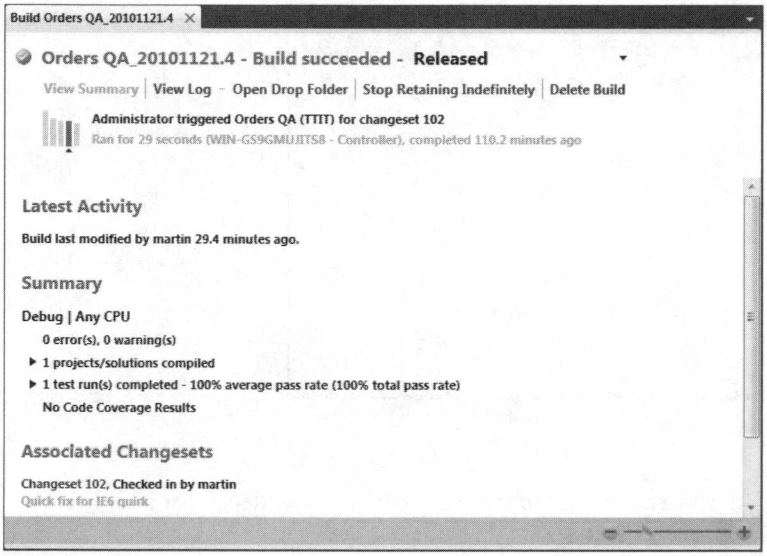

FIGURE 9-25: Build report

The team decides to branch by changeset 102 so as to include all changes up until changeset 102 in the QA branch when creating the Prod branch. To do this, the developer right-clicks on the QA branch in Source Control Explorer, and selects Branching and Merging ⇨ Branch. The developer then changes the "Branch from Version" to Changeset 102, and sets the Target Branch Name to be $/TTIT/Releases/Prod, as shown in Figure 9-26.

Once the branch is created, the version control repository then looks like Figure 9-27.

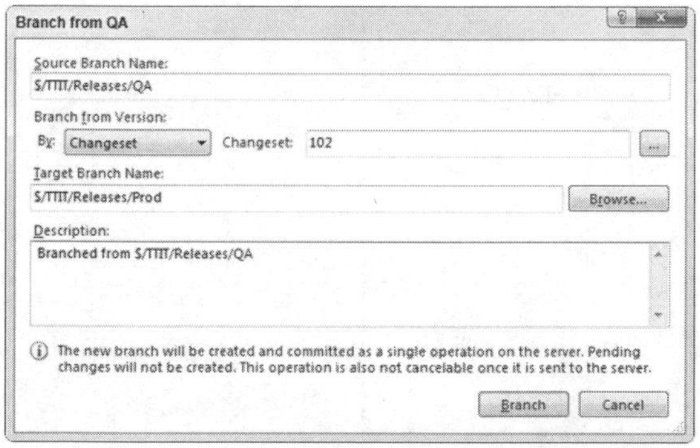

FIGURE 9-26: Branching from a changeset

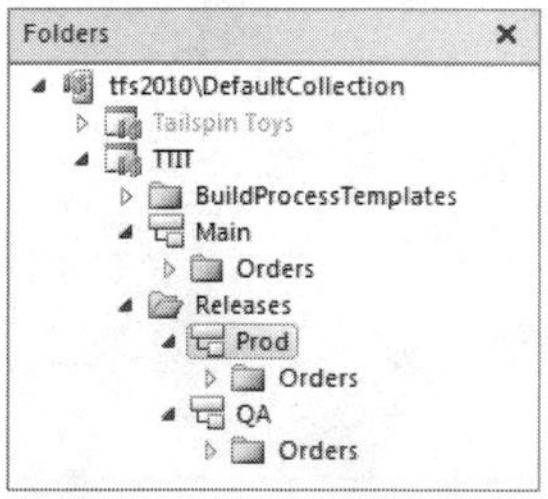

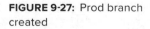

FIGURE 9-27: Prod branch created

If you were to right-click on the Main branch and select Branching and Merging ⇨ View Hierarchy, you could see a visualization of the current branch structure, as shown in Figure 9-28. If you hover over each branch with the mouse, you see a tooltip with the additional metadata about that branch, including any description that you have entered.

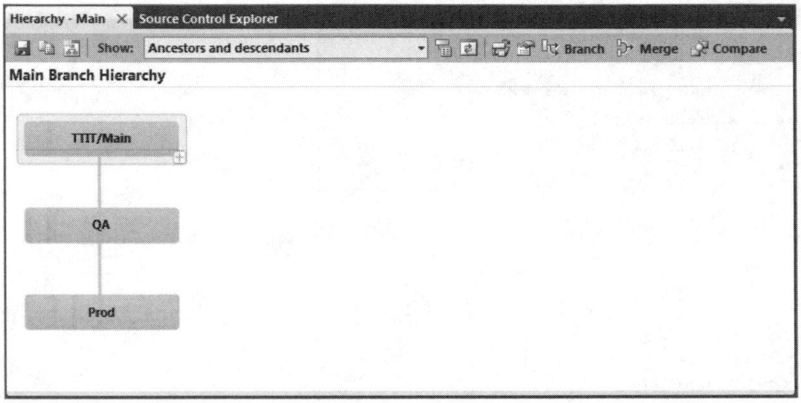

FIGURE 9-28: Current branch hierarchy

At this point, the developer can now create a fix in the `Prod` branch. The developer simply edits the offending `aspx` file and checks it in as changeset `107`. The developer then creates a build and deploys this to production. Now you must ensure that the fix is in the appropriate branches so that it also gets included in the future releases.

To do this, you right-click on the `Prod` branch, and select View History. Then, you right-click on the changeset and select Track Changeset. As before, you select the Check All Visible check box and click Visualize. The change will show in green in the `Prod` branch only, as represented by the bottom box in Figure 9-29.

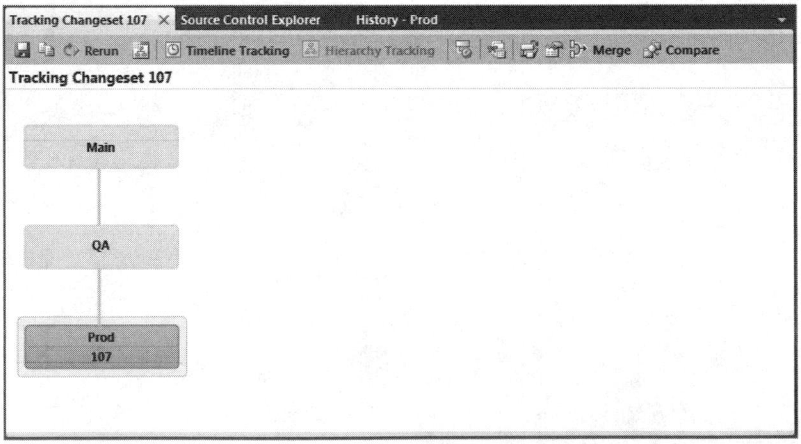

FIGURE 9-29: Change being visualized for the changeset

To merge this change into `Main`, the developer now has two choices: a ladder merge or a baseless merge. If you find that during your branch process you frequently must perform baseless merges or merges through other branches (that is, ladder merges), this is a good indication that the model is no longer optimized for the typical circumstances encountered in your environment, and you may want to revise it.

However, in the Tailspin Toys scenario, making ad hoc changes to production is very much an exception case, so the IT team wants to optimize the branch plan for the usual case of a change starting in Main, getting promoted on to QA, and then to Prod. So, the developer must use a ladder merge or a baseless merge to go from Prod to Main.

Ladder Merge

As shown in Figure 9-29, the team has a change in Prod. To get that fix into Main using standard merges, the developer must first merge it into the QA branch, and then, from there, into Main. This is because in Team Foundation Server, a standard merge can flow from parent to child, or vice versa.

To merge the changes, from the Tracking Changeset view shown in 9-29, the developer simply drags and drops the Prod branch up to the QA branch using the mouse. This will display the standard Merge Wizard shown earlier in Figure 9-18. The developer clicks the "Selected changesets" radio button and clicks Next to display the changeset selection page shown in Figure 9-30.

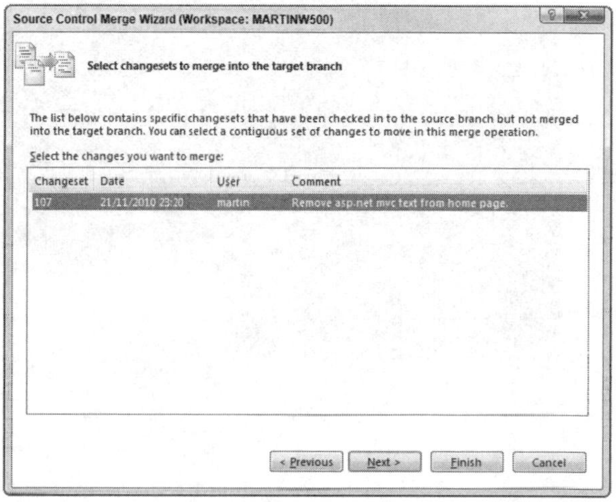

FIGURE 9-30: Merge wizard changeset selection page

On this page, the developer selects the desired changeset (107), and clicks Finish. The developer then checks in the merged file, and clicks the Rerun button in the Tracking Changeset view to show the change in the QA branch. Finally, the developer drags and drops the QA branch to the Main branch, and repeats the process through the Merge Wizard.

In this particular example, because of when the change occurred in production, it actually would have been possible to get the change into Main in this way. However, if the change had been required when there was a different (newer) version of the software in the QA branch, you may have not wanted to merge the changes in this way. Instead, you could have opted to do a baseless merge directly into Main, and then the change would make it back up to the QA branch with the next release to the test team.

Let's take a look at how to plug in that option for the Tailspin Toys example scenario.

Baseless Merge

To perform a baseless merge, the Tailspin Toys IT developer must use the Team Foundation Server command-line client (tf.exe). The developer opens a Visual Studio 2010 command prompt and enters a command similar to the following to merge changeset 107:

```
tf merge /baseless /recursive /version:C107 $/TTIT/Releases/Prod $/TTIT/Main
```

In this example scenario, because development has been ongoing in the Main branch, it is highly likely that a conflict will occur because, during the interim period, someone has modified the same `Index.aspx` page in the `Main` branch, but for a different reason. Therefore, the developer is presented with a Resolve Conflicts dialog, as shown in Figure 9-31.

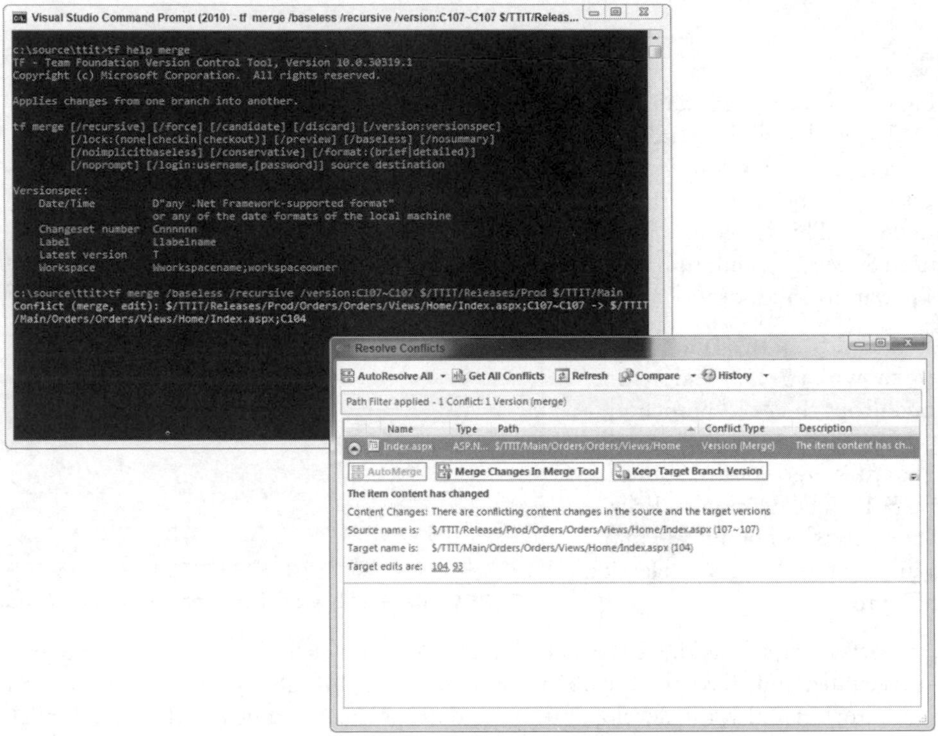

FIGURE 9-31: Resolving baseless merge conflicts

The developer can either keep the target branch version (that is, the version already in `Main`), or merge the changes using a merge tool.

> *External diff and merge utilities can be found in Visual Studio under Tools ⇨ Options ⇨ Source Control ⇨ Visual Studio Team Foundation Server ⇨ Configure User Tools.*
>
> *To find out more about configuring external diff and merge utilities for use with Visual Studio, see* http://msdn.microsoft.com/en-us/library/ms194962(v=VS.100).aspx. *James Manning has a blog post detailing the configuration parameters necessary for many of the common tools at* http://blogs.msdn.com/b/jmanning/archive/2006/02/20/diff-merge-configuration-in-team-foundation-common-command-and-argument-values.aspx.

The Tailspin Toys developer decides to use the built-in merge utility that ships with Visual Studio 2010 and clicks Merge Changes in Merge Tool. This displays the utility shown in Figure 9-32.

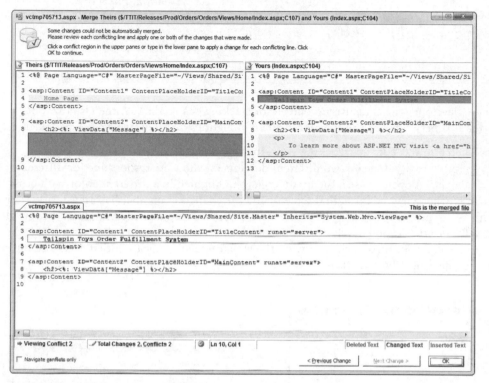

FIGURE 9-32: Standard merge utility

From the conflicting changes at the top of the file, the developer selects the newer title on the right-hand side that had been added in the Main branch, and selects the deletion of text from the left-hand side of the dialog. Note that if this had been a merge with base (that is, the tool had been able to detect the changes since a common shared version), then the changes in this case would not have been flagged as conflicts because those sections changed in one version. This highlights the point that, when you perform baseless merges, you get more conflicts in Team Foundation Server.

Alternatively, developers can simply hand-edit the changes that they wanted to see in the bottom pane, or correct as necessary after clicking the right or left panes.

Once the developer is satisfied that they have completed the resolution actions for each of the conflicts in the file, he clicks OK to save the changes from the merge utility and mark the conflicts as resolved.

The developer can now check in the merge by using the command line or using Visual Studio. Following is the command to execute a check-in from the command line:

```
tf checkin /recursive /noprompt $/TTIT/Main
```

> *For more information on using the* `tf merge` *command to perform merge operations (including additional examples), see the MSDN documentation at* `http://msdn.microsoft.com/en-us/library/bd6dxhfy.aspx`. *For more information about past merges from the command line for a known source and destination branch, see the Help documentation for the* `tf merge` *command on MSDN (*`http://msdn.microsoft.com/en-us/library/656cs2x5.aspx`*) or type* `tf help merges` *at a Visual Studio 2010 command prompt.*

Now, when the developer clicks the Rerun button for tracking changeset 107, the visualization shows a dotted line between `Prod` and `Main` as shown in Figure 9-33, indicating a baseless merge.

You can also switch to the Timeline tracking view. In the example shown in Figure 9-34, the baseless merge was actually done by two different developers who were responsible for different areas of the codebase. As you can see, the first merge is highlighted in a different color with cross-hatching (yellow, when viewing the actual screen), and the changeset number has an asterisk after it (108*). This is because only some of the changes have been merged into the branch in the initial baseless merge. Once the second developer completes the merge in the second changeset (109), the branch goes to a solid color (green when viewing the actual screen), indicating that all the changes in changeset 107 have now been merged.

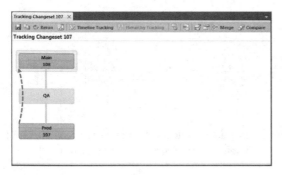

FIGURE 9-33: Baseless merge visualization

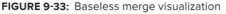

FIGURE 9-34: Timeline view of partial and full merge

Tracking Change Through Branches

As you have seen thus far, the branch visualization tooling in Visual Studio 2010 provides some powerful capabilities for viewing your branch hierarchy, and tracking the progress of changes through it. Using the View Hierarchy functionality, you can immediately see the relationships of the branches in your source tree, and navigate to their locations in the repository. By selecting Track Changeset for a changeset in the History view, you see into which branches that change has been made, and even merge the change into other branches by dragging and dropping between branches.

The Tracking Changeset visualization has some additional features that are not always displayed in simple examples such as the ones presented here. Figure 9-35 shows an example from a more complex branch hierarchy.

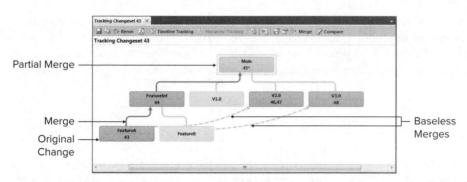

FIGURE 9-35: Complex branch hierarchy in Tracking Changeset visualization

In the example shown in Figure 9-35, the original change occurred in the FeatureA branch as changeset 43. This was reverse-integrated into the FeatureInt branch as a standard merge in changeset 44. That change was then merged into Main. But not all files were copied over as part of the merge as the cross-hatching and the asterisk next to changeset 45 indicate. This should instantly be an area to query to investigate which files were checked in and why. Double-clicking on the branch will show the changeset details to begin the investigation.

Then, rather than a standard merge back down from Main into the V2.0 branch, you can see that two baseless merges have occurred to get all the changes into that branch (changesets 46 and 47). Finally, a single baseless merge took the code into V3.0. Figure 9-35 shows that the changes have yet to make it into the FeatureB branch or into V1.0. Clicking the Timeline Tracking button displays the timeline view for changeset 43, as shown Figure 9-36.

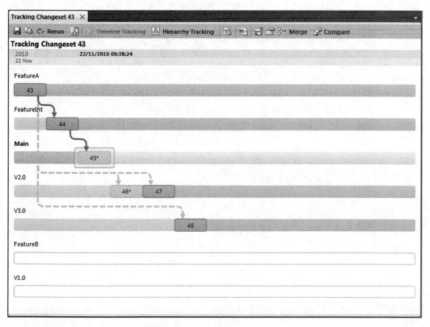

FIGURE 9-36: Complex Timeline Tracking view

This view does not show the relationships between branches (that is, the hierarchy) but instead shows the merges as they happened. The sequence of events around the two partial merges into `Main` and `V2.0`, and the subsequent full merge into `V2.0` are therefore much more clearly represented. Hovering over each branch provides additional metadata, including its owner and description.

SUMMARY

As you can tell from this chapter, the branch and merge capabilities of Team Foundation Server not only allow for some complex software configuration management scenarios, but also provides the tooling to help understand what is happening with changes in your version control repository.

The chapter began by looking at the terminology used in branching, discussed some common branching techniques, and then provided a detailed walkthrough of implementing a basic branching strategy in an organization using the tools provided for Team Foundation Server 2010. Finally, this chapter looked at the changeset tracking functionality available to determine to which branches a particular change has propagated.

Chapter 10 builds on the knowledge built up so far in this book, and provides some best-practice guidance across a few scenarios that are common across development teams (such as how to organize the structure of the repository, manage third-party dependencies, and manage the dependencies for internally developed libraries such as common framework code). Chapter 10 also looks at the practicalities of using Team Foundation Server to manage Team Foundation Server artifacts such as process templates, custom build assemblies, custom tools, and so on.

10

Common Version Control Scenarios

WHAT'S IN THIS CHAPTER?

➤ Organizing folders within the branch structure

➤ Managing and storing third-party dependencies

➤ Managing source code and binaries for internal shared libraries

➤ Storing customization artifacts to manage Team Foundation Server in the version control repository

There are a few scenarios that are common across development teams when managing source code for their applications and managing Team Foundation Server. Organizing and architecting the structure of the version control system can have a direct effect on improving the way applications are managed and built.

This chapter explores some of those scenarios, and discusses possible solutions to tackle each of them.

SETTING UP THE FOLDER STRUCTURE FOR YOUR BRANCHES

One common issue that development teams have centers on the organization of their source control repositories. Over time, these repositories can become unruly and downright difficult to locate. The common question around the office can sometimes be, "Where is that located in source control?"

By providing some organization to the version control repository in Team Foundation Server, you can provide your team with better discoverability of source code assets, as well as introduce best engineering practices that will make it easier to compile your applications locally and on automated build servers.

Figure 10-1 shows a sample folder structure within a branch. Notice how the folders are inside of the folder that is indicated as a branch in Team Foundation Server version control. Essentially, the idea is to store within the same branch all of the artifacts necessary for building, testing, architecting, and so on, the product or product family. This allows you to create as many branches as the team needs to contain everything that is necessary for the development effort.

Later on, when you are creating a build definition that will build the entire product family, it will be useful to scope the build to the branch so that it has access to all of the artifacts that would be necessary to compile, test, and package the product family. Each of these folders and their purposes will be examined in this chapter.

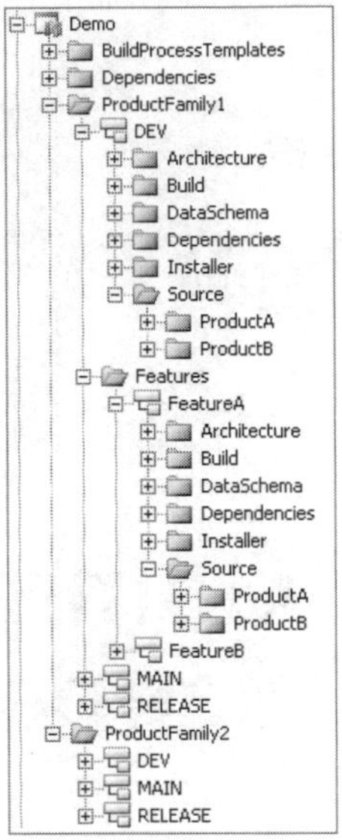

FIGURE 10-1: Sample folder structure within a branch

Application Source Code

The primary version control folder needed for most teams is one that contains the source code for a family of products. This folder is named `Source` in the branch shown in Figure 10-1. Each product can be contained in a separate subfolder, and any shared libraries that are used only by the products in the product family can have subfolders under the `Source` folder as needed.

Additionally, teams may choose to store the source code for the automated unit tests in this folder, since the unit test projects are traditionally included in the same Visual Studio solution as the product's Visual Studio projects. The development team is usually the team that manages artifacts in this version control folder, and the creation and management of unit tests is typically owned by developers.

Automated Tests Source Code

The testing or quality assurance team may end up generating source code for automated tests like Coded UI, web performance, load, and other types of tests. They need a location in which to store the source code that implemented those automated tests, so the version control folder named `Tests` in the branch shown in Figure 10-1 serves that purpose.

By including it in the same branch as the rest of the product family, it can easily be managed across the branching structure, and it can be included to be compiled or even run in automated builds that use the branch as its source.

Architecture Assets

Software architects can create valuable architecture diagrams that might also be helpful to team members implementing and testing the product family. Visual Studio 2010 Ultimate provides some powerful architecture tools, including a new Visual Studio project type for modeling projects that enable the capability to store UML and other architecture diagrams in a meaningful way. The architecture assets also need a version control folder in the branch, which is shown in Figure 10-1 with the name of `Architecture`.

Alternatively, the architecture modeling projects and diagrams can be stored in the `Source` folder mentioned earlier so as to be included in the same Visual Studio solutions. The idea is to ensure that they are included in the same branch alongside the rest of the assets for the product family.

Again, by including them in the same branch, the architecture components and artifacts could be used in an automated build process. Specifically, you could perform architectural validation during compilation using the layer diagrams stored in the Visual Studio architecture modeling projects.

Database Schema

Database developers also produce artifacts to manage the schema and data in the databases that are used in the product family. Their artifacts can be stored in the same branch folder as well. To offer change management for the database schema, Visual Studio 2010 also includes a project type for database schema management that has integration with version control repositories. Thus, to edit a stored procedure, you would use the same version control techniques as editing a source code file for an application.

The folder named `DataSchema` in Figure 10-1 is used to store database schema artifacts in the branch. The automated build process can even use the database schema "source code" contained in this version control folder to compile the schema into a deployable unit.

> *More information about using the database schema change management tools in Visual Studio 2010 can be found in the companion book,* Professional Application Lifecycle Management with Visual Studio 2010 *(Indianapolis: Wiley, 2010).*

Installer Assets

If your development team needs to produce installers for the product to ship to customers, or to internal business users, or even to ease deployment of server or web applications, then a version control folder should be created inside the branch to store the installer artifacts. This particular folder is represented in the example branch in Figure 10-1 as the folder named `Installer`.

This allows for the automated build process to have easy access within the same branch to the source code necessary to compile the merge modules and/or installers.

Build and Deployment Assets

Finally, there may be artifacts that the development team may want to store that are necessary during the build process or for deployment reasons. A version control folder dedicated to these artifacts is helpful. The version control folder for these artifacts is shown in Figure 10-1 with the name of `Build`.

You don't necessarily need to store the build process template `.XAML` file itself in this folder. However, it is certainly an option if your team decides to store build process templates inside the branch. If you store the build process template file inside the branch, then each of those branched build process template files must be registered for use in the build system before they can be used by a build definition.

> *Chapter 16 provides more information about managing and registering build process templates.*

THIRD-PARTY SOURCE CODE/DEPENDENCIES

Traditionally, teams should not store binaries in version control. This best practice has evolved because team members would check-in the `bin` and `obj` folders that are created after compiling a solution or project in Visual Studio. Those folders, and particularly the binaries that get created, should generally not be stored in version control. Problems may arise when storing those folders, because Team Foundation Server marks files coming from version control as read-only, which prevents Visual Studio or MSBuild from being able to overwrite those files.

The idea around this is to only store in version control the source code necessary to create the binaries, and let the automated build system compile the source code into the necessary binaries. The build drop folders can then be stored on a file share that is backed up regularly and retained appropriately.

> *The practice of not storing the binaries in the version control repository can also be generally applied for other types of compiled "outputs," depending on the circumstance. For example, storing the compiled help file (that is, a .CHM file) in the version control repository would generally not be recommended, since it can be compiled during an automated build process. Instead, the source files used for creating the compiled help file would be stored in version control.*

However, the guideline of not storing binaries in the version control repository does not apply when it comes to managing third-party dependencies.

One folder you might have noticed in the branching structure shown in Figure 10-1 that has not been discussed yet is the `Dependencies` folder. This folder is exactly the version control location that can be used to manage the third-party dependencies. Let's take a look at two methods for managing a `Dependencies` folder, and discuss the strengths and weaknesses of both approaches.

Folder Inside Branch

The first approach is based on the premise that everything necessary for the product family is stored inside of the branch folder. This means that a Dependencies folder could be created inside the branch folder, as shown in Figure 10-1, and used to manage the third-party dependencies.

Subfolders can be created to manage the different types of third-party dependencies that might be needed by the products in the product family. For example, a UIControls subfolder can be created to store third-party custom UI controls, or an EnterpriseLibrary subfolder can be created to store the assemblies that come from the Microsoft Enterprise Library. You might even create further subfolders to isolate the different major versions that might become available for the dependency. Separating and organizing the dependencies into subfolders will help ease the management and discoverability of the dependencies over time.

The first benefit that comes from storing the Dependencies version control folder inside of the branch is that it allows the development team to manage changes to dependencies just like any other change to the products. For example, the new version of a dependency could be updated in the DEV branch for developing and testing, but the RELEASE and MAIN branches continue to use the older version until the update is merged and promoted to those branches. This allows for effective source configuration management of the dependencies of your application, because the teams can choose when to "take" changes to the dependencies by performing the updates themselves.

Another benefit is that it allows for relative references to be used in the HintPath property for file references in Visual Studio project files. Visual Studio and MSBuild can use the HintPath property to resolve the references in a project at compile time. Using relative paths in the file reference (instead of an absolute path that may include the branch name) ensures that the reference can be properly resolved by Visual Studio, or automated build servers, no matter what the physical structure ends up being for storing branches in version control.

Listing 10-1 shows how the relative path would be used if the Visual Studio project file for ProductA used a dependency in the Dependencies folder, as shown in Figure 10-1.

LISTING 10-1: HintPath Property in Visual Studio Project File Branch Dependency Folder

```xml
<?xml version="1.0" encoding="utf-8"?>
<Project ToolsVersion="4.0" DefaultTargets="Build" xmlns=
    "http://schemas.microsoft.com/developer/msbuild/2003">
<!-- Section Removed for Brevity -->
  <ItemGroup>
    <Reference Include="EnterpriseLibrary">
      <HintPath>..\..\Dependencies\EnterpriseLibrary.dll</HintPath>
    </Reference>
    <Reference Include="System" />
    <Reference Include="System.Data" />
    <Reference Include="System.Deployment" />
    <Reference Include="System.Drawing" />
    <Reference Include="System.Windows.Forms" />
    <Reference Include="System.Xml" />
    <Reference Include="System.Core" />
    <Reference Include="System.Xml.Linq" />
```

continues

LISTING 10-1 *(continued)*

```
      <Reference Include="System.Data.DataSetExtensions" />
    </ItemGroup>
    <ItemGroup>
  <!-- Section Removed for Brevity -->
  </Project>
```

A drawback to this approach is that each product family's set of branches contained in version control has a copy of dependencies that might be used by multiple product families. This potentially can cause more data storage to be used in the Team Foundation Server database. It also means that, if an update must be committed for all product families, the update must be made in each product family's branching structure independently.

However, the benefits outweigh the potential drawback in this particular case. This also ensures that teams have a better understanding of the dependencies that are used by the products in their product family. Teams can also actively manage the time when new dependencies are integrated into their product family's branch, and actually make the update themselves.

This approach can be considered the preferred method for managing dependencies, since it falls in line with the concept of storing everything needed for an application inside the branch's root folder. It also provides for the minimal amount of drawbacks, which are negligible in the larger view of software development.

Folder at Team Project Level

Another alternative for storing dependencies inside version control is to use a common `Dependencies` version control folder across several product families. This folder is scoped at the team project level, as shown in Figure 10-2.

The main benefits of this approach are that the storage space is not an issue, and teams have the capability to make a change to a dependency that would be picked up by all product families. Even when using this approach, the same type of subfolder organization that was described for the "folder inside branch" option can be used, and is encouraged for the same beneficial reasons described for that option.

Since this common version control folder is used to centrally manage all dependencies, the work of the responsible teams can be affected, and products in the different product families can also be affected if a dependency that is being used causes changes that break the applications. This causes the teams to immediately fix their applications to address the breaking change in each of the branches for their product families. Teams must also address the breaking change in a branch that contains production source code (such as a RELEASE branch) before they can produce a meaningful build that works with the updated dependency. This approach does not allow the development teams to "take" changes as needed, and to fit them into their normal development cycles.

FIGURE 10-2: Common Dependencies version control folder

Another immediate drawback that will surface is that the relative references may not resolve correctly, depending on the physical placement of the branches in the version control repository.

Also, this approach can be susceptible to breaking the file references when renaming or performing organization version control moves in the future.

For example, if a Visual Studio project file in the DEV\Source\ProductA version control folder included a file reference to the Enterprise Library assembly in the common Dependencies version control folder, the HintPath would be listed as a relative path in the project file, as shown in Listing 10-2.

LISTING 10-2: HintPath Property in Visual Studio Project File with Common Folder Dependency

```xml
<?xml version="1.0" encoding="utf-8"?>
<Project ToolsVersion="4.0" DefaultTargets="Build" xmlns=
    "http://schemas.microsoft.com/developer/msbuild/2003">
<!-- Section Removed for Brevity -->
  <ItemGroup>
    <Reference Include="EnterpriseLibrary">
      <HintPath>..\..\..\..\Dependencies\EnterpriseLibrary\
          EnterpriseLibrary.dll</HintPath>
    </Reference>
    <Reference Include="System" />
    <Reference Include="System.Data" />
    <Reference Include="System.Deployment" />
    <Reference Include="System.Drawing" />
    <Reference Include="System.Windows.Forms" />
    <Reference Include="System.Xml" />
    <Reference Include="System.Core" />
    <Reference Include="System.Xml.Linq" />
    <Reference Include="System.Data.DataSetExtensions" />
  </ItemGroup>
  <ItemGroup>
<!-- Section Removed for Brevity -->
</Project>
```

FIGURE 10-3: Features branches

However, if Features branches were created as shown in Figure 10-3, then the HintPath property would no longer be valid, because it would need an extra "..\" to represent the extra path level that the Features branches are now sitting under.

Finally, if you use this approach, ensure that this common Dependencies version control folder is included in the workspace definition for any build definitions, in addition to the branch that contains the source code needed by the automated build, as shown in Figure 10-4.

	Working folders:		
General	Status	Source Control Folder ▲	Build Agent Folder
Trigger	Active	$/Demo/Dependencies	$(SourceDir)\Dependencies
Workspace	Active	$/Demo/ProductFamily1/DEV	$(SourceDir)
Build Defaults		Click here to enter a new working folder	
Process			
Retention Policy			

FIGURE 10-4: Including the Dependencies folder in the workspace definition

INTERNAL SHARED LIBRARIES

Companies may have multiple development teams that all work separately on the product families that each of them owns. At some point, those development teams may come to the realization that they want to have common types and source code to be shared among the products. There are certainly benefits to having one code base for the common library. For example, bug fixes, new functionality, and performance improvements can be introduced to multiple product families easily, and this allows for a common usage patterns across the teams.

The key to a successful shared library strategy is to treat the package of common libraries as a completely separate "product family" internally. This means that it would ideally have its own release cycle (even if it is on the same cadence as another product family), its own product backlog, and it would be owned by a specific team (whether that is a dedicated team, or a team that also works on another product family).

It is essentially treated as though it is third-party dependency by the teams that want to use the shared library. It's just a third-party dependency that is built internally. A large example of this is how the .NET Framework (common library) is developed alongside Visual Studio and Team Foundation Server, both of which have dependencies on the .NET Framework.

For the following discussion, refer to the sample product families and common libraries that are shown in Figure 10-5. You will notice that both product families have a dependency on the shared libraries.

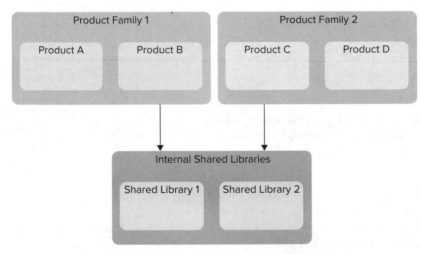

FIGURE 10-5: Product families with a dependency on shared libraries

Choosing a Location in Version Control

The first decision that must be made is the location in version control in which to store the source code for the shared libraries. There are two common choices that come up with Team Foundation Server:

➤ Dedicating a branching structure in the same team project

➤ Dedicating a branching structure in a different team project

Dedicating a Branching Structure in the Same Team Project

If the shared libraries are considered to be grouped together with multiple product families in one team project, you might want to contain the source code for those shared libraries in the same team project. This is especially the case if the release cycle for the shared libraries is on a similar cadence as the other product families in the same team project. The release cycle of the shared libraries just must be set to "release" and stabilized before the release of the other product families. This is to ensure that any bug fixes are included, new features are implemented, and the shared libraries are tested sufficiently before any of the product family teams need to release their products.

Figure 10-6 shows an additional branching structure for the common libraries alongside the other related product families in the same team project. The team that owns the development of the shared libraries now has its own mechanism for managing change in version control.

A different area path node structure can even be created to isolate the work item artifacts related to the shared libraries. This allows managers and executives to still pull reports and work item queries across the entire team project, which provides a high-level view of the progress across multiple product families and the shared libraries. Figure 10-7 shows how those area paths might be defined in the same team project.

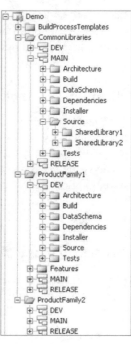

FIGURE 10-6: Branching structure for the common libraries alongside the other related product families in the same team project

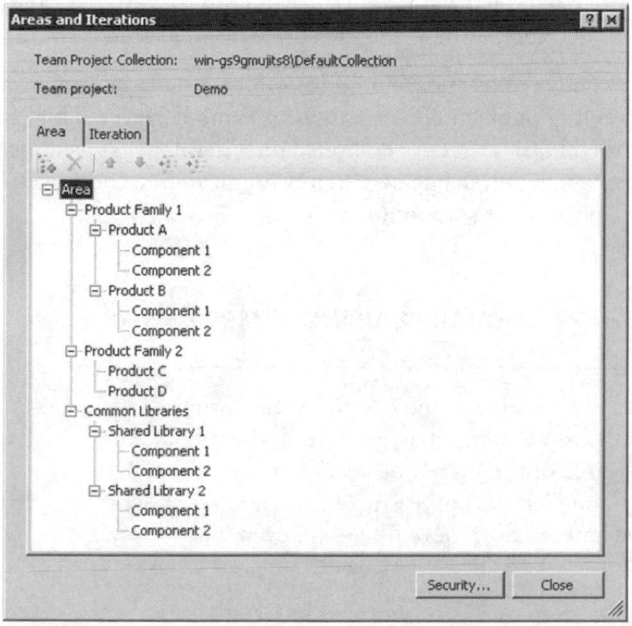

FIGURE 10-7: Area paths defined in the same team project

If this approach is taken, you can also ensure that you have separate build definitions to create the binaries that the other product family teams will end up using as dependencies in their products. Figure 10-8 shows how the build definitions for common libraries might show up alongside the build definitions of other product families in the same team project.

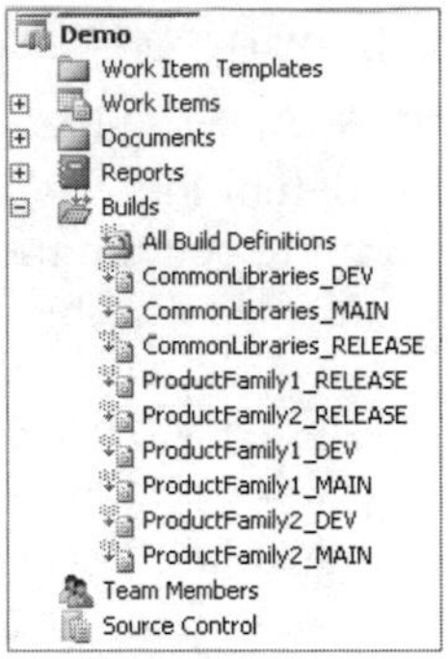

Dedicating a Branching Structure in a Different Team Project

Let's say that the development teams for multiple product families have a dependency on the common libraries, and those product families exist across multiple team projects. In this case, you can either choose one of the existing team projects, or, if needed, create a new team project for managing the source code and release for the common libraries. The concept is essentially the same, except that the new branching structure, build definitions, and area paths would exist in that new team project.

FIGURE 10-8: Build definitions for common libraries

Storing Library Assemblies as Dependencies

Once you have defined the location for the branching structure for the common libraries, and you have created build definitions that run successfully to produce the binaries, the product family teams are ready to take a dependency on those shared libraries in their Visual Studio projects.

The process is very similar to how the team would manage this dependency as any other third-party dependency. Team members would choose when to take a new version of the dependency based on their release schedule, and how they want to support their products against the new version of the shared libraries. They then go to a build with high quality's drop folder to grab the binaries, and check them into the respective Dependencies folder, as described earlier in this chapter.

It is important to ensure that the product family teams choose a build coming from a build definition that is indexing for Source Server and publishing its symbols to Symbol Server. This approach is used as opposed to grabbing the binaries that are compiled on a developer's machine from Visual Studio. This allows the developers to still debug and step through source code, even without having the Visual Studio projects in the same solution.

ENABLING DEBUGGING FOR SHARED LIBRARIES USING SYMBOL AND SOURCE SERVER

One common reason that developers would like to include the Visual Studio projects for the shared libraries in the same solution as their products is to make it easier to step through the source code of the shared libraries at debug time. By taking advantage of Source and Symbol Server support in Team Foundation Server Build and Visual Studio, those developers can achieve that goal, even when using a file reference for the dependency.

To support this, the development team will need to check in a binary that has been produced from a build definition configured for Source Server indexing, and then publish the symbols to Symbol Server. The development team will also need at least read-only access to the branches that contain the source code for the shared libraries — regardless of whether those folders exist in the same team project, or a different team project.

This is one of many scenarios that can be solved by using Source Server and Symbol Server. Chapter 15 provides more information about enabling Source and Symbol Server support in automated builds.

Branching into Product Family Branches

You may also choose to have a separate branching structure in the same or different team project, and then branch the source code folders from the shared library branch into the other product family branches. This allows developers to have copies of the shared library projects inside the same solution, and then use project references to those shared library projects.

To enable this, you must create a branch by selecting Branching and Merging ⇨ Branch from the context menu of the shared library folder, as shown in Figure 10-9.

FIGURE 10-9: Creating a separate branching structure in the same or different team project

Once you select the Branch command, the Branch options dialog shown in Figure 10-10 is displayed. Notice how this branch dialog differs from creating a branch from an actual branch folder, since you are attempting to create a branch inside of an already existing branch root folder. Since the SharedLibrary1 folder is not considered a branch, it will just be created with a version control branching relationship as a folder at the target location.

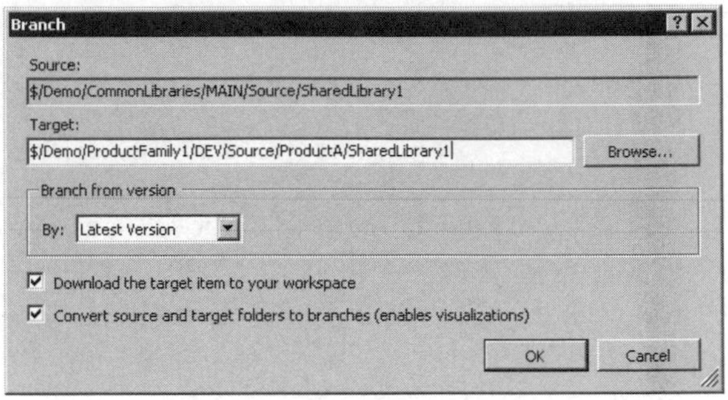

FIGURE 10-10: Branch options dialog

One drawback for this approach is that you will not be able to take advantage of branch or track changes visualizations. It is solely a branching relationship in version control that exists to allow for merging changes into the branching structures of multiple product families.

The team should be careful about how the shared libraries are then deployed, since each would be compiling the shared library separately in the respective build definitions. The team could get in a situation where it is deploying two assemblies with the same name, version number, and so on, but with different content in it.

This also demonstrates another drawback. The shared libraries can start to quickly diverge on different paths if not managed appropriately. For example, one development team may introduce a new exception-handling routine, and another team could introduce a different exception-handling routine at the same time. Later, those two teams could merge their changes back to the original parent branch for the shared library, and end up with two exception-handling routines.

MANAGING ARTIFACTS USING TEAM FOUNDATION SERVER

Team Foundation Server administrators often find that they need a place to organize and store artifacts needed for managing Team Foundation Server. Interestingly, this is where the version control repository can help out those administrators. A dedicated team project can be created to store in one convenient location all of the artifacts that would be necessary to manage Team Foundation Server.

This team project (named, for example, TFS) can be stored in the default team project collection, and its access can be limited to the administrators of the system. For example, you can provide access for this team project only to members of the Team Foundation Server Administrators security group.

From time to time, other developers may help out with some of the custom tools that can be created to extend Team Foundation Server, or build engineers may need access to use or contribute to the master build process templates. In those situations, you can create specific team project security groups to allow privileges on an ad hoc basis without giving full access to the entire team project's repository.

The following sections explore the different types of artifacts that you might organize in this team project. Each suggestion is certainly optional, and depends on your particular scenario. The premise is that you want to effectively organize the artifacts that are necessary to manage Team Foundation Server.

SQL Reporting Services Encryption Key Backup

In disaster-recovery scenarios, one of the commonly misplaced artifacts is a backup of the SQL Reporting Services encryption key. Without this key artifact, you could experience problems with a full restore after a disaster. Therefore, always be sure that a backup of the encryption key is stored in the TFS team project.

The thinking behind storing it in version control is that most companies will ensure that they have a backup of the key Team Foundation Server databases. The databases can be easily restored from those backups, and access to the version control repository can happen early in the disaster-recovery process. At the point when SQL Reporting Services will be restored, the administrator will have access to the encryption key backup file that is available in the newly restored version control repository.

> *To protect the contents of the encryption key, a password is needed when creating the encryption key backup file. Therefore, be sure to make a note of the password in the appropriate location, according to your company's internal security guidelines.*
>
> *It may be acceptable for some employees at some companies to store a text file alongside the encryption key backup file, and check in that text file to the same location in the version control repository. If that option is not an acceptable practice, then ensure that the administrators will have ready access to retrieving the password during a disaster-recovery scenario.*

Figure 10-11 shows the encryption key backup file available in the root of the team project's version control repository folder.

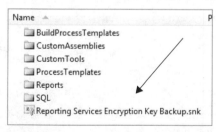

FIGURE 10-11: Location of encryption key backup file

> *Chapter 19 provides more information about disaster-recovery procedures for Team Foundation Server. Also, more information about the procedure for generating an encryption key backup file for SQL Reporting Services is available at* http://msdn.microsoft.com/en-us/library/ms400729.aspx.

Process Templates

A primary reason why administrators want to manage artifacts is to be able to manage the change of process templates used in the team projects on the Team Foundation Server. Work item type definitions are the primary source of changes to the process templates in most organizations.

You should create a folder structure that is set aside especially to manage the changes to the process templates. This allows for each change to go through a check-out/check-in procedure, and is audited to include the date and time the change was made, the user who made the change, and the details about the change (for example, changeset comments and associated work items). This process is very similar to how source code changes would be made to an application being built by a development team.

You can leverage each of the version control features available in Team Foundation Server. For example, you can create two branches to maintain the changes to the process templates. One branch would be for the version of the process templates used on the *testing* Team Foundation Server environment, and one branch would be used to store the version of the process templates used in the *production* Team Foundation Server environment. This allows administrators to make changes that can be tested out first in a separate environment, and then merge those changes to the production branch when the quality of those changes has been determined.

Additionally, the TFS team project can even contain continuous integration build definitions for automatically deploying the changes to the process template's work item type definitions to the appropriate environment whenever the change is checked in to the appropriate branch. One build definition could be created for each branch to deploy to that specific environment (for example, deploy to the production environment when changes are made to the Production branch).

> *Chapter 12 provides more information about process templates, making changes to work item type definitions, and automatic deployment of those changes using a Team Foundation Server build.*

Figure 10-12 shows the branches created for managing process templates in the TFS team project's version control repository.

Custom Build Assemblies

In Team Foundation Server 2010, build servers (specifically build controllers and agents) can monitor a version control folder for custom assemblies that should be used during the build process, and deploy them automatically. This feature is particularly useful for companies that have large numbers of servers in their build farm, and want an effective deployment tool and change control method for the custom assemblies.

These custom assemblies can contain custom build workflow activities, or even custom MSBuild tasks that are used by Visual Studio projects.

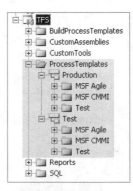

FIGURE 10-12: Branches created for managing process templates

By creating a version control folder in the TFS team project, the custom assemblies can be managed from a central location alongside other artifacts used to manage Team Foundation Server.

Interestingly, this version control folder is not used exclusively by the build servers, but is also used by end-user machines connecting to Team Foundation Server. There could be custom types or custom UI editors used by custom build process parameters that would need to be resolved whenever an end user queues a build manually. The Visual Studio clients will monitor the specified location, and load the assemblies appropriately to resolve those custom types. For this reason, be sure to provide all users of Team Foundation Server read-only access to this version control folder.

> *Chapter 16 provides more information about creating custom build activities and deploying those activities to the servers in the build farm.*

Each build controller should be configured to point to this version control folder for deploying custom build assemblies. Figure 10-13 shows the Build Controller Properties dialog, and the field to set for monitoring the version control folder. The figure also demonstrates how the properties correspond to the version control folder that is created in the TFS team project.

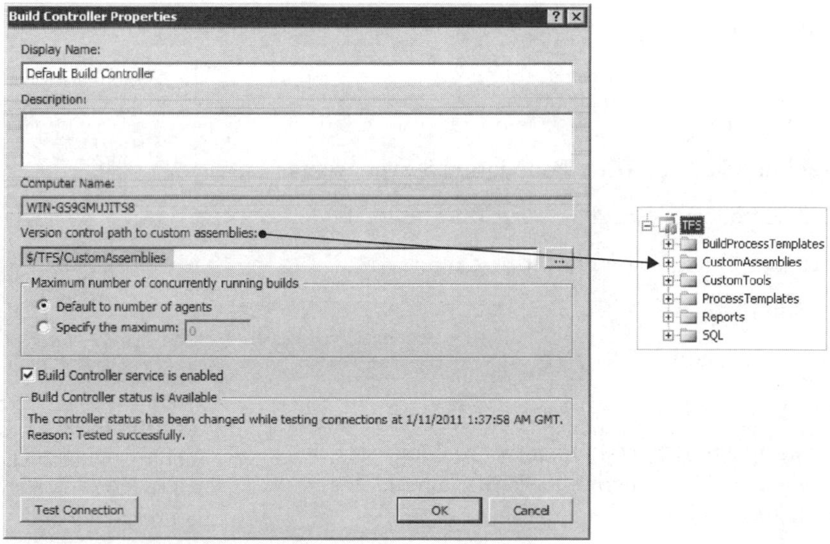

FIGURE 10-13: Build Controller Properties dialog

Master Build Process Templates

Another version control folder that can be created in the TFS team project's version control repository is a folder used to store all of the master build process template .XAML files. After build engineers have architected a build process template that will work for several build definitions, it is nice to have such templates stored and managed from a central location.

Build definitions in the same team project collection can be configured to use the master build process templates, even if those build definitions are defined in a different team project.

 Chapter 16 provides more information about architecting and customizing build process templates.

Source Code for Custom Tools

Custom tools and extensions can be created to further enhance the features available in Team Foundation Server using the Team Foundation Server Software Development Kit (SDK). The TFS team project's version control repository is the perfect location for managing the source code to use for building those custom tools.

Build definitions can be created for the suite of custom tools that compile and package those tools using the source code stored in the TFS team project's version control repository. The work item tracking artifacts in the TFS team project can even be used to manage the releases for the custom internal tools that are built for Team Foundation Server.

Following are examples of the types of tools that could be created and stored in this version control repository:

> ➤ Custom check-in policies

> ➤ Custom build workflow activities and build tasks

> ➤ Custom work item controls

> ➤ Web Service event handlers for Team Foundation Server events

> ➤ Custom testing data collectors (or diagnostic data adapters)

> ➤ Migration utilities and Integration Platform adapters

> ➤ Custom Code Analysis rules

> ➤ Global Code Analysis spelling dictionary

> ➤ Custom IntelliTrace event collectors

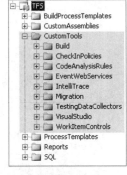

FIGURE 10-14: Version control folders used to store the source code for custom tools

Figure 10-14 shows an example of the version control folders that can be created to store the source code for custom tools that extend Team Foundation Server and Visual Studio.

SUMMARY

The version control repository can quickly become unruly if left up to a team. By introducing some organization (and, specifically, some targeted methods), not only will the discoverability of the source code be improved, but the method in which the application is developed is also improved. This is especially the case when third-party dependencies and internal shared libraries are needed by the application.

Additionally, storing artifacts that are used to manage Team Foundation Server in version control folders will allow administrators to easily access all of those artifacts in one location. The capability to locate key artifacts needed in disaster-recovery scenarios, as well as having a common place to manage source code for extensions to Team Foundation Server and Visual Studio, are also ensured.

This part of the book has explored the features available in the version control repository in Team Foundation Server. The next part of the book introduces the features available in the work item tracking system of Team Foundation Server.

In the next part of the book, you will learn about project management, work item tracking, and reporting capabilities of Team Foundation Server. Chapter 11 introduces you to the concepts of the work item tracking system, and provides the fundamentals for managing projects and work using Team Foundation Server.

PART III
Project Management

11
Introducing Work Item Tracking

WHAT'S IN THIS CHAPTER?

➤ Getting to know the additions and enhancements to project management capabilities in Team Foundation Server 2010

➤ Understanding work items and process templates

➤ Managing and querying work items

In Part II, you learned about the support that Team Foundation Server 2010 has for source control. In Part III, you will learn about how Team Foundation Server 2010 helps with project management.

Project management can involve many aspects of developing software, such as tracking remaining work and open bugs, determining how much work you can commit to with your available resources, and even helping to enforce a standard process of interaction between your team members. You will see that Team Foundation Server 2010 provides capabilities to help you achieve all of these things, and more.

In this chapter, you will start by learning about the enhancements to project management available in this release. This chapter also provides an overview of work item tracking, including some ways to manage and query work items from Visual Studio, Excel, Project, and other clients. You will also learn about the importance of process templates, including an overview of the process templates provided by Microsoft for use with Team Foundation Server 2010.

In subsequent chapters, Part III will also familiarize you with process template customization (Chapter 12) and provide an in-depth look at using reporting and SharePoint dashboards to get real-time insights into how your software development project is going (Chapter 13).

PROJECT MANAGEMENT ENHANCEMENTS IN TEAM FOUNDATION SERVER 2010

Team Foundation Server 2010 delivers a substantial upgrade to the project management capabilities available in prior releases of Team Foundation Server. This section highlights some of the most significant improvements and additions you will find in this release. If you are brand new to Team Foundation Server, concepts such as work items will be explained in greater detail later in this chapter.

Rich Work Item Relationships

According to Microsoft, the top-requested project management feature by users of previous releases of Team Foundation Server was representing rich relationships between work items. In prior releases of Team Foundation Server, it was only possible to relate work items with one another via a simple linking mechanism. But these links didn't provide any explicit meaning, directionality, or cardinality.

For example, a common project management use case for many software development projects is to be able to model parent/child relationships between work items, such as for capturing a feature catalog, or for detailing the tasks required to implement a particular requirement. You could link these work items together using previous releases of Team Foundation Server, but the links didn't carry enough meaning to convey proper parent/child relationships. Without directionality, it's not easy to discern which work item is the parent and which work item is the child in this representation. Furthermore, without cardinality, there isn't a mechanism for restricting that each child work item could only have (at most) one parent work item.

With Team Foundation Server 2010, Microsoft has now introduced rich relational linking between work items. You can now model rich relationships between work items using a variety of link types. These link types can also include directionality and cardinality. Team Foundation Server 2010 ships with the following link types:

➤ *Parent/child* — This is a useful link type for representing hierarchies such as feature catalogs, or for detailing task work items (children) that will be used to implement a requirement or user story (parent). Any work item can have zero or more child work items, and zero or one parent work item.

➤ *Tests/tested by* — This link type is primarily intended to model the relationships between test case work items and the requirements or user stories that they test. This makes it easier to determine the quality of a given requirement or user story by examining the recent results for its related test cases. A work item can test zero or more work items.

➤ *Successor/predecessor* — The successor/predecessor link type is used to indicate work items that have a dependency relationship with one another. For example, designing the user interface for a web page is generally a predecessor to writing the code and markup that will provide the implementation of that web page. A work item can have zero or more successor and/or predecessor links to other work items.

➤ *Related* — The related link type is the same as the legacy linking system found in previous releases of Team Foundation Server. These link types are not directional, and provide no additional context about the type of relationship. If you had linked work items in a project that was upgraded to Team Foundation Server 2010, those relationships will be represented by the related link type.

You will discover that rich work item relationships provide the basis for other new features and enhancements across the project management capabilities of Team Foundation Server 2010, such as enhanced querying and reporting. It is also possible to define your own link types if you wish, although for most teams, the provided link types will be sufficient. More information on creating custom link types can be found at http://msdn.microsoft.com/en-us/library/dd469516.aspx.

> *Team Foundation Server 2010 does not have a mechanism for ensuring that your links are semantically correct. For example, it's possible to create circular chains of successor/predecessor links, or tests/tested by relationships between two work items that don't involve a test case. If you notice that you have invalid link types in your project, you can easily delete them at any time.*

Agile Workbooks

A new set of Excel-bound workbooks are available to help you manage your backlog, iterations, and resources. These workbooks are available if you use the Microsoft Solutions Framework (MSF) for Agile Software Development process template. The workbooks provide both a team- and individual-based view of committed and available resources, and allow you to easily model interruptions such as holidays and illnesses. You will learn more about these workbooks later in this chapter.

Test Case Management

Test cases are now represented as work items in Team Foundation Server 2010. This makes it possible to create rich relationships between the code you are implementing and the results of your quality assurance (QA) efforts.

For example, test case work items can be linked (via a tests/tested by link type) to requirements work items. As tests are run, results can be reported on by querying a given requirement work item, traversing to the related test cases, and viewing the results of recent test runs. Many of the new default reports make use of this information to expose new perspectives on software quality.

> *You learn more about the role that testing plays in Team Foundation Server 2010 in Chapter 22.*

Enhanced Reporting

One of the primary reasons Microsoft designed Team Foundation Server as an integrated solution (including source control, project management, build automation, and so on) is to enable multidimensional views into software development projects. Effectively managing a software project is not unlike managing other complex projects. Making smart decisions requires you to have a rich set of information resources available, usually in real time, which can help to inform resource allocations, prioritizations, cuts, schedule changes, and other important evaluations.

The rich work item relationships that have been added to Team Foundation Server 2010 have enabled Microsoft to significantly enhance the types of reports available. As just one example, parent/child relationships between user stories and tasks can produce a report showing the amount of work required in order to finish implementing any given user story. By further analyzing the tests/tested by links, you can get a view into software quality for those same user stories based on the results of your test cases. There are countless other examples.

In this release, Microsoft has also made it much easier to customize existing reports, or create new ones. The new ad hoc reporting capabilities in this release allow you to create reports from just a work item query.

> *You learn more about reporting with Team Foundation Server 2010 in Chapter 13.*

SharePoint Server Dashboards

Most software development projects involve many stakeholders. In addition to the core programming team, a team may include project managers, business analysts, testers, architects, and so on. There may also be external stakeholders — such as end users or executive management — who have a vested interest in monitoring the progress of your project. Most of these people don't use Visual Studio; so how do you effectively communicate project status to everyone?

Microsoft has integrated Team Foundation Server with SharePoint for this reason. Whenever you create a team project with Team Foundation Server 2010, you can optionally create a new SharePoint site (or use an existing one). This site can be used as a dashboard to provide everybody on your extended team with a view into your project. Your SharePoint site provides a web-based view of reports from your team project, along with a document repository where you can store artifacts such as specifications and storyboards.

> *In Chapter 13, you learn about how these SharePoint dashboards can be used and customized for your team.*

WORK ITEMS

If you're brand new to Team Foundation Server, you may be wondering what exactly a work item is after reading the preceding section. A *work item* is the basic building block of the project management capabilities in Team Foundation Server. Microsoft defines a work item as ". . . a database record that Team Foundation uses to track the assignment and progress of work."

Work Item Types

There are many kinds of work items, known as *work item types*. An instance of a work item type is a work item, in much the same way that, in object-oriented programming (OOP), an instance of a class is an object. A work item can represent explicit work that needs to be completed (or has been completed), such as with a *Task* work item type. Work items can capture details of the software you are building, such as with a *Requirement* or *User Story* work item types. Work items can be used to capture problems, such as the *Bug* work item type (which indicates a problem with your software) or the *Issue* work item type (which might describe a problem with tooling, processes, or people that may be slowing down your project, or even preventing work from happening). Team Foundation Server 2010 includes other default work item types as well, and you can even create your own.

> *You learn more about work item type customization in Chapter 12.*

Work items include a handful of key elements, as shown in Table 11-1.

TABLE 11-1: Work Item Elements

ELEMENT	DESCRIPTION
Field	*Fields* contain the information that can be captured as part of a work item. There are some fields that are shared by all work item types (called *system fields*). Examples of system fields include *Title* (a one-line description of your work item), *ID* (a number that is globally unique across your team project collection), and *Assigned to* (which can be a user, such as a developer, who is working on a fix for a bug work item). Other fields might be specific to a given work item type, such as the *Steps to reproduce* field, which is found in the Bug work item type and describes how a bug was discovered.
Rule	*Rules* can dictate which values are allowed for given fields. For example, you might decide that the *Priority* field for bugs should be assigned a value of 0, 1, or 2 and cannot be left blank.
Form	A *form* describes the way work items are displayed by work item clients such as Visual Studio. (You will learn more about some of the ways to view and interact with work items later in this chapter.)
State	*States* indicate where in your project workflow a work item is. For example, a Bug work item type in the MSF for Agile Software Development process template starts out in an *Active* state when it is first created. Once a developer declares that the code has been written or modified to fix a bug, the developer changes the state of the Bug work item to *Resolved*. If a tester can verify that the bug can no longer be reproduced, the tester changes the bug work item state to *Closed*. But if a tester can still reproduce the bug, it will need to be reactivated (that is, the tester will change the state of the bug back to Active). This signals to the developers that they still have work to do.

continues

TABLE 11-1 *(continued)*

ELEMENT	DESCRIPTION
Transition	*Transitions* are similar to rules, but they define how a work item moves from one state to another. In the previous example, a bug work item must begin in an Active state, and can then move into a Resolved or Closed state. But, from a Resolved state, it is also possible to move back to an Active state. This is all defined by the transition model as part of the work item type. Additionally, transitions can dictate that certain fields should be required in order to move from one state to another. For example, to move a bug from an Active to a Resolved state, a developer must assign a *Reason* (such as Fixed, As Designed, Cannot Reproduce, and so on).
Link	Work items can include *links* to other work items, using any of the link types you read about in the preceding section.
History	Work items also contain a full *history* that includes information about all changes to fields and transitions.

Figure 11-1 shows an example of a bug work item form that has been resolved by the developer. This screenshot is taken from a bug that was created with the MSF for Agile Software Development process template. You will learn more about process templates later in this chapter.

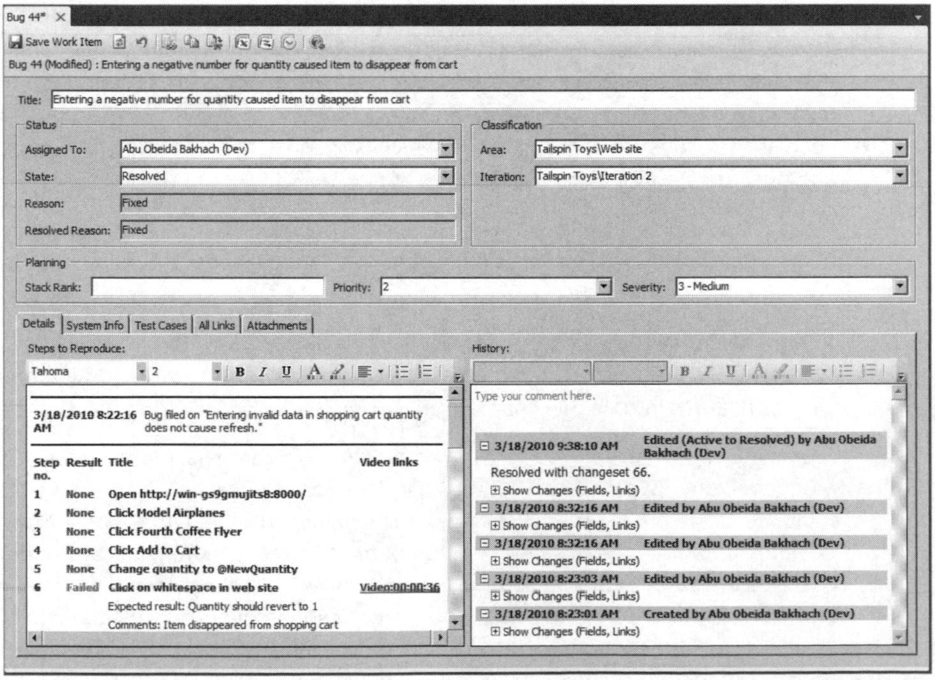

FIGURE 11-1: Bug (Agile) work item form

Figure 11-2 is a state diagram showing the transitions for the default Bug work item type included with the MSF for Agile Software Development process template. State diagrams for each work item type are included with the documentation for the process templates provided by Microsoft. They are useful for understanding how a work item behaves.

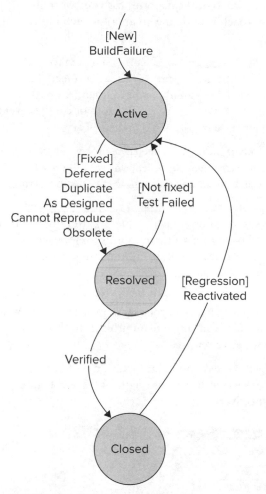

FIGURE 11-2: Bug (Agile) work item type state diagram

> *If you are using a third-party process template, or have customized an existing process template, then you may not have state diagrams for your work items. But Team Web Access (which you learned about in Chapter 4) can generate them for you. Simply open a work item in Team Web Access and click Tools ⇨ State Diagram. Team Web Access will dynamically generate a state diagram like the one shown in Figure 11-2 as an image that you can save a copy of and include in your team's process documentation.*

Areas and Iterations

Most of the system fields available for work items (such as Title and ID) are fairly self-explanatory. But there are two important fields — Area and Iteration — that warrant further discussion.

The *Area* field is a versatile field that can be used to create logical categories for your work items. There are many ways to use areas, but a common approach is to define an area for each logical part of your application.

For example, in Figure 11-1, this bug is assigned to the `Tailspin Toys\Web site` area to indicate that it is part of the web application being developed for the `Tailspin Toys` team project. The complete string that is used for this designation is referred to as an *area path*. Other area paths might include `Tailspin Toys\Database`, `Tailspin Toys\Mobile Application`, or can be several levels deep, such as `Tailspin Toys\Web site\Shopping cart\Update controller`.

The *Iterations* field is useful for project planning, and can indicate a time frame for when you plan to address a work item. In Figure 11-1, this work item is assigned to `Tailspin Toys\Iteration 2`, where `Tailspin Toys` is the name of the team project, and `Iteration 2` is the specific iteration this work item is assigned to.

You can name your iterations whatever you'd like; some teams choose sequential iterations (such as Iteration 1, Iteration 2, and so on), while others choose to map them to milestone releases (such as Beta 1, Beta 2, and so on). You can also create trees of iterations and employ a blend of naming strategies, such as `Tailspin Toys\Version 2.0\Beta 1\Iteration 2`.

You are not required to use iterations and areas to categorize your work items, but they can be very useful for querying, managing, and reporting on your work items as your team project grows. When used effectively, areas and iterations can allow you to employ a single team project for dozens or even hundreds of applications across many years of iterative releases.

A team project administrator can manage the list of valid areas and iterations from within Visual Studio by clicking Team ➪ Team Project Settings ➪ Areas and Iterations. Figure 11-3 and Figure 11-4 show the dialogs for editing areas and iterations, respectively.

FIGURE 11-3: Area administration   **FIGURE 11-4:** Iteration administration

A nice feature of area and iteration administration is that you can use the Security button to define granular permissions for indicating who is allowed to modify or even read work items in each part of your team project. For example, maybe you work for a government security contractor and there are bugs of a sensitive nature that should only be viewed by team members with a certain security clearance. Or, maybe you are building a prototype of the next version of your application and want to restrict access to minimize the potential for leaks that your competitors could get access to. These sorts of restrictions are possible by using iteration and area security settings.

At any time, you can return to the Area and Iteration settings to add, rename, move, or delete areas and iterations. If you rename or move areas or iterations for which there are existing work items, those work items will automatically be reassigned by Team Foundation Server using the new name or location you choose. If you delete an area or iteration for which there are existing work items, you will be prompted for the value that Team Foundation Server should use to replace the iteration or area value in affected work items.

You will discover that work items are used throughout Team Foundation Server. They form the basis of many of the reports you will read about in Chapter 13. They can be linked to changesets (which you read about in Part II) to provide more information about what changes were made to a set of files and why. They can be used by project managers and team leaders for project planning, and they are used to help control which work team members should be focused on, and how they should interact with other team members.

Work items, work item types, and all of the activities involving work items (editing, querying, reporting, and so on) are usually referred to collectively as the *work item tracking* capability of Team Foundation Server. Now that you understand the basics of work items, you are ready to learn about process templates, which include the definitions for work item types.

PROCESS TEMPLATES

A *process template* defines the default characteristics of any new team project. Process templates are a powerful concept in Team Foundation Server. A process template includes the default work item types, reports, documents, process guidance, and other associated artifacts that provide you with everything you need to get started with your software project.

Choosing the right process template is an important step in creating a new team project. You should carefully choose the best process template for your team's preferred work style and the type of project you are working on. This section will help you understand the types of process templates available. While you are reading this section, you should be thinking about the following types of questions:

➤ How does your team work today?

➤ Are there ways about how your team works today that you'd like to change?

➤ Do you need a formal process, or do you work better as a more agile team?

➤ Are there areas of your process where you prefer to be more agile, but other areas where you need to be more formal? (For example, maybe you want to manage your team's iterations in an agile manner, but decisions about requirements require formal negotiations with your customer.)

➤ Do you have resources to invest in and maintain your own custom process template, or would one provided by Microsoft or a reputable third party be a better solution?

➤ What other stakeholders should be involved in the decision-making process for answering these questions?

If answering these questions proves difficult for you or your team, you may want to start with a small pilot project first and see how your team performs when using one of the existing process templates. You can then use the findings from that pilot to determine which process template to start with, and what changes (if any) need to be made to that process template before using it for subsequent projects. Process template customization is covered in Chapter 12.

Embracing the *right* process template can have a transformational effect on an organization by providing everybody on the team with a predictable and repeatable process for capturing and communicating information, making decisions, and ensuring that you are delivering on customer expectations. This, in turn, can drive up software quality and development velocity, which ultimately delivers more value to your customers.

MSF for Agile Software Development

The *MSF for Agile Software Development v5.0* process template included with Team Foundation Server 2010 is designed for teams who are practicing agile methodologies, such as Scrum or eXtreme Programming (XP). These methodologies have their roots in the now-famous Agile Manifesto (www.agilemanifesto.org/).

> *MSF version 1 was introduced by Microsoft in 1993, and version 4 was first codified as a set of process templates with the release of Team Foundation Server 2005. MSF provides guidelines, role definitions, and other materials to help organizations deliver IT solutions, including software development projects. Many of the guiding principles of MSF align closely with those of the Agile Manifesto.*

A key tenet of agile methodologies is that requirements will evolve over time, both as business needs change, and as customers begin to use interim releases of your software. For this reason, the MSF for Agile Software Development process template assumes that teams will be frequently refining requirements and reprioritizing work by maintaining a common backlog of requirements (which are captured as user stories in this template). Periods of work are time-boxed into short lengths of time (iterations). Prior to each iteration, the development team works with the customer to prioritize the backlog, and the top user stories on the backlog are then addressed in that iteration.

Another important aspect of agile methodologies is, as the Agile Manifesto describes it, valuing "individuals and interactions over processes and tools." This doesn't mean that processes and tools shouldn't be used at all, but instead that they sometimes can get in the way of empowering people to communicate and work together in order to make smart decisions.

This is also reflected in the MSF for Agile Software Development process template, which defines a relatively small number of states, fields, transitions, and work item types as compared with other process templates such as the MSF for Capability Maturity Model Integration (CMMI) Process Improvement process template. By keeping the process simple, the goal is to prevent any unnecessary burdens from getting in the way of people making the right decisions.

Following are the work item types available in the MSF for Agile Software Development process template:

➤ Bug

➤ Issue

➤ Task

➤ Test Case

➤ User Story

> *There is a sixth work item in the MSF for Agile Software Development process template — the Shared Steps work item type — which is essentially a special instance of a Test Case. You learn more about shared steps and test cases in Chapter 22. Most team members won't interact with shared steps directly, so they are excluded from the preceding list.*

Another unique aspect of the MSF for Agile Software Development process template in this release of Team Foundation Server is the inclusion of the agile workbooks, mentioned earlier in this chapter. These Excel-bound workbooks are helpful for tasks such as managing your project's backlog, balancing resources across your team, and planning iterations. But there are other similar tools available that can help you perform these functions even if you decide not to use the MSF for Agile Software Development process template (see the section, "Using Third-Party Tools," later in this chapter).

> *You can explore the MSF for Agile Software Development v5.0 process template in depth, including more detail on each of the included work item types, at* http://msdn.microsoft.com/en-us/library/dd380647.aspx.

MSF for CMMI Process Improvement

The *MSF for CMMI Process Improvement v5.0* process template is designed for teams who want to, or may have to, take a more formal approach toward developing software. This process template is based on the Capability Maturity Model Integration (CMMI) for Development, which was developed by the Software Engineering Institute, a part of Carnegie Mellon University. CMMI defines not only a framework for developing software, but also prescribes ways for an organization to constantly improve their processes in an objective and repeatable way. An organization can even become certified by an outside appraiser who can verify whether or not it is performing at one of five CMMI maturity levels.

CMMI is a popular model for developing software by such organizations as systems integrators (SIs) and software factories. There is very little subjectivity in the model, so it allows an organization to represent its services using a standard that is well understood globally, and can be appraised and certified by a neutral third-party organization. CMMI is also used for developing many mission-critical systems, such as by NASA or defense contractors. In fact, the Software Engineering Institute at Carnegie Mellon was originally funded by the United States Department of Defense to help them find better ways of managing their projects.

As you might expect, the MSF for CMMI Process Improvement process template is more complex than its Agile counterpart. The CMMI template includes the following work item types:

➤ Bug

➤ Change Request

➤ Issue

➤ Requirement

➤ Review

➤ Risk

➤ Task

➤ Test Case

> *The Shared Steps work item type is also omitted from this list for the same reason as mentioned previously in the discussion of the MSF for Agile Software Development process template.*

In addition to including three additional work item types, the work item types themselves are also more complex in the CMMI process template than in the Agile process template. Compare the screenshot of a bug work item form from the Agile process template, shown earlier in Figure 11-1, with a bug work item form from the CMMI process template, shown in Figure 11-5. Take note of the additional fields, such as Root Cause, Triage, and Blocked, which were not in the bug work item from the Agile process template. There are also additional tabs across the lower half of the bug work item from the CMMI process template.

The states and transitions of work item types from the CMMI process template are also more complex than in the Agile process template. Now, compare the state diagram of the bug work item type from the Agile process template, shown in Figure 11-2, with the state diagram of the bug work item type from the CMMI process template, shown in Figure 11-6.

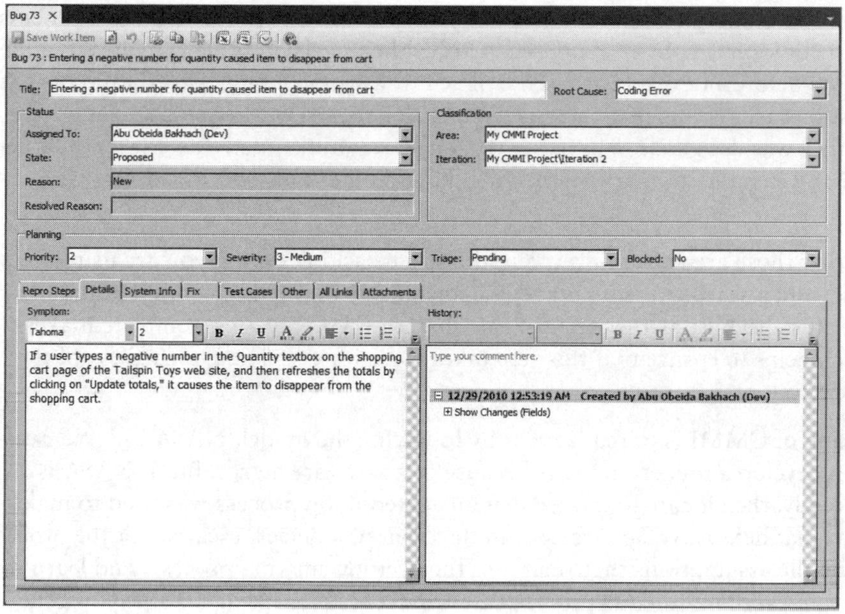

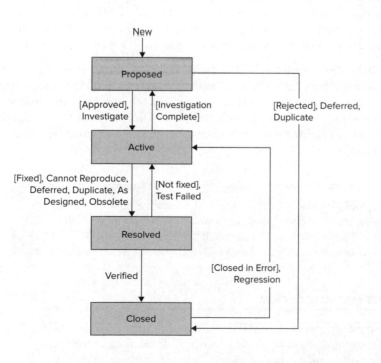

FIGURE 11-5: Bug (CMMI) work Item form

New

Proposed

[Approved], Investigate   [Investigation Complete]   [Rejected], Deferred, Duplicate

Active

[Fixed], Cannot Reproduce, Deferred, Duplicate, As Designed, Obsolete   [Not fixed], Test Failed

Resolved

Verified   [Closed in Error], Regression

Closed

Closed

FIGURE 11-6: Bug (CMMI) work item type state diagram

The key difference you should notice between these two state diagrams is that the CMMI process template introduces an additional state — *Proposed*. This explicit decision stage is required in the CMMI process template before a developer is ever assigned to work on a bug. This should cause the team to ask such questions as, "Is this really a bug, or does this represent a request to change the way certain functionality was designed? Will fixing this bug have unintended side effects on other parts of the software? If we choose to work on this bug, how should it be prioritized against our other work?"

This shouldn't imply that those aren't important questions to be asking even if you are using the Agile process template, and a seasoned team practicing an agile methodology will likely already be mentally following this checklist as they triage bugs. But the CMMI process template makes this step explicit, which helps to ensure that this step takes place for every bug, regardless of the experience level of the development team.

Another way of thinking of CMMI is to realize that by following the model, NASA isn't guaranteed that it will never again develop a rocket that fails because of a software defect. But if NASA is following CMMI correctly, then it can guarantee that an agreed-upon process was used to make decisions leading up to that defect. And conversely, in the event of a defect, it can audit the process that was used, examine the assumptions that went into the decision-making process, and learn from those mistakes in the interest of refining its process and helping to ensure that the same mistake never happens again.

It is also important to point out that using the MSF for CMMI Process Improvement process template alone will not ensure that an organization can successfully pass a CMMI certification audit. This is akin to the fact that simply having a smoke alarm and a fire extinguisher on hand won't keep a family safe if they don't know how to properly use and maintain this equipment.

But Team Foundation Server 2010, along with the MSF for CMMI Process Improvement process template, can be very useful for helping an organization that wants to adopt CMMI as its model of development. Team Foundation Server features such as end-to-end traceability, multidimensional reporting, rich linking (between work items, and with other artifacts such as builds and changesets), and preservation of history are all incredibly useful capabilities that can help an organization to prepare for and pass a CMMI audit.

> *You can explore the MSF for CMMI Process Improvement v5.0 process template in depth, including more detail on each of the included work item types, at* `http://msdn.microsoft.com/en-us/library/dd997574.aspx`.

CMMI DEVELOPMENT METHODOLOGY

There is a common misconception that CMMI dictates a waterfall, or "Big Design Up Front," development methodology. While there is certainly a strong correlation between teams practicing waterfall methodologies and those following a CMMI model, CMMI actually does not define a development methodology. You can choose to use an agile development methodology along with the MSF for CMMI Process Improvement process template if you want to, although you might have a hard time selling agile diehards from your team on the value of the additional rigor imposed by its processes.

As a compromise solution, another approach is to pick and choose the aspects of the CMMI process template that are most interesting to you, and incorporate those into the Agile process template as a custom process template. For example, maybe you like the explicit decision point created by having your bugs begin in a Proposed state before being activated, but you don't see a need for the additional work item types in the CMMI template. In this example, you could start with the Agile process template and import the Bug work item type from the CMMI process template.

Visual Studio Scrum

While there are many development methodologies that make up the agile movement, Scrum has established itself as the most popular for the time being. Scrum defines clear roles, responsibilities, and activities that team members practicing Scrum must follow.

A team practicing Scrum uses a standard vocabulary to define what they are doing. Teams hold daily *stand-ups* (meetings where team members talk about what they did yesterday, what they will do today, and anything that might be blocking them — called an *impediment*). Instead of a project manager, a team practicing Scrum is usually led by a *ScrumMaster*. There are other terms as well, which you can learn about in any of the dozens of books about Scrum, or from the hundreds of Scrum user groups or trainers around the world.

The *Visual Studio Scrum 1.0* process template was introduced specifically to help teams who want to practice Scrum and use Team Foundation Server 2010. It was made available a few months after Team Foundation Server 2010 first shipped, so you'll need to download it at http://msdn .microsoft.com/en-us/vstudio/aa718795 and upload it to your server before you can create a team project that uses it. See the installation instructions on the download site for detailed directions on how to do this.

So, you might now be wondering, if the MSF for Agile Software Development process template is designed to support any of the agile development methodologies — including Scrum — what is the purpose of the Visual Studio Scrum process template? The Visual Studio Scrum process template was created to provide teams practicing Scrum with the *specific* artifacts and terminology used universally by teams who have adopted Scrum.

Instead of User Stories or Requirements, Visual Studio Scrum uses *Product Backlog Item* work item types. Instead of Issues or Risks, Visual Studio Scrum uses *Impediment* work item types. *Sprints* are even represented as work items, and the dates you use to define your Sprints work items are used when rendering your *burndown* and *velocity* reports. In short, if you practice Scrum or are considering practicing Scrum, the Visual Studio Scrum process template is designed to help you do so while making the most of Team Foundation Server 2010.

> *You can explore the Visual Studio Scrum 1.0 process template in depth, including more detail on each of the included work item types, at* http://msdn .microsoft.com/en-us/library/ff731587.aspx.

COMPROMISING WITH SCRUM

If you want to practice Scrum, the Visual Studio Scrum process template provides a great option for doing so. But you shouldn't feel locked into this process template if there are other process templates you like better, such as the MSF for Agile Software Development process template.

For example, you may prefer some of the additional reports that are included with the Agile process template. You can still use the Agile process template and practice Scrum, but you will just need to make some mental translations between the terminology you use as a Scrum team and the way the Agile process template expects you to enter information (such as referring to Product Backlog Items as User Stories).

Third-Party Process Templates

Several third parties provide process templates for use with Team Foundation Server 2010. A list of some of these third-party process templates can be found at http://msdn.microsoft.com/en-us/ vstudio/aa718795 and http://templex.codeplex.com/. Process templates from third parties are usually licensed for free use, and sometimes additional services such as consulting or complementary products are available for purchase from the organizations building those process templates.

There are several great third-party process templates available, but you should carefully consider the support and road map implications of adopting a third-party process template. For example, when the next version of Team Foundation Server is released, will the process template be upgraded to take advantage of new or improved features? And if so, what is the upgrade path for migrating existing projects to the new version of the process template?

If you aren't prepared to take over the maintenance of the process template in the event that the third party chooses to stop investing in it, then you might want to consider one of the aforementioned process templates that are built and supported by Microsoft.

Custom Process Templates

Finally, you might decide that none of the process templates provided by Microsoft or third parties fit the needs of your team or your development project. While you could certainly create your own process template from scratch, a far more common approach is to start with an existing process template and customize it to suit your needs. You can learn about customizing process templates in Chapter 12.

Now that you understand your options for choosing a process template, the next section will introduce you to some of the different ways you can manage your work items.

MANAGING WORK ITEMS

There are many ways of accessing your work items within Team Foundation Server 2010. Since work items will be used by many stakeholders across your team (including programmers, testers, project managers, and so on), and most of these roles don't use Visual Studio as their primary tool, you will discover that Microsoft provides many client options for accessing work items.

In this section you will be introduced to using Visual Studio, Excel, Project, and Team Web Access to access your work items. This chapter won't cover every aspect of accessing work items from each of these clients, but it will give you a better idea of the ways each client can be used, as well as the relative benefits of each, and provide you with pointers to detailed documentation for each client.

The list of clients in this section isn't exhaustive. There are also dozens of third-party clients, a few of which are examined in this section. Testers might use Microsoft Test Manager (discussed in Chapter 22). Eclipse users can utilize Team Explorer Everywhere. You can even write your own clients using the Team Foundation Server object model if you want to.

Using Visual Studio

In Chapter 4, you learned about using Team Explorer to work with Team Foundation Server 2010. Team Explorer not only provides access for Visual Studio users wanting to connect to Team Foundation Server, but it also installs the add-ins required to work with Excel and Project. So, even if you don't plan on using Visual Studio, if you want to use Excel or Project with Team Foundation Server, you should install Team Explorer.

> *The examples in this chapter assume that you are using Team Explorer 2010. While it is possible to use older versions of Team Explorer to connect to Team Foundation Server 2010, you will not be able to access some of the new features in the product. In particular, since earlier editions of Team Explorer aren't aware of the rich relational linking capabilities of Team Foundation Server 2010, you won't be able to manage these link types or use the new querying capabilities to navigate your work items.*
>
> *You can still use older versions of Visual Studio along with Team Explorer 2010. Team Explorer 2010 will be installed "side by side" with your legacy version of Visual Studio, and you can access it by opening the Visual Studio 2010 shell. You can continue to use your legacy Visual Studio client to check in code changes, and then switch to Team Explorer 2010 to update your work items.*

Creating Work Items

Work items are easy to create using Visual Studio. Open the Team Explorer window of Visual Studio 2010 and expand the top-level node for your team project. Now, right-click the Work Items node and place your mouse over the New Work Item menu. The fly-out menu will reveal the work item types that are available in your team project. Click the work item type that you want to create an instance of. An empty work item form will appear, similar to that shown in Figure 11-1.

The new work item form will vary in appearance based on the work item type you chose to create. For the most part, filling out the work item form is self-explanatory, but there are a few things to notice when creating and editing work items.

The first is that your work item won't have an ID until it has been successfully saved for the first time. Remember, the ID is a number that is globally unique across your team project collection, numbered sequentially, starting with 1. This means that the first work item you save within a new team project won't have an ID of 1 if there are existing team projects in your team project collection that also contain work items.

> *Occasionally, you may encounter work item types that you can't edit completely within a particular work item client. The Steps tab of the Test Case and Shared Steps work item types exhibit this behavior; this tab cannot be edited within Team Explorer. The Steps tab is implemented as a custom control, and is designed to be edited by testers with Microsoft Test Manager. (Microsoft Test Manager is discussed in greater detail in Chapter 22.) You will read more about custom controls in Chapter 12. Custom controls must be authored for each type of work item client where it will be used, and since the Steps tab is only applicable to testers, it was only enabled for use within Microsoft Test Manager.*

For now, your work item probably says something like "New Bug 1" at the top of the form. The number 1 isn't your work item's ID; it's just a temporary number used by Visual Studio to track unsaved work items. In fact, until it is saved, Team Foundation Server won't know about your work item.

Before you can successfully save this work item, you will need to assign a Title to it at a minimum. There may be other required fields as well, depending on the work item type you selected. An error message at the top of the form will indicate any remaining fields that you must complete. Some required fields may appear on other tabs.

Another thing you'll notice about work items is that you can't skip states. A work item must be saved in one state prior to moving to the next state. For example, if you refer back to Figure 11-2, you will notice that a bug from the MSF for Agile Software Development process template generally moves from Active to Resolved to Closed.

But you can't immediately create a new bug and save it in the Resolved state, even if you already fixed the bug that you found, and you're just creating the bug work item as a record of what you did. You must first save it in an Active state, then change the state to Resolved, and then save it again.

This may seem cumbersome at first, but the reason is that the work item type may define rules that must be satisfied as a work item transition from one state to another. Additionally, the meaning of some fields changes during its lifecycle, so each time you save in a new state, the available choices for a field may change. For example, when you create a new bug using the Agile process template, the Reason field helps to indicate how a bug was discovered. When you are transitioning the same bug from Active to Resolved, the Reason state indicates why you are doing so (the bug was fixed, or couldn't be reproduced, or was a duplicate, and so on).

The interface for creating and editing work items with Visual Studio is very straightforward. What can be difficult to master is an understanding of all of the fields found throughout the work item types, their transitions, when to use them, and so on.

For the process templates provided by Microsoft, the documentation is very thorough, and is recommended reading to help you decide how to best adopt these process templates within your team. But wholesale adoption of these templates isn't for every team. You should feel empowered as a team to decide which fields are more or less important than others. You may even decide to add to or simplify the work item types to better meet your needs. Process template customization is covered in Chapter 12.

DELETING WORK ITEMS

A common complaint by people who are new to using work items with Team Foundation Server is that work items can't (easily) be deleted. This was a design decision by Microsoft. Organizations do not want bugs, requirements, or other important work items in a project to be accidentally (or maliciously) deleted, so there isn't an option within Visual Studio or the other clients you'll read about in this chapter for deleting work items.

But the Team Foundation Server 2010 Power Tools (available for download from `http://msdn.microsoft.com/en-us/vstudio/bb980963.aspx`) make deletion possible from a command prompt. After installing the Power Tools, open a Visual Studio command prompt and type **witadmin destroywi /?** for the command-line syntax help. This action is not reversible, so take care when using it.

Microsoft's recommended approach is to transition work items as appropriate instead of deleting them. For example, if you examine the state diagram in Figure 11-2, you will see that valid reasons for resolving a Bug work item include indicating that the bug can't be reproduced, it's obsolete (maybe it refers to a feature or functionality that has been removed or changed), or it's a duplicate of a bug that already exists.

While it might be tempting to just want to delete these work items instead of resolving them using one of these reasons, the resolution data might prove useful later for a QA lead to discover that a tester isn't doing his or her job effectively when filing these erroneous bugs. It's easy to generate a report later on showing, for example, all of the bugs created by a tester that were later discovered to be duplicates of existing bugs. But if those same work items are deleted, they won't show up in such a report.

Work Item Queries

Now that you know how to create work items, the next task you should learn about is how to find them. You can always right-click the `Work Items` node within Team Explorer and select Go to Work Item, but this assumes that you know the ID of all of your work items. Chances are you'll want to use queries most of the time.

The process template you are using probably includes some useful built-in queries already. Expand the `Work Items` node of Team Explorer to reveal the `My Queries` and `Team Queries` folders. The `Team Queries` folder is visible to everybody on the team, whereas `My Queries` provides a location to save queries, which may only be useful to you. By keeping specialized queries in `My Queries`, you can avoid creating too much clutter for your fellow team members.

> You should consider using permissions to lock down queries within the shared `Team Queries` node. This will prevent someone from accidentally overwriting a shared query with their own, which might cause unexpected results for others. You can set security on a query or query folder within `Team Queries` by right-clicking it and selecting Security.

If you have an existing query, you can simply double-click it to run it. Your results will vary based on the type of query you run, and the number of matching work items in your team project, but it will look something like the query results shown in Figure 11-7.

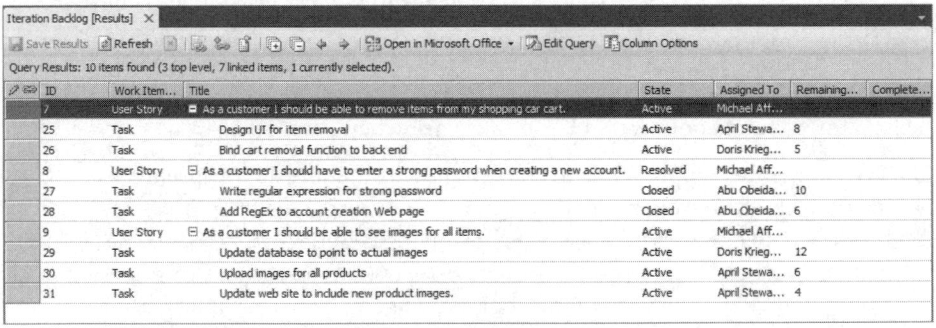

FIGURE 11-7: Results of a tree query

The query results shown in Figure 11-7 are of a "Tree of Work Items" query. This query type returns a list of work items matching your query, and groups them according to their parent/child relationships. In this example, there are top-level User Story work items that are linked to child task work items.

Another type of query is "Work Items and Direct Links." This type of query is similar to the "Tree of Work Items" query, except that you are not limited to parent/child links. For example, you can specify that you want to see all user stories and their test cases as represented by a tested by link type. You can even construct a query that shows all of your user stories that *do not* have linked test cases; this is useful for spotting potential holes in your test plan.

Finally, the *Flat List* query type does not show any link types and is the same type of query found in previous versions of Team Foundation Server.

From within the query results window, you can open a work item simply by double-clicking it. You also have several options available to you from the toolbar located at the top of the query results window. You can place your mouse over these toolbar icons to learn more about them. The available options will vary slightly between query types, but all of them allow you to create new work items (linked to any work items you have highlighted), to open your query results in Microsoft Project or Excel (more on this later), to change which columns are displayed in your query results (and in which order), and to edit the query you are working with.

The query editor shown in Figure 11-8 is the result of having opened the query from Figure 11-7 and clicking Edit Query.

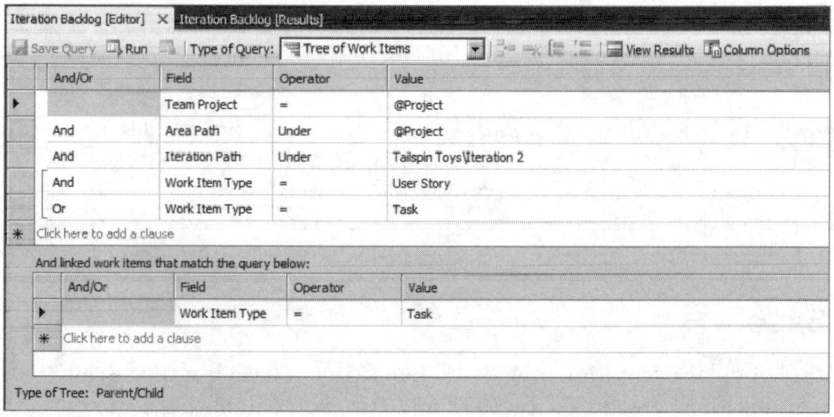

	And/Or	Field	Operator	Value
▶		Team Project	=	@Project
	And	Area Path	Under	@Project
	And	Iteration Path	Under	Tailspin Toys\Iteration 2
	And	Work Item Type	=	User Story
	Or	Work Item Type	=	Task
✳	Click here to add a clause			

And linked work items that match the query below:

	And/Or	Field	Operator	Value
▶		Work Item Type	=	Task
✳	Click here to add a clause			

Type of Tree: Parent/Child

FIGURE 11-8: Query editor

Even if you've never used queries with Team Foundation Server before, this query should be fairly straightforward to reverse-engineer to learn what it does.

The first row (Team Project = @Project) means that your query results should be scoped to the team project where the project is saved. If you delete this row, your results may return work items from the entire team project collection. @Project is a *query variable*. Query variables are converted into their respective values when the query is executed. So, for this project, @Project will resolve to "Tailspin Toys." By using query variables, you can write more flexible queries. The two other query variables available to you are @Me (which is converted into the username of the person running a query) and @Today (which is converted into today's date).

The next row of the query (AND Area Path Under @Project) indicates that work items from any area path of this project can be included, since the area path specified is the top-level area path (for this project, that means that @Project will resolve to the \Tailspin Toys\ area path). You could change this clause to something like AND Area Path Under Tailspin Toys\Web site if you wanted to restrict results to work items related to your website. Since you are using the Under operator, if you had further sub-paths (such as Tailspin Toys\Web site\Shopping cart), these would be included as well. If you wanted to restrict the results so that the area path matched exactly what was specified in the rightmost column, you could change the operator to the equals sign (=).

The third clause (AND Iteration Path Under Tailspin Toys\Iteration 2) is similar to the second clause. This means that work items must be assigned to an iteration of Iteration 2 (or anything under this path).

Clauses four and five are grouped together (as shown by the vertical bracket on the far-left side of the query). This means that they should be interpreted together, in much the same way that math operations within parentheses or brackets are interpreted together. These clauses, when interpreted together, mean *Return work items with a work item type of User Story OR a work item type of Task.*

Finally, because the query type for this query is a "Tree of Work Items," there is a second grid (labeled "And linked work items that match the query below:"), which allows you to specify any constraints on the child work items that are returned. In this example, only task work items will be returned as children.

> *Work item queries can be very powerful, and the options for creating queries are endless. A full guide for understanding how to use queries can be found at* http://msdn.microsoft.com/en-us/library/dd286705.aspx.

Using Microsoft Excel

Microsoft Excel is another popular client for editing work items. If you have installed Team Explorer 2010 on a machine with Microsoft Excel (2007 or 2010), you will have a Team tab available from the Office ribbon, which allows you to interface with Team Foundation Server 2010.

There are two ways of opening work items in Excel. One option is to open query results from within Team Explorer and then, from the query results toolbar, click Open in Microsoft Office ➪ Open in Microsoft Excel. The other approach is to start in Excel, open the Team tab from the Office ribbon, then click New List. You will be prompted to select your Team Foundation Server and team project, along with the query for the work items you want to manage. Or, instead of a query, you can start with an empty list. This allows you to enter new work items, or to select individual work items to add to your list by clicking Get Work Items.

Managing work items in Excel is a fairly rich experience. You can create new work items, make edits to existing work items, and even manage "Trees of Work Items." Figure 11-9 shows the results of the same query you saw earlier. Note that parent/child relationships are represented here as well. Parent work items have their titles listed in the Title 1 column, and their children have their titles listed in the Title 2 column. If you added a third level to the tree, grandchild work items would be listed in a column named Title 3, and so on.

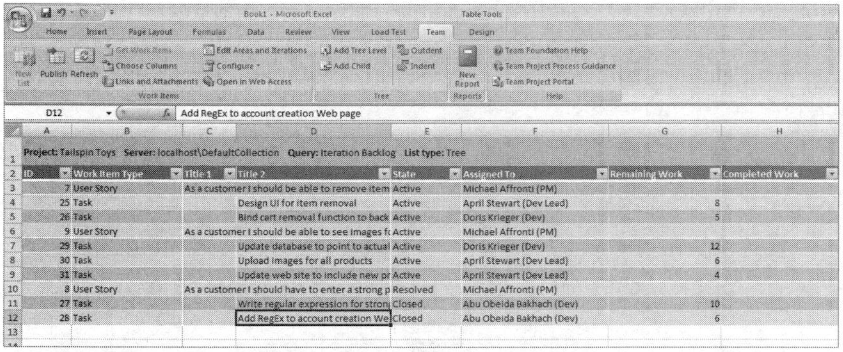

FIGURE 11-9: Work items in Excel

You can make any changes you want to within your Excel grid. You can add new work items for a "Tree of Work Items" query by clicking an existing work item and clicking Add Child from the Team tab of the ribbon. For queries of type Flat List or "Work Items and Direct Links" (which is also compressed to a flat list view in Excel), you can simply place your cursor on a new row at the bottom of your grid, and start typing to begin creating a new work item.

Note, however, that none of your work will be persisted to Team Foundation Server until you click Publish from the Team tab of the ribbon. Even if you save the Excel workbook file, your work items won't be synchronized to Team Foundation Server until you publish them.

> *In order to access the Publish button from the Team tab, your cursor will need to be within a cell that is a part of your work item grid. Otherwise, the Publish button will be disabled.*

You will receive an error message if the values you entered for work items in Excel do not conform to the validation rules or state transition workflow for the work item type. At this point, you can even view the offending work items using the same form view you are familiar with from Visual Studio.

> *Excel is a useful tool for making bulk edits of work items, for quickly importing several work items between team projects, or for people who just prefer working with Excel over Visual Studio. You can read more about using Excel as a work item client at* http://msdn.microsoft.com/en-us/library/ms181695.aspx.

Agile Workbooks

As mentioned earlier, Microsoft has made several Excel-bound workbooks available with the MSF for Agile Software Development process template. These workbooks can make it easier to manage resources, iterations, and your backlog. When you use the MSF for Agile Software Development process template, these workbooks are available under Documents ⇨ Shared Documents. The file Product Planning.xlsm is intended to manage your backlog, and to help you decide which User Story work items you can address in upcoming iterations.

The more interesting workbooks, however, are the iteration workbooks found under the `Iteration` 1, 2, and 3 folders. These workbooks help you to break down the user stories identified for that iteration into their component child tasks. After you have broken down your work into child tasks, you can begin assigning tasks to team members.

> *If you rename the existing iterations (Iteration 1, 2, 3...) or create new iterations, you must manually update the iteration workbooks. You can do this via Team ➪ Configure ➪ List by pointing to an appropriate query for the iteration you are planning.*

Figure 11-10 shows the Capacity tab of the workbook, which allows you to examine (at a glance) the capacity of each of your team members. In this example, it looks like April Stewart might be overcommitted. You can choose to assign her work to somebody who has some spare capacity. Or, you could decide that, as a team, you're just taking on too much work in this iteration, and that some of it needs to be returned to the backlog for a future iteration. The goal of these workbooks is to help you to quickly make resource decisions — perhaps during a weekly planning meeting with your team.

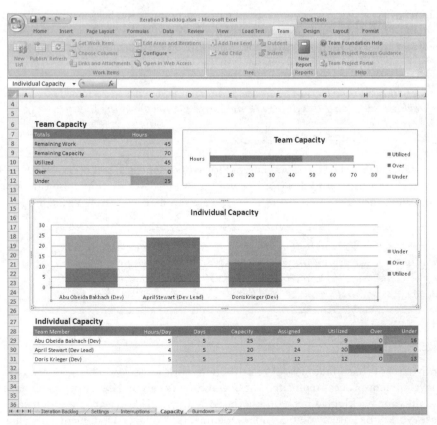

FIGURE 11-10: Agile workbook

After you have balanced the amount of committed work against your available resources, you can publish these changes to Team Foundation Server. If unintended events crop up (such as a team member getting sick), you can always revisit this workbook to examine the impact on your plan and make the proper reallocations.

> *These workbooks can be useful tools, and since they are based on Excel, you can easily customize them to change the way they behave. You can get step-by-step instructions for using these workbooks at* http://msdn.microsoft.com/en-us/library/dd997891.aspx.

Using Microsoft Project

Microsoft Project is one of the most popular project management tools in the world, and supports integration with Team Foundation Server. If you have installed Team Explorer 2010 on a machine with Microsoft Project Professional (2007 or 2010) or Standard, you will have a Team menu that allows you to interface with Team Foundation Server 2010.

As with Excel, you can either start with a query in Team Explorer (and choose Open in Microsoft Office ⇨ Open in Microsoft Project), or you can open Project and use the Team menu to access a query of work items from Team Foundation Server. Figure 11-11 shows work items being managed by Microsoft Project.

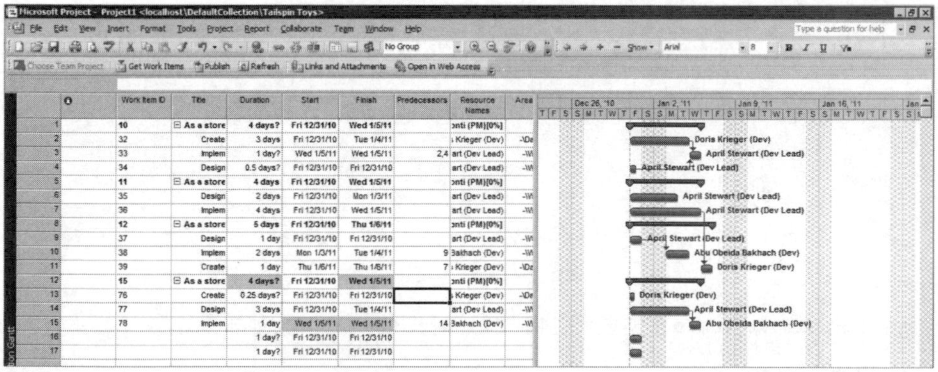

FIGURE 11-11: Work items in Project

Project will also display work items according to their parent/child relationships. A major benefit of using Project to view your work items is that it's easy to visualize dependency relationships (successor/predecessor) using the built-in Gannt chart visualization that Project is popular for. In Figure 11-11, it's easy to see that some work items have dependencies on others, which can be helpful for teams deciding how to prioritize their work.

Like Excel, changes to work items that you make within Project are not synchronized to Team Foundation Server until you click Publish from the Team menu.

> 🖊 *You can learn more about using Project for managing work items at* http://
> msdn.microsoft.com/en-us/library/dd286701.aspx.

Using Team Web Access

Team Web Access provides yet another way of managing your work items. You learned about how to connect to Team Web Access in Chapter 4. Team Web Access provides a rich, web-based way of accessing Team Foundation Server. An obvious benefit of Team Web Access is that users do not need to have any software other than a web browser. Figure 11-12 shows Team Web Access being used to manage work items.

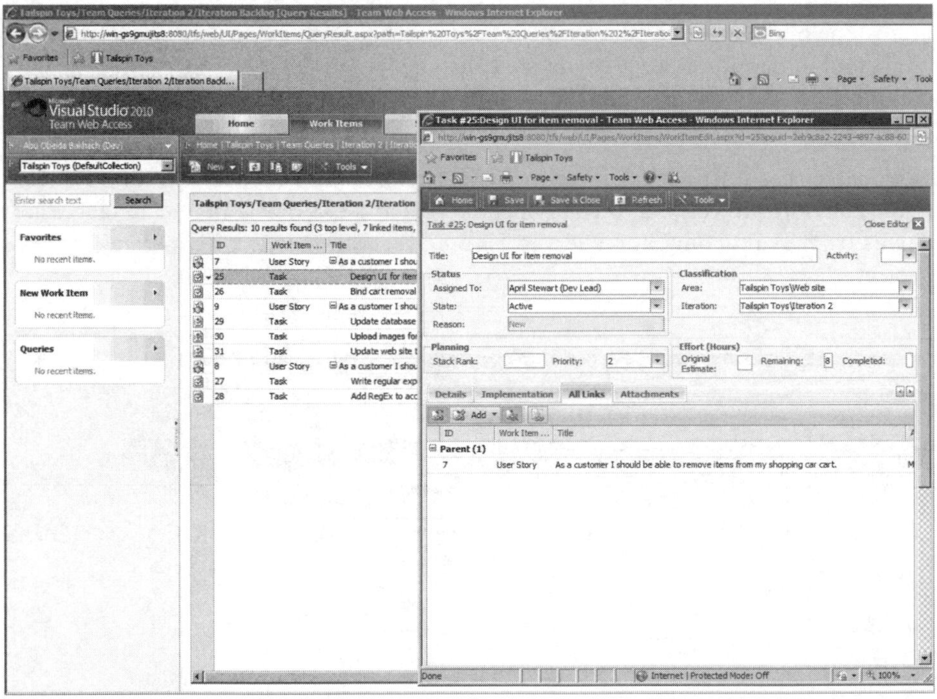

FIGURE 11-12: Team Web Access

Team Web Access provides a surprising number of features for a web-based client. You can even edit queries with it. It also has one unique feature that is currently lacking in the other clients — a full-text work item search. To search for work items using Team Web Access, simply type your search string into the text box in the left-hand margin of the website and click Search.

Team Web Access makes an ideal work item client for users who don't have Team Explorer installed. Some organizations even encourage end users to file bugs and enhancement requests about their software using Team Web Access.

> *You can read more about using Team Web Access as a work item client at*
> http://msdn.microsoft.com/en-us/library/ee523998.aspx.

> *If you are interested in using Team Web Access as a way for end users to file and track bugs and enhancement requests, you should consider the Work Item Only View version of Team Web Access. When users connect to Team Foundation Server using the Work Item Only View, they do not need to have a client access license (CAL) for Team Foundation Server. For more details on enabling Work Item Only View for your end users, see* http://msdn.microsoft.com/en-us/library/cc668124.aspx.

Using Third-Party Tools

In addition to the tools mentioned previously, there are several third-party tools available that integrate with Team Foundation Server 2010 and make use of work items. The following sections examine just a small sampling of the many tools that integrate with Team Foundation Server 2010. A more complete, up-to-date list of tools can be found at www.visualstudiowidgets.com/.

AIT Task Board

The AIT Task Board (built by AIT GmbH & Co.) provides a graphical way of viewing your project's work items and managing them in a visually pleasing manner. If you're familiar with managing projects using sticky notes on a whiteboard, then you will be instantly familiar with the AIT Task Board interface.

The AIT Task Board advertises compatibility with any Team Foundation Server 2010 process template, and can be quickly customized to display your preferred work item types and states.

The AIT Task Board can be downloaded for free at http://tinyurl.com/AITTaskBoard.

TeamSpec

TeamSpec (by TeamSolutions) provides an innovative way of using work items by integrating them directly with Microsoft Word. The makers of TeamSpec recognized that Microsoft Word is the world's most popular tool for capturing and iterating on software requirements. With this in mind, they built TeamSpec to allow business analysts to author requirements in Word, and easily publish them to Team Foundation Server.

TeamSpec uses templates and skins to identify which areas of a Word document should correspond to work item types in Team Foundation Server. When a spec is finished in Word, it can be published to Team Foundation Server, and the appropriate work items are generated automatically. The solution is also bidirectional, meaning that if requirements change in Team Foundation Server, a business analyst can update the Word document, review it with the end users, and ensure that it still meets the users' needs.

You can learn more about TeamSpec at www.teamsystemsolutions.com/teamspec/.

Urban Turtle

Urban Turtle (http://urbanturtle.com/) is another great backlog and iteration planning tool that provides a nice alternative to the agile workbooks provided by Microsoft. It also provides a task board, similar to the one provided by AIT. One of the really nice aspects of Urban Turtle is that it neatly integrates into Team Web Access as a new set of tabs.

PROJECT SERVER INTEGRATION

Earlier in this chapter, you learned about how Microsoft Project can be used to create project plans with your work items in Team Foundation Server 2010. But organizations that utilize Project Server may also be interested in the capability of Team Foundation Server 2010 to integrate with their Project Server 2007 or 2010 deployments.

This integration allows planning and status information from your development team, using Team Foundation Server, to flow through to your project management office, using Project Server. This enables the software development team to use a single tool — Team Foundation Server — for managing their work, while allowing Project Server users to easily report on and participate in project management activities from those same projects.

In order to enable this integration, you must install and configure the Team Foundation Server 2010 and Project Server Integration Feature Pack. This Feature Pack and the accompanying documentation are available via certain MSDN subscription levels. Once installed, you can determine which work items in Team Foundation Server should be synchronized with work in Project Server. You can even decide, for example, that parent user stories should be synchronized between the two systems, but that child tasks should remain in Team Foundation Server.

The integration service can then roll up the remaining and completed work being recorded against those tasks and synchronize that information to the User Story work item when it is updated in Project Server. This provides near real-time information to the project management office without overwhelming them with implementation details about your development project that they may not be interested in.

SUMMARY

In this chapter, you learned about the project management capabilities of Team Foundation Server 2010, with a focus on work item tracking.

You first learned about some of the major new enhancements related to project management that have been introduced in this release. You were introduced to work items, including the key components that make up work item types. You discovered the importance of process templates, which include pre-defined work item types, and you read overviews of several of the most popular process templates available for use with Team Foundation Server 2010. Finally, you were introduced to a variety of ways that you can manage your work items with Team Foundation Server 2010, including from within Visual Studio, Excel, Project, and through integration with Project Server.

In Chapter 12, you will learn about how work items and process templates are defined, and how you can customize them to best suit the needs of your team.

12

Customizing Process Templates

WHAT'S IN THIS CHAPTER?

➤ Understanding the artifacts contained in a process template

➤ Using the Process Template Editor

➤ Learning about custom work item controls

➤ Deploying custom work item controls to client machines

Although Team Foundation Server contains several great out-of-the-box process templates, and several quality third-party process templates exist in the supporting ecosystem, you may find the need to customize the process template in a multitude of different ways. Tools are available for editing the artifacts necessary for customizing a team project's process template.

This chapter introduces you to these tools and the different types of customizations that are available. You will also learn how to easily deploy changes to work item type definitions through the use of the automated build system in Team Foundation Server.

ANATOMY OF A PROCESS TEMPLATE

Process templates are built around the concept that a process should enable you, rather than hinder you. If you implement too little of a process, you must expend significant effort to stay on track. The inroads you make on a project will fully depend on the organizational skills of your team. The infrastructure will not support or enforce your process. Too much process inhibits productivity and velocity.

Process templates in Team Foundation Server 2010 provide a way to introduce the process to the entire team without getting in the way. When you create a new team project, process templates are used to set up the work items, work item queries, several shared documents, dashboards, reports, and more. A process template is a collection of files, including XML files, documents, and spreadsheets.

Before you start exploring the contents of a process template, it will be helpful for you to download an existing one by going to the Process Template Manager. Choose Process Template Manager from the Team Project Collection Settings menu on the team project collection node in the Team Explorer window, as shown in Figure 12-1.

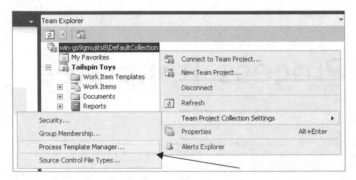

FIGURE 12-1: Downloading a process template

Next, you select a process template, click the Download button, and then choose the location where you want to save the process template files. Figure 12-2 shows the Process Template Manager dialog.

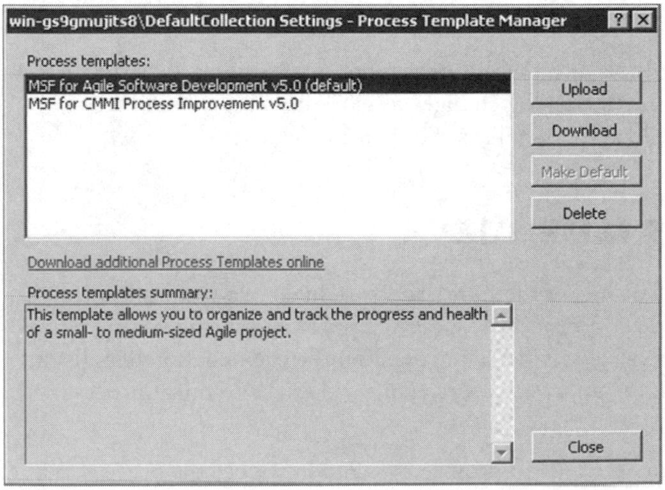

FIGURE 12-2: Process Template Manager dialog

Plug-in Files

Plug-in files are artifacts that are essential to the New Team Project wizard. Each plug-in file defines the tasks that will end up running during the wizard. The displayed screens used for gathering information during the wizard are also defined in the plug-in files.

Each plug-in reads the list of tasks and dependencies, and creates an automation sequence that will run during the team project creation wizard experience.

Table 12-1 lists each of the plug-in folders, plug-in files, and a description of what each file contains. Figure 12-3 also shows the directory layout inside a process template where each of the configuration files is stored.

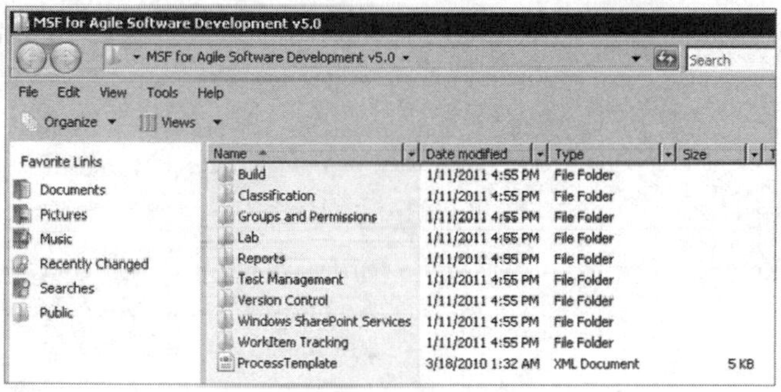

FIGURE 12-3: Directories in Process Template

TABLE 12-1: Process Template Plug-in Files

FOLDER	PLUG-IN FILE	DESCRIPTION
Build	Build.xml	Defines the tasks to configure the initial security permissions that are assigned to identities for Team Foundation Server Build, and uploads the build process template files.
Classification	Classification.xml	Defines the initial iterations and areas of a team project.
Groups & Permissions	GroupsandPermissions.xml	Defines the initial security groups of a team project and their permissions.
Lab	Lab.xml	Defines the tasks to configure the initial security permissions that are assigned to identities for Visual Studio Lab Management.
Reports	ReportsTasks.xml	Defines the initial reports for a team project, and sets up the report site.

continues

TABLE 12-1 *(continued)*

FOLDER	PLUG-IN FILE	DESCRIPTION
Test Management	TestManagement.xml	Defines the test management files to upload, which will create the initial test variables, configurations, settings, and resolution states of a team project. These settings are used by Microsoft Test Manager.
Version Control	VersionControl.xml	Defines the initial security permissions for version control, check-in notes for a team project, and whether exclusive check-out is required.
Work Item Tracking	WorkItems.xml	Defines the initial work item types, queries, and work item instances of a team project.
Windows SharePoint Services	WssTasks.xml	Defines the project portal for the team based on a template for a SharePoint site. Also defines template files and process guidance.

Source: MSDN Library (http://msdn.microsoft.com/en-us/library/ms243856.aspx)

Default Security Groups and Permissions

Each team project can contain security groups, and each has a set of permissions that are scoped to the team project level. The process template can create default team project security groups that can be used for setting permissions in each of the other plug-ins for the team project, as well as which permissions should be initially granted or denied for those security groups. For example, the Microsoft Solutions Framework (MSF) for Agile Software Development v5.0 process template defines the following default team project security groups:

- ➤ Readers
- ➤ Contributors
- ➤ Builders

> *Additionally, the team project creation wizard will create a security group called* Project Administrators *that will be granted all permissions. You do not have to define the group in the process template to be created.*

Figure 12-4 shows an example of what the MSF Agile process template defines for the default security groups.

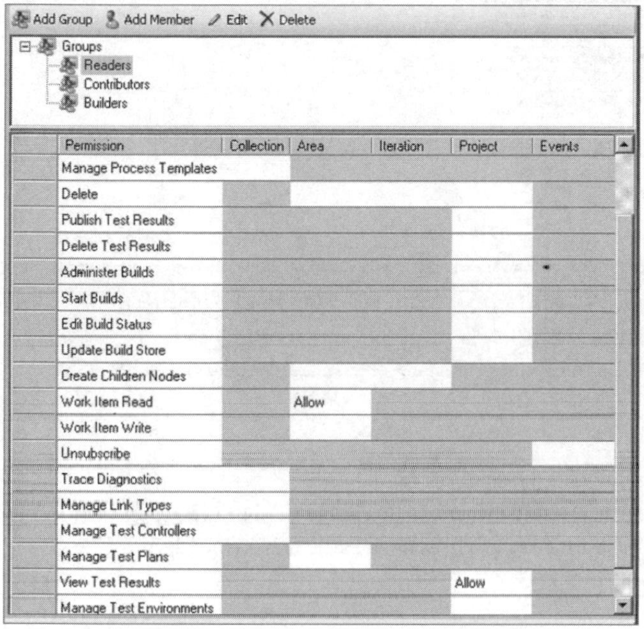

Add Group
Add Member
Edit
Delete
Groups
Readers
Contributors
Builders
Permission
Collection
Area
Iteration
Project
Events
Manage Process Templates
Delete
Publish Test Results
Delete Test Results
Administer Builds
Start Builds
Edit Build Status
Update Build Store
Create Children Nodes
Work Item Read
Allow
Work Item Write
Unsubscribe
Trace Diagnostics
Manage Link Types
Manage Test Controllers
Manage Test Plans
View Test Results
Allow
Manage Test Environments

FIGURE 12-4: Default security group definitions for MSF Agile process template

> *Chapter 20 provides more information about managing security privileges and permissions.*

Initial Area and Iteration Nodes

If there will be standard area path and iteration path nodes that should be available for each new team project, you can define those initial nodes in the process template. Figure 12-5 shows the default iteration nodes that are created when using the MSF Agile process template.

Areas
Iterations
MS Project Mapping
Iteration
Iteration 1
Iteration 2
Iteration 3

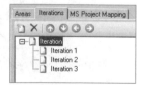

FIGURE 12-5: Default iteration nodes

Work Item Type Definitions

Work item type definitions are the files that contain information about which states, transitions, fields, and form layouts exist on a particular work item type. Work item type definition files are by far the most commonly customized artifacts in a process template. The main process template file lists each of the work item type definitions that should be included, as well as the location of the individual work item type definition files, as shown in Figure 12-6.

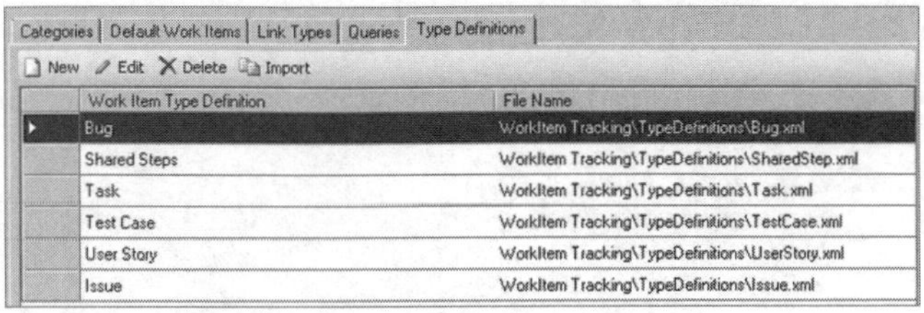

FIGURE 12-6: Work item type definitions to be included and location of files

> *Chapter 11 provides more information about the default work item types that are available in the standard process templates.*

Work Item Fields

One of the defining parts of the work item type definition is the list of fields that are contained for that work item type. Each field can have the attributes shown in Table 12-2 that define it.

TABLE 12-2: Field Attributes

FIELD	DESCRIPTION
Name	This is the friendly name that is used for the work item query. Each field in a team project collection must contain a unique name.
Field Type	This attribute defines the type of data that will be stored in the field. Among all of the types that are available, the following types are commonly used: `String`, `Integer`, `Double`, `DateTime`, `PlainText`, and `Html`. The correct type should be chosen, since it cannot be changed after the field is created in the team project collection.
Reference Name	This attribute defines a longer name for use in organizing multiple fields. Each field in a work item type definition must contain a unique reference name. You will probably want to distinguish your company's custom fields by prefacing the reference name with your company name (for example, `Contoso.MyNewCustomField`).
Help Text	This describes the field's purpose to the end user. The help text is displayed whenever hovering over a field's label on the work item forms.

FIELD	DESCRIPTION
Reportable & Formula	This attribute indicates how the field will be handled when the data warehouse jobs process it. The possible values for this attribute are `None`, `Dimension`, `Detail`, and `Measure`. The correct option should be chosen, since, once it is set to something other than `None`, you won't be able to change it. For example, the number of hours remaining for a task would be defined as a measure, but the task's priority and to whom it is assigned would be defined as dimensions. Fields marked as a `Detail` do not show up in the Analysis Services warehouse cube, but do show up in the relational data warehouse.
Reportable Reference Name	By default, the name that is used for the data warehouse is the *reference name*. However, if fields in multiple team project collections must have a different reference name, but still be reported as the same field, this attribute can be defined. The reportable reference name should be unique for each team project collection.
Reportable Name	In addition to the reportable reference name, a friendly reportable name is offered as well. It is similar to the name of the field, and is used in the warehouse.

> *You must be careful not to create too many fields, but, rather, reuse them across work item types, team projects, and team project collections as necessary. By reusing the same reference names (or reportable names if different) for fields, you also benefit from being able to report the same data across team projects and team project collections, even if they are using different process template types. You can even create work item queries that use the same field across multiple team projects for showing up as a column in the query results.*
>
> *The maximum number of fields for all work item types in a team project collection is approximately 1,000. Additionally, a total of approximately 1,000 reportable fields can be defined across all team project collections for one Team Foundation Server instance. These maximums happen to correspond to the number of columns that can be created in a SQL Server table, less some overhead that is used by Team Foundation Server.*

Work item fields can also contain rules that are applied to the field at run time. Multiple rules can be specified to be applied for a single field. Table 12-3 shows some examples of common field rules that can be used.

TABLE 12-3: Field Rule Examples

RULE	DESCRIPTION
DEFAULT	This rule allows for a value to be specified as the default value for a field. This can be the current date/time, user information, another field's value, or a specified literal value.
ALLOWEDVALUES	This rule indicates a list of values that are allowed for this field. This can be a list of literal values, or an entry for a global list. For example, you might want to constrain the values of a Priority field to the integers 1 through 4.
REQUIRED	This rule indicates that the field is required to contain a value.
VALIDUSER	This rule indicates that the value of the field must contain the name of a valid user who has permissions to access Team Foundation Server.
SERVERDEFAULT	This rule is particularly useful in states and transitions whenever the current user, or the current date and time, should be stored in a particular field.
COPY	This rule can be used to copy a value from another field, date/time from the clock, current user information, or from a specified literal value.
READONLY	This indicates that that field cannot be edited.
ALLOWEXISTINGVALUE	This rule allows for an existing value to still be valid even if it is removed as an allowed value in the future. This applies as long as the field does not change values.

Several rules have optional `for` and `not` attributes that can be specified to indicate whether that rule applies to a security group (`for` attribute), or does not apply to the security group (`not` attribute). For example, a `REQUIRED` rule can be added to a field for the `Contributors` security group by specifying the group in the `for` attribute, but the `Project Administrators` security group can be excluded by specifying the group in the `not` attribute.

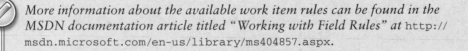

More information about the available work item rules can be found in the MSDN documentation article titled "Working with Field Rules" at `http://msdn.microsoft.com/en-us/library/ms404857.aspx.`

Work Item States and Transitions

Work items can be classified in different states, and a workflow between those states can be defined using transitions. Each transition can contain a *reason* for the transition. For example, a bug can be in the state of Active, and then transitioned to the Resolved state with a reason of Fixed, Duplicate, As Designed, Cannot Reproduce, Deferred, and so on. The combination of state and reason can be used for reporting and for work item queries to further distinguish between work items in the same state.

Each work item can only have one initial transition that can contain multiple reasons. Figure 12-7 shows the states and transitions for the Bug work item type in the MSF Agile process template. Figure 12-7 also shows the available reasons for the transition between the Active and Resolved states.

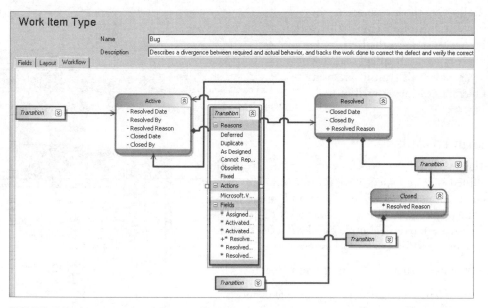

FIGURE 12-7: States and transitions for the Bug work item type

Rules for States and Transitions

Previously in this chapter, you learned that rules can be applied to fields globally for the work item type. Rules can also be applied at the state level or at a particular transition or reason. A combination of all of the rules is applied based on the rules defined at the field, state, transition, and reason scopes. Figure 12-8 shows the different field rules that are specified for the `System .AssignedTo` field on the transition between the Active and Resolved states.

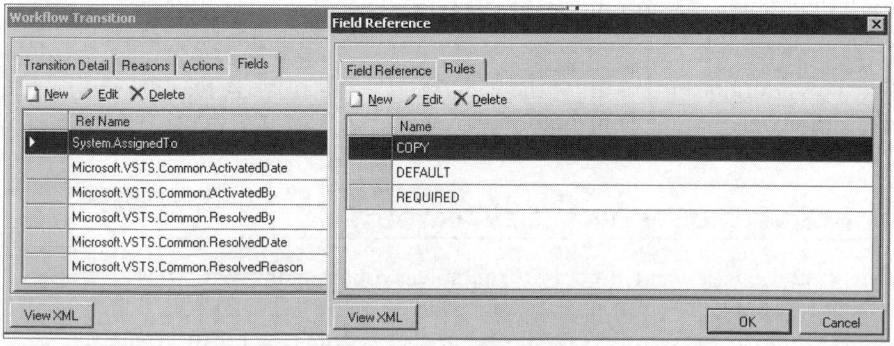

FIGURE 12-8: Different field rules

You can also restrict certain transitions using the same `for` and `not` attributes that are used for certain field rules. Figure 12-9 shows those attributes being specified for transition between the Active and Resolved states. In this case, you are allowing those that are in the Contributors security group to move the work item from the Active state to the Resolved state, but members of the Readers security group can never make this transition, even if they are a member of the Contributors security group.

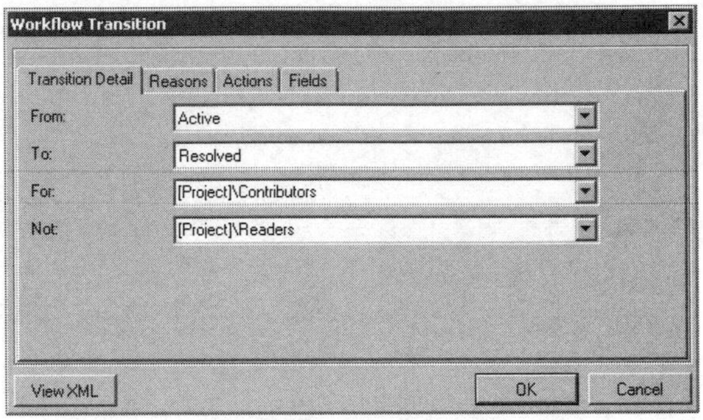

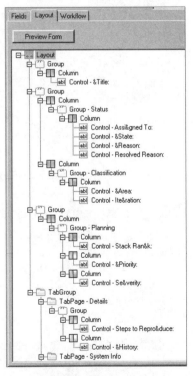

FIGURE 12-9: Attributes being specified for transition

Work Item Form Layouts

Once all of the fields and the workflow of states and transitions have been defined, you can specify what the work item form will look like when it is opened in any of the Team Foundation Server client tools. The layout is specified by using a set of items. Figure 12-10 shows a partial example of a layout for the Bug work item type in the MSF Agile process template.

Following are the items that can be used on the form:

➤ *Group* — This container can include one or more columns, and optionally can specify a display name for the container.

➤ *Column* — A column is contained within a group, and can be either a fixed width, or have a width that is percentage-based relative to the other columns in the same group.

➤ *Control* — This item can be added to other container units, and allows the presentation of a work item control that can edit a field or display other information.

➤ *Tab Group* — This container begins a new grouping of tab pages.

➤ *Tab Page* — This container stores all of the items that would exist inside a particular named tab.

FIGURE 12-10: Layout for the Bug work item type

CONSIDERATIONS FOR DIFFERENT CLIENT LAYOUTS

Work item type definitions can actually specify multiple layout sections that target specific clients. For example, you might specify a particular layout when a work item is opened in Visual Studio Team Web Access, versus one that is displayed for the Visual Studio Team Explorer client. Following are the available work item form layout values:

> ➤ *WinForms* — This layout target is used in the Visual Studio Team Explorer client, and additionally in Microsoft Test Manager.
>
> ➤ *Web* — This layout target is used by Visual Studio Team Web Access.
>
> ➤ *JavaSWT* — This layout target is used by Visual Studio Team Explorer Everywhere that displays within Eclipse-based products.
>
> ➤ *Unspecified* — If no other display targets are specified, then clients can ultimately fall back to using the *Unspecified* layout.
>
> The current version of the Process Template editor does not support editing multiple work item form layouts. If you choose to use multiple work item form layouts, then you must use the XML editing approach described later in this chapter.

Standard Work Item Controls

There are several standard work item controls that are available for displaying and editing fields in the form layout. Table 12-4 describes each of the available standard work item controls.

TABLE 12-4: Standard Work Item Controls

CONTROL	DESCRIPTION
Field	This control is used for standard field editing, and can accommodate many of the different field types without any special editing features.
Date Time	This control has special editing features available for date/time fields. For example, this control can be used to provide a standard calendar control that the user can use to edit a field.
HTML Field	This control allows an end user to edit with rich text for HTML fields. In Visual Studio Team Explorer 2010, a new rich editing toolbar is displayed immediately above the control to allow the end user to easily reach the commonly used rich editing options available for an HTML field.
Links	This control does not specify a particular field to edit, but instead allows a user to edit the different links of multiple link types that are currently set on a work item. The control additionally has filter options to filter certain types of work item link types, work item types, and external link types from showing in an instance of the links control.
Attachments	This control provides the end user with the capability to manage the file attachments on a work item. However, it does not modify a particular work item field.

continues

TABLE 12-4 *(continued)*

CONTROL	DESCRIPTION
Work Item Classification	This control is only used for editing the Area Path and Iteration Path fields, and displays the available nodes in a tree control.
Work Item Log	This control shows a view of the historical revisions for a work item, including the comments for each of the revisions. Additionally, end users can specify a rich-text comment to be stored with a particular revision of the work item as soon as the end user saves the work item changes.
Label	This control allows for a label to be specified on the work item form. The label can specify a plain-text value, and include a link to a static URL or a dynamic-based link that uses several supported macros (such as @ReportServicesSiteUrl, @ReportManagerUrl, @PortalPage, @ProcessGuidance, and @Me.)
Webpage	This control can display literal HTML data, or point to a static or dynamic-based URL that can also use any of the support macros mentioned on the label control. Additionally, the UrlPath attribute can contain string parameters (similar to when using format strings in the .NET method String.Format()), and specify another field's value for use as the parameter to the dynamic URL.
Associated Automation	This control is used on the Test Case work item type to display and/or edit the associated automation for the Test Case work item.
Test Steps	This control is used on the Test Case work item type to show and/or edit the test steps for the Test Case work item. The test steps can only be edited in Microsoft Test Manager, and will be a read-only view of the test steps in the other available clients.

Work Item Categories

Team Foundation Server 2010 introduces a new work item tracking feature called *work item categories*. This feature allows for work item types with different names in different team projects to be used in external tools, in reporting, and in work item queries. For example, one team project may have a work item type with the name of "Bug" where another has a work item type called "Defect" that need to appear together in metrics on reports that pull data from both team projects.

Microsoft Test Manager is one example of an external tool that uses the work item categories to create and select work items based on their categories. Multiple work item types can be included in a work item category, and one is identified as the default work item type for the individual category.

Figure 12-11 shows the default work item categories that are specified in the MSF Agile process template.

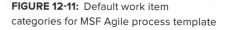

FIGURE 12-11: Default work item categories for MSF Agile process template

Work Item Link Types

Team Foundation Server 2010 also introduces the concept of *rich link types* that can be used throughout Team Foundation Server for reporting and querying work items. These rich link types truly allow full traceability between work items stored in Team Foundation Server. Each link type can have a specific topology, and also have a different name that describes each end of the link.

Table 12-5 shows the standard link types that are available.

TABLE 12-5: Standard Defined Link Types

FORWARD NAME	REVERSE NAME	LINK TYPE REFERENCE NAME	TOPOLOGY
Successor	Predecessor	`System.LinkTypes.Dependency`	Dependency
Child	Parent	`System.LinkTypes.Hierarchy`	Tree
Related	Related	`System.LinkTypes.Related`	Network
Tested By	Tests	`Microsoft.VSTS.Common.TestedBy`	Dependency
Test Case	Shared Steps	`Microsoft.VSTS.TestCase.SharedStepReferencedBy`	Dependency

Source: MSDN Library (http://msdn.microsoft.com/en-us/library/dd293527.aspx)

You can also create custom link types for your own purposes in customized process templates. Following are the different types of link topologies that are available in Team Foundation Server 2010:

➤ *Network* — Link types of this topology have essentially no rules and no directionality. You can have circular relationships, and the link looks the same from both ends. Figure 12-12 shows the network topology.

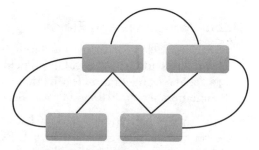

FIGURE 12-12: Network topology

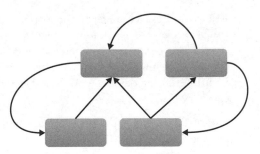
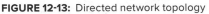

➤ *Directed Network* — Link types of this topology are network links, except that there is directionality. You can specify a name that appears at each link end. In other words, the link looks different depending from which side you view it. Figure 12-13 shows the directed network topology.

FIGURE 12-13: Directed network topology

➤ *Dependency* — Link types of this topology are like directed network links in that they have directionality, but also have an additional constraint to prevent circular relationships. Figure 12-14 shows the dependency topology.

➤ *Tree* — Link types of this topology are essentially trees that enforce a one-to-many relationship, and do not allow circular relationships. Figure 12-15 shows the tree topology.

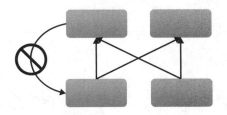

FIGURE 12-14: Dependency topology

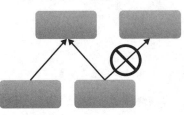

FIGURE 12-15: Tree topology

Global Lists

Global lists are available at the team project collection level to allow for managing common lists that are used in the work item tracking system.

For example, a company might have a list of departments that it would like to use in multiple work item types across several team projects. The company can specify an ALLOWEDVALUES field rule that includes only the values listed in the global list that is created for the departments.

Any time the list must be updated, the global list can be edited, and this does not involve deploying out new work item type definitions to each of the team projects.

Global Workflows and Fields

In Service Pack 1 for Team Foundation Server 2010, a new concept has been introduced to manage global fields and workflows. Global fields and workflows were primarily added to support the Project Server Integration feature that has been released to synchronize changes between Team Foundation Server 2010 and Project Server 2007 or 2010.

You can also take advantage of this new concept if you have upgraded your Team Foundation Server environment to Service Pack 1. Essentially, by defining a global workflow for a team project collection or specific team project, you are defining which fields should exist on all work item types across all of the team projects, or for the specified team project. Additionally, you can define global lists in the global workflow definition.

> You can find more information about global workflows in the MSDN
> documentation article at `http://msdn.microsoft.com/library/gg534720.aspx`.

Initial Work Items

The process template can also contain a list of initial work items that will be initialized during the team project creation process. This is useful if each new team project should contain a certain set of startup work items to kick-start the team project. By default, the standard MSF process templates do not create any default work items.

Work Item Queries and Folders

Certain work item queries and their organizational folder structure should be defined for a new team project in the process template. The standard work item queries should be included. Additionally, the default security and privileges for the work item query folders can be specified.

Figure 12-16 shows the default work item queries and query folders that are specified in the MSF Agile process template.

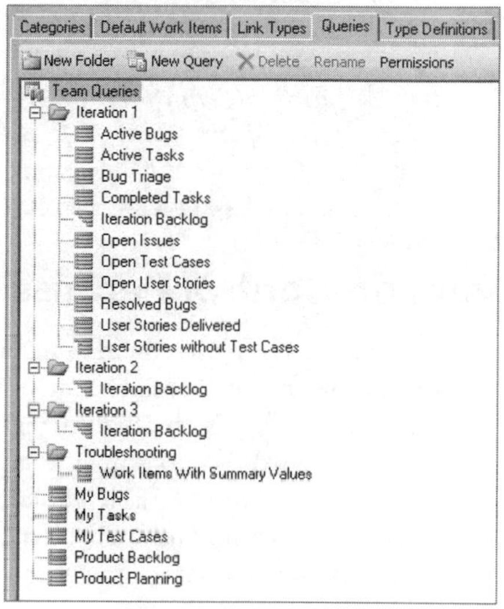

FIGURE 12-16: Default work item queries and query folders

Microsoft Project Column Mappings

The Microsoft Project column mappings file correlates work item fields to fields that are defined in a Microsoft Project file. Figure 12-17 shows the default Project column mappings that are defined in the MSF Agile process template.

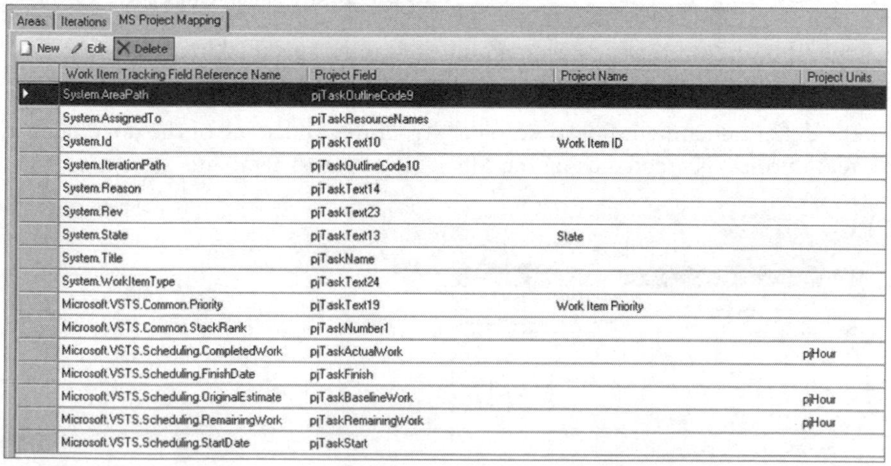

Work Item Tracking Field Reference Name	Project Field	Project Name	Project Units
System.AreaPath	pjTaskOutlineCode9		
System.AssignedTo	pjTaskResourceNames		
System.Id	pjTaskText10	Work Item ID	
System.IterationPath	pjTaskOutlineCode10		
System.Reason	pjTaskText14		
System.Rev	pjTaskText23		
System.State	pjTaskText13	State	
System.Title	pjTaskName		
System.WorkItemType	pjTaskText24		
Microsoft.VSTS.Common.Priority	pjTaskText19	Work Item Priority	
Microsoft.VSTS.Common.StackRank	pjTaskNumber1		
Microsoft.VSTS.Scheduling.CompletedWork	pjTaskActualWork		pjHour
Microsoft.VSTS.Scheduling.FinishDate	pjTaskFinish		
Microsoft.VSTS.Scheduling.OriginalEstimate	pjTaskBaselineWork		pjHour
Microsoft.VSTS.Scheduling.RemainingWork	pjTaskRemainingWork		pjHour
Microsoft.VSTS.Scheduling.StartDate	pjTaskStart		

FIGURE 12-17: Default Project column mappings

Each mapping can additionally specify an `IfSummaryRefreshOnly` optional attribute that indicates that if a Project task is a summary task that it will never publish its value back to Team Foundation Server, but will allow new values in Team Foundation Server to overwrite the value in the Project file. This is particularly useful for calculated fields in Project that should not be pushed back into Team Foundation Server.

> *More information about customizing the Microsoft Project field mappings files can be found in the MSDN Library at* `http://msdn.microsoft.com/en-us/library/ms404684.aspx`.

Version Control Permissions and Settings

The process template can also include the settings and permissions on the version control repository of the team project that is created during the team project creation wizard. For example, the "Enable multiple check-out" setting, "Enable get latest version on check-out" setting, and "Check-in notes" can be provided. Permissions for each group can also be specified.

Figure 12-18 shows the default permissions available to the `Contributors` security group in the MSF Agile process template.

SharePoint Project Team Portal Document Library Settings

If a SharePoint team project portal is created during the team project creation wizard, then the initial

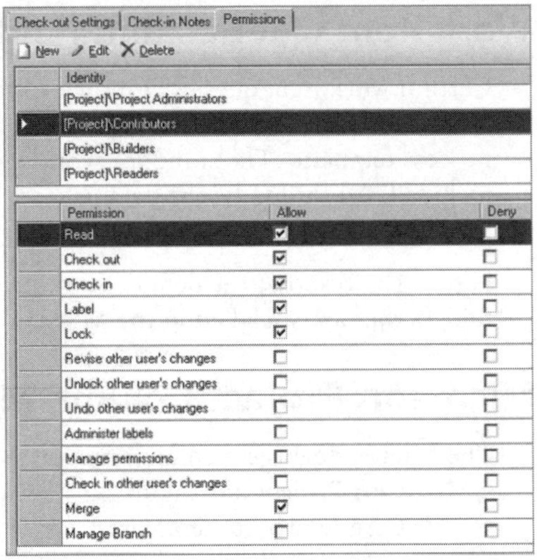

FIGURE 12-18: Default permissions

content for the document libraries in that new SharePoint site can be specified in the process template. Additionally, the process guidance documents for the process template are specified.

Figure 12-19 shows the default document libraries, folder structure, and some of the documents that are available after a team project is created using the MSF Agile process template.

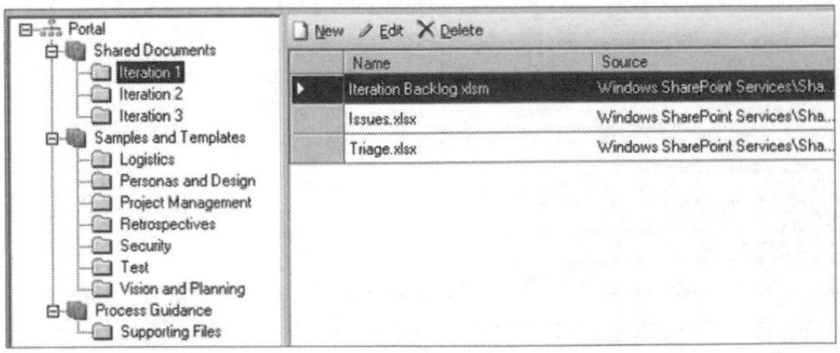

FIGURE 12-19: Default document libraries, folder structure, and some of the available documents

> *You cannot customize the Microsoft Excel report and SharePoint dashboards by customizing the process template files. These artifacts are created for a team project depending on the selection you make in the New Team Project wizard.*

SQL Reporting Services Report Definitions

The initial folder structure and reports in the related Reports site can also be specified in the process template. Figure 12-20 shows the list of each of the folders and SQL Reporting Services report definition files that will be uploaded to the Reports Manager site during the team project creation wizard.

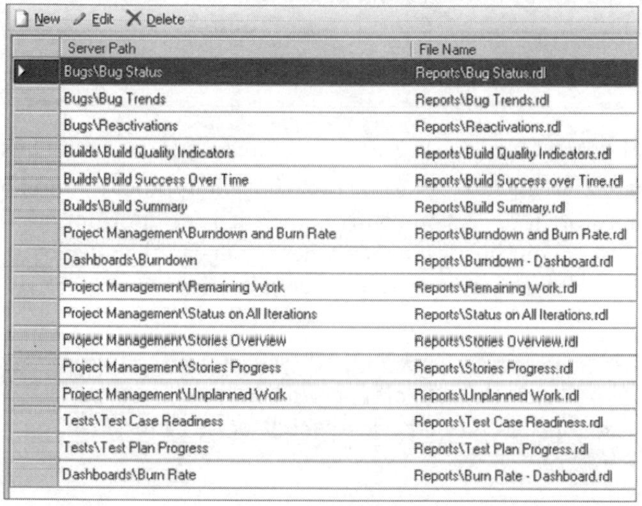

Server Path	File Name
Bugs\Bug Status	Reports\Bug Status.rdl
Bugs\Bug Trends	Reports\Bug Trends.rdl
Bugs\Reactivations	Reports\Reactivations.rdl
Builds\Build Quality Indicators	Reports\Build Quality Indicators.rdl
Builds\Build Success Over Time	Reports\Build Success over Time.rdl
Builds\Build Summary	Reports\Build Summary.rdl
Project Management\Burndown and Burn Rate	Reports\Burndown and Burn Rate.rdl
Dashboards\Burndown	Reports\Burndown - Dashboard.rdl
Project Management\Remaining Work	Reports\Remaining Work.rdl
Project Management\Status on All Iterations	Reports\Status on All Iterations.rdl
Project Management\Stories Overview	Reports\Stories Overview.rdl
Project Management\Stories Progress	Reports\Stories Progress.rdl
Project Management\Unplanned Work	Reports\Unplanned Work.rdl
Tests\Test Case Readiness	Reports\Test Case Readiness.rdl
Tests\Test Plan Progress	Reports\Test Plan Progress.rdl
Dashboards\Burn Rate	Reports\Burn Rate - Dashboard.rdl

FIGURE 12-20: Folders and SQL Reporting Services report definition files

USING THE PROCESS TEMPLATE EDITOR

Instead of editing each XML file by hand, you can use the Process Template Editor that is included with the latest version of the Team Foundation Server Power Tools. The Process Template Editor is comprised of a set of tools integrated into Visual Studio Team Explorer that allow you to edit work item type definitions, process template definition files, export/import work item type definitions, create/modify global lists, and includes a work item field explorer to view details about the fields included in a team project collection.

Installing the Process Template Editor

Before you begin installing the Power Tools, be sure to have all instances of Visual Studio completely closed, since the installer will be setting up and configuring several Visual Studio add-ins. The setup is available on Visual Studio Gallery, and is updated regularly.

The quickest way to find the latest download for the Power Tools installer is to go to your preferred search engine and use the search term "Team Foundation Server Power Tools." Currently, a list of all the Power Tools for the entire Visual Studio product line is listed at `http://msdn.microsoft` `.com/en-us/vstudio/bb980963.aspx`. That particular list is regularly updated, but, after new releases of the Power Tools, may not be completely up to date.

As of this writing, the current version of the Team Foundation Server Power Tools is the September 2010 edition.

> *Always be sure that you are using the latest version of the Team Foundation Server Power Tools. The Team Foundation Server product team at Microsoft continually improves the Power Tools with bug fixes and new features. A new version of the Power Tools is usually released every three to six months.*

Working with a Process Template

Instead of editing work item type definitions directly on the server (which is an option), it is a best practice to download the process template, store it in version control, and then edit it offline. When the changes you have made are ready and tested out in a test environment, you can then deploy those updates to your production Team Foundation Server team project collection(s).

> *Chapter 10 provides more information about storing process templates and managing other Team Foundation Server artifacts in the version control repository.*

Whenever you have the process template stored in an offline location, you can open the `ProcessTemplate.xml` file that is contained in the root folder for a process template, and the Process Template Editor window will display in Visual Studio. Figure 12-21 shows the root Process Template Editor window when opening the MSF Agile process template.

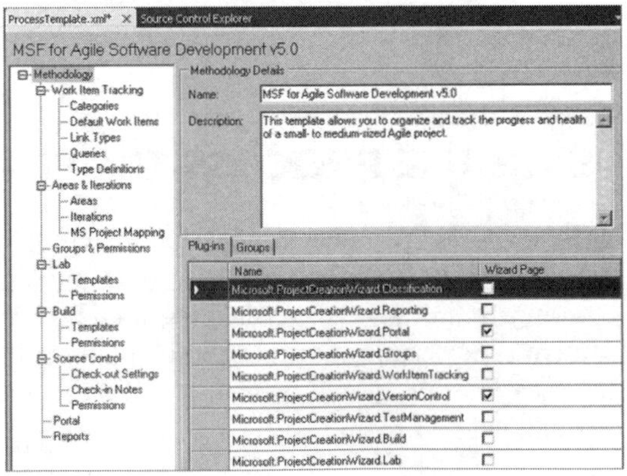

From the root window, you can edit all of the individual parts of the process template easily. For example, you can edit the work item type definitions by navigating to the Methodology ⇨ Work Item Tracking ⇨ Type Definitions node. Then select a work item type and click the Edit

FIGURE 12-21: Process Template Editor window

button. Many of these different parts were shown in earlier figures for this chapter in each heading that discussed the process template artifact types.

> *If you are interested in learning more about using the Process Template Editor, you can read through the help documentation that is included in the Team Foundation Server Power Tools installer. For 64-bit operating systems, the default location for the help documentation is* `C:\Program Files (x86)\Microsoft Team Foundation Server 2010 Power Tools\Help\ProcessEditor.mht.`

Using an XML Editor and WITAdmin

An alternate approach for managing process template and work item type definitions is to edit the XML files with your preferred XML file editor, and then use the command-line tools to export and import the work item type definitions. The XML schema is completely documented in the MSDN Library, and is available in the following locations:

➤ *Process Template Schema Reference* — `http://msdn.microsoft.com/en-us/library/aa395287.aspx`

➤ *Work Item Type Definition Schema Reference* — `http://msdn.microsoft.com/en-us/library/aa337615.aspx`

The command-line tool named `witadmin.exe` is actually a tool that is installed whenever you install Visual Studio Team Explorer (or another Visual Studio 2010 product). From a Visual Studio command prompt window (and with the appropriate permissions), you can perform several administrative functions to manage the work item tracking system.

Table 12-6 shows a few of the available commands, but you can always discover the full list by executing `witadmin.exe /?` at a Visual Studio command prompt window.

TABLE 12-6: Sample Commands for witadmin.exe

COMMAND	DESCRIPTION
`listfields`	This command is particularly useful when you need a list of all of the fields in a team project collection and their details. Each of the entries will even list all of the work item types and team projects that the field is being used by. When used with the `/unused` switch, you can also get a list of fields that exist in the team project collection that are completely unused.
`changefield`	This command allows you to update certain attributes for an existing field after it has been created. For example, you can update any of the name attributes, but you will notice that not all attributes can be changed (such as the field's type once it is created).
`deletefield`	This command will completely remove a field once it is unused by any work item type in any team project in the team project collection. It will also remove the field from the warehouse during the next warehouse processing cycle if this was the last team project collection that was using the specified field to be deleted.

continues

TABLE 12-6 *(continued)*

COMMAND	DESCRIPTION
`listwitd`	This command is helpful for listing the work item types that are available in a team project.
`renamewitd`	This command allows you to rename an existing work item type even if there are already work items of that type that have been created in a team project. For example, you may decide to rename the Requirement work item type to User Story or Feature at some point in the future.
`destroywi, destroywitd`	These commands allow you to completely destroy a particular work item (`destroywi`) or a work item type, and all its existing work items (`destroywitd`), in a team project. The data is not destroyed in the warehouse, and will remain until a full rebuild occurs.
`exportwitd, importwitd`	These commands allow for exporting and importing work item type definitions from a team project. If a work item type currently exists, then it will be replaced with the new work item type definition. Existing work items will use the new definition after it is imported.
`listlinktypes`	This command lists the available set of link types in a team project collection.
`exportlinktype, importlinktype`	These commands allow for exporting (`exportlinktype`) and importing (`importlinktype`) new link types for the team project collection. If the link type already exists, then it will be updated.
`exportcategories, importcategories`	These commands allow for exporting (`exportcategories`) and importing (`importcategories`) new work item category definitions for a specific team project. If the work item category already exists, then it will be updated.
`exportgloballist, importgloballist`	These commands allow for exporting (`exportgloballist`) and importing (`importgloballist`) global list definitions for a team project collection respectively. If a global list has the same name, it will be replaced with the newly imported global list definition.

DEPLOYING UPDATES TO PROCESS TEMPLATES

Now that you have a grasp of how to fully customize your process template, you can use that new process template in several ways. You can deploy your process template in one of two scenarios:

➤ Updating individual components of an existing team project

➤ Using it in the team project creation wizard for new team projects

Uploading Process Templates in Team Foundation Server

To allow project collection administrators to create a new team project using the customized process template, you must add the process template to the available process templates for the team project collection. You can manage the available process templates by using the Process Template Manager window that was described earlier in this chapter (and shown in Figures 12-1 and 12-2).

You will notice that there is an Upload button that is available. During the upload process, the process template will be validated for compliance, and any errors that are encountered during validation will be displayed in a message box.

Editing Work Items on an Existing Team Project

The most common way to deploy updates for a process template for an existing team project is updating the work item type definitions. You can use the `witadmin.exe importwitd` command-line tool option for importing a new definition for an existing work item type definition in a team project.

Concerns

Updating work item type definitions for existing team projects can be particularly risky. You should always ensure that you are testing out your work item type definition updates in a test environment that includes waiting for a successful warehouse processing cycle to occur without any errors from the updates.

Some work item type definition changes have minimal impact, where others might take a little more effort to be fully implemented. For example, adding a new reportable field to an existing work item type definition does not impact the health of the Team Foundation Server, unless it conflicts with a field in another team project collection that has the same name, but different attributes. You will begin seeing a problem whenever the next warehouse processing cycle begins, because the conflicting field definitions will block further warehouse processing.

An additional scenario that has a higher impact would be changing the state name for an existing work item type definition. You must handle all existing work items that are in the old state name. Also, there may be existing work item queries that have used the particular state name, and standard reports that rely on the old state name, all of which must get updated.

> *One method you might use for changing a state name on existing work items is to create a temporary transition from the old state name to the new state name. You can then update the work item type definition with the temporary transition. Then, move all of the work items in the old state to the new state using that temporary transition. Remove the temporary transition and then upload the final work item type definition without the old state and the temporary transition to update the team project.*

When adding additional field rules you will want to think about the impact of those changes on the existing work items in a team project. For example, if you were to add a new REQUIRED field rule, or change the values in the ALLOWEDVALUES rule list, then you could potentially use a combination of ALLOWEXISTINGVALUE and DEFAULT field rules to ensure that the existing work items are still considered valid work items. You can then update all of the existing work items using a tool such as Microsoft Excel to bulk-edit the field value in all of the existing work items.

Using an Automated Build to Deploy Work Item Type Definition Changes

When you are editing source code for an application, it is helpful to have regular builds to compile and deploy the application for testing. Similarly, when making changes to work item type definitions in version control, it is helpful to have an automatic deployment process. You can use a customized build process template that will automatically deploy multiple work item type definitions to multiple team projects. You can create an automatic deployment build for both Production and Test branches that contain the process templates that would deploy to their respective Team Foundation Server environments.

The work item type definition deployment build process template is available with instructions for use at www.edsquared.com/2010/06/18/Deploying+Process+Template+Changes+Using+TFS+2010 +Build.aspx. This automated deployment process has the following features:

➤ Specifies multiple team projects to update

➤ Specifies multiple work item types to update

➤ Backs up each of the existing work item type definitions currently in use

➤ Copies the latest version of the work item type definition and backups to a build drop folder

➤ Indicates errors during the deployment process in the build log

Additionally, the following standard build features are included, since it is an automated Team Foundation Server build:

➤ Build versioning

➤ Labeling the source code for the process template

➤ Getting the latest version of the process template

➤ Associating changesets and work items

➤ Gated check-in, continuous integration, scheduled, and so on

> *Chapter 15 provides more information about automated builds and build process templates.*

COMMON WORK ITEM TYPE CUSTOMIZATIONS

There are certain customizations that are commonly made to the existing process template. The following discussions provide an overview of some of those common customizations.

Adding New States

Teams often might not feel that the states provided in the standard process templates fit well with the team's process. They might decide that a new state should be created in the workflow.

If you can avoid adding too many states, you can make it easier for end users to understand and use these new states during normal day-to-day interaction with work items. This will also reduce the amount of effort required to customize reports to take advantage of each of those states. Instead, you can use the combination of states and reasons to help you distinguish between work items in a specific state when querying or reporting on work items.

Adding a state can be done pretty easily. For example, if you wanted to add a Proposed state to a work item type definition, you might add a snippet similar to following:

```
<WORKFLOW>
  <STATES>
    <STATE value="Proposed">
    </STATE>
    <STATE value="Active">
      <FIELDS>
        <FIELD refname="Microsoft.VSTS.Common.ClosedDate">
          <EMPTY />
        </FIELD>
        <FIELD refname="Microsoft.VSTS.Common.ClosedBy">
  ...
```

You might also want to move around some of the field rules (for example, empty out the Closed Date and Closed By fields), as well as change some of the existing transitions to take advantage of the new state.

> *A full how-to article about adding a new state to a work item type definition is available in the MSDN Library at* http://msdn.microsoft.com/en-us/library/ms404845.aspx.

However, adding a state does mean that certain reports will be affected. For example, some of the following reports in the MSF Agile process template may be impacted:

➤ *Bug Status Report* — This report has a stacked area chart that lists bugs by state, and has a particular color assigned to each state. Additionally, it shows the number of bugs in the Resolved and Active state assigned to each team member.

➤ *Stories Overview Report* — This report shows how many bugs are open for each user story, and displays them in a segmented bar chart by state.

➤ *Status on All Iterations* — This report shows how many bugs exist in each iteration path, and displays them in a segmented bar chart by state.

Displaying Custom Link Types

The new links control allows for rich interaction with the new link types that are available in Team Foundation Server, including any custom link types you create for your process template. You can take advantage of the new links control to create an additional instantiation of a links control on your work item form that filters by work item type, work item link type, and/or external links.

In the MSF Agile process template, you will notice a tab named Implementation exists on a User Story and Task that displays any parent and children tasks and user stories. It also allows for easily creating new links scoped to the particular link type.

One example customization you can make would be to specify a new tab for tracking dependencies between work items. For example, you might add the following XML entry into the form layout for the work item type definition. Notice that the System.LinkTypes.Dependency link type is used for filtering for this particular links control instantiation.

```
<Tab Label="Dependencies">
  <Control Type="LinksControl" Name="Dependencies">
    <LinksControlOptions>
      <LinkColumns>
        <LinkColumn RefName="System.Id" />
        <LinkColumn RefName="System.WorkItemType" />
        <LinkColumn RefName="System.Title" />
        <LinkColumn RefName="System.AssignedTo" />
        <LinkColumn RefName="System.State" />
        <LinkColumn RefName="Microsoft.VSTS.Scheduling.OriginalEstimate" />
        <LinkColumn RefName="Microsoft.VSTS.Scheduling.RemainingWork" />
        <LinkColumn RefName="Microsoft.VSTS.Scheduling.CompletedWork" />
        <LinkColumn RefName="Microsoft.VSTS.Scheduling.StartDate" />
        <LinkColumn RefName="Microsoft.VSTS.Scheduling.FinishDate" />
        <LinkColumn LinkAttribute="System.Links.Comment" />
      </LinkColumns>
      <WorkItemLinkFilters FilterType="include">
        <Filter LinkType="System.LinkTypes.Dependency" />
      </WorkItemLinkFilters>
      <ExternalLinkFilters FilterType="excludeAll" />
      <WorkItemTypeFilters FilterType="includeAll" />
    </LinksControlOptions>
  </Control>
</Tab>
```

Figure 12-22 shows how this might look when added to the form layout, and then the work item type definition updated for a team project.

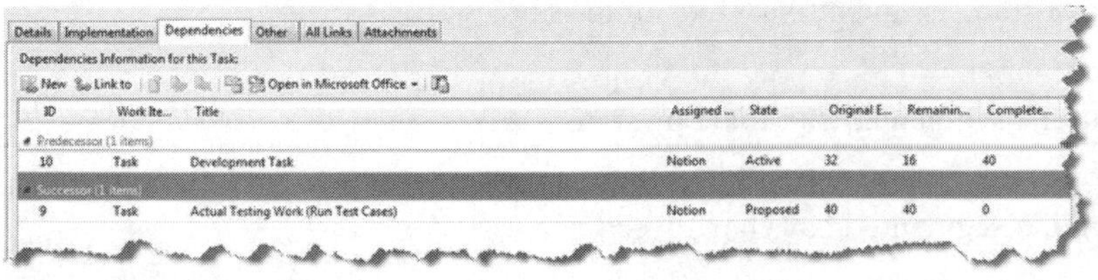

FIGURE 12-22: Specifying a new tab

Using Display Name Changes (New syncnamechanges attribute)

For work item fields that contain names of people, handling name changes can be particularly tricky. The names that are used for fields like the Assigned To field are actually the display names for each Active Directory account, and are synchronized from Active Directory.

You can specify a new attribute on work item fields named `syncnamechanges` and set its value to `True` to indicate that the particular field should be automatically updated any time the display name in Active Directory changes. This should help the management of work items tremendously, and ensure that work items are not orphaned to users who have experienced name changes.

The following XML excerpt for a field definition demonstrates the use of this attribute:

```
<FIELD name="Assigned To" refname="System.AssignedTo" type="String"
    syncnamechanges="true" reportable="dimension">
  <VALIDUSER />
  <HELPTEXT>The person currently working on this bug</HELPTEXT>
</FIELD>>
```

You can also use the `witadmin.exe changefield` command-line tool option to update an existing field's `synchnamechanges` value.

> Team Foundation Server can actually detect if multiple accounts use the same display name in Active Directory. The display name that is used in work item fields in this case would be a disambiguated name that is a combination of the Active Directory display name, and the full username, in the format of DOMAIN\user.

Using a Rich-Text Description

An out-of-the-box process template includes a plain-text description field for each of the work item type definitions. There is a rich-text capability including a new HTML Editor control, but the plain-text fields continue to be included for backward compatibility, since you cannot change a field's type once it has been created. To handle this situation, you can remove the existing `System .Description` field that is defined and then add a new HTML field.

The following code snippet shows an example of a new rich-text description field:

```
<Field refname="CompanyName.Description.Rich"
    name="Description - Rich" type="HTML" />
```

Also, be sure to update the form's layout to use the newly defined field, and ensure that its control type is set to use the HTML editor control, as shown in the following code snippet:

```
...
<TabGroup>
  <Tab Label="Details">
    <Group>
```

```
        <Column PercentWidth="50">
            <Control FieldName="CompanyName.Description.Rich"
                Type="HtmlFieldControl" Label="&amp;Description:"
                LabelPosition="Top" Dock="Fill" />
        </Column>
        <Column PercentWidth="50">
            <Control FieldName="System.History" Type="WorkItemLogControl"
                Label="&amp;History:" LabelPosition="Top" Dock="Fill" />
        </Column>
      </Group>
    </Tab>
  ...
```

INTRODUCING CUSTOM WORK ITEM CONTROLS

The standard work item controls provide plenty of functionality for editing the work item fields that can be created in Team Foundation Server. However, there may be additional functionality that you would like to add to the work item forms or custom editors for the work item fields. You can do this by creating custom work item controls and deploying them to all of the end users' machines to use while editing work items.

Custom work item controls do not have to edit a work item field at all. Several of the standard work item controls (such as the `Webpage` control) do not contain any fields and only display information. An example of this would be a custom work item control to pull information from an external system that is related to the opened work item.

Work Item Clients

A different implementation of the custom work item control must be created based on the client that will be displaying the work item control. The following clients are currently available for displaying custom work item controls.

➤ *Visual Studio Team Explorer* — Windows Forms control

➤ *Microsoft Test Manager* — Windows Forms control

➤ *Visual Studio Web Access* — ASP.NET control

➤ *Visual Studio Team Explorer Everywhere* — Java SWT control

Preferred and Fallback Control

If a particular client does not have an implementation of the custom control, or cannot locate the custom control, you can specify a control in the work item form's layout section of the work item type definition to be used. You can then specify the preferred control to use if it is deployed.

The following work item form layout excerpt demonstrates the use of the preferred control attribute:

```
<Control Type="FieldControl" PreferredType="MyCustomControl"
    FieldName="System.AssignedTo" Label="Assigned To" LabelPosition="Left" />
```

> ⊗ Note, *however, that the preferred control method is not supported by Visual Studio Team Web Access, which will always use the standard control that is defined.*

Work Item Control Interfaces

To create a custom work item control for Windows Forms, you must essentially create a new Windows Forms control that implements specific interfaces in the Team Foundation Server 2010 SDK. The following sections describe some of the most common interfaces that can be implemented for work item controls.

IWorkItemControl

The IWorkItemControl interface is actually the primary interface to be implemented, and is required for custom work item controls. It contains the base functionality for a custom work item control, and its members are used by the work item form in Visual Studio Team Explorer.

Listing 12-1 shows the full signature for the IWorkItemControl interface.

LISTING 12-1: IWorkItemControl Interface Definition

```
// C:\Program Files (x86)\Microsoft Visual Studio 10.0
    \Common7\IDE\PrivateAssemblies
    \Microsoft.TeamFoundation.WorkItemTracking.Controls.dll

using System;
using System.Collections.Specialized;

namespace Microsoft.TeamFoundation.WorkItemTracking.Controls
{
    public interface IWorkItemControl
    {
        StringDictionary Properties { get; set; }
        bool ReadOnly { get; set; }
        object WorkItemDatasource { get; set; }
        string WorkItemFieldName { get; set; }

        event EventHandler AfterUpdateDatasource;
        event EventHandler BeforeUpdateDatasource;

        void Clear();
        void FlushToDatasource();
        void InvalidateDatasource();
        void SetSite(IServiceProvider serviceProvider);
    }
}
```

Table 12-7 shows common members that are used to provide the base functionality for the work item control.

TABLE 12-7: Common Members Used to Provide Base Functionality

MEMBER	DESCRIPTION
WorkItemDatasource	This property contains a reference to the actual `WorkItem` object (and must be cast properly to the `Microsoft.TeamFoundation.WorkItemTracking.Client.WorkItem` type). It can end up being `null` during initialization, so be sure to handle the situation gracefully.
WorkItemFieldName	This property contains the name of the field that is used by the work item control for editing. This is something that is defined in the work item type definition's form layout section in the control definition. Not all controls need to edit work item fields, so the value for this property could be empty.
Properties	This collection provides all of the properties that are defined in the work item type definition's control item. In Team Foundation Server 2010, you can even use a `CustomControlOptions` type that contains custom properties to be used by the control.
ReadOnly	This property specifies whether the control should render itself as read-only to the end user.
BeforeUpdateDatasource/ AfterUpdateDatasource	These events should be implemented and raised before and after data is flushed to the data source (the work item).
Clear	This method may be called by the work item system. It indicates to the control that the control should be cleared.
FlushToDatasource	This method is called by the work item system to indicate that the value stored by the control should be saved to the work item object immediately. This often occurs when the end user chooses to save the work item.
InvalidDatasource	This method is called by the work item system to indicate to the control that it should redraw itself. Typically, the control will refresh its display by reading the data from the work item object.
SetSite	The method provides a pointer to the `IServiceProvider` object that allows you to take advantage of Visual Studio services such as the `DocumentService` or the `IWorkItemControlHost` service. You do not have to store this service provider reference if you will not be using any of the services provided by Visual Studio.

IWorkItemToolTip

The label for the custom control can display a tooltip with information about the work item field or the custom control. You can decide what and how to display the tooltip implemented by the `IWorkItemToolTip` interface.

Listing 12-2 shows the full interface signature for the `IWorkItemToolTip` interface.

LISTING 12-2: IWorkItemToolTip Interface Definition

```
// C:\Program Files (x86)\Microsoft Visual Studio 10.0
    \Common7\IDE\PrivateAssemblies
    \Microsoft.TeamFoundation.WorkItemTracking.Controls.dll

using System.Windows.Forms;

namespace Microsoft.TeamFoundation.WorkItemTracking.Controls
{
    public interface IWorkItemToolTip
    {
        Label Label { get; set; }
        ToolTip ToolTip { get; set; }
    }
}
```

Once each member is set, you can then make a call to `ToolTip.SetToolTip(string)` to provide a meaningful tooltip when the end user hovers over the label.

IWorkItemUserAction

The `IWorkItemUserAction` interface is implemented when the control requires some type of user action (such as the control or work item field being in a bad state, and you want to prevent the user from saving the work item).

Listing 12-3 provides the full interface definition for the `IWorkItemUserAction` interface.

LISTING 12-3: IWorkItemUserAction Interface Definition

```
// C:\Program Files (x86)\Microsoft Visual Studio 10.0
    \Common7\IDE\PrivateAssemblies
    \Microsoft.TeamFoundation.WorkItemTracking.Controls.dll

using System;
using System.Drawing;

namespace Microsoft.TeamFoundation.WorkItemTracking.Controls
{
    public interface IWorkItemUserAction
    {
        Color HighlightBackColor { get; set; }
        Color HighlightForeColor { get; set; }
        string RequiredText { get; set; }
        bool UserActionRequired { get; }

        event EventHandler UserActionRequiredChanged;
    }
}
```

Following are some of the interface members:

➤ `RequiredText` — This property stores the friendly error message that is displayed to the end user about what action needs to be taken. It is commonly displayed in an information bar in Visual Studio at the top of the work item form.

➤ `HighlightBackColor/HighlightForeColor` — These properties store the background and foreground colors that should be used in your custom control to stay consistent with the theme of the work item form.

➤ `UserActionRequired` — This property indicates to the work item form whether the control needs input from the user.

➤ `UserActionRequiredChanged` — This event should be raised any time the `UserActionRequired` property is changed by the control.

IWorkItemClipboard

The `IWorkItemClipboard` interface provides functionality to your control for integrating with the clipboard functionality in Visual Studio.

Listing 12-4 provides the full interface definition for the `IWorkItemClipboard` interface.

LISTING 12-4: IWorkItemClipboard Interface Definition

```
// C:\Program Files (x86)\Microsoft Visual Studio 10.0
    \Common7\IDE\PrivateAssemblies
    \Microsoft.TeamFoundation.WorkItemTracking.Controls.dll

using System;

namespace Microsoft.TeamFoundation.WorkItemTracking.Controls
{
    public interface IWorkItemClipboard
    {
        bool CanCopy { get; }
        bool CanCut { get; }
        bool CanPaste { get; }

        event EventHandler ClipboardStatusChanged;

        void Copy();
        void Cut();
        void Paste();
    }
}
```

Each of the methods should be implemented and should handle the appropriate user-initiated command. If any of the Boolean properties (such as `CanCopy`) are changed, the `ClipboardStatusChanged` event should be raised to indicate to the work item form that the clipboard status for the control has been updated.

> *A group of developers have teamed together and released a set of commonly requested custom work item controls (including their source code) on a CodePlex project available at* http://witcustomcontrols.codeplex.com/.

Deploying Custom Controls

Once you have implemented the appropriate interfaces on your work item control, you must compile the .NET project and deploy both the compiled assembly that contains the custom work item control, and a work item custom control deployment manifest file. Each of the artifacts should be deployed to one of the following locations for Visual Studio 2010 and Microsoft Test Manager 2010 clients:

➤ *Value Name Entries in Registry* — If you want to store the artifacts in a custom folder, you can add a custom value list to the following registry key to point to that custom folder:

```
[HKEY_LOCAL_MACHINE\SOFTWARE\Microsoft\VisualStudio\10.0
    \WorkItemTracking\WorkItemTracking\CustomControls\LookInFolders]
"C:\\CustomControls\\MyCustomLocation"=""
```

➤ *Common Application Data 2010-Specific Location* — For example, C:\ProgramData\ Microsoft\Team Foundation\Work Item Tracking\Custom Controls*10.0*\.

➤ *Local Application Data 2010-Specific Location* — For example, C:\Users\UserName\ AppData\Local\Microsoft\Team Foundation\Work Item Tracking\Custom Controls*10.0*\.

➤ *Visual Studio Private Assemblies Location* — For example, C:\Program Files (x86)\ Microsoft Visual Studio 10.0\Common7\IDE\PrivateAssemblies\.

➤ *Common Application Data Location* — For example, C:\ProgramData\Microsoft\Team Foundation\Work Item Tracking\Custom Controls\.

➤ *Local Application Data Location* — For example, C:\Users\UserName\AppData\Local\ Microsoft\Team Foundation\Work Item Tracking\Custom Controls\.

Work Item Custom Control Deployment Manifest

The work item custom control deployment manifest file has a .wicc extension. It contains the full class name for the custom work item control, as well as the name of the assembly that contains the custom work item control. That is the filename for the file where .wicc is the file's extension, as in MyCustomControl.wicc.

The contents of the custom control deployment manifest would contain something similar to Listing 12-5.

LISTING 12-5: Work Item Custom Control Deployment File

```xml
<?xml version="1.0"?>
<CustomControl xmlns:xsi="http://www.w3.org/2001
    /XMLSchema-instance" xmlns:xsd="http://www.w3.org/2001/XMLSchema">
  <Assembly>Wrox.CustomWorkItemControl.dll</Assembly>
  <FullClassName>Wrox.CustomWorkItemControl.MyCustomControl</FullClassName>
</CustomControl>
```

Using the Custom Control in the Work Item Type Definition

Once the work item custom control artifacts have been deployed to each of the client machines, you can then configure the control definition in the work item type definition's form layout section by setting the `Type` attribute as shown here. The value for this attribute is the filename of the custom work item control deployment manifest, without the `.wicc` extension.

```xml
<Control Type="MyCustomControl" FieldName="System.AssignedTo"
    Label="Assigned To:" LabelPosition="Left" />
```

SUMMARY

Process templates are the most customized part of Team Foundation Server. They allow teams to easily modify their process and have the tool help them with day-to-day activities for managing their process. In this chapter, you learned about the different artifacts that make up a process template, how to deploy changes to the work item type definitions, and how to edit work item type definitions to include common customizations.

You also learned about custom work item controls and the specific Team Foundation Server SDK interfaces that should be implemented when creating the custom work item control. Deployment of those work item controls to each of the client machines was also covered.

In Chapter 13, you will learn about different reporting capabilities, as well as the interaction with SharePoint products and Team Foundation Server.

13
Reporting and SharePoint Dashboards

WHAT'S IN THIS CHAPTER?

➤ Learning about the changes and new features

➤ Understanding the Team Foundation Server data warehouse

➤ Understanding the tools available to create and manage reports

➤ Creating and customizing reports using Excel

➤ Extending and customizing the data warehouse and dashboards

One of the key value propositions for Team Foundation Server has always been the reporting features that it provides. When you have your source control, work item tracking, build and test case management systems all integrated in a system like Team Foundation Server, the reporting can provide powerful insight into the status of your projects. The data collected and the reports provided by Team Foundation Server gives your projects a level of transparency that allows you to react and adjust to changing conditions.

In this chapter, you will first learn about changes in the integration with SharePoint 2010 designed to support multiple team project collections on a single server and, thus, improve reporting capabilities. You will then learn about the three data stores in the Team Foundation Server data warehouse. This chapter also provides an overview of how to set up and configure the integration with SharePoint, and how to take advantage of the excellent reporting features. Finally, you will learn how to customize project portals and warehouse adapters.

WHAT'S NEW IN TEAM FOUNDATION SERVER 2010

As discussed elsewhere in this book, Team Foundation Server 2010 includes significant architectural changes to facilitate support of multiple team project collections on a single logical server. Following are the biggest changes for reporting and SharePoint integration since the 2008 release:

➤ Cross-collection reporting is now supported.

➤ A relational warehouse schema is now supported.

➤ The Analysis Services cube schema is more usable.

➤ An optional, but richer, SharePoint integration is now supported.

➤ New Excel-based reporting features have been included.

Cross-Collection Reporting Support

Team Foundation Server 2008 allowed a single relational warehouse and cube per server. Ironically, organizations that were large enough to need multiple Team Foundation Servers were the same organizations that most needed aggregated reporting across their entire organizations.

Team Foundation Server 2010 allows organizations like this to consolidate their multiple separate servers into a single logical server. Now that they have a single logical server, they also have a single data warehouse across which they can do reporting.

Team project names are unique within a team project collection. Because of this, the data warehouse schema was modified to support a hierarchy of collections and projects.

None of the reports included with the out-of-box process templates are configured for cross-project or cross-collection reporting. However, it is possible to modify the Team Project filter on the reports to select multiple projects.

Changes to the Relational Warehouse

Before Team Foundation Server 2010, customer feedback reflected that the latency for reporting from the cube was too high. Customers wanted their work item updates to be available in reports almost immediately.

A common example was a daily stand-up meeting, whereby the team would be looking at the Remaining Work report and question why the report showed that an individual or team hadn't made any progress. Often, it turned out that they had, in fact, updated their work items, but those updates hadn't been processed in the cube before the report was rendered.

Until the 2010 release, reporting against the relational warehouse was not supported. With the 2010 release, that is no longer the case. There are now several views on top of the warehouse to support reporting. These views make it easier to query for data and keep compatibility with future versions. Additionally, the naming conventions have been standardized to help differentiate fact tables and dimension tables. For example, `dbo.Work Item` is now called `dbo.DimWorkItem`, which identifies it as a dimension table.

> *A more detailed discussion about fact tables and dimensions is provided later in this chapter.*

Along with supporting queries against the relational warehouse, the work item tracking warehouse adapters were updated for improved performance. The new adapters are now capable of moving data from the operational store to the relational warehouse much faster than in previous releases. The goal for the adapters was to keep the latency for work item tracking less than five minutes during normal operations.

Changes to the Analysis Services Cube

Although the cube in Team Foundation Server 2005 and 2008 provided useful data, and was reasonably well-used by customers, there was room for improvement. Along with supporting the architecture improvements, the changes in Team Foundation Server 2010 improve usability, query performance, and processing performance.

The main changes to the cube schema include the following:

➤ The `Current Work Item` and `Work Item History` measure groups were combined into the `Work Item` measure group. Now you just include the `Date` measure to show historical trends.

➤ Area and iteration dimensions have been folded into the `Work Item` dimension as true hierarchies.

➤ Some dimension names have been updated to make them more meaningful, and provide context, especially when looking at the entire list. For example, `Platform` is now `Build Platform`.

➤ Dimensions starting with `Related...` have been moved to the `Linked Work Item` dimension.

A more detailed discussion of measures is presented later in this chapter.

The main additions to the cube schema include the following:

➤ Work item hierarchy and linking are now supported in the cube through the `Linked Work Item` and `Work Item Tree` dimensions.

➤ Work item types can now be grouped into categories. For example, the Bug category can group Bug and Defect work item types together. This is useful if you have different terminology across your team projects and need a meaningful report across all of them.

➤ `Area Path` and `Iteration Path` are now available as attributes on the `Work Item` dimension. This allows you to show a flat string (rather than a hierarchy) on your reports.

➤ As shown in Figure 13-1, display folders have been added to the `Work Item` dimension to make it easier to group fields, rather than display one long list.

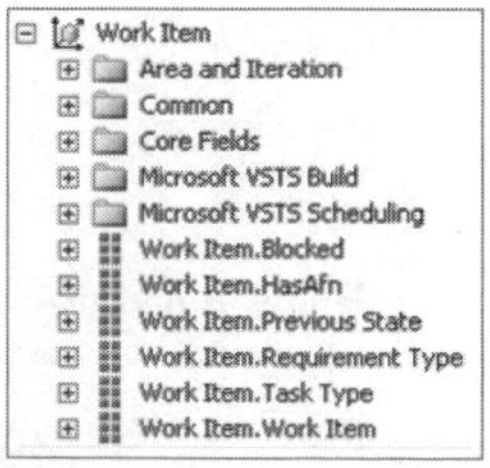

FIGURE 13-1: Display folders on the Work Item dimension

> *For more information on the data warehouse changes and the reasons behind them, refer to John Socha-Leialoha's three-part blog post titled "Upgrading Team Foundation Server 2008 Reports to 2010" (Part I at* `http://tinyurl` *`.com/UpgradeReports1`; Part II at `http://tinyurl.com/UpgradeReports2`; and Part III at `http://tinyurl.com/UpgradeReports3`). Also see the official MSDN documentation, "Changes and Additions to the Schema for the Analysis Services Cube," at* `http://msdn.microsoft.com/en-us/library/ff472574.aspx`.

Optional and Richer SharePoint Integration

Integration with SharePoint is an important feature for Team Foundation Server. However, the installation and configuration of the integration was a significant source of problems. Along with the other architectural changes in this release designed to support different server topologies, SharePoint integration is now optional.

If you want to use the SharePoint integration features, you can configure SharePoint at install time or at a later time. The configuration options are designed to be flexible.

Team Foundation Server 2010 integration is available with both SharePoint 2007 and SharePoint 2010.

> *The reporting features are not available when Team Foundation Server is configured as a Basic configuration, or when installed on a client operating system (such as Windows 7). If you have either of these configurations, and would like to enable the reporting features, you must use a Standard or Advanced configuration on a server operating system.*

TEAM FOUNDATION SERVER DATA WAREHOUSE

The Team Foundation Server reporting and data warehouse features are comprised of three data stores, as shown in Table 13-1.

TABLE 13-1: Team Foundation Server Reporting Data Stores

DATA STORE	DATABASE NAMES	CHARACTERISTICS
Operational	`Tfs_Configuration,` `Tfs_Collection`	Now normalized, optimized for retrieving the most recent data, and transactional.
Relational warehouse database	`Tfs_Warehouse`	Has a star schema, and includes all historical data designed to be used for analysis.
Analysis Services cube	`Tfs_Analysis`	Data is pre-aggregated, pre-indexed, and includes advanced analysis features.

Along with these three data stores, there is a set of scheduled jobs that move data between the stores:

➤ Warehouse adapter jobs (sometimes called *sync jobs*) periodically copy changes from the operational store to the relational database.

➤ Analysis processing jobs instruct the cube to begin either an incremental or full process.

Figure 13-2 shows a high-level representation of this data movement and processing.

FIGURE 13-2: High-level architecture of the Team Foundation Server data warehouse

Operational Stores

The operational stores in Team Foundation Server 2010 are nothing more than the databases that support the normal day-to-day operations of the server. In previous versions of Team Foundation Server, there were different databases for the different feature areas (for example, the `TfsWorkItemTracking` and `TfsVersionControl` databases). In Team Foundation Server 2010, the contents of these databases are merged into a single `Tfs_Collection` database for each team project collection.

The schema of these databases is optimized for Team Foundation Server commands, rather than reporting. The data in these databases is changing all the time, and does not lend itself to historical reporting and analysis.

The operational stores should not be accessed directly. The only supported interface for accessing them is through the Team Foundation Server object model.

Relational Warehouse Database and Warehouse Adapters

Each component in Team Foundation Server has different requirements for storing data in the relational warehouse database. The warehouse adapters for each operational store are responsible for transferring data to the data warehouse for their store.

Although the warehouse adapters are set to run on a schedule, they are also triggered and run on-demand when data changes. This keeps the latency in the relational warehouse low.

The warehouse adapters are also responsible for making schema changes in the relational warehouse and cube. For example, when you add a new field to a work item type and mark it as reportable, the warehouse adapter will perform a schema change and add a new column to the relational warehouse, as well as make changes to the cube definition.

The dynamic nature of these data adapters allows the structure and mechanics of the data warehouse to be hidden from project administrators. This is one of the unique benefits of reporting in Team Foundation Server. You can define your work item types in a single place using a relatively straightforward schema and tools. You then automatically get access to rich reporting features based on these customizations. You never have to deal with database schema changes or updating cube structures.

The downside of this, however, is that if you want to make customizations to either the relational warehouse or cube, you must deploy them as a custom warehouse adapter. If you don't, your customizations will be lost when the warehouse is rebuilt.

The relational warehouse database stores data in a set of tables organized in a star schema. The central table of the star schema is called the *fact table*, and the related tables represent *dimensions*. For example, the `dbo.FactCurrentWorkItem` table has one row for every work item stored in the work item tracking operational store. A dimension table stores the set of values that exist for a given dimension. For example, a `Person` dimension is referenced by the `Work Items` fact table for the `Assigned To` and `Closed By` properties.

You'll learn more about fact tables and dimensions later in this chapter.

Querying the Relational Warehouse Database

For the first time, writing reports against the relational warehouse database using Transact-SQL (TSQL) queries is officially supported. As a rule of thumb, you'll generally want to use the cube for historical reports, or reports that require a lot of slicing and dicing using parameters or aggregate data. The cube is pre-aggregated, indexed, and is ideal for this sort of reporting.

The relational warehouse, on the other hand, allows you to create reports that pull loosely related data together in ways not possible with the cube.

Following are the nine views that you can query and write reports against with some level of assurance that they will work when the server is upgraded to a future version of Team Foundation Server:

➤   `CurrentWorkItemView`

➤   `WorkItemHistoryView`

➤   `BuildChangesetView`

➤   `BuildCoverageView`

➤   `BuildDetailsView`

➤   `BuildProjectView`

➤   `CodeChurnView`

➤   `RunCoverageView`

➤   `TestResultView`

The other views that begin with v and end with Overlay are used for processing the cube, and, as such, aren't meant for use in your own reports.

The relational warehouse is an ideal store to use if you require reports with a lower latency than the cube can provide.

> *As with previous versions of Team Foundation Server, fields that have the* Html *data type are not stored in the relational warehouse. Therefore, they are not available in the cube. For reporting against those fields, you must use the Work Item Tracking object model to query and retrieve them.*

Querying the Current Work Item View

Using the CurrentWorkItemView, you can query the relational warehouse and retrieve a list of work items without using the Work Item Tracking object model.

For example, following is a Work Item Query (WIQ) that returns all non-closed bugs assigned to John Smith in the Contoso project:

```
SELECT
[System.Id],
[Microsoft.VSTS.Common.StackRank],
[Microsoft.VSTS.Common.Priority],
[Microsoft.VSTS.Common.Severity],
[System.State], [System.Title]
FROM WorkItems
WHERE [System.TeamProject] = 'Contoso'
AND  [System.AssignedTo] = 'John Smith'
AND  [System.WorkItemType] = 'Bug'
AND  [System.State] <> 'Closed'
ORDER BY
[System.State],
[Microsoft.VSTS.Common.StackRank],
[Microsoft.VSTS.Common.Priority],
[Microsoft.VSTS.Common.Severity],
[System.Id]
```

And here's an equivalent query that retrieves the same data from the relational warehouse:

```
SELECT
[System_Id],
[Microsoft_VSTS_Common_StackRank],
[Microsoft_VSTS_Common_Priority],
[Microsoft_VSTS_Common_Severity],
[System_State],
[System_Title]
FROM CurrentWorkItemView
WHERE [ProjectNodeGUID] = 'a6fc4213-94c0-4361-87bf-9520e07eb096'
AND  [System_AssignedTo] = 'John Smith'
AND  [System_WorkItemType] = 'Bug'
```

```
AND  [System_State] <> 'Closed'
ORDER BY
[System_State],
[Microsoft_VSTS_Common_StackRank],
[Microsoft_VSTS_Common_Priority],
[Microsoft_VSTS_Common_Severity],
[System_Id]
```

Querying the Work Item History View

You can construct an "as of" query that returns only the last records for each work item that was modified before a certain date. For example, the following "as of" query returns the remaining work as of the end of December 2010:

```
SELECT System_Id, Microsoft_VSTS_Scheduling_RemainingWork
FROM WorkItemHistoryView WHERE System_ChangedDate < '1/1/2011'
AND System_RevisedDate >= '1/1/2011'
AND RecordCount > 0
AND ProjectNodeGUID = 'A393845-EA29-6D4A-68AE-D46EDAA37897'
```

Other Considerations for Querying the Relational Warehouse

The relational warehouse is not suitable for all queries and, therefore, some will be faster using the Work Item Tracking object model that uses the operational store. Team Foundation Server 2010 has multiple project collections, and these collections share the same relational warehouse and cube.

There are three important considerations to keep in mind when writing queries against the views:

> Use `ProjectNodeGUID` as the filter. A team project's name is not necessarily unique across multiple collections on the same logical server, whereas a project's GUID is unique.

> Use unique keys for joins. For example, a work item ID is no longer guaranteed to be unique within the warehouse.

> Be aware of compensating records. Whenever a work item is updated, a pair of records is added to the warehouse. The first record negates the previous record. This makes querying the relational warehouse faster for some types of queries.

> *For more information on compensating records see "Compensating Records" on MSDN at* http://msdn.microsoft.com/en-us/library/ee939347 .aspx#RelationalDB, *and "Work Item Tracking Compensating Records" at* http://tinyurl.com/WITCompensating.

Analysis Services Cube

The fact tables in the relational warehouse are suitable for reporting on current information. However, reporting on historical trends of data over time requires duplicating the data for every time interval that you want to report on.

Each time the cube is processed, the relational warehouse data is aggregated, summarized, and stored. The cube is a single central store to report against without having to aggregate across the different operational stores.

The cube contains *dimensions*, *facts*, *attributes*, and *measures*. Table 13-2 and Figure 13-3 show the definitions and the relationships of these.

TABLE 13-2: Cube Terminology

TERM	DESCRIPTION
Dimension	Dimensions enable the data to be sliced in many ways. Data values are associated with a set of dimensions, allowing you to show aggregate results sliced using a specific set of dimension values.
Fact	Facts are data that can be associated with multiple dimensions. This data may also be aggregated. Fact tables hold these values.
Attribute	Under each dimension, you'll find a set of attributes, and possibly hierarchies (areas and iterations are hierarchies). Each attribute is connected to a column in the corresponding dimension table in the relational warehouse.
Measure	Measures are values that correspond to columns in the corresponding fact table.

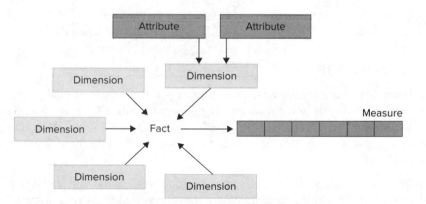

FIGURE 13-3: Relationships of objects in the cube

> For more information, see "Cube Definition: Measure Groups and Metrics Provided in the Analysis Services Cube for Team System" on MSDN at http://msdn.microsoft.com/en-us/library/ms244710.aspx.

Cube Perspectives

In the cube, *perspectives* are groups of related dimensions and measure groups. A perspective is a subset of the features and objects of a cube. They are useful because you don't have to scroll through the whole `Team System` cube to get to where you need to be.

They are only available when you are using the Enterprise or Datacenter edition SQL Server Analysis Services. Only a license for Standard edition is included with Team Foundation Server, so you'll need to license one of the other editions separately if you want to use cube perspectives.

Cube Processing

The Analysis Services cube is processed periodically on a schedule. The processing is triggered by two built-in Team Foundation Server jobs that correspond to the two different processing types:

➤ *Full Process* — Re-creates the cube from its definition, and processes every object in the cube. The default processing interval is every day at 2:00 a.m. for a full process.

➤ *Incremental Process* — Processes only objects that have changes since the last full or incremental process. The default processing interval is every two hours for an incremental process.

If the previous cube process failed, or the cube schema has changed, the next process is upgraded from an incremental process to a full process.

> *If you would like to change the processing interval, see the "Change a Process Control Setting for the Data Warehouse or Analysis Services Cube" article on MSDN at* http://msdn.microsoft.com/en-us/library/ms244694.aspx.

Data Warehouse Permissions

Users within Team Foundation Server are not automatically granted access to the relational warehouse or cube. They must be explicitly granted access. The reason for this is because there are no fine-grained permissions provided or security trimming performed in the warehouse. When users have permission to view the warehouse, they have full access to the warehouse data for all team projects in all team project collections.

In some organizations, it is perfectly acceptable to allow any individual with work item access in a particular project to have access to the whole data warehouse. However, in other more regulated industries and organizations, these permissions are reserved for a smaller subset of users.

To grant access, the `TfsWarehouseDataReader` role exists in both the `Tfs_Warehouse` relational database and the `Tfs_Analysis` cube. Users and groups can be added to these roles to allow them access to the resources.

> *For more information, see the article "Grant Access to the Databases of the Data Warehouse for Visual Studio ALM" at* http://msdn.microsoft.com/en-us/library/bb737953.aspx.

SHAREPOINT INTEGRATION

Once you have the standard reporting features working correctly, you can optionally configure integration with SharePoint. SharePoint integration is comprised of two parts:

➤ Team Foundation Server Extensions for SharePoint

➤ Excel Services and dashboard compatibility

SharePoint Extensions

In order for a team project to have SharePoint integration, the Team Foundation Server must have an association with a SharePoint web application. In order for this association to be configured, the SharePoint server must have the Team Foundation Server Extensions for SharePoint Products installed and configured.

There is no requirement that SharePoint be installed on the same server as Team Foundation Server, or even managed by the same people. Many organizations already have an existing SharePoint farm, and Team Foundation Server can integrate with the farm, as long as the Extensions are installed and configured.

The Extensions include site templates, web parts, and SharePoint timer jobs that maintain the associations between team projects and project portals, among other things.

> *For more information, see "Extensions for SharePoint Products" at* http:// msdn.microsoft.com/en-us/library/bb552177.aspx.

Excel Services and Dashboard Compatibility

Excel Services is a feature of the Enterprise edition of SharePoint. It allows an Excel workbook to be rendered on the SharePoint server and presented to the user as a web page. This is incredibly useful because of the following:

➤ For report producers, pivot tables and pivot charts can easily be created in Excel.

➤ For report consumers, no extra software is required. The reports are simply web pages.

> *For detailed instructions on manually integrating Team Foundation Server and SharePoint, you should consult some articles on MSDN. See "Add Integration with SharePoint Products to a Deployment of Team Foundation Server" at* http://msdn.microsoft.com/en-us/library/ee462861.aspx, *"Integrate Team Foundation Server with SharePoint Products without Administrative Permissions" at* http://msdn.microsoft.com/en-us/library/ee462864 .aspx, *and "Configure Settings for Dashboard Compatibility" at* http://msdn .microsoft.com/en-us/library/ee462863.aspx.

SharePoint Configuration Tool

As an alternative to the rather arduous manual configuration, you can use a configuration tool officially named "Visual Studio Team Foundation Server 2010 Pre-configuration Tool for Office SharePoint Server 2007 and SharePoint Server 2010" that automates many aspects of the configuration. It is available for download from http:// go.microsoft.com/fwlink/?LinkId=199082.

You can use this tool to configure an existing installation of SharePoint Server 2007 or 2010, for use with Team Foundation Server 2010. As you can see in Figure 13-4, the tool prompts for a few configuration settings before attempting to configure the integration.

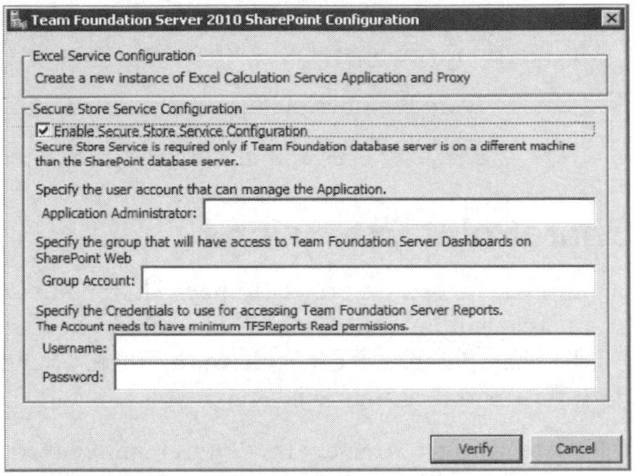

FIGURE 13-4: SharePoint configuration tool

For more information about how to use this tool, download and run the installer. Then open the instructions document from the installation folder, which by default is: `C:\Program Files\ Microsoft Team Foundation Server 2010 SharePoint Configure`.

For troubleshooting configuration issues, the tool also generates log files and saves them at `%TEMP%\ TfsMossConfigure_%DATETIME%.log`.

ADDING A PROJECT PORTAL AND REPORTS TO AN EXISTING TEAM PROJECT

For a number of reasons, you might not have a project portal or reports associated with your team project, such as in the following scenarios:

➤ The server or team project collection may not have had reporting or SharePoint integration configured when the team project was created.

➤ The process template used to create the team project may not have included the reporting or SharePoint tasks.

➤ Creating a SharePoint site might have been skipped during the project creation wizard.

➤ The connection between the team project and project portal may have been removed, or been invalid, before an upgrade.

➤ The 2008 server may have been imported rather than upgraded, which doesn't maintain the project portal and reporting settings.

Fortunately, with the help of the Team Foundation Server Power Tools, it's easy enough to add either a project portal or the default reports from a process template after the fact. From a Visual Studio command prompt, you can use the following two commands:

> ➤ `tfpt addprojectportal` — Create a project portal for an existing team project that doesn't currently have one.
>
> ➤ `tfpt addprojectreports` — Create (or overwrite) the reports for an existing team project.
>
> ➤ Additionally, you can open Team Explorer and navigate to `Team Project Settings` and then `Portal Settings` to modify the association of a team project with a SharePoint site at any time.

CREATING REPORTS

Reporting is a powerful feature in Team Foundation Server. It breaks down the usual barrier within teams that is often caused by a lack of information. Team Foundation Server provides a powerful set of reports out-of-the-box, and provides the capability to add additional reports based on your needs.

Tools

Since reporting in Team Foundation Server is based upon SQL Server, any tool that can produce reports from SQL Server can be used. Following are the three main tools that Team Foundation Server is designed to work with:

➤ Excel for pivot tables, pivot charts, and dashboards

➤ SQL Server Report Builder

➤ SQL Server Business Intelligence Development Studio (BIDS)

Each of these tools has different capabilities, as well as an associated learning curve. Figure 13-5 shows this comparison.

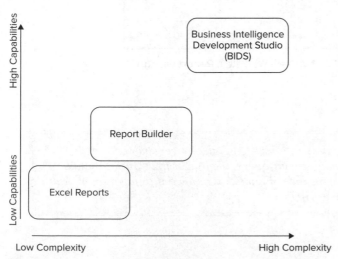

FIGURE 13-5: Comparison of report authoring tools

Excel Reporting from a Work Item Query

Creating reports with Excel has the lowest barrier to entry. It's powerful enough for most purposes, and leverages a tool that most people are already familiar with.

Perhaps the most impressive new reporting feature in Team Foundation Server 2010 is the capability to create reports from Work Item Queries.

Although many people working with previous versions of the product used Excel to create reports based on the cube, it was still not approachable for many. You first had to be given access to the cube, then be told the server name, and then wade through all the dimensions to find the ones you wanted in your report.

With Team Foundation Server 2010, you can go from a Work Item Query to a pivot chart report in as little as two steps. No special knowledge is required.

To do this, open Team Explorer and start by expanding either the `Team Queries` or `My Queries` folder. Then, right-click a query and select Create Report in Microsoft Excel, as shown in Figure 13-6.

The first thing that happens is that Excel translates the Work Item Query into a query for the Analysis Services cube. After that, it presents a New Work Item Report dialog, as shown in Figure 13-7. From this dialog, you select which fields that you would like to pivot by, as well as the type of reports to generate.

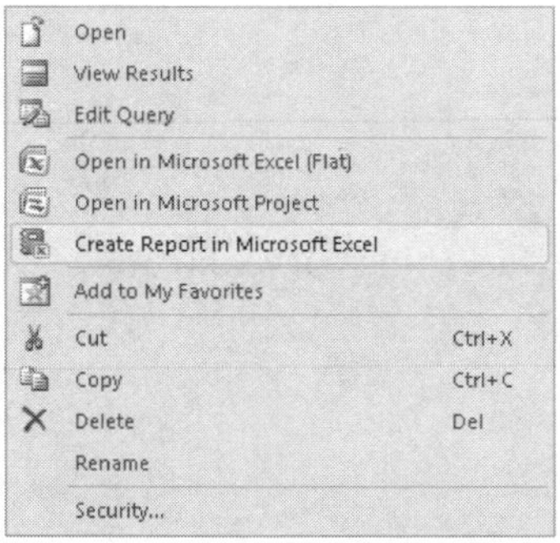

FIGURE 13-6: Selecting the Create Report in Microsoft Excel option

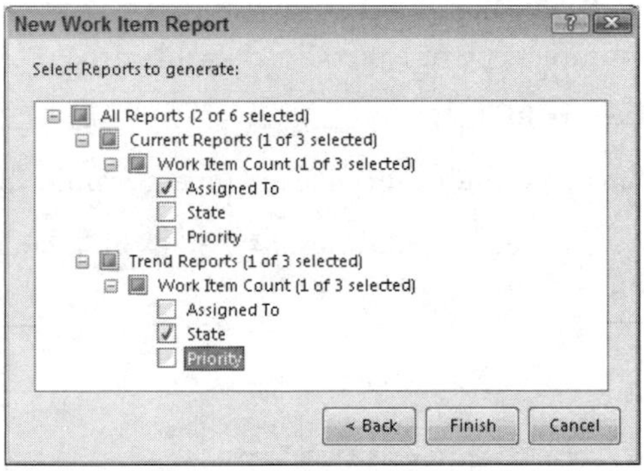

FIGURE 13-7: New Work Item Report dialog

Sometimes translating the Work Item Query can take longer than expected. The more columns that you have in your query, the longer the translation will take. It's a good idea to only have the columns that you want to pivot on in your query before you try generating a report.

There are two different types of reports:

➤ *Current reports* show the current state of the work items. These are represented as pie charts, as shown in Figure 13-8.

➤ *Trend reports* show the historical trend of the work items. These are represented as area charts, as shown in Figure 13-9.

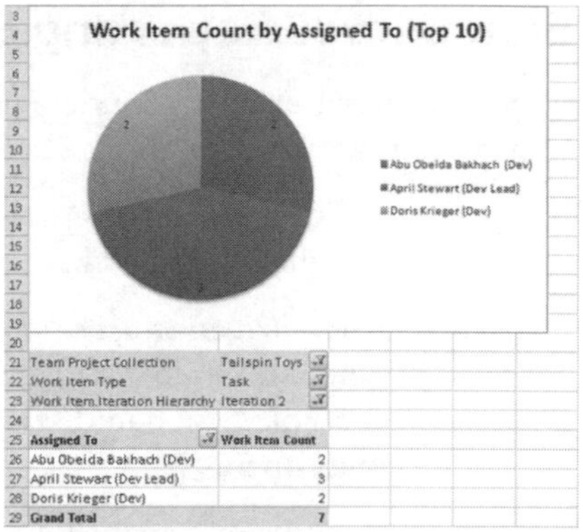

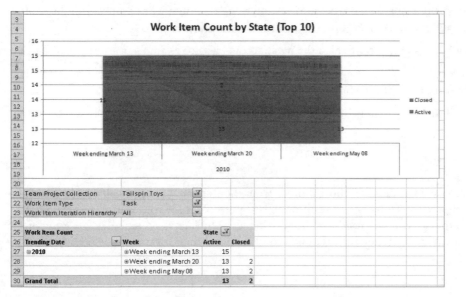

FIGURE 13-8: Current Report pivoted by the Assigned To field

FIGURE 13-9: Trend Report pivoted by State

Once the reports are generated, you have a workbook that is pre-populated with the Analysis Services database connection. You can further filter and customize the automatically generated reports, or create entirely new reports.

For more information, see "Creating Reports in Microsoft Excel by Using Work Item Queries" at http://msdn.microsoft.com/en-us/library/dd433251.aspx.

SQL Server Reporting Services Reports

SQL Server Reporting Services provides a powerful reporting platform. Along with allowing you to run rich reports, Reporting Services also provides the following features:

➤ *Subscriptions* — Reports can be executed on a regular schedule, and the results can be e-mailed to the team (for example, a weekly progress report).

➤ *Data-driven subscriptions* — Reports can be executed and the parameters or delivery schedule can be dynamically changed based upon the results of a database query. For example, you could send a daily e-mail to team members who have high-priority bugs open.

➤ *Caching and snapshots* — If a report is particularly complex, or is refreshed regularly, you can configure caching and snapshots to improve performance.

➤ *Linked reports* — By using linked reports, you can create multiple reports with different parameters off a single base report (for example, a remaining work report with different area and iteration parameters for different teams within a project).

These Reporting Services reports are also the most accessible. For example, they are available from the following:

➤ Directly from the Report Manager website

➤ Integrated in Visual Studio Team Explorer

➤ As web parts on the SharePoint project portal

Permissions

Before you can access SQL Server Report Builder from the Report Manager website, you must be granted the appropriate permission. In addition to this permission, if you want to publish your report for others to use, you will need that permission as well. The `Team Foundation Content Manager` role is created as part of Team Foundation Server configuration, and includes both of these permissions.

> *For more information, see "SQL Server Reporting Services Roles" at* `http://msdn.microsoft.com/en-us/library/bb558976.aspx`.

SQL Server Report Builder

Report Builder provides a Microsoft Office–like report authoring environment. Using the tool, you can create and edit reports directly from the Reporting Services server.

You can download and install Report Builder 2.0 from `http://go.microsoft.com/fwlink/ ?LinkID=130666`. Once it is installed, you can access Report Builder from the Start menu under the `Microsoft SQL Server Report Builder 2.0` folder.

To build a simple report, open Report Builder and select the Chart wizard icon on the design surface. Then, on the Data Source Connections screen, select Browse. When the Select Data Source screen appears, select the `Tfs2010OlapReportDS` shared data source from your Reporting Services Server, as shown in Figure 13-10.

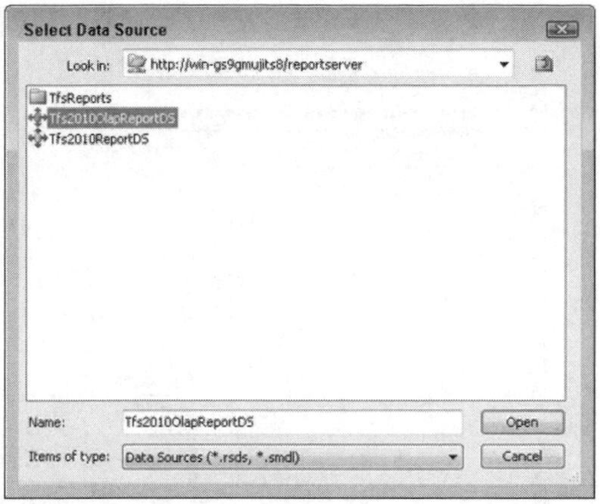

FIGURE 13-10: Select Data Source screen

On the "Design a query" screen shown in Figure 13-11, drag the `Work Item.Area Path` dimension attribute and the `Work Item Count` measure onto the query pane.

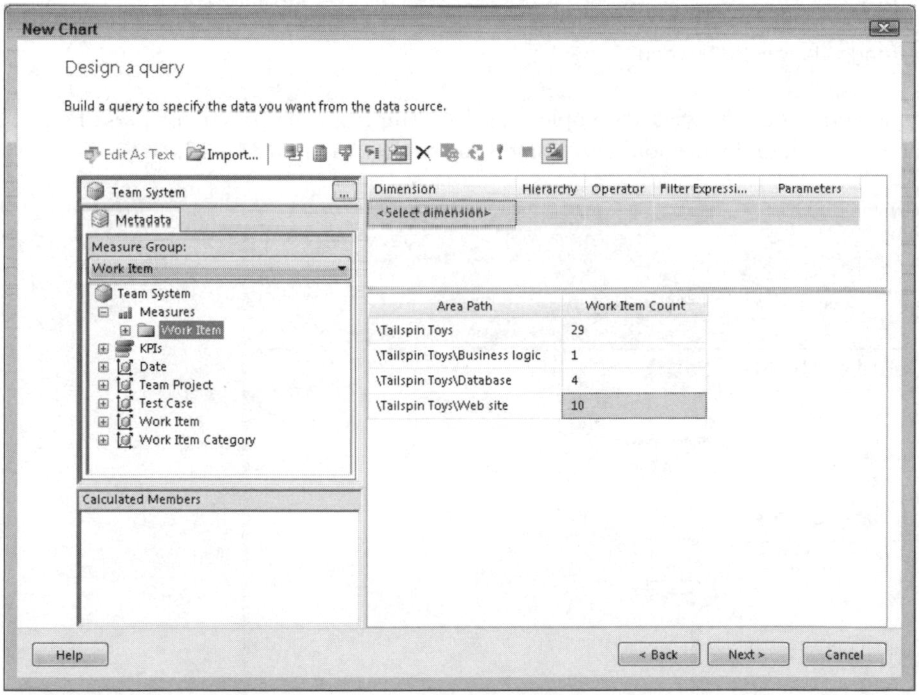

FIGURE 13-11: "Design a query" screen

On the "Choose a chart type" screen, select a Column or Bar chart. On the "Arrange chart fields" screen shown in Figure 13-12, drag `Area_Path` from the available fields list to the Categories list. Then drag `Work_Item_Count` to the Values list.

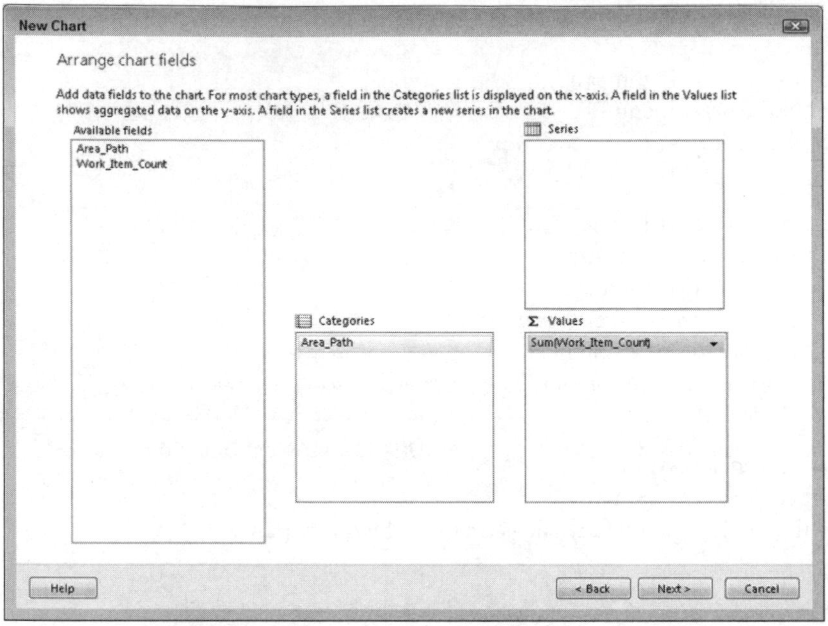

FIGURE 13-12: "Arrange chart fields" screen

Select a chart style and, when the wizard completes, select Run from the ribbon (or press F5). The report should be rendered, and you should see something similar to Figure 13-13.

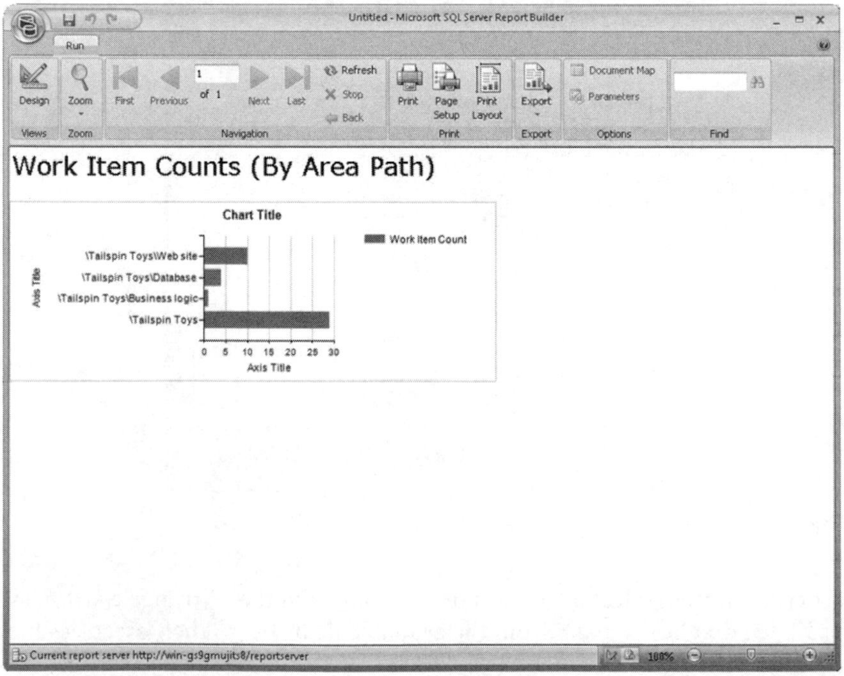

FIGURE 13-13: Example report created with Report Builder

When you are finished with your report, you can save it to your Reporting Services server and share it with other team members.

> For more information, see "Report Builder 2.0 How-to Topics" at `http://msdn`
> `.microsoft.com/en-us/library/dd220513.aspx`.

> SQL Server 2008 R2 includes Report Builder 3.0. This version includes new wizards and many other improvements over the 2.0 version that make it a compelling choice for report authors. Unfortunately, Team Foundation Server 2010 only includes a license for SQL Server 2008 and Report Builder 2.0. This means that you'll need to license SQL Server 2008 R2 separately to use the latest version of Report Builder. SQL Server Report Builder 3.0 for Microsoft SQL Server 2008 R2 can be downloaded from `http://go`
> `.microsoft.com/fwlink/?LinkID=186083`.

SQL Server Business Intelligence Development Studio

Business Intelligence Development Studio (BIDS) is an integrated environment for developing cubes, data sources, and reports. To install BIDS, run the Setup program for SQL Server, and select the Client Components check box when you specify the components to install. Since BIDS is an add-in to Visual Studio 2008, it will install the Visual Studio 2008 shell if you don't already have it installed. This can be installed side by side on a computer with Visual Studio 2010.

If you need to create complex and rich reports like the ones that are included with the product, you should refer to the whitepaper by John Socha-Leialoha. The paper is called "Creating Reports for Team Foundation Server 2010" and it's available at `http://msdn.microsoft` `.com/en-us/library/ff730837.aspx`.

In the paper, Socha-Leialoha mentions that he was responsible for revising the reports in the standard process templates for 2010 and previous releases. A little piece of trivia about Socha-Leialoha is that he is the original author of the product known as Norton Commander. He even has his own Wikipedia page at `http://en.wikipedia.org/wiki/John_Socha`.

SETTING DEFAULT REPORT PARAMETERS WITH LINKED REPORTS

The reports that are included in the Agile and CMMI process templates are very powerful, while, at the same time, very generic. (These process templates are examined in more detail in Chapter 12.)

For them to be generic, a lot of their behavior is driven through parameters. For example, there are parameters for areas, iterations, and work item types. Without

continues

(continued)

any customization, each time someone opens the report, they must select the correct parameters before the report is meaningful to them.

If you have multiple teams using a team project, and they are using different area paths to keep their work items separate, the default parameter settings of the reports can be frustrating. Even if you're the only team working in a team project, you might want quick access to reports with preconfigured iteration parameters.

With the use of linked reports, you can predefine a set of parameters for a report, and have it appear as a new report, without creating an actual copy of the original report.

For more information, see the following blog posts:

➤   "Customizing Report Parameters — Cube Reports" at `http://tinyurl`
    `.com/ReportParams1`

➤   "Customizing Report Parameters — SQL Reports" at `http://tinyurl`
    `.com/ReportParams2`

SharePoint Dashboards

SharePoint dashboards are a new feature available with Team Foundation Server 2010 when it is integrated with either SharePoint 2007 or SharePoint 2010. Each dashboard is made up of three different types of web parts:

➤   *Team Foundation Server web parts* — These web parts access the operational store, and show the current data in the system. They are interactive, and can be used to update work items.

➤   *Page Viewer web parts* — These web parts display SQL Server Reporting Services reports. They pass through parameters and cache results.

➤   *Excel Services web parts* — These web parts render charts from Excel workbooks stored in a SharePoint document library. They use the Single Sign-On (SSO) or Secure Store Service (SSS) to authenticate to the cube server.

When Team Foundation Server is integrated with the Enterprise edition of SharePoint (which includes Excel Services), the dashboards will display Excel Services web parts. For servers that don't have Excel Services available, the dashboards will use Page Viewer web parts and display Reporting Services reports.

Both the Agile and the CMMI process templates come with the following dashboards. However, only the first two dashboards are available on a server without Excel Services.

➤   *My Dashboard* — Quickly access work items that are assigned to you.

➤   *Project Dashboard* — Review progress with the team. Shows the Task Burn Down and Burn Rate reports.

➤ *Progress Dashboard* — Track progress toward completing an iteration.

➤ *Bugs Dashboard* — Monitor bug activity.

➤ *Build Dashboard* — Monitor code coverage, code churn, and build activity.

➤ *Quality Dashboard* — Troubleshoot software quality issues with the team.

➤ *Test Dashboard* — Monitor test progress and find gaps in test coverage.

> *For more information including detailed descriptions and samples of each of the dashboards, see "Dashboards (Agile)" at* http://msdn.microsoft.com/en-us/library/dd380719.aspx. *and "Dashboards (CMMI)" at* http://msdn.microsoft.com/en-us/library/ee461578.aspx.

Accessing Dashboards

The easiest way to access dashboards for a team project is to right-click on the team project in Team Explorer and select Show Project Portal, as shown in Figure 13-14. This will then open the default web browser and navigate to the SharePoint site associated with that team project.

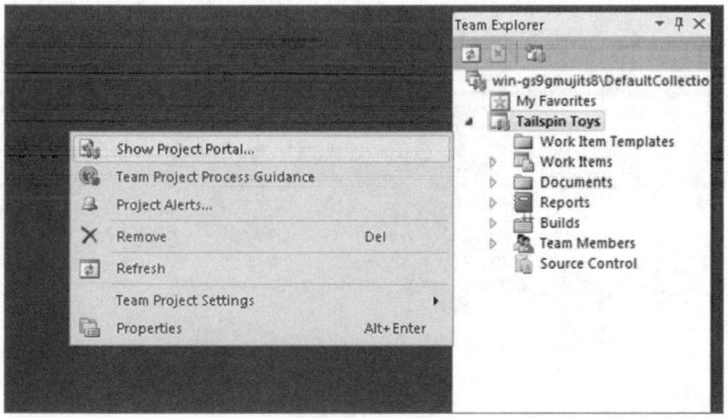

FIGURE 13-14: Show Project Portal option in Team Explorer

If there is no project portal associated with the team project, then the option will not be available on the context menu.

Customizing a Dashboard

The default dashboards have no filters applied and, therefore, the first customization you'll want to make is to scope them to the area and iteration that your team is currently using.

To create a customized dashboard for your team, follow these steps:

1. Browse to an existing dashboard on your project portal site.

2. Select the Copy Dashboard button in the site toolbar, as shown in Figure 13-15.

FIGURE 13-15: Toolbar showing Copy Dashboard button

3. On the Copy Dashboard Page screen shown in Figure 13-16, enter a Dashboard File Name and Title for the new dashboard. Then, click the Copy Dashboard button.

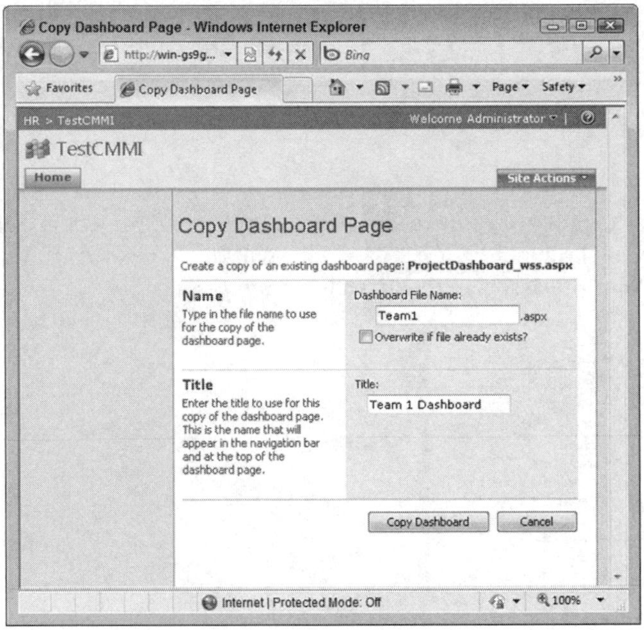

FIGURE 13-16: Copy Dashboard Page screen

Now you can modify the web parts on the dashboard to show details specific to your team.

ADVANCED CUSTOMIZATION

Let's take a brief look at a few advanced customization topics, including the following:

➤ Customizing project portals

➤ Customizing warehouse adapters

➤ TfsRedirect.aspx

Customizing Project Portals

Project portals are designed to be customized to the team or the organization's needs. Beyond the simple customization available within SharePoint, you can modify the process template to change project portals created in the future. Following are a few scenarios that you might want to do this for:

➤ Your organization has an existing SharePoint site template, and you want to modify it to include the Team Foundation Server dashboards.

➤ You want to modify the existing Team Foundation Server site templates to include your customizations for future project portals.

➤ You want to change the visual appearance of the portal site.

> For more information, refer to the whitepaper, "Customizing Team Foundation Server Project Portals," by Phil Hodgson at `http://msdn.microsoft.com/en-us/library/ff678492.aspx`.

Customizing Warehouse Adapters

As discussed earlier, if you want to make customizations to either the relational warehouse or cube that are beyond simple field changes, you must deploy them as a custom warehouse adapter. If you don't deploy the changes as an adapter, your customizations will be lost when the warehouse is rebuilt.

A custom adapter must know how to do the following:

➤ Create the schema in the relational warehouse.

➤ Retrieve and transform data from the operational store, and load it into the relational warehouse.

➤ Create the schema in the analysis database.

➤ Create a warehouse adapter sync job and schedule it.

> For more information, refer to the Team Foundation Server 2010 sample warehouse adapter from Nick Ericson in the MSDN Code Gallery at `http://code.msdn.microsoft.com/Tfs2010SampleAdapter`.

TfsRedirect.aspx

If you look at the Link property for the Page Viewer web parts on the dashboards, you'll see that they're set to a value like the following:

```
/sites/DefaultCollection/Tailspin Toys/_layouts/TfsRedirect.aspx?tf:Type=Report&tf:
    ReportName=Dashboards/Burndown&tf:ShowToolbar=0&Width=381pt&Height=180pt
```

TfsRedirect.aspx is a special piece of glue that helps SharePoint, Reporting Services, and Team Foundation Server work together. For example, there are several items on a project portal that point to other related resources:

➤ Team Web Access

➤ Process Guidance

➤ Reports on the dashboard pages

Since these settings are only stored in Team Foundation Server and can be changed at any time, SharePoint uses the TfsRedirect.aspx page to retrieve them.

By specifying the tf:Test parameter, you can see the underlying settings, which may be useful in debugging project portal configuration problems. For any existing project portal, simply append the following to the site URL:

```
/_layouts/TfsRedirect.aspx?tf:Type=ReportList&tf:Test=1&tf:clearcache=1
```

 For more information, see "Using TfsRedirect to Display Reports in TFS 2010 Dashboards" at http://tinyurl.com/TfsRedirect.

SUMMARY

In this chapter, you learned about the compelling new reporting features in Team Foundation Server 2010, as well as about the major changes incorporated into this release. You also learned about the various data stores in the system and how data flows between them.

This chapter covered the two main reporting technologies (Reporting Services and Excel Services), along with the tools to create and customize the reports. This chapter also described how to quickly and easily create a report from a simple Work Item Query. Finally, this chapter looked briefly at some advanced customization topics.

Chapter 14 takes a look at automating your build system using Team Foundation Build. It discusses what build automation is, and the benefits that it brings.

PART IV
Team Foundation Build

Overview of Build Automation

WHAT'S IN THIS CHAPTER?

➤ Getting to know build automation

➤ Scripting a build

➤ Using build automation servers

➤ Adopting build automation

After version control, automating the build is the second most important thing you can do to improve the quality of your software.

This chapter defines build automation, discusses the benefits of it in general, and examines why it benefits the software engineering process overall. This is followed by a look at the high-level capabilities and limitations of Team Foundation Server, and a comparison with other common build systems in use today. Finally, some general advice is provided to assist in adopting build automation in your environment today.

Subsequent chapters of this book dive deeper into Team Foundation Server's build capabilities, discuss how to customize the build process, and demonstrate this by working through a series of common build customizations used in real-world scenarios.

LET'S BUILD SOMETHING

Imagine building a house. You visit the site every day and see nothing but a muddy field. The construction team tells you, "Yup, we're making excellent progress. The doors are all done and look great. Walls are 80 percent there. Plumbing is ready to go, and the kitchen is ready to drop in." Every day you visit you see that same muddy field. The construction teams tell you how well progress is going. Sometimes they regale you with stories about how they decided the doors were not going to be up to the job, so they threw them on a bonfire and built new ones from scratch that can open both ways, and even have little flaps ready should you ever decide to get a cat.

But you never see any progress — just a muddy field with lots of busy people running around looking stressed.

Then, the day before you are due to move in, everything arrives on site at the same time. Things are stuck together in a hurry — but it takes longer than everyone seemed to think it would. The day draws on, night begins to fall, and everyone gets tired, but they heroically continue trying to get the thing to fit together.

In the morning, you take a look at your house. It's a house for sure. A couple of the rooms are not quite finished yet, because they didn't fit when they arrived onsite. A few of the screws are missing, none of the paint is the color you would have chosen, and many things aren't exactly how you'd envisioned them when you drew up the plans six months ago. You can't help wondering why they spent all that time putting cat flaps in your doors when you are allergic to cats, but they didn't manage to get your bathroom finished.

Now, try to imagine how your customers feel when dealing with something as ephemeral as software. How do you show progress to a customer? How do you know how complete you are? How do you know if everything works? How do you know if you are done with a particular feature, or if a feature is done enough to move onto the next one?

The only way to know all this is to assemble your software together and try it out as a whole, to run your application, or to visit your website. Sure, some areas are missing, or not quite functional yet. But once you are able to see your application running, you know how close you are to finishing, and it is also very easy for your customer to know how things are going. Once the customer sees it for real, he or she might say that a particular feature you thought was only partially implemented is actually enough to do what he or she wanted. The customer can suggest some course corrections early on, which will make everyone happier with the end result. But you didn't have to change too much to get there.

The problem is that assembling your application can take time. But by making an investment in automating this experience as you go through the software development process, you not only ensure that you can accurately measure and demonstrate progress, but you remove a huge source of error when it comes to that last-minute push to completion.

If you are serious about the quality of the software you deliver, then you need to be serious about build automation.

WHAT IS BUILD AUTOMATION?

Build automation is the process of streamlining your build process so that it is possible to assemble your application into a usable product with a simple, single action. This entails not just the part of code a particular developer is working on, but other typical activities such as the following:

➤ Compiling source code into binaries

➤ Packaging binaries into installable modules such as MSI files, XAP files, JAR files, DMG images, and so on

➤ Running tests

➤ Creating documentation

➤ Deploying results ready for use

Only once the parts of your application come together can you tell if your application works and does what it is supposed to. Assembling the parts of an application is often a complex, time-consuming, and error-prone process. There are so many parts to building the application that, without an automated build, the activity usually falls on one or two individuals on the team who know the secret. Without an automated build, even they sometimes get it wrong, with show-stopping consequences that are often discovered very late, making any mistakes expensive to fix.

Imagine having to recall an entire manufacturing run of a DVD because you missed an important file. Worse still, imagine accidentally including the source code for your application in a web distribution, or leaving embarrassing test data in the application when it was deployed to production. All these things made headlines when they happened to organizations building software, yet they could have easily been avoided.

Integration of software components is the difficult part. Developers work on their features in isolation, making various assumptions about how other parts of the system function. Only once the parts are assembled together do the assumptions get tested. If you integrate early and often, these integrations get tested as soon as possible in the development process — therefore reducing the cost of fixing the inevitable issues.

It should be trivial for everyone involved in the project to run a copy of the latest build. Only then can you tell if your software works and does what it is supposed to. Only then can you tell if you are going to have your product ready on time. A regular, automated build is the heartbeat of your team.

In Visual Studio 2010, a developer can usually run his or her application by pressing the famous F5 key to run the code in debug mode. This assembles the code together on the local workstation and executes it. This makes it trivial for the developer to test his or her part of the code base. But what it doesn't do is ensure that the code works with all the latest changes committed by other members of the team. In addition, pressing the F5 key simply compiles the code ready for manual testing. As part of an automated build, you can also run a full suite of automated tests, giving you a high degree of confidence that no changes that have been introduced have broken something elsewhere.

Pressing the F5 key is easy for a developer. You want your automated build to make it just as easy to run your application — if not easier. This is where a build automation server plays a part.

The build automation server is a machine that looks for changes in version control and automatically rebuilds the project. This can be on demand, on a regular schedule (such as nightly or daily builds), or can be performed every time a developer checks in a file — a process that is often referred to as *continuous integration.*

> **MARTIN FOWLER ON CONTINUOUS INTEGRATION**
>
> The term *continuous integration* (CI) emerged from Agile software development methodologies such as Extreme Programming (XP) at the turn of the millennium. Martin Fowler's paper on continuous integration from 2000 is still worth reading today at `www.martinfowler.com/articles/continuousIntegration.html`.
>
> Note that, as originally described, the term refers to increasing the speed and quality of software delivery by decreasing the integration times, and not simply the practice of performing a build for every check-in. Many of the practices expounded by Fowler's paper are supported by tooling in Visual Studio 2010 Team Foundation Server — not simply this one small feature of the build services. However, the term *continuous integration* has come to be synonymous with building after a check-in has occurred and is, therefore, used by Team Foundation Server as the name for this type of trigger, as discussed in Chapter 15.

However, before you can run your build on a build server, you must script your build so that it can be run with a single command.

SCRIPTING A BUILD

The most basic form of build automation is to write a script that performs all the operations necessary for a clean build for you. This could be a shell script, batch file, PowerShell script, and so on. However, because of the common tasks that you perform during a build (such as dependency tracking, compiling files, batching files together, and so on), a number of specialized build scripting languages have been developed over the years.

Make

The granddaddy of specialized build scripting languages is *Make*. Originally created at Bell Labs by Dr. Stuart Feldman in 1977, Make is still commonly used on UNIX-based platforms to create programs from source code by reading the build configuration as stored in a text-based file called *makefile*. Normally, to build an executable, you had to enter a number of commands to compile and link the source code, also ensuring that dependent code has been correctly compiled and linked. Make was designed specifically to help C programmers manage this build process in an efficient manner.

A makefile defines a series of targets, with each command indented by a tab inside the target.

```
#Comment
target: dependencies
<TAB>command
```

For example, a simple `Hello World` application could have the following makefile:

```
# Define C Compiler and compiler flags
CC=gcc
```

```
CFLAGS=-g

# The default target, called if make is executed with no target.
all: helloworld

helloworld: helloworld.o
    $(CC) $(CFLAGS) -o $@ $<    # Note: Lines starts with a TAB

helloworld.o: helloworld.c
    $(CC) $(CFLAGS) -c -o &@ $<

clean:
    rm -rf *o helloworld
```

Note that one of the main features of Make is that it simplifies dependency management. That is to say that to make the executable `helloworld`, it checks if the target `helloworld.o` exists, and that its dependencies are met. `helloworld.o` is dependent on the C source file `helloworld.c`. Only if `helloworld.c` has changed since the last execution of Make will `helloworld.o` be created and, therefore, `helloworld`.

The previous script is the same as typing the following commands in sequence at the command line:

```
gcc -g -c -o helloworld.o helloworld.c
gcc -g -o helloworld helloworld.o
```

In a simple makefile like the one shown previously, everything is very readable. With more complex makefiles that do packaging and deployment activities, it can take a while to figure out which commands are executed in which order. Make uses a declarative language that can be difficult to read for developers used to coding in more imperative languages (like most modern program languages are). For many developers, it feels like you must read a makefile slightly backward — that is, you must look at the target, then follow all its dependencies and then their dependencies, to track back what will actually occur first in the sequence.

Since its inception, Make has gone through a number of rewrites and has a number of derivatives that have used the same file format and basic principles, as well as providing some of their own features. There are implementations of Make for most platforms, including nmake from Microsoft for the Windows platform.

Apache Ant

Ant is a build automation tool similar to Make, but it was designed from the ground up to be a platform-independent tool. James Duncan Davidson originally developed Ant at Sun Microsystems. It was first released in 2000. According to Davidson, the name "Ant" is an acronym for "Another Neat Tool." It is a Java-based tool and uses an XML file, typically stored in a file called `build.xml`. With its Java heritage and platform independence, Ant is typically used to build Java projects.

Ant shares a fair number of similarities with Make. The build file is composed of a project that contains a number of targets. Each target defines a number of tasks that are executed and a set of dependencies. Ant is declarative and does automatic dependency management. For example, a simple `Hello World` application in Java could have the following `build.xml` to compile it using Ant:

```xml
<?xml version="1.0" encoding="utf-8"?>
<project name="helloworld" basedir="." default="package">

    <target name="compile">
        <mkdir dir="${basedir}/bin" />
        <javac srcdir="${basedir}/src"
                destdir="${basedir}/bin"
                debug="on"
                includeAntRuntime="false"/>
    </target>

    <target name="jar">
        <jar destfile="${basedir}/helloworld.jar"
            basedir="${basedir}/bin" />
    </target>

    <target name="clean">
        <delete file="helloworld.jar" />
        <delete dir="${basedir}/bin" />
    </target>

    <target name="package" depends="compile,jar">
        <!-- Comments are in standard XML format -->
    </target>


</project>
```

The tasks in Ant are implemented as a piece of compiled Java code implementing a particular interface. In addition to the large number of standard tasks that ship as part of Ant, a number of tasks are available in the Open Source community. Manufacturers of Java-related tooling will often provide Ant tasks to make it easier to work with their tools from Ant.

Ant scripts can get quite complex, and because the XML used in an Ant script is quite verbose, scripts can very quickly get very large and complicated. Therefore, for complex build systems, the main `build.xml` file can be broken down into more modular files.

Ant is so common among the Java community that most of the modern IDEs ship with a version of Ant to allow automated builds to be easily executed from inside the development environment, as well as with tooling to help author Ant scripts.

Apache Maven

Maven is an Open Source project management and build automation tool written in Java. It is primarily used for Java projects. The central concept in Maven is the Project Object Model (`pom.xml`) file that describes the project being built. While Maven is similar in functionality to Make and derivations such as Ant, it has some novel concepts that make it worth discussing in this book.

Make and Ant allow a completely free-form script to be coded, and for you to have your source files located in any manner. Maven takes the not-unreasonable assumption then you are performing a build, and uses conventions for where files should be located for the build process. It applies the "Convention over Configuration" software design paradigm to builds. The main advantage of this is that is makes it easy to find your way around a Maven project, because they all must follow certain patterns to get built (at the disadvantage of losing some flexibility).

The other main difference between Maven and the Make-inspired build tools is that it takes dependency management to the next level. While Make and Ant handle dependencies inside the project being built, Maven can manage the dependencies on external libraries (which are especially common in many Java projects). If your code takes a dependency on a certain version of a library, then Maven will download this from a project repository and store it locally, making it available for build. This helps the portability of builds because it means that all you need to get started is Java and Maven installed. Executing the build should take care of downloading everything else you need to run the build.

 For more information about Maven, visit http://maven.apache.org/.

NAnt

NAnt (http://nant.sourceforge.net/) was inspired by Apache Ant, but written in .NET and designed to build .NET projects. Like Ant, it is also an Open Source project and was originally released in 2001. Interestingly, according to the NAnt FAQ, the name NAnt comes from the fact that the tool is "Not Ant," which, to extract Ant from its original acronym, would mean that NAnt was "Not Another Neat Tool." But, in fact, NAnt was a very neat way of performing build automation, and was especially useful in early .NET 1.0 and 1.1 projects.

Syntactically very similar to Ant, NAnt files are stored with a `.build` suffix such as `nant.build`. Each file is composed of a project that contains a number of targets. Each target defines a number of tasks that are executed and a set of dependencies. There are tasks provided to perform common .NET activities such as `<csc />` to execute the C# command-line compiler tool.

The main problem with NAnt files is that they were not understood by Visual Studio as of this writing, and so changes made to the Visual Studio solution files (`.sln`) and project files must also be made in the NAnt file; otherwise, the dependencies would not be known to the automated build script. To execute a build using the `.sln` file or the `.vbproj`/`.csproj` files, you must install Visual Studio on the build server and use the `devenv` task to drive Visual Studio from the command line, which most people therefore avoid.

MSBuild

MSBuild is the build system that has been used by Visual Studio since Visual Studio 2005. However, the MSBuild platform is installed as part of the .NET Framework, and it is possible to build projects using `MSBuild.exe` from the command line without using the Visual Studio IDE.

Visual Studio keeps the MSBuild file up to date for the project. In fact, the .csproj and .vbproj files that are well known to developers in Visual Studio are simply MSBuild scripts.

MSBuild was heavily influenced by XML-based build automation systems such as Ant or NAnt, but also by its predecessor nmake (and therefore Make). MSBuild files typically end with a *proj extension (for example, TFSBuild.proj, MyVBProject.vbproj, or MyCSharpProject.csproj). The MSBuild file follows what should by now be a familiar pattern. It consists of a project, and inside the project, a number of properties and targets are defined. Each target contains a number of tasks.

Following is an example of a simple MSBuild script that you could execute from a Visual Studio command prompt with the command msbuild helloworld.proj:

```
<?xml version="1.0" encoding="utf-8"?>
<Project xmlns="http://schemas.microsoft.com/developer/msbuild/2003"
         DefaultTargets="SayHello" >

  <PropertyGroup>
    <!-- Define name to say hello to -->
    <Name>World</Name>
  </PropertyGroup>

  <Target Name="SayHello">
    <Message Text="Hello $(Name)!" />
  </Target>


</Project>
```

However, MSBuild has some notable exceptions. As well as simple properties in a PropertyGroup as shown previously (which can be thought of as key-value pairs), there is also a notion of an Item. Items are a list of many values that can be thought of as similar to an array or enumeration in programming terms. An Item also has metadata associated with it. When you create an Item, it is actually a .NET object (implementing the ITaskItem interface). There is a pre-defined set of metadata available on every Item, but you can also add your own properties as child nodes of the Item in the ItemGroup.

Another way that the use of MSBuild differs from things like Ant or NAnt is that Visual Studio and Team Foundation Server ship with a number of templates for the build process. These are stored in an MSBuild script with a .targets extension. These are usually stored in %ProgramFiles%/MSBuild or in the .NET Framework folder on the individual machine. The actual build script created by Visual Studio usually just imports the relevant .targets file and provides a number of properties to customize the behavior of the build process defined in the .targets file. In this way, MSBuild shares some slight similarities to Maven in that a typical build pattern is presented, which the project customizes to fit.

In an MSBuild script, reading the file from top to bottom, the last place to define a property or target wins (unlike in Ant, where the first place defined is the winner). This behavior means that anything you write after you import the .targets file in your MSBuild script will override behavior in the imported build template.

The standard templates provided by Microsoft include many .targets files that are already called in the standard template prefixed with Before or After, which are designed as hook points for your own custom logic to run before or after these steps. A classic example would be BeforeBuild and AfterBuild. It is considered good practice to only override targets that are designed to be overridden like this, or to override properties that are designed to control the build process. The imported .targets files are typically well-commented, and can be read if you would like to learn more about what they do.

Following is a basic .vbproj file as generated by Visual Studio 2010 for a simple Hello World style application. Hopefully, you will now recognize and understand many of the elements of the file. Notice that is doesn't contain any actual Targets — these are all in the imported Microsoft .VisualBasic.targets file, including the actual call out to the Visual Basic compiler. The .vbproj file just contains properties and ItemGroups, which configure how that .target file behaves.

```xml
<?xml version="1.0" encoding="utf-8"?>
<Project ToolsVersion="4.0" DefaultTargets="Build"
    xmlns="http://schemas.microsoft.com/developer/msbuild/2003">
  <PropertyGroup>
    <Configuration Condition=" '$(Configuration)' == '' ">Debug</Configuration>
    <Platform Condition=" '$(Platform)' == '' ">x86</Platform>
    <ProductVersion>
    </ProductVersion>
    <SchemaVersion>
    </SchemaVersion>
    <ProjectGuid>{D36961BC-0340-4462-A7A9-A5C766F37176}</ProjectGuid>
    <OutputType>Exe</OutputType>
    <StartupObject>HelloWorld.Module1</StartupObject>
    <RootNamespace>HelloWorld</RootNamespace>
    <AssemblyName>HelloWorld</AssemblyName>
    <FileAlignment>512</FileAlignment>
    <MyType>Console</MyType>
    <TargetFrameworkVersion>v4.0</TargetFrameworkVersion>
    <TargetFrameworkProfile>Client</TargetFrameworkProfile>
  </PropertyGroup>
  <PropertyGroup Condition=" '$(Configuration)|$(Platform)' == 'Debug|x86' ">
    <PlatformTarget>x86</PlatformTarget>
    <DebugSymbols>true</DebugSymbols>
    <DebugType>full</DebugType>
    <DefineDebug>true</DefineDebug>
    <DefineTrace>true</DefineTrace>
    <OutputPath>bin\Debug\</OutputPath>
    <DocumentationFile>HelloWorld.xml</DocumentationFile>

<NoWarn>42016,41999,42017,42018,42019,42032,42036,42020,42021,42022</NoWarn>
  </PropertyGroup>
  <PropertyGroup Condition=" '$(Configuration)|$(Platform)' == 'Release|x86' ">
    <PlatformTarget>x86</PlatformTarget>
    <DebugType>pdbonly</DebugType>
    <DefineDebug>false</DefineDebug>
    <DefineTrace>true</DefineTrace>
    <Optimize>true</Optimize>
    <OutputPath>bin\Release\</OutputPath>
    <DocumentationFile>HelloWorld.xml</DocumentationFile>
```

```xml
<NoWarn>42016,41999,42017,42018,42019,42032,42036,42020,42021,42022</NoWarn>
  </PropertyGroup>
  <PropertyGroup>
    <OptionExplicit>On</OptionExplicit>
  </PropertyGroup>
  <PropertyGroup>
    <OptionCompare>Binary</OptionCompare>
  </PropertyGroup>
  <PropertyGroup>
    <OptionStrict>Off</OptionStrict>
  </PropertyGroup>
  <PropertyGroup>
    <OptionInfer>On</OptionInfer>
  </PropertyGroup>
  <ItemGroup>
    <Reference Include="System" />
    <Reference Include="System.Data" />
    <Reference Include="System.Deployment" />
    <Reference Include="System.Xml" />
    <Reference Include="System.Core" />
    <Reference Include="System.Xml.Linq" />
    <Reference Include="System.Data.DataSetExtensions" />
  </ItemGroup>
  <ItemGroup>
    <Import Include="Microsoft.VisualBasic" />
    <Import Include="System" />
  </ItemGroup>
  <ItemGroup>
    <Compile Include="Module1.vb" />
    <Compile Include="My Project\AssemblyInfo.vb" />
    <Compile Include="My Project\Application.Designer.vb">
      <AutoGen>True</AutoGen>
      <DependentUpon>Application.myapp</DependentUpon>
    </Compile>
    <Compile Include="My Project\Resources.Designer.vb">
      <AutoGen>True</AutoGen>
      <DesignTime>True</DesignTime>
      <DependentUpon>Resources.resx</DependentUpon>
    </Compile>
    <Compile Include="My Project\Settings.Designer.vb">
      <AutoGen>True</AutoGen>
      <DependentUpon>Settings.settings</DependentUpon>
      <DesignTimeSharedInput>True</DesignTimeSharedInput>
    </Compile>
  </ItemGroup>
  <ItemGroup>
    <EmbeddedResource Include="My Project\Resources.resx">
      <Generator>VbMyResourcesResXFileCodeGenerator</Generator>
      <LastGenOutput>Resources.Designer.vb</LastGenOutput>
      <CustomToolNamespace>My.Resources</CustomToolNamespace>
      <SubType>Designer</SubType>
    </EmbeddedResource>
  </ItemGroup>
  <ItemGroup>
```

```
                    <None Include="My Project\Application.myapp">
                      <Generator>MyApplicationCodeGenerator</Generator>
                      <LastGenOutput>Application.Designer.vb</LastGenOutput>
                    </None>
                    <None Include="My Project\Settings.settings">
                      <Generator>SettingsSingleFileGenerator</Generator>
                      <CustomToolNamespace>My</CustomToolNamespace>
                      <LastGenOutput>Settings.Designer.vb</LastGenOutput>
                    </None>
                  </ItemGroup>
                  <Import Project="$(MSBuildToolsPath)\Microsoft.VisualBasic.targets" />
                  <!-- To modify your build process, add your task inside one of
                          the targets below and uncomment it.
                      Other similar extension points exist, see Microsoft.Common.targets.
                  <Target Name="BeforeBuild">
                  </Target>
                  <Target Name="AfterBuild">
                  </Target>
                  -->

                </Project>
```

Windows Workflow Foundation

Although this chapter has familiarized you with specialized build scripting languages, so far no mention had been made of other programming and scripting methods that could also be used to create a build (such as PowerShell, batch files, or even UNIX shell scripts). But one such general-purpose framework is worth mentioning here because of its use by the build automation functionality in Team Foundation Server 2010 — *Windows Workflow Foundation* (WF).

WF is a programming framework from Microsoft used for defining and executing workflows. Introduced in .NET Framework 3.0, the version used by Team Foundation Server is version 4.0, and is part of the .NET Framework 4.0. Version 4.0 was a major revision of WF. It can be coded using the XML-based XAML markup or in any .NET language directly against the Windows Workflow Foundation APIs, which ship with the .NET Framework.

Unlike the specialized build languages, WF contains no functionality built in for dependency management — or even methods for mass manipulation of files. Therefore, its use by Team Foundation Server for build automation might seem a little odd at first. However, WF provides a couple of capabilities that traditional build scripting languages do not.

The build scripting languages do not typically store state between instances, but workflow is all about state. WF maintains state, gets input and sends output to the world outside of the workflow engine, provides the control flow, and executes the code that makes up the work.

In addition, most build scripting languages control the execution on a single machine. The state persistence nature of WF brings with it the capability to take components of the build and deploy them across multiple machines. This means that you can split some of the workload of your build across several machines, and bring the results back together before proceeding with the rest of the build process. For example, you could perform compilation on one machine, while generating documentation from the source on another, and bring them both together when you package your build. This capability provides another weapon in your arsenal when trying to reduce the overall time for a build to complete, and thus tightening the feedback loop for your builds.

For activities that require more traditional build capabilities (such as amassing a bunch of files together and compiling them), the WF templates used by Team Foundation Server rely on the traditional build scripting languages — typically MSBuild.

The next two chapters of this book explain more about WF and how it is used by Team Foundation Build. The rest of this chapter looks in more detail at the concept of a build automation server.

USING BUILD AUTOMATION SERVERS

Once you have a single command that can run your build, the next step is to run it periodically. This ensures that the product in version control is always in a runnable state, but also removes yet another manual step in the chain, and fully automates the build process. Having the build runnable on a server ensures that the build is repeatable on a machine other than the one used by the developer to code the project. Just this simple act of separation helps to ensure that all dependencies are known about and taken account of in the build — which is what helps build repeatability.

In the earliest days of build automation, the build was performed periodically (typically weekly, nightly, or daily) using a simple cron job or scheduled task.

Building on every single check-in to the version control system requires a machine with dedicated build server logic. It was exactly this logic that was built for a project being implemented by a company called ThoughtWorks (an IT consultancy focused on Agile software development practices). The Continuous Integration (CI) build server logic was then later extracted into a standalone project, which became CruiseControl.

CruiseControl

CruiseControl (http://cruisecontrol.sourceforge.net/) is an Open Source build server implemented in Java. Therefore, it runs on many platforms, including Windows and Linux. At the heart of CruiseControl is the build loop that periodically checks the configured version control system for changes to the code, and, if a change is detected, it will trigger a new build. Once the build is complete, a notification can be sent regarding the state of the build.

Configuration of CruiseControl is performed using a single `config.xml` file. Because of its long life as a vibrant and active Open Source project, there are many extensions that have been contributed to CruiseControl over time. Many different version control systems (including Team Foundation Server) can be queried by CruiseControl, and equally many different notification schemes (including e-mail, a web-based console, instant messenger, or even a system tray application in Windows).

Output from the build (including results of unit tests, code coverage reports, API documentation, and so on) are all available via the Web interface.

While any build process can, in theory, be executed by CruiseControl, it is typically used to automate Ant builds. Therefore, it is typically used to build Java projects.

As discussed, Team Foundation Server is supported by CruiseControl as a version control repository. However, data about the build and build notifications are kept within the CruiseControl system.

CruiseControl.NET

CruiseControl.NET (http://ccnet.thoughtworks.com/) is an Open Source build server, but, as the name suggests, is implemented using .NET. It was loosely based on the original Java version of CruiseControl, and was also originally developed by the same ThoughtWorks consultancy.

Configuration of CruiseControl.NET is typically performed by editing of an XML file called ccnet.config. It is also capable of working with a number of version control systems, including Team Foundation Server, but because of its focus on .NET developers, it is capable of building .NET projects by using NAnt or MSBuild scripts and notifying the developers of the results.

Hudson

Hudson is another Open Source build server implemented in Java. In recent years, it has become a popular alternative to CruiseControl, not least because of an easy-to-use web-based interface for configuring new builds, rather than relying on manual editing of XML files.

While Hudson is capable of building a number of projects (including Ant, and even MSBuild), it has some special features for handling Maven builds and tracking dependencies between the builds for Maven projects, which is what makes it worth calling out in particular in this book.

Hudson is capable of working with many version control tools, including Team Foundation Server. However, like all external build systems, data about these builds is kept inside the Hudson system, though it does have some useful build reporting capabilities.

Team Foundation Server

Build automation is so vital to improving the quality of software development that, since its original release in 2005, Team Foundation Server has included build automation capabilities. Internally, the feature was known by the name "Big Build," but people refer to the build automation component of Team Foundation Server as Team Build or Team Foundation Build.

MSBuild first shipped with Visual Studio in 2005, and the original incarnation of Team Foundation Build in 2005 was based heavily around MSBuild. A build was defined by an MSBuild script called TFSBuild.proj located in a folder under $/*TeamProject*/TeamBuildTypes/*BuildTypeName* in Team Foundation Server version control.

When a build was triggered, the TFSBuild.proj file was downloaded to the build server and executed. Results were published back to the server, and, importantly, metrics about the build were fed into the powerful Team Foundation Server data warehouse. The build was automatically linked with Team Foundation Server work item tracking.

However, in the original 2005 release, the capabilities of Team Foundation Build were very limited. There was no built-in process for triggering builds — they had to be triggered manually, or users had to configure their own jobs to trigger builds periodically, or listen for check-ins and trigger continuous integration builds.

Thankfully, the 2008 release of Team Foundation Server saw huge improvements in the build capabilities. In fact, Team Foundation Build was probably the single biggest reason to upgrade from

Team Foundation Server 2005. In 2008, you had the capability to trigger builds by one of several trigger types, including scheduled builds and continuous integration style builds.

The 2010 release saw even more improvements to Team Foundation Server's build capabilities. The biggest of these was the move from a totally MSBuild-based solution to one using WF as the build orchestration engine. This had several important advantages, including the capability to easily surface common build configuration properties about the build into the user interface in Visual Studio or Eclipse, as well as the capability to distribute a build across multiple servers (or Build Agents).

While you get very rich integration in Team Foundation Server between the version control, build, and work item tracking functionality, it is important to note that the build automation capabilities of Team Foundation Server can only be used with Team Foundation Server version control. While this should not be an issue to readers of this book, it is an important element to factor in when planning your migration to Team Foundation Server. Only once your source code is in Team Foundation Server does it make sense to switch on its build automation capabilities.

ADOPTING BUILD AUTOMATION

Hopefully, by now, you are suitably convinced that build automation is something that you want to do. But how should you go about adopting build automation as a practice?

The first step is to ensure that you have a single command that you can run to fully build and package your product ready for deployment. If you use Visual Studio, then this is very easy, because most Visual Studio project types are easily built using MSBuild. However, if you have components developed in Java or other software languages, then you will need to do some work to put together your build script using the most appropriate scripting language (such as Ant or Maven).

Next, you should ensure that everyone knows how to build the project, and that all the developers can run this from their machines.

Once the build is easily runnable, the next step is to periodically run the build to ensure that you always have a clean code base. If you have sufficient resources, and your build is fast enough, then strive for a continuous integration style of build and ensure that you have a fast (and hopefully fun) method of notification to tell the developers when the build has been broken. A simple e-mail notification will suffice, and should be used at a minimum, but you can be more creative if you would like.

BRIAN THE BUILD BUNNY

Some ways of making the team pay attention to the state of the build are more imaginative than others. A popular way of encouraging the team to pay attention to the current state of the build is to create creative and eye-catching build status notification mechanisms. While wall displays and lava lamps are a good way of communicating this information to the team, one of the authors of this book has even gone so far as to connect a talking, moving robot rabbit into Team Foundation Server. For more information on this project (including a prize-winning YouTube video and full source code), see www.woodwardweb.com/gadgets/brian_the_build_1.html.

Just this simple step of running the build regularly will hugely affect the productivity of your team. No longer will developers need to roll back changes they have downloaded, because they do not compile in their environment. At this point in your adoption of build automation, the trick is to keep things fun, but to gradually introduce a little peer pressure to ensure that the build status is usually good. If a build fails for some reason, that build failure should be the team's immediate priority. What change to the system made the build fail? Who just broke the build? Fix the build and then resume normal work.

If you are developing a website, then make your build automatically deploy to a server so that people can easily play with the latest version of the code. If you are building a client-side application, then try to package it so that it can easily be executed by anyone involved in the project. Using MSI files or ClickOnce installers are good ways of doing this on Windows, but DMG images for the Mac, RPM/DEB files on Linux, or Eclipse Update sites for Eclipse developers are all great ways of making it easy to run the latest build.

Once the team has become familiar with the notion of builds happening automatically, and gotten into the habit of ensuring that the build is "good" at all times, you can gradually raise the bar on determining what makes a good build.

To begin with, simply being able to compile the build and package it ready for deployment is good enough. Next, you want to introduce things such as automated unit tests (again slowly at first) so that, not only does the build compile, but it also actually works as originally intended. You can also introduce other code-quality indicators at this point, such as ensuring that code meets team-wide coding standards. Over time, you can introduce targets such as 20 percent of code should be covered by the unit tests, and then gradually increase this.

The trick is to be constantly improving the quality of your builds, but still ensuring that checking in and getting a clean build is fast and easy. By keeping the feedback loop between a check-in and a working, deployable product to test as short as possible, you will maximize the productivity of your team, while also being able to easily demonstrate progress to the people sponsoring the development activity in the first place.

SUMMARY

This chapter explained what build automation is, and the benefits it brings. You learned about some of the various ways to script an automated build, and how to run that build periodically using a build automation server. Finally, tips were provided on how to adopt build automation in general inside the organization.

Once you have migrated your source code into Team Foundation Server, getting builds configured is an important next step. As discussed in this chapter, if you are already using an existing build automation server, then most of these are already able to use Team Foundation Server as a version control repository from which to draw when automating the build. However, there are several advantages for using Team Foundation Server's built-in build automation capabilities — primarily the integration you get between the version control and work item tracking systems, but also the excellent reporting capabilities provided by Team Foundation Server. The regular builds act as a heartbeat to which you can track the health of your project once all the data from version control, work item tracking, and build automation is combined in the reports provided by Team Foundation Server.

Things have been deliberately generalized in this chapter because build automation is important regardless of the technology or platform you choose to use. However, Team Foundation Server has some innovative features around build automation.

Chapter 15 describes in detail how to create automated builds inside Team Foundation Server. It describes all the features that Team Foundation Server provides, and highlights new features in the 2010 release. You will learn about the architecture of the Team Foundation Build system and how to work with builds. Finally, the build process will be examined in detail, describing what it does and how it works.

15

Using Team Foundation Build

WHAT'S IN THIS CHAPTER?

➤ Getting to know the build automation features provided by Team Foundation Server

➤ Understanding the Team Foundation build architecture

➤ Installing a build controller and build agent

➤ Working with builds

➤ Understanding the build process

➤ Editing build process parameters

➤ Building both .NET and Java projects with Team Foundation Server

This chapter introduces the build automation capabilities of Team Foundation Server 2010, the core concepts, and how to install the build server functionality. You will learn how to create your own builds based on the standard build process templates, along with how to use and manage them.

> *For information on customizing the standard build process, see Chapter 16.*

INTRODUCTION TO TEAM FOUNDATION BUILD

The build automation capabilities of Team Foundation Server have probably undergone the most significant change since the initial release of Team Foundation Server 2005. Originally, the build functionality simply extended MSBuild to allow for a basic level of build automation integrated with Team Foundation version control and work item tracking.

In the 2008 release, the build system came of age in its own right as a fully enterprise-ready build automation system. That release introduced new first-class concepts into Team Foundation Server, such as the build definition and build agent, and also had powerful build triggering functionalities provided out-of-the-box. However, the build process was still tightly tied to MSBuild.

The 2010 release introduced even more features into the build automation area. The biggest change was the introduction of Windows Workflow 4.0 as the main build orchestration mechanism. The actual build of solutions is still handled by the specialized build language (such as MSBuild for .NET solutions, but also Ant or Maven for Java-based projects). However, the rest of the process is governed by a build process template written using Windows Workflow 4.0.

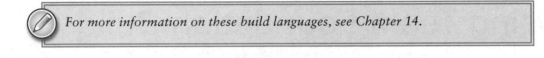

For more information on these build languages, see Chapter 14.

Other notable features new in the 2010 release include gated check-in support, private builds, build notifications, common build customization properties, integration with Symbol and Source servers, enhanced build deletion capabilities, and the introduction of a new concept called the *build controller*.

TEAM FOUNDATION BUILD ARCHITECTURE

Figure 15-1 shows several of the logical components that are critical in the Team Foundation Build architecture.

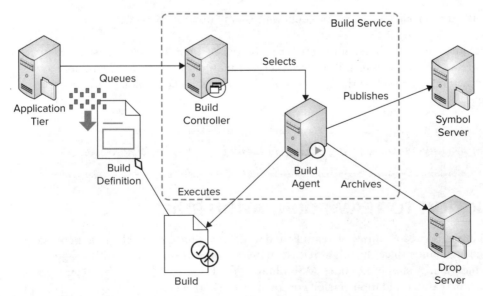

FIGURE 15-1: Team Foundation Build logical architecture

A build is defined by a *build definition,* which describes the build in detail, including what should be built, how, and when. More information about build definitions, as well as how to create and manage them, is provided later in this chapter.

The build definition belongs to a team project in Team Foundation Server. When the application tier determines that a build for the build definition should be performed, it sends a build request to a web service running on the *build controller.*

The build controller then downloads the Windows Workflow-based build process template defined for the build definition, and executes it. By default, this causes a build to be run on the next available *build agent* in the controller's pool of agents.

A build agent is the actual machine that performs the build. Each build agent has a build controller as a parent, but one build controller can have multiple build agents that it can use for the build. Each build controller must be assigned to a single project collection.

The build agent executes the main part of the build process as described in the build definition's process template — including calling MSBuild to perform the actual compilation and test steps. The build agent also exposes a number of web services that are used to control the operation of the build by the build controller.

Once the build agent has successfully executed the build, the default build process template then archives the build results (such as the website, executable files, assemblies, and so on) to the Windows-based file share provided as the *drop location.* It will also publish any symbols to the *symbol server* (if configured).

All the information about the resulting build (including the build number, status, and information on the individual build's progress for a particular build definition) are called the *build details.* These details are displayed in a *build report.*

Note that the build controller and build agent processes are hosted by the *build service.* The web services used by the controller and agent are using Windows Communication Foundation (WCF), and, therefore, Internet Information Services (IIS) is not required on the build machines.

The build controller and build agent may live on the same machine. However, it is recommended that they do not reside on the same machine as the Team Foundation Server application tier in a production configuration. A build is very CPU- and disk I/O-intensive. Therefore, the operation of builds could affect the performance of your application tier if running on the same machine, which could reduce the productivity of your entire development group.

SETTING UP THE TEAM FOUNDATION BUILD SERVICE

This section details how to set up the build service to enable build automation. This is useful for those administering a Team Foundation Server instance. If you already have a build controller for your project collection, then you may wish to skip this section and go straight to the section, "Working with Builds," to discover how to create new build definitions and manage them.

> *The build service for Team Foundation Server is installed from the Team Foundation Server media. This section briefly touches on installing the build service, but, for the most recent information on how to install and configure the build service, as well as the list of supported hardware and software, see the "Team Foundation Server Installation Guide." The guide is included in the install media for Team Foundation Server, but the latest version is published at* http://go.microsoft.com/fwlink/?LinkId=127730. *Microsoft continues to update the "Installation Guide" download to include extra guidance or any new issues that surface. Therefore, it is always worth working from the downloaded version. After you download the "Installation Guide," you cannot view its contents unless you right-click the* .chm *file, click Properties, and then click Unblock. As an alternative, you can double-click the* .chm *file to open the Open File-Security Warning dialog box, clear the "Always ask before opening this file" checkbox, and then click Open.*

As discussed, for production use, it is recommended to install the build service on a separate machine from the application tier. However, a build machine (that is, any machine running the build service in either the build controller or build agent role — or both) is well-suited to installation in a virtual machine. In the case of a build agent machine it is particularly important that the virtual machine has fast disk access and plenty of CPU resources allocated.

Hosting the build agent in a virtual machine has several advantages that come along with the technology, such as the capability to rapidly add machines to the available pool of build agents for a controller, and manage those agents across the physical hardware hosting them. Because a build process requires access to the machine to run any code that may execute as part of the build and test scripts, running in virtualization also provides for a degree of isolation between build agents to ensure that the actions of one build do not affect the outcome of another. Another benefit of virtualization worth mentioning is that the build agent can easily be restored to a known clean state at any time — again, ensuring a clean build environment.

You must have local administrative permissions to install the build controller or agent services on a machine. As part of the installation, you must provide a service account under which the installed services will run. This user is often referred to as the TFSBUILD user.

If standard builds are required, and the policy in your company permits it, then it is recommended to use the machine's Network Service account. This will avoid issues encountered when using a real domain user account such as expiring passwords, and so on. The Network Service option is only available when running the build services as a Windows service in a domain environment where the build agent and the application tier machine are in the same domain, or have a trusted domain relationship.

If you need to manually add a Network Service account to a group such as the Project Collection Build Service Accounts, then the format to use is DOMAIN\MACHINE_NAME$, where DOMAIN is the build server's domain name, and MACHINE_NAME is the name of the build server.

If the user performing the installation is also part of the Project Collection Administrators group on the project collection to which you will be attaching the build service, this installation process will automatically add the TFSBUILD user to the appropriate Build Services group in the project collection. Otherwise, you must manually add the TFSBUILD user to the group. (See the "Team Foundation Server Installation Guide" for more information.)

Just as with the Team Foundation Server installation, setting up the build service is done in two parts: installation and configuration.

Installing Team Foundation Build

From the Team Foundation Server installation media, navigate to the appropriate 32-bit or 64-bit version of the setup.exe file in the TFS-x86 or TFS-x64 folders and run it. You will then be prompted with the usual Welcome page and License Terms page, which you must accept to proceed. On the Team Foundation Server 2010 Setup Options Page, select the Team Foundation Build Service and click Install, as shown in Figure 15-2.

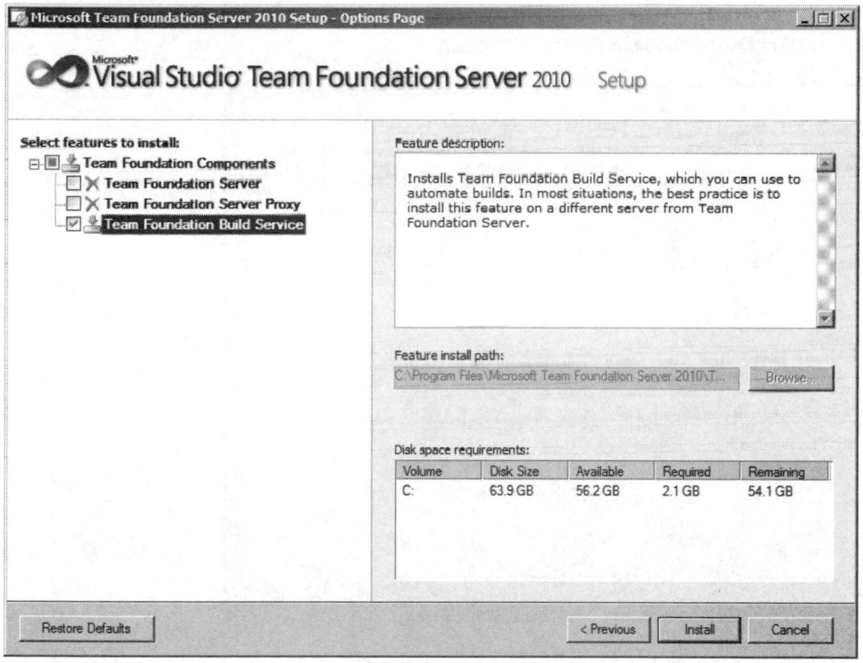

FIGURE 15-2: Installing the Team Foundation Build Service

The installation will then proceed. Depending on the prerequisites required, you may be forced to do a reboot as part of the installation process. Note that the install will add prerequisites (such as .NET 4.0) to do a basic build. However, if you wish to perform more advanced operations (such as test impact analysis), you must install a suitable version of Visual Studio (such as Visual Studio Ultimate or Visual Studio Premium) onto the build agent machine as well.

> *While the installation process will install .NET Framework 4.0 as part of the setup, the build service also requires .NET Framework 3.5 to be available. To install this on Windows Server 2008 R2, go to Server Manager ⇨ Features ⇨ Add Feature and select .NET Framework 3.5 or appropriate version, and allow required role services to be installed.*

Once the installation has completed (and you have restarted, if necessary), ensure that the Launch Team Foundation Server Configuration Tool check box shown in Figure 15-3 is selected, and click Configure.

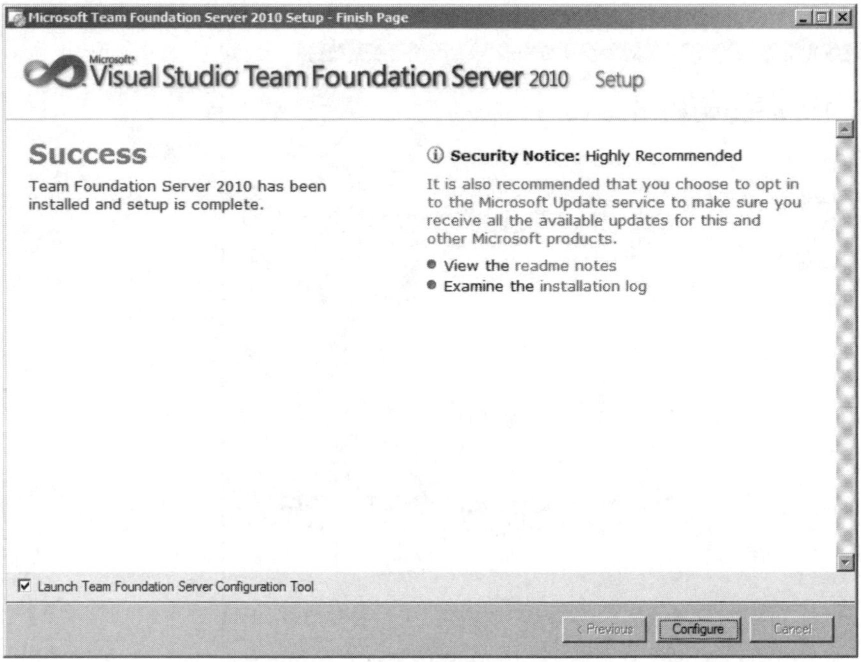

FIGURE 15-3: Launch Team Foundation Server Configuration Tool check box

Configuring the Team Foundation Build Service

If the check box was not selected at the time of installation, or if you wish to configure the build service after installation, then you can access it by running the Team Foundation Server Administration Console from the Start menu. Click Build Configuration ⇨ Configure Installed Features ⇨ Configure Team Foundation Build Service and click Start Wizard.

Regardless of whichever way you get into it, you will be presented with the Welcome screen, which you should read before clicking Start Wizard.

After reading the next Welcome screen and opting to send any setup information to Microsoft, click Next to go to the Select a Team Project Collection screen of the wizard, as shown in Figure 15-4.

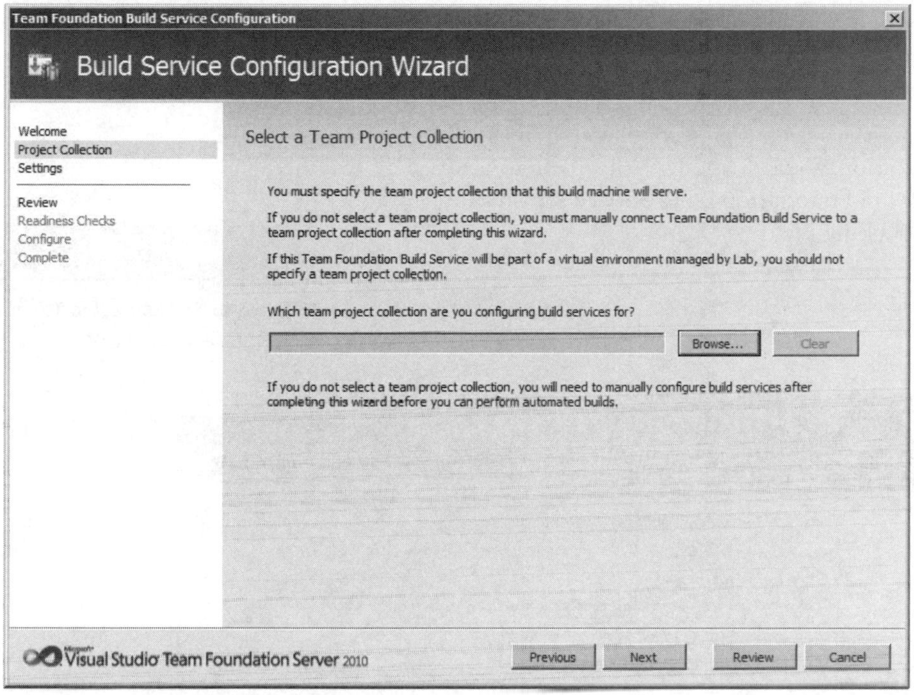

FIGURE 15-4: Build Service Configuration Wizard

Here you must define the project collection to which the build service is bound. Note that this can be one (and only one) project collection per build service instance. If you have many project collections in your organization, but want them to share the same build hardware, you should utilize virtualization to host several virtual machines running the build controllers for each project collection.

> While it is not a supported configuration, it is possible to run multiple build services on a single machine. For more information, see http://blogs.msdn.com/b/jimlamb/archive/2010/04/13/configuring-multiple-tfs-build-services-on-one-machine.aspx. But this is not recommended. Virtualization is the preferred option to achieve this result.

Click the Browse button shown in Figure 15-4 to select the server and project collection. If the server drop-down in the Connect to Team Project Collection dialog shown in Figure 15-5 is empty, or does not display the server you need to talk to, then clicking the Servers button will allow you to add a new server instance first, and then select the project collection.

Clicking the Connect button on the dialog shown in Figure 15-5 will then populate the selected project collection in the Build Service Configuration Wizard, and will allow you to proceed to the Configure Team Foundation Build Service screen shown in Figure 15-6 by clicking Next.

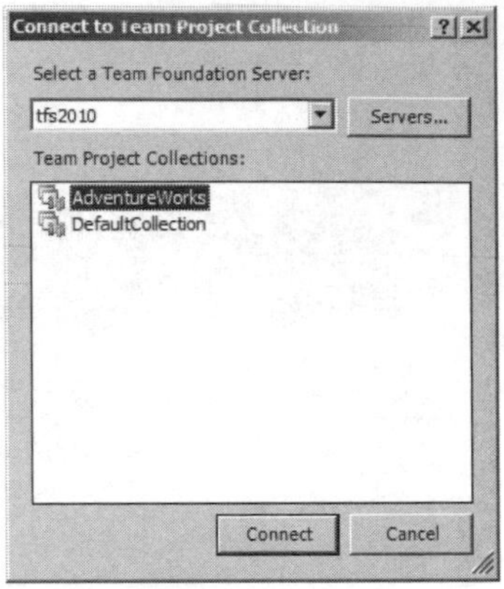

FIGURE 15-5: Connect to Team Project Collection dialog

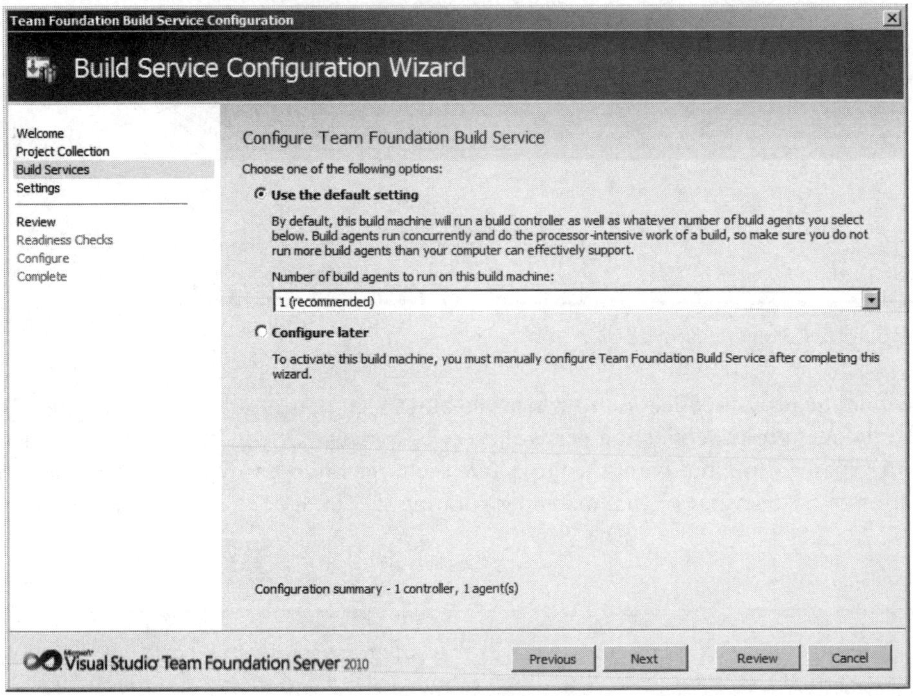

FIGURE 15-6: Configure Team Foundation Build Service screen

Depending on the number of processors that you have available, you may wish to configure multiple build agents to run on the same machine under the build service. This allows for parallel building of projects on the same machine. However, you should be sure that your build server has sufficient CPU resources and fast enough disks to ensure that it can perform adequately in this way. The default setting (and likely most appropriate for a virtualized build server) is to have one build agent per CPU. A single core virtual machine is shown in Figure 15-6 which is why a single agent is shown as the default.

Note that, if you have selected a project collection that already has a build controller, the Configure Team Foundation Build Service screen will look as shown in Figure 15-7. In that instance, if you wanted to add the current machine as a build agent to the selected build controllers pool, you could do so, or you could replace the existing controller with this current machine, or simply reserve the machine for use with Lab Management.

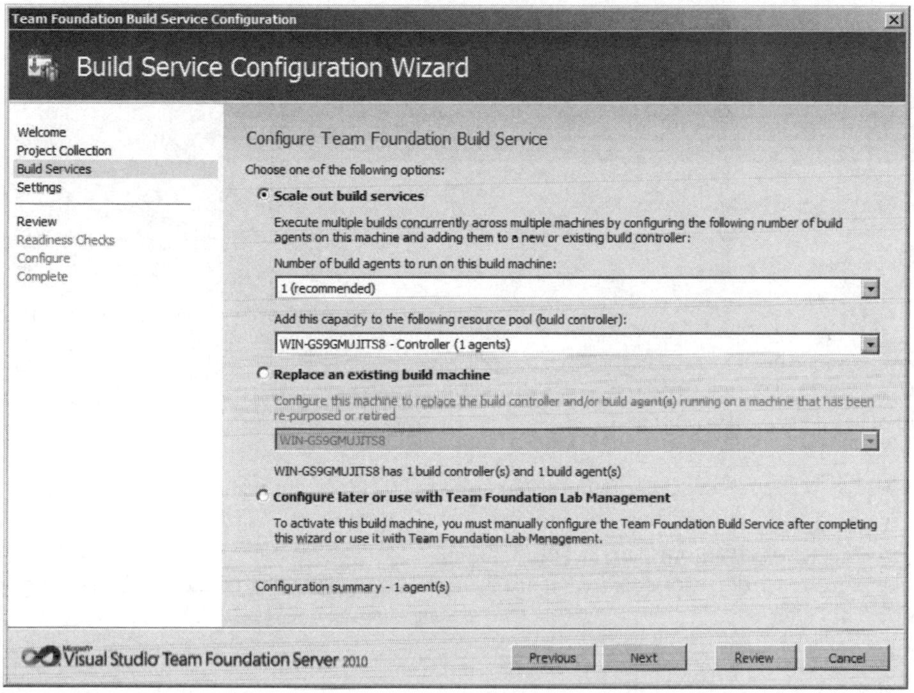

FIGURE 15-7: Alternate Configure Team Foundation Build Service screen

> For more information on Team Foundation Lab Management, see Chapter 22. For more information on configuring this machine as an additional build agent, see the "Team Foundation Server Installation Guide."

Either way, you will now be prompted for some additional information. First, you will need to provide a build service account (the TFSBUILD user). Second, you will need to provide the port for the application tier to communicate with the build service (Figure 15-8).

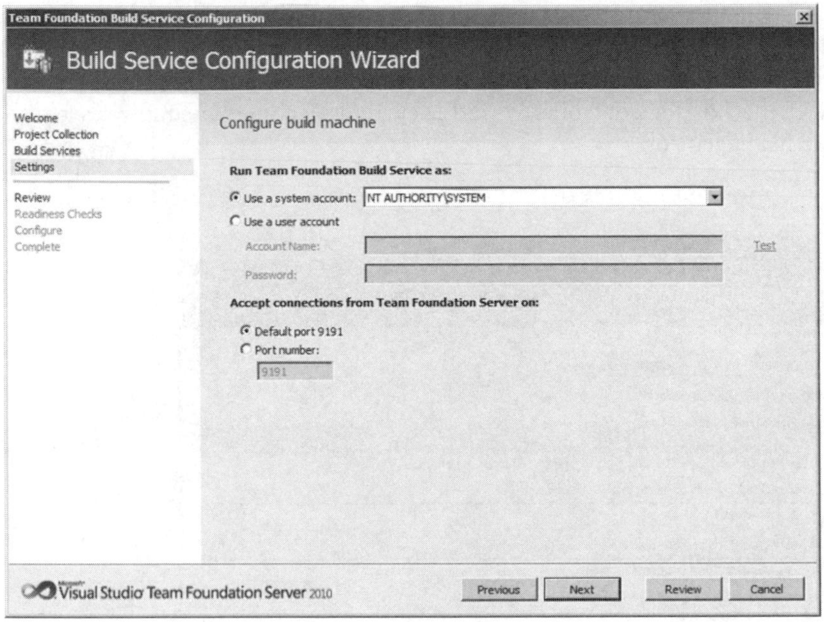

FIGURE 15-8: Configure build machine screen

Click Next to proceed to the review page, where you can check the configuration that is about to occur. You may also set additional properties for any build controller (Figure 15-9) and build agent(s) (Figure 15-10) being created at this point. You can access these dialogs again either from the Team Foundation Administration Console or Visual Studio. The various settings will be covered in more detail later in this chapter.

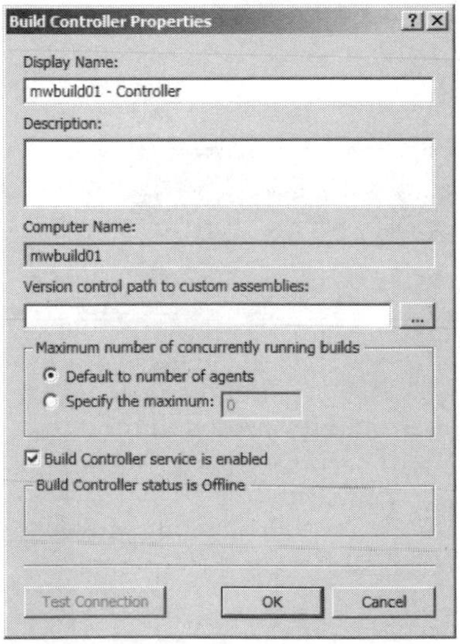

FIGURE 15-9: Build Controller Properties dialog

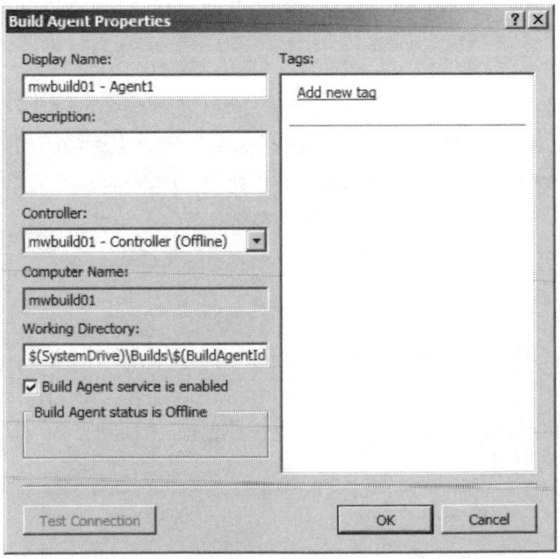

FIGURE 15-10: Build Agent Properties dialog

Clicking Next will perform the readiness checks. If you need to correct any errors, do so then click the link at the bottom of the dialog saying "Click here to rerun Readiness Checks," as shown in Figure 15-11. Once everything has passed, click Configure to actually begin the build agent configuration process. When this has completed successfully, finish the wizard and your configuration will be complete.

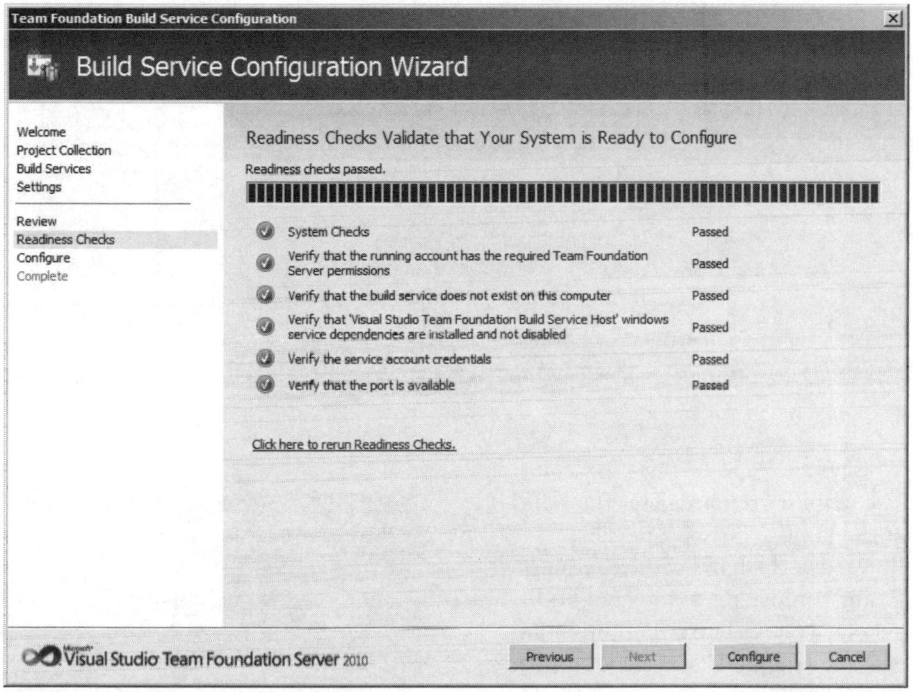

FIGURE 15-11: "Click here to rerun Readiness Checks" link

You will now be presented with the Team Foundation Server Administration Console. Viewing the Build Configuration screen shown in Figure 15-12 will allow you to check the status of the build service and the defined controller and agent(s).

The top part of the Build Configuration screen shown in Figure 15-12 controls the actual build service that is hosting the build controller and/or build agent(s). You can control the service from here by starting, stopping, or restarting it. The same could also be done using the usual Windows Services section of Server Manager in Windows Server, and selecting the Visual Studio Build Service Host service, or by issuing the typical `net start "Visual Studio Build Service Host"` commands from an Administrative command line. For example, you might need to restart the build service to pick up any changes such as modifications to system environment variables.

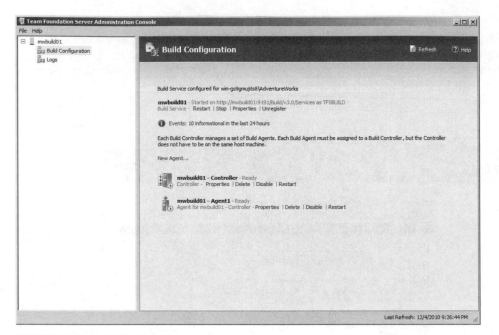

FIGURE 15-12: Build Configuration screen

More useful is the capability to unregister the build service and adjust the build service properties. Unregistering will remove the build service from the project collection, and remove the associated build controller and agents if you wish to decommission the build machine. Once the build service is stopped, clicking the Properties for the build service will show the Build Service Properties dialog, as shown in Figure 15-13.

In the dialog as shown in Figure 15-13, you have the capability to change the project collection to which the build services are connected, which is useful if the URL to access the project collection changes because of a move of that collection to a new application tier. You can also specify the web service endpoint for the build services. By clicking Change, you can adjust the configuration to a different port, force SSL, and optionally require client certificate authentication in the instances where you want a cryptographically secure link between the application tier machine and the build service.

FIGURE 15-13: Build Service Properties dialog

The Build Service Properties dialog also allows you to specify that the build service host process be run as an interactive process, rather than a Windows service, if a session with a desktop login is required (such as when running coded UI tests).

RUNNING THE BUILD SERVICE HOST AS AN INTERACTIVE PROCESS

There are instances when it is necessary to run the build service host as an interactive process with a real domain user account. The most common example is when you require the build agent to interact with a running application through the desktop, such as when you want to run coded UI tests without a full test agent. There are several steps to ensure this kind of configuration is as reliable as possible.

The first is to configure the build service host to run as an interactive service using the Build Service Properties dialog, as shown in Figure 15-13.

Next, you should configure the build service user as an auto-logon account for the server. This will ensure that when the machine reboots because of Windows updates requiring restarts or other events, it will go straight to an interactive session for the build user. For more information, see `http://support.microsoft.com/kb/310584`.

You should then ensure that the screen saver is disabled for the build user account to prevent it from locking the session.

Note that all these options degrade the security of the build agent machine, because anyone with physical access to the machine would then be able to interact with it as the logged-on build user. Therefore, any build agent configured in this way should be placed in an environment with the appropriate level of physical security.

For more information on coded UI tests and test agents, see Chapter 22.

Additional Software Required on the Build Agent

To perform basic compilation and unit tests of many project types in Visual Studio, no additional software is required on the build agent after installing the build service. However, you must install a suitable Visual Studio edition for other types of projects and activities. For example, to build an ASP.NET Web Application project or a C++ project, you must have Visual Studio 2010 installed on the build agent computer.

Additionally, you may need to install third-party component libraries if they are required to be in the Global Assembly Cache (GAC) by your projects. If your build process requires additional functionality to be present (such as the Build Extensions power tool, along with Java and Ant or Maven to build Java projects), these must also be installed.

WORKING WITH BUILDS

Now that you have configured a build controller and build agent, you can go about automating the build of your project. This section focuses primarily on building Visual Studio projects and managing the build automation from within the Visual Studio IDE. For information on building Ant or Maven projects, see the section, "Building Ant and Maven Projects with Team Foundation

Server" later in this chapter. Many of the tools and windows are identical (or at least very similar) in Eclipse for Java-based projects, so the following is still relevant.

This discussion assumes that you have a project that cleanly builds in Visual Studio, that you are sharing the source for the build in version control with the rest of your team, and that you want to automate in the build process for that project.

Creating a Build Definition

As previously mentioned, the build definition defines how, what, when, and where to perform your build. You create a new build definition in Visual Studio from Build ⇨ New Build Definition, or by right-clicking the `Builds` node in Team Explorer for the team project and selecting New Build Definition, as shown in Figure 15-14.

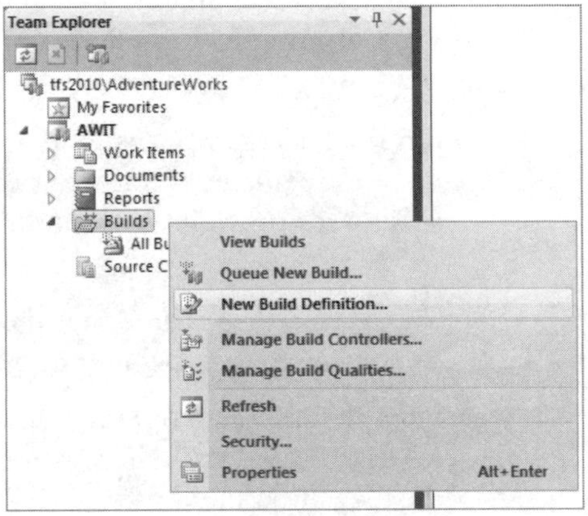

This will then show the build definition editor. In Visual Studio, it will show in the main document (Figure 15-15), and in Eclipse it is a new modal dialog box. The build definition editor is divided into two parts. The area on the left shows the various sections of the build definition, and the area on the right is the form for that section.

FIGURE 15-14: Creating a New Build Definition

Note that, when you first create the build definition, a number of warning triangles appear on the left-hand side of the dialog. This is completely normal, and just indicates which sections have data that must be filled out before proceeding. However, it is a good practice to go through every section and fill in the relevant data, because the defaults are not always what you might want.

> 🖉 *In Visual Studio 2010, if you have the solution open for which you wish to automate the build, then when you create the new build definition, it will default a number of values into the build definition form for you (such as the build definition name, the workspace template, and which solution to build). You can still edit these as you go through the form, but having the solution open before creating the new build definition can save you some time.*

General Section

The General section shown in Figure 15-15 allows you to set the build definition name, description, and optionally disable the build. Note that the current version of Team Foundation Server does not allow you to place the build definitions into folders in Team Explorer — they all live directly under the `Builds` node. Therefore, you may want to use a naming convention such as `MyProject CI`, `MyProject QA`, and so on, to distinguish between multiple builds related to each other. It is very easy to rename a build at any point in the future, so do not worry too much at this point about what naming convention to use if you do not have one already.

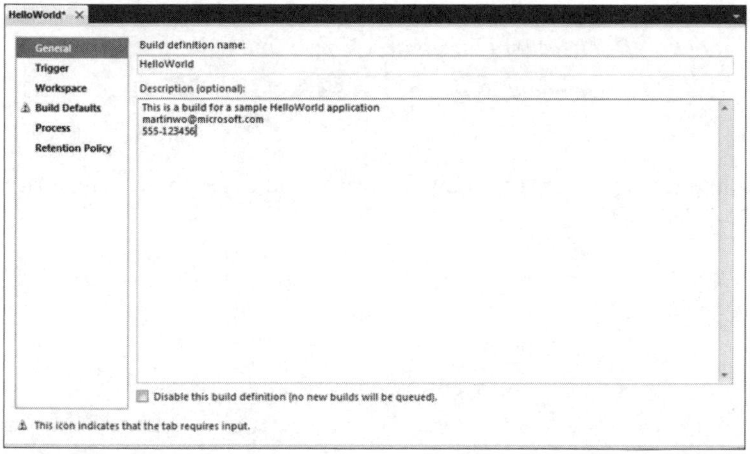

FIGURE 15-15: General section

For the description of the build, it is a good practice to provide a short (one-line) description of what the build is for, as well as contact details for the build owner or "build master." The first three lines of the build descriptions are displayed in other dialogs in Team Foundation Build without scrolling, and are, therefore, quite useful to add data to in order to make your development system more discoverable and easy to use for new team members.

Trigger Section

The Trigger section controls *when* the build should be run. As shown in Figure 15-16, there are a number of triggers defined that can allow a build to run. Note that these are the only built-in triggers in Team Foundation Server, and they are not extensible. Therefore, if they do not meet your needs, you must create your mechanism for queuing the build using the extensibility APIs for Team Foundation Server. For an example of using the extensibility API to queue a build, see the blog post at www.woodwardweb.com/dotnet/tfs_build_api_b.html.

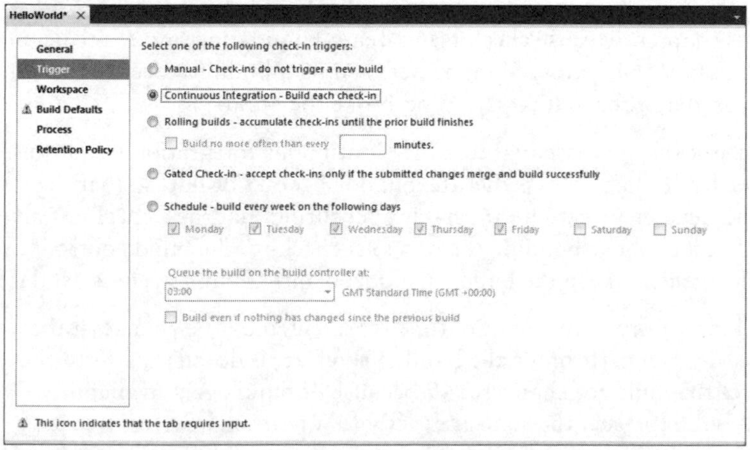

FIGURE 15-16: Trigger section

See Chapter 25 for more details on Team Foundation Server extensibility.

However, the following built-in trigger types are very comprehensive, and cover the vast majority of build scenarios:

➤ Manual

➤ Continuous Integration

➤ Rolling Builds

➤ Gated Check-in

➤ Schedule

Manual

The Manual trigger was the only trigger available in Team Foundation Server 2005. When a build is manually triggered, it will be run only when the build is explicitly queued by a user in Visual Studio, Eclipse, by the tfsbuild.exe command, or by other code using the extensibility APIs for Team Foundation Server.

Manual builds are very useful when first creating the build definition to ensure that everything is working correctly before turning to one of the other triggers. They are also commonly used for a QA build — that is, a build that is performed when the team wishes to push code to a QA environment. The QA build might perform additional automated tests and documentation activities that take a significant amount of time, and would be overkill for a standard development build, but only necessary when creating a build that may be used in production.

Continuous Integration

The Continuous Integration trigger monitors every check-in affecting the build files and causes a new build to be queued. The folders and files that trigger the build are determined by the Workspace definition examined later in this chapter. Because check-ins to Team Foundation Server are denoted by the changeset number as a single atomic transaction, by performing a build for every check-in, it is easy to see which check-in caused a problem (that is, "Who broke the build?").

For systems that have a lot of check-ins, it is essential that the Continuous Integration build runs as quickly as possible to provide feedback as to whether the build is "good" or not, so that the feedback loop is maintained and developers get into the habit of ensuring that their check-ins always result in good builds. If a build agent is busy building the previous check-in, the build controller will look for the next available build agent, or keep the builds in a queue until a build agent is available.

The state of the version control repository at the point of time represented by the changeset that triggered the build is what is used when performing the build. Therefore, it doesn't matter if the build for changeset 17 runs after the build for changeset 19 because of build agent availability or build priorities — the builds will represent the state at exactly that point in time.

Because of the precise nature of Continuous Integration builds — and the clear way in which they indicate which check-in broke the build — they are the preferred trigger to use for a standard development automated build.

> To prevent a check-in from triggering a build, simply insert the text ***NO_CI*** anywhere in the comment string. This special string indicates the check-in should be ignored by the build system triggers.

Rolling Builds

A Rolling Build trigger is similar to the build trigger called Continuous Integration by Team Foundation Server. However, it will group together several check-ins to ensure that the build controller never has a large queue of builds waiting to be processed. Optionally, a time interval can be specified to control the minimum duration that must have passed before a new build is triggered. This is the type of trigger that was first used by the Continuous Integration build servers such as CruiseControl or CruiseControl.NET.

Rolling builds reduce the number of builds performed and, therefore, can guarantee a time in which the results of a particular check-in will be known. However, the grouping of check-ins from several developers can make it difficult to identify which change was responsible for any build failure.

A build definition with a Rolling Build trigger can also be used in conjunction with a Continuous Integration build. Both can build the same resources. However, the Continuous Integration build can be responsible for providing a quick check on quality for the build, whereas the Rolling Build can perform additional activities such as running a full UI automation pass, generating code documentation, packaging the build into MSI installers and ISO images ready for distribution, or even deploying the build into a test environment ready for evaluation.

Gated Check-in

The Gated Check-in trigger is new to Team Foundation Server 2010. It is similar to a Continuous Integration trigger, but with a twist. When a check-in is performed into the area covered by a Gated Check-in build definition, the developer is presented with the dialog as shown in Figure 15-17.

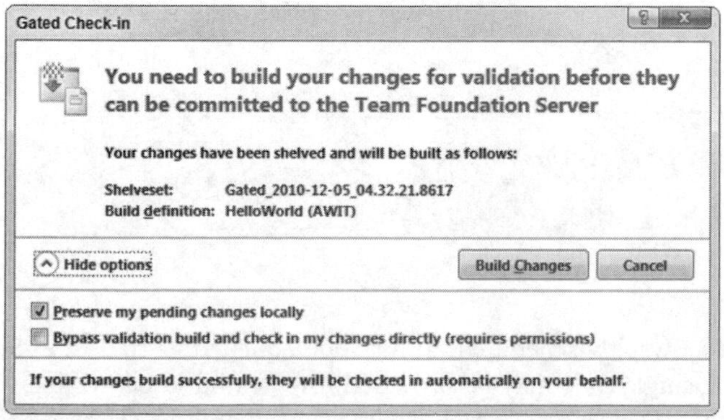

FIGURE 15-17: Gated Check-in dialog

Any check-ins are first stored as a shelveset. The build server then merges the code as it was before the check-in was attempted with the code stored in the shelveset. Only if the build is successful are the changes then committed to the version control repository by the build controller on behalf of the person performing the check-in (but with the addition of ***NO_CI*** appended to the end of the check-in comment to ensure a subsequent build is not required). If the merge of the shelveset with the latest version of source control is not possible due to a merge conflict then the build will fail. If the build fails for any reason then no code is checked in but the shelveset is kept on the server for remediation.

The user will be notified of the check-in build completion via the build notification tool running in the system notification area on Windows, or via the Gated Check-ins view in Eclipse. At this point, the user may *reconcile* his or her workspace — that is, remove the pending changes that were committed as part of the build from the current pending changes list.

If there is more than one build definition that is affected by a gated check-in, the user will be prompted to select the one he or she wishes to use to validate the build in the gated check-in warning dialog shown in Figure 15-17.

Because gated check-ins require the code to be automatically merged as part of the build process, this has two important effects:

➤ The actual code checked in may differ slightly from the code submitted as part of the shelveset.

➤ Even though Team Foundation Server 2010 has built-in agent pooling capabilities, only one build of a gated check-in may be executed at a time to prevent merge conflicts.

Gated check-ins are useful in organizations that have very large numbers of developers working in the same codebase where traditional gated Continuous Integration builds are failing too often because of a natural human error rate. (Even the best developer might break the build once or twice a year, but if you have 300 developers checking into the same tree, that means the build breaks at least every day.)

The more common case where gated check-in is used is when organizations wish to ensure that code committed to the main codebase meets certain requirements, such as code quality, test coverage, and so on. These factors can sometimes be determined by deploying custom check-in policies to every developer machine. However, that may require significant overhead, and make for a very complex check-in experience. Gated check-ins move all the check-in validation to a centralized server infrastructure.

> *For more information on using gated check-ins to ensure code quality, see Chapter 7.*

Schedule

The Schedule trigger can define a time on a weekly schedule that a build is queued — that is, a daily, nightly, or weekly build. Note that only a single time may be provided for each build definition, and that time is used on the chosen days of the week repeated weekly. This time should be selected so that it does not conflict with any ongoing backup or other maintenance jobs in the network, and ideally should also be selected so that, when the build is due to complete, there are people available to help fix the build if any errors have occurred.

The time in which the build is run is converted to the time zone for the application tier when the build definition is saved, but is always displayed in the local time zone of the user editing the build definition. Therefore, there can be some confusion around periods when daylight savings is in operation in one of those times zones and not the other.

If a more complex schedule is required (such as every second Thursday or the last Tuesday of the month), then it may be preferable to create a build definition using a Manual trigger, and then set up a Windows Scheduled Job to run on the defined schedule that will queue the build using the tfsbuild.exe command line.

MANAGING BUILDS FROM THE COMMAND LINE WITH TFSBUILD.EXE

Visual Studio Team Explorer installs a number of command-line tools, one of which is the tfsbuild.exe command. The command can be used to perform a limited number of Team Foundation Build tasks, and is also useful in scripting scenarios where full access to the Team Foundation extensibility APIs is not required.

For example, to trigger a build, a command similar to the following could be used:

```
tfsbuild start http://tfs2010:8080/tfs/DefaultCollection
        AdventureWorks "My Build Definition"
```

In this example, http://tfs2010:8080/tfs/DefaultCollection is the URL for the team project collection, AdventureWorks is the name of the team project, and My Build Definition is the name of the build definition for which you wish to queue a build.

For more information on the tfsbuild command, open a Visual Studio 2010 command prompt and type TFSBuild help, or visit http://msdn.microsoft .com/en-us/library/aa337622.aspx.

Workspace Section

The Workspace section shown in Figure 15-18 allows you to define the working folder mappings that should be used for your build. This determines not only where the files should be placed on the disk to perform the build, but also which files are relevant to the build definition and, therefore, should be included in any build label, or monitored as part of the build trigger.

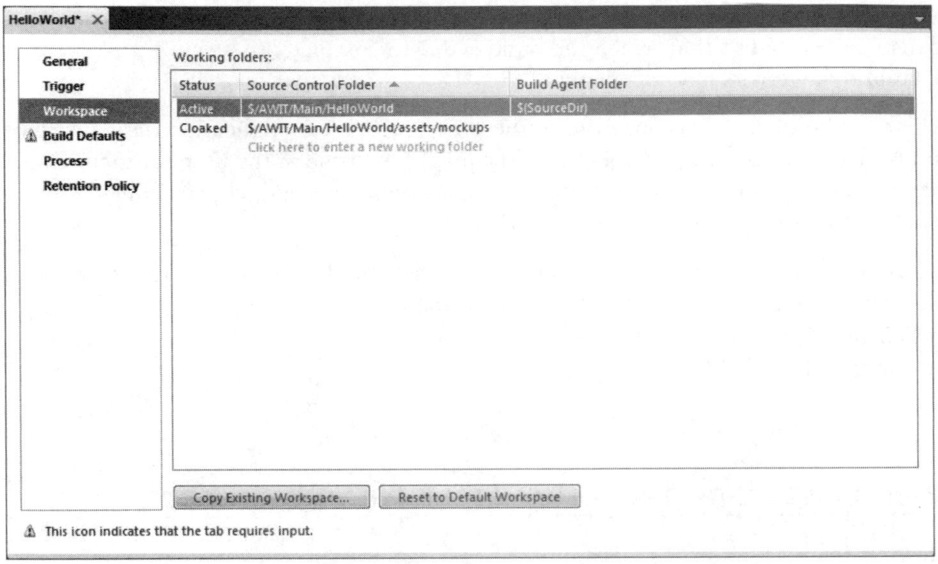

FIGURE 15-18: Workspace section

The default working folder mapping is usually given as the root of the team project (for example, $/AdventureWorks) mapped to the sources directory represented by the environment variable $(SourceDir). This is almost always too broad of a mapping, and covers many files that should not be part of your build. It has the effect of triggering builds when they should not be, and slowing down the build process (because files outside the area of source that you are interested in must be downloaded).

The working folder mappings should be altered to include an active mapping with as fine of a granularity as possible (usually the folder containing the solution to be built inside the branch you wish to build, as shown in Figure 15-18). Also, any files or folders that should not trigger a build should be cloaked.

In the example in Figure 15-18, a directory containing a series of UI mockup images is excluded from the build because, while they are checked in alongside the source tree, the files do not make up part of the software being built. (They are for reference by the development team during development and would take a significant amount of time to download in each build because of their large size.)

> *For more information on working folder mappings and cloaked mappings, see Chapter 6.*

Build Defaults Section

On the Build Defaults section shown in Figure 15-19, you select which controller you wish to be responsible for the build definition by default, and where you want the results of the build to be staged after they have been built (that is, the drop location).

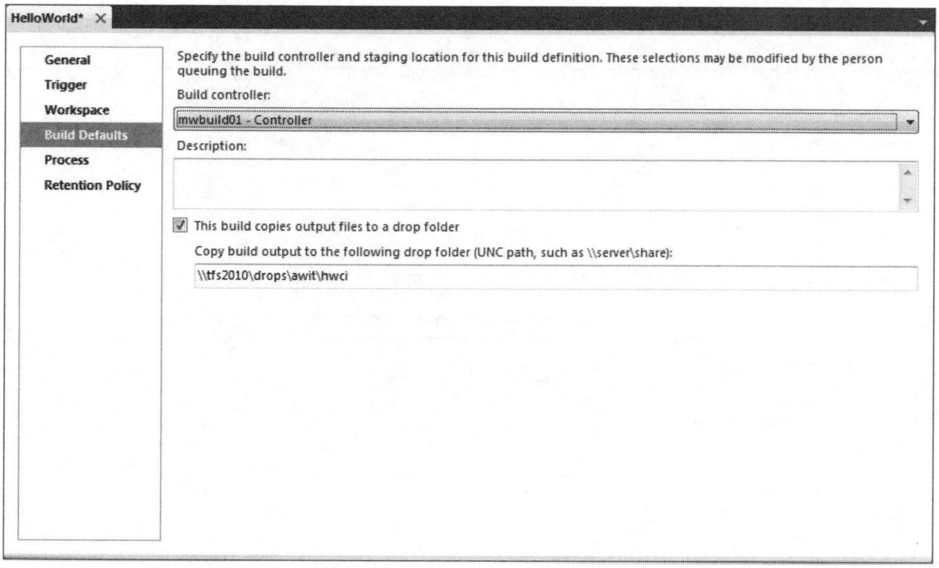

FIGURE 15-19: Build Defaults section

In Team Foundation Server 2010, installing the build service host registers the build controller with the server. If there are no build controllers present in the drop-down, you do not have one installed for your current project collection. See the section, "Setting Up the Team Foundation Build Service," earlier in this chapter for details on how to do this.

The Description field shows the description assigned to the build controller (useful for conveying information about who owns the controller, or what it should be used for), and is read-only in this section. To edit the description, see the Build Controller Properties dialog (Figure 15-9).

The drop location must be a UNC path to a Windows file share on the network. The build agent machine must have network access, and the user running the build service must have permission to write to that location, because files are copied directly from the build agent to the drop location as part of the build. There is a 260-character limit to the full path of all files copied to the drop location, so you should ensure that the server name and path are reasonably short, leaving you the maximum space for your output. However, you should put builds in directories in the drop location that correspond to the build definition to help keep them organized.

Process Section

The Process section determines which of the registered build process templates should be used for the build definition, and what properties should be passed into that Windows Workflow 4.0 process when it is started, as shown in Figure 15-20.

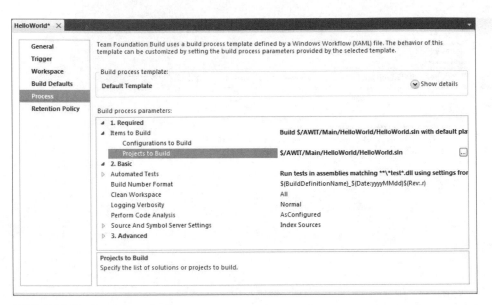

FIGURE 15-20: Process section

Each process can define a number of customizable properties to control how the build behaves. Properties that are mandatory but not populated are marked with a warning triangle when the build definition is created. If the build definition was created while a solution was open in Visual Studio, this solution will be pre-populated in the "Projects to Build" area. If this occurs, ensure that this is the correct solution or project that you wish to build.

Note that the Process section is one area that differs greatly when creating Java-based builds from Eclipse using Team Explorer Everywhere. For more information, see the section, "Building Ant and Maven Projects with Team Foundation Server," later in this chapter.

The build process, along with more details on the various properties used by the main process templates that ship out-of-the-box, is described in more detail later in this chapter in the section, "Understanding the Build Process."

Retention Policy Section

The Retention Policy section shown in Figure 15-21 specifies the rules by which builds should be retained automatically, and what should be deleted for builds that fall outside of the retention policy.

Once you start building on every check-in, the number of builds created by the system can rapidly increase. However, not all of the builds are relevant for very long once the status (passed or failed) is known. Finding the build that you are looking for can get complicated, but also the disk space required to store all the build results grows for each build retained.

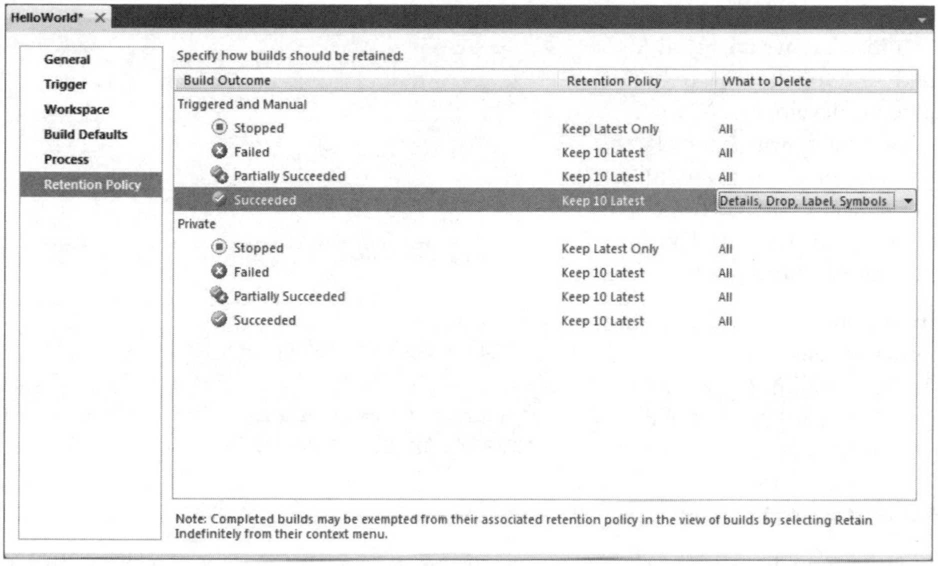

FIGURE 15-21: Retention Policy section

With Team Foundation Server a build may finish in one of four states:

➤ *Succeeded* — Succeeded is when everything in the build is good and is what you want to see.

➤ *Partially Succeeded* — Partially Succeeded is the default state given to a build that has passed compilation but something else has gone wrong during the build (such as unit tests failing). In the case of unit test failures, it is possible to completely fail the build. (See the "Build Process Parameters" section later in this chapter for more information.)

➤ *Failed* — A Failed build is one that has completely failed for some reason.

➤ *Stopped* — A Stopped build is one that has been terminated manually while it was running.

The retention policy controls how many results you would like to keep by default for each type of build result. At any time, from the context menu of the build details, or from the build report, you can indicate that a particular build should be marked Retained Indefinitely (or Keep Forever). Marking a build as Retain Indefinitely means that it will be excluded from the automatic retention policies.

> For teams that are making use of Microsoft Test Manager to record fast-forward test executions, deleting test results will destroy the action recordings required for fast-forwarding. Therefore, be careful with the retention policy settings for build definitions that are used by your test teams. You may alter the retention policy to exclude test results from the items deleted, as shown in Figure 15-21, or mark any builds used by your test teams as Retain Indefinitely. For more information, see Chapter 22.

There are separate retention policies for both the team builds that are triggered (or manually queued) and for the private builds queued by individual developers. More information is given on private builds later in this chapter. Changing the private build retention policy affects all the developers performing private builds for that definition — not just the developer editing the setting.

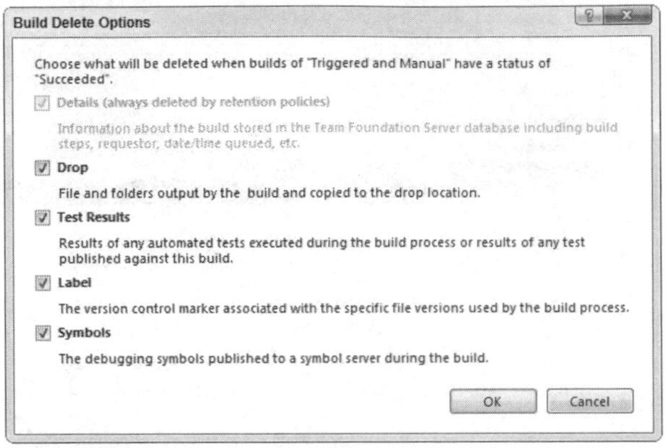

For each retention policy, you can determine what is automatically deleted by selecting the "What to Delete" column. Selecting <Specify What to Delete> displays the dialog shown in Figure 15-22, which allows a custom setting to be applied when the build is automatically deleted from that point onward.

FIGURE 15-22: Build Delete Options dialog

For more information on what each of the delete options means, see the section, "Deleting Builds," later in this chapter.

Saving the Build Definition

Once you are happy with the settings for the build definition, you can save it by clicking the Save button or pressing *Ctrl+S*. In Eclipse, click the OK button to save the changes to the server.

Queuing a Build

When you have created a new build definition, you should manually queue the build the first time to ensure that it is working as desired. The latest successful build for a build definition is used to determine which changesets and work items will be associated with the subsequent build, so this first build will be the baseline by which the next triggered build is compared.

To manually queue a build in Visual Studio, go to Build ➪ Queue New Build. Alternatively, in either Eclipse or Visual Studio, you can right-click on the build definition in the `Builds` node of Team Explorer and select Queue New Build.

You will then be presented with the Queue Build dialog, as shown in Figure 15-23.

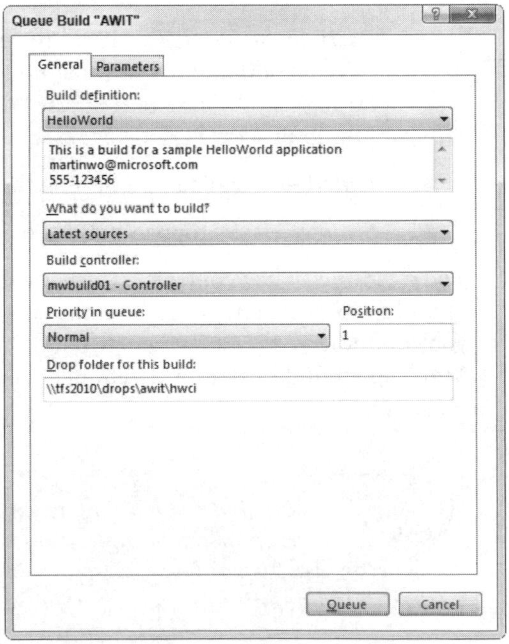

FIGURE 15-23: Queue Build dialog

Understanding the Queuing Process

When you manually queue a build, you may specify on which controller you would like this to run (overriding the default, which is used for a triggered build). Additionally, you can set the priority of the queued build and get an indication as to where in the queue this priority would put you when submitting the build.

Builds that are triggered using one of the build definition triggers are done so with a priority of Normal. You can set this to High, Above Normal, Normal, Below Normal, or Low, depending on the priority of your manual build request. Click Queue to trigger the build at this point and take you to the Build Explorer to see the results.

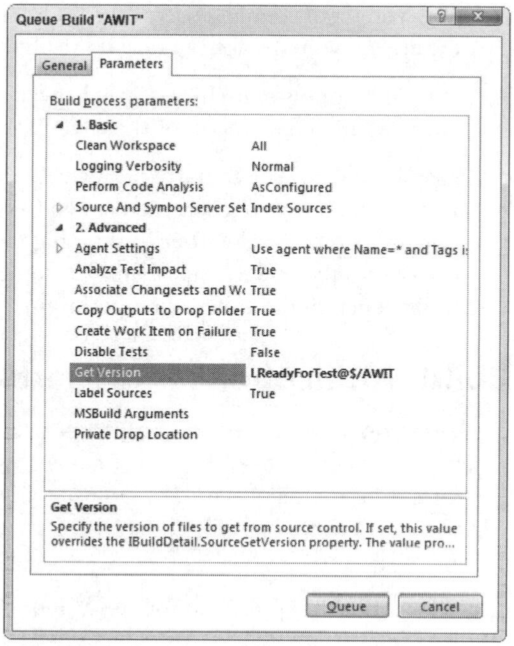

When queuing a build, there is an additional Parameters tab that is new for builds queued against Team Foundation Server 2010. There you will find a customizable list of properties as defined by the build process template, allowing you to alter the value of that property for this single invocation of the build.

For example, if you wanted to manually queue a build of the source tree based on the label `ReadyForTest`, then you could manually specify the Get Version property for the build to be `LReadyForTest@$/AWIT` (where L specifies that this is a Label version specification, and `@$/AWIT` specifies that this label was in the scope of a Team Project folder called `$/AWIT` in version control), as shown in Figure 15-24.

Private Builds

A new feature in Team Foundation Server 2010 is the capability to request that a build be performed using the latest sources merged with a shelveset specified by the developer as a *private build* (sometimes called a *buddy build*). You do this from the Queue Build dialog when manually queuing a build by changing the "What do you want to build option" to "Latest sources with shelveset," and then specifying the shelveset, as shown in Figure 15-25.

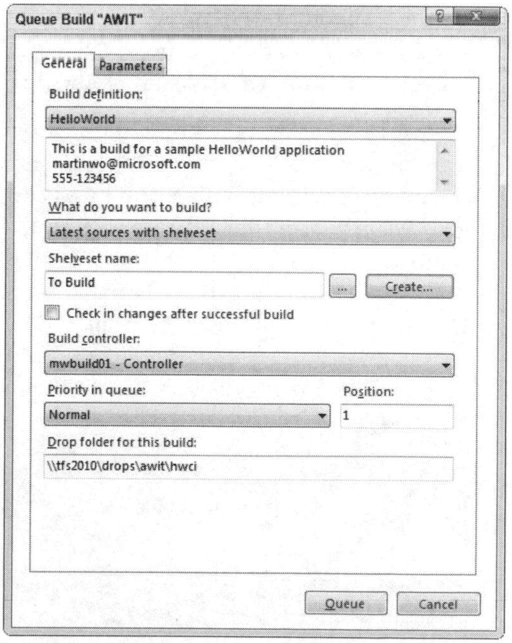

Private builds are useful when you want to ensure that you are including all the changes necessary to successfully perform the build on a different machine before committing the changes to the main source repository. They are also very useful

FIGURE 15-24: Manually queuing a build from a Label

FIGURE 15-25: Manually queuing a private build

when you want to make use of the build process set up on the server to test and create all the build output, but you are not yet sure if the change you are proposing should be included in the codebase.

A private build is similar to a gated check-in, except for the fact that the use of shelvesets is not enforced, and checking in of the code in the shelveset after a successful build is optional.

Private builds (those that are performed without selecting the check-in option) do not follow the same build numbering scheme defined for the regular team builds, and have separate retention policies, as discussed earlier in this chapter. The results of the private build are shown to that developer only, and are not displayed to the entire team. However, build alerts may notify of private builds depending on their configuration.

Build Notifications and Alerts

Team Foundation Server exposes a powerful eventing model and extensibility APIs that allow for custom integrations of any imaginable application or device for notification of build results, from standard e-mail alerts to lava lamps, confetti-filled leaf blowers, build status screens, and even talking robot rabbits. However, there are two main notification systems exposed to the developer out-of-the-box:

➤ Build notification tool on Windows

➤ E-mail alerts

Build Notification Tool

The notification tool is a small application that runs in the system notification area on Windows. In the 2008 release, this was provided as part of the Team Foundation Server Power Tools, but ships with Visual Studio and Visual Studio Team Explorer in the 2010 release.

Figure 15-26 shows the build notification tool running and displaying a notification to the user as an Outlook style pop-up message in the bottom right-hand corner of the screen. It can be configured to run on login, but will be run by Visual Studio if a gated check-in is requested. In the case of a gated check-in, if the build is successful, then the notification tool will display a dialog to the users (Figure 15-27) asking them if they would like to Reconcile their workspaces. The build notification tool works by polling Team Foundation Server at a regular interval and therefore notifications may take up to two minutes to be displayed to the user after the build has been completed.

FIGURE 15-26: Notification tool pop-up

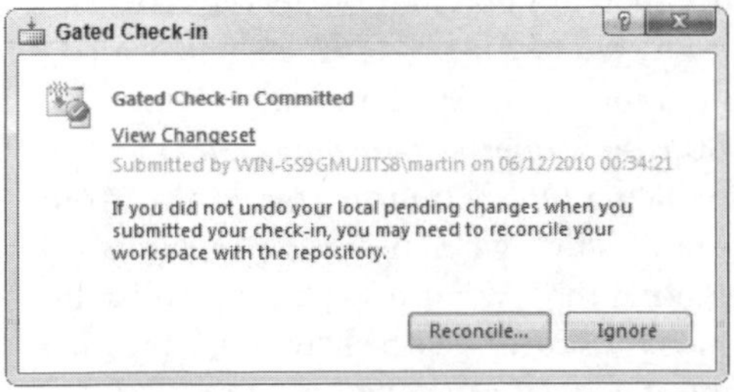

FIGURE 15-27: Notification prompting for reconciliation of workspace

> *For more information on gated check-ins and reconciling the local workspace, see Chapter 7.*

E-mail Alerts

Basic e-mail alerts can be configured from the Team ⇨ Project Alerts menu in Visual Studio once the selected team project has been highlighted in Team Explorer. Using the interface shown in Figure 15-28, e-mail alerts can be enabled when a build quality changes, when any build completes, or when builds are initiated by the developer.

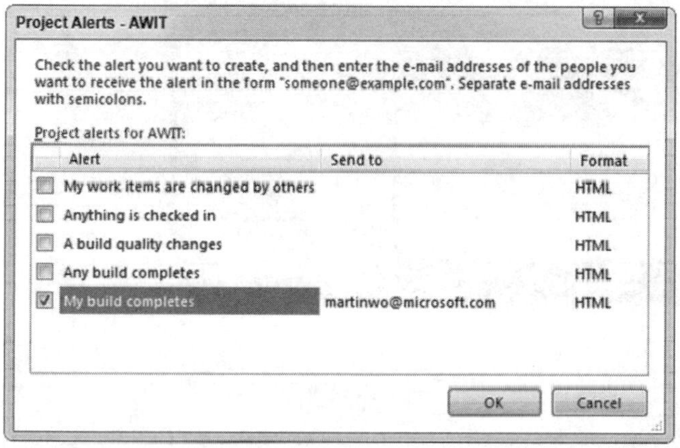

FIGURE 15-28: Enabling e-mail alerts

In the Team Foundation Power Tools, a more flexible Alerts Editor is available by right clicking on the root Team Project Collection node in Team Explorer of Visual Studio. This provides a greater degree of control over which events and what event values cause an e-mail alert to be dispatched.

E-mails can be sent to any e-mail address, including team aliases, provided the Team Foundation Server application tier is configured with the correct SMTP server details to send the messages. However, the e-mail alerts belong to the user who created the alert, and that user must delete or edit the alert through the Visual Studio interface.

On the Team Foundation Server application tier machine, the BisSubscribe.exe command is available in the Team Foundation Server\Tools folder, and can be used to script the creation of project alerts for a team project.

Managing Builds

The main build management activities are performed using the Build Explorer in Visual Studio or Eclipse, which is accessed by double-clicking on the Builds node in Team Explorer, or from Build ⇨ View Builds in Visual Studio. Figure 15-29 shows the Build Explorer.

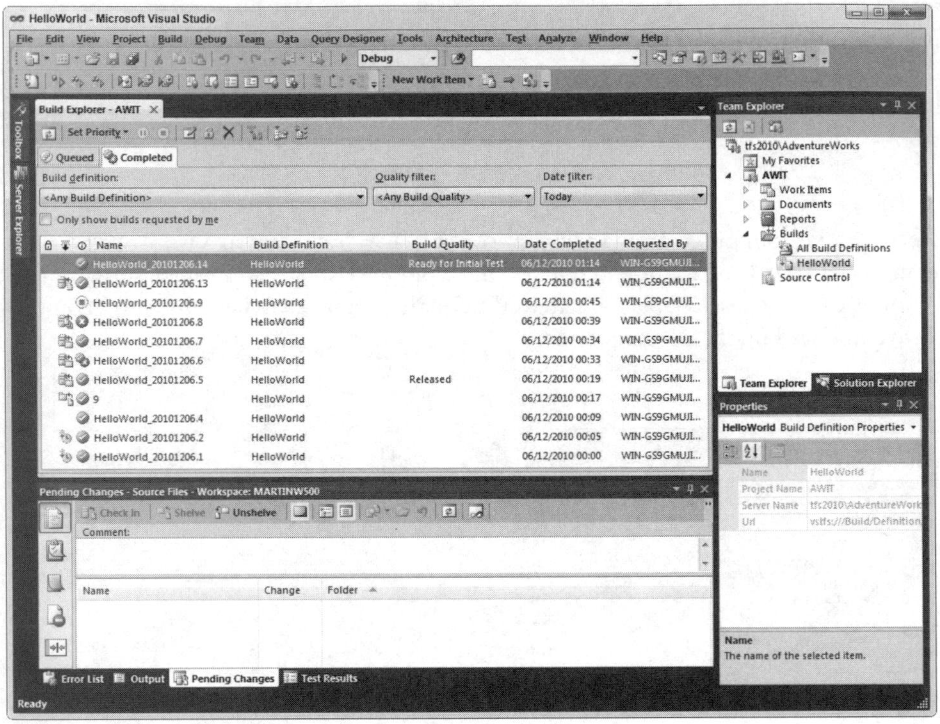

FIGURE 15-29: Build Explorer

All the build definitions for a particular team project are listed under the `Builds` node in Team Explorer. There is no capability to order the builds into folders, so a naming convention may be needed to keep the various build definitions organized if there are many for a particular team project.

Build Explorer

The Build Explorer allows access to builds that the system is aware of, those that have run, are running, or are waiting to run. The Build Explorer is organized into two tabs:

➤ Queued builds

➤ Completed builds

Queued Builds

From the Queued builds tab shown in Figure 15-30, you can cancel, pause, or change the priority of any build that is currently waiting to be built. You can also stop builds that are currently executing. By default, the Queued builds tab will also show you builds that have completed in the last five minutes.

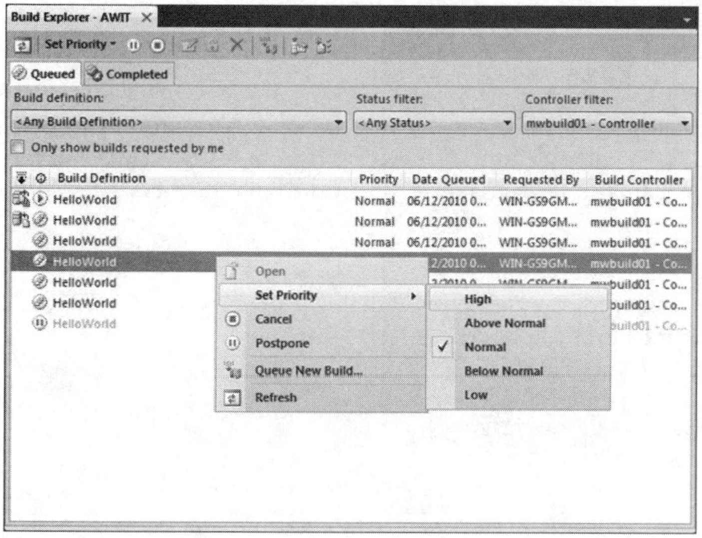

FIGURE 15-30: Queued builds tab

Completed Builds

The Completed builds tab shown in Figure 15-31 displays builds that have completed (that is, have finished execution, and are Successful, Partially Successful, Failed, or Stopped). An icon shows the status of the build, with another icon to the left showing the build reason (that is, scheduled build, Continuous Integration, rolling build, private build, gated check-in, and so on). Hovering over an icon will display a tooltip with a full description.

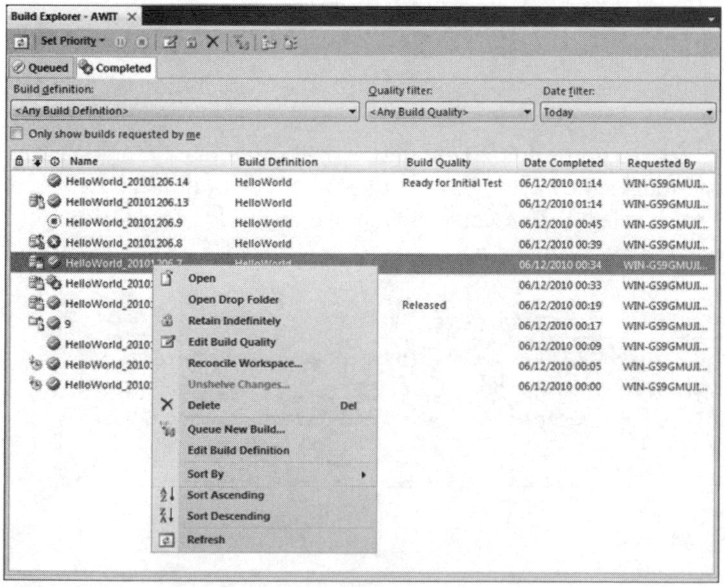

FIGURE 15-31: Completed builds tab

The builds are filtered by the criteria at the top of the Completed builds tab — by default, showing all builds for that day by everyone on the team. You can constrain the list to show only your builds, or show a greater date range, and so on, by adjusting the options.

The Completed builds tab is where much of the build management is performed for individual build details. You can mark a build to Retain Indefinitely to prevent it from being included in the automatic retention policy rules. You can also delete builds and edit the build quality.

Deleting Builds

If you delete the build, you are presented with the Delete Build dialog shown in Figure 15-32, which allows you to control which parts of the build you wish to delete.

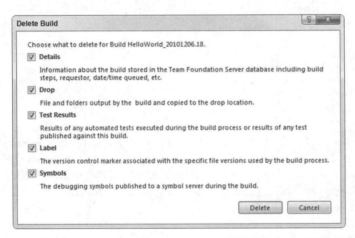

FIGURE 15-32: Delete Build dialog

You can delete the following:

➤   *Details* — This is the build record in the Team Foundation Server database, and deleting this means that the build no longer shows in the Build Explorer. The build is actually still in the database, just marked as deleted. To completely remove the build record, you must destroy it using the `tfsbuild.exe` command line.

> *For more information about this, as well as what information does and doesn't get deleted and why, see Adam Root's blog post at* `http://blogs.msdn.com/b/adamroot/archive/2009/06/12/working-with-deleted-build-data-in-team-foundation-server-2010-beta-1.aspx`.

➤ *Drop* — These are all the build outputs that were copied to the network share. These can be very significant in size, and, therefore, the most likely thing that you wish to delete. Using this dialog is a quick way to clean up the drop location without removing the rest of the data for the build.

➤ *Test Results* — This includes all the test results from test management and any associated test data (including video files and action recordings). Be careful when deleting test data, because that may impact testers.

> *For more information, see Chapter 22.*

➤ *Label* — This is the label associated with the build in version control. For auditing and tracking purposes, it is common to leave the label for all builds.

➤ *Symbols* — If you are using the Symbol and Source servers, then you may have configured your build to have symbol files stored on a Symbol server that may take up significant space. However, if you have released this build to anyone, you might want to keep the symbols around for debugging purposes.

It is worth noting that the "Found in Build" and "Fixed in Build" fields that are used by some of the process templates in Team Foundation Server work item tracking make use of a global list in the work item system. There is no option to automatically delete the corresponding entry to the build from this global list. So, it will still appear in the work item tracking drop-downs, unless it is manually removed from the global list in the team project.

> *For more information on managing global lists, see Chapter 12 and the MSDN documentation at* http://msdn.microsoft.com/en-us/library/ms404878. aspx.

Build Details View

When you double-click a build in the Build Explorer, you can see a report of the build details, as shown in Figure 15-33. This is known as the Build Details View or the Build Report.

When the build is executing, you will see the build log periodically refreshing to show the latest results of the build. A small bar chart in the top left-hand corner of the build shows the build duration in comparison with the previous builds to give you an indication of how much longer the build is likely to run.

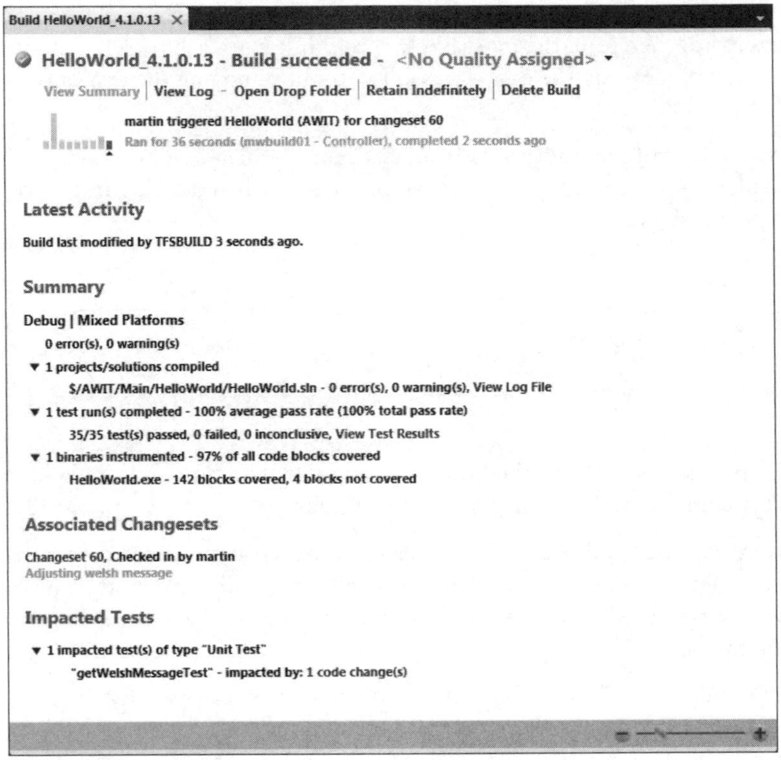

FIGURE 15-33: Report of the build details

As the build progresses, more information is added to the build log. If you scroll to the bottom of the build log, the view will maintain that bottom scroll position, and the results will scroll up as the build proceeds further.

The information is displayed in a hierarchical tree, with the duration of each step displayed in the top right-hand side of that node. For steps that create additional log files (such as MSBuild, Ant, or Maven that perform the actual compilation of the code), you can click on the report to download it from the drop location and view it.

Once the build has completed, you will see the build summary view by default (Figure 15-33). This shows all the compilations, test runs, and any unit test results, code coverage, and test impact analysis data. You will also see information regarding the changesets included since the last successful build of that build definition, along with any work items that were associated with those changesets as they were checked in.

In this way, you can see how the full requirements traceability data is being tracked by Team Foundation Server, and why the build automation system completed the feedback loop for the development process. By performing the build, you can see which code was changed, what work items that change was associated with, and what build the changes went into. You can also see which unit tests were run, what the code coverage was, which tests might be impacted by the code that was changed, and so on. All this data is being stored in the Team Foundation Server data warehouse, and is available for later analysis.

From the Build Details View, you can open the drop location to view the actual outputs of the build (that is, the website or executable files). You can also mark the build to be retained indefinitely, and set the build quality. You can even delete the build from this view.

Managing Build Quality Descriptions

For each build, you can set a *build quality* from the Completed builds tab or from the build report. The build quality is a text string that allows the team to tag the build with additional metadata, and is useful for communicating the quality of the build with the rest of the team. For example, you can easily identify builds that have been released, or are ready for testing. Note that, in addition to setting the build quality, you may want to mark the build to be retained indefinitely in those cases.

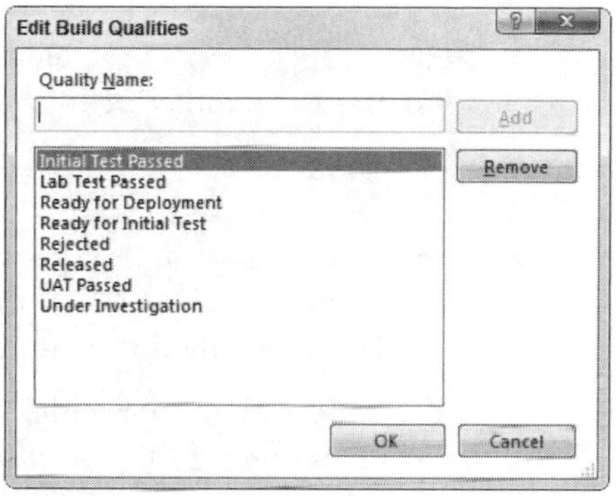

To manage the options available for the build quality, go to Build ⇨ Manage Build Qualities in Visual Studio, or right-click the `Builds` node in Team Explorer in Visual Studio or Eclipse and select Manage Build Qualities. This displays the Edit Build Qualities dialog shown in Figure 15-34, which you can use to add new entries and remove ones that are not used.

FIGURE 15-34: Edit Build Qualities dialog

Managing Build Controllers and Build Agents

The build controllers and agents can be managed from the Team Foundation Administration Console on the build controller machine or application tier. However, the controller and agent properties are also available from Visual Studio by going to Build ⇨ Manage Build Controllers, or by right-clicking the `Builds` node in Team Explorer and selecting Manage Build Controllers, which displays the Manage Build Controllers dialog. Selecting a build controller and clicking Properties will show you its Properties dialog (Figure 15-9), and selecting an agent and clicking Properties will show you its properties (Figure 15-10).

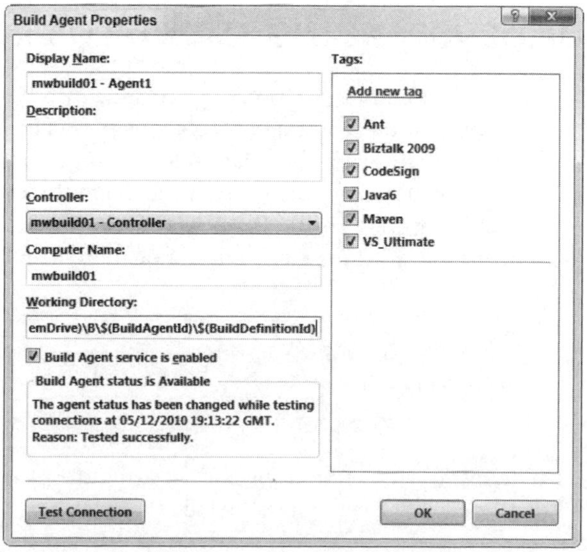

From the Build Agent Properties dialog, you can add a number of tags to the agent to signify capabilities of that agent, as shown in Figure 15-35. For example, you could use CodeSign if you have the projects code signing certificate installed on that machine, DataCenter1 if it is located in your main data center, or Ireland if it is located remotely.

FIGURE 15-35: Build Agent Properties dialog

As part of the build process, you can then filter by these tags to ensure that you are allocated a build agent that meets the requirements necessary for the build. For more information on this, see the section, "Understanding the Build Process," later in this chapter.

MINIMIZING THE BUILD PATH

Because of limitations in the way that the tools interact with the filesystem, there is a 260-character limit on the full path of files that make up the build process. In previous versions of Team Foundation Server, the initial working directory for a build agent was in the build service users profile directory, which significantly reduced the number of characters in the path available for your build files.

In Team Foundation Server 2010, the build working folder was reduced to `$(SystemDrive)\Builds\$(BuildAgentId)\$(BuildDefinitionPath)`, which, for a typical build, is something like `C:\Builds\1\Team Project\Build Definition Name\`. While this is much improved, you may still run into issues with build path length and need to reduce it further.

The shortest common build path can be created by setting the build agent working directory to something like `$(SystemDrive)\B\$(BuildAgentId)\$(BuildDefinitionId)`, which will create a typical build working folder of `C:\B\1\42\`, leaving you with some valuable additional characters if you find yourself pushing the 260-character limit. Using the `BuildDefinitionId` also guarantees that each new working folder created is unique, and prevents any workspace issues that sometimes happen when deleting and then adding a build definition with the same name for a team project.

UNDERSTANDING THE BUILD PROCESS

The end-to-end build process performed by a build is defined in a Windows Workflow 4.0 XAML file stored in the version control repository. The initial build process templates available are defined by the overall Team Foundation Server process template, and are created as part of the Team Project creation process. Any time after the Team Project is created, new build process templates can be created, registered with Team Foundation Server, and stored in version control. Those files can be modified to adjust the behavior of new builds for that particular process template.

> *For more information on customizing the build process templates, see Chapter 16.*

The rest of this section focuses on using the process templates that ship in the box with Team Foundation Server. These include the following:

➤ `DefaultTemplate` — This is the default template for all new builds created for Team Foundation Server 2010. This is the template that will be the primary focus of discussion in the remainder of this section.

➤ UpgradeTemplate — This is the template used for builds using the MSBuild-wrapped approach that was utilized in previous versions of Team Foundation Server, and also used for non .NET compilation projects such as VB6, C++ and also Java-based builds with Ant or Maven. The UpgradeTemplate is used by any existing build definitions that existed in a Team Foundation Server 2008 instance that was upgraded to Team Foundation Server 2010. UpgradeTemplate basically performs some simple housekeeping functionality that used to previously be hard-coded into the build agent process in earlier versions of Team Foundation Server. It then wraps the call to the MSBuild file called TFSBuild.proj that controls the rest of the MSBuild-based build process.

In addition, the LabDefaultTemplate may also be present for use by the Lab Management functionality described in Chapter 22.

As stated previously, all the build process templates are stored as XAML files in version control. By default, they will live in a folder called BuildProcessTemplates in the root of the team project (that is, $/TeamProject/ BuildProcessTemplates). However, custom process templates may be located inside your team project branching structure if created in that way.

DefaultTemplate Process

The DefaultTemplate process as defined in the file DefaultTemplate.xaml is used for most new, un-customized build definitions in Team Foundation Server 2010. The process is described at a high level in Figure 15-36. To view the process template in Visual Studio, double-click the DefaultTemplate.xaml file in the BuildProcessTemplates directory inside your team project.

DefaultTemplate Process

- Get the Build Detail
- Update Build Number
- Create Drop Folder
- Get Build Agent

Run On Agent
- Get Build Directory
- Initialize Workspace
- Get Source
- Create Label
- Compile
- Test
- Associate Work Items
- Calculate Impacted Tests
- Index Sources
- Publish Symbols
- Copy Build Outputs to Drop Folder

- Check in any Gated Changes

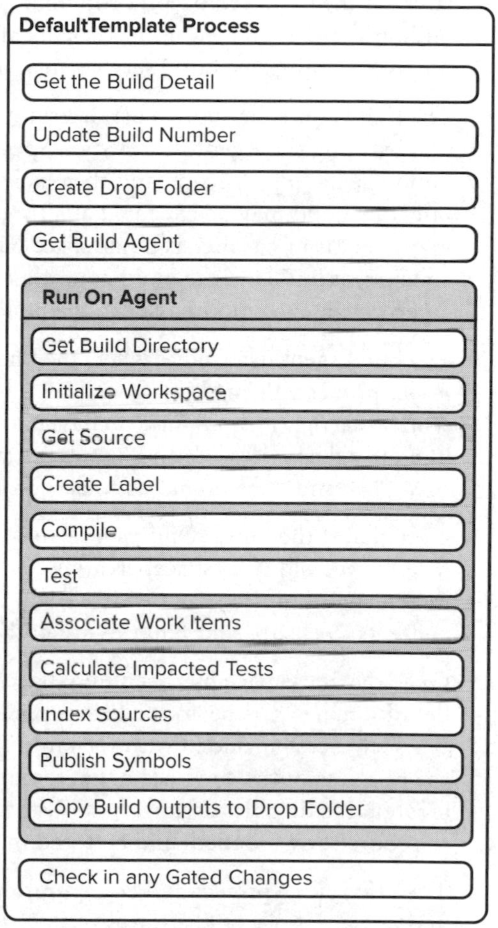

FIGURE 15-36: DefaultTemplate process

Chapter 16 describes in more detail how to edit a build process template. However it is worth noting at this point that, while you can edit the DefaultTemplate from Visual Studio, the best practice is to create a new process template from the Process section of the Build Definition editor based on the DefaultTemplate and edit this file. All builds in the team project sharing the same build process template will be affected by a change to that template. Therefore, it is good to leave the standard un-edited DefaultTemplate.xaml file alone in version control to avoid confusing team members who expect the DefaultTemplate to perform the same between systems using Team Foundation Server.

Understanding the Process

On the build controller the BuildDetail object corresponding to this running instance of the build is populated from the Team Foundation Server application tier machine and stored in a variable for later use. Then the build number is created based on a passed build number format (more on that later). If the build requires a drop folder, the next thing to occur is that a folder corresponding to the build number is created in the drop location specified by the build definition. This is the reason why the user running the build service must have write permission to the drop location network share.

The build controller now must determine on which build agent to execute the actual build. It does this by using the Agent Reservation Spec property described later in this chapter to determine which build agents to pick from, and then picks the next available build agent. If this is a gated build, only one build may be executed at a time. Otherwise, the build controller will attempt to run as many builds in parallel as it has spare build agents (unless constrained to a maximum number of concurrent builds in the build controller properties shown in Figure 15-9). Once the agent has been determined, execution passes to the build agent.

The build agent determines where the build directory should be located based on the agent working folder property defined in Figure 15-35. It then determines the name of the Team Foundation Server workspace that it should use on the build agent to download the sources into. Then the build agent initializes the workspace and figures out what the root Sources directory should be, along with the Binaries and Test Results folders — creating them if they do not already exists.

Note that if the build requires a clean workspace, the initialization process would have consisted of deleting the old workspace, creating a new one, and setting up the folder structure again. Equally, if incremental builds are not enabled, the Test Results and Binaries folders will be cleaned of all contents to ensure that binaries are built fresh for every build.

Once the workspace has been initialized as per the working folder template defined in the build definition, a Get is performed from version control to download the source files to the build agent. If a shelveset is included with the build (for example, for a gated check-in, or for a private build), the contents of the shelveset are automerged with the source code at this point. If a label should be created (the default for most builds), the label name is generated (created based on the version of the source downloaded) and is stored in the build details.

Then, for every project and configuration in the build definition, MSBuild is executed to compile and test the project. The status of the compilation and test phases of the build are also stored in the build details. At this point, if the build has been defined to treat test failures as build failures, the build will fail here if any failed tests have been detected. By default, a build will carry on from this point regardless of test status. If the build had a successful compilation, but any other phase of the build resulted in an error being thrown, the build will complete with a status of Partially Successful.

The changesets included in the build since the last successful build label was created are recorded. Each of the changesets is analyzed to determine which work items were associated with those changesets. These associated work items are recorded in the build details. If any of the work items were resolved as a result of one of these changesets, the "Fixed in Build" field for the work item will be updated to inform anyone investigating the resolved work item which build to test to validate that it was indeed fixed.

Next, the tests impacted by the changes included in the build are determined and stored in with the build details. The sources are indexed, and symbols are published to the Symbol server if specified.

Finally, the binaries generated by the build are copied over to the drop folder created by the build controller. If the build is still successful, then any changes that were being built as part of a gated check-in validation are checked in to version control on the triggering user's behalf.

Build Process Parameters

As you may have noticed already, there are lots of variables in the build process that can control how the build performs. These are stored as workflow parameters that are passed into the build as it is queued, based on the parameters defined in the build definition editor, and any parameters modified when manually queuing a build.

Figure 15-37 shows the parameters available when editing the build definition.

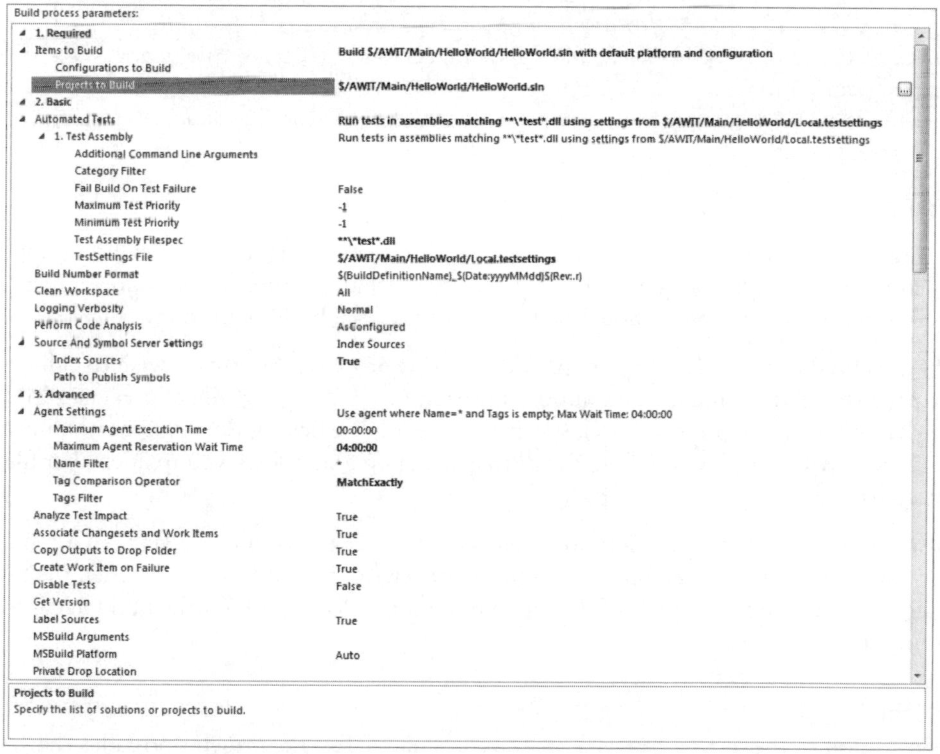

FIGURE 15-37: Parameters available when editing the build definition

Parameters are ordered into groups: Required, Basic, and Advanced. For more information on a particular parameter, select it in the build definition editor; the help section at the bottom of the Process section will show more information about that parameter, as shown at the bottom of Figure 15-37.

In the Required section of the `DefaultTemplate`, the items to build are specified. These are made up of the Configurations to Build and the Projects to Build.

Configurations to Build

The default Visual Studio build configuration to use is the default build configuration for the selected solution. However, you can override this — for example, if you would like to do a Release build on the build server, but the default in the solution is a Debug build.

To modify the configuration, use the Configurations dialog that is displayed when you click the "..." button in the Configurations to Build parameter.

> *Team Foundation Build typically deals with solution configurations. These allow you to specify a named collection of project-level platforms and configurations that should be built. For more information on solution configurations, see a blog post by Aaron Hallberg (former lead of the Team Foundation Build team at Microsoft) at* http://blogs.msdn.com/aaronhallberg/archive/2007/06/25/ solution-configurations.aspx.

Projects to Build

The Projects to Build parameter was discussed earlier in this chapter when the build definition was created. This parameter describes which MSBuild project files (that is, `.vbproj` or `.csproj` files) or Visual Studio Solution files (`.sln` files) should be built as part of the build definition.

Projects will be executed in the order they are provided in this property. So, if you wish to call a project after performing the build of the solution (for example, a `.wixproj` file to create an MSI installer using the Open Source project WiX), specify that second. Clicking the "..." button in the Projects to Build parameter displays the Solutions/Projects dialog and allows you to add other files to the list, and control the order.

The server paths to the projects to build are provided. These server paths must be mapped by the working folder template defined in the build definition. Otherwise, the build will fail when the build agent attempts to convert the server path of the file to build into a local path on the build agent to use when running the build.

Automated Tests

Under the Basic section of the `DefaultTemplate`, the Automated Tests parameter provides the tests that will be executed as part of the build. By default, this is set to execute all tests found in an assembly created by the build matching the pattern `*test*.dll` — that is, `HelloWorldTests.dll` would be inspected for tests implemented using the Microsoft test framework.

Clicking the ". . ." button in the Automated Tests parameter allows you to specify more tests that should be run, and their configuration, as shown in Figure 15-38. When editing a particular set of tests, you can control if the build should fail if those tests fail execution.

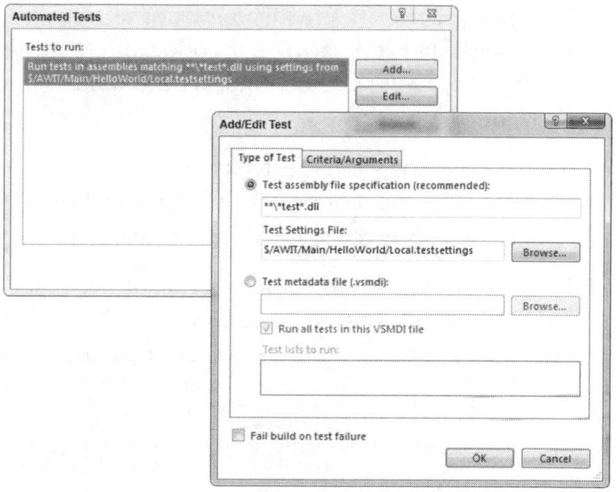

Tests can be filtered based on the test category or test priority using the Criteria/Arguments tab for the test, as shown in Figure 15-39. By categorizing your unit tests, you could set up your build verification tests differently from your coded UI or integration tests. Build verification tests (signified by a category of BVT) could fail the build, whereas failures in integration tests or coded UI tests (which are more prone to failure from external factors) may simply be recorded and the build marked as Partially Successful. An example of filtering based on category is shown in Figure 15-39.

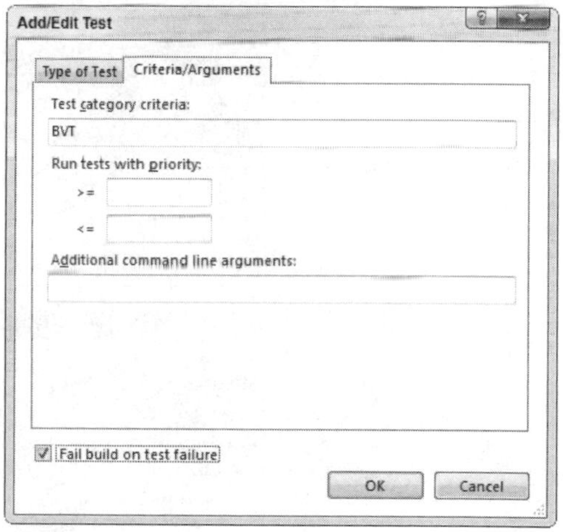

FIGURE 15-38: Specifying more tests should be run

Another example of using this functionality is that you may set up a build so that all tests with a priority of 1 or less are run as part of the standard Continuous Integration build, but all tests are run in an additional build definition triggered as a rolling build set to build no more often than once every 30 minutes. That way, the Continuous Integration build can give rapid feedback on the approximate build quality, but the rolling build can come along later and do a final check that everything is satisfactory.

The Automated Tests section also specifies the `TestSettings` file to be used for a test run. In the example shown in Figure 15-38, this is set to `$/AWIT/`

FIGURE 15-39: Criteria/Arguments tab

`Main/HelloWorld/Local.testsettings`. Your Visual Studio solution can contain a number of `.testsettings` files to control the behavior of the test environment, and to enable configuration settings such as code coverage and test impact analysis as part of the test run. If you have unit tests executing as part of the build, it may be very useful to enable these.

Code coverage tracks how much of the application code is being tested by the tests under execution. Test impact analysis determines which tests were affected by the changes since the last successful build — which gives an important indication to your testers about the impact of a particular change, and which tests should be revisited first when testing a build.

It is best practice to create a new test settings file specifically for your build server settings. That way, developer test settings used locally by the development team and the actual build server test settings are kept separate, but are available to the developer team to validate against locally if needed.

To create a new server test settings file, open the `Local.testsettings` file in the Solution Items. Then change the name in the General section to `Build Server` and click the Save As button to save the file as `BuildServer.testsettings`.

In the Data and Diagnostics section of the Test Settings dialog, check both the Code Coverage and the Test Impact options, as shown in Figure 15-40. Note that this is also where IntelliTrace can be enabled to get a rich diagnostic trace of any test failures, as well as many other test settings.

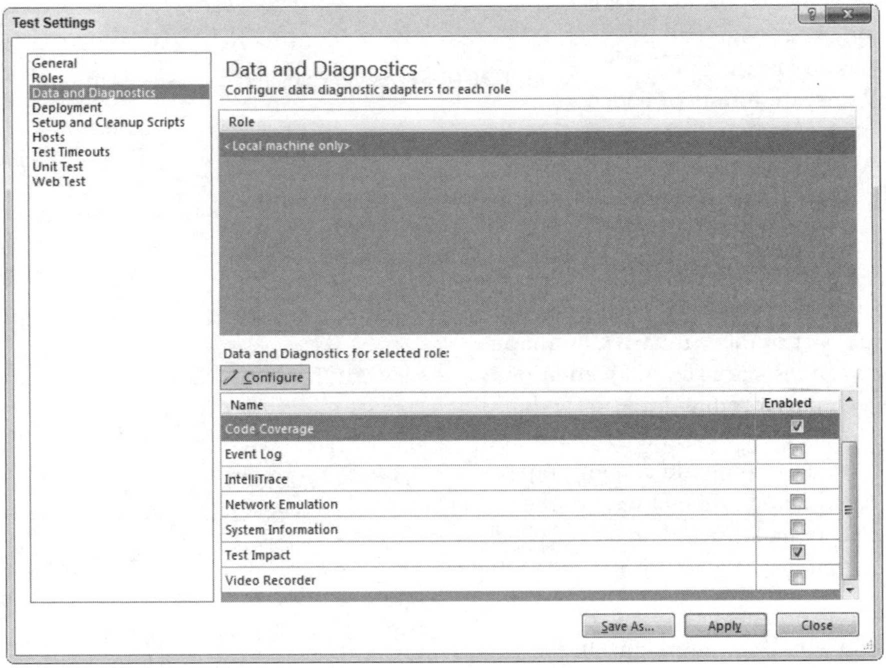

FIGURE 15-40: Test Settings dialog

With the Code Coverage option selected, click the Configure button highlighted in Figure 15-40. This displays the Code Coverage Detail dialog, and allows you to determine which assemblies make up the product under test (that is, excluding any unit test assemblies or Framework assemblies tested by other builds). Check the assemblies to have the code coverage measure, as shown in Figure 15-41, and click OK.

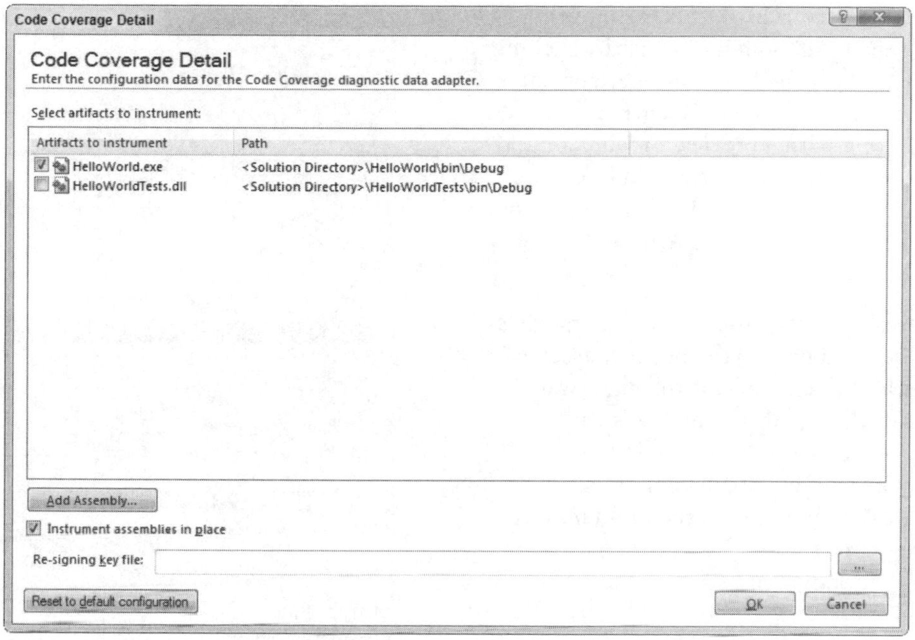

FIGURE 15-41: Selecting the assemblies to have the code coverage measure

Once configured, save the test settings file and check in to version control. Then, edit the TestSettings File parameter for the test assembly to point to the `BuildServer.testsettings` file.

> To record code coverage as part of the build, Visual Studio Premium or Visual Studio Ultimate must be installed on the build agent.

Build Number Format

Also in the Basic section of the `DefaultTemplate`, the Build Number Format parameter controls the format used when creating the build number at the beginning of the build process. By default, builds are created with the number format of `$(BuildDefinitionName)_$(Date:yyyyMMdd)$(Rev:.r)`. For example `HelloWorld_20101206.18`, where this is the 18th build for the HelloWorld build definition on 6 December 2010. Build numbers must be unique across a team project, and, therefore, this format serves as a good default. However, it is common that users wish to customize the build numbering.

In Team Foundation Server 2010, this is simply a matter of editing the build number format by clicking the ". . ." button to show the BuildNumber Format Editor. Initially, the dialog shows the current build number format, along with a preview of what a build number generated with this format would look like. Clicking the Macros button expands the dialog to show a number of available macros, as shown in Figure 15-42.

A common number format to use is one that matches the version numbers baked into the product assemblies as part of the build. For example, if the build was for version 4.1.0 of the product (where 4 is the major version, 1 is the minor version, and 0 is the servicing version), and the revision number is incremented for each build, then the build number format should be set to `$(BuildDefinitionName)_ 4.1.0$(Rev:.r)`, as shown in Figure 15-42.

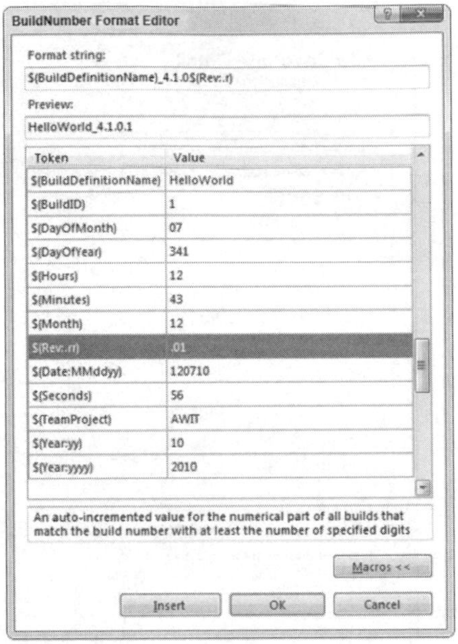

FIGURE 15-42: BuildNumber Format Editor dialog

> See Chapter 16 for an example of how to then customize the build process template to add this build number into the assemblies as the build is being performed.

Clean Workspace

By default, the Clean Workspace parameter in the Basic section is set to `All`, meaning that all existing build outputs and sources for that build definition will be deleted at every build. This is the safest option, but it is also the slowest, because it means that all files must be downloaded from version control, and everything built each time, regardless of how little changed between each build.

If you have a lot of source files, and you are not manipulating those source files in situ as part of the build (for example, you are not editing the `AssemblyInfo` files to include the build version number), you can set the value of the Clean Workspace parameter to `Outputs`. This will simply delete the build outputs every time a build is performed, but will keep the version control workspace between runs of the build, and so will only get the files that have changed between builds.

As discussed in Chapter 6, Team Foundation Server manages workspaces to ensure that files are deleted, moved, and renamed as they are deleted, moved, and renamed in version control, thus ensuring that there are no orphaned files. Therefore, enabling the workspace to be maintained between builds can dramatically improve build performance, especially for Continuous Integration builds, where the changes between each build are typically small.

If you set the value of the Clean Workspace parameter to `None`, neither the sources nor the build outputs will be deleted at the start of a build. Only the files that have been modified in version control will be updated, and only the items that have changed will be recompiled.

In a typical Continuous Integration build where the scope of changes between builds is typically small, this setting gives a further performance increase. In addition, it can also be useful for ASP.NET-based websites. In that case, you might only subsequently publish the items that have changed between the build output and your website to minimize the upgrade impact of a new version, thus better facilitating continuous deployment.

Logging Verbosity

By default, only messages above the Normal priority will be included in the build log. However, by editing the Logging Verbosity parameter in the Basic section, you can adjust the logging priority to change the level of the detail recorded.

The more information that is recorded, the slower the build is to perform. This results in it taking longer to download the results to display in Visual Studio, as well as using more memory. Therefore, Logging Verbosity is a parameter that is usually left at Normal in the build definition, but can be manually set to a lower level (such as Detailed or even Diagnostic) when manually queuing a build definition that has been causing issues.

Perform Code Analysis

Static code analysis allows you to provide a set of rules that can be checked during a build to ensure that code conventions are being adhered to, and common bugs and security issues are avoided. The Managed Code Analysis tool (otherwise known as FxCop) is a tool used by Visual Studio to analyze code against a library of rules. Nearly 200 rules are provided out-of-the-box based on the .NET Framework Design Guidelines. They are organized into a series of rule sets and groups.

By default, the use of code analysis is set at the project level in Visual Studio. However, the Perform Code Analysis parameter in the Basic section of the build parameter can set the code analysis to be run Always, Never, or AsConfigured in the Visual Studio project.

If set to Always then code analysis will force all projects in the solution to be analyzed. If a code analysis Rule Set has not been defined for a particular project then the default Rule Set (Microsoft Minimum Rules) will be used.

> *For more information on using static code analysis with Visual Studio projects, see Chapter 8 of the book* Professional Application Lifecycle Management with Visual Studio 2010 *(Indianapolis: Wiley, 2010).*

Source And Symbol Server Settings

A Symbol server is simply a file share that is used to store the symbols or program database (.pdb) files for your executable binaries in a defined layout. Visual Studio can then be configured with the details of this server. From then on, when debugging code live or using the advanced historical debugging features (IntelliTrace), Visual Studio is capable of taking you directly to the version of the source code that was used to create the binary being debugged.

The configuration of the Symbol server is performed by providing the Windows file location to be used for the Symbol store in the Path to Publish Symbols parameter of the Source And Symbol Server Settings within the Basic section of the DefaultTemplate.

> *For more information on what every developer should know about symbol files, see the blog post by John Robbins at* http://www.wintellect.com/CS/blogs/ jrobbins/archive/2009/05/11/pdb-files-what-every-developer-must- know.aspx.

Agent Settings

The Agent Settings are located in the Advanced section of the build parameters in the DefaultTemplate. In addition to controlling how long a build may execute before being cancelled, and the maximum time a build may wait for an available agent, the Agent Settings provides for a Name and Tag filter. These can be used by the build controller to restrict the selection of agents when determining on which agent the build should execute.

Specifying a full name of a build agent allows you to force it to run on a particular machine. If you adopt a naming convention for your build agents such as TeamXAgent1, then using wildcards for the name filter will allow scoping to a particular set of build agents (for example, TeamX*).

A more flexible way is to use build agent tagging as shown earlier in this chapter in the "Managing Build Controllers and Build Agents" section. In this way, you can tag a build agent with its capabilities, and then use the Tags filter to specify the tags that you require (such as VS_Ultimate to indicate a machine that has that version of Visual Studio installed, and is, therefore, suitable for running a build requiring code coverage). You can then change the Tag Comparison Operator from the default of MatchExactly to MatchAtLeast, which means that you will accept any build agent that has the VS_Ultimate tag, regardless of the other tags it might have.

Analyze Test Impact

If the .testsettings file provided for the test run indicates that test impact analysis should be performed, the default setting of True for the Analyze Test Impact parameter in the Advanced section of the DefaultTemplate means that the analysis will be performed. Setting this to False means that the impact analysis will not be performed, regardless of the .testsettings.

Associate Changesets and Work Items

By default, the Associate Changesets and Work Items parameter of the DefaultTemplate is set to True, which means that the work will be performed to understand which changesets were included since the last successful build label, and which work items they are related to.

This analysis can take a long period of time, and can require several server calls, which will impact the performance of your Team Foundation Server instance. Therefore, if you decide that you do not require that functionality for a particular build definition, you can disable it by setting the value to False.

Copy Outputs to Drop Folder

If a drop location has been provided, then the outputs in the Binaries folder for the build definition will be copied to the drop location, unless the Copy Outputs to Drop Folder parameter in the Advanced section of the DefaultTemplate is set to False.

Create Work Item on Failure

When a build fails, the default behavior is to create a work item assigned to the person for whom the build was running (the person that checked in files, for example, in the case of a Continuous Integration triggered build definition). Set the Create Work Item on Failure parameter in the Advanced section of the `DefaultTemplate` to `False` if you do not require work items to be created automatically.

Disable Tests

By default, the tests specified in the Automated Tests setting will be executed unless the Disable Tests parameter in the Advanced section of the `DefaultTemplate` is set to `True`. This is usually performed when manually queuing a build that you wish to have a one-off run without tests (for example, to expedite the build process temporarily).

Get Version

By default the Latest version of source is used to perform a build. However, you may wish to create a build definition that always builds the files with a particular label — for example, `QARelease` in the project `MyTeamProject`. Setting the Get Version parameter in the Advanced section of the `DefaultTemplate` to `LQARelease@$/MyTeamProject` would force the build definition to only get files with this label. Because labels can be edited in Team Foundation Server, you can now label the versions and files that make up that QA release, and know that they will be included in the build once triggered.

An alternative approach to using Get Version in this way would be to have a branch in version control representing the files that were in QA and merge changes into this branch to be included in that build. For more information on branching see Chapter 9.

Label Sources

By default, the Label Sources parameter in the Advanced section of the `DefaultTemplate` is set to `True`, which means that the sources in the workspace of the build are labeled at the `start` of the build process so that the exact versions included in the build can be easily determined. Set this to `False` if you do not require a label to be created. However, be warned that this also disables much of the change analysis functionality that relies on the last successful build label to determine the differences between builds.

MSBuild Arguments

Use the MSBuild Arguments parameter in the Advanced section of the `DefaultTemplate` to pass additional command-line argument to `MSBuild.exe` whenever it is invoked in the build process.

MSBuild Platform

By default, the MSBuild platform used to execute the build process is auto-detected, based on the current operating system of the build agent. However, this parameter in the Advanced section of the `DefaultTemplate` can be set explicitly to say `x86` if an explicit platform is required (for example when the project is calling assemblies that are not `x64` compatible and so you need to force them to be loaded into the correct version of the CLR).

Private Drop Location

Use the Private Drop Location parameter in the Advanced section of the `DefaultTemplate` to specify an alternate default drop location to use when performing private or buddy builds. If not specified (which is the default), then private build results are dropped to the same location as the default drop location specified for the build definition.

Building Ant and Maven Projects with Team Foundation Server

A standard build agent may perform basic build and test activities for most .NET project types. Visual Studio Ultimate or Visual Studio Premium is required on the build agent to perform advanced .NET builds with features such as code coverage or static code analysis.

It is also possible to execute Java builds from the Team Foundation build agent by installing the Build Extensions Power Tool on the build agent, along with a suitable Java Development Kit (JDK) version, as well as Ant and/or Maven. The latest version of the Build Extensions Power Tool can be found at `http://go.microsoft.com/fwlink/?LinkID=185588`.

This Power Tool provides a set of Workflow Activities and MSBuild tasks that wrap the calling of Ant or Maven by a Java build definition. The results of the build tool are then interpreted and published back to Team Foundation Server by the build agent, along with any JUnit test results. The data for the Java build process is then available in Team Foundation Server in just the same way as Visual Studio builds are.

The easiest way to create a Java-based build definition is to create it from Eclipse using Team Explorer Everywhere. Right-click the `Builds` node in Team Explorer and follow the build definition creation process as outlined earlier in the chapter. The only significant difference is that, instead of the Process section described earlier, the build definition in Eclipse requests that a project file be created.

Click the Create button to display the Create Build Configuration Wizard shown in Figure 15-43, and then select the Ant `build.xml` or Maven `pom.xml` file that you wish to use to perform the build.

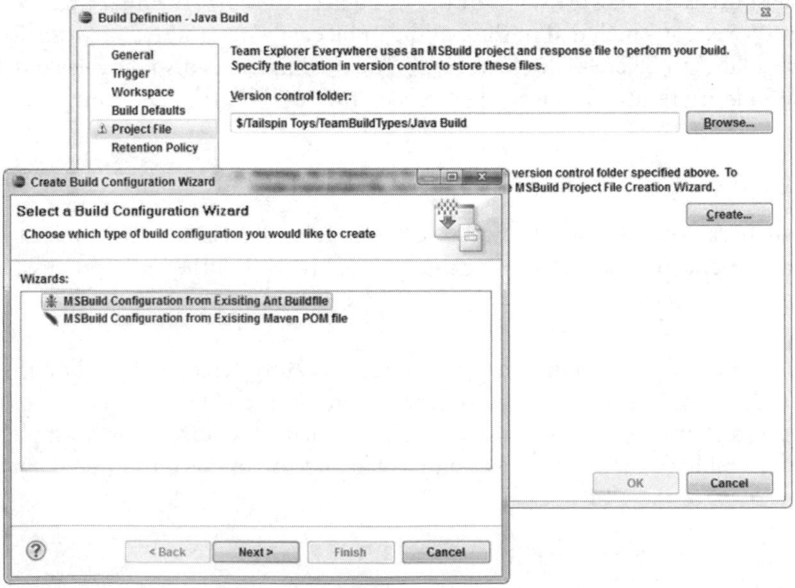

FIGURE 15-43: Create Build Configuration Wizard

Note that this creates a build using the `UpgradeTemplate` process template, with all the functionality controlled by a `TFSBuild.proj` file with an MSBuild-based wrapping script. In this way, the build functionality can be easily edited from Eclipse or cross-platform where a suitable Windows Workflow 4.0 editor is not easily available.

SUMMARY

This chapter was all about using the build functionality provided by Team Foundation Server. You learned about installation of the build services, and about the creation of a build definition. You became familiar with the tools and windows used to manage builds with Team Foundation Server. Finally, the chapter described the build process, provided a detailed examination of the available configuration parameters for the `DefaultTemplate`, and described how to build Java projects (as well as Visual Studio ones) with Team Foundation Server.

Chapter 16 examines customization of the build process in more detail, and presents some examples of common build customizations.

16

Customizing the Build Process

WHAT'S IN THIS CHAPTER?

➤ Getting to know Windows Workflow Foundation

➤ Creating custom process parameters

➤ Reviewing standard workflow activities

➤ Reviewing standard Team Foundation Server activities

➤ Creating custom activities

➤ Reviewing other extensibility options

As you learned in Chapter 15, Team Foundation Server includes a rich set of features for automated builds that are based on the Windows Workflow Foundation 4.0 technology included in the .NET Framework. The main functionality for an automated build is included in the default build process template that is available in the standard process templates. More than likely, however, you will find yourself needing to customize that functionality, or add actions for your build process.

In this chapter, you will learn the fundamentals for working with Windows Workflow Foundation 4.0 and how to customize the build process template using the workflow designer tools available in Visual Studio 2010. Additionally, you will learn how to create custom build workflow activities that can be deployed to build machines and used by your automated builds.

INTRODUCTION TO WINDOWS WORKFLOW FOUNDATION

Windows Workflow Foundation (WF) is a framework that is included in the .NET Framework to assist with managing workflows in applications. Your team can even use it to manage workflows in your custom applications. Thankfully, a lot of the normal heavy lifting has been done by the Team Foundation Server Build developers. So, you can take advantage of the customization and extensibility that WF provides in your automated build process. In this section, you will learn about the basic tenets of WF as it is used in Team Foundation Server for automated builds.

At a high level, WF workflows describe the process of doing something by using a sequence of activities, and providing a run time for executing a described sequence. Workflows are stored in XAML files that describe the sequence of those activities, as well as the parameters that are exposed by the workflow, and the local variables that are declared and used during the workflow.

The entire workflow definition is serialized and then evaluated at run time. Because it can be serialized, the framework even allows sending parts of the workflow to another process hosting the workflow run time. This is how the build controller is able to send a part of the workflow to another build machine running as a build agent to execute its portion of the workflow, and even receive updates about the progress of the workflow on the remote machine.

Figure 16-1 shows the beginning of the default build process template as it is shown in the workflow designer. This displays the initial workflow activities.

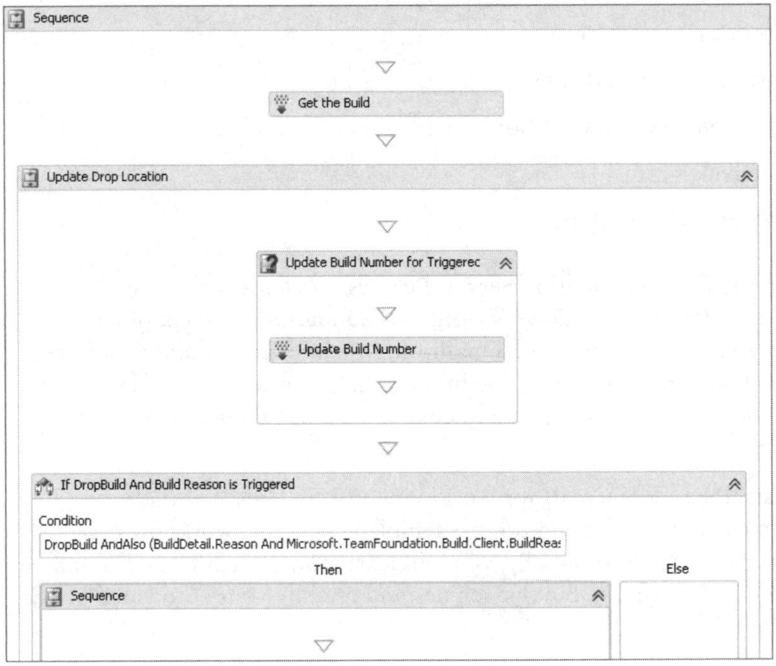

FIGURE 16-1: Beginning of the default build process template

You can edit a workflow file by opening it in Visual Studio 2010. For example, the build process templates that are available out-of-the-box are stored in the version control repository, usually in a subfolder of the team project with a folder name of `BuildProcessTemplates`. For example, you should find the default build process template available named `DefaultTemplate.xaml`, which you can open from Source Control Explorer directly to view the default workflow.

Visual Basic.NET Expressions

You can use Visual Basic.NET expressions in several locations in the workflow to assist with automation. These expressions are parsed and then evaluated at run time. For example, Figure 16-2 shows how the `If` activity is using features available in the .NET Framework (in this case, the `String` `.IsNullOrEmpty` function) for its `Condition` parameter. The workflow editor provides the capability to be more productive as well by including the IntelliSense feature, because developers are familiar with IntelliSense when using Visual Studio.

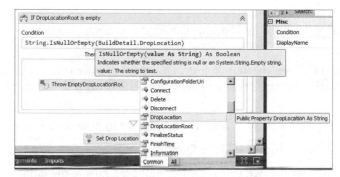

FIGURE 16-2: If activity in the .NET Framework

If you want to use a particular type from a namespace in the .NET Framework, you can also add an entry into the `Imports` list for the workflow, as shown in Figure 16-3. The list can be edited by clicking the Imports tab in the lower-left corner of the workflow editor window. This is very similar to adding an `Imports` statement in a Visual Basic.NET source code file, or a `using` statement in a Visual C# source code file.

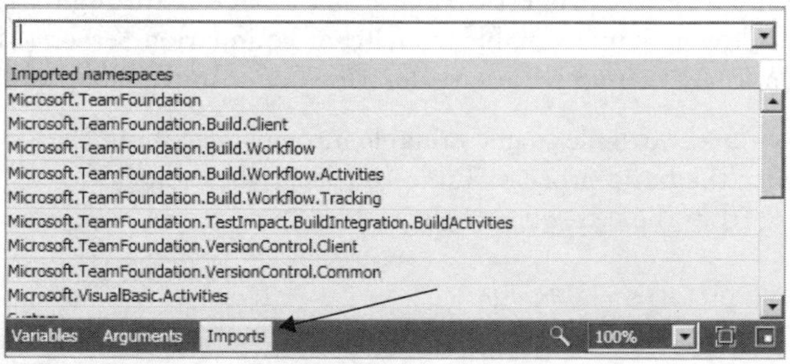

FIGURE 16-3: Adding an entry into the Imports list for the workflow

Custom Workflow Variables

Just as you might declare local variables inside a method or function, you might want to store values as local variables for use during the workflow. Workflow variables are defined by clicking the Variables tab in the lower-left corner of the workflow editor window, as shown in

Figure 16-4. Local variables have a name, .NET type, scope, and a default value.

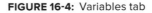

Name	Variable type	Scope	Default
BuildDirectory	String	Run On Agent	*Enter a VB expression*
LabelName	String	Run On Agent	BuildDetail.BuildNumber
WorkspaceName	String	Run On Agent	*Enter a VB expression*
SourcesDirectory	String	Run On Agent	*Enter a VB expression*
BinariesDirectory	String	Run On Agent	*Enter a VB expression*
TestResultsDirectory	String	Run On Agent	*Enter a VB expression*
BuildDetail	IBuildDetail	Sequence	*Enter a VB expression*
Create Variable			
Variables Arguments Imports			🔍 100%

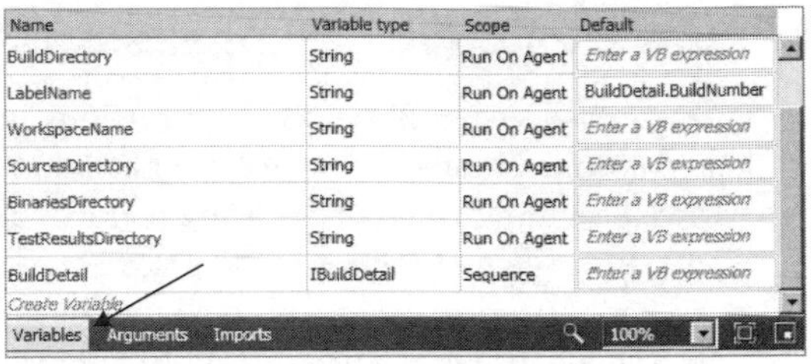

FIGURE 16-4: Variables tab

The default value can be a literal value, variable, parameter, or any .NET expression that returns an object of the type of the variable that was defined. The variable can also only be used while it is in scope as it is specified.

Following are some of the common variables that you can use from the build process template:

➤ `SourcesDirectory` — The local path on the build agent that is used to download the source code.

➤ `BinariesDirectory` — The local path on the build agent that is used to store the compilation outputs. This is also the directory that will get copied to the drop folder that is created for the build process.

➤ `TestResultsDirectory` — The local path on the build agent that is used to store the test results.

➤ `Workspace` — The workspace definition for the build definition.

➤ `WorkspaceName` — The name of the workspace that is created and used during the build process on the build agent.

➤ `BuildDetail` — Stores information about the current build.

➤ `BuildAgent` — Stores information about the build agent that is being used by the current build.

These workflows provide information back to the Team Foundation Server Build service about the build through the use of a globally scoped variable named `BuildDetail` that has a type of `Microsoft.TeamFoundation.Build.Client.IBuildDetail`. For example, the build can pass back the final status (Succeeded, Failed, Partially Succeeded) of the build, or even just the compilation or testing status. This is done by setting the appropriate properties on the `BuildDetail` through the use of the `SetBuildProperties` workflow activity available from Team Foundation Server. (This activity and other common Team Foundation Server activities are described later in this chapter.)

More commonly, you can use the `BuildDetail` variable to get valuable information about the current build that can be used to customize the build process. Table 16-1 describes some of the information artifacts that you can use from the `BuildDetail` variable.

TABLE 16-1: Information Artifacts to Use from BuildDetail Variable

ARTIFACT	DESCRIPTION
`BuildNumber`	This property is the unique number that is generated for the build to identify the build.
`BuildDefinition`	This allows you to get information about the build definition for the current build.
`TeamProject`	This property returns the name of the team project of where the build definition of the current build is stored.

ARTIFACT	DESCRIPTION
BuildServer	This property gives you the IBuildServer object that contains information about the build system, and even the team project collection for the current build.
DropLocation	This property returns the unique drop folder location that will be used by this specific build.
Status	This property returns the overall status for the current build (that is, In Progress, Succeeded, Partially Succeeded, Failed, and so on). You can use the SetBuildProperties activity to change this property.
CompilationStatus	This property returns the specific compilation status for the current build (that is, Succeeded, Failed, or Unknown). You can use the SetBuildProperties activity to change this property.
TestStatus	This property returns the specific test run status for the current build (that is, Succeeded, Failed, or Unknown). You can use the SetBuildProperties activity to change this property.
Reason	This property returns the reason the current build was started. For example, you can find out whether this is a gated check-in, private, scheduled, manually queued, rolling Continuous Integration, or individual Continuous Integration build. If there is certain functionality that should be run (or not run) based on the reason the build was started, you can use the InvokeForReason composite workflow activity, as described later in this chapter.
ShelvesetName	If the current build is a gated check-in or private ("buddy") build, then this property will return the name of the shelveset that is being used.
StartTime	This property returns the starting time of the current build.
SourceGetVersion	This property returns the version of the source code used during the current build.
Quality	The SetBuildProperties activity can be used to specify the initial build quality for the current build by using this property.
KeepForever	The SetBuildProperties activity can be used to specify whether the current build should be retained indefinitely, and be exempt from build retention policies by using this property.

Custom Build Parameters

Workflows can specify arguments as a means of exposing certain parameters that can be passed into and used by the workflow. Workflow arguments are similar to workflow variables in that they have a name, .NET type, direction, and a default value, but they can be used anywhere in the entire workflow.

Workflow arguments are defined by clicking on the Arguments tab in the lower-left corner of the workflow editor window, as shown in Figure 16-5. You may also recognize several workflow arguments that are defined in the default build process template as discussed in Chapter 15. The values for these arguments can also be used when customizing your build process templates.

Name	Direction	Argument type	Default value
BuildSettings	In	BuildSettings	New Microsoft.TeamFoundation.Build.Workflow.Activities.BuildSettir
TestSpecs	In	TestSpecList	New Microsoft.TeamFoundation.Build.Workflow.Activities.TestSpecL
BuildNumberFormat	In	String	"$(BuildDefinitionName)_$(Date:yyyyMMdd)$(Rev:.r)"
CleanWorkspace	In	CleanWorkspaceOption	Microsoft.TeamFoundation.Build.Workflow.Activities.CleanWorkspac
RunCodeAnalysis	In	CodeAnalysisOption	Microsoft.TeamFoundation.Build.Workflow.Activities.CodeAnalysisOp
SourceAndSymbolServerSettings	In	SourceAndSymbolServerSettings	New Microsoft.TeamFoundation.Build.Workflow.Activities.SourceAnc
AgentSettings	In	AgentSettings	New Microsoft.TeamFoundation.Build.Workflow.Activities.AgentSett
AssociateChangesetsAndWorkItems	In	Boolean	True

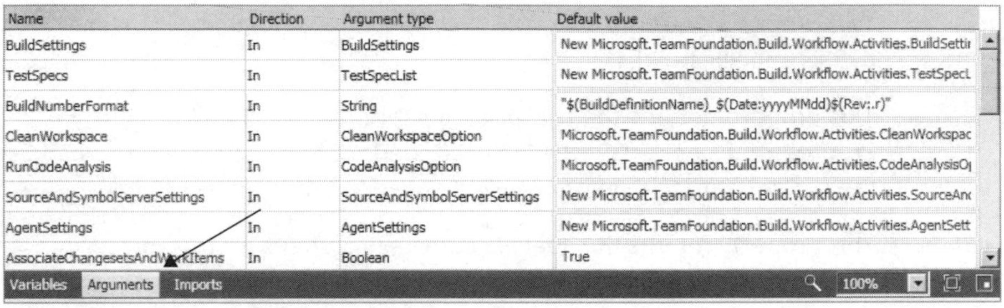

Variables | Arguments | Imports   🔍 100% ▼ 🔲 🔳

FIGURE 16-5: Arguments tab

Normally, a workflow can provide values back to the process hosting the workflow run time as output parameters. In this case, that would be the Team Foundation Server Build service, which does not use the workflow's parameters as a means to provide data back to Team Foundation Server. It instead stores information on the `BuildDetail` object for the current build, as described in the previous section. Therefore, when specifying custom build process workflow arguments, the direction is usually defined as `In`.

Specifying Metadata

As you learned in Chapter 15, process parameters that are exposed by the build process templates are used by the Build Definition Editor and the Queue New Build dialog windows to allow an end user to modify the parameters. To enable the editor and dialog to display friendly information and provide extra details in those standard Team Foundation Server user interface windows, you provide metadata for the custom process parameters that are included in your build process template.

The custom parameter metadata is stored as a workflow argument named `Metadata`, which is a collection of `ProcessParameterMetadata` entries. The `Metadata` argument is easily editable by clicking the edit button for the default value of the argument, as shown in Figure 16-6.

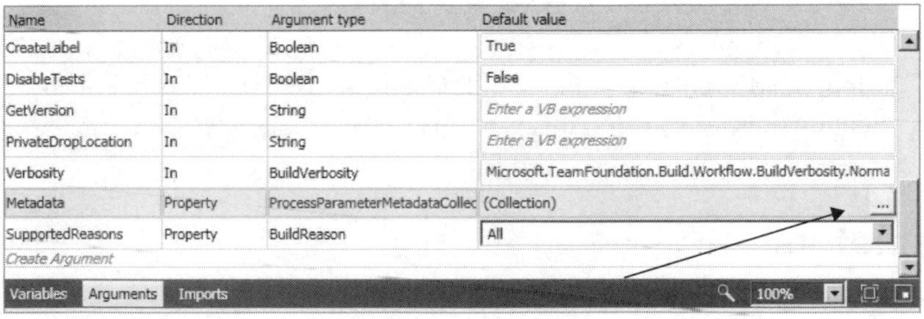

Name	Direction	Argument type	Default value
CreateLabel	In	Boolean	True
DisableTests	In	Boolean	False
GetVersion	In	String	Enter a VB expression
PrivateDropLocation	In	String	Enter a VB expression
Verbosity	In	BuildVerbosity	Microsoft.TeamFoundation.Build.Workflow.BuildVerbosity.Norma
Metadata	Property	ProcessParameterMetadataCollec	(Collection) ...
SupportedReasons	Property	BuildReason	All
Create Argument			

Variables | Arguments | Imports   🔍 100% ▼ 🔲 🔳

FIGURE 16-6: Edit button for the default value of the argument

A Process Parameter Metadata Editor dialog enables you to edit the `Metadata` collection, as shown in Figure 16-7.

Each custom parameter should be specified using the name as defined in the workflow `Arguments` list. Instead of showing the argument's name in the Process Parameter Metadata Editor, you can specify a friendly name and description to be shown for more information. Figure 16-8 shows the custom parameter as defined from Figures 16-6 and 16-7 named `MyCustomParameter`.

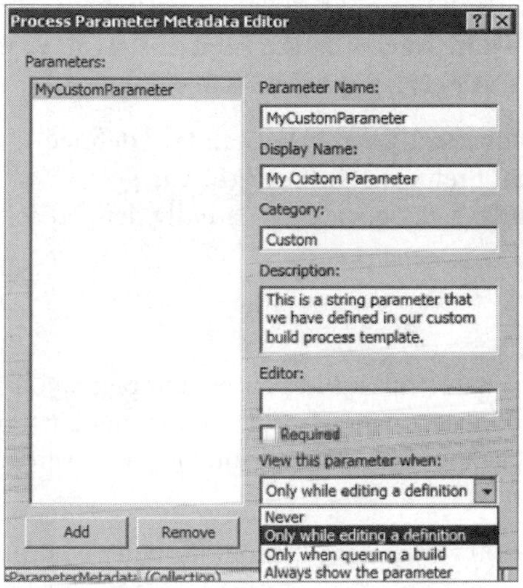

FIGURE 16-7: Process Parameter Metadata Editor dialog

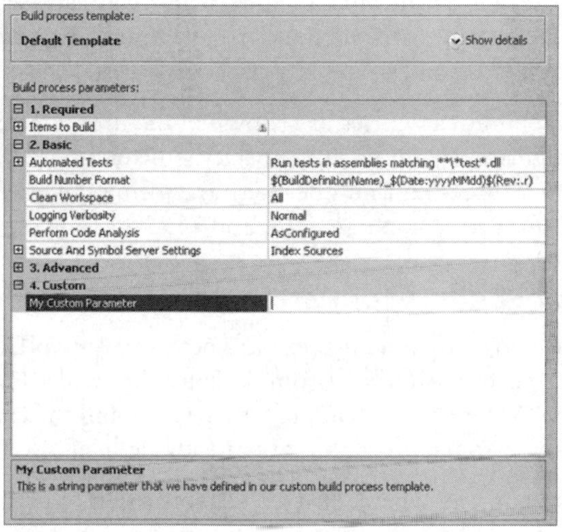

FIGURE 16-8: Custom parameter named MyCustomParameter

> *You can override the default metadata for any of the standard build process parameters by including an entry for each one that should be overridden in the `Metadata` collection. You might want to override the visibility, category, display name, custom editor, and so on.*

Parameter Visibility

You can specify when a parameter should be shown to end users by updating the "View this parameter when" property for the metadata entry. This is very helpful for hiding parameters from some end users (such as those who do not have permissions to edit build definitions), and allowing some parameters to be changed for manually queued builds. Following are the available values for this property:

➤ *Never* — The parameter will never be shown, and the default specified in the build process template will always be used.

➤ *Only while editing a definition* — The parameter will only be shown and editable from the build definition editor.

➤ *Only when queuing a build* — The parameter will only be shown and editable when queuing a new build manually in the Queue New Build dialog on the `Parameters` tab.

➤ *Always show the parameter* — The parameter will be shown while editing a build definition and queuing a build manually.

Parameter Categories

If you end up with lots of custom parameters, you should group parameters together using the category property in the metadata item. There are already several that will be used by the build definition editor according to the standard build process parameters. Those categories are `Required`, `Basic`, and `Advanced`. You can use any of those, or you can specify a custom category such as `Deployment`.

By default, categories are shown in the user interface alphabetically after the standard defined categories. If you want to specify a different order, you can prefix the name of the category with a three-digit number with the format #nnn. The standard categories are actually defined as `#010Basic`, `#020Required`, and `#030Optional`.

Custom Editors for Parameters

Since you can add custom parameters of any .NET type to a custom build process template, you may need to offer a custom designer that will allow the end user to specify a value for that custom type. Most of the standard .NET types and those that are custom for Team Foundation Server Build have custom editors that are already defined.

For example, when editing the Items to Build parameter, you can use the custom designer Microsoft has created for the `Microsoft.TeamFoundation.Build.Workflow.Activities.BuildSettings` type by clicking the button with the ellipsis, as shown in Figure 16-9, to display the custom editor dialog shown in Figure 16-10.

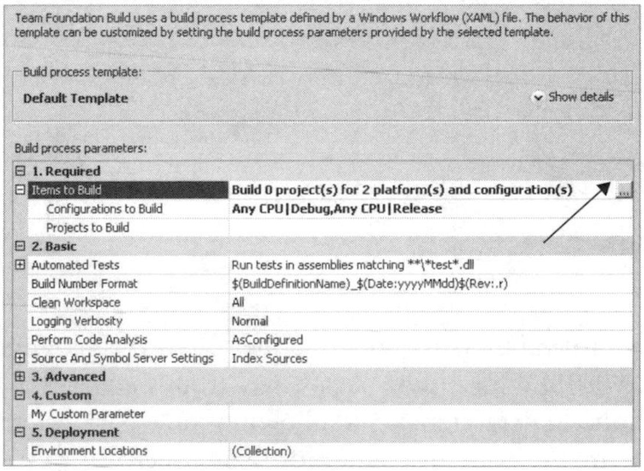

FIGURE 16-9: Ellipsis button

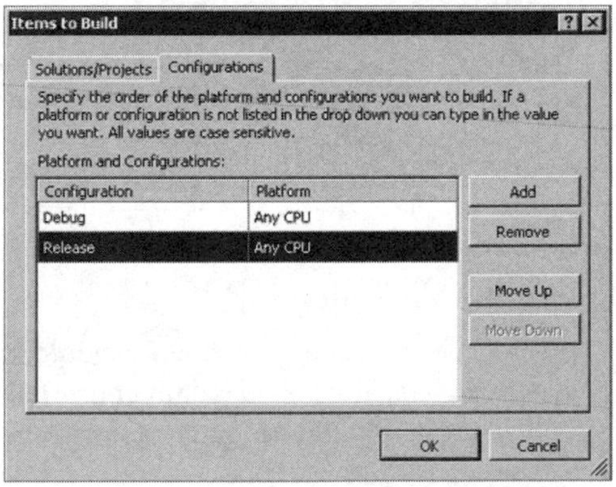

FIGURE 16-10: Custom editor dialog

The custom editor dialog is essentially a Windows Form that is used to edit the object of the custom type, and then can pass back to a custom editor class that inherits from the `System.Drawing.Design.UITypeEditor` class.

For example, let's say that you were to create a custom build process parameter as shown in Figure 16-11 with the name of `EnvironmentLocations` that is of type `System.Collections.Generic.Dictionary<string, string>` to store the locations of the different environments along with the name of the environment as the key. You must then create a custom editor for the `Dictionary` type, since one is not included for your end user to be able to edit the values for the parameter.

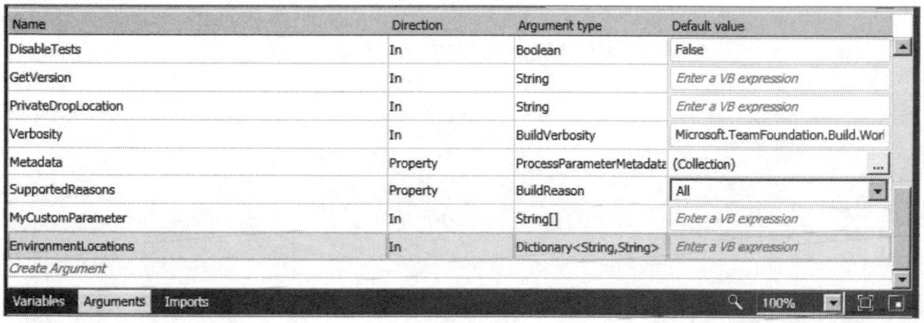

Name	Direction	Argument type	Default value	
DisableTests	In	Boolean	False	
GetVersion	In	String	Enter a VB expression	
PrivateDropLocation	In	String	Enter a VB expression	
Verbosity	In	BuildVerbosity	Microsoft.TeamFoundation.Build.Wor	
Metadata	Property	ProcessParameterMetadata	(Collection)	...
SupportedReasons	Property	BuildReason	All	
MyCustomParameter	In	String[]	Enter a VB expression	
EnvironmentLocations	In	Dictionary<String,String>	Enter a VB expresssion	
Create Argument				

Variables   Arguments   Imports   100%

FIGURE 16-11: Custom build process parameter

Listing 16-1 shows a sample custom editor for editing the `EnvironmentLocations` parameter.

LISTING 16-1: Sample Custom Parameter Editor Implementation

```
using System;
using System.ComponentModel;
using System.Collections.Generic;
using System.Drawing.Design;
using System.Windows.Forms;
using System.Windows.Forms.Design;
using Microsoft.TeamFoundation.Build.Client;

namespace Wrox.Build.CustomEditor
{
    public class EnvironmentsCustomEditor : UITypeEditor
    {
        public override object EditValue(ITypeDescriptorContext context,
            IServiceProvider provider, object value)
        {
            if (provider != null)
            {
                IWindowsFormsEditorService service =
                    (IWindowsFormsEditorService) provider.GetService
                    (typeof(IWindowsFormsEditorService));
                IBuildDefinition buildDefinition = (IBuildDefinition)
                    provider.GetService(typeof(IBuildDefinition));

                if (service != null)
                {
                    Dictionary<string, string> environments =
                        (Dictionary<string, string>) value;
```

continues

LISTING 16-1 *(continued)*

```
                using (EnvironmentsDialog dialog = new
                    EnvironmentsDialog(environments))
                {
                    DialogResult result = dialog.ShowDialog();

                    if (result == DialogResult.OK)
                    {
                        value = dialog.Environments;
                    }
                }
            }
        }

        return value;
    }

    public override UITypeEditorEditStyle
        GetEditStyle(ITypeDescriptorContext context)
    {
        return UITypeEditorEditStyle.Modal;
    }
    }
}
```

You will notice in Listing 16-1 that the real work is ultimately done by a custom Windows Form that you create to present the user interface. In this example, the Windows Form type name is EnvironmentsDialog.

After you have created the custom editor, you can specify the full name for the editor in the Metadata argument dialog, as shown in Figure 16-12. You use the following format, where the first entry is the full type name, and the second entry is the assembly's full name:

```
Wrox.Build.CustomEditor.EnvironmentsCustomEditor, Wrox.Build.CustomEditor
```

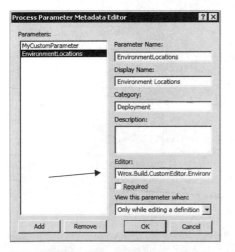

FIGURE 16-12: Full name for the editor in the Metadata argument dialog

Alternately, if you have created a custom type instead of using a standard .NET type, you can add the `System.ComponentModel.EditorAttribute` attribute to your type to indicate which custom editor should be used if a parameter is defined with that custom type.

```
[Serializable, Editor("Wrox.Build.CustomEditor.MyCustomTypeEditor,
    Wrox.Build.CustomEditor", typeof(UITypeEditor))]
public class MyNewCustomType
{
    // Implementation
}
```

Workflow Activities

Workflow activities are the basic building blocks of the build process template. Activities can be either simple or composite. A *composite activity* is one that can contain other activities. For example, the entire build process workflow begins with a `Sequence` workflow activity, which is a type of composite activity that executes contained activities in a specified sequence. Alternately, a *simple activity* is an activity that does not contain other activities.

Each activity exposes parameters that can be edited by using the Properties window in Visual Studio. You can use literal values, expressions, variables, workflow arguments, and so on. One important property is the display name for an activity, because it is what ends up being used in the build log. Each activity contains a displayed name property on it.

Figure 16-13 shows the available activities displayed in the Visual Studio Toolbox window. You can drag and drop activities onto your build process template file, similar to adding new controls to an ASP.NET page or Windows Forms form.

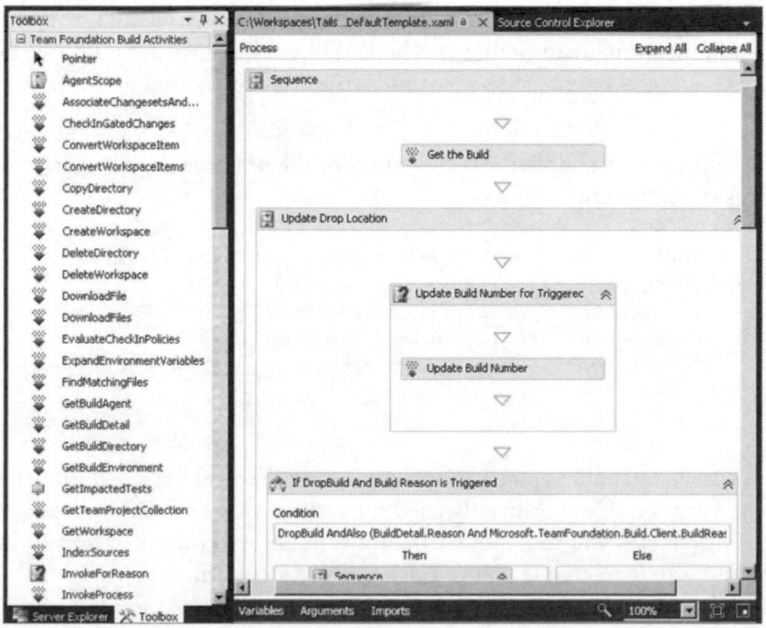

FIGURE 16-13: Activities that are available as displayed in the Visual Studio Toolbox

Notable Workflow Framework Activities

Build process workflows can use any workflow activity. There are several standard workflow activities from the .NET Framework that you can use in your build process templates. This section covers some of the common workflow activities.

If

The `If` composite activity allows you to have a conditional switch based on an expression property exposed by the activity. There are two branches that the workflow can take, depending on whether the expression evaluates to `True` or `False`. You can use any valid expression, including using standard .NET methods like `System.IO.File.Exists`.

This is an extremely useful activity for segmenting optional parts of the build process. For example, you may define a Boolean process parameter named `Deployment` with a default value of `False`. You can then wrap the deployment functionality of the build inside an `If` activity that uses the parameter value for the expression. The deployment functionality will run whenever the parameter is specified as `True`, and will be skipped if it is not set.

Sequence

The `Sequence` composite activity contains other activities, and will run each activity in order from top to bottom. Some other composite activities can only contain one activity (such as the `If` activity). So, if you need to use more than one activity in those circumstances, you can insert a `Sequence` activity, and then include the desired activities inside of the `Sequence` activity.

Assign

The `Assign` activity is one of the simple workflow activities that allow you to assign one value to a workflow variable or argument. One of the nice features about the `Assign` activity is that the value to be used can use any expression including using .NET methods. For example, you might use the `System.String.Format` or `System.IO.Path.Combine` methods to initialize a variable using other argument or variable values.

For example, if you wanted to initialize a variable for the location of the `witadmin.exe` utility, you might use an expression such as the following:

```
System.IO.Path.Combine(If(String.IsNullOrEmpty(Environment.GetFolderPath
(Environment.SpecialFolder.ProgramFilesX86)),
Environment.GetFolderPath(Environment.SpecialFolder.ProgramFiles),
Environment.GetFolderPath(Environment.SpecialFolder.ProgramFilesX86)),
"Microsoft Visual Studio 10.0\Common7\IDE", "witadmin.exe")
```

Exception Handling

The three activities that are available to enable you to handle exceptions are `Rethrow`, `Throw`, and `TryCatch`. The `TryCatch` composite activity is primarily used for setting up a try-catch-finally block around a set of activities. It enables you to handle different types of exceptions by specifying multiple `catch` blocks. `Throw` and `Rethrow` enable you to raise a new exception, or re-throw an existing exception that was caught.

Parallel

The `Parallel` composite activity allows for running multiple activities in parallel simultaneously. This is a very useful activity for speeding up the build process. You will notice several locations in the default process template that use a `Parallel` activity to speed up the entire build process.

You might also use a `Parallel` activity to run multiple `AgentScope` activities (which are discussed later in this chapter) to have multiple build servers running parts of the build process in parallel. For example, you might configure the build process to compile the `Debug` configuration on one build machine simultaneously with compiling the `Release` configuration on a different build machine.

ForEach<T> and ParallelForEach<T>

The `ForEach<T>` composite activity allows you to define a for-each loop over a collection or any type that implements the `IEnumerable` interface. For example, the default build process template uses this activity to iterate over the solutions to build collections. It will go through each item in the collection, and run the same routine using the item.

The `ParallelForEach<T>` works similarly to the `ForEach<T>` activity, except that it attempts to run each of the iterations in parallel.

InvokeMethod

The `InvokeMethod` activity allows you to call any .NET method, and allows you to store the return value into a workflow variable. This can be useful when operating on strongly typed variables and workflow arguments defined in your build process.

Notable Team Foundation Server Activities

In addition to the standard workflow activities that are available, Team Foundation Server provides a set of workflow activities specifically designed to be used during the build process. This section covers some of the common Team Foundation Server activities used during a build workflow.

> *For more information and documentation on the standard Team Foundation Server workflow activities, see the MSDN documentation article at* http:// msdn.microsoft.com/en-us/library/gg265783.aspx.

AgentScope

The `AgentScope` composite activity performs the activities contained inside of it on a build agent. It performs all of the necessary steps to reserve an available build agent matching the reservation specifications that are passed into the activity by using the `ReservationSpec` property on the activity. If an available agent that matches the reservation specifications isn't available, the activity will wait until one is available (up until the time when it is set for the `MaxWaitTime` property on the activity).

> *It is important to ensure that most work done during a build process is done inside of an* AgentScope *activity. Activities outside of an* AgentScope *activity will actually be performed on the build controller, instead of a build agent. If the activity is anything extensive, it will add extra load to the build controller, which can slow down the entire build farm.*

Additionally, any workflow arguments or variables that are changed inside of an AgentScope activity will not retain their values once the build process leaves the scope. Any data that you want to continue passing on will need to be stored on the IBuildDetail object, or as build information nodes for the build process (which is available on the IBuildDetail object). *Build information nodes* are the internal structures for each build detail that contain data about the build. For example, each of the messages that is displayed in the build log is a type of build information node.

MSBuild and MSTest

The MSBuild and MSTest activities allow you to call MSBuild.exe to compile a solution or project, or to call MSTest.exe to run a set of tests during the build process. You will notice that each is used in the default build process template in the appropriate location during the build workflow.

WriteBuildMessage, WriteBuildWarning, and WriteBuildError

The WriteBuildMessage, WriteBuildWarning, and WriteBuildError activities allow you to add messages, warnings, and errors, respectively, to the build log. The main property for these activities is the Message property that indicates the message to be included in the build log.

One additional property that should be set for the WriteBuildMessage activity is the build message Importance. If your build is using the Normal build verbosity level, then you will want to set the WriteBuildMessage's Importance property to High if you want the message shown in the build log. Setting the build verbosity to a higher value such as Detailed or Diagnostic will show the build messages with Importance values of Normal and Low, respectively.

InvokeProcess

The InvokeProcess composite activity is used to handle calling a command-line utility, batch script, PowerShell script, and so on. This activity is a basic building block for customizing the build process, since there are command-line utilities that are usually used during a build process. For example, you might use the InvokeProcess activity to call the vsdbcmd.exe utility to publish the changes for a database project's schema to a development database server.

The InvokeProcess activity is a composite activity because it defines two locations where you can specify what do to with the standard output of the process and the error output. You might use a WriteBuildMessage activity for the standard output, and a WriteBuildError activity for the error output. If a command-line utility does not write to STDERR, you will want to use the Result property for the activity to get the return code for the command-line utility. You could then compare that to what you are expecting. If an error code is returned, you can handle it appropriately.

UpdateBuildNumber

The `UpdateBuildNumber` activity allows for the build process to update its build number using the build format string provided.

> See Chapter 15 for more information on the build number format string.

SetBuildProperties and GetBuildDetail

The `SetBuildProperties` activity is available for setting different properties on the `IBuildDetail` object. This is used in several locations during the default build process template to store permanent information, such as the build's drop folder or its final status.

Alternately, if there is a particular build property that cannot be set using the `SetBuildProperties` activity, you can store additional information on the `IBuildDetail` object. You do this by getting a reference to it using the `GetBuildDetail` activity, and then setting the appropriate properties using an `Assign` activity, or by adding build information nodes inside of a custom build workflow activity.

CopyDirectory, DeleteDirectory, and CreateDirectory

The `CopyDirectory`, `DeleteDirectory`, and `CreateDirectory` activities will help you handle common directory manipulation tasks. For example, you might use the `CopyDirectory` activity to help you copy the compiled output for your web application project from the `_PublishedWebsites` folder inside of the local output directory (stored in a build variable called `BinariesDirectory`) to your development web server.

ConvertWorkspaceItem and ConvertWorkspaceItems

The `CovertWorkspaceItem` and `ConvertWorkspaceItems` activities are extremely useful for converting an item specified using a server path location in the Team Foundation Server version control repository to its local path location, or vice versa. This allows you to define a build workflow argument that asks for a server path location (for example, to a configuration file), and the activities can convert it into its local location on the build agent. You can then use that local location in other activities that need the local location.

FindMatchingFiles

The `FindMatchingFiles` activity allows you to get a list of files that match a certain pattern expression. For example, if you wanted to find all of the `AssemblyInfo` files in the sources directory, you might specify the following match pattern expression:

```
String.Format("{0}\**\AssemblyInfo.*", SourcesDirectory)
```

You must also ensure that you have a variable of type `IEnumerable<String>` defined for the result property of the activity.

SharedResourceScope

There are times when certain functionality can only occur once across multiple builds that may be running. Similar to using the `lock` statement in C#, you can use the `SharedResourceScope` composite activity to define a scoped set of activities that can only be run based on a shared resource key. The shared resource key is used across build definitions in a team project collection. A build that is running will not enter the scope if another build using the same resource key in the team project collection is currently inside of the scope.

For example, Symbol server only permits one build process to publish symbols to the file share at a time. The default build process template keeps this in mind, and includes a `SharedResourceScope` activity with the shared resource key set to the Symbol server path. If another build in the same team project collection is publishing to the same Symbol server path, the build will wait until that other build has exited the scope.

There are certain routines that must run in isolation on the same build machine because of tools that are not meant to be run simultaneously. This can pose a problem if you have multiple build agents defined per build machine. To ensure that those routines do not run at the same time in multiple builds that could be running on the same build machine, you can use the build machine's name as the shared resource key — for example, `BuildAgent.ServiceHost.Name`.

GetBuildEnvironment

The `GetBuildEnvironment` activity is used to get a reference to the `BuildEnvironment` object. The `BuildEnvironment` object is typically used to find out whether the current section of the build process is running on a build controller or a build agent. It also has a `CustomAssemblyPath` property to get the path to the assemblies folder that contains the custom activities on the build agent.

InvokeForReason

The `InvokeForReason` composite activity defines a scope of activities that should only be run if the build was started for a particular reason, as described earlier in this chapter. An example usage for this activity is the functionality for checking in the changes included in the shelveset used for a gated check-in build, as defined in the default build process template. The `InvokeForReason` activity's `Reason` property would be set to `CheckInShelveset` to ensure that it is run only if the build is triggered as a gated check-in build.

Build Log Verbosity

You may not want every activity to show up in the build log using its display name. For example, the `If` activity may not be an activity that you necessarily want to log all the time.

You can lower the tracking priority for an activity, but it is not a property that you can edit using the workflow designer. If you open the process template using an XML editor, you can add the following attribute to any activity:

```
mtbwt:BuildTrackingParticipant.Importance="Low"
```

Following are the available values that are recognized:

➤ `None` — This activity will never be logged.

➤ `Low` — This activity will be logged if the build verbosity is set to `Detailed` or `Diagnostic`.

➤ `Normal` — This activity will be logged if the build verbosity is set to `Normal`, `Detailed`, or `Diagnostic`.

➤ `High` — This activity will always be logged.

Since you may need to troubleshoot builds by setting the build verbosity to `Diagnostic`, you should not use the `None` value, and opt for using `Low` for hiding activities during normal verbosity builds. This will allow you to at least see the activities (and their corresponding input and output values) whenever the build verbosity is set to `Diagnostic`.

> *Jason Prickett has an excellent blog post about reducing the build log noise where you can find out more information about this topic. See* `http://blogs`
> `.msdn.com/b/jpricket/archive/2010/12/09/tfs-2010-making-your-build-`
> `log-less-noisy.aspx.`

WHEN TO USE MSBUILD VERSUS WF

In general, you should consider using the default build process template based on WF for all new build definitions, instead of the MSBuild-based upgrade process template that is used for build scripts created for earlier versions of Team Foundation Server.

You might be wondering when is it appropriate to add build functionality using MSBuild versus WF. In general, anything that occurs inside of the compilation process (and that should be run on developer machines) should be defined by using MSBuild and customizing the Visual Studio project files (which are MSBuild scripts). Otherwise, you should take advantage of WF for all of the build functionality that should occur outside of the compilation process.

> *Jim Lamb has an excellent blog post article about deciding when to use MSBuild or WF in Team Foundation Server 2010 builds. See* `http://blogs.msdn.com/b/`
> `jimlamb/archive/2010/06/09/windows-workflow-vs-msbuild-in-tfs-2010`
> `.aspx.`

CUSTOM BUILD WORKFLOW ACTIVITIES

There are a lot of great workflow activities available in the .NET Framework and provided by Team Foundation Server. However, there may be times when there is certain functionality that you need to perform and cannot use the standard workflow activities that are available. However, creating custom workflow activities is one of the extensibility points for Team Foundation Server.

> **COMMUNITY TEAM FOUNDATION SERVER BUILD ACTIVITIES AND EXTENSIONS**
>
> A group of Microsoft employees, Visual Studio ALM Rangers, and Microsoft MVPs for Team Foundation Server have grouped together to start a CodePlex project of commonly requested custom workflow activities for Team Foundation Server Build. You might find an activity that you currently need on the CodePlex project.
>
> The source code for all the activities is available and is licensed under the Microsoft Permissive License, which allows you to use the activities for commercial purposes. For more information about the project, to request new custom activities, or to vote on current requests, visit http://tfsbuildextensions.codeplex.com.

How to Create a Custom Build Activity

Following are several options available to you for creating custom workflow activities:

- ➤ Declarative activities
- ➤ Native activities
- ➤ Code activities
- ➤ Asynchronous activities

More commonly, you will create *declarative activities* (which are a collection of several activities composed into one activity) or *code activities* (which allow you to specify exactly what should be executed using .NET code). Each of these types is included as a Visual Studio item template inside of a workflow activity library project.

To get started, create a new activity library project in Visual Studio by heading to File ➪ New Project and choose the Activity Library project type, as shown in Figure 16-14. If you created a team project for managing artifacts for Team Foundation Server as described in Chapter 10, you can use the location specifically for the source code for custom build extensions. You might also create an automated build using the Visual Studio solution you create in this procedure.

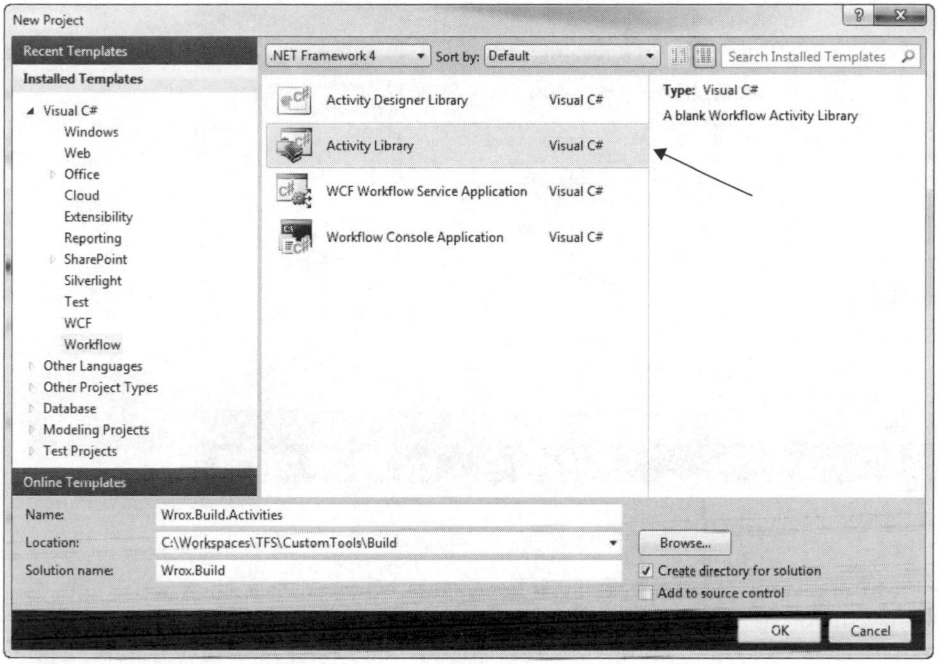

FIGURE 16-14: Choosing the Activity Library project type

After creating the project, you will want to change the project's target framework from the default of ".NET Framework 4 Client Profile" to ".NET Framework 4." You can do this by editing the `Target Framework` property on the `Application` tab of the Visual Studio Project Properties window.

After setting the .NET Framework target level, you will want to add the following references to the Team Foundation Server Build SDK assemblies:

➤ `Microsoft.TeamFoundation.Build.Client` — Available from the folder at `C:\Program Files (x86)\Microsoft Visual Studio. 10.0\Common7\IDE\ReferenceAssemblies\v2.0`

➤ `Microsoft.TeamFoundation.Build.Common` — Available from the folder at `C:\Program Files (x86)\Microsoft Visual Studio. 10.0\Common7\IDE\ReferenceAssemblies\v2.0`

➤ `Microsoft.TeamFoundation.Build.Workflow` — Available from the folder at `C:\Program Files (x86)\Microsoft Visual Studio 10.0\Common7\IDE\PrivateAssemblies`.

Start a new code activity by using the Code Activity item template available from the Add ➪ New Item context menu option off of the Visual Studio project node in Solution Explorer. Figure 16-15 shows the Add New Item dialog with the Code Activity item template.

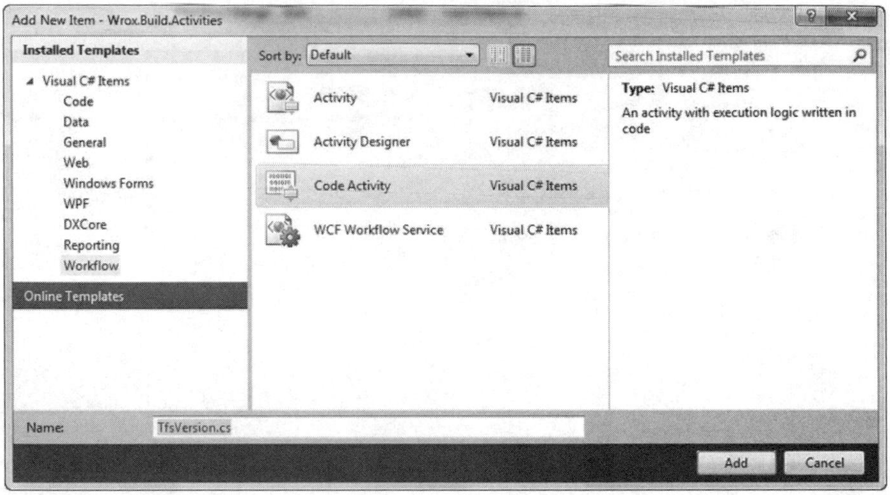

FIGURE 16-15: Add New Item dialog

If you will be creating several code activities, it is beneficial to create a base class activity that can store some common methods you might use in your activities. Listing 16-2 shows a good example of a base code activity class from the community Team Foundation Server build extensions mentioned in the sidebar, "Community Team Foundation Server Build Activities and Extensions."

LISTING 16-2: Custom Build Workflow Base Code Activity Class

```csharp
//---------------------------------------------------------------------
// <copyright file="BaseCodeActivity.cs">(c)
// http://TfsBuildExtensions.codeplex.com/. This source is subject to the
// Microsoft Permissive License. See
// http://www.microsoft.com/resources/sharedsource/licensingbasics/
// sharedsourcelicenses.mspx. All other rights reserved.</copyright>
//---------------------------------------------------------------------
namespace Wrox.Build.Activities
{
    using System;
    using System.Activities;
    using System.ComponentModel;
    using System.Diagnostics;
    using System.Globalization;
    using System.Text;
    using Microsoft.TeamFoundation.Build.Client;
    using Microsoft.TeamFoundation.Build.Workflow.Activities;

    /// <summary>
    /// Provides a base class to all Activities which supports remoting
    /// </summary>
    public abstract class BaseCodeActivity : CodeActivity
    {
        private bool failingbuild;

        /// <summary>
```

```csharp
/// Set to true to fail the build if the activity logs any errors.
/// Default is false
/// </summary>
[Description("Set to true to fail the build if errors are logged")]
public InArgument<bool> FailBuildOnError { get; set; }

/// <summary>
/// Set to true to fail the build if the activity logs any errors.
/// Default is false
/// </summary>
[Description("Set to true to make all warnings errors")]
public InArgument<bool> TreatWarningsAsErrors { get; set; }

/// <summary>
/// Set to true to log the entire stack in the event of an exception.
/// Default is false
/// </summary>
[Description("Set to true to log the entire stack in the event of an
    exception")]
public InArgument<bool> LogExceptionStack { get; set; }

/// <summary>
/// Variable to hold CodeActivityContext
/// </summary>
protected CodeActivityContext ActivityContext { get; set; }

/// <summary>
/// Entry point to the Activity. It sets the context and executes
/// InternalExecute which is implemented by derived activities
/// </summary>
/// <param name="context">CodeActivityContext</param>
protected override void Execute(CodeActivityContext context)
{
    this.ActivityContext = context;
    try
    {
        this.InternalExecute();
    }
    catch (Exception ex)
    {
        if (!this.failingbuild)
        {

            if (this.LogExceptionStack.Get(context))
            {
                this.LogBuildError(ex.Message + " Stack Trace: " +
                    ex.StackTrace);
            }
        }

        throw;
    }
}

/// <summary>
```

continues

LISTING 16-2 *(continued)*

```
/// InternalExecute method which activities should implement
/// </summary>
protected abstract void InternalExecute();

/// <summary>
/// Logs a message as a build error
/// Also can fail the build if the FailBuildOnError flag is set
/// </summary>
/// <param name="errorMessage">Message to save</param>
protected void LogBuildError(string errorMessage)
{
    Debug.WriteLine(String.Format("BuildError: {0}", errorMessage));
    if (this.FailBuildOnError.Get(this.ActivityContext))
    {
        this.failingbuild = true;
        var buildDetail =
            this.ActivityContext.GetExtension<IBuildDetail>();
        buildDetail.Status = BuildStatus.Failed;
        buildDetail.Save();
        throw new Exception(errorMessage);
    }

    this.ActivityContext.TrackBuildError(errorMessage);
}

/// <summary>
/// Logs a message as a build warning
/// </summary>
/// <param name="warningMessage">Message to save</param>
protected void LogBuildWarning(string warningMessage)
{
    if (this.TreatWarningsAsErrors.Get(this.ActivityContext))
    {
        this.LogBuildError(warningMessage);
    }
    else
    {
        this.ActivityContext.TrackBuildWarning(warningMessage);
        Debug.WriteLine(String.Format("BuildWarning: {0}",
            warningMessage));
    }
}

/// <summary>
/// Logs a generic build message
/// </summary>
/// <param name="message">The message to save</param>
/// <param name="importance">The verbosity importance of the
/// message</param>
protected void LogBuildMessage(string message, BuildMessageImportance
    importance = BuildMessageImportance.Normal)
```

```
        {
            this.ActivityContext.TrackBuildMessage(message, importance);
            Debug.WriteLine(String.Format("BuildMessage: {0}", message));
        }
    }

    internal static class StringExtension
    {
        public static string AppendFormat(this string originalValue,
            IFormatProvider provider, string format,
            params object[] args)
        {
            if (String.IsNullOrEmpty(format) || args == null)
            {
                return originalValue ?? String.Empty;
            }

            StringBuilder builder = new StringBuilder(originalValue ??
                String.Empty);
            builder.AppendFormat(provider, format, args);
            return builder.ToString();
        }

        public static string AppendFormat(this string originalValue,
            string format, params object[] args)
        {
            return AppendFormat(originalValue, CultureInfo.CurrentCulture,
                format, args);
        }
    }
}
```

You will notice that the base code activity class inherits from the CodeActivity class defined in WF. The particular method that is overridden from the CodeActivity class is the Execute public method, which is used to provide the main functionality of a workflow code activity. In the base code activity class implementation shown in Listing 16-2, a protected abstract method named InternalExecute is defined that is meant for inheriting types to implement, instead of the public Execute method.

Additionally, the base code activity class implementation shown in Listing 16-2 includes some helper functions for exception handling, and logging messages, warnings, and errors to the build log. The context argument of the Execute method has some extension methods available for you to use the same functionality for logging using the build tracking participant as the standard Team Foundation Server workflow activities. This makes it extremely easy for you to add to the build log inside of a custom activity.

To create a new code activity that inherits from the base code activity implementation, perform the code activity library template creation steps mentioned earlier in this section, and then inherit from BaseCodeActivity instead of the standard CodeActivity base class that is included in the item template.

The build controllers and agents can use activities that are marked specifically for use by Team Foundation Server build. You indicate this by adding the `Microsoft.TeamFoundation.Build` `.Client.BuildActivityAttribute` attribute to the workflow activity class. The attribute takes in one parameter that describes where the activity should be able to run. Following are available options for that parameter:

➤ `HostEnvironmentOption.Agent` — Indicates that the activity can only run in the context of a build agent (that is, inside of a `BuildAgentScope` activity).

➤ `HostEnvironmentOption.Controller` — Indicates that the activity can only run in the context of a build controller (that is, outside of a `BuildAgentScope` activity).

➤ `HostEnvironmentOption.All` — Indicates that the activity can run either on a build controller or a build agent.

➤ `HostEnvironmentOption.None` — Indicates that the activity can never be run in a Team Foundation Server build workflow.

An activity may need to make updates to source code files, or be extensive in its processing. In most cases, you will want to specify those heavy-lifting activities as only being able to run on a build agent to prevent too much work from being done on the build controller.

> *By default, the Team Foundation Server Build service on the build machines will only load assemblies that contain at least one activity that is marked with the* `BuildActivity` *attribute.*

Listing 16-3 shows an example build custom workflow activity available from the community Team Foundation Server build extensions CodePlex project (as mentioned in the sidebar, "Community Team Foundation Server Build Activities and Extensions"). The `TfsVersion` activity that is included in Listing 16-3 is a partial implementation for brevity purposes based on the full version of the activity available on the CodePlex project.

LISTING 16-3: TfsVersion Custom Workflow Activity (Partial Implementation)

Available for download on Wrox.com

```
//-----------------------------------------------------------------------
// <copyright file="TfsVersion.cs">(c) http://TfsBuildExtensions.codeplex.com/.
// This source is subject to the Microsoft Permissive License. See
// http://www.microsoft.com/resources/sharedsource/licensingbasics/
// sharedsourcelicenses.mspx. All other rights reserved.</copyright>
//-----------------------------------------------------------------------
namespace TfsBuildExtensions.Activities.TeamFoundationServer
{
    using System;
    using System.Activities;
    using System.Collections.Generic;
    using System.Globalization;
    using System.IO;
    using System.Text;
```

```
using System.Text.RegularExpressions;
using Microsoft.TeamFoundation.Build.Client;

public enum TfsVersionAction
{
    SetVersion
}

[BuildActivity(HostEnvironmentOption.Agent)]
public sealed class TfsVersion : BaseCodeActivity
{
    private const string AppendAssemblyVersionFormat = "\n[assembly:
        System.Reflection.AssemblyVersion(\"{0}\")]";
    private const string VBAppendAssemblyVersionFormat = "\n<assembly:
        System.Reflection.AssemblyVersion(\"{0}\")>";
    private const string AppendAssemblyFileVersionFormat = "\n[assembly:
        System.Reflection.AssemblyFileVersion(\"{0}\")]";
    private const string VBAppendAssemblyFileVersionFormat = "\n<assembly:
        System.Reflection.AssemblyFileVersion(\"{0}\")>";
    private const string AppendAssemblyDescriptionFormat = "\n[assembly:
        System.Reflection.AssemblyDescription(\"{0}\")]";
    private const string VBAppendAssemblyDescriptionFormat = "\n<assembly:
        System.Reflection.AssemblyDescription(\"{0}\")>";
    private Regex regexExpression;
    private Regex regexAssemblyVersion;
    private Regex regexAssemblyDescription;
    private Encoding fileEncoding = Encoding.UTF8;
    private bool setAssemblyFileVersion = true;
    private TfsVersionAction action = TfsVersionAction.SetVersion;

    /// <summary>
    /// Set to True to set the AssemblyDescription when calling SetVersion.
    /// Default is false.
    /// </summary>
    public bool SetAssemblyDescription { get; set; }

    /// <summary>
    /// Specifies the action to perform
    /// </summary>
    public TfsVersionAction Action
    {
        get { return this.action; }
        set { this.action = value; }
    }

    /// <summary>
    /// Set to True to set the AssemblyVersion when calling SetVersion.
    /// Default is false.
    /// </summary>
    public bool SetAssemblyVersion { get; set; }

    /// <summary>
    /// Set to True to set the AssemblyFileVersion when calling SetVersion.
```

continues

LISTING 16-3 *(continued)*

```csharp
        /// Default is true.
        /// </summary>
        public bool SetAssemblyFileVersion
        {
            get { return this.setAssemblyFileVersion; }
            set { this.setAssemblyFileVersion = value; }
        }

        /// <summary>
        /// Set to true to force SetVersion action to update files that do not
        /// have AssemblyVersion | AssemblyFileVersion
        /// | AssemblyDescription present.  Default is false.  ForceSetVersion
        /// does not affect AssemblyVersion when
        /// SetAssemblyVersion is false or AssemblyDescription when
        /// SetAssemblyDescription is false.
        /// </summary>
        public bool ForceSetVersion { get; set; }

        /// <summary>
        /// Sets the file encoding. Default is UTF8
        /// </summary>
        public InArgument<string> TextEncoding { get; set; }

        /// <summary>
        /// Sets the files to version
        /// </summary>
        public InArgument<IEnumerable<string>> Files { get; set; }

        /// <summary>
        /// Gets or Sets the Version
        /// </summary>
        public InOutArgument<string> Version { get; set; }

        /// <summary>
        /// Gets or Sets the AssemblyDescription.
        /// </summary>
        public InArgument<string> AssemblyDescription { get; set; }

        /// <summary>
        /// Sets the AssemblyVersion. Defaults to Version if not set.
        /// </summary>
        public InArgument<string> AssemblyVersion { get; set; }

        /// <summary>
        /// Executes the logic for this workflow activity
        /// </summary>
        protected override void InternalExecute()
        {
            switch (this.Action)
            {
                case TfsVersionAction.SetVersion:
                    this.SetVersion();
```

```
                    break;
                default:
                    throw new ArgumentException("Action not supported");
            }
        }

        private void SetVersion()
        {
            // Set the file encoding if necessary
            if (!string.IsNullOrEmpty(this.ActivityContext.GetValue
                (this.TextEncoding)) && !this.SetFileEncoding())
            {
                return;
            }

            if (string.IsNullOrEmpty(this.ActivityContext.GetValue(this.Version)))
            {
                this.LogBuildError("Version is required");
                return;
            }

            if (this.ActivityContext.GetValue(this.Files) == null)
            {
                this.LogBuildError("No Files specified. Pass an Item Collection of
                    files to the Files property.");
                return;
            }

            if (string.IsNullOrEmpty(this.ActivityContext.GetValue
                (this.AssemblyVersion)))
            {
                this.ActivityContext.SetValue(this.AssemblyVersion,
                    this.ActivityContext.GetValue(this.Version));
            }

            // Load the regex to use
            this.regexExpression = new Regex(@"AssemblyFileVersion.*\(.*""" +
                ".*" + @""".*\)", RegexOptions.Compiled);
            if (this.SetAssemblyVersion)
            {
                this.regexAssemblyVersion = new Regex(@"AssemblyVersion.*\
                    (.*""" + ".*" + @""".*\)", RegexOptions.Compiled);
            }

            if (this.SetAssemblyDescription)
            {
                this.regexAssemblyDescription = new
                    Regex(@"AssemblyDescription.*\
                    (.*\)", RegexOptions.Compiled);
            }

            foreach (string fullfilename in
                this.ActivityContext.GetValue(this.Files))
            {
```

continues

LISTING 16-3 *(continued)*

```
FileInfo file = new FileInfo(fullfilename);
this.LogBuildMessage(string.Format(CultureInfo.CurrentCulture,
    "Versioning {0} at {1}", file.FullName,
    this.ActivityContext.GetValue(this.Version)));
bool changedAttribute = false;

// First make sure the file is writable.
FileAttributes fileAttributes = File.GetAttributes(file.FullName);

// If readonly attribute is set, reset it.
if ((fileAttributes & FileAttributes.ReadOnly) ==
    FileAttributes.ReadOnly)
{
    this.LogBuildMessage("Making file writable",
        BuildMessageImportance.Low);
    File.SetAttributes(file.FullName, fileAttributes ^
        FileAttributes.ReadOnly);
    changedAttribute = true;
}

// Open the file
string entireFile;
using (StreamReader streamReader = new
    StreamReader(file.FullName, true))
{
    entireFile = streamReader.ReadToEnd();
}

// Parse the entire file.
string newFile = this.regexExpression.Replace(entireFile,
    String.Format(@"AssemblyFileVersion(""{0}"")",
        this.ActivityContext.GetValue(this.Version)));

if (this.SetAssemblyFileVersion)
{
    if (this.ForceSetVersion && newFile.Equals(entireFile,
        StringComparison.OrdinalIgnoreCase) &&
        newFile.IndexOf("AssemblyFileVersion",
        StringComparison.OrdinalIgnoreCase) < 0)
    {
        switch (file.Extension)
        {
            case ".cs":
                newFile =
                    newFile.AppendFormat
                    (AppendAssemblyFileVersionFormat,
                    this.Version);
                break;
            case ".vb":
                newFile =
                    newFile.AppendFormat
                    (VBAppendAssemblyFileVersionFormat,
                    this.Version);
                break;
```

```
            }
        }
    }

    if (this.SetAssemblyVersion)
    {
        string originalFile = newFile;
        newFile = this.regexAssemblyVersion.Replace(newFile,
            String.Format(@"AssemblyVersion(""{0}"")",
            this.ActivityContext.GetValue
            (this.AssemblyVersion)));
        if (this.ForceSetVersion && newFile.Equals(originalFile,
            StringComparison.OrdinalIgnoreCase) &&
            newFile.IndexOf("AssemblyVersion",
            StringComparison.OrdinalIgnoreCase) < 0)
        {
            switch (file.Extension)
            {
                case ".cs":
                    newFile =
                        newFile.AppendFormat
                        (AppendAssemblyVersionFormat,
                        this.AssemblyVersion);
                    break;
                case ".vb":
                    newFile =
                        newFile.AppendFormat
                        (VBAppendAssemblyVersionFormat,
                        this.AssemblyVersion);
                    break;
            }
        }
    }

    if (this.SetAssemblyDescription)
    {
        string originalFile = newFile;
        newFile = this.regexAssemblyDescription.Replace(newFile,
            String.Format(@"AssemblyDescription(""{0}"")",
                this.ActivityContext.GetValue
            (this.AssemblyDescription)));
        if (this.ForceSetVersion && newFile.Equals(originalFile,
            StringComparison.OrdinalIgnoreCase))
        {
            switch (file.Extension)
            {
                case ".cs":
                    newFile =
                        newFile.AppendFormat
                        (AppendAssemblyDescriptionFormat,
                        this.AssemblyVersion);
                    break;
                case ".vb":
                    newFile =
                        newFile.AppendFormat
```

continues

LISTING 16-3 *(continued)*

```
                                   (VBAppendAssemblyDescriptionFormat,
                                   this.AssemblyVersion);
                           break;
                   }
               }
           }

           // Write out the new contents.
           using (StreamWriter streamWriter = new
               StreamWriter(file.FullName, false, this.fileEncoding))
           {
               streamWriter.Write(newFile);
           }

           if (changedAttribute)
           {
               this.LogBuildMessage("Making file readonly",
                   BuildMessageImportance.Low);
               File.SetAttributes(file.FullName, FileAttributes.ReadOnly);
           }
       }
   }

   /// <summary>
   /// Sets the file encoding.
   /// </summary>
   /// <returns>bool</returns>
   private bool SetFileEncoding()
   {
       switch (this.ActivityContext.GetValue(this.TextEncoding))
       {
           case "ASCII":
               this.fileEncoding = System.Text.Encoding.ASCII;
               break;
           case "Unicode":
               this.fileEncoding = System.Text.Encoding.Unicode;
               break;
           case "UTF7":
               this.fileEncoding = System.Text.Encoding.UTF7;
               break;
           case "UTF8":
               this.fileEncoding = System.Text.Encoding.UTF8;
               break;
           case "BigEndianUnicode":
               this.fileEncoding = System.Text.Encoding.BigEndianUnicode;
               break;
           case "UTF32":
               this.fileEncoding = System.Text.Encoding.UTF32;
               break;
           default:
               throw new ArgumentException(string.Format
                   (CultureInfo.CurrentCulture,
                   "Encoding not supported: {0}",
```

```
                    this.ActivityContext.GetValue
                    (this.TextEncoding)));
            }

            return true;
        }
    }
}
```

In this example, the `TfsVersion` activity allows you to specify a version string to the `Version` parameter on the activity. That can then be used to stamp the assembly information files for the `AssemblyFileVersion` attribute of the assembly. Similar parameters are available on the custom activity for stamping the `AssemblyVersion` and `AssemblyDescription` attributes as well. You could even easily modify the partial implementation to allow setting the `AssemblyInformationVersion` attribute.

Later in this chapter, you will learn about the process of using the custom build number format string to generate a standard version that can then be used on the build agent to stamp that version number appropriately.

Integrating Activity into the Build Process Template

Interestingly, if you want to use a custom build activity, the best way to integrate it into the build process to ensure that the references in the build process template to the activity are correct, you must load the build process template and edit it from a different Visual Studio project that has a reference to the activity library project in the same solution. You will not be able to store the process template inside of the same activity library project because a reference to the activity inside of the build process template file will be incorrect whenever it runs on the build machines.

Let's walk through the process for getting a separate Visual Studio project created so that you can use it for editing test versions of the build process templates. Follow these steps:

1. From the context menu on the solution file in Solution Explorer, click Add ⇨ New Project, as shown in Figure 16-16.

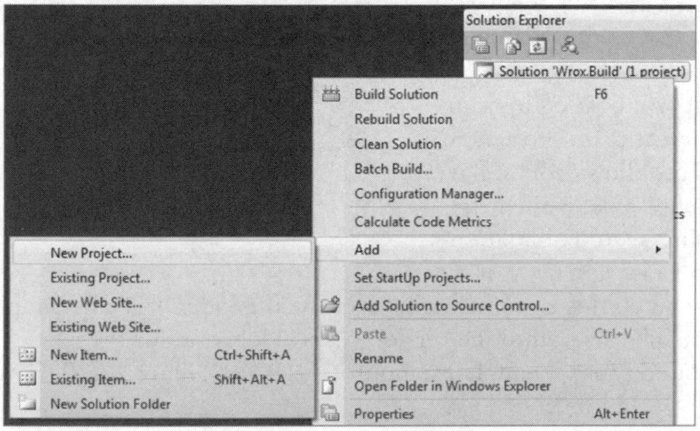

FIGURE 16-16: Accessing the Add New Project dialog from the context menu

2. At this point, you can choose to use any type of project. However, since you might be creating unit tests for your custom workflow activities, choose to use the Test Visual Studio project type, as shown in Figure 16-17.

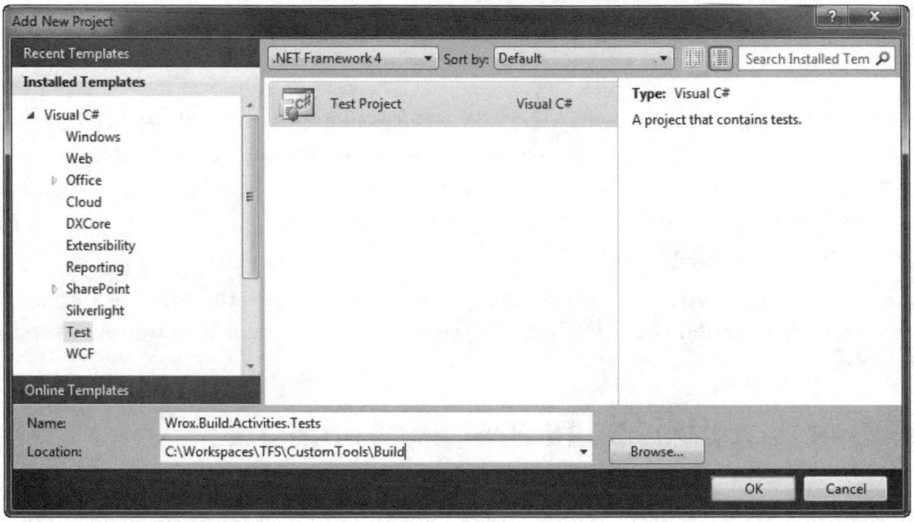

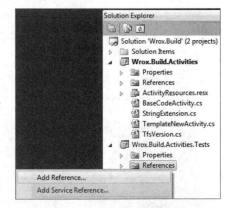

FIGURE 16-17: Choosing the Test Visual Studio project type

3. To ensure the appropriate assembly signature in the process templates when you edit them, add a project reference to the new project to use the workflow activities library project, as shown in Figure 16-18.

4. At this point, you will want to include a copy of the custom build process templates that you want to edit using the custom workflow activities you created in the new project. However, instead of creating a copy, you can create a branch from the "golden" process template location that will be used by your production build definitions in the team projects in the same project collection. This allows you to have a linked copy for test build definitions, while being able to merge any changes using Team Foundation Server version control to the production copy of the

FIGURE 16-18: Adding a project reference

build process templates. You can do this by branching either the individual process template files, or the build process template folder, into the version control location for the new project that will contain the build process templates. Figure 16-19 and Figure 16-20 show the latter method.

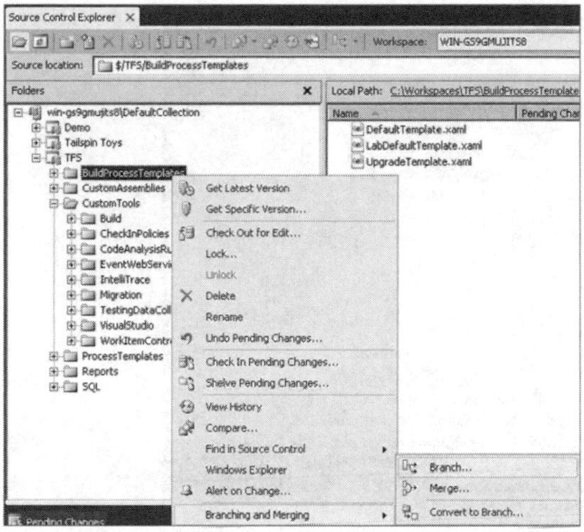

FIGURE 16-19: Selecting the Branch option from the context menu

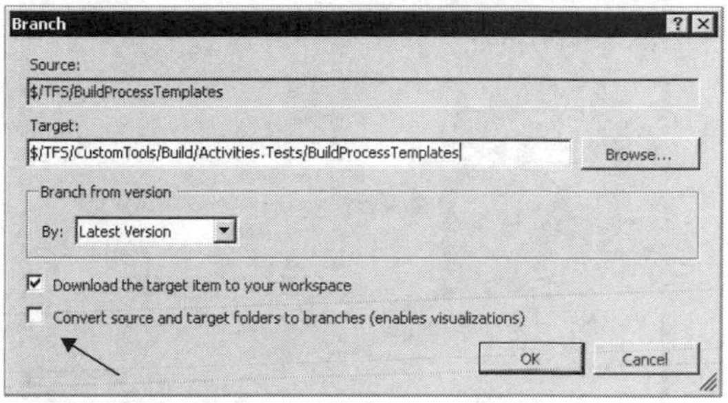

FIGURE 16-20: Branching the build process template folder

5. Now that the build process templates have been branched into the proper version control location, you can add them to the new Visual Studio project. You can do that by choosing the new Visual Studio project in the Solution Explorer window, and then clicking the Show All Files button in the Solution Explorer window's toolbar, as shown in Figure 16-21.

6. Once you perform that step, you will see all of the files and folders existing on the file system that are not included in the project. You can right-click the build process templates folder or files, and choose Include In Project from the context menu, as shown in Figure 16-22.

7. If you were to attempt to compile the solution at this point, you would end up with some compilation errors. This is because, by default, XAML files that are added to a Visual Studio project are set to compile. Some walkthroughs available about this topic would instruct you to add the appropriate references to ensure that they compile correctly. However, you can instead instruct

FIGURE 16-21: Show All Files button in the Solution Explorer window's toolbar

MSBuild to ignore the build process template files altogether, and simply copy them to the output directory. You can do this from the Properties window in Visual Studio by setting the Build Action property to `None` and the Copy to Output Directory property to `Copy always`, as shown in Figure 16-23.

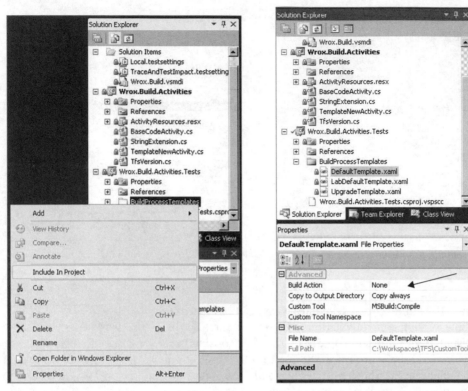

FIGURE 16-22: Choosing Include In Project from the context menu

FIGURE 16-23: Copying the build process template files to the output directory

It has taken a bit to get to this point, but you should be able to compile the entire solution successfully. You can edit process template files from now on by opening the solution and opening the process template files from their location in the Visual Studio project. When you do that, the activities in the activity library project show up in the Visual Studio Toolbox for the workflow designer, as shown in Figure 16-24.

Dragging one of the custom activities and dropping it to the workflow will add it appropriately, and will ensure that the reference to the custom workflow activities assembly will be correct when it is used by Team Foundation Server Build. Even better, after you have made all of the necessary modifications and tested them out sufficiently, you can use the merging functionality from Team Foundation Server version control to merge those changes to the production copies of the build process templates, as shown in Figure 16-25.

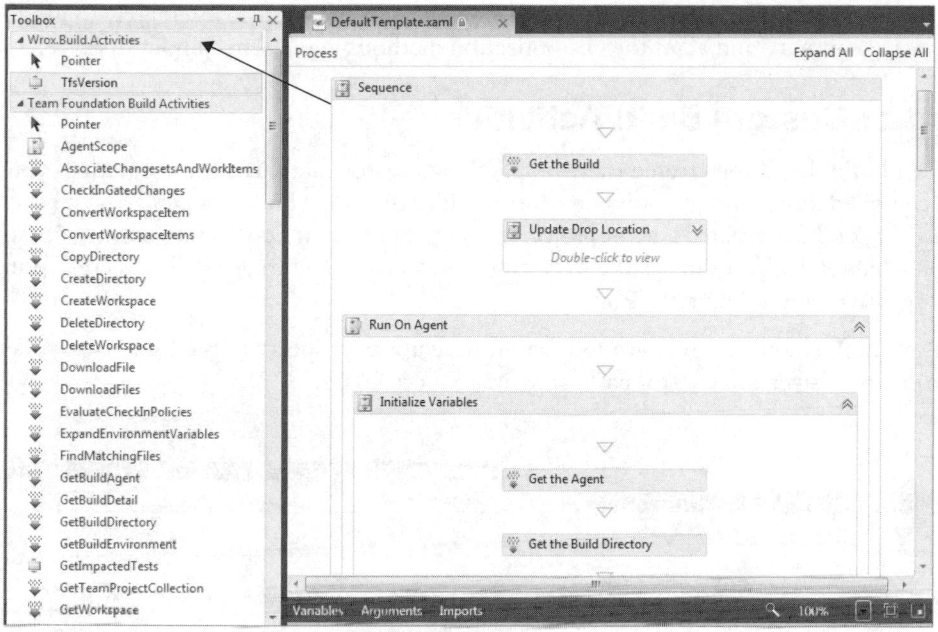

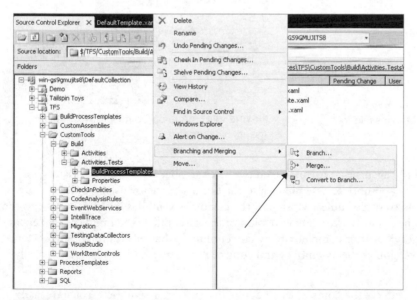

FIGURE 16-24: Activities in the activity library project

FIGURE 16-25: Merging changes to the production copies of the build process templates

Later in this chapter, you will learn how to customize the default build process template to use the `TfsVersion` custom activity and all of the customization methods you learned about in this chapter.

Deployment of Custom Build Activities

Once you have a build definition created that compiles your custom activity library solution, you can store the compiled assemblies in a version control folder that your build controllers can be specified to use. If you have created a team project for managing Team Foundation Server artifacts as described in Chapter 10, you can use the `$/TFS/CustomAssemblies` folder that was created just for this purpose, as shown in Figure 16-26.

You can then set the Version Control Path to Custom Assemblies property in the Build Controller Properties dialog to this version control path, shown in Figure 16-27.

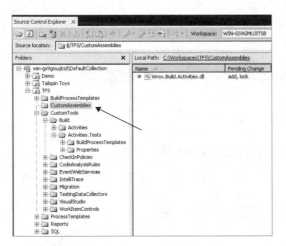

FIGURE 16-26: CustomAssemblies folder

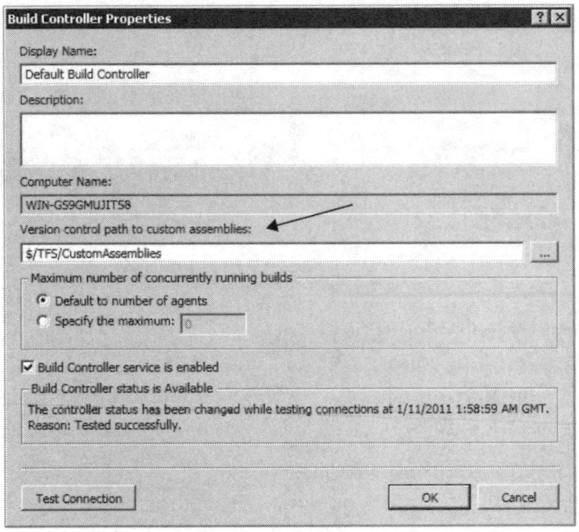

FIGURE 16-27: Version Control Path to Custom Assemblies property

The build controller and the agents that are managed by the controller will monitor this version control folder and load any appropriate assemblies into the build service for use by build process templates. All you must do to deploy a new version of the custom assemblies is check them into the version control folder. When you check in a new version of the assemblies, the build controllers and agents will restart their services after completing any current builds that are running by the agents. They then load the new version of the assemblies and continue with any builds that are currently in the build queue.

This process significantly reduces the complexity of deploying custom assemblies. You can easily add additional build machines to the build farm without having to worry about how to deploy the appropriate custom assemblies to them.

There is one key point to remember from earlier in this chapter. Assemblies that have at least one activity that has the `BuildActivity` attribute added to the class will be loaded by the build controllers and build agents. You might have external references from the custom activity assemblies that do not have any build activities included in it. Therefore, these activities would not be loaded by the build services, even if they are included in the version control folder of the custom assemblies. If they are not loaded, you will likely notice "Cannot find reference" errors from your custom activities.

However, you can specify assemblies that should be loaded by the build service that do not have custom activities included in it. You can do this by checking in an XML file with the filename of `CustomActivitiesAndExtensions.xml` that specifies the assemblies to load, as shown in Listing 16-4.

LISTING 16-4: Example CustomActivitiesAndExtensions.xml File

Available for download on Wrox.com

```xml
<?xml version="1.0" encoding="utf-8"?>
<Assemblies>
  <Assembly FileName="AssemblyWithoutBuildActivities.dll">
    <Extensions>
      <Extension FullName="AssemblyWithoutBuildActivities.SomeSetOfEventArgs" />
    </Extensions>
  </Assembly>
  <Assembly FileName="AnotherReferencedAssembly.dll">
    <Extensions>
      <Extension FullName="AnotherReferencedAssembly.MyCustomException" />
    </Extensions>
  </Assembly>
</Assemblies>
```

You must also specify a public class with a parameter-less constructor in each of the assemblies you intend to include in the file. The best candidates that meet these requirements are custom exception and event argument classes.

CUSTOMIZING THE BUILD REPORT OUTPUT

Custom build workflow activities are not the only extensible points for Team Foundation Server Build. You can also customize what is displayed in the build report and log, including displaying custom information types and summary sections.

Creating a Log Data Visualizer

You can create a custom visualization for data that is included in the build log for either standard build information node types, or custom build information node types. You simply create a custom build information converter to display a custom Windows Presentation Foundation Paragraph, as shown in Figure 16-28.

FIGURE 16-28: Creating a custom build information converter

> ✎ *Jason Prickett has an excellent walkthrough that shows you how to create a custom build information converter on his blog, available at* `http://blogs` `.msdn.com/b/jpricket/archive/2009/12/22/tfs2010-changing-the-way-` `build-information-is-displayed.aspx.`

Build Summary Report Custom Section

Additionally, you may want to add a custom section to the build summary view to display information that was captured during the build process, where a build was deployed, or other important information that you might want to display to users who open the build report. Figure 16-29 shows an example of a simple custom build summary report section.

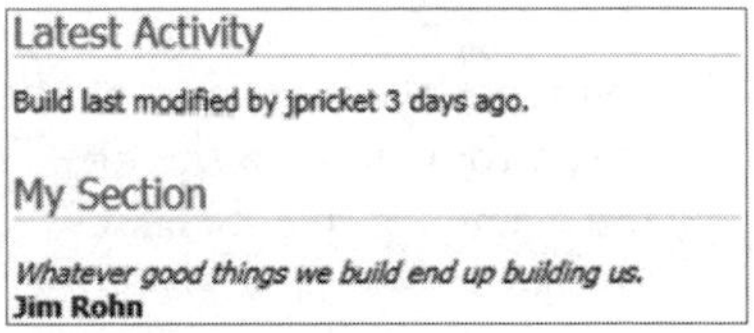

FIGURE 16-29: Simple custom build summary report section

> ✎ *Jason Prickett also has an excellent walkthrough that shows you how to create a custom build summary report section on his blog, available at* `http://blogs` `.msdn.com/b/jpricket/archive/2010/08/09/tfs2010-customizing-the-` `build-details-view-summary-view.aspx.`

CUSTOMIZING THE BUILD PROCESS TO STAMP THE VERSION NUMBER ON ASSEMBLIES

At this point, you can use all of the build customization and extensibility methods that you learned in this chapter for an end-to-end customization to stamp an incrementing version number to the assembly information files. These files are used for the versioning of assemblies when they are compiled by MSBuild. Open the build process template you want to add this functionality to, and follow the upcoming procedures.

Defining Custom Build Process Parameters

To allow build definition editors the option to turn this functionality off, and to also create a file specification, you can expose custom build process parameters for use inside of the build process template. To begin, create the build process parameters that are listed in Table 16-2 using the method for creating custom workflow arguments specified earlier in this chapter.

TABLE 16-2: Custom Build Process Parameters

NAME	DIRECTION	ARGUMENT TYPE	DEFAULT VALUE
StampVersionNumber	In	Boolean	True
AssemblyInfoFileSpec	In	String	"*AssemblyInfo*.*"

Next, you specify the appropriate metadata to display to the end user, including a custom category of "Versioning," as shown in Figure 16-30.

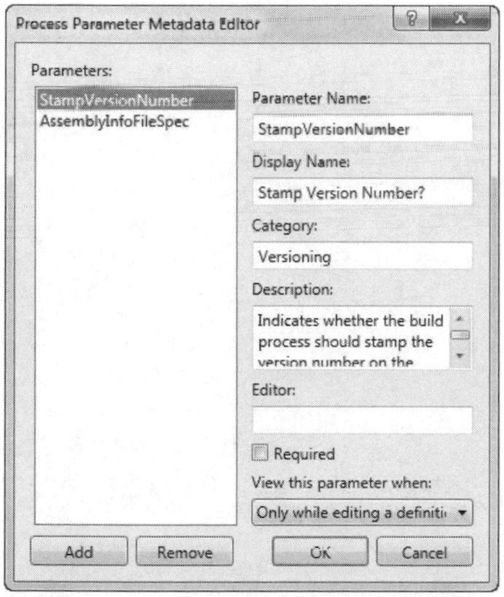

FIGURE 16-30: Specifying the appropriate metadata to display to the end user

Additionally, since you want to use a four-part version number that is standard for .NET assemblies, change the default for the BuildNumberFormat workflow argument to the following:

```
"$(BuildDefinitionName)_$(Year:yy).$(Month).$(DayOfMonth)$(Rev:.r)"
```

This provides a four-part version number that uses the year, month, and day of the month integers as the first three parts of the version number, and an incrementing revision number for the fourth part. You could easily change any of the first three parts as shown in the following example, and you could always rely on the person editing the build definition to set his or her own custom build number format string:

```
"$(BuildDefinitionName)_1.0.0$(Rev:.r)"
```

Allowing the Functionality to Be Optional

Now it is time to add the custom functionality to the custom build process template itself. The most appropriate location for stamping the assembly information source code files would be right after the get latest version from version control, and before any compilation occurs. If you are using a custom build process template that is based off of the default build process template, then you will find it right after the `Sequence` activity with the display name of `Initialize Workspace` inside of the `AgentScope` activity.

You can start by allowing the build process to completely skip the functionality you will be adding for stamping the version assemblies by using the `StampVersionNumber Boolean` workflow argument you created as the `Condition` parameter on a new `If` workflow activity. Remember, the `If` activity only allows one activity to be included in each of the drop locations in the designer. Therefore, you can add a new `Sequence` activity to the drop location, as shown in Figure 16-31.

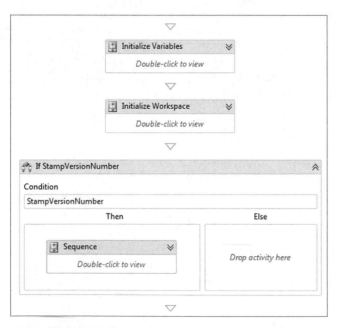

FIGURE 16-31: Adding a new Sequence activity to the drop location

Remember that, if you do not want the `Sequence` activity to show up in the build log, you can mark it with a build tracking importance attribute of `Low`, as mentioned earlier in this chapter. You might also change the display parameter of `Sequence` to something similar to "Stamp Version Numbers Sequence."

Defining Local Workflow Variables

There will be some variables that you will want to use during the stamp version numbers sequence but that are not needed later in the build process. Select the `Sequence` activity that you added previously and add the custom workflow variables listed in Table 16-3. For the scope of the variables, use the display name of the `Sequence` activity that you added previously so that the variables can only be used inside of the `Sequence` activity.

TABLE 16-3: Custom Workflow Variables

NAME	VARIABLE TYPE	DEFAULT
VersionNumberRegularExpression	String	"\d+\.\d+\.\d+\.\d+"
VersionString	String	
FullAssemblyInfoFileSpec	String	
AssemblyInfoFiles	IEnumerable<String>	

Initializing the Local Workflow Variables

Before you can meaningfully use these variables, you must initialize them to their appropriate values. The `Assign` workflow activity is a perfect candidate for initializing workflow variables. Add a new `Assign` activity inside the `Sequence` activity created earlier and set its `To` parameter to the `VersionString` variable. Set the `Value` parameter on the activity to the following:

```
New System.Text.RegularExpressions.Regex
    (VersionNumberRegularExpression).Match(BuildDetail.BuildNumber).Value
```

This creates a new regular expression using the workflow variable that contains the version number regular expression pattern, and then attempts to match it against the build number as it is stored on the `BuildDetail` variable available in the build process. The `VersionString` workflow variable should now be initialized to just a four-part version string.

Now, add another `Assign` activity immediately following the previous one, and set its `To` parameter to the `FullAssemblyInfoFileSpec` variable. Set the `Value` parameter on the activity to the following:

```
System.IO.Path.Combine(SourcesDirectory, "**", AssemblyInfoFileSpec)
```

This is using the local `Sources` directory on the build server and combining it with the `AssemblyInfoFileSpec` workflow argument that has been defined so that it can be used appropriately in the next step.

Finding Matching Assembly Info Files

Now you can add the standard Team Foundation Server `FindMatchingFiles` workflow activity to find the appropriate files to stamp with the version number. Add a new `FindMatchingFiles` activity immediately after the initialization, and set its `MatchPattern` parameter to the `FullAssemblyInfoFileSpec` variable that you just initialized.

The activity returns an `IEnumerable<String>` object with each of the files, along with the full path that corresponds with the match pattern. Therefore, to use that return value, set the `Result` parameter for the activity to the `AssemblyInfoFiles` workflow variable that was defined earlier.

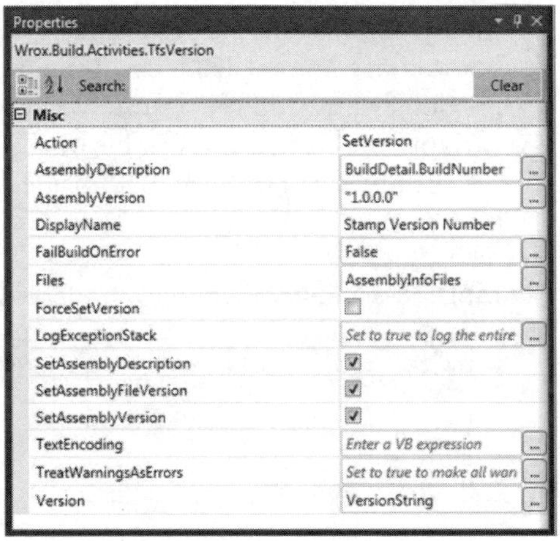

Adding the Custom TfsVersion Activity

You now have all of the information required in this part of the build process to add the custom `TfsVersion` activity from the Toolbox. Once you add it, set all of the parameters of the activity instance similar to what is shown in Figure 16-32.

You will see that the `Version` parameter is set to the `VersionString` variable that contains the extracted four-part version number from the full build number for this build. The `AssemblyVersion` parameter is set to a static value, since, normally, the `AssemblyFileVersion` is changed (which is what is stamped using this custom activity) and the `AssemblyVersion` attribute stays the same for a major version of a .NET assembly.

Additionally, the full build number is stamped as the `AssemblyDescription`, which is helpful when you look at assemblies created during the automated build process, and you want to trace back to the original Team Foundation Server build.

Finally, notice that the activity will take action on each of the files by passing in the `AssemblyInfoFiles` variable as the `Files` parameter on the activity. The full implementation of all of these customization steps is shown in Figure 16-33.

FIGURE 16-32: Setting the parameters of the activity instance

FIGURE 16-33: Implementation of the customization

After checking in all of the modifications to the build process, simply merge the changes to the production build process template version control folder, and use it as the process template file for the build definitions that you want to take advantage of this functionality.

SUMMARY

In this chapter, you learned how to customize the automated build process by using standard workflow activities available from the .NET Framework, as well as activities provided from Team Foundation Server. You reviewed the essential functionality from Windows Workflow Foundation (WF) that is leveraged in Team Foundation Server Build, including creating local workflow variables, and exposing custom build process parameters that can be provided by end users, and then acted on during the build process.

Finally, you surveyed several customization options that are available to you if the default functionality is not what you are looking for, including how to create custom workflow activities that can be deployed to build machines automatically, build report summary sections, and build log visualizations.

In the final part of the book, you will learn about all of the different topics for administering Team Foundation Server. In Chapter 17, you will be introduced to Team Foundation Server, including an overview of the different parts of the server, as well as the tools and utilities that will be beneficial for administration.

PART V
Administration

17

Introduction to Team Foundation Server Administration

WHAT'S IN THIS CHAPTER?

➤ Understanding the architecture of the system

➤ Getting to know the administration console

➤ Using the command-line tools

➤ Getting to know other administration tools

Team Foundation Server is a system with lots of moving parts, and lots of integration with other systems. For the person (or persons) charged with administering all this, it can be quite a daunting task at first. For someone not familiar with developer tools, there are lots of new concepts and different things to consider while administering the server.

Don't be discouraged though! As with many products, the administration tools have evolved over time. There was a huge investment in improving the administrative experience for the 2010 release. The biggest improvement was the streamlined setup and installation experience. These investments also led to the creation of the Team Foundation Server Administration Console, along with the powerful command-line equivalent `TfsConfig.exe`.

Before you get started with learning about Team Foundation Server administration, it's important to understand the different types of administrators for a Team Foundation Server environment.

ADMINISTRATOR TYPES

There are many different administrative roles in Team Foundation Server. Each of these roles has slightly different responsibilities, and deals with a different part of the overall system. In smaller organizations, all of these roles may be performed by the same person. In larger organizations with an IT department, these roles may be performed by many different people and groups.

Infrastructure Administrator

Infrastructure administrators are responsible for anything with a power cord. They manage the physical servers, the networks, and the storage. In some cases, there is a separate database administrator who manages the database servers, but in any case, the two roles work closely together.

An infrastructure administrator is concerned with reliability, availability, performance, disaster recovery, and security. The infrastructure administrator ensures that the servers are running smoothly, and that Team Foundation Server works within the requirements of the organization.

Team Foundation Server Administrator

Team Foundation Server administrators are responsible for configuring and managing the software that is running on the server. They have the expertise in running software configuration management for the organization, and often have specialized knowledge about how to operate Team Foundation Server.

This administrator is concerned with the performance of the application, and the smooth operation of version control, work item tracking, data warehouse, and any other related applications. Typically, this person acts as a bridge between the development and infrastructure teams. The Team Foundation administrator handles the delicate balance and needs of both groups. Sometimes these administrators coordinate upgrades and patches to the server, since it's a critical piece of infrastructure for the teams.

Project Administrator

A server will contain collections that house team projects. For each project, there will be someone performing this role who has the capability to change the structure and permissions within that project. In some cases, a project administrator might be a project collection administrator, and have the capability to create new team projects and manage multiple projects.

The project administrator role is an important one, because it is the closest to the users of the server. People in this role manage groups and permissions for their projects. They have the capability to change the work item type definitions, and modify areas and iterations for their projects.

LOGICAL ARCHITECTURE

Before discussing administering Team Foundation Server, it's helpful to understand the architecture of the system. As shown in Figure 17-1, Team Foundation Server contains three logical tiers:

- ➤ Client tier
- ➤ Application tier (AT)
- ➤ Data tier (DT)

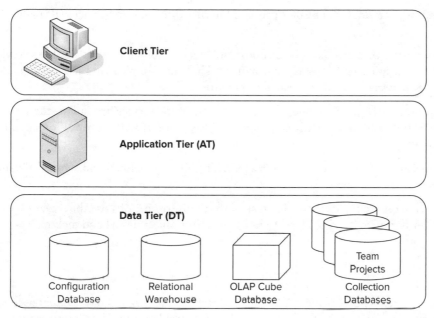

FIGURE 17-1: Logical three-tier architecture

These logical tiers might be deployed across two or more computers.

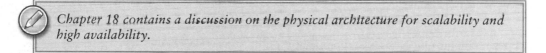

Chapter 18 contains a discussion on the physical architecture for scalability and high availability.

Client Tier

The client tier is any computer that contains tools for accessing the server. An installed application such as Visual Studio Team Explorer or Team Explorer Everywhere can be used as a client. A web browser and Visual Studio Team Web Access can also be used. Additionally, any application that uses the Team Foundation Server object model or web services is considered a client of the system.

Application Tier

The application tier is commonly referred to as the "AT." It includes the Team Foundation Server Web Application, which hosts a number of different web services, including the following:

➤ Version control

➤ Work item tracking

➤ Lab management

➤ Framework services

These all run on Windows Server 2003 or 2008 running Internet Information Services (IIS) and ASP.NET.

The Visual Team Foundation Background Job Agent (or "job agent," for short) is a Windows service that executes Team Foundation Server jobs asynchronously. These jobs implement the `Run` method in `ITeamFoundationJobExtension` and are loaded as plug-ins.

The job agent runs continuously on the application tier using the same service account as the web application. You should not need to manually stop or start this service. It will restart automatically when a server is restarted.

There is no direct configuration required for the job agent. The jobs are defined and scheduled using either the client or server object models.

The job agent has direct access to the data tier. Because of this, most of the jobs use the server object model to access the data tier directly, as opposed to using the client object model and making web requests.

Data Tier

The data tier is commonly referred to as the "DT." It includes the databases and data warehouse infrastructure. The data tier runs on SQL Server 2008 SP1 or R2, and hosts the databases for the system.

Configuration Database

The `Tfs_Configuration` database stores information that is central to a Team Foundation Server instance, as seen in Table 17-1.

TABLE 17-1: Contents of the Configuration Database

COMPONENT	DESCRIPTION
Team Project Collection connection strings	The SQL connection strings for the collections associated with this instance.
Registry	Team Foundation Server 2010 has a registry service for storing key and value pairs. This is different from the Windows registry.
Catalog	The catalog is a hierarchical store that describes team projects and all their properties.
Job history	History about when a job was executed and the result of the job is recorded here.
Identity cache	Identities are shared across all team project collections. The identity tables in the configuration database are the master store.

Relational Warehouse and OLAP Cube Database

The `Tfs_Warehouse` database and `Tfs_Analysis` cube are the key stores that support the data warehouse and reporting capabilities of Team Foundation Server. These are discussed in more detail in Chapter 13.

Team Project Collections

In Team Foundation Server 2008 and earlier, there were seven different databases that made up a server. For Team Foundation Server 2010, these databases have been folded together into a single collection database. Note the following key points:

➤ These databases are the main store for all data in Team Foundation Server.

➤ A collection is almost entirely self-contained within a single database.

➤ A server can have one or more collection databases attached to it.

➤ One database contains a group of coupled team projects.

➤ A collection can exist on a different physical SQL server than the configuration database.

BUILT-IN ADMINISTRATION TOOLS

There are a number of built-in administration tools with Team Foundation Server 2010. This section examines both the Administration Console and the command-line equivalent.

Team Foundation Administration Console

The Team Foundation Administration Console is new in Team Foundation Server 2010. It's the centralized management tool for server administrators.

The tool was originally implemented as a Microsoft Management Console (MMC) snap-in. However, there were limitations with what was possible in this implementation, as well as the version of the .NET Framework that the snap-in could use.

Perhaps the biggest limitation of the tool (and most of the built-in administration tools) is that it must be run on the application tier server itself. Although you can use Remote Desktop and tools like `PSExec.exe` to connect to the server remotely, the tools still must execute on the server.

After logging on to your application tier server, click Start, point to All Programs, and then click Microsoft Team Foundation Server 2010. Click Team Foundation Administration Console and the administration console will open.

Any user who has access to log on to the server can open the administration tool. However, you must be a member of the Team Foundation Administrators group to change anything.

License Information

When Team Foundation Server 2010 and previous versions were released, they were first made available to download as a 180-day trial. The availability of the final version wasn't available through licensing programs for a few weeks. This meant that a lot of people installed or upgraded using the time-limited version with the plan to enter their license keys before the trial expired.

However, some people got a rude shock when their trial expired and the server suddenly started refusing commands 180 days later. One of the reasons this occurred was because it wasn't easy to determine whether you were running a trial license, and when that license might expire.

Figure 17-2 shows how you can see your current license type and when it will expire. To see your current license information, open the Team Foundation Server Administration Console from the Start menu. Select your server name in the tree view on the left. You will then see the licensing information on the right. This screen allows you to enter a product key to upgrade to the full version. In addition to this dialog, the Administration Console will also warn you that your trial is about to expire when you open it.

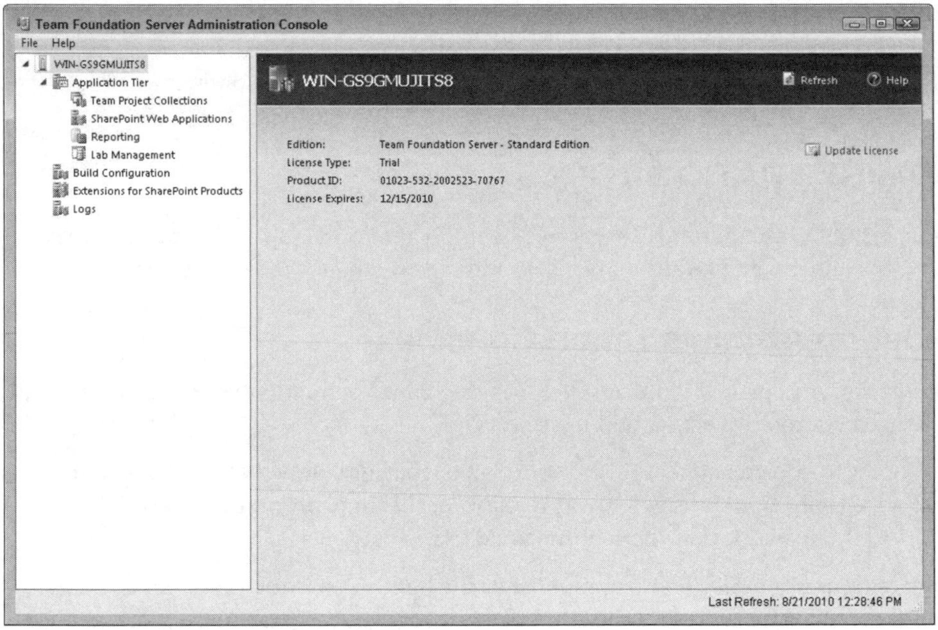

FIGURE 17-2: License information screen

Managing Application Tiers

Possibly the most commonly used dialog of the Administration Console, the Application Tier section of the Console contains all the configuration settings pertinent to the installation, as shown in Figures 17-3 and 17-4. From this section you can perform most of the common administrative tasks. Table 17-2 describes each of the settings.

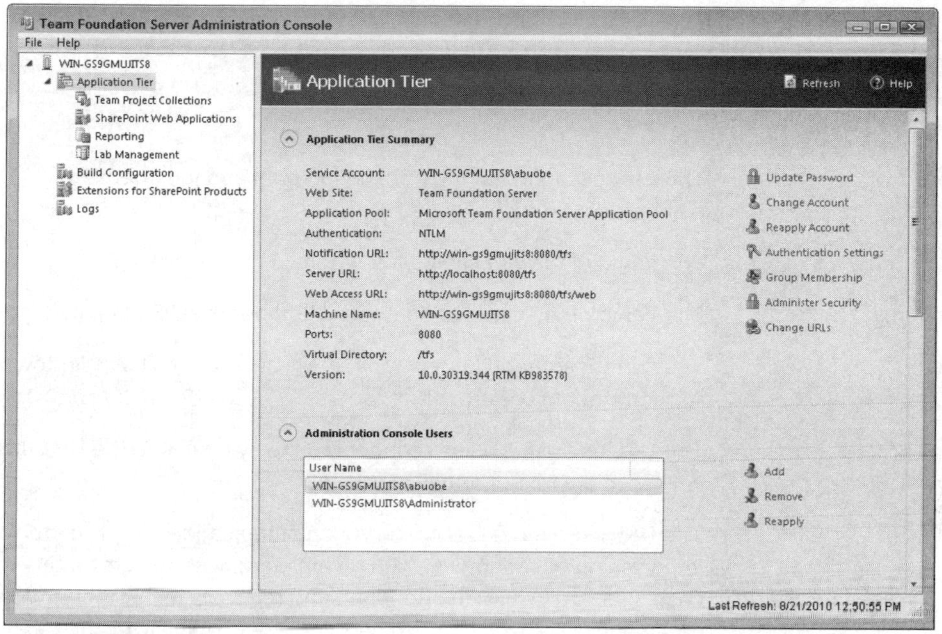

FIGURE 17-3: Application Tier screen

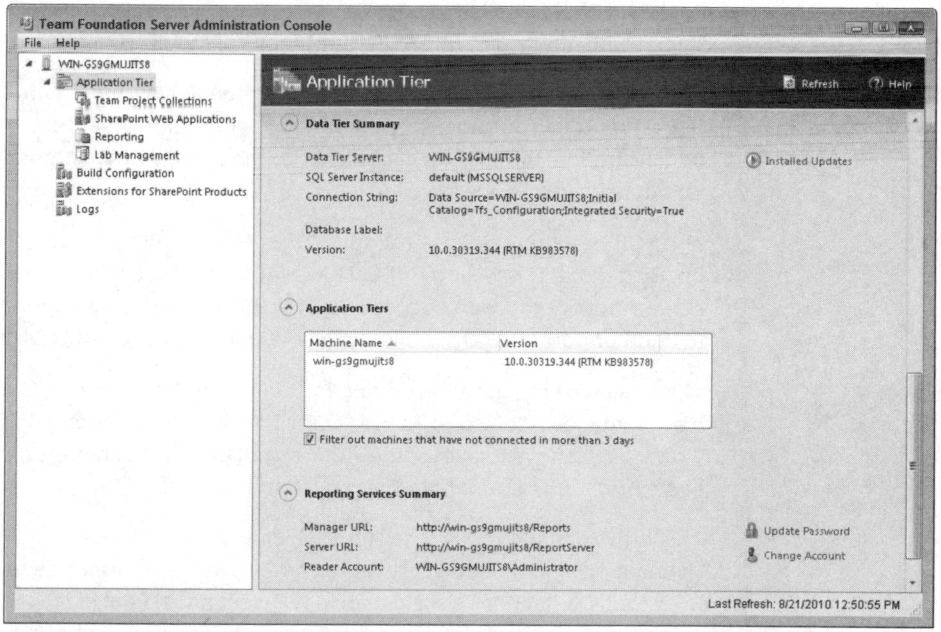

FIGURE 17-4: Continuation of the Application Tier screen

TABLE 17-2: Settings Displayed on the Application Tier Section

SETTING	DESCRIPTION
Application Tier Summary	
Service Account	The user account that the application pool and job agent are configured to run as.
Web Site	The name of the website as it appears in IIS Manager.
Application Pool	The name of the application pool as it appears in IIS Manager.
Authentication	The current authentication mode. It will be either NTLM (Windows Authentication) or Kerberos.
Notification URL	The URL that users use to connect to the system, and the URL that is used in the text of e-mail alerts.
Server URL	The URL used for server-to-server communication. This is especially important in environments with multiple application tiers. In this case, you don't want one node making requests to another node that the first node could have handled itself. That is why the default is localhost, and it's recommended for most configurations.
Web Access URL	The URL that web access should identify itself as. This is used when the Team Explorer client generates web access links, such as in the "Open with Microsoft Office Outlook" feature.
Machine Name	The name of the computer that the application tier is running on. Since the Administration Console doesn't allow remote server administration, this is always going to be the same as the computer that the console is open on.
Port	The TCP port that the application is currently accepting requests on. By default, this will be 8080. However, it may be port 443 for servers configured with secure SSL (HTTPS). Or, it may be changed to another port that is friendlier with your company's firewall policy.
Virtual Directory	This is a new configuration setting in Team Foundation Server 2010. It's sometimes referred to as the "vdir." The purpose of adding the virtual directory is to allow other future applications to share the same port, and differentiate them by their URLs.
Version	This is the definitive way to identify which version of Team Foundation is running on this server, as well as the current patch level that's installed. This is useful in two scenarios. First, it is an easy way to check whether you have a service pack or hotfix installed. Second, if you are thinking about moving a collection from another server, this is where you can check that the versions match.

SETTING	DESCRIPTION
Administration Console Users	
User Names	The list of individuals who have been granted administrative access to the Team Foundation Server environment, including SharePoint Services, Reporting Services, and SQL Server databases. You can add and remove administrative users by selecting the Add or Remove links. The Reapply link will re-apply the permissions for those users.
Data Tier Summary	
Data Tier Server	The SQL Database Server that is currently running the `Tfs_Configuration` database for this Team Foundation Server environment.
SQL Server Instance	SQL Server can have multiple instances running on the same server, differentiated by the instance name. This shows the instance that Team Foundation Server is configured to use.
Connection String	The connection string is the combination of the server name, instance name, and `Tfs_Configuration` database name that allow the application to connect to the database.
Database Label Version	The server has a version of code it is running, and the `Tfs_Configuration` database has a version stamp in the extended properties. This shows what that stamp is, and it must match the application version.
Application Tiers	
Machine List	The list of application tier servers that have ever been associated with this Team Foundation Server environment. If a server has not been active in the last three days, it can be filtered out of the list by selecting the checkbox.
Reporting Services Summary	
Reporting Services Manager URL	The URL to the root folder of the web-based report manager.
Reporting Services Server URL	The URL to the root of the Reporting Services web services.
Reader Account	Team Foundation Server uses two reporting data sources that allow reports to connect to the data warehouse as the account specified here.

Update Service Account Password

Team Foundation Server allows you to use a built-in Windows account as the service account, such as `NT AUTHORITY\Network Service` or `NT AUTHORITY\Local Service`. These special built-in accounts don't require manual password changes, and are a good choice to minimize the administrative overhead. However, for an environment with multiple application tiers, using a built-in Windows account is not supported, and you'll have to update the password on the server when it is changed.

Some corporate environments have password policies that require passwords to be changed every month. This requirement can make changing passwords for applications a very common administrative task.

Fortunately, it's very simple to do in Team Foundation Server 2010. After clicking the Update Password link in the Administration Console, you are presented with the dialog shown in Figure 17-5 that allows you to enter the new password and test it to ensure that it's correct.

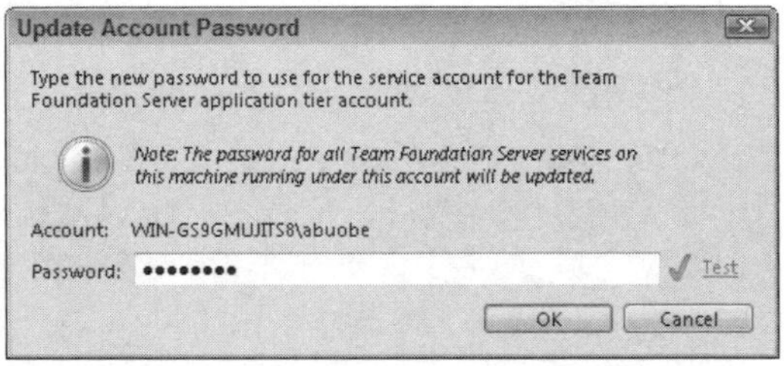

Once you click OK, the dialog again verifies that the password is correct and changes the password in all the locations it's used on the current server.

FIGURE 17-5: Update Account Password dialog

Figure 17-6 shows an example of a successful password change. If you have multiple application tier servers, you'll need to perform these same steps one at a time on each server.

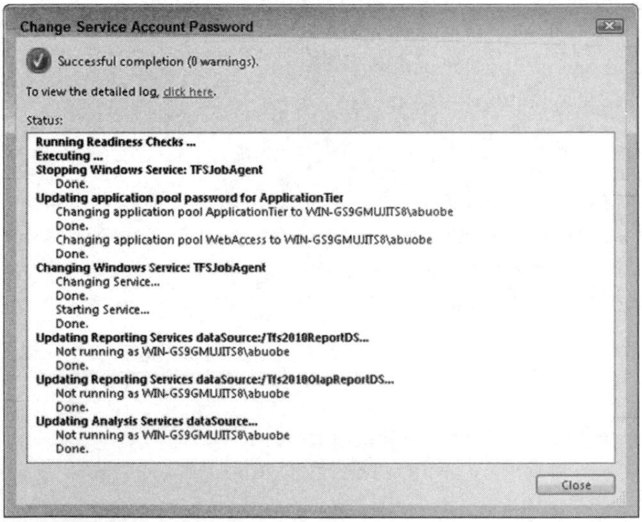

FIGURE 17-6: Change Service Account Password dialog

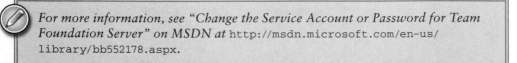

For more information, see *"Change the Service Account or Password for Team Foundation Server"* on MSDN at `http://msdn.microsoft.com/en-us/library/bb552178.aspx`.

Change Service Account

Changing the service account that Team Foundation Server runs as is not a very common task. Changing it is as simple as clicking the Change Account link in the Administration Console. In the resulting dialog shown in Figure 17-7, you either select a built-in system account, or enter the credentials for a domain account. Similar to changing passwords, it's also possible to verify the credentials before attempting to apply them by clicking the Test link.

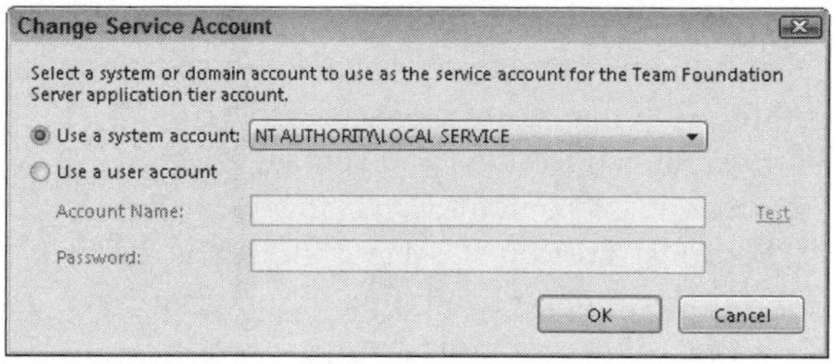

FIGURE 17-7: Change Service Account dialog

Reapply Service Account

In some cases, a server may have had its service account configuration changed manually. This means that the service accounts might not match across the different components, and this would put the server in an inconsistent state. To return the server to a consistent state, you can choose the Reapply Account link from the Administration Console. This will set the service account of all components to the currently configured service account, and reset the correct permissions. Similar to Figure 17-8, you should see all changes that were made, along with the successful completion message.

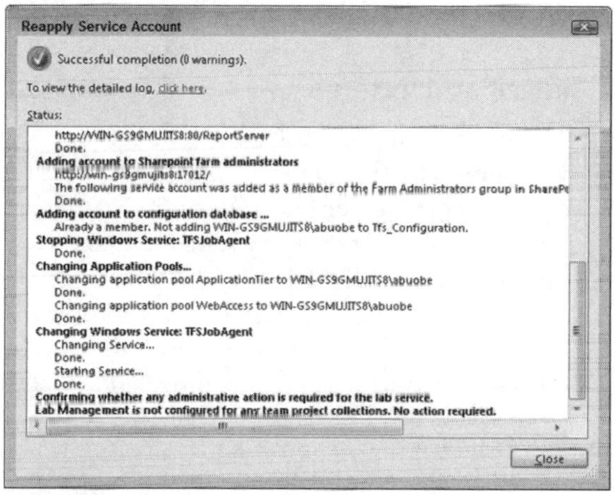

FIGURE 17-8: Reapply Service Account dialog

Change URLs

When Team Foundation Server makes requests to itself, it should use localhost. However, if you are using multiple application tiers, or you have a DNS alias configured for your server, then the Server URL setting may need to be changed.

After clicking the Change URLs link in the Administration Console, you are presented with a dialog similar to Figure 17-9 that allows you to change the two URLs used by the system.

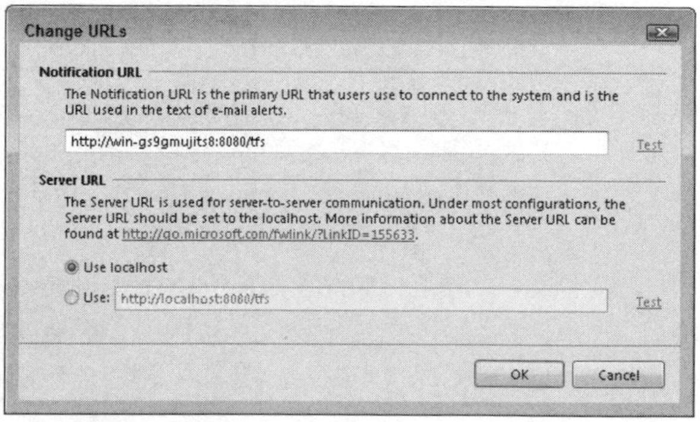

FIGURE 17-9: Change URLs dialog

Add Team Foundation Server Administration Console User

Users who aren't Team Foundation Server administrators can be given access to open the Administration Console, as well as to create collections and change service accounts. By default, anyone who is an administrator on the server already is a Team Foundation Server administrator. However, it's possible to remove this permission.

By clicking the Add link under Administration Console Users, you can give users administrative access in Team Foundation Server. Figure 17-10 shows you the advanced options available to restrict the permissions.

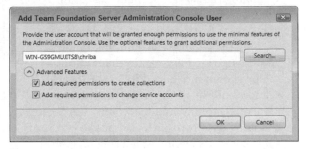

FIGURE 17-10: Add Team Foundation Server Administration Console User dialog

Installed Updates

The main Administration Console screen will show you the currently installed version of the server. Server patches are cumulative, which means that every new patch includes all the patches released before it. There are some cases where you might want to know each individual patch that has been installed on a server, and when it was installed.

By clicking the Installed Updates link in the Administration Console, you can see all the installed patches, as shown in Figure 17-11.

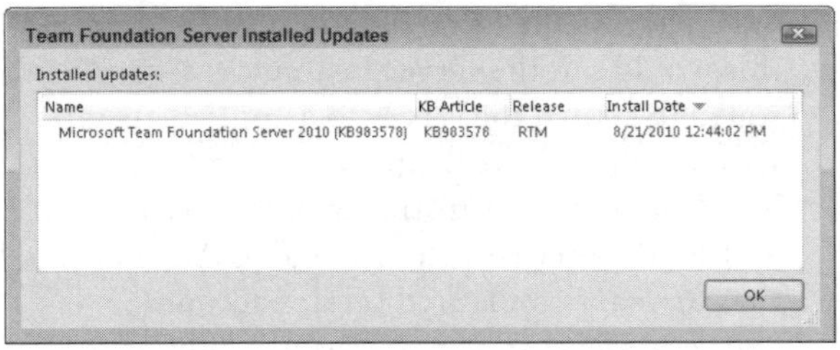

FIGURE 17-11: Team Foundation Server Installed Updates dialog

---

VIEWING THE CURRENT VERSION OF AN UNCONFIGURED SERVER

If your server is installed but not yet configured, you will not be able to see the current version or installed updates through the Administration Console. Therefore, you must check the file version of `Microsoft.TeamFoundation.Admin .dll` to determine what updates are already installed. Follow these steps:

1. Open Windows Explorer, and browse to `\Program Files\Microsoft Team Foundation Server 2010\Tools`.

2. Right-click `Microsoft.TeamFoundation.Admin.dll`, and then click Properties.

3. Click the Details tab, and review the information under File Version. For example, if the File Version field shows a value of `10.0.30319.1`, you are running the initial release of Team Foundation Server 2010.

4. When you have finished viewing the file version, click OK.

Managing Team Project Collections

The Team Project Collections section is perhaps the second-most used section of the Administration Console. This section of the Console allows you to perform all tasks that relate to collections. The tasks range from creating new collections to managing security, moving collections, and viewing collection logs.

To get to the Team Project Collections section of the tool, log on to your application tier server, click Start, point to All Programs, and then click Microsoft Team Foundation Server 2010. Click Team Foundation Administration Console and the administration console will open. You can then expand the tree in the left pane to show Application Tier and then Team Project Collections. As shown in Figure 17-12, you will see a list of the Team Project Collections available in your environment.

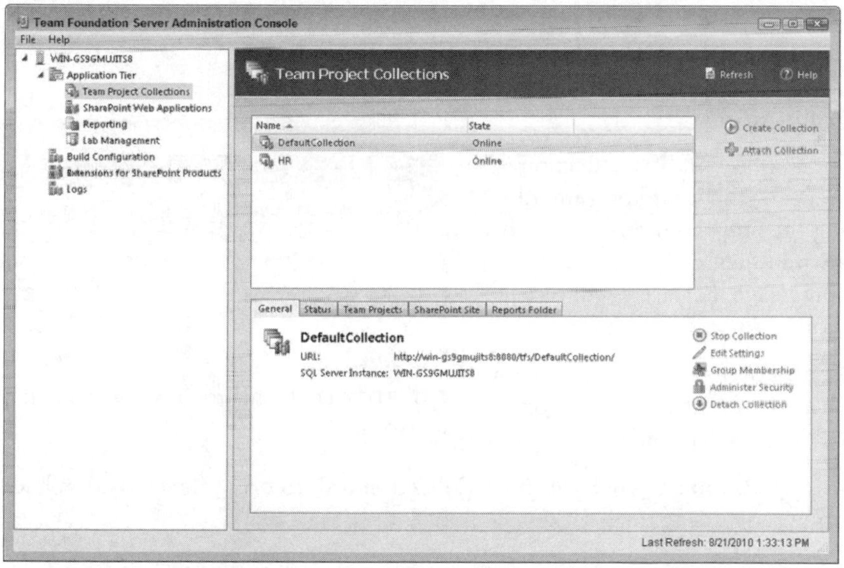

FIGURE 17-12: Team Project Collections

> If you are using a Basic configuration of Team Foundation Server, or your application tier is running on a client operating system (such as Windows 7), then the SharePoint and Reporting tabs described shortly won't be available.

General Tab

The General tab shows the full URL of the collection that can be used to connect from Visual Studio 2005 and 2008 clients.

In Team Foundation Server 2010, each collection can reside on a different SQL Server Instance to the central Tfs_Configuration database. The General tab shows the instance for the currently selected collection.

As shown in Figure 17-13, you can also view or edit the description of the collection from the General tab, and administer the group membership and permissions for users and groups in the collection.

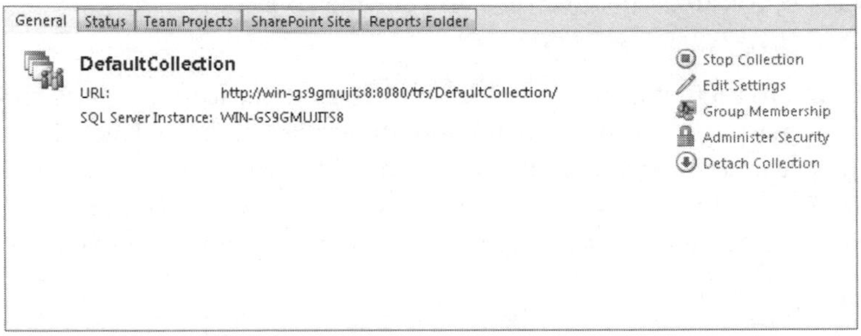

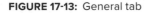

| General | Status | Team Projects | SharePoint Site | Reports Folder |

DefaultCollection
URL: http://win-gs9gmujits8:8080/tfs/DefaultCollection/
SQL Server Instance: WIN-GS9GMUJITS8

⊙ Stop Collection
✎ Edit Settings
👥 Group Membership
🔒 Administer Security
⊙ Detach Collection

FIGURE 17-13: General tab

Stop and Start a Collection

From the General tab of a collection, if a collection is currently running, you can stop it and prevent all new requests by clicking the Stop Collection link. This presents the dialog shown in Figure 17-14, which allows you to specify a message that users will receive when they attempt to connect to the collection.

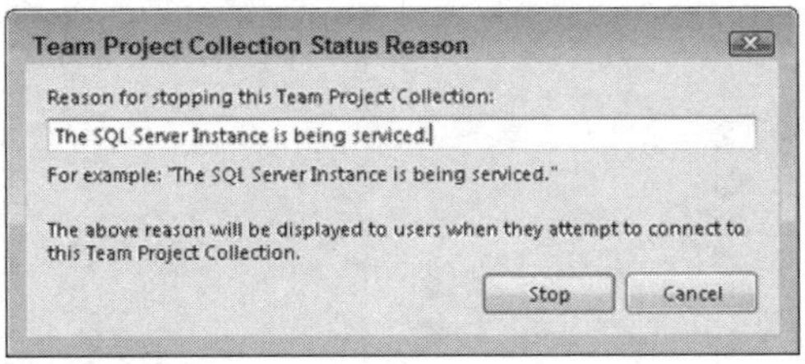

This is useful if you need to perform maintenance on the underlying SQL server, or for any other reason that you need to take a single collection offline.

Team Project Collection Status Reason

Reason for stopping this Team Project Collection:

The SQL Server Instance is being serviced.

For example: "The SQL Server Instance is being serviced."

The above reason will be displayed to users when they attempt to connect to this Team Project Collection.

[Stop] [Cancel]

FIGURE 17-14: Team Project Collection Status Reason dialog

Once the collection is stopped, you can click the Start Collection link to bring the collection back online and start accepting requests again.

Status Tab

As shown in Figure 17-15, the Status tab displays each of the jobs that have been executed for that collection. You can open the log for any of these jobs by double-clicking the entry.

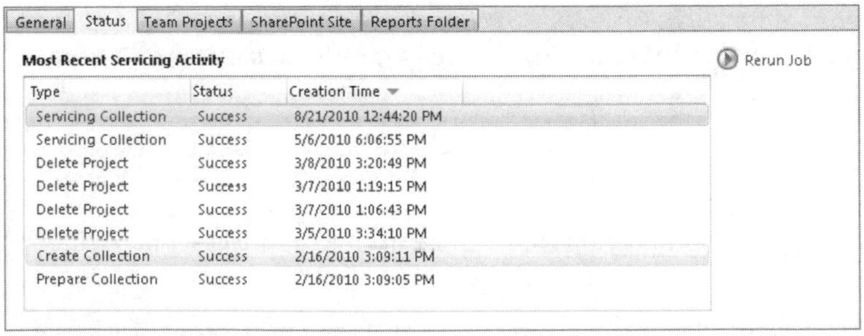

| General | Status | Team Projects | SharePoint Site | Reports Folder |

Most Recent Servicing Activity   ⊙ Rerun Job

Type	Status	Creation Time ▼
Servicing Collection	Success	8/21/2010 12:44:20 PM
Servicing Collection	Success	5/6/2010 6:06:55 PM
Delete Project	Success	3/8/2010 3:20:49 PM
Delete Project	Success	3/7/2010 1:19:15 PM
Delete Project	Success	3/7/2010 1:06:43 PM
Delete Project	Success	3/5/2010 3:34:10 PM
Create Collection	Success	2/16/2010 3:09:11 PM
Prepare Collection	Success	2/16/2010 3:09:05 PM

FIGURE 17-15: Status tab

In some circumstances, a job may fail. This could be because of an interrupted patch installation, a mismatched server and collection version, or a timeout. In these cases, it is possible to attempt the job again by clicking the Rerun Job link. You can view the current progress of a running job by double-clicking the entry.

When you are performing a server upgrade, it's possible to close the upgrade wizard before all the collections have finished upgrading. Additionally, when you are performing a collection import, the import process is command-line only, and it can be difficult to gauge the progress of the import. In these cases, you can also double-click the job to view the current progress of the upgrade or import job.

Team Projects Tab

This tab displays the list of team projects in the collection, along with their descriptions.

Because of the existing implementation of the Project Creation Wizard, it's not possible to add new team projects through the Administration Console. You still must use Team Explorer 2010 to create new team projects in a collection.

From the Team Projects tab shown in Figure 17-16, an administrator can delete a team project. Once a project is selected, the Delete link is available.

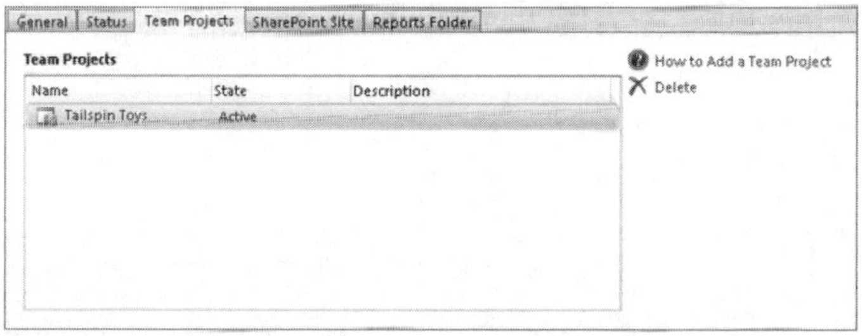

FIGURE 17-16: Team Projects tab

After clicking the Delete link, you can optionally delete lab management, reporting, and build artifacts that relate to the team project. Figure 17-17 shows the dialog you would use to do this. Additionally, you can optionally delete the version control workspace associated with the project.

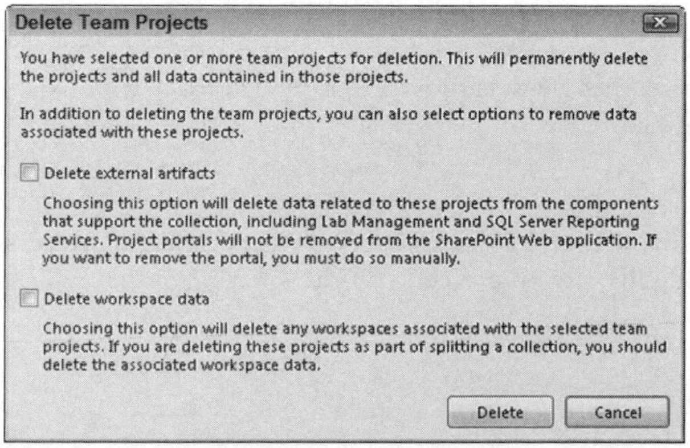

FIGURE 17-17: Delete Team Projects dialog

DATA MAY REMAIN UNDELETED AFTER DELETING A TEAM PROJECT

Deleting a team project can leave remnants of the team project in the system. For example, the team project data will remain in the data warehouse until it is rebuilt. Work item tracking metadata that is shared between other team projects is not deleted. Version control shelvesets that contain code from other team projects are also not deleted.

For more information on deleting a team project, see "TFSDeleteProject: Deleting Team Projects" on MSDN at `http://msdn.microsoft.com/en-us/library/ms181482.aspx`.

SharePoint Site Tab

Team Foundation Server 2010 allows you to configure any SharePoint site for your team project's project portal. As shown in Figure 17-18, this tab shows you the default site location that will be used to create project portals for new team projects. When you create a team project or configure a project portal for an existing team project, this is the URL that will be used by default.

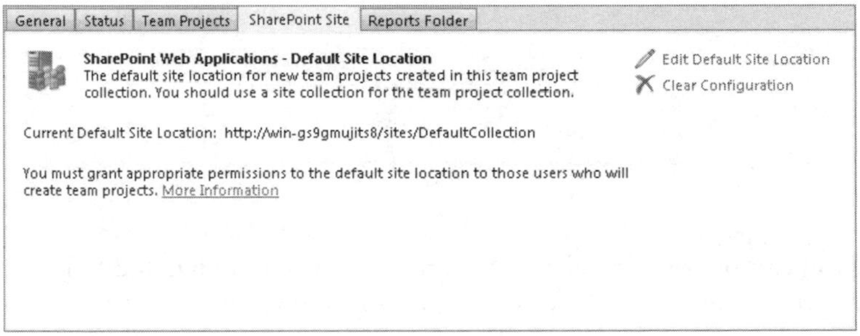

| General | Status | Team Projects | SharePoint Site | Reports Folder |

SharePoint Web Applications - Default Site Location
The default site location for new team projects created in this team project collection. You should use a site collection for the team project collection.

✎ Edit Default Site Location
✖ Clear Configuration

Current Default Site Location: http://win-gs9gmujits8/sites/DefaultCollection

You must grant appropriate permissions to the default site location to those users who will create team projects. More Information

FIGURE 17-18: SharePoint Site tab

If you don't specify a default site location here, then no default will be provided for new or existing team projects when they are created or modified.

Reports Folder Tab

As shown in Figure 17-19, this tab displays the path under which report folders for team projects will be created by default. If you create or modify a team project, you can specify another folder, but this root path will be used as the default.

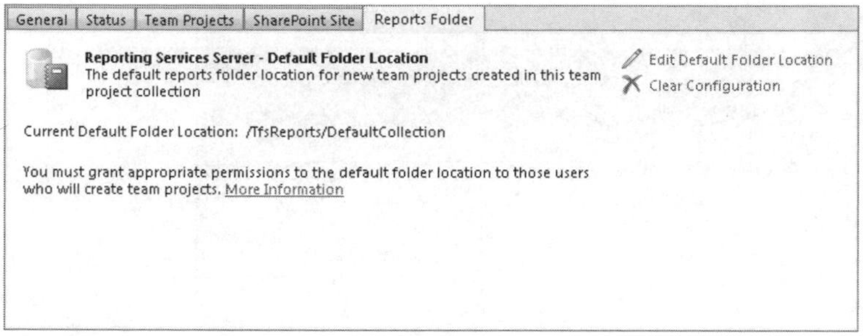

FIGURE 17-19: Reports Folder tab

Create a Team Project Collection

This is also the section where you create new team project collections. To do so, click the Create Collection link as shown on the right side of Figure 17-12. A dialog is displayed as shown in Figure 17-20. After you specify a name for the collection and an optional description, a series of readiness checks are run to confirm that a collection can be created on the specified server.

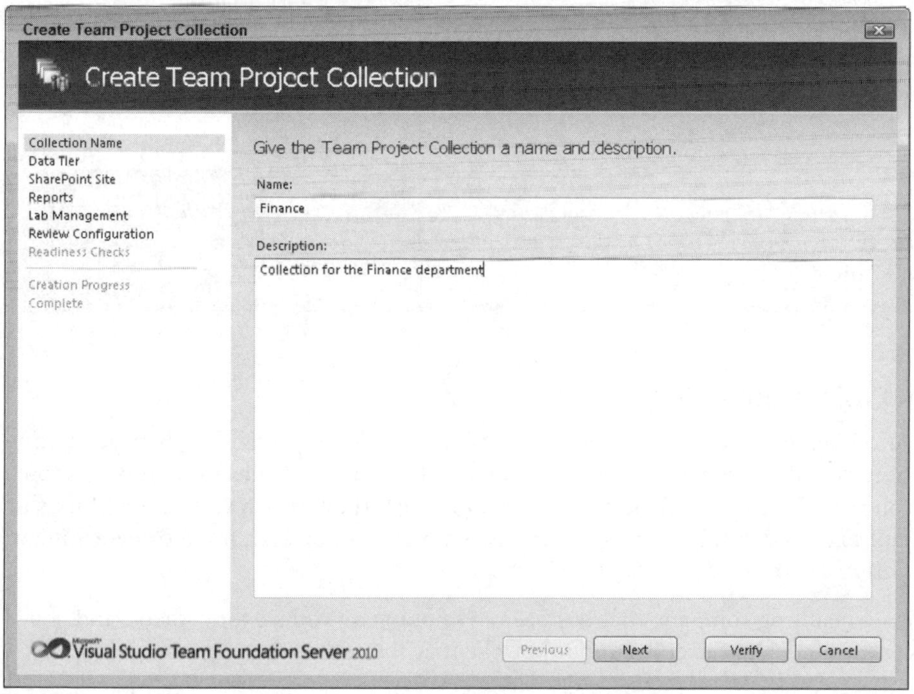

FIGURE 17-20: Create Team Project Collection name and description screen

Once the checks pass and you proceed with the wizard, you should receive eight green checkmarks as shown in Figure 17-21. In the background, a Create Collection job was queued on the server and the collection was created by the background job agent.

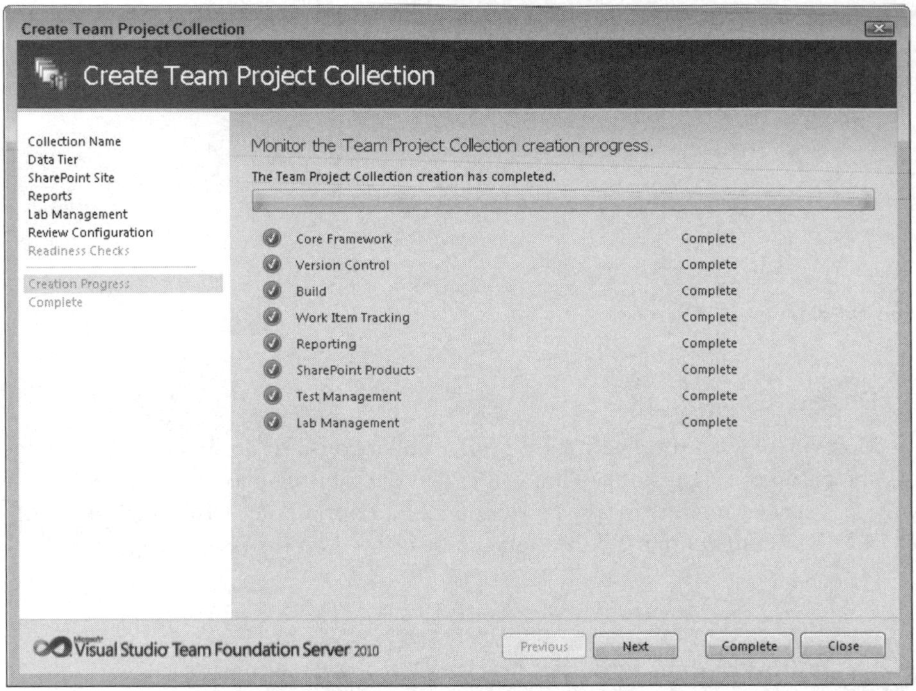

FIGURE 17-21: Successful creation of a Team Project Collection

> For more detailed instructions on this process, see "Create a Team Project Collection" page on MSDN at `http://msdn.microsoft.com/en-us/library/dd273726.aspx`.

Move a Team Project Collection

In Team Foundation Server 2010, it's very easy to move a team project collection between two servers of matching versions. To detach a collection, click the "Detach Collection" link as shown in Figure 17-13 on the General tab. To attach a collection, click the "Attach Collection" link shown on the right side of Figure 17-12. Following are the two most common scenarios for detaching a collection:

➤ You are a consulting company that has been developing a product for a client, and you want to deliver the code and the collection to the client at the end of the project.

➤ The organizational structure has changed, or the company has been acquired, and you must move the collection to a different Team Foundation Server.

The process is quite safe and relatively straightforward.

> For more detailed instructions, see "Move a Team Project Collection" on MSDN
> at http://msdn.microsoft.com/en-us/library/dd936138.aspx.

Detach a Team Project Collection

Each collection has shared information (such as identities) that is stored in the instance's
Tfs_Configuration database. Because of this, it's necessary to detach a collection before it can be
attached to another server.

This detach process copies the shared information into the collection database before disconnecting
it from the instance. The database remains online on the SQL server, but it is not associated with
the Team Foundation Server anymore.

To start the detach process, click Detach Collection from the General tab for the Team Project
Collection node in the admin console. For the relatively short duration (typically a few minutes)
while the detach operation is in progress, the collection will be offline.

The wizard allows you to optionally specify a message that will be displayed to users that connect
during this period, as shown in Figure 17-22. However, once the detach operation finishes, the
collection effectively doesn't exist on the server anymore, and this message won't be displayed to
users. Instead, they will receive a message indicating that the collection couldn't be found.

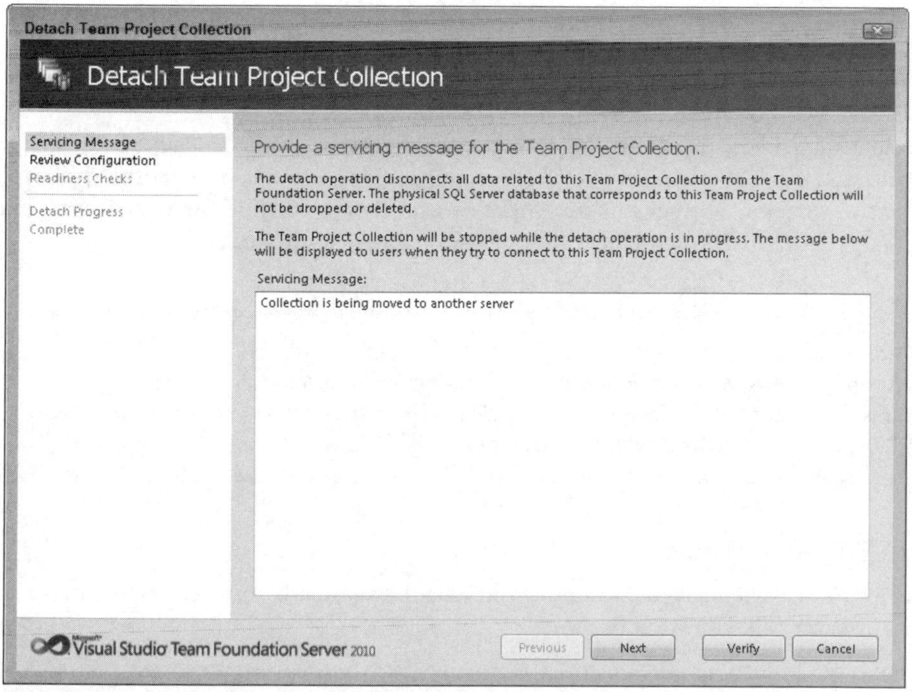

FIGURE 17-22: Detach Team Project Collection servicing message

Once you proceed with the wizard, a series of jobs are executed by the background job agent. After a short period, you should receive five green checkmarks, as shown in Figure 17-23.

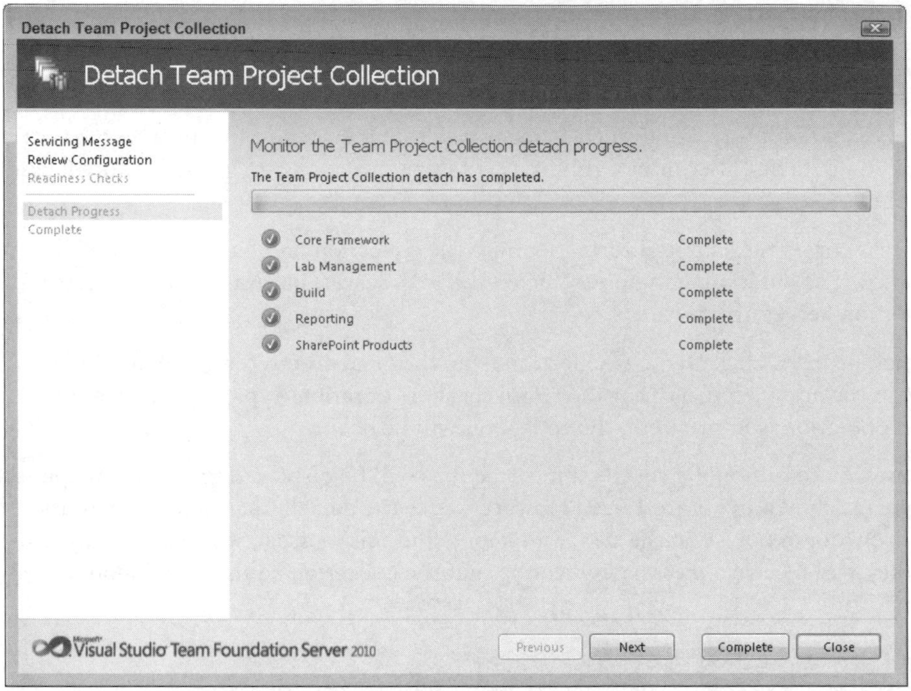

FIGURE 17-23: Successful Detach of a Team Project Collection

Once the database is detached, you can use SQL Server Management Studio to back up the collection database and move it to another SQL server, or provide the backup to another person. Remember to treat this backup with care, since anyone with access to the file can restore it to Team Foundation Server, and that person will have administrator access to the collection.

> *Detaching a collection requires additional steps beyond just clicking Detach Collection in the Administration Console. To achieve full fidelity, you must save the reports from Reporting Services, delete any Lab Management resources, and rebuild the data warehouse as part of any detach operation.*

Attach a Team Project Collection

Before attaching a previously detached collection, you must have already restored the database backup to the SQL server that you want to use.

To start the process, click the Attach Collection link from the Administration Console on the Team Project Collections node, as shown in Figure 17-12. When the dialog appears, specify the SQL Server Instance, as shown in Figure 17-24.

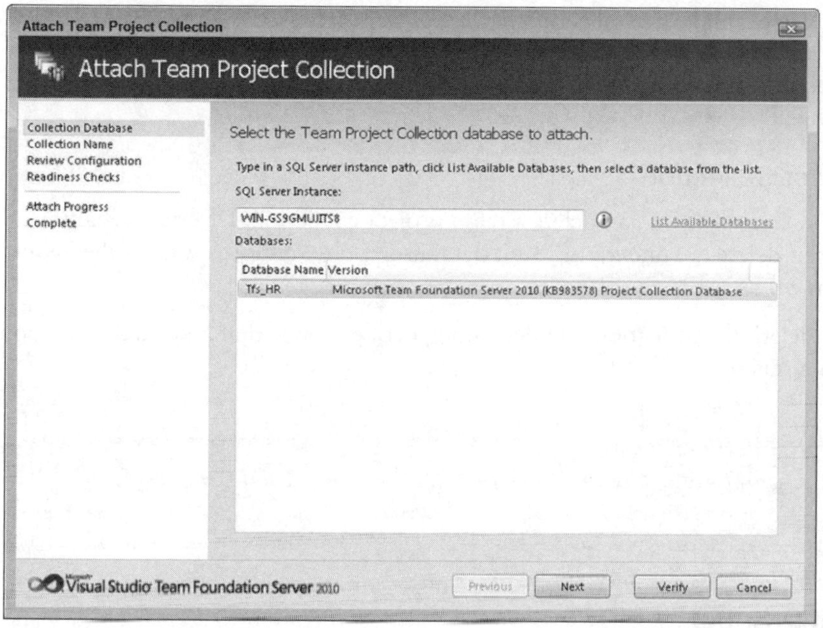

FIGURE 17-24: Specifying a SQL Server instance and database to attach

Once the collection is verified and you proceed with the wizard, a job is executed on the background job agent. This job copies the shared data out of the collection database and places it in the Tfs_Configuration database for the instance. As shown in Figure 17-25, once the job is completed, the collection is brought online and users can begin accessing it.

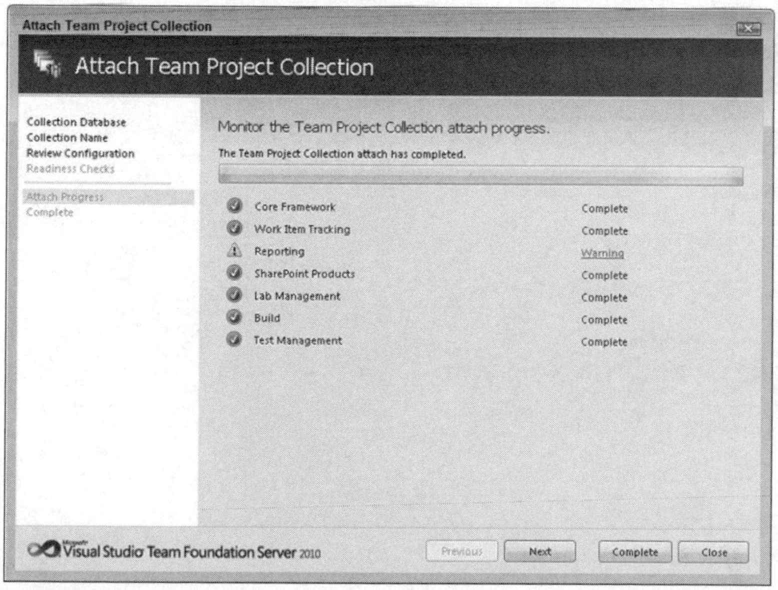

FIGURE 17-25: Successful Attach of a Team Project Collection

Every Team Foundation Server and each collection has a unique instance ID. As part of the attach process, the server will check the instance ID of the collection and ensure that it doesn't conflict with an existing collection on the server. If a conflict is detected, then the new collection's instance ID is automatically changed.

Delete a Team Project Collection

Using the Administration Console, you can delete a team project collection. Deleting a team project collection does not delete the underlying SQL database; it only removes it from the Team Foundation Server instance.

The difference between deleting a collection and detaching a collection is that a deleted collection cannot be reattached to a server.

> *For more details, see "Delete a Team Project Collection" on MSDN at* `http://msdn.microsoft.com/en-us/library/dd312130.aspx`.

Managing SharePoint Products

As you can see in Figure 17-26, this section is where you establish the connection between your Team Foundation Server instance and your SharePoint web applications. If you already have a SharePoint server configured, or you'd like to allow project portals on an additional server, you can add that server here.

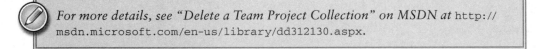

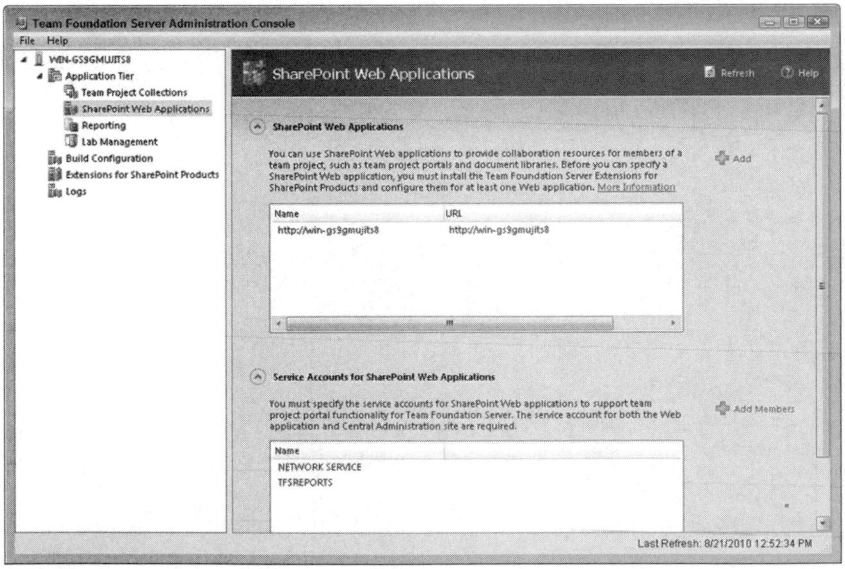

FIGURE 17-26: SharePoint Web Applications section

Managing Reporting

As you can see in Figure 17-27, this section is where all the Reporting settings are configured for your Team Foundation Server instance. The main screen shows you the current settings, which you can change by clicking the Edit link.

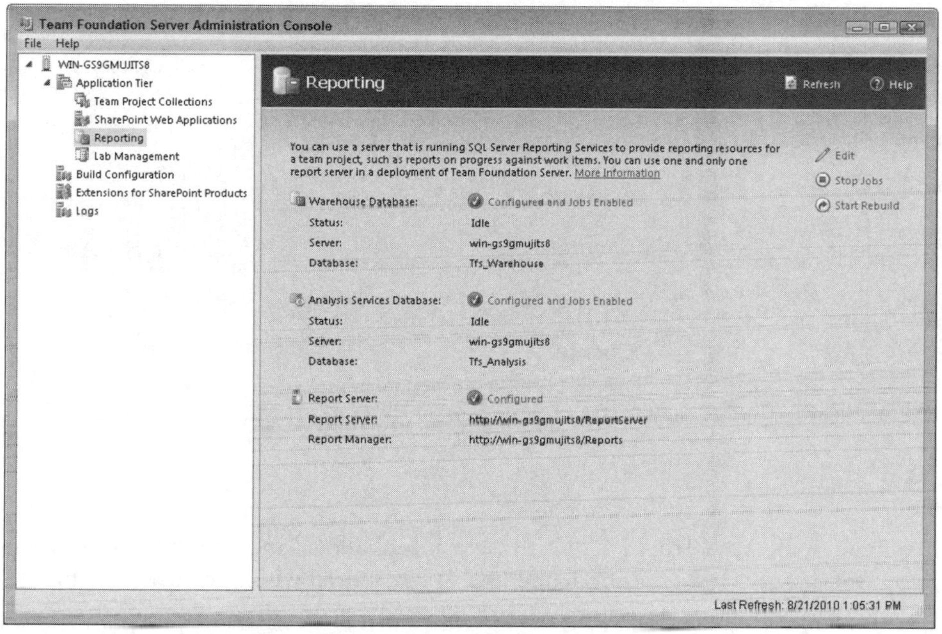

FIGURE 17-27: Reporting section

For a more detailed look at the administration aspects of reporting, see Chapter 13.

Other

For details on the other options available in the Administration Console, refer to the chapters shown in Table 17-3.

TABLE 17-3: Parts of the Administration Console Covered in Other Chapters

SECTION	REFER TO
Build Configuration	Chapter 15
Lab Management	Chapter 22
Logs	Chapter 21

Command-Line Configuration Tools

There are quite a few command-line configuration tools available in Team Foundation Server. In the latest version, a number of disparate tools were consolidated into two. For example, the WITImport .exe, WITExport.exe, and WITFields.exe tools are now commands that are available in the WITAdmin.exe tool.

Many of the administration tools are examined in other chapters of this book, and you should refer to the chapters shown in Table 17-4 for more details.

TABLE 17-4: Command-Line Configuration Tools Covered in Other Chapters

TOOL	REFER TO
TFSSecurity.exe	Chapter 20
WITAdmin.exe	Chapter 12
TF.exe Proxy	Chapter 24
TF.exe Permission	Chapter 20

TFSConfig.exe

New in Team Foundation Server 2010, the TFSConfig.exe tool allows an administrator to perform most server configuration tasks from the command line. When paired with a remote execution tool such as PSExec.exe (which is available at http://technet.microsoft.com/en-us/sysinternals/ bb897553.aspx), TFSConfig.exe can help you achieve remote server administration. The biggest gap in this command-line configuration tool is the reporting settings. These still must be configured using the Administration Console.

Table 17-5 provides an overview of each of the commands available with TFSConfig.exe and what they can be used for.

TABLE 17-5: Commands Available with TFSConfig.exe

COMMAND	DESCRIPTION
Accounts	Allows you to update passwords, change service accounts, add new service accounts, remove service accounts, and reset database ownership.
Authentication	Allows you to view or change the current authentication settings (NTLM or Kerberos) for the server.
Certificates	Configures how client authentication certificates are used when Team Foundation Server connects to itself using a secure (HTTPS) connection.

COMMAND	DESCRIPTION
ChangeServerID	Initializes the Team Foundation Server instance and all of its collections with a new instance ID. This command is required when you restore a copy of your server while the original copy remains online. Without changing the instance ID of the new server, clients will be confused and will communicate with the original server instead of the new server.
Collection	Attaches, detaches, or deletes a team project collection from the server.
ConfigureMail	Changes the e-mail From address and the SMTP host used by the server to send notifications.
Diagnose	Diagnoses software update problems that might prevent Team Foundation Server from working correctly. This command inspects the system to find any service level (patch) mismatches between the application tier and the collection databases.
Identities	Lists the status or changes the security identifiers (SIDs) of identities stored by the server. This command is used when you move a server from one domain to another where the usernames match, but the SIDs are different.
Import	Imports databases from either a 2005 or 2008 data tier as a new project collection. This command is used when you want to consolidate multiple Instances onto a single instance, and don't want to perform an in-place upgrade first.
Jobs	Allows you to retrieve the logs or retry a job on a single, or all, collection(s).
Lab	Configures Lab Management and manages host group and library share assignments for a collection.
License	Used to display or modify Team Foundation Server licensing information. Using this command, you can extend your trial period by an additional 30 days.
Perfcounters	Installs Windows Performance Counters used by Team Foundation Server.
PrepareClone	Prepares an existing configuration database after cloning. This will reset the SharePoint and Reporting Services URLs to the local machine, and create the required SQL roles in the master database.
PrepSql	Prepares a SQL Server instance by installing the error messages and SQL roles required to host Team Foundation Server databases.
RebuildWarehouse	Rebuilds the Analysis Services database and the relational database of the warehouse. Unlike the Start Rebuild link in the Administration Console, you can specify the /analysisServices parameter, which will only rebuild the Analysis Services database without rebuilding the relational database.

continues

TABLE 17-5 *(continued)*

COMMAND	DESCRIPTION
Recover	Recovers lost team projects or team project collections after a disaster recovery with loss of data. There are no guarantees with this command, but it may be able to attach a collection database to an instance if it wasn't detached correctly. This is useful in situations where the backups of the configuration database and collection database are not synchronized.
RegisterDB	Changes the database the application tier uses. This command is usually used when you restore a set of databases and want to connect them to new application tier.
RemapDBs	Enumerates the databases in the specified SQL instances, and validates that the connection strings match the locations of the found databases.
Repair	Re-creates all stored procedures, functions, indexes, constraints, and tables in the configuration and collection databases. It doesn't repair any of the data, only the structure of the databases.
Settings	Manages the notification and server URL settings for the server.
Updates	Reapplies software updates that are required to synchronize the service level of the databases for Team Foundation Server to the level of the application tier.
Setup	Used for unconfiguring a Team Foundation Server. After running this command, you can open the Administration Console and run the server configuration wizard again.

> *For more details on this command-line tool, see "Managing Server Configuration with TFSConfig" on MSDN at* `http://msdn.microsoft.com/en-us/library/ms253116.aspx`.

TFSServiceControl.exe

The `TFSServiceControl.exe` tool is used to stop or start all of the services and application pools that Team Foundation Server uses on a server. If you have multiple application tier servers, you will need to run this command on each server to completely start or stop the environment.

The `quiesce` option will gracefully stop all related services on the server, and the `unquiesce` option will restart them again.

OTHER ADMINISTRATION TOOLS

As with most products, there are gaps in functionality. Team Foundation Server 2010 is no exception, and there are many Microsoft-sponsored and non-Microsoft-sponsored utilities available. This section examines the ones released outside Microsoft's normal release cycle, as well as a useful tool developed by another company.

Team Foundation Server Power Tools

Power Tools are extra features that are developed by Microsoft outside of the normal release cycle. They are always "additive," which means that they are extensions of the shipping product and don't change any core functionality. Typically, they are used to temporarily address customer pain points and adoption blockers. In an ideal world, all the Power Tool features would eventually make it in to the normal product, but that can take some time.

The Power Tools include some useful utilities for administrators, such as the Alerts Explorer (for creating e-mail and SOAP subscriptions to events), the Process Editor (for managing work item types and fields), and the Best Practices Analyzer.

> *The latest version of the Team Foundation Server Power Tools can be downloaded from* http://msdn.microsoft.com/en-us/vstudio/bb980963.

Best Practices Analyzer

Perhaps the most useful Power Tool for administrators is the Best Practices Analyzer (BPA). The BPA is the same tool that is used by the Microsoft Support team when customers call with a server problem.

The health check scan types have hundreds of rules and alerts built in. These check all the different configuration settings in an environment against expected settings, and generate warnings or errors when something doesn't look correct.

In addition to one other scan that collects statistics of your server, the following are the seven different variations of the health check scan:

- ➤ Team Foundation Server Complete Health Check
- ➤ Team Foundation Server Framework Health Check
- ➤ Team Foundation Server Warehouse Health Check
- ➤ Team Foundation Build Health Check
- ➤ Visual Studio Lab Management Health Check
- ➤ SharePoint Products Health Check
- ➤ Team Foundation Server Statistics

Team Foundation Server Complete Health Check is the most comprehensive scan, and will take the longest to run. As you can see in Figure 17-28, it enumerates all the servers in an environment (including build agents and lab management components), and performs the health check scan on them. If you have an environment with more than a few build servers, then this scan type is probably not very useful because it will take a very long time to run and scan all your servers.

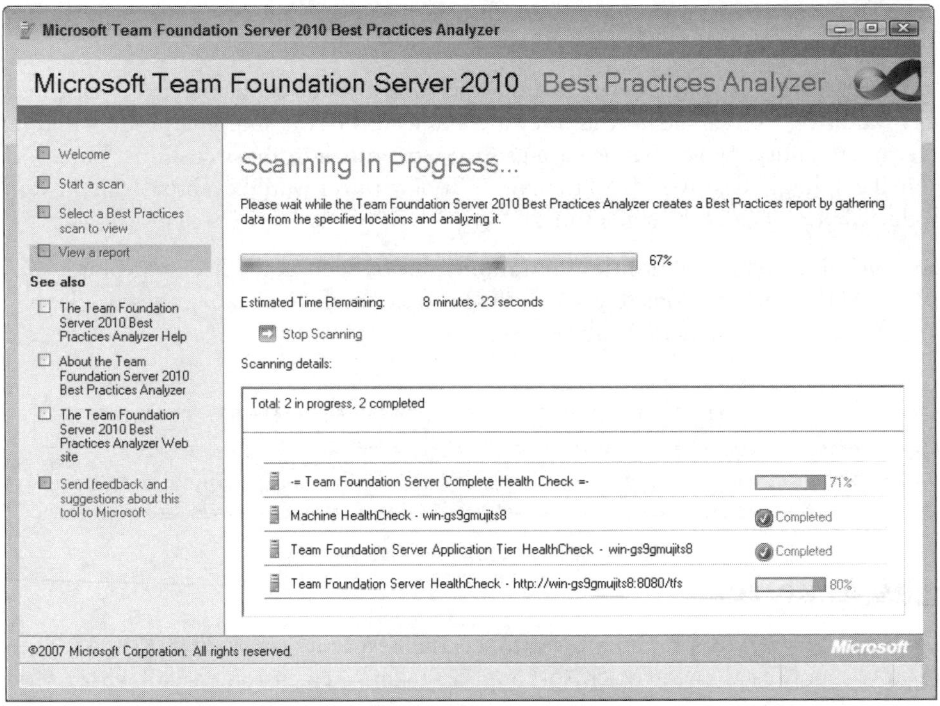

FIGURE 17-28: Microsoft Team Foundation Server 2010 Best Practices Analyzer

Additionally, if you are having a problem with a particular component (such as the Warehouse or SharePoint Products), you can just run the health check for those components.

Once the scan completes, you can select each issue and click the "Tell me more about this issue and how to resolve it" link shown toward the bottom of Figure 17-29. This will display the documentation for that particular check, and describe the steps to resolve the issue. This is an often overlooked and very valuable resource for diagnosing and troubleshooting Team Foundation Server configuration issues.

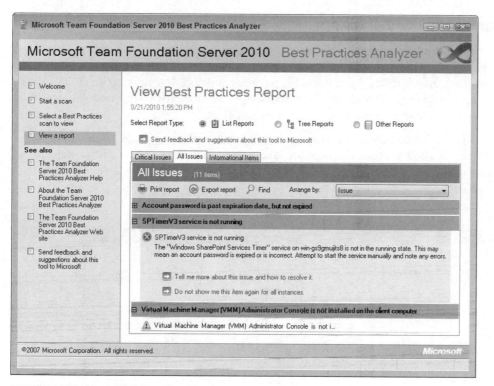

FIGURE 17-29: View Best Practices Report

It's not very well known, but you can actually run the BPA tool from the command line using the TfsBpaCmd.exe tool. With this functionality, you might consider running it once a week as a scheduled task to proactively detect any server configuration issues.

> *Chapter 21 covers the usage of the BPA tool in more detail.*

Team Foundation Server Administration Tool

Team Foundation Server includes integration with SharePoint Products and SQL Reporting Services. However, this integration isn't as great as it could be for project or server administrators. Permissions between Team Foundation Server and these other systems aren't integrated. This means that you have to manage the permissions and group memberships separately through each system's own administration interface.

> *Fortunately, this permission integration issue was identified as an early gap for administrators, and the Team Foundation Server Administration Tool was created. This tool will be discussed further in Chapter 20.*

Team Foundation Sidekicks

As a Team Foundation Server administrator, you may be required to venture beyond SQL servers, application tiers, collections, and team projects. If you must delete old workspaces or unlock files from users who are on vacation, you can use the tf.exe command-line tools to do so. For those who are not intimately familiar with the client tools, this can be a little tricky, and you would be much more comfortable in a graphical user interface (GUI).

The Attrice Corporation has created a freeware suite of tools called the Team Foundation Sidekicks. The tools allow server administrators and advanced users to use a GUI to perform many administrative and advanced version control tasks. Figure 17-30 shows an example of the Workspace sidekick.

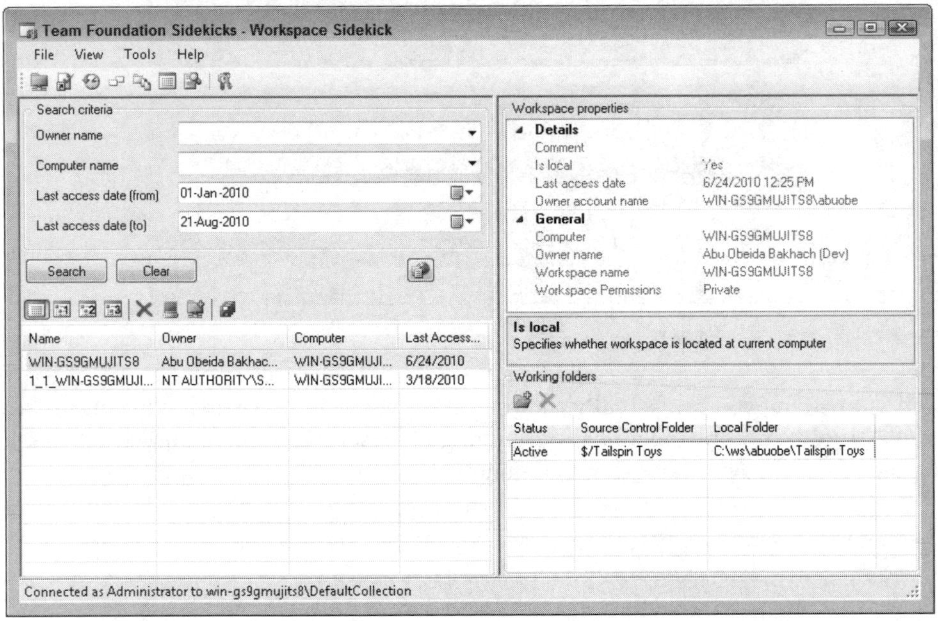

FIGURE 17-30: Team Foundation Workspace Sidekick

The standalone edition of the tool suite provides a GUI for managing different parts of Team Foundation Server. Table 17-6 provides a brief description of each sidekick.

TABLE 17-6: Team Foundation Sidekicks Available in the Standalone Version

SIDEKICK	DESCRIPTION
Workspace Sidekick	View, search, delete, and modify workspaces.
Status Sidekick	View pending changes, and unlock locked files and folders.
History Sidekick	View, search, and compare the history of files and folders, along with their associated branches and merges.
Label Sidekick	View, search, and compare labels, along with any linked changesets and work items.
Shelveset Sidekick	View, delete, compare, and download the contents of a shelveset, along with any linked work items and check-in notes.
Permission Sidekick	View a user's effective global, project-specific, and file permissions.
Users View Sidekick	Display and search all valid users in the system.

These sidekicks are a very useful addition to any Team Foundation Server administrator's toolkit, and will save plenty of time.

SUMMARY

Along with a brief look at the server architecture, this chapter was all about tools for administrators. The chapter provided a walkthrough of all the different screens and functionality of the new Team Foundation Server Administration Console.

This chapter also provided a brief look at the command-line administration tool, TFSConfig.exe, and its 23 different commands. You learned that from this tool, you can change almost any setting in the server.

You also learned about some additional tools that aren't included in the product, but are very useful to a server administrator. You learned that the Best Practices Analyzer is great for identifying server misconfigurations, and that the Team Foundation sidekicks allow you to manage workspaces and shelvesets on behalf of other users as well as other administrative and version control focused tasks.

Chapter 18 covers two important topics for server administrators: scalability and high availability. Along with a look at the physical architecture of the system, Chapter 18 includes guidance from several lessons learned while running the servers at Microsoft for many users.

18

Scalability and High Availability

➤ Understanding architectural changes

➤ Understanding scale limitations

➤ Exploring availability solutions

➤ Exploring load balancing

➤ Getting to know configuration best practices

Scalability and high availability are very involved topics, and a whole book could be written on each of them. Every Team Foundation Server environment is unique, and every organization has a different usage pattern and availability requirements.

It's not the purpose or intent of this chapter to provide prescriptive guidance on exact configurations to support your environment or usage pattern. Rather, this chapter is intended to give you insight into the different factors that affect scalability, and to offer some solutions to consider in your overall environment design.

> *If you need advice specifically tailored to your organization's needs, your best option is to contact Microsoft Support or a Microsoft Certified Partner in your area. These people have deep knowledge and ample hands-on experience to best meet your needs.*

WHAT'S NEW IN TEAM FOUNDATION SERVER 2010?

Team Foundation Server 2010 introduced some significant architecture and infrastructure changes. On the product team, these product changes were referred to as Enterprise TFS

Management (ETM). It was a significant and necessary investment of effort to allow the product to handle the future scale demands of enterprises and the Internet.

The introduction of team project collections was perhaps the largest architectural change. This innovation took the seven databases that used to make up a server and "folded" them into a single database that represents a collection. This database becomes the unit of isolation, and a collection can be detached and moved between different servers. Collections enable the following:

- ➤ The consolidation of multiple instances onto a single shared instance
- ➤ The scale-out of a single instance to multiple physical servers

Team Foundation Server 2008 and previous releases included many built-in assumptions about your deployment. For example, you could only have a single application tier. This application tier couldn't be installed on a 64-bit operating system. Analysis Services had to be installed on the same server as SQL Server (although you could move it later if you wanted to). These restrictions made the initial installation and any future configuration changes to the server quite fragile and error-prone.

One of the core deliverables of ETM was to enable configuration flexibility and remove these limitations. Team Foundation Server 2010 now supports the following features critical to scalability and availability:

- ➤ Configuration flexibility
- ➤ Multiple application tiers with load balancing
- ➤ 64-bit application tier installation
- ➤ Stateless application tier and web access

On top of all these infrastructure improvements, there was also a huge investment in the setup, configuration, and administration experiences. All this investment makes Team Foundation Server 2010 the most robust and scalable release yet.

Much of this chapter is relevant to only the largest Team Foundation Server environments. However, since Team Foundation Server is built on top of Microsoft technologies, you might find these suggestions useful for scaling your own applications.

RESOURCE GOVERNOR AT MICROSOFT

While running the internal servers for the Developer Division at Microsoft, the team constantly battled to keep the server performance ahead of user demand. It seemed that no matter how many optimizations and hardware upgrades they did, the gains were quickly eroded. This was usually because of the sheer growth of data in the system, or, more commonly, a misbehaving tool.

This problem was tackled in two ways. The first approach was to do some analysis on the server's activity logs and identify the tools or users generating the most load. In one case, a single user was responsible for more than 50 percent of the load on the system. Once identified, the team worked with the tool owners to understand their requirements, and made suggestions for using the object model more efficiently.

This effort yielded some great results, but left the team vulnerable and waiting for the next rogue tool to hit the system.

Toward the end of the 2010 release, the team implemented a resource governor with a default policy. Every command in the system is assigned a cost based on how intensive it is. Once the total cost of all the commands executing hits a configurable limit, future requests are queued until a slot becomes available. Each individual command can have a limit on its concurrency as well.

As an example, the `Merge` command is assigned a cost of 5. The default limit for a server is 200. This means that, by default, each application tier will only allow 40 `Merge` operations to execute concurrently.

This resource governor prevents the server from becoming overwhelmed with a large number of requests, and overloading the SQL server.

LIMITING FACTORS

Implementing a system that scales is all about finding the biggest bottleneck, removing it, and finding the next one. In a system with as many moving parts as Team Foundation Server, there are many opportunities for bottlenecks. Even when you manage to remove the biggest bottlenecks, there are still some inherent limitations in the architecture to consider.

Microsoft Recommendations

The officially tested and recommended system configurations for deploying Team Foundation Server 2010 are detailed in the Installation Guide at `http://go.microsoft.com/fwlink/?LinkId=127730`.

As you can see in Table 18-1 (which is culled from the Installation Guide), the hardware requirements for a small team are quite modest. It's perfectly reasonable to run a server that supports 250 users on a single core machine that has a reasonable hard disk. You should, however, consider these as recommendations. In general, the bigger your team is, the greater your need will be for robust hardware.

TABLE 18-1: Recommended Hardware Configurations

NUMBER OF USERS	CONFIGURATION	CPU	MEMORY	HARD DISK
Fewer than 250 users	Single-server (Team Foundation Server and the Database Engine on the same server)	1 single core processor at 2.13 GHz	2GB	1 disk at 7.2K rpm (125GB)
250 to 500 users	Single-server	1 dual core processor at 2.13 GHz	4GB	1 disk at 10K rpm (300GB)
500 to 2,200 users	Dual-server (Team Foundation Server and the Database Engine on different servers)			
	Application tier	1 dual core Intel Xeon processor at 2.13 GHz	4GB	1 disk at 7.2K rpm (500GB)
	Data tier	1 quad core Intel Xeon processor at 2.33 GHz	8GB	SAS disk array at 10K rpm (2TB)
2,200 to 3,600 users	Dual-server			
	Application tier	1 quad core Intel Xeon processor at 2.13 GHz	8GB	1 disk at 7.2K rpm (500GB)
	Data tier	2 quad core Intel Xeon processors at 2.33 GHz	16GB	SAS disk array at 10K rpm (3TB)

As discussed later in this chapter, the number of team project collections in an environment will affect the performance of the system. These hardware recommendations don't give an indication of how many collections they can support, only the number of users.

One important distinction for the number of collections is the number of active collections compared to the number of dormant collections. An *active collection* is one that will be accessed on a daily basis. When a collection is automatically marked as *dormant* in the system, it will have most of its background jobs paused. This frees up available memory for active collections.

Table 18-2 describes the maximum number of active collections per SQL server based upon total available memory.

TABLE 18-2: Active Collections per SQL Server

SQL SERVER RAM	ACTIVE COLLECTIONS
8GB	30 to 75
16GB	40 to 90
32GB	50 to 125
64GB	75 to 195

For a recommendation of the number of collections per SQL server, you should refer to the "Visual Studio 2010 Quick Reference Guidance" at http://vs2010quickref.codeplex.com/. More specifically, you should refer to the "Capacity Planning Quick Reference Poster" and the "Capacity Planning Companion Workbook," which are available as downloads from the aforementioned site.

This planning workbook lets you enter the maximum expected users and the current number of users for your environment. Using the official hardware recommendations from Table 18-1, it will tell you the recommended configuration for your expected number of users and a maximum number of active collections it can support.

Data Tier

The vast majority of work in Team Foundation Server happens in the data tier. Therefore, it makes sense that the most common bottlenecks are found in the data tier. Team Foundation Server performance is directly proportional to the performance of your SQL server. For a large environment, you must pay the same level of attention that you pay to other critical database applications in your organization, such as your Human Resources, Finance, or Sales databases.

There are quite few opportunities for bottlenecks in the data tier:

➤ Storage performance

➤ TempDB storage performance

➤ SQL plan cache

➤ SQL buffer cache

➤ Storage size and growth

Storage

The single biggest factor that contributes to server performance is the performance of the storage. If your storage isn't matched to the demands of the system, then everything will suffer. Team Foundation Server makes heavy use of SQL Server's TempDB database for large version control commands, so that is a common source of bottlenecks.

SQL Query Plan Cache

SQL-stored procedures have query plans. These query plans are pre-compiled, and the server uses them to work out how it needs to execute a particular query. Some commands (like `Merge`) in Team Foundation Server contain some very complex logic. This makes the query plans quite detailed, and their size adds up. Since each project collection is a separate database, there is a separate plan cached in SQL for each stored procedure.

The limitation here is that the plan cache is shared among all databases on the same SQL instance. The plan cache is sized according to this formula:

➤   75 percent of visible target memory from 0 to 4GB

➤   + 10 percent of visible target memory from 4GB to 64GB

➤   + 5 percent of visible target memory greater than 64GB

This means that as you add more collections to a SQL server, there will be more contention in the plan cache. When a stored procedure's plan isn't in the cache, it must be recalculated and recompiled. Although this is not a significant overhead, it's not optimal to be recompiling plan caches all the time.

> For more information on how the SQL plan cache works, see the "Plan Caching in SQL Server 2008" whitepaper from Greg Low at http://msdn.microsoft .com/en-us/library/ee343986(SQL.100).aspx.

SQL Buffer Cache

The SQL buffer cache is where frequently accessed database pages are kept in memory. Having pages in memory is a good thing, because this results in the fastest performance.

Work item tracking uses a series of tables to store work items with a set of views over those tables. When you run a query from Team Explorer, that query is translated into a SQL query and executed in the database. Because work item tracking is completely customizable and has a dynamic schema, it performs best when all the tables are in the buffer cache.

The buffer cache is shared across all databases on a SQL server. So, if your work item tracking tables are competing in the buffer cache with other tables, then they may get pushed out. When they get pushed out, work item query performance will suffer.

This can be observed as you add more project collections to a server, or your collections get bigger. If you look at the SQL Server "Memory Manager\Buffer Cache Hit Ratio" performance counter, it will drop and performance may start to suffer. In particular, work item queries that use the `contains` clause will suffer the most noticeable effects, since they require a table scan. If the pages aren't in the buffer cache, then SQL must fetch them from disk.

To summarize, the size of the SQL buffer cache (which is calculated based upon total server memory) will limit the size of the project collections that a SQL server can support while maintaining reasonable performance.

Application Tier

You're more likely to encounter bottlenecks in the data tier than the application tier. There are, however, two main scale limitations that affect the application tier:

➤ Memory

➤ ASP.NET worker threads configuration

Memory

Access control for version control is performed on the application tier. At a high level, this is the way that it works:

1. The client makes a Get request to the application tier.

2. The application tier runs the prc_Get stored procedure on the data tier.

3. The data tier executes the request and returns all the relevant files, regardless of the permissions of the requesting user.

4. The application tier then retrieves the permissions associated with the paths returned. If the permissions are in the cache, then the cached permissions are used. If the permissions are not in the cache, they are requested from the data tier.

5. The application tier then evaluates the permissions of the requesting user against the path permissions. Any file that the user does not have access to is removed from the response.

6. The application then sends the trimmed response to the client.

What's important here is that each application tier server keeps a cache of all version control path permissions that it has evaluated. The cache is not persisted and is reset every time the application pool restarts. Cached permissions are also invalidated when the permissions change.

Version control uses Access Control Entries (ACEs) on paths to define which users and groups have access to which files and folders. By default, these permissions are inherited to subdirectories. However, you can set explicit permissions on subdirectories. Each of these explicit permissions results in an additional ACE that the server must store, evaluate, and cache.

To summarize, if you have lots of paths, or lots of paths with explicitly set permissions, then you may run into issues where the cache isn't big enough. In this scenario, the application tier will be constantly retrieving permissions from the data tier, and this may affect version control performance.

ASP.NET Worker Threads Configuration

ASP.NET 2.0 introduced the processModel/autoConfig configuration element that defines how many worker threads should be running to serve requests. The default configuration setting may not work for everyone, since it limits the number of concurrently executing requests per CPU to 12.

This works well for websites with low latency. But in an application like Team Foundation Server that has large operations and higher latency, it may become a bottleneck. If ASP.NET has reached these limits, then users may receive intermittent timeout or "Server does not exist" error messages.

Web Access

In previous versions of Team Foundation Server, the web access component was available as a Power Tool. This meant that it was possible to set up additional servers and install the web access components on them. Using this configuration, you could then implement load balancing and effectively have a load-balanced farm of web access servers.

In the 2010 release, web access is integrated into the product, and runs in the same web application as the web services. It is not possible to install web access by itself, or separate it out from the rest of the web services.

Warehouse

As discussed at the beginning of this chapter, Team Foundation Server 2010 introduced some major architectural changes to support server consolidation and scale-out. One of the commonly requested features from large organizations was the capability to do cross-server (and, therefore, in 2010, cross-collection) reporting. Users wanted the capability to roll up metrics into a company-wide view.

This requirement drove the architectural decision to have a single, shared relational data warehouse and Analysis Services Online Analytical Processing (OLAP) cube per Team Foundation Server instance. This, in itself, is not a big problem. The limitations of the architecture start to emerge when you have multiple project collections attached to an instance that would, by themselves, strain a dedicated data warehouse per collection architecture.

Following are the main limitations with the data warehouse in Team Foundation Server 2010:

> ➤ The relational warehouse has a limit of approximately 1,000 unique reportable fields across all project collections. This is the limit of columns in a SQL Server table, less some overhead.

> ➤ The time to process the OLAP cube is proportional to the number of reportable fields.

> ➤ Different field data types will be expanded out to more than one dimension in the cube. For example, a `datetime` field is expanded out to six dimensions to support the different data slicing requirements of a date: Year Month Date, Year Week Date, Date, Month, Week and Year.

> ➤ Analysis Services does not have a scale-out solution for processing a single cube. You can add additional query servers, or process multiple cubes on separate processing servers and swap them in later. But you cannot process a single cube across multiple servers.

In summary, if your SQL Server hardware and application tier server are not scalability bottlenecks in your environment, there are some architectural limitations in the data warehouse that may affect you.

Team Foundation Proxy

The Team Foundation Proxy is a very effective method of increasing version control performance for users, and reducing the load on the application tier servers.

Following are the biggest limitations in the performance of the proxy server:

➤ Network latency and throughput

➤ Disk size and throughput

➤ Processor speed

Network Performance

The largest factor to influence performance of the proxy server is the network performance between the proxy server and the clients. If the clients are separated from the proxy by a slow link, then the proxy may not provide any benefit at all compared to accessing the application tier directly.

Storage Performance

The amount of disk space available for the version control cache is the next most important factor. If the cache size isn't large enough, then the proxy will be constantly cleaning up and refilling the cache.

Periodically, the cleanup job will scan the entire directory and look for files that have not been accessed recently (more than 14 days by default). The cleanup job will then delete these files.

For caches with large numbers of files, the cleanup algorithm can be quite inefficient and take many hours to identify and clean up stale files. It's important that your disks can handle the normal proxy load in addition to this cleanup load.

To get an estimate of how long this cleanup identification process takes, you can open a command prompt and run a directory listing of your cache directory. Follow these steps:

1. Open a command prompt.

2. Change to your cache directory by typing the following (all on one line):

```
CD /D "C:\Program Files\Microsoft Team Foundation Server 2010\
    Application Tier\Web Services\_tfs_data"
```

3. Perform a directory listing by typing the following:

```
dir /s > NUL
```

This will retrieve the file descriptors of every file in the cache directory, and redirect the output to the NUL device so that it doesn't flood your console. The time it takes for this command to return is roughly the same time it takes for the proxy to identify files for cleanup.

In the case of a cache miss, the proxy server streams the content from the SQL server and writes the stream to the cache drive simultaneously while sending it to the client. In the case of a cache hit, the proxy server streams the content from disk to the client. This means that the memory and processor demands of the proxy server are relatively moderate. Therefore, if the network speed is not a bottleneck, the throughput of the proxy server is directly proportional to the performance of the disks.

MICROSOFT DEVELOPER DIVISION ADOPTION

The adoption of Team Foundation Server at Microsoft is something that has steadily increased since the early days of the product's development. Brian Harry and others on the product team have been blogging the internal adoption numbers over the years and sharing them with the public. You can see an example of these numbers at `http://tinyurl.com/DogfoodStats`.

The Developer Division is the division in which the Team Foundation Server product group works. Until the release of Team Foundation Server 2008, the usage was limited to the product group, and the larger division used the existing Microsoft-only internally developed tools (Product Studio and Source Depot).

Once the division had shipped the 2008 wave of developer tools, there was a huge push to move all the people and systems over to Team Foundation Server. It's fair to say that this was not without its challenges, and the server was constantly patched to meet the scalability demands of the division's 4,000 users and build lab.

These patches made up the majority of the performance-related improvements in Team Foundation Server 2008 Service Pack 1. You can get an overview of these improvements on Harry's blog under the "Performance & Scale" heading at `http://tinyurl.com/TFS2008SP1Changes`.

Although the use of these systems was painful at times for people in the division and across the company, it has pushed the product team to ensure the product scales well. The widely varied usage patterns and user base has proven that the product can scale in real-world use far beyond what any load simulation can do.

PRINCIPLES

If you are in the process of designing a new Team Foundation Server 2010 environment, or you anticipate having to scale your existing installation, there are a number of principles that can be applied generally. When implemented, these principles will also help you achieve your goals of high availability.

Following are the principles:

➤ Spread the components out over multiple servers.

➤ Eliminate single points of failure.

➤ Anticipate growth.

➤ Keep it simple.

The first principle is to spread out the different components that make up a Team Foundation Server environment over multiple physical or virtual servers. The biggest benefit of doing this is to allow each component to make maximum use of the hardware that it sits on without competing with other components. As bottlenecks develop, the hardware for that single component can be scaled up or scaled out, without touching the other components. It's much easier for users to accept "Reporting won't be available this weekend while we upgrade the reporting server hardware" than it is "The whole server won't be available this weekend while we upgrade the hardware." This reduces overall risk, and increases the capability to react to changing usage patterns.

The second principle is the well-known formula for achieving high availability. By introducing redundancy in the environment and eliminating single points of failure, you reduce the chances that a failed component will impact the overall availability of the service. Depending on your goals for availability, this can be the most costly principle to implement. However, for some organizations, the impact of a failure greatly outweighs the infrastructure cost to avoid that failure, and it's an easy decision to make.

The third principle can be a difficult one to gauge and plan for. Team Foundation Server 2010 is a powerful system with some very compelling features. Without proper planning and preparation, the use of these features can overwhelm the planned capacity of the system. The most common limitation that people encounter in a successful Team Foundation Server environment is the lack of storage space. Once people discover the value of an integrated version control, work item tracking, build, and test case automation system, the storage requirements start to grow rapidly. Without careful growth estimates and foresight in the storage design, this can have a dramatic impact on the stability of the system.

The final principle applies not just to Team Foundation Server, but any system. Keep it simple. Simple things are easy to get right, and they usually cost less to set up and maintain.

SOLUTIONS

Now that the limitations have been covered, it's time to discuss some of the solutions. This section covers the different components of Team Foundation Server and some strategies to increase the availability and scalability of them.

Data Tier

If scalability and high availability are important to you, then the data tier is where you will need to invest most of your resources.

High Availability

Availability is not only impacted by unexpected failures, but also expected failures or maintenance work. Without a redundant system in place that can respond to requests while the primary system is undergoing maintenance, the system will be unavailable.

When planning for high availability, the most important database is the `Tfs_Configuration` database. Within the current architecture of the system, this is a single point of failure. An issue with this database will cause the entire instance to be unavailable. Because of this, some people opt to place the configuration database on its own failover cluster and each collection database on a single SQL server. If there is an issue with a single SQL server, it only affects that collection, rather than the whole instance.

SQL Server Failover Clustering

The Microsoft recommendation for implementing high availability on a SQL Server is to use the failover clustering features included in the Enterprise and Data Center editions of Windows Server. *Failover clustering* is the capability for multiple independent servers to work together to increase the availability of applications and services. An application can be moved from one server (or cluster node) to another, as required.

One constraint of clustering is that it requires shared storage attached to each node of the cluster. The storage device must support being connected to one or more servers. When a node fails and the resources are moved to another node, the storage is taken offline from one node, and brought online on the other node.

This attribute of clustering means that having a geographically distributed cluster can be expensive, and you must include the hardware vendor in any issues encountered. The most common solution to this requirement is to use a third-party storage replication product. These products will mirror changes from one storage system to a duplicate storage system at another site to achieve cross-site redundancy.

> *For more information, see Windows clustering and geographically separate sites at* http://support.microsoft.com/kb/280743.

Failover Topologies

One of the drawbacks of clustering is that it requires completely redundant hardware to achieve the increased availability. With the growing trend to increase server utilization and reduce power consumption in data centers, it can be difficult to justify having two identical servers. These servers can only achieve a maximum combined utilization of 50 percent and an ideal utilization of 25 percent (50 percent of one node).

There are two common types of failover clusters:

➤   Single failover cluster instance two-node cluster

➤   Multi-instance cluster

The first type was commonly referred to as an "Active/Passive" cluster. However, this is no longer accurate when you install more than one SQL instance on each node. The second type was referred to as an "Active/Active" cluster, since each node in the cluster would run an instance of SQL.

One solution to increase the utilization of the hardware is to use the second type of failover clusters. In this configuration, you run multiple instances of SQL Server or Analysis Services and configure them to run on each node of the system. In the event of a failure on one of the nodes, the services are moved to another node in the cluster until the original node is available again.

> *For more information, see the "SQL Server 2008 Failover Clustering" whitepaper at* http://tinyurl.com/SQL2008Clusters.

BE CAREFUL OF THE COMPLEXITY

Although a multi-instance cluster is a possible and fully supported configuration, it violates the fourth principle of achieving high availability: "Keep it simple." The Developer Division server at Microsoft used to run a two-node, two-instance cluster configuration with SQL Server running on one node and Analysis Services running on the other. This worked fine until it came time to upgrade from SQL Server 2005 to SQL Server 2008.

The upgrade wizard supported failover cluster upgrades, but it did not support an online upgrade of a failover cluster with multiple resource groups. Because this wasn't a commonly used scenario, it wasn't supported. In the end, moving Analysis Services out of the cluster and off to its own dedicated hardware kept the configuration simple, and allowed the team to utilize the online upgrade capabilities of the upgrade wizard.

In a more complex example of clustering, you could have 10 servers in a multi-instance cluster with each node only 90 percent utilized. Then, when one server fails, one ninth of its load can be distributed to each of the remaining servers. This allows you to increase the utilization of all the servers and maintain the availability goals.

> *For more details on this configuration, see the "SQL Server Consolidation in Microsoft IT" article at* http://msdn.microsoft.com/en-us/library/dd393309.aspx.

SQL Server Database Mirroring

Similar to clustering, mirroring can also be used to meet the availability goals for a Team Foundation Server environment. The advantage of mirroring is that the mirrored server doesn't have to be in the same data center as the primary server. Additionally, the storage isn't shared between the two servers, which means that the expensive and complicated storage replication software isn't required. The replication is handled by SQL Server at the transaction log level.

The drawback of SQL Server mirroring is that Team Foundation Server doesn't support automatic failover from a primary to a mirrored partner server. This means that the recovery time from a failure is limited to how quickly an operator (or some custom developed automation scripts) can bring the mirror server online and instruct Team Foundation Server to use it.

If clustering isn't something that your operations team is familiar with or your hardware supports, then you might want to consider mirroring.

> **DATABASE MIRRORING AT MICROSOFT**
>
> The CodePlex team at Microsoft uses a combination of network load balancing and database mirroring to achieve availability requirements. Team Foundation Server is configured to connect to the virtual name of the load balancer. This means that when they fail-over the mirror from the primary node to the partner node, they don't have to reconfigure the application tier servers for the new server name.
>
> Failover clustering could achieve similar results, but mirroring allows increased flexibility and imposes less strict hardware compatibility requirements.

Scalability

Earlier in this chapter, storage performance was identified as the biggest potential bottleneck of Team Foundation Server performance. In general, the same recommendations that apply for SQL Server also apply for Team Foundation Server.

You should start with the SQL Server Customer Advisory Team (CAT) "Storage Top 10 Best Practices" at `http://tinyurl.com/SQLStorageTop10`. Following are the most important of these ten best practices:

➤ More or faster spindles are better for performance.

➤ Isolate transaction log files from data files at the physical disk level.

➤ Consider the configuration of the `TempDB` database.

➤ Don't overlook some of SQL Server basics.

➤ Don't overlook storage configuration basics.

Physical disks have physical limitations with the performance they can provide. The only way to increase your storage performance is to have faster spindles, or to have more of them to spread the load out onto.

It's fairly common knowledge that SQL transaction logs, data files, and `TempDB` files should reside on physically separate drives. Since all of these are used at the same time, you don't want contention for resources among them. The aforementioned article includes this advice, along with many other storage configuration best practices.

When you have multiple data files for a database, SQL Server uses a proportional fill algorithm when writing to them. This means that if you have two files and one of them is 10 percent full and the other 40 percent full, SQL Server will favor the first file. This leads to unbalanced load among the files and the devices that they reside on.

Your storage is the most critical component of your Team Foundation Server environment. You must collaborate with your storage administrators and vendors to ensure that the storage is optimally configured for your needs.

A STORAGE MISCONFIGURATION

An upgrade of the particularly large Developer Division server at Microsoft occurred in the fall of 2008. In the weeks leading up to the upgrade, the storage vendors had identified an issue on the storage array that required a firmware update. This update was supposed to have minimal impact on storage performance, and the team was told that it could be done while the server was online.

Unfortunately, this was not the case. It turns out that the firmware update resets the configuration back to factory defaults. It disabled the write cache setting on the array. It wasn't until halfway through the upgrade that a team member noticed the storage wasn't performing as expected. After some frantic phone calls and support investigations from the vendor, the missed configuration setting was identified and restored. The upgrade still failed for other reasons, but it certainly taught the team to keep the storage administrators close by during critical times.

SQL Server Enterprise and Data Center Editions

If you separately license one of these high-end SQL Server editions, Team Foundation Server can make use of the extra features that they provide. These features can be used to increase the availability and scalability of the system.

> *For more information on the features available, see "Compare Edition Features" at* www.microsoft.com/sqlserver/2008/en/us/editions-compare.aspx.

Following are the additional features in these editions that Team Foundation Server has been designed to make use of:

➤ Online index operations

➤ Page compression

➤ Table and index partitioning

➤ Larger read-ahead buffering

➤ Cube perspectives

Index rebuilds and reorganizes will be automatically done using the WITH ONLINE condition as part of the Optimize Databases job. Normally, indexes are taken offline, and operations that rely on those indexes are blocked while they are rebuilt.

Page compression can yield significant storage savings and increased storage performance. However, compression increases processor utilization, so be sure that you have enough available capacity. When you create a new collection on a SQL Server Enterprise edition server, the majority of the version control tables are enabled for compression. With page compression on these tables, storage usage can be reduced to a quarter of the uncompressed size.

UPGRADING TO ENTERPRISE OR DATA CENTER EDITION

If you upgrade an existing SQL Server instance that hosts Team Foundation Server databases, compression will not be automatically used for existing collections. Existing collections will need to have compression enabled and their indexes rebuilt to see the benefits of compression. This process isn't documented by Microsoft, so you will need to contact Microsoft Support and they will guide you through. Newly created collections will have compression enabled automatically.

If you are using SQL Server 2008 R2 Data Center edition, it's a new edition that includes all the Enterprise edition features. It was released after Team Foundation Server 2010, which means that the additional capabilities aren't detected or utilized. If you find yourself in this situation, you will need to install Team Foundation Server 2010 Service Pack 1.

On large systems with many files and workspaces, the `tbl_LocalVersion` table can become very large and unwieldy. At Microsoft, this table peaked at 5 billion rows. This caused all kinds of problems, most notably that it would take more than a week to rebuild the index. If it finished rebuilding, it would need to start again because of the high churn in the table. The obvious solution to this was to implement table partitioning and split the table into more manageable chunks. Since this isn't documented, if you have a need for table partitioning, you must contact Microsoft Support and they will guide you through the process.

Enterprise edition uses 1024KB read-ahead buffering compared to 64KB in Standard edition. This increased buffering makes some of Team Foundation Server's expensive queries faster.

A *cube perspective* is a definition that allows users to see the cube in a simpler way. If you are using the Enterprise edition of Analysis Services, Team Foundation Server defines individual perspectives for work items, builds, and so on, in addition to the Team System cube.

Application Tier and Web Access

As discussed at the beginning of this chapter, there have been some significant changes to the architecture of the system. These changes enable the application tier to be scaled out and meet your scalability and high-availability requirements.

Stateless

Besides the change to support 64-bit architectures, changing web access to be stateless was the biggest change in the application tier from previous versions. Before this change, users would lose their sessions, as well as the page they were on or the changes they were making. The lost session was usually triggered by a timeout, an application pool recycle, or by being directed to a different back-end server by a load balancer. This was extremely frustrating.

The stateless implementation of web access dehydrates and rehydrates the client's session as needed. This eliminates the session timeouts, and allows any application tier to serve a user's request.

Load Balancing

Load balancing is an important feature for scalability and high availability. It allows the load to be spread across multiple servers. This increases the number of requests that can be handled by the system, as well as providing protection against planned and unplanned server downtime.

There are many load-balancing options. Whether you use Windows Network Load Balancing, the IIS Application Request Routing (ARR) extension, or a third-party load-balancer device, there are some settings that you need to consider. Table 18-3 provides an overview of these settings and their recommended configurations.

TABLE 18-3: Recommended Load Balancer Configuration Settings

SETTING	DESCRIPTION
Idle timeout	60 minutes
Affinity or Stickiness	No Affinity
IP Pass Through	Enabled

Idle Timeout

Most load balancers have an idle connection timeout setting. This is because every connection consumes memory, and they want to close the connection if it's idle. The usual default setting of 5 minutes can cause problems with version control in Team Foundation Server.

If the client sends a request that takes a long time to calculate in SQL Server (such as a large Get), there will be no data transferred over the connection and it will appear to be idle. If the setting is not long enough, then the load balancer will close the connection and the client will get an error like "The connection was forcibly closed by the remote server." In this scenario, you want to match the idle timeout setting of the load balancer with the request timeout setting of Team Foundation Server, which is 60 minutes.

Affinity

Affinity is the setting that determines if a client should be routed to the same back-end server for successive requests.

Some operations in Team Foundation Server can take a long time to process. Some operations (such as downloading version control file content) will use multiple threads. If you have affinity enabled, then it's possible that the load won't be evenly distributed between your back-end servers. In the case of a two-server load-balanced instance, it's possible for one server to be overloaded processing most of the requests, while the other server is sitting idle. For this reason, you may want to disable affinity.

Unfortunately, some load-balancing technologies don't handle authentication well. Users may receive generic authentication errors if they were authenticated against one back-end server, but then are load-balanced to another back-end server. In this scenario, you will need to fix the authentication issues or enable affinity.

IP Pass Through

One of the useful diagnostic tools in Team Foundation Server is the activity log. (See Chapter 21 more information on this.) The activity log records the IP address of each request in the system. The use of a load balancer can mask the actual IP address of the client. In this case, the activity log will show that the load balancer is the only client of the system.

To avoid this masking, you will want to enable the IP pass-through setting or some equivalent setting. If the load balancer sets the `X-Forwarded-For` HTTP header with the actual client IP address, then the activity log will show this address.

Advanced Load Balancing

One of the limitations discussed earlier was the cache of ACEs on the application tier. One way to overcome this is to minimize the number of paths that an application tier needs to cache.

Web service requests for each project collection are prefixed with the collection name. If your load balancer supports it, you can work around this limitation by directing traffic to different application tiers based on the collection in the URL requested. For example, requests to `/Collection1` get sent to `Server1`, and requests for `/Collection2` and `/Collection3` get sent to `Server2`.

ASP.NET Worker Threads

As discussed earlier, the default configuration of ASP.NET limits the number of concurrently executing requests per CPU to 12. You can check to see if you are reaching this limit by monitoring the ASP.NET Applications\Requests in Application Queue performance counter. If this is a non-zero value, then it means you definitely have a performance problem.

To enable increased concurrency, you can follow the guidance in the KB821268 article at `http://support.microsoft.com/kb/821268`. This describes the steps to change the `maxWorkerThreads` and `maxIoThreads` settings.

If your bottleneck is the throughput of your SQL server, then the majority of the concurrent requests will be sitting idle waiting for a response from the data tier. In this scenario, you can safely increase the settings to allow more concurrent connections.

Version Control Cache Directory

If you have a large or busy server, the version control cache directory is going to be important for you. By default, it lives in the `\Web Services\_tfs_data` directory where Team Foundation Server is installed. This directory can become very large, very quickly, and you should consider moving it to its own drive. There are two ways to move this directory.

The first way doesn't require any Team Foundation Server configuration changes. You can use the Disk Management administrative tools and use a mount point to mount the available drive to the `_tfs_data` path.

The second way is to follow these steps:

1. On the application-tier server, create a cache folder.

2. Right-click the folder, and click Properties. The Properties dialog box for the folder opens.

3. Click the Security tab, and click Add.

4. Add the local group TFS_APPTIER_SERVICE_WPG, and click OK.

5. Select both the Read and Write check boxes, clear all other check boxes, and click OK.

6. Open Windows Explorer, and browse to C:\Program Files\Microsoft Team Foundation Server 2010\Application Tier\Web Services.

7. Open the Web.config file in a text or XML editor, and locate the <appSettings> section.

8. Add a new line within the <appSettings> section and change the value to match the new location:

```
<add key="dataDirectory" value="D:\Cache" />
```

9. Save and close the Web.config file. The application pool will be recycled automatically. The next time a file is downloaded from the application tier, it will be cached to this new location.

Team Foundation Proxy

The proxy server is completely stateless, and has always supported being in a load-balanced configuration. If your proxy server is overloaded, the simplest solution is to set up an additional server and configure network load balancing.

When designing a proxy server for scalability, you should prioritize the following things:

1. Proximity to build servers and users

2. Storage size

3. Storage performance

If your application tier is in another building or another city, then having a proxy server in the same building as your biggest users is important. You want to keep the latency low for the most benefit.

Given the choice of storage size or storage speed, you should prioritize for storage size. For example, there's no point having high-performance solid-state drives for your proxy if they're not big enough to hold a day's worth of files.

The more storage that the proxy server can use, the more files and versions of files it can store. This increases the chance of a cache hit, and decreases the number of times a file must be downloaded from the main server.

Like the application tier, you should also change the version control cache directory for the proxy server to be a dedicated drive.

 For more information, see "How to: Change Cache Settings for Team Foundation Server Proxy" at http://msdn.microsoft.com/en-us/library/ms400763.aspx.

Virtualization

Virtualization can be a great solution for achieving your high-availability goals. You can configure your application tier and data tier servers as virtual machine guests on a highly available host machine. If the underlying host requires planned or unplanned maintenance, you can perform a quick migration of the guest machines to another host without interruption.

> *This configuration is beyond the scope of this chapter, and you should refer to the article "Virtualization: Achieving High Availability for Hyper-V" at* http:// technet.microsoft.com/en-us/magazine/2008.10.higha.aspx *along with Using Hyper-V and Failover Clustering at* http://technet.microsoft.com/ en-us/library/cc732181(WS.10).aspx.

Microsoft supports virtualization of Team Foundation Server in supported virtualization environments. For more information, see the following pages on the Microsoft website:

➤ Microsoft server software and supported virtualization environments at http:// go.microsoft.com/fwlink/?LinkId=196061

➤ Support policy for Microsoft software running in non-Microsoft hardware virtualization software at http://go.microsoft.com/fwlink/?LinkId=196062

➤ Support partners for non-Microsoft hardware virtualization software at http:// go.microsoft.com/fwlink/?LinkId=196063

➤ Server Virtualization (officially supported products) at http://go.microsoft .com/fwlink/?LinkId=196072

You should also read the best practices and performance recommendations on "Running SQL Server 2008 in a Hyper-V Environment" at http://tinyurl.com/SQLHyperV. Regardless of your virtualization technology, the tests and recommendations are very relevant.

SUMMARY

This chapter explored some of the limitations of Team Foundation Server 2010, as well as the issues faced by large and busy environments. You learned that the performance of Team Foundation Server is tied directly to the performance of SQL Server. Finally, solutions and best practices were discussed for overcoming these limitations to meet your scalability and high-availability goals.

Chapter 19 discusses another important aspect of Team Foundation Server administration — disaster recovery.

19

Disaster Recovery

WHAT'S IN THIS CHAPTER?

➤ Using the backup-and-restore wizard

➤ Walking through step-by-step examples of how to back up and restore your Team Foundation Server environment

➤ Learning about backup plan considerations

Disaster recovery is an important topic, but it is too broad to cover in a single chapter. The purpose of this chapter is to prompt you to think about what your disaster-recovery plan is and how it relates to Team Foundation Server.

> For more information, see "Proven SQL Server Architectures for High Availability and Disaster Recovery" at http://tinyurl.com/SQLDR.

BUSINESS CONTINUITY AND RECOVERY GOALS

Before discussing disaster recovery in detail, let's establish some goals. You should consult with the team who will be using Team Foundation Server and ask some important questions. The answer to each question has an effect on the cost and complexity of your solution. Following are examples of some questions to ask:

➤ In the event of a hardware failure (for example, a hard drive crash or a network outage), how quickly must service be restored?

➤ In the event of a major disaster (for example, a hurricane or an earthquake), how quickly must service be restored?

> ➤ If the service is unavailable for a period of time, what is the cost to the business?

> ➤ What is an acceptable level of data loss (for example, 15 minutes or 15 hours)?

> ➤ How long and how often should backup copies be kept (for example, seven days, seven weeks, or seven years)?

> ➤ When can backup media be overwritten? When should backup media be retired? How is backup media retired?

> ➤ Where are backups kept (for example, on-site, in another building, another city, or another continent)?

> ➤ Who should have access to the backups? Are they encrypted?

The answers to these questions will be different for every organization. At one end of the scale will be the highly regulated financial and engineering industries. At the other end of the scale will likely be the small companies and individuals. With different needs and requirements, the costs will be very different depending on the chosen solution.

DEFINING RESPONSIBILITIES

Having a robust and reliable disaster-recovery plan is an important responsibility of any Team Foundation Server administrator. In large organizations, this responsibility may fall on a central business continuity team, or maybe the database administration team.

Regardless of who is responsible, as the Team Foundation Server administrator, it is your responsibility to ensure that the implementation of the plan is supported by Team Foundation Server. Backups that were not taken correctly, or that cannot be restored, are a risk to the business and effectively useless. For this reason, it's important to not only have a backup plan, but to regularly test that plan to ensure that it's working for when you need it.

BACKING UP TEAM FOUNDATION SERVER

Team Foundation Server includes many components. There's the data tier, application tier, Reporting Services, SharePoint server, Lab Management environment, and Team Build.

The single most important component to back up is the set of databases on the data tier. These are the "crown jewels" of Team Foundation Server, where the majority of the information is kept. If you are unable to recover at least these databases in the event of a disaster, it's time to look for a new job.

For example, if you are able to recover a collection database, the relational warehouse and Online Analytical Processing (OLAP) cube can be rebuilt from the original data. It takes time, but it's possible. As another example, if you can restore the source control data, then you can re-create a build from that source.

Components to Back Up

Table 19-1 provides an overview of the different components that should be backed up.

TABLE 19-1: Components to Back Up

COMPONENT	ARTIFACTS
Data Tier	Configuration database, collection databases, warehouse database, Reporting Services databases, Reporting Services encryption key
Application Tier	Configuration settings, usernames and passwords, custom controls
SharePoint	SharePoint products configuration databases, site collection custom controls, encryption keys databases
Lab Management	System Center Virtual Machine Manager (SCVMM) configuration, virtual machines, lab environments, VM templates
Team Build	Server configurations, custom activities
Clients	No client-side backups required, although you might want to use shelvesets for saving in-progress work to the server

SharePoint Products

For the officially supported procedures to back up SharePoint products that are associated with a Team Foundation Server, you should refer to "Backup and recovery overview" at `http://tinyurl .com/SharePointBackup`. In particular, if you have any customizations to SharePoint products, you must also back those up so that they can be reproduced on a new server.

Reporting Services Encryption Key

Reporting Services uses an encryption key to encrypt data source connection strings, report credentials, and shared data source credentials. You should include the encryption key backup and the associated password to restore the key in your backup plan.

> *For more information, see "Back Up the Reporting Services Encryption Key" at* `http://msdn.microsoft.com/en-us/library/ms400729.aspx`.

YOU LOST THE REPORTING SERVICES ENCRYPTION KEY?

An encryption key? That must be important, right? Have you ever wondered what would happen if you didn't back it up and you lost it? Or, even worse, what if you did back it up, but you don't know the password to restore it.

It turns out that it's not the end of the world. If you are unable to restore the encryption key, you will have to use the Reporting Services Configuration Manager to delete the encrypted data. After you delete the encrypted content, you must create the encrypted data again.

continues

(continued)

Without re-creating the deleted data, the following will happen:

➤ Connection strings in shared data sources are deleted. Users who run reports get the error, "The ConnectionString property has not been initialized."

➤ Stored credentials are deleted. Reports and shared data sources are reconfigured to use prompted credentials.

➤ Reports that are based on models (and require shared data sources configured with stored or no credentials) will not run.

➤ Subscriptions are deactivated.

For more information, see the "Deleting and Re-creating Encryption Keys" article on MSDN at `http://msdn.microsoft.com/en-us/library/ms156010.aspx`.

Lab Management

If you are using Lab Management in your Team Foundation Server environment, you will need to include backups of your SCVMM environment.

> *For more information, see "Backing Up and Restoring the VMM Database" at* `http://go.microsoft.com/fwlink/?linkid=150302`.

Types of Database Backups

SQL Server has the following recovery modes, which are set on a per-database basis:

➤ *FULL recovery mode* — In this mode, each transaction is kept in the transaction log until the log is backed up and a checkpoint is set.

➤ *SIMPLE recovery mode* — In this mode, each transaction is written to the transaction log, but it can be overwritten at a later time.

The default recovery mode used by SQL Server for all user databases is FULL. The recovery mode of a database can be changed at any time without impacting currently running commands.

TRANSACTION LOG GROWING OUT OF CONTROL?

In FULL recovery mode, without transaction log backups, the log will continue to grow until it reaches the configured limit. If the log is set to AUTOGROW, it will continue growing until the disk is full if no limit is set.

When either the database or transaction log is full, users will receive a "Database is full" message when performing operations in Team Foundation Server.

If your database recovery targets are met without doing transaction log backups, then you may want to change your databases to SIMPLE recovery mode. This means that the transaction logs will only grow to the size of your largest transaction.

Full Database Backups

At least one full database backup is required to restore a database. A full database backup includes the entire contents of the database at the time the database backup finished. It does not include any uncommitted transactions.

Typically, full backups are performed once a month or once a week, depending on the rate of data change.

For more information, see "Full Database Backups" on MSDN at `http://go.microsoft.com/fwlink/?LinkId=115462.`

DATABASE EDITIONS AND VERSIONS

When you use the built-in native SQL Server backup and restore functions, you should be aware of the version compatibility. For example, a database backup from SQL Server 2008 R2 cannot be restored to a server with a down-level version, like SQL Server 2008 SP1.

Additionally, if you create a backup with compression enabled, it can only be restored on a server that also has compression available. This can be a problem when moving a database from a SQL Server Enterprise server to a SQL Server Standard server.

Differential Database Backups

A *differential backup* includes everything that has changed since the last full backup. This is sometimes referred to as a "diff" or *incremental backup*. Since a differential backup is only recording differences, it usually takes less time and uses less storage than a full backup.

Over time, as more data changes in the database since the last full backup, the differential backup will become larger. At some point, the differential backup may become larger than the original full backup, and it will be more efficient to run a new full backup. Typically, differential backups are performed once per day.

For more information, see "Differential Database Backups" at `http://go.microsoft.com/fwlink/?LinkId=158819.`

Transaction Log Backups

When a database is in FULL recovery mode, the transaction log contains all the data changes in the database. By performing transaction log backups (along with full and differential backups), you can later restore a database to a point in time, or a specific transaction. Typically, transaction log backups are performed anywhere from every 5 minutes to every 60 minutes, depending on data recovery goals.

> *For more information, see "Working with Transaction Log Backups" at* `http://go.microsoft.com/fwlink/?LinkId=115463`.

Important Considerations

Team Foundation Server has two types of databases: the `Tfs_Configuration` database and the collection databases. Every user who has access to Team Foundation Server has their name, e-mail, and group memberships synchronized with Active Directory. Rather than synchronizing this information with each individual collection, it is stored in the configuration database.

Because of this dependency between the databases, it is vital that the configuration database and collection databases are backed up in a way that they can be restored to a common point in time. Achieving this can become more difficult when your configuration database is on a different server or instance than your collection databases.

If this synchronization between the databases is not maintained, then it is possible that an identity is referenced in a collection database that doesn't exist in the configuration database. Team Foundation Server does not handle this scenario well, and the databases will be in an inconsistent state. Users may lose their permissions to their projects and other data inconsistencies may be seen.

> *If you do find yourself in the situation where your configuration and collection backups are out of sync, you should contact Microsoft Support (*`http://support.microsoft.com`*). There are some cases where the identity data can be reconstructed to overcome the inconsistencies. However, you should design your backup plan to avoid this situation.*

SQL Marked Transactions

The SQL Server solution to ensure synchronization across databases and database servers is to use marked transactions. By establishing a transaction that spans all the databases in the environment, it provides a common point that can be restored to and ensure synchronization.

New Collections

Each time a new collection is created on a Team Foundation Server instance, a new database will be created. You must ensure that this database is added to your backup plan. It's best if new databases are backed up automatically by your backup scripts, so that they aren't accidentally excluded.

Virtualization and Backups

If you are virtualizing your data tier, you can back up the entire virtual machine that your SQL server is running in. But you should consider SQL database backups as well. Depending on the virtualization backup technology used, it may not ensure transactional consistency within the database. If transactional consistency is not maintained, then it is not safe to restore from your virtual machine backups, and you may encounter data loss.

In an environment with multiple SQL servers, it's impossible to keep the database backups synchronized without using marked transactions. Additionally, transaction log backups can be run much more frequently than a backup of a virtual machine, and they allow a much finer-grained recovery point.

Data Security

One of the most common breaches of data security is mishandled backup media. After you have defined how you are going to run your SQL backups, you must define how you are going to store them to meet your retention and off-site backup requirements.

Since a database backup contains all of your data, it would be a big problem if it weren't adequately protected and an untrusted person was able to restore it. This person could restore the data to another server and use his or her own administrative credentials to access the contents of the databases.

For this reason, it's important to consider the security of your backups in the same way you consider the security of your server itself. Consider using encryption, as well as secure transport, handling, and storage of your backups.

Software Versions, Installation Media, and License Keys

In the event of a major disaster or a hardware failure, the backups by themselves are not usually enough to bring the server back online. You will also need software installed to restore those backups to. You should consider the following software in your backup plan:

➤ Windows installation media and product keys

➤ Drivers for the server and storage hardware

➤ Team Foundation Server installation media and product key

➤ SQL Server installation media and product keys

➤ Third-party backup software (if you are not using SQL Server backups)

➤ Service Packs for Windows, SQL Server, and Team Foundation Server

CREATING A BACKUP PLAN

Creating a reliable backup plan can be quite a daunting task. Fortunately, the Team Foundation Server team has made it simple by making a backup-and-restore wizard available as a Power Tool.

> *Power Tool releases are small releases that are made available between major releases to address customer adoption blockers and gaps in the product. Typically, they ship every three to six months. They are releases that don't change core functionality of the main product. They don't go through the same level of testing as the major releases. The latest version of the Team Foundation Server Power Tools can be downloaded from* http://msdn.microsoft.com /en-us/vstudio/bb980963.

The Team Foundation Server backup-and-restore Power Tool takes care of two of the important backup considerations discussed earlier:

➤ It configures and uses SQL marked transactions to keep the databases in sync.

➤ It automatically adds new collections to the backup plan so that they don't miss out on backups.

To access the Backup Plan wizard, open the Team Foundation Server Administration Console. As seen in Figure 19-1, when you select the Team Foundation Backups option for the first time, there is a link to create a backup plan.

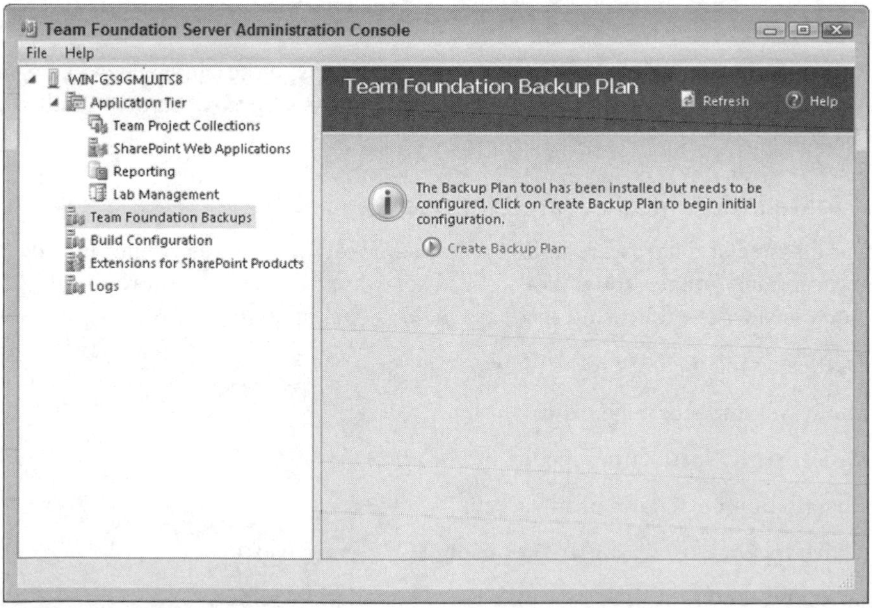

FIGURE 19-1: Team Foundation Server Administration Console

Once you click the link, the Backup Plan Wizard appears. Figure 19-2, shows that the wizard is very similar to the configuration wizard that you used to configure Team Foundation Server for the first time. The left pane shows each of the wizard pages, and the wizard ends with a Review screen before making any changes.

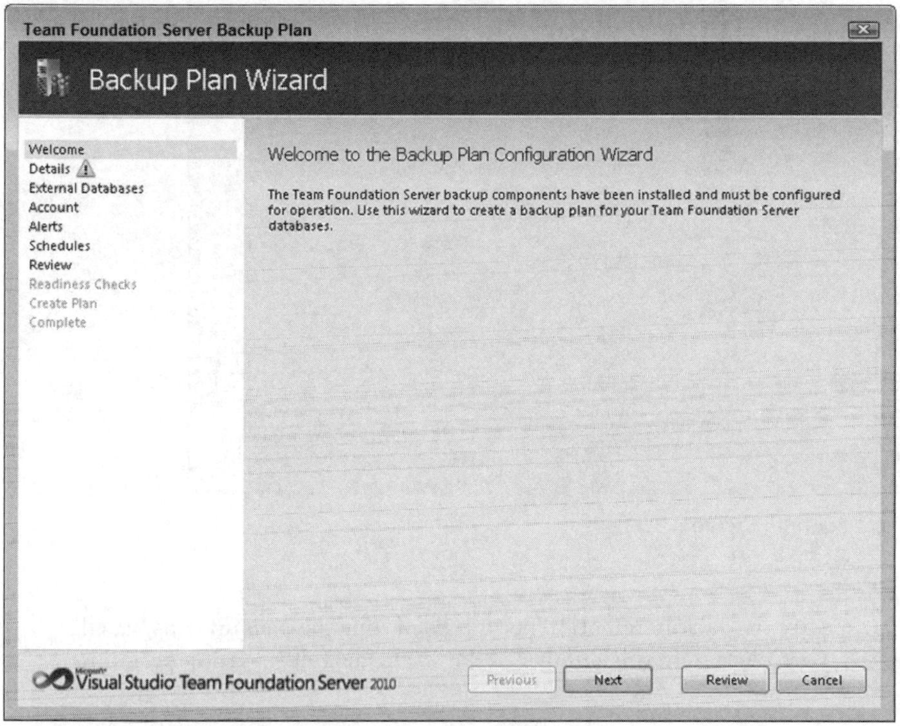

FIGURE 19-2: Backup Plan Wizard

The first step of the wizard allows you to specify a location to store the backups. This is specified as a UNC network path, which means that the share must already exist. When you specify the backup account later in the wizard, it will be given read and write access to the share.

Even though the wizard asks for a Network Backup Path, it is possible to back up to the local machine. To do this, you must create a share that is accessible by the backup account, and then specify the local machine as backup path. For example, in Figure 19-3, the path specified refers to the name of the SQL server itself. The advanced options allow you to use an alternate file extension for the backup files. By default, full backup files have the extension .bak and transaction log backups have the extension .trn.

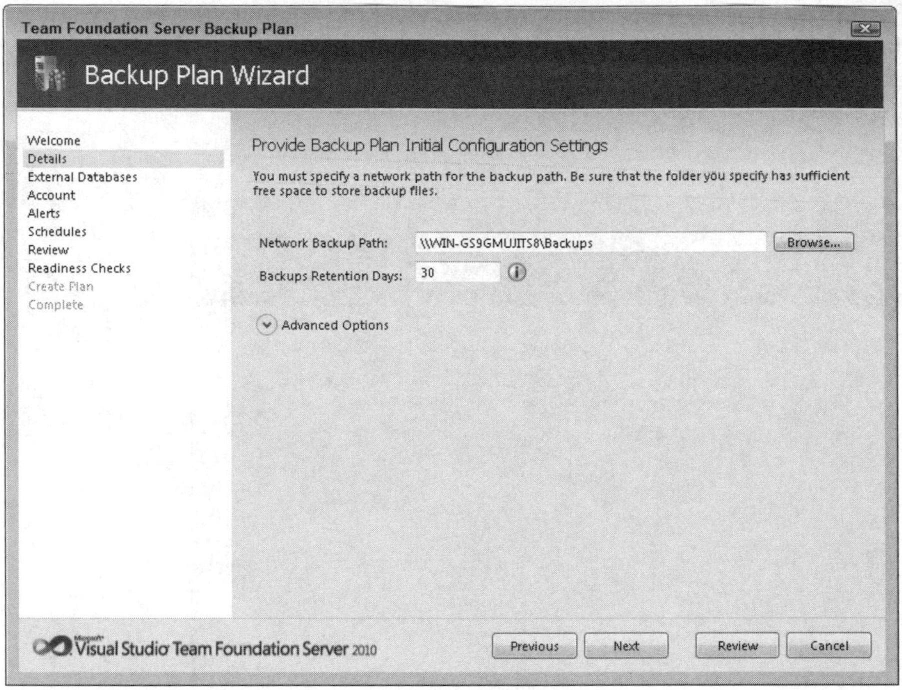

FIGURE 19-3 Initial configuration screen

It is also possible to specify the backup retention period. Each time the backup runs, it will delete any backups that are older than this number of days. The default retention period is one month.

If you have Team Foundation Server installed on a server operating system and you are not using the "Basic" configuration of the server, you will have the option to back up the SharePoint Products and Reporting Services databases, as shown in Figure 19-4. These databases may be located on the same SQL server as your Team Foundation Server, or on a remote instance. After selecting the instance, you must choose the SharePoint configuration database that you wish to include in your backup plan.

The Team Foundation Server backup plan runs as a scheduled task on the application tier that you ran the wizard from. As part of setting up the backup plan, the wizard will add a table to each database included in the plan. This table is required to establish a marked transaction that spans multiple databases.

To add this marked transaction table, the backup account specified in Figure 19-5 will be given the instance-level permission of ALTER ANY DATABASE. Additionally, the account will be given read and write access to the network backup path specified earlier in the wizard.

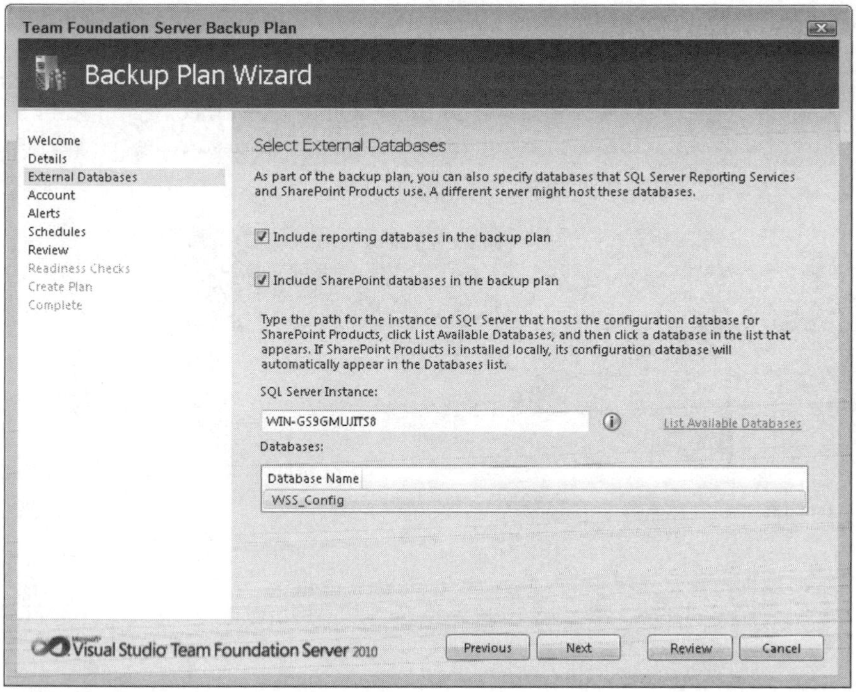

FIGURE 19-4: External database selection screen

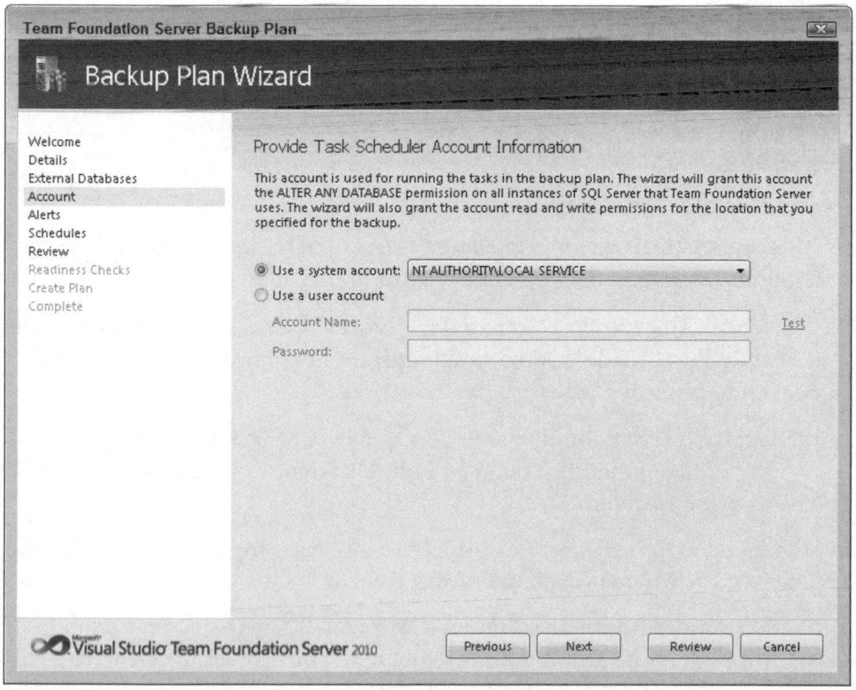

FIGURE 19-5: Account information screen

As an administrator, you will want to know when the backup fails so that you can investigate and fix it. The Alerts page of the wizard (shown in Figure 19-6) allows you to specify an e-mail address to send alerts to. Since the Backup Plan Wizard has access to the Team Foundation Server configuration database, it can retrieve the e-mail server settings from the instance. If you want to change the e-mail server or the From address, then you must change it before starting the Backup Plan Wizard.

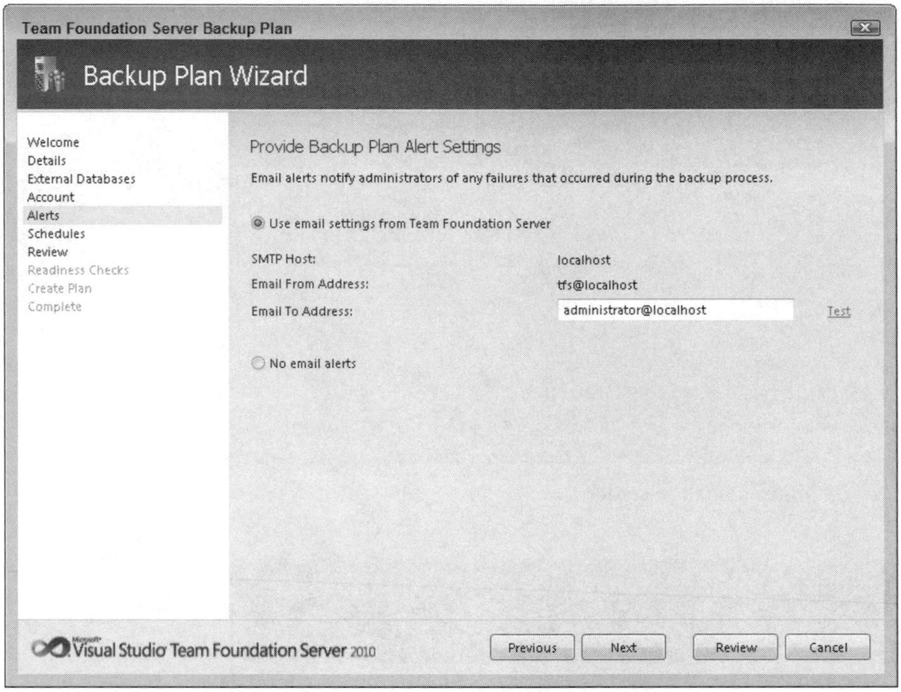

FIGURE 19-6: Alert configuration screen

As discussed earlier in this chapter, there are three different types of SQL Server backups. You can choose one of these three options from the Backup Plan Wizard dialog shown in Figure 19-7:

➤ If it's acceptable to your business to lose up to a day's worth of data and your database is not very big, the Nightly Full Schedule is the simplest option to choose. This will schedule a full database backup to happen once every day.

➤ If you have a large database with a lot of changes every day, and you need the capability to restore to the latest possible point in time, the "Full, Differential, and Transactional Schedule" is the best option to choose.

➤ If you don't use the server very often, or you don't have any need for a regularly scheduled backup, you can choose the Manual Backup Only option.

Similar to the server configuration wizard, the Backup Plan Wizard allows you to review and confirm your settings (Figure 19-8) before any changes are made to your server. Review the settings and, if they are correct, click Verify to start the verification process.

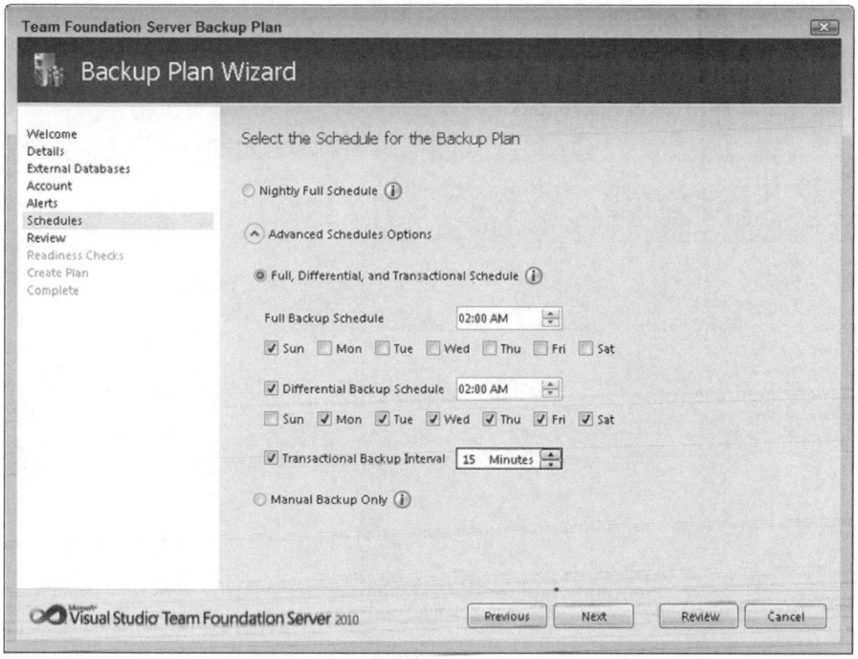

Team Foundation Server Backup Plan

Backup Plan Wizard

Welcome
Details
External Databases
Account
Alerts
Schedules
Review
Readiness Checks
Create Plan
Complete

Select the Schedule for the Backup Plan

○ Nightly Full Schedule ⓘ

⌄ Advanced Schedules Options

◉ Full, Differential, and Transactional Schedule ⓘ

Full Backup Schedule   02:00 AM

☑ Sun ☐ Mon ☐ Tue ☐ Wed ☐ Thu ☐ Fri ☐ Sat

☑ Differential Backup Schedule   02:00 AM

☐ Sun ☑ Mon ☑ Tue ☑ Wed ☑ Thu ☑ Fri ☑ Sat

☑ Transactional Backup Interval   15   Minutes

○ Manual Backup Only ⓘ

Visual Studio Team Foundation Server 2010

Previous   Next   Review   Cancel

FIGURE 19-7: Backup schedule screen

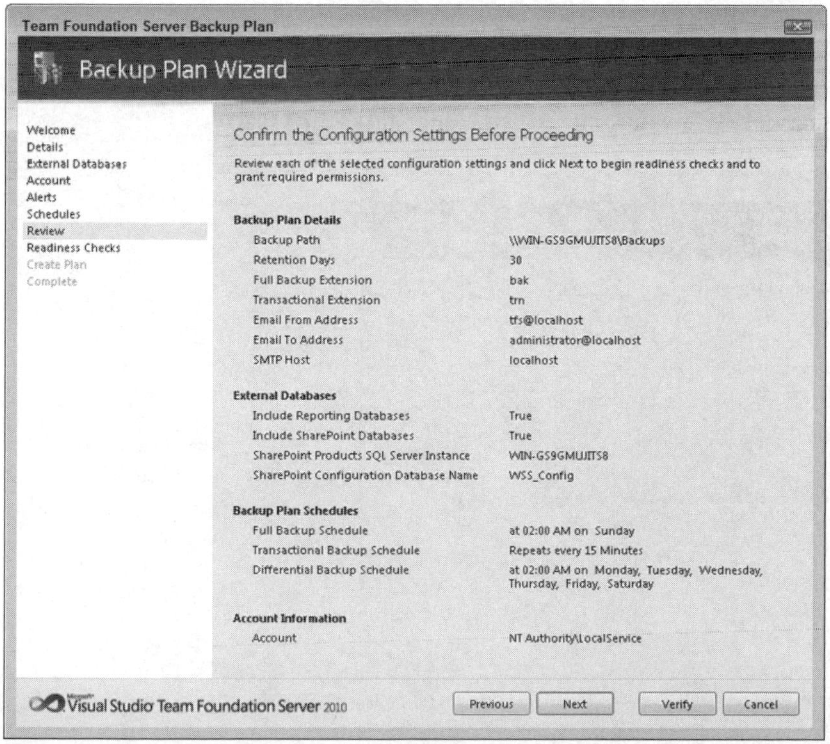

Team Foundation Server Backup Plan

Backup Plan Wizard

Welcome
Details
External Databases
Account
Alerts
Schedules
Review
Readiness Checks
Create Plan
Complete

Confirm the Configuration Settings Before Proceeding

Review each of the selected configuration settings and click Next to begin readiness checks and to
grant required permissions.

Backup Plan Details

Backup Path	\\WIN-GS9GMUJITS8\Backups
Retention Days	30
Full Backup Extension	bak
Transactional Extension	trn
Email From Address	tfs@localhost
Email To Address	administrator@localhost
SMTP Host	localhost

External Databases

Include Reporting Databases	True
Include SharePoint Databases	True
SharePoint Products SQL Server Instance	WIN-GS9GMUJITS8
SharePoint Configuration Database Name	WSS_Config

Backup Plan Schedules

Full Backup Schedule	at 02:00 AM on Sunday
Transactional Backup Schedule	Repeats every 15 Minutes
Differential Backup Schedule	at 02:00 AM on Monday, Tuesday, Wednesday, Thursday, Friday, Saturday

Account Information

Account	NT Authority\LocalService

Visual Studio Team Foundation Server 2010

Previous   Next   Verify   Cancel

FIGURE 19-8: Configuration review screen

Without making any changes to the system, the Readiness Checks screen shown in Figure 19-9 verifies that the configuration changes can be made and the backup plan can be set up without any problems. If any of the checks don't pass, then you must address them before you can continue. When you are ready to create the backup plan, click Create Plan.

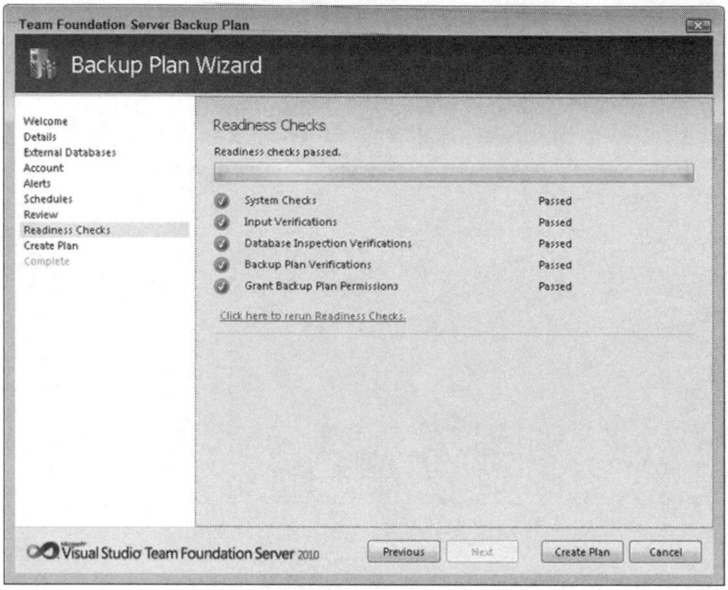

FIGURE 19-9: Readiness Checks screen

The final stage of the wizard (shown in Figure 19-10) is where the server permissions are set, the tables for marked transactions are created, and the scheduled tasks are created.

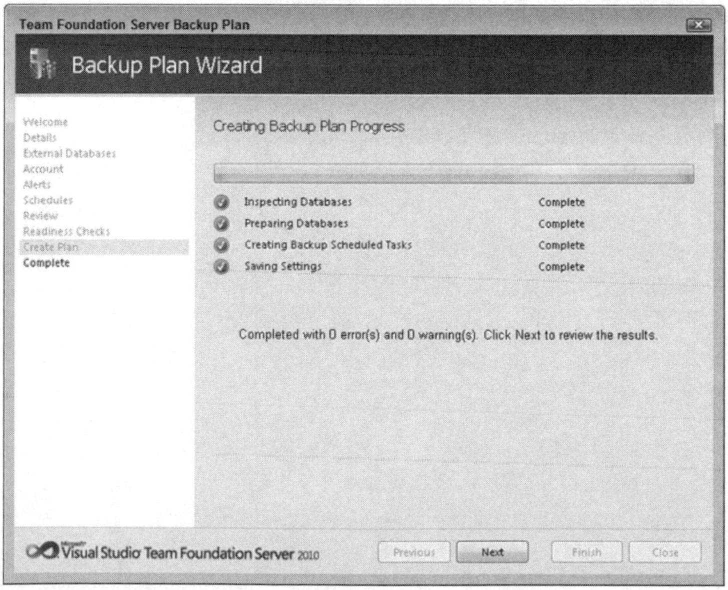

FIGURE 19-10: Backup plan progress screen

Team Foundation Server Backup Plan Details

Once you have configured a backup plan, the Team Foundation Backups tab in the Team Foundation Server Administration Console will show the details of the backup plan. The details screen in Figure 19-11 shows configuration settings such as the account the backup will run as and the path that backups are being sent to, along with the databases and SQL servers that are included in the backup plan.

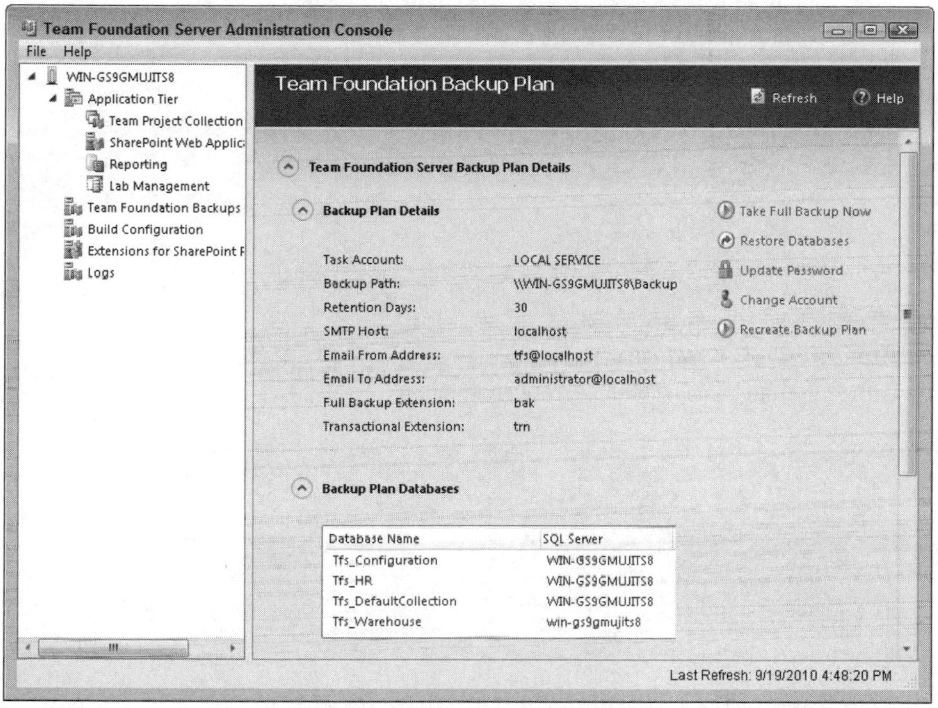

FIGURE 19-11: Team Foundation Backup Plan details

As shown in Figure 19-12, the lower half of the Backup Plan Details screen shows you the scheduled tasks information. This is the same information you will see if you open Task Scheduler from the Control Panel in Windows. It shows you each of the scheduled tasks that were created as part of the plan, when they are scheduled to run, when they last ran, and the result of the previous run.

The backup scripts are executed using the Task Scheduler service that is built into Windows (Figure 19-13). This is a service that exists on all versions and editions of Windows (unlike the SQL Job Agent, which isn't available in SQL Server Express Edition). This means that the backup plan can be used even if you are using SQL Server Express for your databases.

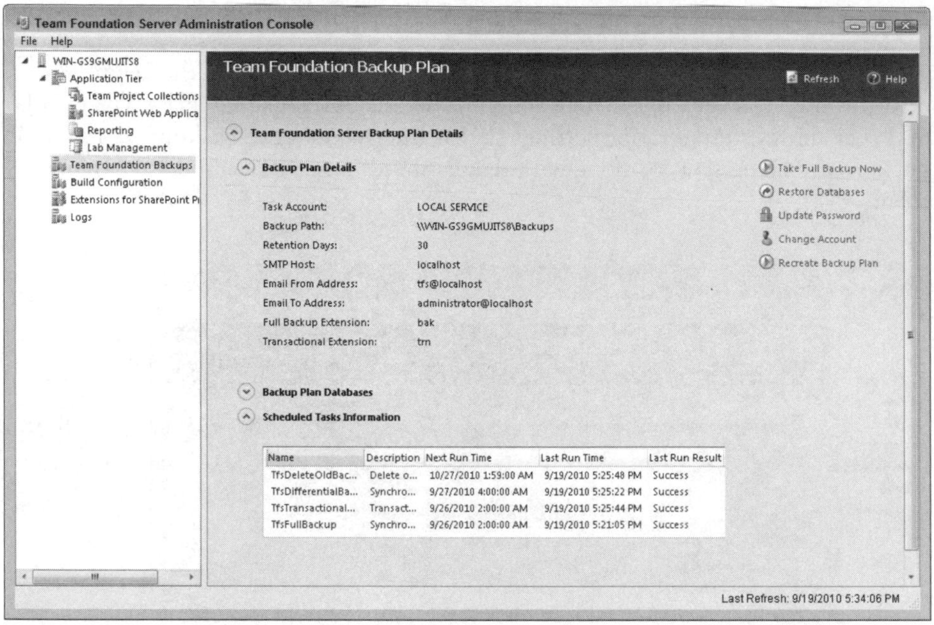

FIGURE 19-12: Backup Plan Details with scheduled task information

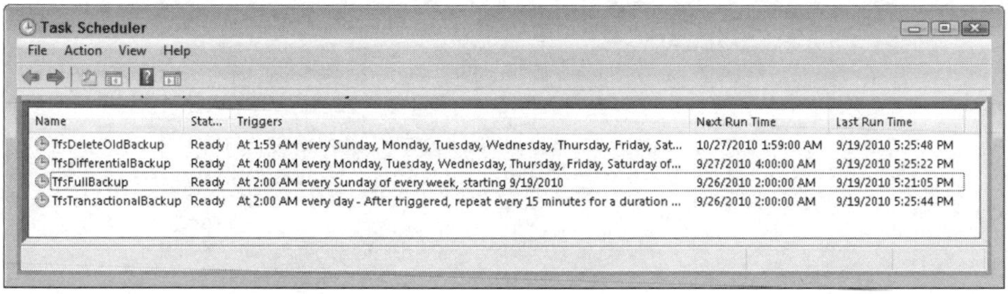

FIGURE 19-13: Windows Task Scheduler

TfsConfigPT.exe and ConfigPT.xml

If you look at the actions associated with each of the scheduled tasks, you will find that they are each running the same command with a parameter. Following are the parameters:

➤   `TfsFullBackup`

➤   `TfsDifferentialBackup`

➤   `TfsTransactionalBackup`

➤   `TfsDeleteOldBackup`

The first three of these options run the three different types of database backups, and the fourth option will scan and delete backups that are older than the configured retention period.

The `ConfigPT.xml` file can be found in the configured UNC network backup location that you specified earlier, as shown in Figure 19-3. It includes the databases that will be backed up, the retention period, backup file extensions, and the e-mail settings.

From the Backup Plan Details screen, there are a number of links on the right-hand side that let you reconfigure the backup plan, change accounts and passwords, start the database restore wizard, and manually start a backup.

Take Full Backup Now

Once you've created a backup plan, regardless of which schedule option you chose, you can manually take a full database backup at any time. This is done by clicking "Take Full Backup Now" in the Backup Plan Details pane. Once you select it, a dialog similar to Figure 19-14 will allow you to monitor the progress of the backup. As discussed earlier, for a valid backup, it's required to have a marked transaction that spans all databases in the backup. After completing the full backup, it will automatically create a marked transaction and perform a transaction log backup that includes the marked transaction.

Tfs Backup Plan

Successful completion.

To view the detailed log, click here.

Status:

```
    Database WSS_Content. Percent completed: 44%
    Database WSS_Content. Percent completed: 50%
    Database WSS_Content. Percent completed: 61%
    Database WSS_Content. Percent completed: 73%
    Database WSS_Content. Percent completed: 82%
    Database WSS_Content. Percent completed: 91%
    Database WSS_Content. Percent completed: 100%
    Backup for database WSS_Content completed successfully
Waiting for any backup tasks running...
Taking full backup of new databases
Marking all databases..
Taking transactional backup...
    Taking transactional backup of database Tfs_Configuration
    Database Tfs_Configuration. Percent completed: 100%
    Backup for database Tfs_Configuration completed successfully
    Taking transactional backup of database Tfs_HR
    Database Tfs_HR. Percent completed: 100%
    Backup for database Tfs_HR completed successfully
    Taking transactional backup of database Tfs_DefaultCollection
    Database Tfs_DefaultCollection. Percent completed: 100%
    Backup for database Tfs_DefaultCollection completed successfully
    Taking transactional backup of database Tfs_Warehouse
    Database Tfs_Warehouse. Percent completed: 100%
```

Close

FIGURE 19-14: Manual backup progress screen

Update Account Password

If you configured the backup plan to use an account that requires a password, you will need to update that password in the backup configuration whenever it changes. You can do this from the Backup Plan Details screen by clicking Update Password on the right side of the pane.

If you are using a built-in system account such as

Update Account Password

The password cannot be set for system accounts.

Note: The password for the Team Foundation Server services running under this account will be not be updated.

Account: LOCAL SERVICE
Password: _____   Test

OK   Cancel

FIGURE 19-15: Update Account Password dialog

NETWORK SERVICE, LOCAL SYSTEM, or LOCAL SERVICE, you will never need to update the password and the password field will be disabled, as shown in Figure 19-15.

Change Account

If you need to change the account used by the backup plan, you can choose the Change Account link from the Backup Plan Details screen. If you select a non-system account, you will need to specify an account name and password, as shown in Figure 19-16. You can test that the username and password is correct in the dialog, and it will also be validated when you click OK.

FIGURE 19-16: Backup Plan Change Account dialog

Restoring a Backup to the Original Server

Even with the backup-and-restore wizards, there are a lot of steps to follow when restoring database backups. To restore a backup of Team Foundation Server, you should refer to the official documentation, "Backing Up and Restoring Your Deployment" on MSDN at http://go.microsoft.com/fwlink/?LinkId=178514.

At a high level, following are the steps from the official documentation that you will need to perform to successfully restore your deployment from a database backup:

1. Stop services that Team Foundation Server uses.

2. Restore Team Foundation databases.

3. Clear the version control cache.

4. Update all service accounts.

5. Rebuild the warehouse.

6. Restart services that Team Foundation server uses.

Stop Services That Team Foundation Server Uses

Team Foundation Server has an application pool and a job agent. If you restore a backup while either of these is running, the restore may fail, or you may end up in an inconsistent state.

To safely stop the services, you should use the TFSServiceControl.exe command with the quiesce option that is in the Tools directory of each application tier. This utility stops the application pool and the job agent. You must run it on every application tier in your deployment.

For more information, see "TFSServiceControl Command" at http://msdn
.microsoft.com/en-us/library/ff470382.aspx.

> **QUIESCE COMMAND FAILED?**
>
> In certain situations in the final release of Team Foundation Server 2010, the `quiesce` command may fail. If the application pool takes too long to stop, then the `TFSServiceControl.exe` command may time out and display an error message. Additionally, if the Team Foundation job agent is currently executing a long-running job, the command may also time out.
>
> In either of these situations, you should try to run the `quiesce` command a second time. If that does not work correctly, then you can run `IISReset` and use Task Manager to end the `TFSJobAgent.exe` process.

Restore Team Foundation Databases Using the Restore Wizard

Once you have stopped the Team Foundation services, it's time to restore the databases from backups. The Restore Wizard will not let you overwrite an existing database, so you will need to delete them or move them out of the way first.

> *If you have SQL Server Management Studio installed, you can use it. For more information, see "How to: Delete a Database" at* `http://msdn.microsoft.com/en-us/library/ms177419.aspx`*. If you are using SQL Server Express, then you will need to download and install SQL Server Management Studio Express from* `http://go.microsoft.com/fwlink/?LinkId=144346` *before you can delete the database.*

To start the wizard, follow these steps:

1. Log on to your Team Foundation Server application tier.
2. Start the Team Foundation Server Administration Console from the Start menu.
3. Select Team Foundation Server Backups.
4. Select the Restore Databases link from the Backup Details pane.

When the wizard starts as shown in Figure 19-17, you'll see that it has a similar look and feel to the server configuration wizard and the Backup Plan Wizard. Click Next to continue and move to the next screen.

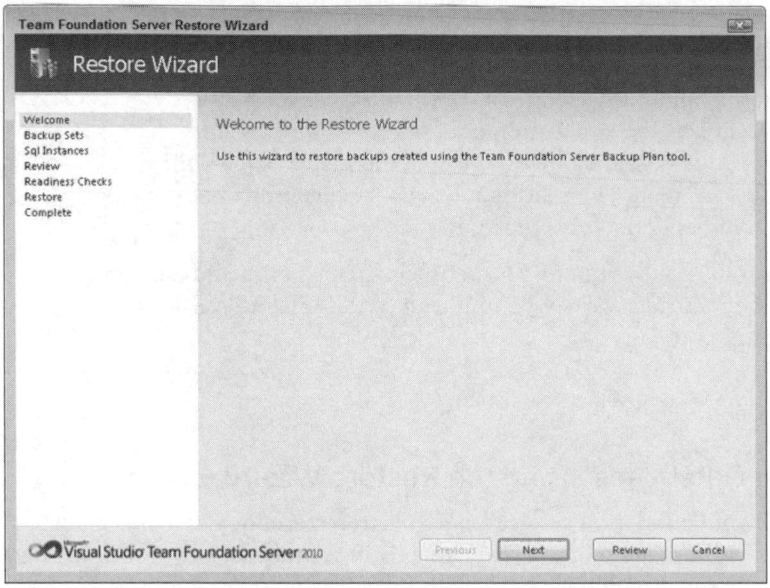

FIGURE 19-17: Team Foundation Server Restore Wizard

The first page of the Restore Wizard allows you to select a UNC network backup path and a backup set to restore. By default, the backup path is the same as the one that the backup plan is configured for. You may choose a different path if you have a backup stored elsewhere that you want to use. When you select the List Backups link, the wizard will look on the share for any backup sets and display them in the list, as shown in Figure 19-18. Once you have selected the backup set from the date that you want to restore to, click the Next button.

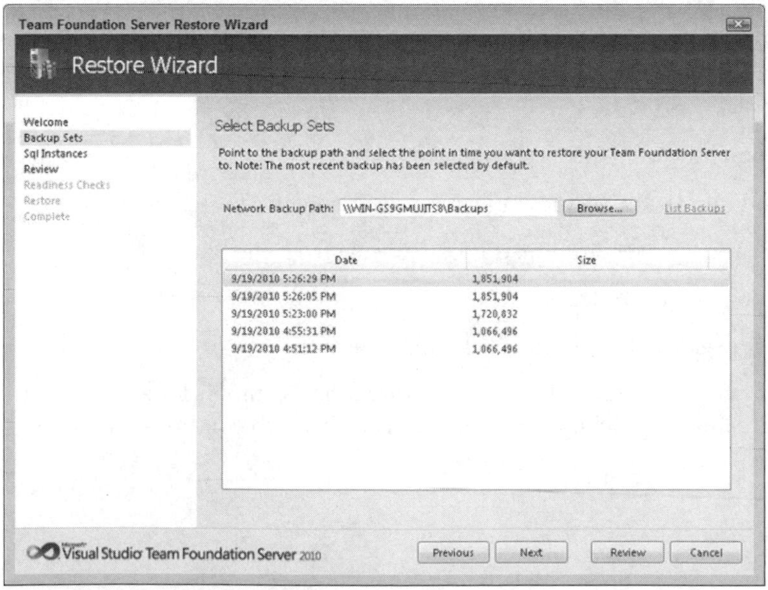

FIGURE 19-18: Select Backup Sets screen

On the Select SQL Instances screen shown in Figure 19-19, you can select which databases you want to restore and which SQL server you want to restore them to. By default, the SQL Server field for each database will be the original server that the backup was taken on. If you want to restore a database to a different SQL server, you should enter its name before clicking Next.

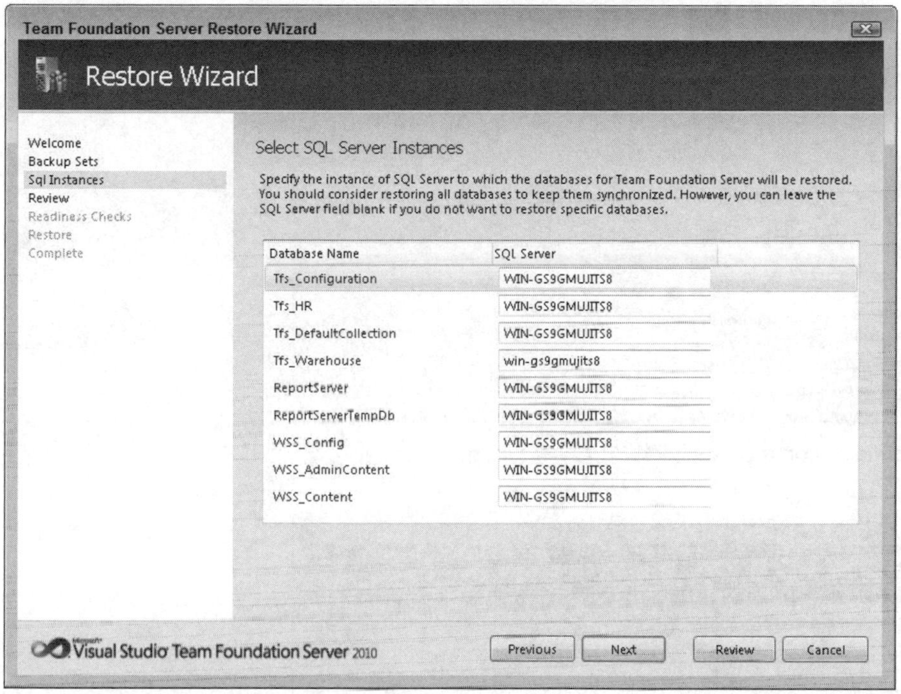

FIGURE 19-19: Select SQL Server Instances screen

Just like the other wizards in Team Foundation Server, the review screen shown in Figure 19-20 allows you to confirm all the configuration settings before making any changes to your server. When you click the Verify button, the wizard will start performing readiness checks.

If the destination databases already exist, or the destination SQL server is not accessible, then the readiness checks will fail, as shown in Figure 19-21. You will need to address the errors and rerun the readiness checks.

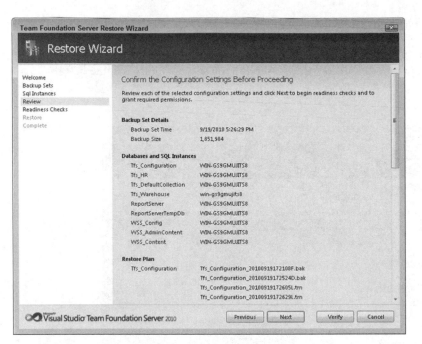

FIGURE 19-20: Configuration review screen

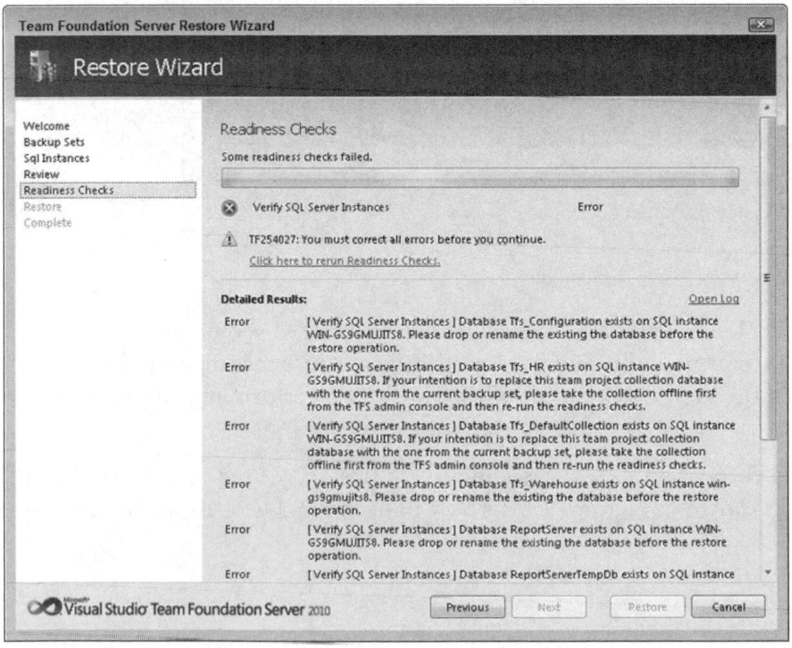

FIGURE 19-21: Readiness Checks screen with errors

Once the readiness checks pass and the configuration details are verified as shown in Figure 19-22, you can click the Restore button to begin the database restore process.

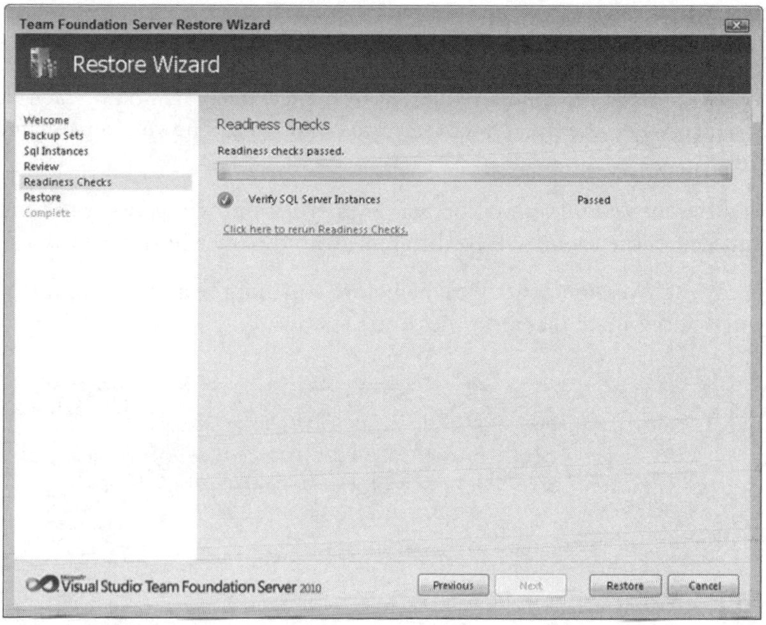

FIGURE 19-22: Readiness Checks screen

Depending on the size of your backup and the speed of your hardware, the restore process may take some time. Once the restore is complete as shown in Figure 19-23, you can close the wizard and continue with the other steps required to restore your Team Foundation Server.

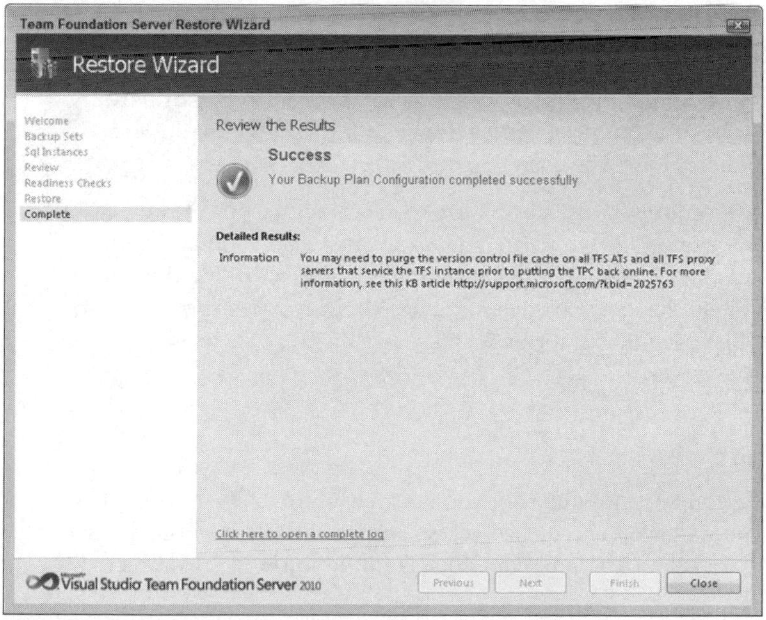

FIGURE 19-23: Successful restore screen

Clear the Version Control Cache

Each application tier and Team Foundation Proxy server includes a version control cache. The version control cache keeps a copy of every file that is requested by a user. Each version of each file has a unique `FileID` that is assigned when the file is checked in the first time. The version control cache uses this `FileID` to store the files.

If you restore a backup from a different Team Foundation Server or from a previous point in time, it's likely that the `FileID` of the files in the cache will be different from the ones in the database.

It's very important that you purge each version control cache before starting the server again. If you don't, then users will unknowingly download incorrect files and versions.

> *For more information on the procedure, you should refer to the KB2025763 article at* `http://support.microsoft.com/kb/2025763`. *Essentially it involves deleting the contents of the version control cache directory on each application tier and proxy server.*

PURGING LARGE VERSION CONTROL CACHES

On application tiers and proxy servers with a large drive for the version control cache, there will be a large number of cached files. Deleting all of these files individually will take a considerable amount of time, and will increase the time it takes to bring the server back online.

There are two ways to mitigate this and allow you to bring the server back online sooner:

➤ *Format the drive* — If you have configured the cache directory on a separate partition or a separate drive, the fastest way is to perform a Quick Format of the drive. After formatting the drive, you will need to re-create the top-level cache directory and configure the correct permissions.

➤ *Rename the cache directory* — By moving the cache directory out of the way, it allows the server to start with an empty directory. Since renaming a directory is a metadata-only operation on a single folder, it will be done almost instantly. Then you can start deleting the old directory in the background after bringing the server back online.

Update All Service Accounts

Once you restore Team Foundation Server databases, you must ensure that the current Team Foundation Server service accounts have the required access and permissions on the databases. This is done by using the `TfsConfig.exe` command, which is found in the `Tools` directory of your application tier.

> *For more information on this procedure, refer to the "Restore Data to the Same Location" article on MSDN at* http://msdn.microsoft.com/en-us/library/ms252458.aspx.

Rebuild the Warehouse

If you restored the `Tfs_Warehouse` relational database to the same point in time as your other databases, then it should be in sync already. The only remaining step is to re-create the `Tfs_Analysis` analysis services database. You can do this by following these steps:

1. Log on to one of your application tier servers.

2. Open a command prompt.

3. Change directories to `\Program Files\Microsoft Team Foundation Server\Tools`.

4. Type the following command:

```
TfsConfig rebuildwarehouse /analysisServices
```

This will drop the Analysis Services database if it exists and create a new one from the operational store. This is slightly different to selecting the Start Rebuild link from the Reporting view in the Administration Console. That link will drop the relational warehouse as well as the Analysis Services Cube, and your rebuild will take much longer.

> *For more information, see "Manually Process the Data Warehouse and Analysis Services Cube for Team Foundation Server" at* http://msdn.microsoft.com/en-us/library/ff400237.aspx.

Restart Services That Team Foundation Server Uses

The last step to bring the server back online is to restart the application pool and job agent. Using a similar procedure to when you stopped the services, you can do this by running the `TFSServiceControl.exe` command with the `unquiesce` option on each application tier server in your deployment.

> *For more information, see "TFSServiceControl Command" at* http://msdn.microsoft.com/en-us/library/ff470382.aspx.

Restoring to Different Hardware

If you have suffered a hardware failure, or you just want to move to a new server, you will need to restore backups to the new server. The steps for restoring data to different hardware are not the same as the steps to restore to the same hardware.

For the officially supported procedures, you should refer to the following documents:

➤ "Restore a Single-Server Deployment to New Hardware" at `http://msdn.microsoft.com/en-us/library/ff459215.aspx`.

➤ "Restore Data to a Different Server or Instance" at `http://msdn.microsoft.com/en-us/library/ms252516.aspx`.

SUMMARY

This chapter started with the important questions to ask when defining your disaster-recovery plan. It highlighted that it is the responsibility of a Team Foundation Server administrator to make sure that the server is correctly backed up.

The main part of the chapter covered a walkthrough with screen-by-screen examples of how to back up and restore your Team Foundation Server environment. It also discussed the important considerations that your backup plan must take into account, such as the use of SQL marked transactions to synchronize backups.

Chapter 20 examines all things related to security and permissions in Team Foundation Server. The chapter will take a look at all the different places that security can be set, along with some best practices for avoiding a permissions mess.

Security and Privileges

WHAT'S IN THIS CHAPTER?

➤ Getting to know the different types of users and groups

➤ Understanding the new and interesting permissions

➤ Using tips for managing security

➤ Learning about useful tools

When you first start looking at security, groups, and permissions in Team Foundation Server, it can be very daunting. This is a large system with many different features. A large part of the customer base also demands fine-grained controls in order to meet their compliance goals. Combined, these two things make managing security a sometimes tricky task.

However, by understanding some basic principles and avoiding some of the traps, Team Foundation Server security can be wrangled to achieve your security objectives. This chapter examines those principles and provides the information you'll need to avoid common pitfalls.

USERS

The first concept to understand in Team Foundation Server security is that there are a couple of different types of users, including the following:

➤ Domain users

➤ Local users

Domain Users

A *domain* in a Windows network usually means an Active Directory (AD) domain. AD is a directory and authentication service that comes with Windows Server. User accounts that are created in the directory are called *domain users*. In the directory, each user object has a set of properties, including a unique identifier (called a security ID, or SID), a display name, and an e-mail address.

Service Accounts

A *service account* is nothing more than just another domain user. The main difference is that a domain user is usually a real person. A service account is a domain account created and used specifically for the purpose of running a Windows service or other application.

It's generally considered a bad practice to run services as accounts that real people use for their day-to-day work. A service account usually has elevated privileges compared to a normal user. For this reason, the service account passwords are often randomly generated strong passwords, and are kept a closely guarded secret by the owners.

Machine Accounts

There are three accounts built into a Windows computer:

➤ `Local System`

➤ `Local Service`

➤ `Network Service`

The first two accounts cannot be used to authenticate to other computers. `Local System` is an administrator on the system. `Local Service` has limited privileges, and is designed for running Windows services. Similarly, `Network Service` has limited local privileges. However, it is capable of connecting to other computers on the domain.

When a computer is joined to a domain, a trust relationship is established between the computer and the domain. Once this trust is established, the computer is essentially under the control of the domain. This allows domain policies to be applied and enforced from the central directory service.

When the domain join occurs, a special domain account called a *machine account* is created with an automatically generated password. As long as the computer remains in contact with the domain, this password will change periodically, and the trust relationship will remain. If the computer does not connect to the domain controller for a period of time, the account will be disabled, and the trust relationship will be voided.

A machine account is represented as a domain user followed by $ in its account name, as shown in the following example:

```
MYDOMAIN\MYCOMPUTER$
```

To give the `Network Service` account permissions on the machine itself, you can use either the `Network Service` account or the machine account. To give the `Network Service` account permissions on a remote resource, you must use the machine account.

Local Users

If you install Team Foundation Server on a computer that isn't joined to a domain, it is considered to be running in *workgroup mode*. In workgroup mode, there is no domain, so the only users that exist are users on that local computer. These users are called *local users*.

Even if your computer is installed on a domain, you can still have local users. However, these local users cannot be added to domain groups, or used for authenticating to other computers in the domain.

> **SHADOW ACCOUNTS**
>
> If you have computers in different domains, or computers that are not part of any domain, there are cases where you want to be able to authenticate between them. When connecting to a remote machine, normally you must provide a username and password to an account on that machine.
>
> There is a trick called "shadow accounts" that you can use to avoid being prompted for credentials.
>
> To use shadow accounts, you establish a local account on both machines with a matching username and password. When the user from one machine tries to connect to the other machine, it first tries to connect using the current username and password. Since the usernames and passwords match on both machines, this works without prompting for credentials.

Identity Synchronization

Team Foundation Server synchronizes some properties of every user that is a member of a group in the system. This is so that domain group membership changes are reflected in the system, and other property changes (such as display names and e-mail addresses) are kept up to date.

Identity Synchronization Job

The Team Foundation Background job agent on each application tier periodically executes the Identity Synchronization job. By default, it runs once per hour, and it is also triggered when a new domain group is added to Team Foundation Server.

The job agent runs as the Team Foundation Server service account. This will be either a domain user, `Network Service`, or a local user (in the case of a server running in workgroup mode).

Domains and Trusts

Since the Identity Synchronization job runs on the job agent, it accesses AD using these credentials. If the appropriate domain trusts aren't in place, or the account doesn't have permissions to list users in the directory, those users will not be able to access Team Foundation Server.

There are lots of different permutations on domain topologies, firewalls, and trust relationships.

> *For more information on what is supported by Team Foundation Server, see "Trusts and Forests Considerations for Team Foundation Server" at* http://msdn.microsoft.com/en-us/library/ms253081.aspx.

Handling Display Name Changes

One of the big changes in Team Foundation Server 2010 is that the server will now update your display name when it changes in AD. This is a fairly common scenario similar to when people get married and change their names from their maiden names to married names.

In Team Foundation Server 2008, even though the change was made in AD, Team Foundation Server would keep using the old name. In Team Foundation Server 2010, the change is detected as part of the identity synchronization job, and updated throughout the environment.

> *For more information on these changes, see "Automatic Update of Work Item Fields that Store Person Names" at* http://msdn.microsoft.com/en-us/library/dd286632.aspx.

Display Name Disambiguation

Another big change in Team Foundation Server 2010 is something called *display name disambiguation*. In the 2008 version, if you had two different user accounts with the same display name, that display name would show only once in people fields like the "Assigned To" field. There was no way to distinguish which user account was actually being referred to. Some people tried to solve this by changing the display name of one of the users in AD, but without the previously mentioned display name changes feature, this didn't solve the problem.

With the disambiguation feature, if two user accounts with the same display name exist within the same team project collection, the identity synchronization job will append the domain and account name to the end.

For example, imagine two users that have the same display name `John Smith`. One user's account is `MYDOMAIN\JSmith`, and the other user's account is `MYDOMAIN\JohnS`. Team Foundation Server 2010 will disambiguate these and show them as two separate entries in the "Assigned To" field, as shown here:

➤ `John Smith (MYDOMAIN\JSmith)`

➤ `John Smith (MYDOMAIN\JohnS)`

In a large organization where you have many domains and trusts, sometimes a user will be moved to or re-created in a different domain. Think of the example where someone moves from a position in Australia to a position in Seattle, and the organization has an AD domain for each region. If both users still exist (whether disabled or not) and continue to be members of a group in Team Foundation Server, this will also be disambiguated to the following:

➤ `John Smith (AUSTRALIA\JSmith)`

➤ `John Smith (USA\JSmith)`

If you want to remove this artifact of disambiguation in the display name, you have two options:

➤ Change the display name of one of the users in AD.

➤ Remove one of the users from all groups in that team project collection.

Alias Mode

Some organizations don't set the display name field in AD to a useful value. Instead, they use it to store an employee ID or something like that. In these environments, it's not very easy to run a work item tracking query looking for bugs assigned to `Grant Holliday` when you have to specify it as assigned to `GH31337`.

Fortunately, there is a privately supported feature called *alias mode*. When this feature is enabled, Team Foundation Server will use the username for the "Assigned To" field instead of the display name. Of course, this is not useful if your account name is also meaningless, but it is useful in some environments.

To enable alias mode, you will need to contact Microsoft Support. It also must be done before you install Team Foundation Server for the first time.

GROUPS

Another Team Foundation Server security concept you should be familiar with is all the different types of groups. These include the following:

➤ Domain groups

➤ Distribution groups

➤ Local groups

➤ Team Foundation Server groups

Domain Groups

Like domain users, *domain groups* are groups that exist in AD. Sometimes they are also referred to as *security groups*. They can contain other domain users, groups, and machine accounts.

Distribution Groups

In an AD environment that also has Microsoft Exchange mail configured, you can create *distribution groups*. These distribution groups can be used to send mail to a list of recipients.

Distribution groups cannot be used to secure resources; only domain groups can be used for that. If you want a group that can be used to secure resources as well as receive mail, you can have a *mail-enabled security group*.

Local Groups

Like local users, *local groups* only exist on a single machine. These can only be used to secure resources that exist on that machine. One feature of local groups is that they can contain domain users and groups as members.

This is useful, for example, if you want to allow administrative access to your machine to members of a domain group. You can add a domain group called `MYDOMAIN\MyGroup` to the `BUILTIN\Administrators` local group on your computer.

Team Foundation Server Groups

Team Foundation Server also has its own application group structure. There are groups at three different levels within the system:

- ➤ Server groups
- ➤ Team project collection groups
- ➤ Team project groups

Server Groups

The default server groups (as shown in Table 20-1) have hard-coded names that cannot be changed or removed from the server.

TABLE 20-1: Built-in Team Foundation Server Groups

GROUP NAME	GROUP DESCRIPTION	GROUP MEMBERS
Team Foundation Administrators	Members of this group can perform all operations on the Team Foundation Application Instance.	By default, this group contains the Local Administrators group (`BUILTIN\Administrators`) for any server that hosts the application services for Team Foundation Server. This group also contains the members of the Service Accounts server group.
Team Foundation Proxy Service Accounts	This group should only include service accounts used by Team Foundation Server Proxy.	
Team Foundation Service Accounts	Members of this group have service-level permissions for the Team Foundation Application Instance. This is for service accounts only.	This group contains the service account that the server is currently running as.

GROUP NAME	GROUP DESCRIPTION	GROUP MEMBERS
Team Foundation Valid Users	Members of this group have access to the Team Foundation Application Instance.	Members of this group have access to Team Foundation Server. This group automatically contains all users and groups that have been added anywhere within Team Foundation Server. You cannot modify the membership of this group.
Work Item Only View Users	Members of this group can only use the Work Item Only View feature in Web Access.	
SharePoint Web Application Services	This application group should only contain service accounts for SharePoint web applications.	If your Team Foundation Server is configured for integration with SharePoint Products, the SharePoint Web Application service account will be a member.

To modify the group memberships or permissions of server groups, you will need to use the Team Foundation Server Administration Console or the TFSSecurity.exe command-line tool.

Team Project Collection Groups

The default team project collection groups are created as part of the collection-creation process. Table 20-2 shows each of the groups and their members.

TABLE 20-2: Default Team Project Collection Groups

GROUP NAME	GROUP DESCRIPTION	GROUP MEMBERS
Project Collection Administrators	Members of this application group can perform all privileged operations on the team project collection.	By default, this group contains the Team Foundation Administrators server group. It also contains the Project Collection Service Accounts group and the user who created the team project collection.
Project Collection Build Administrators	Members of this group should include accounts for people who should be able to administer the build resources.	

continues

TABLE 20-2 *(continued)*

GROUP NAME	GROUP DESCRIPTION	GROUP MEMBERS
Project Collection Build Service Accounts	Members of this group should include the service accounts used by the build services set up for this project collection.	
Project Collection Proxy Service Accounts	This group should only include service accounts used by proxies set up for this team project collection.	This group contains the Team Foundation Proxy Service Accounts server group. This allows a proxy server access to all collections in an environment.
Project Collection Service Accounts	This application group contains Team Project Collection service accounts.	This group contains the Team Foundation Service Accounts server group.
Project Collection Test Service Accounts	Members of this group should include the service accounts used by the test controllers set up for this project collection.	
Project Collection Valid Users	This application group contains all users and groups that have access to the team project collection.	This group automatically contains all users and groups that have been added anywhere within the team project collection. You cannot modify the membership of this group.

To modify a team project collection group's memberships or permissions, you can use the Team Foundation Server Administration Console, Visual Studio Team Explorer, or the TFSSecurity.exe command-line tool.

Team Project Groups

Team project groups are initially defined in the process template and created as part of the team project creation wizard. Table 20-3 shows the default groups that are included with the Microsoft Solutions Framework (MSF) for Agile Software Development and MSF for Capability Maturity Model Integration (CMMI) Process Improvement process templates.

TABLE 20-3: Default Team Project Groups

GROUP NAME	GROUP DESCRIPTION	GROUP MEMBERS
Builders	Members of this group can create, modify, and delete build definitions, as well as manage queued and completed builds.	
Contributors	Members of this group can add, modify, and delete items within the team project.	
Project Administrators	Members of this group can perform all operations in the team project.	The user who created the team project.
Readers	Members of this group have access to the team project.	

PERMISSIONS

Rather than providing a listing of the more than 80 different permissions that are available in Team Foundation Server, this section focuses on the permissions that are new in the 2010 version, or are otherwise ambiguous or interesting. In particular, this discussion examines the following:

➤ Server permissions

➤ Team project collection permissions

➤ Team project permissions

> *For a comprehensive list of all the permissions available, refer to "Team Foundation Server Default Groups, Permissions, and Roles" at* http://msdn .microsoft.com/en-us/library/ms253077.aspx.

Server Permissions

The Team Foundation Administrators group, along with the Team Foundation Service Accounts group, has hard-coded permissions. This is to prevent an administrator from being inadvertently locked out of the system. Table 20-4 shows some of the interesting server-level permissions.

TABLE 20-4: Server Permissions

PERMISSION NAME	COMMAND-LINE NAME	DESCRIPTION
Make requests on behalf of others	`Impersonate`	Users who have this permission can perform operations on behalf of other users or services.
Edit instance-level information	`GENERIC_WRITE`	Users with this permission can start and stop a collection, edit the description, manage the group memberships, and manage the permissions for users and groups in a collection. It's a powerful permission.
View instance-level information	`GENERIC_READ`	Users who have this permission can view server-level group membership and the permissions of those users.

Team Project Collection Permissions

In Team Foundation Server 2010, most of the permissions that used to be at the server level in Team Foundation Server 2008 are now at the team project collection level. This is useful when you have many collections running on a single consolidated and shared server instance. In this kind of environment, you can delegate permissions that allow someone to create team projects within a collection without having to grant them full server administrator rights.

Table 20-5 shows some of the permissions that are available at the collection level.

TABLE 20-5: Team Project Collection Permissions

PERMISSION NAME	COMMAND-LINE NAME	DESCRIPTION
Edit collection-level information	`GENERIC_WRITE`	Users who have this permission can edit collection-level permissions for users and groups in the team project collection. They can add or remove collection-level Team Foundation Server application groups from the collection.
View collection-level information	`GENERIC_READ`	Users who have this permission can view collection-level group membership and the permissions of those users.

PERMISSION NAME	COMMAND-LINE NAME	DESCRIPTION
Manage build resources	`ManageBuildResources`	Users who have this permission can manage the build computers, build agents, and build controllers for the team project collection. These users can also grant or deny the "View build resources" and "Use build resources" permissions for other users.
Use build resources	`UseBuildResources`	Users who have this permission can reserve and allocate build agents. This permission should be assigned only to service accounts for build services.
View build resources	`ViewBuildResources`	Users who have this permission can view build controllers and build agents that are configured for the collection. To use these resources, you need additional permissions.
Manage test controllers	`MANAGE_TEST_ CONTROLLERS`	Users who have this permission can register and de-register test controllers for the team project collection.
View test runs	`VIEW_TEST_RESULTS`	Users who have this permission can view test plans in this node.
Manage work item link types	`WORK_ITEM_WRITE`	Users who have this permission can add, remove, and change the types of links for work items.

The "Manage build resources" permission can cause some angst for organizations that are using Team Foundation Build. There are three problems with this permission:

➤   It is very broad and powerful.

➤   It is required to be able to connect a build agent to a collection.

➤   When you configure a build server, if you do not have the "Edit collection-level information" permission, configuration will fail.

These three things work against each other when you want to allow people to run their own build agents without making everybody a project collection administrator.

Fortunately, there is a reasonable solution. Before anyone runs the Team Foundation Build configuration wizard, the service account they want to run the build service as can be added to the Project Collection Build Services group. This avoids the second and third problems.

If you force people to use `Network Service` or a service account as the account for their build service, you can avoid the problem of having normal user accounts as project collection administrators.

Team Project Permissions

As shown in Table 20-6, Team Foundation Server 2010 includes several new team project level permissions that control access to some of the Microsoft Test Manager assets.

TABLE 20-6: Team Project Permissions

PERMISSION NAME	COMMAND-LINE NAME	DESCRIPTION
Create test runs	PUBLISH_TEST_RESULTS	Users who have this permission can add and remove test results, as well as add or modify test runs for the team project.
Delete test runs	DELETE_TEST_RESULTS	Users who have this permission can delete a scheduled test for this team project.
Manage test configurations	MANAGE_TEST_CONFIGURATIONS	Users who have this permission can create and delete test configurations for this team project.
Manage test environments	MANAGE_TEST_ENVIRONMENTS	Users who have this permission can create and delete test environments for this team project.
View test runs	VIEW_TEST_RESULTS	Users who have this permission can view test plans in this node.
Delete team project	DELETE	Users who have this permission can delete from Team Foundation Server the project for which they have this permission.
Edit project-level information	GENERIC_WRITE	Users who have this permission can edit project-level permissions for users and groups on Team Foundation Server.
View project-level information	GENERIC_READ	Users who have this permission can view project-level group membership, and the permissions of those project users.

Let's take a closer look at a couple of those permissions.

View Project-Level Information

When users have the "View project-level information" permission, they are able to see that the project exists in the collection, as well as list the project's group memberships and permissions.

Prior to Team Foundation Server 2010, the Valid Users group was given this permission for every team project by default. This meant that users could see all the projects that existed on a server. It also made the list of projects in the team project connect dialog quite long on a server with many projects.

In the 2010 version, this is no longer the case. However, if your server was upgraded from an earlier version, these permissions will still exist.

If you want to trim down the projects that users see when they connect to the server, you can remove this permission for them.

Edit Project-Level Information

The "Edit project-level information" permission is also very generic, and it's not very clear from the name what a user with this permission can do. To clarify, a user with this permission can do the following:

➤ Edit areas and iterations.

➤ Change the version control check-in policies enabled for a project.

➤ Create and modify team queries, team query folders (discussed later in this chapter), and the team query folder permissions.

➤ Modify group memberships and project-level permissions.

Work Item Tracking

Within the work item tracking components of Team Foundation Server, there are three different sets of permissions that can be managed. There are permissions on the following:

➤ Areas

➤ Iterations

➤ Team query folders

Areas

Area path permissions can be applied to any node in the tree. The permissions on a parent node can be inherited to the child nodes if inheritance is enabled.

The available permissions fall into two categories:

➤ Permissions to modify work items *in* area paths.

➤ Permissions to modify the area paths *themselves*.

The permissions shown in Table 20-7 are particularly interesting, because they can be used to hide or lock down parts of the tree for different sets of users.

TABLE 20-7: Selected Area Level Permissions

PERMISSION NAME	COMMAND-LINE NAME	DESCRIPTION
Edit work items in this node	WORK_ITEM_WRITE	Users who have this permission can edit work items in this area node.
View work items in this node	WORK_ITEM_READ	Users who have this permission can view, but not change, work items in this area node.

For example, say you had a large team project that your whole organization shared. You might do this if you wanted to all work with one set of work items, instead of having projects in silos. If there was a super-secret product that a team was working on, and you didn't want anyone else in the organization to see those work items, you could remove the "View work items in this node" permission.

Another example might be a change request area path. Your team could have a set of area paths, and one of those area paths could be called \Change Requests. You could configure the permissions so that anyone on the server could create a work item in just that area path.

Iterations

The permissions for iterations are much the same as those for area paths. The notable difference though, is the lack of the "View work items in this node" and "Edit work items in this node" permissions. This means that you cannot control who can move work items into iteration paths. You can only control modifications to the iteration path structure itself.

Team Query Folders

Team query folders are a new feature in Team Foundation Server 2010. Before these folders, you could only have a flat list of queries. Some people tried to work around this by coming up with elaborate naming schemes. Others used a SharePoint document library with folders and *.WIQ files in each folder to achieve the same thing.

Team query folders were actually available before 2010 on an internal release of Team Foundation Server that was built especially for the Windows and Office organizations at Microsoft. The feedback from teams using the folders was that there needed to be permissions on them. Because of this feedback, the team added the permissions shown in Table 20-8 before including the feature in the final Team Foundation Server 2010 release.

TABLE 20-8: Team Query Folder Permissions

PERMISSION NAME	DESCRIPTION
Read	View this folder and its contents.
Contribute	View and edit this folder and its contents.
Delete	View, edit, and delete this folder and its contents.
Manage Permissions	Manage permissions for this folder and its contents.
Full Control	View, edit, delete, and manage permissions for this folder.

BYPASS RULES AND THE FORCING ROLLBACK ERROR

Team Foundation Server has a `ClientService.asmx` web service. This is the same web service that the Team Foundation object model uses.

If you are migrating work items from another system, you will likely need to save work items with invalid values. Team Foundation Server provides a mechanism for doing this, which is commonly called *Bypass Rules*.

By calling the web service directly from your own code, you can set the `BypassRules` flag and submit an XML package that includes the values that you want to set. Only members of the Project Collection Service Accounts group are able to use this functionality, since it can put a work item into an invalid state.

If you try to use this functionality and you're not in the correct group, you'll receive a very cryptic `SoapException`:

```
Forcing rollback ---> Forcing rollback ---> Forcing rollback
```

This indicates that SQL was trying to apply your changes, but found that you didn't have the required permissions.

Team Web Access and Work Item Only View

Work item only view (WIOV) allows users in your organization to create and view work items *that you created* in Team Web Access without having a client access license (CAL). This is useful if you want to allow others to log bugs about your product directly into Team Foundation Server.

 For more information, see the "Visual Studio 2010 Licensing White Paper" at http://go.microsoft.com/fwlink/?LinkId=191417.

To access WIOV, you must be a member of the Work Item Only View Users server group. To create and modify work items that are assigned to you, you must also be a member of the Contributors group, or have the "View work items in this node" and "Edit work items in this node" permissions.

The great thing about this feature is that you can create a linked work item from a bug submitted by an end user. The end user cannot see the work item and the discussion that happens for that bug. When the work is complete and the bug is resolved, the end user can see that his or her feedback was addressed.

Version Control Permissions

The biggest change for version control permissions in Team Foundation Server 2010 is that branching and merging are now separate permissions from the check-in permission. This can be seen in Table 20-9.

TABLE 20-9: New and Interesting Version Control Permissions

PERMISSION NAME	COMMAND-LINE NAME	DESCRIPTION
Merge	tf: Merge	Users who have this permission for a given path can merge changes into this path.
Manage branch	tf: ManageBranch	Users who have this permission for a given path can convert any folder under that path into a branch. Users with this permission can also take the following actions on a branch: edit its properties, re-parent it, and convert it to a folder. Users who have this permission can branch this branch only if they also have the Merge permission for the target path. Users cannot create branches from a branch for which they do not have the "Manage branch" permission.
Check In other user's changes	tf: CheckinOther	Users who have this permission can check in changes that were made by other users. Pending changes will be committed at check-in.

When your server is upgraded from the 2008 version to the 2010 version, folders that were branches are detected and automatically converted to real branches. If you previously had Read and CheckIn permissions on that folder, you are grandfathered in, and given the Merge and ManageBranch permissions.

CHECK-IN ON BEHALF OF ANOTHER USER

In some scenarios, you may want to check in some changes using one account, but record that another user actually made the changes. An example of this is a shared workstation used for generating hotfixes. Each user would log on to the machine and access the server using a shared username. Then, after the user makes the fix, he or she checks it in and specifies that his or her username is the actual author of the change.

To do this, you must specify the `/author` flag on the `TF.exe checkin` command line:

```
C:\Code\MyProject> tf checkin * /author:jsmith
Checking in add: MyFolder

Changeset #11 checked in.
```

If you want to see who checked in a changeset on behalf of another user, unfortunately, you will have to use the command-line tools. To do this, specify the `/noprompt` flag on the `TF.exe changeset` command:

```
C:\Code\MyProject> tf changeset 11 /noprompt
Changeset: 11
User: jsmith
Checked in by: Administrator
```

Check-In Policies

The check-in policy settings for a team project are stored as a version control annotation. Annotations aren't part of the public API, and, in Team Foundation Server 2010, are superseded by the properties API. Annotations are like properties, in that they are extra metadata that is attached to a particular path in version control.

Since the annotation is on the root version control folder for each team project, users will need at least Read permissions on that folder. Without this permission, they will get an error message similar to, "$/MyProject does not exist or you don't have access to it." This can be quite confusing when the user is trying to check into some other path that the user actually does have permission to.

Branching and Permissions

When you branch a folder, the permissions from the source folder are copied to the target. In most cases, this is acceptable. However, there are other cases (such as when creating a maintenance or release branch) that you don't want to copy the permissions to. In these cases, you'll have to lock down the permissions after creating the branch. Then, as people need to check in patches, you can grant them the PendChange and Checkin permissions.

The reverse is also true. For example, your Main branch might have very restrictive permissions to prevent people from making changes directly. When you create a branch of Main, those restrictive permissions will also be copied. In this case, you'll have to add the extra permissions after creating the branch.

HOW TO UNDO CHANGES FROM ANOTHER USER

A very common question on the support forums and e-mail lists concerns when someone has a set of files checked out and locked, and the person goes on vacation or is otherwise unavailable. Until these locks are removed, no one else can check in these files.

Fortunately, it's fairly simple for someone with the "Administer workspaces" permission to undo changes for another user.

One option is to use the TF.exe command-line tool, as shown here:

```
tf undo "$/MyProject/VersionX/Utils/file.cs"
/workspace:MyWorkspace;Domain\User/collection:http://server:8080/
tfs/Collection
      /recursive
```

Another option is to use the Team Foundation Power Tools. Follow these steps:

1.   Open Source Control Explorer.

2.   Right-click the item on which checkout is to be undone (or a parent folder of multiple files to be undone).

3.   Select Find in Source Control ➪ Status.

4.   In the Find in Source Control dialog, leave the Status check box marked.

5.   Optionally, enter a value for the Wildcard text box.

6.   Optionally, enter a username in the "Display files checked out to" text box and select that radio button.

7.   Click Find. This will result in a list of files.

8.   Select the items to undo.

9.   Right-click and select Undo.

10.   Click Yes when prompted with "Undo all selected changes?"

Destroy

When you delete a file in version control, it is just a "soft" delete. The file contents and all the previous revisions still exist, and anyone with Read permissions can still retrieve the file or undelete it.

To permanently delete a file from version control and remove all previous versions of it, you can use the TF.exe destroy command. Since this is a potentially very destructive operation, you must be a member of the Team Foundation Administrators server group.

Once a file is destroyed, the only way to recover it is to restore a backup of your server to a previous point in time. Each time a file is destroyed, a message is logged to the Application event log on the application tier that the destroy command ran on.

Reporting

By default, users do not have access to query the relational warehouse database or the Analysis Services cube. If you want to allow users to use the Excel reporting features of Team Foundation Server 2010, you must grant them access to at least the Analysis Services cube.

The Analysis Services cube contains aggregated and summarized data from all team projects in all team project collections in an environment. There is no security filtering based on your permissions within Team Foundation Server. If a user has Read access to the cube, then that user can query the summarized data from all projects. If this is a concern for you, then you may want to consider limiting the users who have access to the cube and its data.

If you have a more relaxed security policy, and all users can see all work items, then you should consider giving all users access to the warehouse and cube. This will allow them to leverage the useful metrics that the data warehouse provides. To do this, you must add the users (or a security group) to the roles shown in Table 20-10.

TABLE 20-10: Team Foundation Server Reporting Roles

COMPONENT	DATABASE NAME	ROLE
Relational warehouse database	Tfs_Warehouse	TfsWarehouseDataReader
Analysis Services cube	Tfs_Analysis	TfsWarehouseDataReader

For more information, see the following articles on MSDN:

➤ "Grant Access to the Databases of the Data Warehouse for Visual Studio ALM" at http://msdn.microsoft.com/en-us/library/bb737953.aspx.

➤ "Assigning Permissions to View and Manage Reports for Visual Studio ALM" at http://msdn.microsoft.com/en-us/library/bb649553.aspx.

SECURITY MANAGEMENT

If you ever have to manage security and permissions in a Team Foundation Server environment, there are a few general principles that you'll want to follow.

Deny, Allow, and Unset Permissions

A deny permission takes precedence over all other permission settings, including an allow permission. Consider the example where a user is a member of two groups. One group has a permission set to deny, and the other group has the same permission set to allow. In this case, the user will be denied that permission.

Since the deny permission takes precedence, a common practice is to instead not set any explicit permissions at all. If permissions are neither set to allow or deny, an implicit permission of deny is applied. This setting is referred to as "unset."

> For more information, see "Team Foundation Server Permissions" at http://msdn.microsoft.com/en-us/library/ms252587.aspx.

Use Active Directory Groups

Before Team Foundation Server is introduced into an organization, there is usually a process (whether formal or informal) whereby people can be given access to different network resources. The easiest way to manage this is by creating security groups in AD and applying the permissions to the group.

Some organizations have self-service tools with built-in approval processes that allow users to join groups. One such example of a product that provides this service is Microsoft Forefront Identity Manager.

Some organizations have Help Desk processes that allow people to join groups. The Help Desk staff has training in the AD tools, and can move users in and out of groups.

As discussed earlier, Team Foundation Server has its own concept of groups and tools for managing those groups. A lot of organizations keep the Team Foundation Server groups very simple and put a single AD group in each of them. This allows the existing group management processes to be used without having to train people on how Team Foundation Server groups work.

Avoid Granting Individual User Permissions

To make permission and security management easier, you should avoid setting explicit user permissions. Instead, identify the role of the user and create a group for that role. Then apply permissions to the role.

With this process, it's much easier to give other people the same permissions. For example, when someone changes roles within the organization or gets a promotion, that person can easily be added to the "Branch Admins" or "Build Masters" group to provide the required access for his or her new responsibilities.

With that said, though, you want to avoid a proliferation of groups and nesting of groups. If you want to find out how a user has access to a file, you don't want to be hunting through five different nested groups. Keep the nesting shallow.

Use Inheritance

Where possible, you should set permissions at a high level, and enable inheritance for the sub-items. This is especially true for version control, since the files in every command must have its security permissions checked.

If you have many individually set permissions throughout your version control tree, that means lots of work for the application tier to validate them and trim the results. You will see increased CPU load on your application tiers, and sometimes poor response times.

By setting permissions higher in the tree, they can be cached and files can be transferred with very little overhead.

TOOLS

There are a few tools that people use to manage permissions in Team Foundation Server. Visual Studio Team Explorer and the Team Foundation Server Administration Console are the most common. If you do a lot of security management in Team Foundation Server, you will want to become familiar with some of the command-line and third-party tools.

Command-Line Tools

TFSSecurity.exe is included with a Visual Studio Team Explorer installation. If you're comfortable with the command line, this is a very powerful tool that is much faster than clicking through menus and dialogs in Visual Studio.

Perhaps the most useful application of this tool is the /imx command. Using this option, you can list the expanded group memberships of any user or group within the system. This is great for working out how a user is nested in a group.

To run the command, you must specify a server to run it against, and a user or group to look up.

```
TFSSecurity.exe /collection:http://server:8080/tfs/Collection
    /imx n:DOMAIN\user
```

You can also use the tool with the /g+ command to add team project groups to server groups, which is something that you cannot do through Visual Studio.

> *For more information, see "Changing Groups and Permissions with TFSSecurity" at* http://msdn.microsoft.com/en-us/library/ms252504.aspx.

TFSSecurity.exe is not the only tool. Table 20-11 shows some other included command-line tools.

TABLE 20-11: Other Command-Line Tools

TOOL NAME	MORE INFORMATION
TF.exe Permission	http://msdn.microsoft.com/en-us/library/0dsd05ft.aspx
TFSLabConfig.exe Permissions	http://msdn.microsoft.com/en-us/library/dd386318.aspx

Team Foundation Server Administration Tool

In a standard installation of Team Foundation Server, Reporting Services is available for reports, and SharePoint Products is available for team portals and documents. The unfortunate gap in the included tools is that Team Explorer is not capable of managing permissions across these other systems. You are expected to manage permissions for those other products using their permissions tools.

Fortunately, there is an alternative. The Team Foundation Server Administration Tool is an extremely useful and free third-party tool. This tool is capable of working with the Team Foundation Server, Reporting Services, and SharePoint Products APIs to manage permissions across these services in one view (as shown in Figure 20-1).

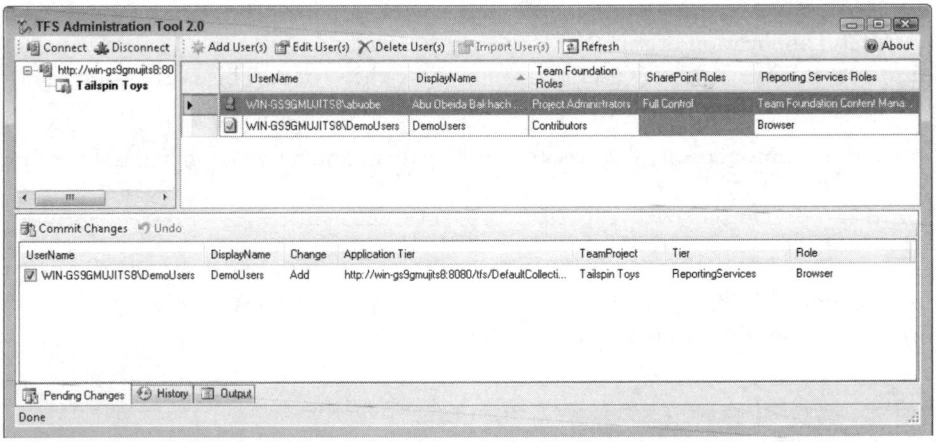

FIGURE 20-1: The main screen of the Team Foundation Server Administration Tool

You can download the latest release of the tool from the CodePlex site at http://tfsadmin.codeplex.com/.

SUMMARY

This chapter started with an overview of the different types of users and groups that you'll encounter when managing a Team Foundation Server 2010 environment. Following this, you caught a glimpse into some of the new and interesting permissions that are available in Team Foundation Server. Some ambiguous permissions purposes were also clarified.

After taking a look at the different parts that make up security, the rest of the chapter covered some tips for managing security, along with some tools to make things easier, such as the Team Foundation Server Administration Tool.

Chapter 21 covers all things related to monitoring the server health and reporting on the performance of Team Foundation Server. The chapter will introduce you to the Best Practices Analyzer and the System Center Operations Manager management pack. It will also cover some of the rich activity logging details that the server collects over time.

21

Monitoring Server Health and Performance

WHAT'S IN THIS CHAPTER?

➤ Understanding factors that affect Team Foundation Server health

➤ Monitoring SQL Server health

➤ Learning useful queries for investigating SQL Server performance

➤ Learning about data sources available for monitoring Team Foundation Server

➤ Using valuable tools and reports

The health of a Team Foundation Server can be broken down into three components:

➤ System health

➤ SQL Server health

➤ Team Foundation Server health

The health and performance of Team Foundation Server is largely dependent upon the health and performance of the underlying components. For example, if the storage subsystem is not performing well, then SQL Server performance will likely suffer and, in turn, affect the performance of Team Foundation Server commands.

This chapter provides an overview of how you can monitor the health and performance of Team Foundation Server.

> *While Team Foundation Server was being developed, the entire Developer Division at Microsoft started using the server as its primary source control and bug tracking system. This onboarding process continued through the 2008 release, and the overall size and usage of the server increased. As more teams were moved on to the server, performance issues with the application were identified and fixed.*
>
> *Because of this aggressive internal usage over an extended time period, the 2010 release is highly tuned based upon real-world usage, rather than synthetic load tests. This level of tuning means that, in most cases, the cause of a performance problem in the server is likely to be a configuration or hardware problem in the underlying systems, rather than in Team Foundation Server itself.*

SYSTEM HEALTH

Server health refers to the health of the operating system and the underlying hardware. The easiest and most reliable way to monitor and measure server health is through the use of Windows performance counters.

Performance counters are generally considered to be an accurate representation of system performance. Performance counters are understood across different disciplines (development, testing, and operations) and across different groups (customers, vendors, and product teams). This makes them very useful for understanding the performance of a system.

If you don't already have a system (such as System Center Operations Manager) for collecting and analyzing performance counters, it's fairly easy to get started.

You can configure a performance counter log to capture a core set of counters, once a minute, to a circular log file on each server. This will prove invaluable when you get the inevitable phone call asking, "Why is the server slow?"

To configure a performance counter log in Windows 2008, see the "Create a Data Collector Set from a Template" article at `http://technet.microsoft.com/en-us/library/cc766318.aspx`.

Storage System Health

In large applications and database applications, the most common source of slow system performance or high response times is the performance of the storage system. To determine if you are having an issue with storage latency you should use the following performance counters:

- ➤ *Object* — `Physical Disk` or `Logical Disk`
- ➤ *Counter* — `Avg. Disk Sec/Transfer`
- ➤ *Instance* — Ideally, you should collect this for individual disks. However, you may also use `_Total` to identify general issues. If `_Total` is high, then further collections can be taken to isolate the specific disks affected.

➤ *Collection Interval* — Ideally, you should collect at least every 1 minute (but no more than every 15 seconds). The collection should be run for a significant period of time to show it is an ongoing issue, and not just a transient spike. The minimum suggested interval is 15 minutes.

When looking at the results, the following are the thresholds (in seconds) that you should consider:

➤ `< 0.030` — This is normal, and no storage latency issues are apparent.

➤ `> 0.030` to `0.050` — You may be somewhat concerned. Continue to collect and analyze data. Try to correlate application performance issues to these spikes.

➤ `> 0.050` to `0.100` — You should be concerned, and should escalate to your storage provider with your data and analysis. Correlate spikes to application performance concerns.

➤ `> 0.100` — You should be very concerned, and should escalate to your storage provider. Correlate spikes to application performance concerns.

With this data and these thresholds, you should be able to confidently identify a storage issue, and work with either your server administrators or storage providers to get the issue resolved.

In large organizations, the storage will usually be provided from a Storage Area Network (SAN). There are usually SAN administrators who work with the SAN vendors to ensure optimal configuration and performance. The administrators have many knobs they can tweak, and quite often it's just a matter of allocating more bandwidth and processing power from the SAN controller to your server. Sometimes, however, there just may not be enough disks available to meet the performance demands. If this is the case, it will require a redesign and a data migration to new SAN drives.

SQL SERVER

The majority of the Team Foundation Server application logic is in SQL Server as stored procedures. The application tier itself is responsible for very little processing. For source control, the application tier performs caching and security checks. For work item tracking, the majority of the requests are passed directly to SQL Server.

Because of this, the health of Team Foundation Server can largely be determined using the tools and functions provided by SQL Server.

Dynamic Management Views (DMV)

Dynamic management views (DMVs) return server state information that can be used to monitor the health of a server instance, diagnose problems, and tune performance. To use them, you must have the `VIEW SERVER STATE` permission on the SQL server, or be a member of the `sysadmins` database role.

If DMVs are new to you, the easiest way to get started is to download the sample script from Jimmy May's blog at `http://tinyurl.com/SQLDMVAllStars`. Following are the five examples included in this script:

➤ Expensive Queries (CPU, reads, frequency, and so on)

➤ Wait Stats

➤ Virtual File Stats (including calculations for virtual file latency)

➤ Plan Cache

➤ Blocking (real time)

Each of these queries has a series of commented-out WHERE and ORDER BY clauses that can be uncommented to surface different information.

> *For more information and examples, see "Dynamic Management Views and Functions (Transact-SQL)" at* http://msdn.microsoft.com/en-us/library/ms188754.aspx.

Currently Running Processes

The query examined here is perhaps the single most useful query for identifying performance problems within SQL Server. It uses a combination of the dm_exec_requests, dm_exec_sql_text and dm_exec_query_memory_grants DMVs to discover problems in real time. This query is not specific to Team Foundation Server, and can be used on any SQL server to see what SQL is doing.

As shown here, the query will return interesting details (explained in Table 21-1) about all non-system processes. It also excludes the process running the query, and sorts all the processes with the longest-running ones at the top.

```
SELECT
@@SERVERNAME as ServerName,
a.session_id,
datediff(ss, a.Start_Time, getdate()) as seconds,
a.wait_type,
a.wait_time,
m.requested_memory_kb / 1024 as requestedMB,
a.granted_query_memory,
m.dop,
a.command,
d.Name as DBName,
a.blocking_session_id as blockedby,
LTRIM(b.text) as sproc,
substring(b.text, a.statement_start_offset / 2,
CASE WHEN
  (a.statement_end_offset - a.statement_start_offset) / 2 > 0
  THEN
    (a.statement_end_offset - a.statement_start_offset) / 2
  ELSE 1
END) as stmt,
a.last_wait_type,
a.wait_resource,
a.reads,
a.writes,
a.logical_reads,
```

```
    a.cpu_time
FROM
    sys.dm_exec_requests a with (NOLOCK)
OUTER APPLY sys.dm_exec_sql_text(a.sql_handle) b
LEFT JOIN
    sys.dm_exec_query_memory_grants m (NOLOCK)
    on m.session_id = a.session_id
    and m.request_id = a.request_id
LEFT JOIN
    sys.databases d
    ON d.database_id = a.database_id
WHERE
    a.session_id > 50
    AND a.session_id <> @@spid
ORDER BY
    datediff(ss, a.Start_Time, getdate()) DESC
```

TABLE 21-1: Description of the Columns Returned by the Currently Running Processes Query

COLUMN	DESCRIPTION
ServerName	The name of the server that the query was executed on. When using SQL Server Management Studio to connect to multiple servers, this column is useful to verify that the query was executed against the correct server.
session_id	The ID of the SQL process. This is commonly referred to as a SPID, as in a *SQL Process ID*. It is unique while the process is running, and can be reused by another process later.
seconds	Total seconds since the query was started.
wait_type	See the section, "SQL Wait Types," later in this chapter.
requestedMB	Memory requested by the query.
granted_query_memory	Memory allocated to the query.
dop	The degree of parallelism (DOP). This indicates how many CPU cores this process is using.
command	Command that the query is running (for example, SELECT, INSERT, UPDATE, DELETE or BACKUP DATABASE).
DBName	Name of the database that the query is running on.
blockedby	The ID of the process that this process is blocked by or waiting for.
sproc	The text of the currently running query.

continues

TABLE 21-1: *(continued)*

COLUMN	DESCRIPTION
stmt	The currently executing statement within the currently running query.
last_wait_type	The wait type that the process was previously waiting for.
wait_resource	The resource that the process is currently blocked by or waiting for.
reads	Physical read operations of the process.
writes	Physical write operations of the process.
logical_reads	Logical read operations of the process.
cpu_time	CPU time (in milliseconds) that is used by the process.

The detailed information provided by this query can be used to identify many common SQL Server issues.

Long-Running Processes

The seconds column will tell you how long a process has been running.

Team Foundation Server has a default SQL timeout setting of 1 hour (3,600 seconds). If there are processes running against the Tfs_Configuration or Tfs_Collection databases that are anywhere near 3,600 seconds, then you likely have a problem.

Once a Team Foundation Server process runs for 3,600 seconds in SQL, it will be cancelled on the application tier, and clients will receive an error message. The exception to this is queries executed by the Team Foundation Server Background Job Agent. These queries usually have a much longer timeout.

> *There may be processes that Team Foundation Server did not start, and that run for longer than 1 hour. An example is a SQL backup or other database maintenance task.*

High Memory Usage

The granted_query_memory column tells you how much memory SQL has allocated to a specific process. Each process will require different amounts of memory to perform its work.

In general, the commonly executed Team Foundation Server commands use less than 4GB of memory, and anything consistently higher is worth further investigation. If a process is using large amounts of memory, it can mean that SQL has chosen an inefficient query plan. If the total of the column is close to the total physical memory of the server, then you may want to consider adding more memory.

UPGRADES AND SQL QUERY PLANS

When SQL compiles a stored procedure, it uses the query optimizer engine to generate a query plan. Upon execution, the query plan is used to determine the most efficient way to run the query. Based upon index statistics, data histograms, and other metrics, it determines things like whether it is more efficient to use a scan (iterate through all rows) or a seek (skip to a specific location based upon an index).

As a SQL developer, you can set query hints in your stored procedure that force the query optimizer to choose a specific plan.

Although the SQL team strives to ensure that query plans remain stable, many things can cause SQL to pick a new query plan.

During the development of Team Foundation Server 2010, there were a couple of events that caused query plan instability on the busy internal servers.

The first was a hardware and operating system upgrade. The SQL server was moved from a 32-bit to a 64-bit machine with more capable storage.

The second change was an upgrade from SQL Server 2005 to SQL Server 2008. Changes in the query optimization engine caused SQL to over-estimate memory for some of the important commands. For example, Get commands started consuming 10GB of memory each. Get was the most commonly executed command, and there was only 64GB of memory available on the server. This meant that everything ground to a halt until the inefficient query plan was identified, and a query hint was added to force the old behavior.

Sometimes other changes such as index fragmentation and growing data sizes will cause a query plan to be inefficient over time.

Fortunately, most of these types of issues have been flushed out through Microsoft's own internal usage, and you are unlikely to encounter them on your own server. In other cases, a restart of SQL server or DBCC FREEPROCCACHE will cause the query plans to be flushed and regenerated.

For much more detailed information on how SQL Server allocates memory for plan caching, see the "Plan Caching in SQL Server 2008" white paper by Greg Low at http://msdn.microsoft.com/en-us/library/ee343986.aspx.

High Processor Usage

The dop column indicates the degree of parallelism for a query. A value of 0 indicates that the process is running in parallel on all processors. SQL Server has a setting for the maximum degree of parallelism (referred to as MAXDOP). This controls how many processors any individual process can use. The default setting is zero, meaning all processors.

If a process is using all processors, it means that it is making the most of the CPU hardware available. This is great. However, it also reduces the concurrency of the system, and will block other processes from running until it is finished.

On busy servers, you may want to reduce the MAXDOP setting to allow increased concurrency. For example, do you want one large Merge command to block all the smaller commands while it executes? Or, could you live with a slightly slower Merge command that doesn't block all the other smaller commands?

> *For more information, see the "max degree of parallelism Option" article at* http://msdn.microsoft.com/en-us/library/ms181007.aspx.

Performance Problems in a Specific Collection Database

The DBName column indicates which database the process is currently executing in. If you are experiencing a performance problem for a particular team project collection, this column will help you identify what commands are currently running for that collection.

Blocking Processes

The blockedby column indicates the ID of the process that this process is waiting for. If one process has a lock on a table or an index, and another process requires that same lock, it will be blocked until the first process releases the lock.

An example of this is a check-in lock. Since all check-ins are serialized, there must be a lock until SQL has committed the changes. If a check-in is large and requires lots of processing, it can hold the lock for a period of time. This can frustrate users who are just trying to check in a single file.

Another example is a lock in the tbl_LocalVersion table. If a user has a large workspace with many files, a DeleteWorkspace command may cause blocking of other commands such as a Get. This is because SQL Server does lock escalation. Team Foundation Server will request row-locks (which only lock the affected rows), but SQL may determine that a page lock (which affects all rows on the same page) or a table lock (which affects all rows in the table) is more efficient.

Locking (and, therefore, blocking) was a significant problem during the internal usage of Team Foundation Server 2008 and 2010. The 2010 release eliminated the most common causes of blocking (for example, undo, edit, and check-in commands), which results in a much improved user experience.

Resource Contention

The wait_resource column is an identifier for what resource the process is waiting for. If the wait_type is PAGIOLATCH_*, this value will likely be a set of three colon-separated numbers like 6:1:35162.

> ➤ The first number is the database ID.
>
> ➤ The second number is the physical file ID.
>
> ➤ The third number is the page number.

You can look up the name of the database from the database ID by running the following query:

```
SELECT database_id, name FROM sys.databases
```

You can look up the physical file path by running the following query:

```
USE [Database_Name]
GO
SELECT file_id, type_desc, name, physical_name
FROM sys.database_files
```

> *For large operations, Team Foundation Server makes heavy use of SQL's* TempDB. *The database ID of* TempDB *is usually* 2. *If you see processes waiting on* TempDB *as a resource, this may indicate that you have a storage throughput problem. The general scalability recommendation for* TempDB *is that you should have one equal-sized data file per CPU.*

SQL Wait Types

A SQL process will either be running or waiting. When the process is waiting, SQL will record the wait type and wait time. Specific wait types and times can indicate bottlenecks or hot spots within the server.

The wait_type column of the currently running requests query will indicate what each process is waiting for (if anything). If you see many processes with the same value, this may indicate a system-wide bottleneck.

If it's not clear from the list of processes, you can also use the dm_os_wait_stats DMV, which collects cumulative wait statistics since the server was last restarted (or the statistics were reset). The following command will give you an output similar to Table 21-2.

```
-- What is SQL waiting for the most?
SELECT TOP 5 wait_type, wait_time_ms
FROM sys.dm_os_wait_stats
ORDER BY wait_time_ms DESC
```

TABLE 21-2: Sample Output from dm_os_wait_stats

WAIT_TYPE	WAIT_TIME_MS
FT_IFTS_SCHEDULER_IDLE_WAIT	2669883
DISPATCHER_QUEUE_SEMAPHORE	2316915
BACKUPBUFFER	2029392
CXPACKET	1292475
XE_TIMER_EVENT	932119

You can also manually reset the wait statistics for a server by running the following command:

```
-- Clear wait stats for this instance
DBCC SQLPERF ('sys.dm_os_wait_stats', CLEAR)
```

By looking at the results of the dm_os_wait_stats DMV, you can determine what the most likely bottleneck in the system is. Table 21-3 describes the common wait types.

TABLE 21-3: Common Wait Types

WAIT TYPE	DESCRIPTION
CXPACKET	Indicates time spent waiting for multiple processors to synchronize work. You may consider lowering the degree of parallelism, or increasing the number of processors if contention on this wait type becomes a problem.
PAGEIOLATCH_*	Indicates time spent waiting for storage operations to complete. You may have a storage throughput problem if this is consistently high.
LOGBUFFER	Indicates time spent waiting for the transaction log. Consistently high values may indicate that the transaction log devices cannot keep up with the amount of logging being generated by the server. You will also see this wait type if your transaction log is full and has triggered an auto-grow. In this case, you should check that your transaction log backups are working and correctly truncating the log files.

> *For more information and a description of each of the wait types, see "sys
> .dm_os_wait_stats" at* http://msdn.microsoft.com/en-us/library/ms179984
> .aspx.

Storage Health

SQL Server provides the dm_io_virtual_file_stats DMV for keeping track of various storage metrics. The following query will list each of the physical database files in descending latency order:

```
SELECT
    --virtual file latency
    vLatency
      = CASE WHEN (num_of_reads = 0 AND num_of_writes = 0)
             THEN 0 ELSE (io_stall/(num_of_reads + num_of_writes)) END
  , vReadLatency
        = CASE WHEN num_of_reads = 0
               THEN 0 ELSE (io_stall_read_ms/num_of_reads) END
  , vWriteLatency
        = CASE WHEN num_of_writes = 0
               THEN 0 ELSE (io_stall_write_ms/num_of_writes) END
```

```
--avg bytes per IOP
, BytesperRead
    = CASE WHEN num_of_reads = 0
          THEN 0 ELSE (num_of_bytes_read/num_of_reads) END
, BytesperWrite
    = CASE WHEN num_of_writes = 0
          THEN 0 ELSE (num_of_bytes_written/num_of_writes) END
, BytesperTransfer
    = CASE WHEN (num_of_reads = 0 AND num_of_writes = 0)
          THEN 0 ELSE (
          (num_of_bytes_read+num_of_bytes_written)/
          (num_of_reads + num_of_writes)) END

, LEFT(mf.physical_name,2) as Drive
, DB_NAME(vfs.database_id) as DB
, vfs.*
, mf.physical_name
FROM sys.dm_io_virtual_file_stats(NULL,NULL) as vfs
  JOIN sys.master_files as mf
  ON vfs.database_id = mf.database_id AND vfs.file_id = mf.file_id
ORDER BY vLatency DESC
```

In the results of this query, you should pay particular attention to the vLatency and physical_ name columns. The vLatency column indicates the combined average read and write latency for a file (in milliseconds). The physical_name column indicates which database file the results are for.

Following are some general points to consider when looking at these results:

➤ A latency of more than 30 milliseconds is something worth investigating for large databases with lots of activity.

➤ Latency in TempDB will affect overall server performance.

➤ High write latency (greater than 50 milliseconds) may be an indication that write caching is disabled or not working correctly. If this is the case, you will need to work with either your server administrators or storage providers to get the issue resolved.

Memory Contention

SQL Server (and, therefore, Team Foundation Server) performs best when the data pages that it requires are in memory. SQL Server maintains a buffer pool of pages. You can see how much of each database is available in the buffer pool by using the dm_os_buffer_descriptors DMV. If your database is not in the buffer pool, or it is lower than you expect, you may need to add more memory to your SQL Server. As another option, you could move the database to a new SQL Server.

The following query produces an output similar to Table 21-4.

```
-- How much of the databases are in memory?
SELECT
db_name(database_id) as dbName,
COUNT(*)*8/1024 as BufferPoolMB
FROM sys.dm_os_buffer_descriptors
GROUP BY db_name(database_id)
ORDER BY 2 DESC
```

TABLE 21-4: Example Output of dm_os_buffer_descriptors

DBNAME	BUFFERPOOLMB
Tfs_Collection1	92251
Tfs_Collection2	15252
Tempdb	2914
Tfs_Warehouse	1175
Tfs_Configuration	231
Tfs_Collection3	129
ReportServer	27
Master	2
ReportServerTempDB	2
Model	0

TEAM FOUNDATION SERVER

Ever since the very first release of Team Foundation Server, the server has included rich command logging and tracing functionality. This level of logging and tracing is invaluable in identifying and measuring server performance.

Command Log

The application tier keeps track of who executed what command at what time. It logs information such as the username, IP address, user agent, execution time, and execution count for each request.

In the 2005 and 2008 versions, this data was recorded in the TfsActivityLogging database. In Team Foundation Server 2010, the tables were moved into the Tfs_Configuration and Team Project Collection databases. Following are the two tables that are used to record this data:

➤ tbl_Command

➤ tbl_Parameter

Approximately every 30 seconds, the application tier flushes recent requests to the command log tables in the database, where they can be queried. There is also a nightly scheduled job that trims the command log to the last 14 days of data.

> If you would like to change the default retention period of 14 days, see the "TFS2010: Update Activity Logging Cleanup Interval" blog post at http://tinyurl.com/TFS2010Cleanup.

To show all the commands run by a particular user in the last 24 hours, you can run the following query:

```
-- Recent commands from a particular user
USE [Tfs_DefaultCollection]
GO
SELECT *
FROM [dbo].[tbl_Command] WITH (NOLOCK)
WHERE StartTime > DATEADD(HOUR, -24, GETUTCDATE())
AND IdentityName = 'DOMAIN\Username'
ORDER BY StartTime DESC
```

For commands that run longer than 30 seconds, the parameters are also logged to tbl_Parameter. This is useful to identify if the user is trying to do something unreasonable. One such example is a QueryHistory call of the root folder ($/) with the Recursive flag set. To retrieve the parameters for the command, you must join or filter on the CommandId column, as shown in the following example:

```
-- Parameters for a particular CommandId
USE [Tfs_DefaultCollection]
GO
SELECT *
FROM tbl_Parameter WITH (NOLOCK)
WHERE CommandId = 12345678
ORDER BY ParameterIndex
```

The data in the command log is useful for seeing how many users actively use the server. For example, if you want to know how many distinct users have actively used the server in the last seven days, you can run the following query:

```
-- Recent active users
USE [Tfs_DefaultCollection]
GO
SELECT
  COUNT(DISTINCT IdentityName) as DistinctUsers,
  SUM(ExecutionCount) as TotalExecutionCount
FROM [dbo].[tbl_Command] WITH (NOLOCK)
WHERE StartTime > DATEADD(DAY, -7, GETUTCDATE())
AND Command IN ('UpdateLocalVersion', 'PendChanges', 'Update', 'GetWorkItem')
```

This will include any user who has refreshed his or her workspace, checked out a file, saved a work item, or opened a work item. For measuring active users, it's important to filter based upon the command. Otherwise, if a user happens to select a collection in the "Connect to Team Foundation Server" dialog, he or she will be included in the count, even though that user is not actively using that collection. This can lead to inflated numbers.

The command log is incredibly useful for identifying performance problems for particular commands. For example, you can use the ExecutionTime and ExecutionCount columns to determine the average response time for each command. So, if you want to know the top ten slowest commands for the last seven days, you can run the following query:

```
-- Top 10 commands with the highest average response time
USE [Tfs_DefaultCollection]
GO
SELECT TOP 10
  Application,
  Command,
  ROUND(SUM(Cast(ExecutionTime AS float) / 1000000) / SUM(ExecutionCount),3)
    AS ResponseTimeSeconds
FROM [dbo].[tbl_Command] WITH (NOLOCK)
WHERE StartTime > DATEADD(DAY, -7, GETUTCDATE())
GROUP BY Application, Command
ORDER BY
  SUM(Cast(ExecutionTime AS Float) / 1000000) / SUM(ExecutionCount) DESC
```

Using the information within the command log, you can help determine whether user complaints of slow performance are widespread, on the client side, or specific to a particular user.

> The ExecutionTime in the command log starts when the server received the first byte of the request. It finishes when the server starts transmitting the last packet of the response to the client.
>
> Because of this, it only shows the server's view of the request, and there may be additional time spent on the client to complete processing of a request. For a more accurate view from a particular client, you can use client-side tracing.

Active Server Requests

Team Foundation Server provides a web service that lists the currently executing requests on an application tier server. This web service can be used to see real-time blocking, as well as which users are currently using the server.

The Team Foundation Server URL for the web service is `http://localhost:8080/tfs/TeamFoundation/Administration/v3.0/AdministrationService.asmx`.

> If you have multiple application tiers in a network load-balancing configuration, you will need to query each server. The active requests are local to each server, and are not aggregated between servers.

There are no tools provided with Team Foundation Server for calling this web service. You will need to write your own, or use another method. The simplest (but not necessarily the prettiest) way to view the requests is to user Microsoft PowerShell 2.0.

> *Windows PowerShell 2.0 is included with Windows 7 and Windows Server 2008 R2. For other operating systems, it is available for download from* http://go.microsoft.com/fwlink/?LinkID=151321.

The following script will dynamically generate a web service proxy object, execute the request, retrieve the results, and print them out (as shown in Figure 21-1).

```
$tfsadmin = New-WebServiceProxy -UseDefaultCredential
    -URI http://tfsserver:8080/tfs/TeamFoundation/administration
    /v3.0/AdministrationService.asmx?WSDL
$tfsadmin.QueryActiveRequests($null, "False") | %{ $_.ActiveRequests } |
    sort StartTime | ft StartTime,UserName,MethodName,RemoteComputer
```

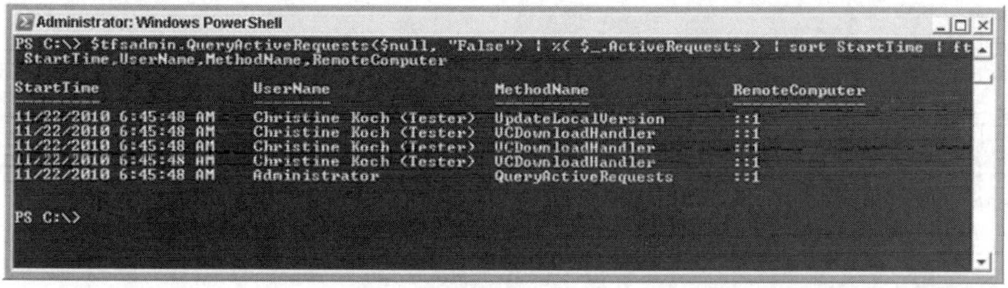

FIGURE 21-1: Example output from PowerShell script

If you are not a member of the Team Foundation Server Administrators group, then you will only see your own requests. Otherwise, you will see the requests for all users in all collections.

Server Tracing

Team Foundation Server also includes low-level tracing for diagnosing complex server problems. Typically, this is only used by Microsoft support personnel when investigating a bug or strange behavior.

> *For more information, see "How to: Use Web Services to Enable and Configure Trace for Team Foundation Server Components" at* http://msdn.microsoft .com/en-us/library/ms400797.aspx.

Client Performance Tracing

Similar to server tracing, tracing is also available in the client object model.

> *For more information on enabling client-side tracing, see the "Team Foundation Server Client Tracing" blog post at* http://tinyurl.com/TFSClientTracing.

If you want a convenient way to see the web service calls your application (or Visual Studio) is making to the server, you can enable the `PerfTraceListener` trace listener on your client. This is done by adding the following configuration in the appropriate `app.config` file:

```
<configuration>
  <system.diagnostics>
    <switches>
      <add name="TeamFoundationSoapProxy" value="4" />
    </switches>
    <trace autoflush="true" indentsize="3">
      <listeners>
        <add name="perfListener" type="Microsoft.TeamFoundation.Client
            .PerfTraceListener,Microsoft.TeamFoundation.Client,
            Version=10.0.0.0, Culture=neutral,
PublicKeyToken=b03f5f7f11d50a3a"/>
      </listeners>
    </trace>
  </system.diagnostics>
</configuration>
```

Once the trace listener is enabled and the application is started, a dialog will appear, as shown in Figure 21-2. In the dialog, you'll see how long each call takes (in milliseconds), the number of calls made, and the average time for each call.

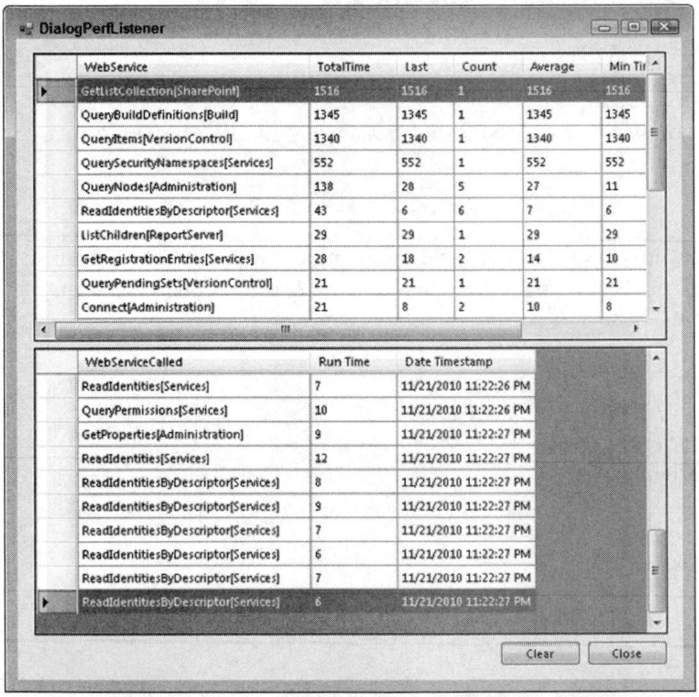

FIGURE 21-2: Example of the performance trace listener dialog

The top section of the dialog shows the aggregated information. The bottom section of the dialog shows the list of web service methods in the order in which they were called, the elapsed time in milliseconds, and the time of day when the method completed execution. If the method has not completed, it will display Running for the completion time. If you move the mouse over the entries in the bottom section, a tooltip will show you the stack trace, so you can see what part of the application made the call.

> *For more information on how to interpret the results of the dialog, see Buck Hodges's blog post, "How to see the TFS server calls made by the client," at* http://tinyurl.com/TFSPerfListener.

Job History

Team Foundation Server 2010 includes a background job agent. Jobs are defined in the configuration and in each collection database. The history for each of these jobs is stored in the configuration database. The supported way of accessing this history is through the object model.

To list the currently defined jobs for a server, you can use the following PowerShell script. The output will be similar to that shown in Figure 21-3.

```
[Reflection.Assembly]::Load("Microsoft.TeamFoundation.Client,
    Version=10.0.0.0, Culture=neutral, PublicKeyToken=b03f5f7f11d50a3a");

# Modify the collection URL as necessary.
$tpc = new-object Microsoft.TeamFoundation.Client.TfsTeamProjectCollection
    "http://localhost:8080/tfs/DefaultCollection"

$jobService = $tpc.GetService([Microsoft.TeamFoundation
    .Framework.Client.ITeamFoundationJobService])

# List all the jobs and their JobIds
$jobService.QueryJobs() | sort Name | select JobId, Name | ft -a
```

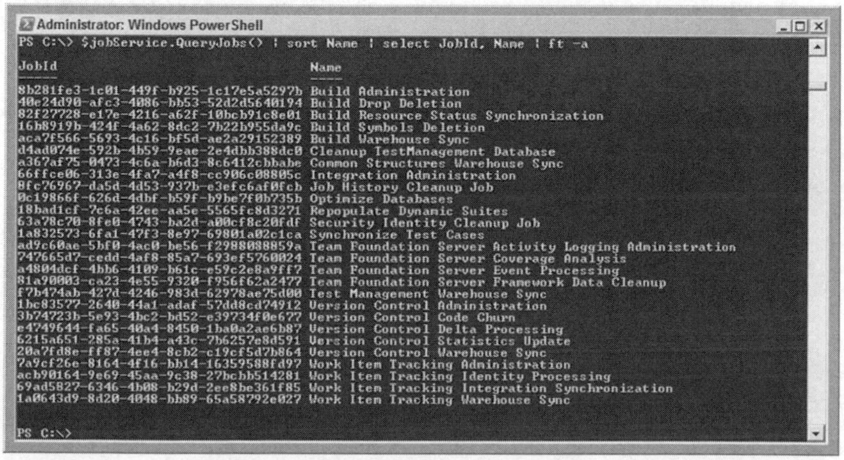

FIGURE 21-3: PowerShell example of currently defined jobs

To get the recent execution history of a job as shown in Figure 21-4, you can use the following PowerShell command after running the previous one:

```
# Get the 20 latest execution results for a particular JobId
$jobService.QueryJobHistory([Guid[]] @('a4804dcf-4bb6-4109-b61c-e59c2e8a9ff7'))
    | select -last 20 | ft ExecutionStartTime,Result,ResultMessage
```

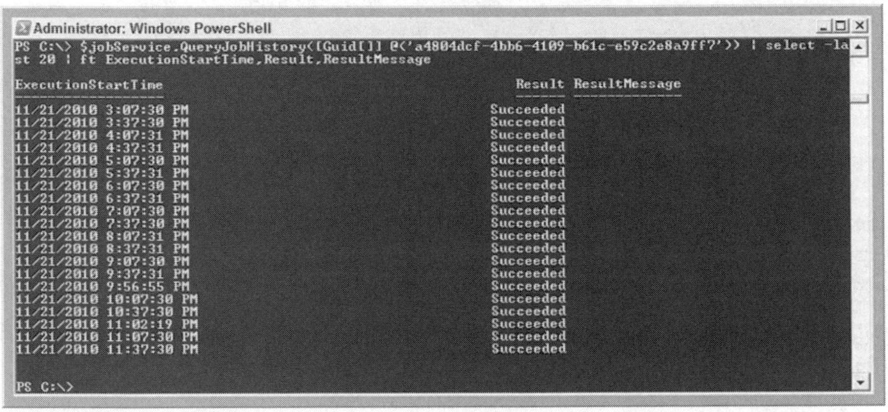

FIGURE 21-4: PowerShell example of recent job history

> *For more information, see Chris Sidi's blog post, "TFS 2010: Introducing the TFS Background Job Agent and Service," at* http://tinyurl.com/TFSJobAgent.

Storage Usage

With a system like Team Foundation Server, it's not uncommon for the storage usage to grow rapidly as people discover the value of the system and start using it for more things.

As a Team Foundation administrator, you may want to know what is causing your databases to grow. Since all Team Foundation Server data is stored in SQL Server, you can use the SQL sp_spaceused stored procedure to identify where the data growth is occurring.

The following script will list the total database size and the top ten largest tables. You will need to run it for each collection database.

```
-- Database total space used
EXEC sp_spaceused

-- Table rows and data sizes
CREATE TABLE #t (
  [name] NVARCHAR(128),
  [rows] CHAR(11),
  reserved VARCHAR(18),
  data VARCHAR(18),
  index_size VARCHAR(18),
  unused VARCHAR(18)
```

```
)
INSERT #t
EXEC [sys].[sp_MSforeachtable] 'EXEC sp_spaceused ''?'''
SELECT TOP 10
  name as TableName,
  Rows,
  ROUND(CAST(REPLACE(reserved, ' KB', '') as float) / 1024,2) as ReservedMB,
  ROUND(CAST(REPLACE(data, ' KB', '') as float) / 1024,2) as DataMB,
  ROUND(CAST(REPLACE(index_size, ' KB', '') as float) / 1024,2) as IndexMB,
  ROUND(CAST(REPLACE(unused, ' KB', '') as float) / 1024,2) as UnusedMB
FROM #t
ORDER BY CAST(REPLACE(reserved, ' KB', '') as float) DESC

DROP TABLE #t
```

You can then use the information in Table 21-5 to match table names to their purposes, and implement strategies to reduce the storage used and control the growth.

TABLE 21-5: Largest Tables within a Collection Database

TABLE NAME	USED FOR	HOW TO REDUCE
tbl_Content	Version control file content	Destroy content or delete team projects.
tbl_LocalVersion	Version control workspaces	Delete workspaces or reduce the number of folders that they have mappings for. Upgrade to a SQL Server edition that supports compression.
tbl_PropertyValue	Version control code churn metrics	Upgrade to a SQL Server edition that supports compression.
Attachments	Test Case Management test result attachments	Delete test results.
WorkItemsWere	Work item tracking historical revisions	Destroy work items.
WorkItemLongTexts	Work item tracking long text field data	Destroy work items.
WorkItemsLatest	Work item tracking latest revisions	Destroy work items.
WorkItemsAre	Work item tracking latest revisions	Destroy work items.
tbl_AttachmentContent	Work item tracking attachments	Remove work item attachments. Limit the maximum work item attachment size.
tbl_tmpLobParameter	Temporary storage for large in-progress check-ins	N/A.

Data Warehouse

One of the key components of Team Foundation Server is the data warehouse. In general, people don't have a problem with the performance or operation of the data warehouse. However, there are two classes of problems that you're more likely to run into as your servers grow larger:

➤ *Processing time* — As the number of reportable fields increases, the number of dimensions that Analysis Services must process also increases. This increases the time it takes to process the cube and, therefore, the latency of the data is higher.

➤ *Schema conflicts* — In the simple case, when there are two fields in different collections (for example, `Priority`) with the same name, but a different type (for example, `String` versus `Integer`), this results in a schema conflict. That project collection is then blocked from processing warehouse updates, and the data in the relational warehouse and cube become stale.

There are two reports ("Cube Status" and "Blocked Fields") that you can use to monitor the health and performance of the Team Foundation Server data warehouse. They display the following information:

➤ Recent processing times

➤ Current status (whether the cube is processing now and, if not, when it is scheduled to process next)

➤ Schema conflicts

➤ Most recent time that each warehouse adapter successfully ran

> *For more information on how to download, install and interpret the reports, see "Administrative Report Pack for Team Foundation Server 2010" at* http://tinyurl.com/WarehouseReports *and "Monitoring the TFS Data Warehouse — FAQ" at* http://tinyurl.com/WarehouseReportsFAQ.

TOOLS

There are a few tools that are useful for monitoring server health and performance. Some are specific to Team Foundation Server, and some are not.

Performance Analysis of Logs (PAL) Tool

The Performance Analysis of Logs (PAL) tool knows how to analyze a performance counter log file, look for threshold violations, and produce a server health report. It is not specific to Team Foundation Server, and it can identify SQL Server issues.

The tool encapsulates the collective wisdom of Microsoft engineers and other experts to identify possible problems with your servers. Figure 21-5 shows an example of a CPU utilization threshold violation. You can use this report to identify potential problems that might need to be looked at on the server, or deeper in SQL Server and Team Foundation Server.

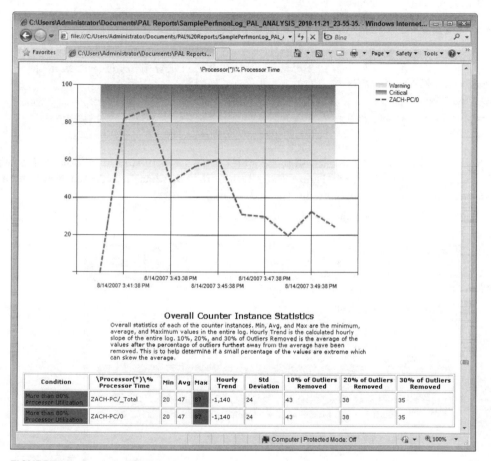

FIGURE 21-5: Example PAL report

> For more information and to download the tool, see the PAL project site on CodePlex at http://pal.codeplex.com/.

Team Foundation Server Best Practices Analyzer (BPA)

The Team Foundation Server Best Practices Analyzer (BPA) is a tool used by Microsoft support personnel to help diagnose customer issues. When executed, the BPA tool will connect to your Team Foundation Server and download the event logs and command logs, and run queries against the database. With each Power Tool release, the tool is updated to include rules that detect the causes of common support requests.

For the most complete results, you should run the tool as an administrator on one of your application tier servers. It can also be run remotely if you are an administrator and remote administration is enabled for Windows and SQL Server.

> *To run the BPA tool, you must download and install the latest Team Foundation Server Power Tools from* http://msdn.microsoft.com/en-us/vstudio/ bb980963.aspx.

Once it has finished collecting the data, it will parse it and run a series of rules that look for known problems. It displays a report similar to Figure 21-6. Each of the rules has an expected result and a help topic that describes how to rectify an unexpected result.

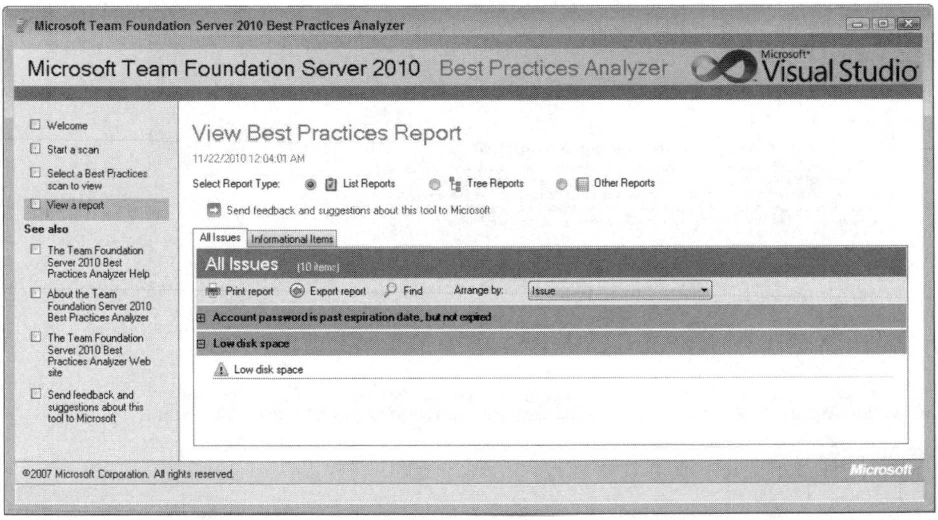

FIGURE 21-6: Best Practices Analyzer scan report

When you run the scan, you can also choose a scan type of Team Foundation Server Statistics. This will run a set of SQL queries on each collection database, and capture general usage statistics of the server. Figure 21-7 shows an example of the statistics.

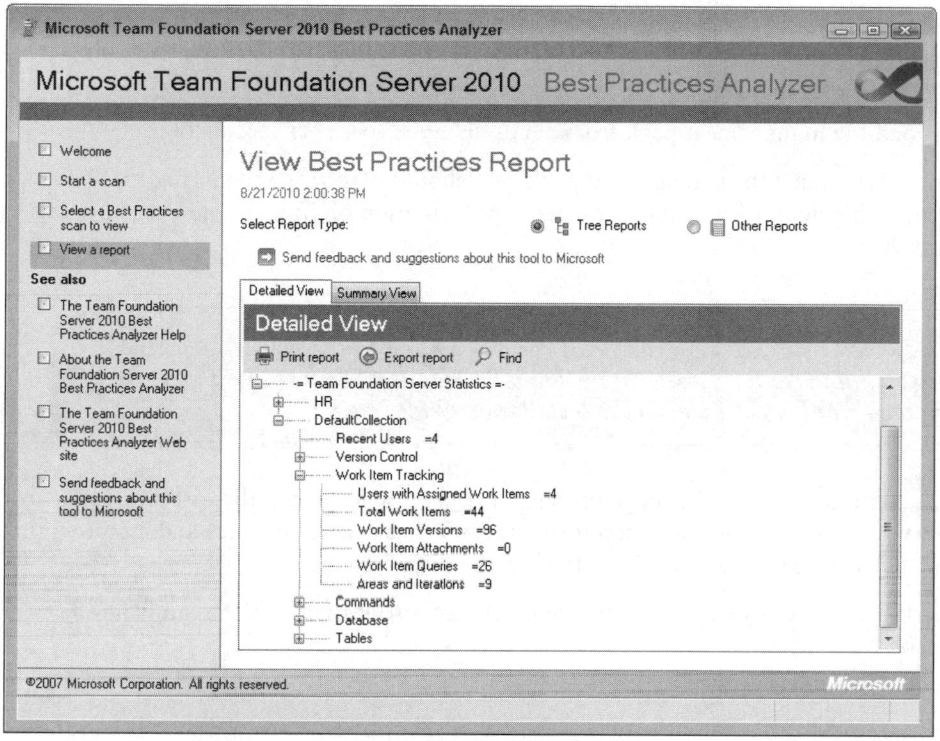

FIGURE 21-7: Team Foundation Server statistics scan

It's a good practice to periodically run the latest BPA tool against your server and review the results. One way to achieve this is to set up a scheduled task to run the command-line version of the BPA tool once a week. To run the BPA tool and perform a health check from the command line, you can use the following commands:

```
"%ProgramFiles%\Microsoft Team Foundation Server 2010 Power Tools
    \Best Practices Analyzer\TfsBpaCmd.exe" -GS TFSServerURL
    http://localhost:8080/tfs
```

To run a statistics scan, add -r Statistics to the end of the command line.

Team Foundation Server Management Pack for System Center Operations Manager (SCOM)

System Center Operations Manager (SCOM) is an enterprise-level monitoring product from Microsoft. A management pack defines monitors and rules for monitoring specific applications.

The Team Foundation Server 2010 management pack provides both proactive and reactive monitoring of Team Foundation Server 2010. It monitors application tier servers, team project collections, build servers, and proxy servers.

You can download the management pack from `http://tinyurl.com/TFS2010SCOM`.

Once you have downloaded the management pack, you should review the `TFS2010MPGuide` `.docx` document. This document includes important information on how to set up and use the management pack.

> *You will need to create a* `Run As Profile` *and an associated* `Run As Account` *that has administrative access within Team Foundation Server to be able to use the management pack. Refer to the installation guide.*

If everything is configured correctly, the management pack will automatically discover Team Foundation Server instances, and start monitoring them. It has a series of rules and monitors that look for problems in the event log and check the health of the system.

When the Best Practices Analyzer tool is installed, you can also initiate a BPA scan from the Operator Console.

SUMMARY

In this chapter, you learned about the factors that influence the health of Team Foundation Server. You learned that Windows performance counters are a useful way to record system health. This chapter covered how to use the built-in SQL Server Dynamic Management Views to understand many aspects of SQL Server Performance.

This chapter covered the different data sources available within Team Foundation Server, along with some useful queries and reports for determining the health of the system. Finally, this chapter covered three useful tools for monitoring server health and performance.

Chapter 22 takes a look at the new Testing and Lab Management features, and how they can be used to build high-quality software.

Testing and Lab Management

Across the Visual Studio 2010 family of products, Microsoft has made significant investments to better support software testing activities. This is arguably *the* single biggest investment Microsoft has made for application lifecycle management in this release, and many software development and testing organizations have already shown great results by embracing these capabilities.

While many of these enhancements include tooling features that are outside the scope of a book about Team Foundation Server, there are several testing technologies and workflows that, in one way or another, involve Team Foundation Server. In this chapter, you will become more familiar with the testing capabilities of the Visual Studio 2010 product line, and the impact that adopting these technologies will have as you plan, implement, and manage your Team Foundation Server deployment.

As you will see in this chapter, there is a high potential for complexity as you begin embracing Visual Studio 2010 as your software testing solution. Many factors will influence the complexity of your specific environment, such as which capabilities you want to use, how much you wish to automate, and your organization's network topology. For this reason, every effort has been made in this chapter to provide you with a broad overview of the topics you will need to consider, with links to supporting documentation and blog posts that provide more detailed guidance.

> For more information about how to use the specific testing technologies included across the Visual Studio 2010 family of products, see the book Professional Application Lifecycle Management with Visual Studio 2010 (Indianapolis: Wiley, 2010). Parts II and III of that book detail the different testing tools and technologies that can be found throughout the Visual Studio 2010 product line.

SOFTWARE TESTING

It should go without saying that the role of software testing in any development process is to ensure a high level of quality for any software by the time it is released to end users. There are numerous studies to suggest that software defects discovered in production are exponentially more expensive to identify and correct than if those same defects had been discovered and fixed during the development or testing phases of a project, prior to release. Hence, it stands to reason that most investments in software testing will more than pay for themselves in the long run.

> Steve McConnell's Code Complete Second Edition (Redmond, WA: Microsoft Press, 2004) cites data from several interesting studies that exhibit the high cost of quality issues once they are discovered downstream. See Chapter 3, "Measure Twice, Cut Once: Upstream Prerequisites," for examples.

Many approaches to software testing have been developed over the years to address the variety of defects that can be found in software. The field of software testing can be divided into areas such as functional testing, regression testing, scalability testing, acceptance testing, security testing, and so on. But, in your role as a Team Foundation Server administrator, there are generally two major categorizations of software testing you should be familiar with:

➤   *Manual testing* is by far the most common type of testing employed across the software testing field. As the name implies, manual testing involves human labor — testers interacting with software, usually in the same way as the end user is expected to, with the purpose of validating functionality and filing bugs for any defects they discover.

➤   *Automated testing* involves writing and running software, which, in turn, inspects the software you are testing. The obvious advantage of automated tests is that they can run quickly, frequently, and involve little or no human interaction. But an investment is usually required to author and maintain automated tests.

It may seem counterintuitive that the software industry — which has a reputation for automating everything from banking to automobile assembly — would rely so heavily on manual testing. But the reality is that early on, as a software project is evolving and undergoing a heavy degree of churn, manual testing provides the flexibility required to adapt to rapid changes. However, keeping automated tests up to date during those early stages of implementation may be cost-prohibitive.

Manual testing also provides the added insurance policy of a set of human eyes analyzing an application and spotting defects that an automated test may not be programmed to look for.

Investment in automated tests usually becomes attractive only after an application or set of functionality has matured and stabilized.

Later in this chapter, you will learn more about how the Visual Studio 2010 family of products addresses both manual and automated testing.

Test Case Management

Test case management is a discipline of software engineering much like requirements management, project management, or change management. Effective test case management ensures that the right sets of tests are designed and executed in order to validate that an application behaves as it should. This is based on the explicit set of requirements that have been defined by, or on behalf of, its users. Test case management should also account for implicit requirements — those requirements that may not have been stated up front by a user, but are understood to be important (such as making sure that the user interface is easy to read, text is spelled properly, and the application doesn't crash when Daylight Savings Time goes into effect).

Test case management is a new feature of Team Foundation Server 2010. Test plans and their associated artifacts (which you will learn about later in this chapter) can be stored in Team Foundation Server and linked to other artifacts, such as requirements and builds. By centralizing all of these artifacts, Team Foundation Server allows you to track your test plans alongside your implementation.

For any given feature, you can already ask, "How long before this feature is done being coded?" With the addition of test case management to Team Foundation Server, you can now ask questions such as, "How many tests have we written? For last night's build, how many tests have been run? Did those tests pass or fail? For the tests that failed, what types of bugs did we generate?"

Visual Studio 2010 also introduces a new family member — Microsoft Test Manager — which can be used by testers and test leads to manage and execute test plans. You will learn more about Microsoft Test Manager later in this chapter.

Lab Management

Gone are the days when the typical installation procedure for an application was to "xcopy deploy" it to the system and launch an executable. Nowadays, most applications require an increasingly complex installation procedure that could involve deploying software packages across multiple machines, and require a long list of prerequisite software.

Conversely, removing a piece of software from a machine isn't always straightforward, and commonly leaves behind unwanted artifacts, making it difficult to clean a test machine for subsequent deployments. This complicates the process of effectively testing your software, especially when this deployment procedure must be repeated to accommodate daily (or even hourly) changes being checked in by your development team.

Advances to virtualization technology have helped to alleviate this problem. Virtualization provides an easy mechanism for staging test environments, creating snapshots of them at some known state (such as when the latest updates and prerequisites have been applied), and restoring them to that known state to prepare to deploy a new build. Although virtualization solves some of these problems today, orchestrating an automated workflow for building, deploying, and testing your software across these virtual environments often requires a great deal of manual effort, or expensive automation investment.

Lab Management is designed to address this problem. Lab Management is another new capability of Team Foundation Server 2010 that you will learn about in this chapter. Lab Management provides an out-of-the-box solution for automating a build-deploy-test workflow for your software project.

Imagine having your software automatically built and deployed to one or more virtual environments, each environment consisting of one or more virtual machines. Each virtual environment might represent a different configuration under which your software needs to be tested. Automated tests are run, defects are noted, and environments are readied for use by manual testers to complete the test pass and scour for additional defects. As bugs are found, snapshots of a virtual environment can be created again so that developers can instantly see a bug for themselves without having to re-create it in their own environments. Visual Studio 2010 Lab Management makes all of this possible.

TESTING ARCHITECTURE

In Part I of this book, you learned about the possible configurations for installing and configuring Team Foundation Server. In Part IV, you learned about how build controllers and build agents can be used to provide build automation capabilities to Team Foundation Server. If you intend to use the software testing capabilities covered in this chapter, there are a few other components you should begin to familiarize yourself with. Figure 22-1 shows an example of a topology that utilizes all of the software testing capabilities covered in this chapter.

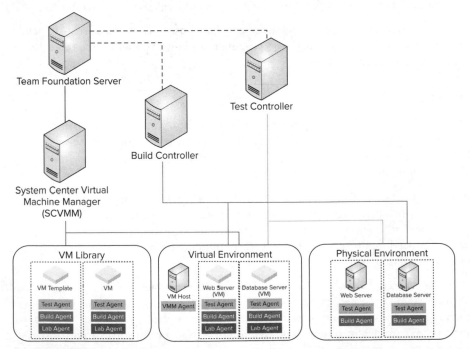

FIGURE 22-1: Testing architecture

The first thing to notice is that (not surprisingly) Team Foundation Server is at the heart of this solution. Team Foundation Server is ultimately responsible for orchestrating such activities as test automation, lab deployments, and test result collection, although it does get some help from other servers and services that facilitate these tasks.

For example, in Part IV you learned about how builds can be delegated to the build controller, which, in turn, finds an available build agent to execute the build workflow. Build agents can also participate in deployments when configured in a build-deploy-test workflow, which you will learn more about later.

The remaining components in the test architecture are as follows:

➤   A *test controller* is responsible for orchestrating one or more *test agents* in order to execute automated tests. A test controller also collects test result data from test agents after a test run has finished. This data can then be stored in Team Foundation Server for reporting purposes.

➤   *System Center Virtual Machine Manager* (*SCVMM*) is required to orchestrate virtual machine (VM) operations (such as deployment, snapshots, and state management) across one or more physical machines. An SCVMM server is required in order to configure Lab Management with Team Foundation Server.

➤   A *VM library* is used by SCVMM to store *VMs* and *virtual machine templates* (*VM templates*). Once a VM or VM template is available in a VM library, it can be deployed as a running instance to a *VM host*. You will learn more about VMs and VM templates later in this chapter.

➤   A *virtual environment* is a collection of one or more deployed VMs. Lab Management treats a virtual environment as a single entity that can be deployed, snapshotted, or rolled back together as a single collection of machines. A virtual environment can be used to simulate a real environment, which might contain a web server, a database server, and a client machine with a web browser. Virtual environments are deployed to VM hosts, which are, in turn, managed and monitored by SCVMM. A *VMM agent* can be installed on a physical machine, enabling that physical machine to act as a VM host and to communicate with the SCVMM server.

➤   A *physical environment* can also play an important role in your testing architecture, especially when virtualization is not an option (such as to support tests that require special hardware not accessible from a virtual machine). You will learn more about the capabilities and limitations of physical environments as compared with virtual environments later in this chapter.

➤   Finally, a *lab agent* can be deployed to a set of VMs in order to provide advanced *network isolation* capabilities to a virtual environment. Network isolation allows you to establish virtual environments with their own private virtual network, without fear of machine name conflicts or IP address collisions.

One important limitation to be aware of in this architecture is that a test controller can be bound to just one team project collection. If your Team Foundation Server deployment includes multiple team project collections that need test controllers, you must install those test controllers on separate physical or virtual machines. This same limitation exists for build controllers, but there is a workaround described in Part IV of this book.

> *Detailed instructions for installing and configuring test controllers, build controllers, and their respective agents can be found at* `http://msdn.microsoft` `.com/en-us/library/dd648127.aspx.`

MICROSOFT TEST MANAGER

Microsoft Test Manager is a new member of the Visual Studio 2010 product family. It was built from the ground up to provide software testers and test leads with a dedicated tool for managing and executing test plans. These test plans and associated artifacts are stored in Team Foundation Server 2010. Figure 22-2 shows Microsoft Test Manager. Microsoft Test Manager is included with Visual Studio 2010 Ultimate and Visual Studio Test Professional 2010 editions.

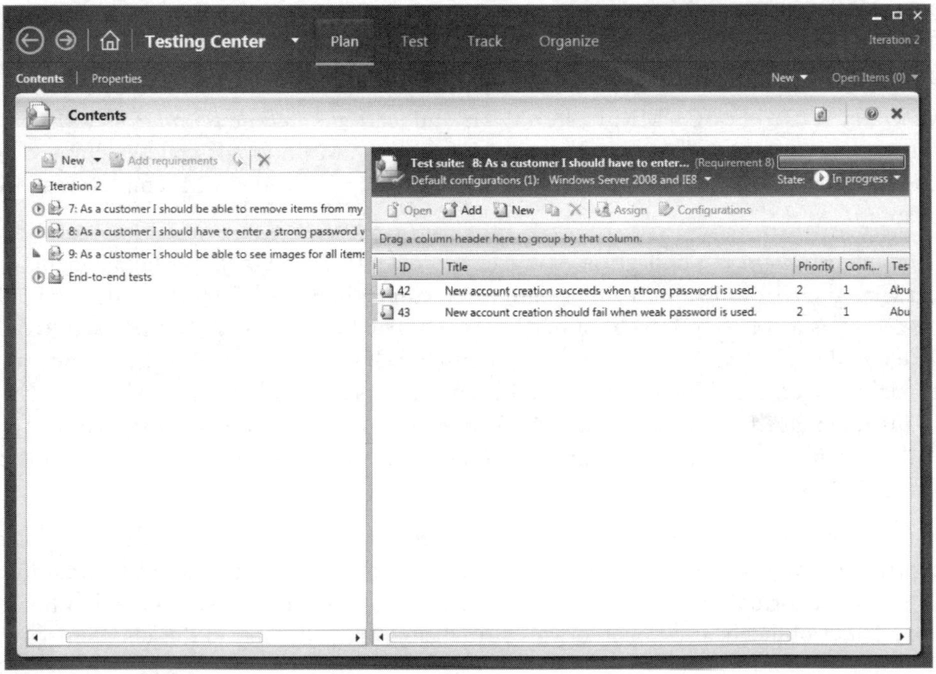

FIGURE 22-2: Microsoft Test Manager

This section provides a brief overview of the terminology and artifacts used by Microsoft Test Manager, along with a few key settings that you should be aware of as a Team Foundation Server administrator.

> You can learn much more about Microsoft Test Manager from Part III of Professional Application Lifecycle Management with Visual Studio 2010 (Indianapolis: Wiley, 2010), and from the MSDN Library at http://msdn.microsoft.com/en-us/library/ms182409.aspx.

Test Plans

A *test plan* is used by Microsoft Test Manager to define and track everything that is being tested for a given software project. A testing team will usually create a test plan that corresponds to each development iteration. This is so that the tests they are designing and running ensure that the features the development team is implementing work as expected.

Test Suites

Test suites are used to organize your test cases. There are three types of test suites in Microsoft Test Manager:

> ➤ *Requirements-based test suite* — This includes any test cases that are linked to requirement work items via a "Tests" relationship. For any given iteration of an application's development, you will usually want to start by adding to your test plan all of the requirements that are being implemented in that iteration. By linking test cases with requirements, you can later report against an individual requirement to determine whether it is working as expected.

> ➤ *Query-based test suite* — This allows you to specify a dynamic work item query for selecting test cases. For example, you might want to include all test cases with a priority of 1, even if they are for requirements that were implemented and already tested in earlier iterations. This can help ensure that critical functionality that used to work doesn't break (or regress) as development progresses.

> ➤ *Static test suite* — This is simply a list of test cases that can be added manually to the suite. A static test suite can also be used as a container for other test suites, giving you a hierarchical option for organizing your tests.

Test Cases

A *test case* is used to describe a set of actions a tester should perform in order to validate that an application is working as expected. For example, a simple test case might confirm that a user can visit a web page and create a new user account using a strong password. Likewise, another test case may validate that, if a user tries to create a new account with a weak password, the application prevents the user from doing so. Figure 22-3 shows an example test case.

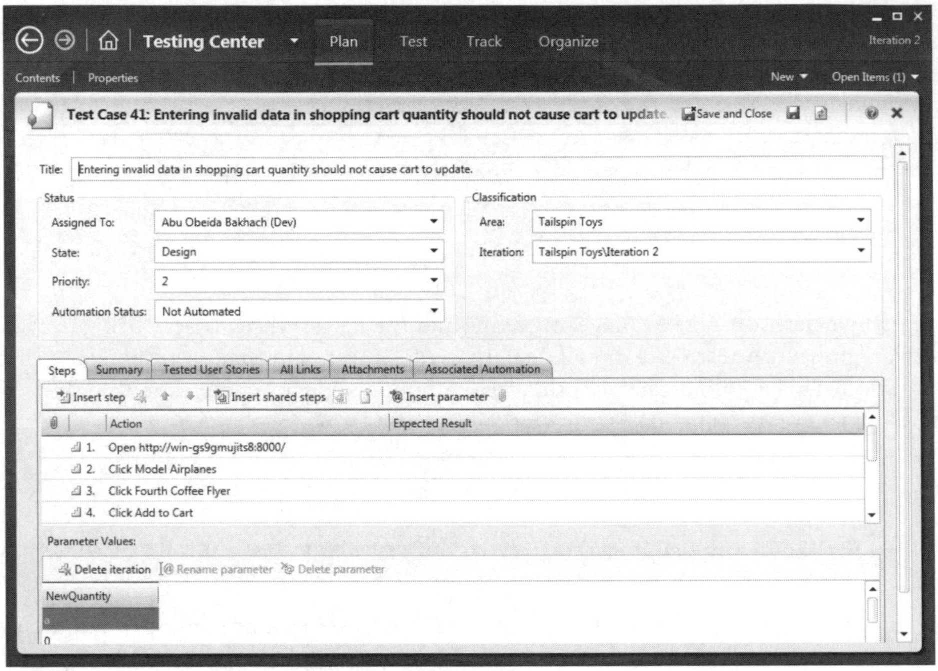

FIGURE 22-3: Test case work item

The structure of a test case should look familiar to you. A test case is stored as a work item in Team Foundation Server 2010. It contains all of the core work item fields (Title, Iteration, Area, Assigned To, and so on). But a test case also has a Steps tab that contains the individual test steps testers should perform when they exercise this test case. A major advantage of a test case being represented as a work item within Team Foundation Server is that it can be linked to other work items (such as the relationship with requirements described earlier) and reported on.

A *shared step* is another work item type that can be used to consolidate a series of test steps that may be shared across multiple test cases. Shared steps allow you to centrally manage changes to commonly used parts of your application (such as user sign-in, account creation, and so on).

Test Runs

Microsoft Test Manager provides testers with the capability to run test cases from a test plan. Microsoft Test Manager will guide a tester, step by step, through test case execution, alerting the tester about what he or she should expect to see in order to validate an application's intended behavior. Testers can even file bugs directly from this interface. Figure 22-4 shows a test case being run.

FIGURE 22-4: Test case execution

Actionable Bugs

Many software projects fall prey to an all-too-common scenario in which the tester finds and documents a defect, but the developer is unable to reproduce it. This is known as the "No Repro" scenario, and is the source of the adage, "It works on my machine." To address this problem, Microsoft's test architecture is capable of capturing rich data about a test run. This happens automatically, without any additional work required by the tester. When a tester files a bug, Microsoft Test Manager can automatically include rich details such as system information (operating system, service pack level, total memory, available memory, and so on), event logs, and even a video recording that shows exactly what a tester did as he or she ran a test case.

Even if a developer can't reproduce the same problem on his or her machine, the developer can at least get proof that a defect exists, along with a set of data used to look for clues about why the problem occurred in the tester's environment. The set of data that is collected during a test run is configured by test settings.

Test Settings

Test settings can be configured per test plan to describe what information should be collected while a tester is running a test. Collecting the right set of information can be invaluable for developers as they analyze bugs to determine why a problem occurred.

However, as a Team Foundation Server administrator, you should also be aware that test settings have the potential to occupy a lot of disk space. Figure 22-5 shows the test settings configuration dialog from within Microsoft Test Manager, along with a list of *diagnostic data adapters* that can be enabled and configured to collect a variety of details from a test run.

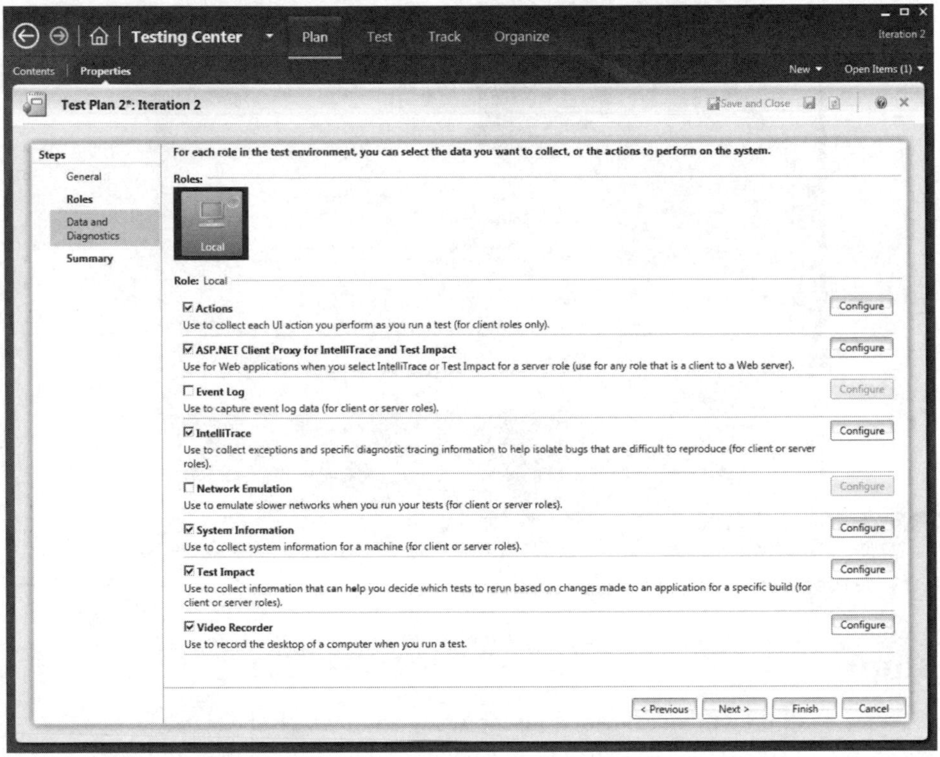

FIGURE 22-5: Test settings

There is a temptation to want to collect everything, all of the time, from every test run, to avoid missing key pieces of information if a bug is discovered. However, this can impact test run performance, and could quickly consume all of the available disk space on your Team Foundation Server instance.

Therefore, it's important for test leads and development leads to work together to construct test settings that thoughtfully capture the *right* information. You can also have multiple test settings, such as one called "Full Diagnostics" and another called "Lightweight Diagnostics." Testers can run with the Lightweight Diagnostics test settings for the majority of their work, and, if they encounter a bug, they can re-run a test with the Full Diagnostics and add the additional details to the same bug.

The exact amount of disk space required per test setting will vary, based on the length of your test runs, the complexity of the application being tested, and the number of machines in a test environment from which you are gathering information. But, generally speaking, from a resource perspective, the two diagnostic data adapters to pay special attention to are IntelliTrace and Video Recorder.

IntelliTrace can provide extremely rich, historical debugging data about .NET applications, which can help developers understand exactly what was happening during the execution of an application. Developers can analyze IntelliTrace files using Visual Studio 2010 Ultimate edition, but testers running Microsoft Test Manager can capture IntelliTrace files during test execution.

> *You can read more about using IntelliTrace at* http://msdn.microsoft.com/en-us/library/dd264915.aspx.

Left unchecked, the IntelliTrace files themselves can quickly consume tens or even hundreds of megabytes of disk space. The good news is that the maximum size of an IntelliTrace file can be limited by configuring that particular diagnostic data adapter, and for successful test runs (where a test cases passes), IntelliTrace files will be discarded. But, from a resource perspective, this is the most important diagnostic data adapter to pay attention to.

Video recordings can also consume about a megabyte of disk space per minute of test execution. MB/min If enabled, video recordings will always be attached to test results if a test case fails. You can optionally configure video recordings to be saved even if a test case passes. This can be useful for auditing third-party testing organizations, to ensure that they are running test cases properly. It can also be useful for capturing ad hoc video "documentation" of your application, which can easily be shared with business stakeholders to show them the progress of your development.

> *You can learn more about configuring test settings at* http://msdn.microsoft.com/en-us/library/dd286743.aspx.

Test Attachments Cleaner

If you are making effective use of the diagnostic data adapters to collect rich, actionable information about your test runs, eventually you will probably want to clean up old test run data in order to reclaim disk space. Microsoft has created the Test Attachments Cleaner to aid with this process. This is a command-line tool that you can configure to clean up test attachments based on age, size, attachment type (such as IntelliTrace files or video files), and so on.

> *The Test Attachments Cleaner can be downloaded from* http://tinyurl.com/TestAttachmentsCleaner.

Assigning a Build to a Test Plan

Another challenging aspect of any test team's job is determining which builds they should test. A development team will likely produce several builds during the course of a week, and perhaps even multiple builds during a given day, especially if they are embracing continuous integration. It is usually impractical to expect that a test team will install and test every build. But Microsoft Test Manager can help test teams with this process.

Since Team Foundation Server already contains rich information about builds and the work items that have been incorporated into each build (such as which bugs are fixed, or which requirements are implemented), this information can be used by a test team to determine which builds are worth testing. Figure 22-6 shows the Assign Build dialog within Microsoft Test Manager.

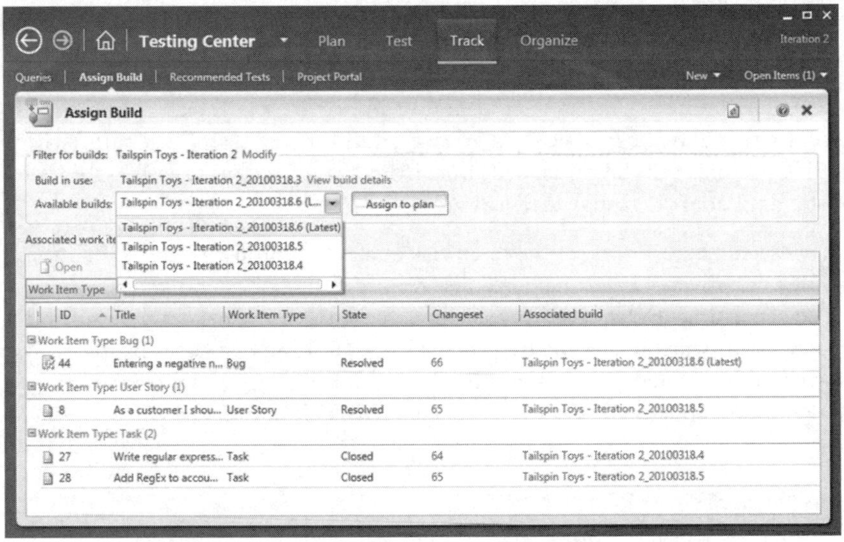

FIGURE 22-6: Assigning a build to a test plan

The build currently in use can be compared with newer builds to determine what has changed in a given build, and to help determine whether a newer build is worth adopting. For example, maybe a bug has been resolved by a developer, but must be validated by a tester. Or, maybe a requirement has been coded and is ready for testing.

> *The cadence of your builds is something you should think about when configuring your test plans. For example, you probably don't want every single continuous integration build to show up in the list of available builds. Instead, you might consider creating a dedicated build definition that produces nightly builds, and linking that build definition to your test plan. Having a consolidated number of builds on a predictable cadence will also make your build quality reports easier to read.*

Analyzing Impacted Tests

Test impact analysis is a powerful new feature that can help improve the productivity of testers by allowing them to quickly identify tests to re-run based on changes to code. Test impact analysis can be enabled to run in the background while tests are being executed. This feature records which methods of code are executed while each test is run. These can be automated tests (for example, unit tests, load tests, or coded UI tests), as well as manual tests, but the code you are analyzing must be managed code (that is, based on .NET Framework 2.0 and above).

Microsoft Test Manager can provide testers with a list of impacted tests whenever they select a new build. In order to support this capability, you must be using the Test Impact diagnostic data adapter during your test runs (as configured by your test settings), and your build definition must be configured with test impact analysis enabled as described in Part IV of this book.

Build Retention

In Part IV of this book, you learned how to define build definitions, trigger a build, delete builds, and set build retention policy. Most of the time, accidentally deleting a build (or inadvertently losing a build because of an aggressive retention policy) does not create much of a problem for a software development team, since you can just re-create a build based on an older changeset. But if you are conducting manual testing with Microsoft Test Manager, improperly deleting a build can cause you to lose the test results run against that build.

When test runs are stored in Team Foundation Server, they are stored along with the associated build they were run against. This can include artifacts such as video recordings, IntelliTrace files, or action recordings (which can be used to partially or fully automate test execution). If a developer needs any of this information to diagnose a problem, and the build was deleted along with the test results, he or she may lose valuable information to help reproduce and debug a problem. Likewise, if testers are using action recordings to fast-forward test execution (a feature of Microsoft Test Manager), deleting test results will destroy the action recordings required for fast-forwarding. These same action recordings can be used to create fully automated, coded UI regression tests as well.

To avoid this problem, be very careful when deleting builds that may have been used by your test team. This is another good reason to follow the build cadence described earlier for the builds you will test with.

You can periodically clean up your irregular continuous integration builds without jeopardizing the test results from the builds that your testing team may have used. You should then disable the retention policy from deleting builds from your testing build definition, or at least configure the retention policy to preserve test results when builds are deleted. If disk space becomes scarce, you can then use the Test Attachments Cleaner to selectively delete old testing artifacts (such as video recordings and IntelliTrace files) without jeopardizing important test results that may still be useful. Keep in mind that action recordings may be useful long after a feature is considered "done," since a test team may occasionally re-test older features to ensure that nothing has regressed in a recent build.

Custom Work Item Types

You have seen how Microsoft Test Manager uses requirements, test cases, shared steps, and bugs, all of which are stored in Team Foundation Server as work items. But if you want to customize your process template, or use a third-party process template, how does Microsoft Test Manager know which work item type is the equivalent of a "requirement" or a "bug" and so on? The answer is to use categories to define the roles for each of your work item types to Team Foundation Server.

> *More information on using categories to define work item roles can be found at* http://tinyurl.com/MTMWITCategories. *More information on customizing your process template can be found in Chapter 12.*

TEST AUTOMATION

This chapter has mostly dealt with manual testing, but Visual Studio also provides support for automated tests. As mentioned previously, automated tests are beneficial because they have the capability to run quickly and repeatedly, without human interaction, in order to surface regressions that indicate to a development team that (for example) the last change they made to the code broke a feature that was working in last night's build.

Table 22-1 shows several types of automated test types supported by Visual Studio 2010.

TABLE 22-1: Automated Test Types

TEST	DESCRIPTION
Coded UI	This test provides the capability to author tests that automatically interact with the user interface of an application and verify some expected result, and file bugs if an error is encountered. Coded UI tests typically evolve from test cases that were previously run manually, once the application's user interface (UI) has mostly stabilized. You can even use action recordings from manual test runs as the basis for creating new coded UI tests.
Unit	These low-level tests verify that target application code functions as the developer expects.
Database unit	Visual Studio 2010 also provides the capability to write unit tests against database code (for example, T-SQL code within a SQL Server database).
Web performance	This test is used primarily to test performance of a web application. For example, you may create a web performance test capturing the web requests that occur when a user shops for items on your website. This web performance test could be one of a suite of web performance tests that you run periodically to verify that your website is performing as expected.

TEST	DESCRIPTION
Load	These tests verify that a target application will perform and scale as necessary. A target system is stressed by repeatedly executing a variety of tests. Visual Studio records details of the target system's performance, and automatically generates reports from the data. Load tests are frequently based on sets of web performance tests. However, even non-web applications can be tested by defining a set of unit tests or database unit tests to execute.
Generic	These tests enable calling of alternative external testing systems, such as an existing suite of tests leveraging a third-party testing package. Results of those tests can be automatically parsed to determine success. This could range from something as simple as the result code from a console application, to parsing the XML document exported from an external testing package.
Ordered	Essentially containers of other tests, these establish a specific order in which tests are executed, and enable the same test to be included more than once.

Each of these test types is described in detail in Parts II and III of *Professional Application Lifecycle Management with Visual Studio 2010* (Indianapolis: Wiley, 2010). As a Team Foundation Server administrator, you should familiarize yourself with how automated tests can be run as part of a build definition, which was described in Part IV of this book. You should also familiarize yourself with test controllers and agents, introduced earlier in this chapter (see the section, "Testing Architecture"). When configuring test agents, some test types (such as coded UI tests) will require you to configure the test agent to run as an interactive process so that it has access to the desktop.

Automated tests can also be run as part of a build-deploy-test workflow in a Lab Management environment. You will learn about Lab Management next.

VISUAL STUDIO 2010 LAB MANAGEMENT

Visual Studio 2010 Lab Management is a powerful new capability of Team Foundation Server 2010 that allows you to orchestrate physical and virtual test labs, automate build-deploy-test workflows, and enhance developer-tester collaboration. This section provides an overview of the components required to enable Lab Management, along with their associated capabilities.

This section also provides you with a starting point as you plan your adoption of Lab Management, considerations for maintaining your testing environment, and troubleshooting tips. Several URLs have been provided throughout this section, as well as links to supporting documentation, all of which dive deeper into these topics.

> **CHALLENGES OF CONFIGURING LAB MANAGEMENT**
>
> It should be stated up-front that configuring Lab Management (especially for the first time) can be overwhelming and even frustrating at times. While the Lab Management technology is capable of doing a lot of heavy lifting for you, there are always going to be areas that you must customize for your own environment, to suit your individual process, and to meet the requirements of your existing IT infrastructure. Stick with it, because the benefits of Lab Management often far outweigh the initial investment. You can read about some teams who have already adopted Lab Management and their results at `http://tinyurl .com/LabManagementStories`.
>
> Configuring Lab Management also requires a mixture of disciplines across development, build engineering, testing, and IT. So, be prepared to immerse yourself in the documentation, then buy some doughnuts and assemble a virtual team with the right level of expertise.

Installing and Configuring Lab Management

Earlier in this chapter (in the section, "Testing Architecture"), you learned about the components that make up a testing environment that makes use of physical and virtual environments. A solid understanding of these components and how they integrate with one another is important for configuring and administering Lab Management.

> *Before configuring Lab Management on your production Team Foundation Server instance, you should consider setting up an evaluation environment where you can become familiar with the installation procedure and experiment with the capability. Microsoft even provides a pre-configured virtual hard disk (VHD) file that you can download, along with walkthroughs and a sample application, so that you can begin evaluating Lab Management without needing to invest a lot of time configuring it yourself. To download the VHD and access these walkthroughs, visit* `http://go.microsoft.com/fwlink/?LinkID=195885`.

When you are ready to install Lab Management in your own environment, you should start with the MSDN Library documentation at `http://msdn.microsoft.com/en-us/library/dd380687.aspx`. This help topic provides step-by-step instructions for configuring your environment for the first time. Read the documentation end-to-end before getting started, and be prepared for this to take several hours.

> *The documentation provides information about the "update for Visual Studio 2010 Lab Management" (also sometimes referred to as the "Lab Management GDR"). When Visual Studio 2010 was officially released in April 2010, the Lab Management functionality was declared to be in a Release Candidate (RC) state, since the team was still incorporating important customer feedback at that time. The update was released in August 2010, and should be applied in your environment so that you can benefit from these enhancements and fixes. The update applies to many components, including Team Foundation Server, Microsoft Test Manager, test controllers and agents, build controllers and agents, and lab agents. Be sure to install this update on any of those components that are in your environment today, as well as any new components that are added later. Alternatively, Visual Studio 2010 Service Pack 1 also includes this update, and can be installed instead of the update.*

When you are finished, you will have added the Lab Management capability to Team Foundation Server, and have configured an SCVMM server, along with a VM library share and one or more VM hosts. You are then ready to begin preparing virtual machines, defining virtual environments, and configuring build definitions to support build-deploy-test workflows.

The remainder of this section covers additional considerations you may need to account for in your environment, as well as optimizations and best practices to be aware of, which can save you time and enhance the quality of your Lab Management deployment.

Ports and Protocols

Unless you are the system administrator for your organization's IT department, you may need to request that certain ports and protocols be enabled to support your testing architecture. This becomes especially important if your solution will span multiple networks, such as if your existing test lab infrastructure is separate from your Team Foundation Server instance.

> *A detailed description of the ports and protocols required to support the testing architecture described in this chapter can be found at* http://msdn.microsoft .com/en-us/library/ms252473.aspx.

Capacity Planning

There are many factors that will affect the hardware requirements in order for your team to utilize Lab Management capabilities. These factors include variables such as the following:

➤ At any given time, how many testers will need access to their own individual virtual environments to run tests?

➤ At any given time, how many developers will need access to virtual environments (for analyzing bugs reported by testers)?

➤ How many VMs are required in each virtual environment? In other words, does your software run on a single server, or will your tests involve multiple servers?

➤ What are the system requirements of each VM in your virtual environments (disk space, memory usage, processing power)?

➤ How often will you run your build-deploy-test workflow, and how long will you need to retain historical snapshots containing older builds?

➤ How many VMs and VM templates do you need to store in your VM library, and what is the size of those files?

➤ Do you need multiple testing environments in order to support geographically distributed teams?

The answers to these questions will begin to form the hardware requirements of your testing environment. This will allow you to calculate the answers to questions such as the following:

➤ How many VM host servers do I need?

➤ What kinds of servers should I buy?

➤ How much storage capacity do I need?

> *The Lab Management product team has compiled guidelines to help you answer these questions. You can access these guidelines at* `http://tinyurl .com/LabManagementCapacityPlanning`*.*

Managing Host Groups and Library Shares

The basic infrastructure of any Lab Management deployment will consist of an SCVMM server, one or more library shares, and one or more VM hosts (which are organized along with other VM hosts into *host groups*). The SCVMM server coordinates the deployment of VMs from a library share to a VM host by examining the available resources on each VM host within a host group to determine to which physical machine a VM should be deployed.

There are several techniques you can use to optimize the performance of your Lab Management deployment. For example, ensuring that your library share is on the same network switch as your VM hosts can substantially reduce the amount of time required to deploy VMs to hosts. Another technique is to allow unencrypted file transfers between your library share and the VM hosts.

> *The Lab Management team has compiled guidelines to help you better understand the way SCVMM host groups and libraries interact with Team Foundation Server's Lab Management capability. These guidelines also provide best practices for optimizing your host groups and library shares. You can find the guidelines at* `http://tinyurl.com/LabManagementHostsAndLibraries`*.*

Creating VMs and VM Templates

Creating VMs and VM templates for your SCVMM library can be a time-consuming (but important) step in building out your Lab Management environment. Depending on the requirements of the software you are testing, you may need to create multiple VM templates that correspond to different operating system editions, languages, browser versions, and so on. In addition to creating these environments, you must also install the agents required to support a build-deploy-test workflow. This includes the test agent, build agent, and lab agent.

> *The Lab Management team has built a tool to simplify the creation of your VMs. The VM Prep Tool can be downloaded at* http://code.msdn.microsoft .com/vslabmgmt. *This tool will automatically install and configure all of the required agents on your VMs, apply the Lab Management General Distribution Release (GDR), and sysprep your VM. The end result is a VM that can be stored in your SCVMM library as a VM template that is ready for use in your Lab Management environment.*

CHOOSING BETWEEN A VM AND VM TEMPLATE

You may be wondering what the difference is between a VM and a VM template, and when you should use each.

A *VM* can be stored in an SCVMM library by starting with a running VM, shutting it down, saving it to the SCVMM library share, and registering it with the SCVMM server. When it is later deployed from the library to a VM host, it will have the same machine name and other configuration properties as it did when it was originally saved to the library. The obvious downside with this approach is that if you deploy this VM more than once, you may experience machine name conflicts on your Lab Management network. The solution to this is to utilize VM templates.

A *VM template* has gone through a sysprep step to essentially remove its machine name, domain memberships, and other uniquely identifying properties. When a VM template is later deployed from the library to a VM host, you can specify its machine name (or use a randomly chosen GUID), domain memberships, and so on. This provides you with protection from machine name collisions, and even allows you to use the same VM template more than once in a given virtual environment.

Generally speaking, you should use VM templates whenever you can. The major exception to this rule is if your test environments require software that is not supported with sysprep. For example, SQL Server 2008 did not support sysprepping, but SQL Server 2008 R2 does provide this support. If you are forced to use VMs, be sure to create virtual environments that utilize network isolation. This won't prevent machine name collisions within a virtual environment (you will have problems if you have two VMs with the same name in the same virtual environment), but it will provide isolation between different virtual environments.

Working with Virtual Environments

After you have populated your SCVMM library with VMs and/or VM templates, you can use Microsoft Test Manager to define virtual environments. A virtual environment consists of one or more VMs or VM templates, and you can use the same VM template twice within a given virtual environment. (This will customize the VM template twice, creating two instances of running VMs.) After you have defined your virtual environments, you can then deploy those to VM host groups.

> *For more information on creating virtual environments, see* http://msdn
> .microsoft.com/en-us/library/dd380688.aspx.

DETERMINING VM RAM

When you are configuring and deploying virtual environments, you can decide how much RAM to assign to each VM within each virtual environment. Remember that the more RAM you assign to each VM, the more RAM will be required by your VM host groups.

If you multiply the number of VMs in each virtual environment by the number of simultaneous virtual environments you need to support, you may discover that trimming even a few hundred megabytes of RAM off of each VM can represent a substantial resource savings for your environment. Therefore, it's important to understand what the minimum RAM requirements can be for the VMs in your test environments without sacrificing the performance or accuracy of your testing efforts.

Defining a Build-Deploy-Test Workflow

Although you can choose to use Lab Management purely for managing a lab of VMs to conduct manual testing, the real power of Lab Management is unlocked when you begin to take advantage of the automation support for building your software, deploying it to an environment, and running your automated tests in that environment. This is known as a *build-deploy-test workflow*.

Imagine the benefits of this workflow by considering the following hypothetical scenario. The software you create consists of a website, powered by a database, which needs to be accessed by people running multiple supported web browsers. Your web application needs to work with Internet Information Services (IIS) 6 and IIS 7, and you support both SQL Server and Oracle for the database tier.

Just deploying the dozens of machines required to support each of these configurations alone can be time-consuming. After the machines are ready, you then must deploy the software, and then run your tests. Now, consider repeating this process every night in order to support the daily changes coming from the development team.

Of course, some organizations have already invested heavily in scripts to automate some or all of this workflow, but the cost of doing so can be quite high. Development and testing teams should not be in the business of maintaining this type of infrastructure — they should be spending their time building and testing great software.

Once you have installed and configured your Lab Management infrastructure, you can easily create a new build definition using Team Build, which allows you to establish a build-deploy-test workflow. You can create multiple definitions to support multiple environments. (For example, you might create one workflow to test a SQL Server deployment with IIS 6, and a separate workflow to test an Oracle deployment with IIS 7.) Imagine arriving to work in the morning and being able to instantly discover that last night's build caused a failure in the account authorization logic, which only occurs with SQL Server 2005 SP1.

This is the type of rapid, iterative feedback that can allow teams to identify and fix bugs well before a release is ever distributed to customers. Figure 22-7 shows an example of a typical build-deploy-test workflow enabled by Lab Management. This workflow can be customized and extended to suit your specific requirements.

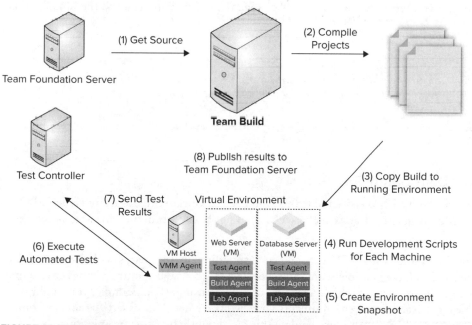

FIGURE 22-7: Build-deploy-test workflow

> To get step-by-step instructions for configuring a build-deploy-test workflow with Team Build and Lab Management, visit http://msdn.microsoft.com/ en-us/library/ee471614.aspx (for build and deployment) and http://msdn .microsoft.com/en-us/library/ee702477.aspx (for test automation).

Note that, in order to run automated tests as part of a build-deploy-test workflow, you must create automated tests (such as coded UI tests or unit tests), store these tests in Team Foundation Server version control, and associate these tests with test case work items. These test case work items must, in turn, be part of a test plan. Admittedly this will require a bit of up-front work to create these associations, but the end result is that you will get rich reporting data that links your builds with your test plans, test cases, and, ultimately, the requirements being tested.

> *To learn how to associate automated tests with test cases, visit* http://msdn .microsoft.com/en-us/library/dd380741.aspx.

Lab Management Permissions

There are several permissions to be aware of when you are configuring Lab Management. You may want to consider using these permissions to govern, for example, who has the capability to modify virtual environment definitions. Since your build-deploy-test workflow will depend on these definitions, it is important that users only change them if they understand the implications of their changes.

> *To learn about the granular permissions you can assign related to Lab Management activities, visit* http://msdn.microsoft.com/en-us/library/ dd380760.aspx.

Geographically Distributed Teams

You may have geographically distributed teams who need to work with Lab Management. But the size of Lab Management artifacts such as VMs can put heavy strain on wide area networks (WANs).

You should consider co-locating VM hosts and corresponding library shares with the testing teams who need them. If you have multiple teams who need access, consider naming virtual environments appropriately to indicate to users which ones they should be using. (For example, you might prepend your Chicago-based virtual environments with "CHI," New York-based virtual environments with "NYC," and so on.) You can even regulate this more tightly by using permissions.

Physical Environments

There may be times when virtualization isn't an option for your testing. A good example is if your tests require access to hardware that cannot be accessed virtually, such as a specialized imaging device that attaches to the serial port. In these cases, it is still possible to use some (but not all) of the same capabilities that Lab Management enables for virtual environments.

You can easily use the test controller and agent infrastructure to run automated tests across your physical machines. With additional work, you can also configure a build-deploy-test workflow by customizing the Team Build workflow in order to support the deployment of your application's components to physical environments.

The key capabilities you would not be able to take advantage of with physical environments are snapshots, and the capability to use the lab environment viewer integrated with Microsoft Test Manager for remotely accessing virtual environments. Instead, you can use software such as Remote Desktop to access these machines.

VMware

VMware is a popular virtualization technology, and a common query centers on whether the Lab Management infrastructure supports VMware images. The answer is, "It depends on what you want it to do."

Out of the box, Lab Management capabilities will only work with Microsoft's Hyper-V virtualization technology. But, similar to physical environments, it is possible to enable a build-deploy-test workflow with VMware deployments by essentially treating them as physical environments.

However, despite VMware being a virtualization technology, Lab Management does not provide any workflow activities for accessing VMware snapshotting capabilities. It is possible to author these activities and integrate them with Team Build's build-deploy-test workflow, but, as of this writing, there are no community projects to support this, so you would be faced with writing these activities yourself. Alternatively, there are several free tools available that can be used to help you convert existing VMware images that you might be using into Hyper-V images.

> *Microsoft has provided more details about the level of support for physical and VMware-based environments with Lab Management at* `http://msdn .microsoft.com/en-us/library/dd997438.aspx`.

Advanced Topologies

Your existing IT infrastructure requirements (such as whether you have multiple domains), your Team Foundation Server topology (such as whether you have a single AT/DT server, or a scale-out infrastructure), and other factors can have an impact on how you configure your Lab Management infrastructure. If you believe that your implementation might be nonstandard, you should read about the advanced topologies with which Lab Management has been tested and documented. This is available as a four-part blog series at the following locations:

- ➤ `http://tinyurl.com/LabTopology1`
- ➤ `http://tinyurl.com/LabTopology2`
- ➤ `http://tinyurl.com/LabTopology3`
- ➤ `http://tinyurl.com/LabTopology4`

Maintaining a Healthy Test Lab

An effective Lab Management infrastructure can be a powerful tool for development and testing teams alike to automate the delivery of their iterative software changes into environments that can be tested and, if defects are discovered, debugged. But this environment will require some level of administration to ensure that it remains healthy, and that resources are utilized effectively. This section highlights a few things to consider as your test lab starts to light up with activity.

Instilling Good Citizenship

Lab Management allows testers to easily deploy multiple virtual environments, often consisting of multiple VMs, across numerous physical VM hosts, with just a few clicks of their mouse. But Lab Management does not have a mechanism to enforce that testers shut down environments they are no longer using. Left unchecked, you may find that your VM hosts are running out of disk space, processing power, or (most likely) RAM. There is no substitute for educating testers about the resource constraints of the environment, and instructing them to power down environments that they aren't actively using. If an environment is obsolete, it should be deleted.

Lab Management allows you to pause an environment, which will prevent that environment from consuming any CPU cycles on its VM hosts. But this will not free allocated RAM. If testers wish to retain the state of VMs that they aren't actively using, a better approach is to create a snapshot of the environment. After a snapshot is taken, the environment can be powered off completely. When testers are once again ready to resume working with that virtual environment, they can restore it to the previous snapshot, and it will be restored to the state it was in prior to being powered off.

Finally, Lab Management allows testers to mark a virtual environment as "In Use" to signal that they are actively working with it, or planning on working with it soon. This indicates to other testers that they should not try to connect to that virtual environment. Administrators will then know that running environments *not* marked "In Use" can probably be powered off if they need to reclaim VM host resources. Of course, testers should also be instructed to unmark virtual environments that they are no longer using. If you notice that a tester has an unusually high number of virtual environments in use, then this may indicate that he or she is claiming more resources than should be necessary.

Managing Snapshots

Snapshots are a great benefit of virtualization that allows you to easily store the state of a VM at any point in time, and easily restore that state in the future. Snapshots have several uses in a Lab Management environment.

You can use snapshots to capture the baseline system state of a virtual environment prior to deploying your builds. You can again use snapshots to capture the state of the virtual environment after the build has been deployed, but before any of your tests have been run. Finally, if you find a defect, a tester can create a snapshot of an entire virtual environment and share a pointer to that snapshot when he or she creates a bug. This way, a developer can easily restore an environment back to the state it was in when the tester found the bug.

> *You can learn more about using snapshots within Microsoft Test Manager at* http://msdn.microsoft.com/en-us/library/ff427550.aspx.

But snapshots also have the capability to consume hefty amounts of disk space on your VM hosts. Additionally, Lab Management does not have a built-in retention policy to prune older snapshots — this will need to be done manually. Even if you set a retention policy in your build definition using Team Build, the process of deleting a build from here will not modify any virtual environments. Obsolete snapshots will need to be managed by the testers utilizing the virtual environments, or by a lab administrator.

> *Another reason to prune your snapshots is that Hyper-V has a built-in limitation of 50 snapshots per VM. Depending on how you use Lab Management, this limitation could be something to watch for, especially if you build and deploy multiple times per day.*

While it is possible to manage snapshots via the SCVMM Administration Console, this is not recommended. SCVMM is only aware of individual VMs. It doesn't understand the composition of VMs in virtual environments, since this level of organization is maintained by Lab Management. Therefore, it is best to manage snapshots using Lab Management via the Microsoft Test Manager interface.

Another important consideration regarding snapshots is that of password expiration. Since snapshots can date back many months, password expiration policies can cause authentication to fail if appropriate precautions are not taken to prevent this from happening. The documentation at http://msdn.microsoft.com/en-us/library/ff427550.aspx provides a detailed explanation of this process, along with preventative measures to keep it from impacting your virtual environments.

Workflow Customizations

The default build-deploy-test workflow provided with Lab Management is a powerful workflow, but there may be times when you want to customize this to add new activities, or change existing ones. Since the Lab Management workflows are built on Team Build, and Team Build in this release utilizes Windows Workflow, there are endless possibilities for extending and customizing the built-in workflows.

> *To read more about customizing the built-in Lab Management workflow, see* http://msdn.microsoft.com/en-us/library/ff934561.aspx. *This article also details the Lab Management activities that are provided out of the box, and can easily be added to existing workflows with very little additional work. Also, a blog post at* http://tinyurl.com/LabManagementBDTSnapshot *details how to use the Lab Management activities to automatically create a snapshot to reference from a bug if part of a build-deploy-test workflow fails.*

Patching of VMs and VM Templates

Many of the snapshots you create as part of your experience using Lab Management will be short-lived. Snapshots are commonly created when a new build is deployed, or when a bug is discovered. But a week or two later, older snapshots may be cleaned up in favor of newer builds, and as bugs are resolved. However, some VM artifacts — such as the VMs and VM templates in your VM library, or the baseline snapshots of virtual environments that you use as part of your build-deploy-test workflows — may last for months, or even years. Usually, you will want to keep these artifacts up to date with the latest security updates and other patches from Windows Update, but manually maintaining all of the VMs in your environment may prove to be very painstaking.

The recommended solution to this is to use the Virtual Machine Servicing Tool available at `http://technet.microsoft.com/en-us/library/cc501231.aspx`. This tool can be scheduled to automatically patch your VMs and VM templates with the latest updates from Windows Update. The use of this tool will require that you host and maintain Windows Server Update Services (WSUS) locally. This is a free download from Microsoft that allows you to specify which patches you wish to incorporate into your environments.

Troubleshooting

As you have seen in this chapter, utilizing the software testing capabilities of Visual Studio 2010 can involve many moving parts, long-running workflows, complex topologies, and many stakeholders from across your development and testing teams. The Lab Management product team diligently manages a list of evolving troubleshooting techniques, along with an active forum, on MSDN at `http://msdn.microsoft.com/en-us/library/ee853230.aspx`.

SUMMARY

In this chapter, you learned about the testing capabilities of Visual Studio 2010, and the impact that adopting these tools can have on your Team Foundation Server planning and administration. You learned about the architecture of Team Foundation Server when configured in concert with test controllers and agents, SCVMM, VM hosts, VM libraries, and both physical and virtual environments. Finally, you learned some key areas to consider as you build and scale out your Lab Management environment, as well as some tips to maintain this environment over time.

In Chapter 23, you will learn about upgrading from earlier editions of Team Foundation Server to Team Foundation Server 2010.

Upgrading from Earlier Versions

Instead of installing a brand-new Team Foundation Server 2010 instance, you may have an earlier version of Team Foundation Server internally and want to upgrade to Team Foundation Server 2010. Thankfully, Microsoft has provided the means to upgrade an existing server to the latest version. However, as a Team Foundation Server administrator, you will actually have several additional tasks to complete to ensure that end users are able to leverage the new features.

The upgrade wizard in Team Foundation Server 2010 allows upgrading from the following legacy versions:

➤ Team Foundation Server 2005

➤ Team Foundation Server 2005 with Service Pack 1

➤ Team Foundation Server 2008

➤ Team Foundation Server 2008 with Service Pack 1

In this chapter, you will learn about the different approaches to take for upgrading from an earlier version of Team Foundation Server, as well as what is involved with performing an upgrade for each part.

UPGRADING FROM TEAM FOUNDATION SERVER 2005 AND 2008

Getting the software and database schema from earlier versions of Team Foundation Server upgraded to Team Foundation Server 2010 could not be easier. However, you will discover that the upgraded Team Foundation Server 2010 environment will essentially work as though it were a Team Foundation Server 2008 instance that is now running in Team Foundation Server 2010. It will be your job to enable any new features that you desire for the legacy team projects that exist prior to upgrade.

There will be several aspects of an upgrade to take into consideration. In this section, you will learn about some of those aspects to ensure that your team can go through a smooth upgrade experience.

In-Place Upgrades Versus Migrating to New Hardware

The first major decision is whether you want to perform an in-place upgrade on the current hardware where Team Foundation Server is installed, or move to new hardware (including any environment topology changes, such as splitting to a dual-tier configuration).

The upgrade wizard in the configuration utility enables you to connect to a set of Team Foundation Server 2005 or 2008 databases and upgrade the schema and data appropriately.

During an in-place upgrade, the former versions of the software are uninstalled, and then Team Foundation Server 2010 is installed. The upgrade wizard then targets the existing database server, and the new databases are created in-place.

For a hardware migration-based upgrade, the legacy databases are fully backed up and then restored to the new hardware environment. The upgrade wizard is then pointed to the new database server instance. It will discover the legacy version, and appropriately upgrade the database schema to Team Foundation Server 2010.

> **DIFFERENCE BETWEEN MIGRATIONS AND UPGRADES**
>
> Moving to new hardware is considered a *hardware migration-based upgrade*, which should not be confused with another option that some may describe as "migrating to Team Foundation Server 2010." Note that despite having a similar name, a migration-based upgrade is *not* a migration.
>
> The approach that others have described (that is not recommended) would involve setting up a brand-new Team Foundation Server 2010 environment with new databases, creating new team projects, and then migrating the source code and work items using a tool such as the Team Foundation Server Integration platform.
>
> That approach will end up with many side effects, and is considered a *low-fidelity data transfer*. This is because the data has changed (such as changeset and work

item ID numbers) and this approach doesn't move over other data such as reporting, security privileges, and build information. By taking the actual upgrade route (which is described in this chapter), the configuration wizard will upgrade the database schema and keep all of the data as it existed from the Team Foundation Server 2008 environment. For that reason, this is considered a *high-fidelity upgrade*.

For more about these differences, you can read Matt Mitrik's articles about this topic here:

➤ `http://blogs.msdn.com/b/mitrik/archive/2010/01/25/upgrade-vs-migration-definitions.aspx`

➤ `http://blogs.msdn.com/b/mitrik/archive/2010/01/26/upgrade-vs-migration-upgrading-to-a-newer-version-of-tfs.aspx`

There are several advantages and disadvantages to both an in-place upgrade and a hardware migration-based upgrade. The main disadvantage to performing a hardware migration is the fact that you will need to acquire new hardware (whether physical or virtual machines). The nice thing, though, is that, after the upgrade is completed and verified, you will be able to retire the legacy hardware and repurpose it for some other use.

Following are the advantages of performing a hardware migration-based upgrade:

➤ *Testing the upgrade* — Having a separate Team Foundation Server environment allows you to perform the upgrade steps while the production environment is still running. This allows you to perform the upgrade to test it before going through with the final upgrade run.

➤ *Having a rollback plan* — One of the main advantages of performing a hardware migration-based upgrade is the fact that you have a rollback plan already in place in case the upgrade is not successful, or in case it cannot be verified. By keeping up the legacy hardware environment, you can have users continue to connect to the old environment (if needed) while researching any upgrade issues in the new hardware environment.

➤ *Taking advantage of new operating system versions* — If the legacy environment is using Windows Server 2003 or Windows Server 2008, you can take advantage of newer operating system versions (such as Windows Server 2008 R2) by ensuring that the new hardware has the latest versions installed. Otherwise, the final upgrade plan would require you to upgrade the operating system as well, which can affect your rollback plan.

➤ *Taking advantage of a 64-bit application tier* — Earlier versions of the Team Foundation Server application tier software only supported installation on 32-bit operating systems. By moving to new hardware, you can install the Team Foundation Server 2010 application tier software on a 64-bit version of either Windows Server 2008 R2 or Windows Server 2008.

➤ *Installing new copies of prerequisite software* — As discussed later in this chapter, you will end up needing to ensure that SQL Server and SharePoint are upgraded to newer versions for Team Foundation Server 2010. Acquiring new hardware allows you to install each of the prerequisite software fresh, instead of worrying about having to upgrade the software during the final upgrade.

Planning Upgrades

There are additional aspects to account for with the upgrade process that are different from a fresh Team Foundation Server 2010 installation. Let's take a look at a few of those.

Connection URL

Hopefully, the person setting up the earlier version of Team Foundation Server used fully qualified, friendly DNS names for each of the subsystems of Team Foundation Server as described in Chapter 2. After the upgrade is complete, you should ensure that the friendly DNS entries are changed to point to the new hardware environment. When users start connecting to the Team Foundation Server environment using the friendly DNS entries, they will automatically be pointing to the new environment that is fully upgraded without having to make any additional changes.

If friendly DNS names were not used in the previous setup, then it is recommended that you use the concepts described in Chapter 2 to allow for smoother upgrades in the future. Future Team Foundation Server administrators will thank you for it!

Also, remember that some versions of Visual Studio clients and other tools that connect to Team Foundation Server 2010 may need to include the team project collection name and the virtual directory in the connection URL. Chapters 4 and 17 provide more information about these changes.

Other Servers in Team Foundation Server Environment

Remember that there might be other servers that should be upgraded before they can be fully utilized. For example, all of the build servers will need to be upgraded to the latest version, as well as proxy servers.

Legacy versions of the build software cannot be used with a Team Foundation Server 2010 environment. The software is incompatible, and the application tier server will indicate that it is not able to connect to the legacy build servers until they are upgraded to use the latest version of the Team Foundation Server build software.

After testing the upgrade in a separate environment, you will want to establish downtime for the Team Foundation Server environment to be unavailable to end users while the upgrade wizard is processing the legacy databases and moving the information into the new databases. The amount of time necessary depends on the amount of data that is currently stored in the legacy databases. The amount of time is extremely variable and dependent on hardware, disk speed, available memory, and so on. This is also another great reason for doing a hardware migration based-upgrade!

When the cut-off time arrives, make sure that users are no longer using the environment and take the full backup. Any changes made to the legacy environment after the full backup occurs will not be available on the upgraded server.

After the upgrade has been successfully completed, there will be a different set of databases that are used by the Team Foundation Server 2010 environment. Legacy SQL Server backup plans may be looking for the legacy database names, so you will want to ensure that any relevant backup plans are reviewed and modified accordingly.

Chapter 19 provides more information about disaster recovery with Team Foundation Server 2010.

UPGRADING PREREQUISITES

Team Foundation Server 2010 drops support for several pieces of prerequisite software that were formerly supported with earlier versions of Team Foundation Server. Before running the upgrade wizard, you will want to ensure that all prerequisite software has been upgraded to the supported versions, since the upgrade wizard will block you from continuing if those conditions have not been met.

Team Foundation Server 2010 continues to support the 32-bit versions of Windows Server 2003 and Windows Server 2008. However, it also adds 64-bit support for Windows Server 2008 R2 and Windows Server 2008 to the list of supported operating systems. You will notice that the 64-bit versions of Windows Server 2003 are specifically *not* supported. Additionally, Team Foundation Server 2010 supports installing on Windows 7 and Windows Vista, although the reporting and SharePoint integration features will be disabled if you install on either of the supported client operating systems.

SQL Server

Team Foundation Server 2005 and 2008 both initially only supported using SQL Server 2005 on the data tier. SQL Server 2008 was added as a supported edition when Service Pack 1 for Team Foundation Server 2008 was released.

Additionally, Team Foundation Server 2010 supports using the Express version of SQL Server 2008 R2 or SQL Server 2008 if you would like to take advantage of a lighter-weight version of SQL. The Reporting Services and Analysis Services features are not available if you use SQL Express. This configuration is common if you choose to use the Basic configuration wizard. However, if you are upgrading a server, you will be using the Upgrade configuration wizard.

Virtualization of the server that has SQL Server installed is not recommended, because it can lead to data loss and severe performance problems. If you choose to use virtualization of the SQL Server machine, be sure to configure the virtual machine for top performance when working with Team Foundation Server. See the discussion about virtualization in Chapter 2 for more information.

SharePoint

Team Foundation Server 2005 and 2008 both supported using Windows SharePoint Services 2.0 for the team project portal sites. Unfortunately, if you are still using Windows SharePoint Services 2.0, you must upgrade to one of the following versions of SharePoint products and technologies that are supported by Team Foundation Server 2010:

➤ Windows SharePoint Services 3.0 (*no licensing cost*)

➤ Microsoft Office SharePoint Server 2007

➤ SharePoint 2010 Foundation (*no licensing cost*)

➤ Office SharePoint 2010 Server

> *For more information about upgrading the SharePoint products and technologies for a Team Foundation Server 2010 environment, see the related topic and step-by-step instructions available on MSDN at* `http://go.microsoft.com/fwlink/?LinkId=167252`*.*

USING THE CONFIGURATION UTILITY

The latest version of the *Team Foundation Server 2010 Installation Guide* has a step-by-step list of instructions and a checklist that details how to upgrade using either upgrade approach (in-place upgrade or hardware migration-based upgrade). You will want to make sure that you follow each part of the checklist to ensure the smoothest upgrade possible.

If you are following the hardware migration-based upgrade approach, you will essentially back up the databases on the old database server instance, and then restore them on the new database server instance. Once you have upgraded all of the prerequisite software and restored a full backup of all of the Team Foundation Server databases as listed in the *Installation Guide*, you are ready to go through the Team Foundation Server upgrade wizard.

As mentioned in Chapter 3, the setup configuration process has been split into two parts. There is an installation phase that puts all of the necessary software on the application tier server. There is not a separate data tier server install as there was in Team Foundation Server 2005. Once the software is installed, you configure it with a separate configuration utility. This segmented approach resolves the legacy issue introduced in earlier versions of Team Foundation Server (that is, an installation that was successful, but whose configuration failed). In those cases, all of the software was removed from the server, even though it was correctly placed. Now you are able to get everything installed, and a rich user interface (UI) can let you know if there are any problems during the configuration phase, instead of it occurring inside of an installer.

Interestingly, another benefit of this two-phase approach is that Microsoft can release service packs and patches that will easily fix problems with the configuration utility!

Upgrade Wizard

Instead of taking the approach of installing a new server as described in Chapter 3, you will instead need to run the upgrade wizard once to get the database schema upgraded to the version used by

Team Foundation Server 2010. The Upgrade wizard option is available in the configuration utility, as shown in Figure 23-1.

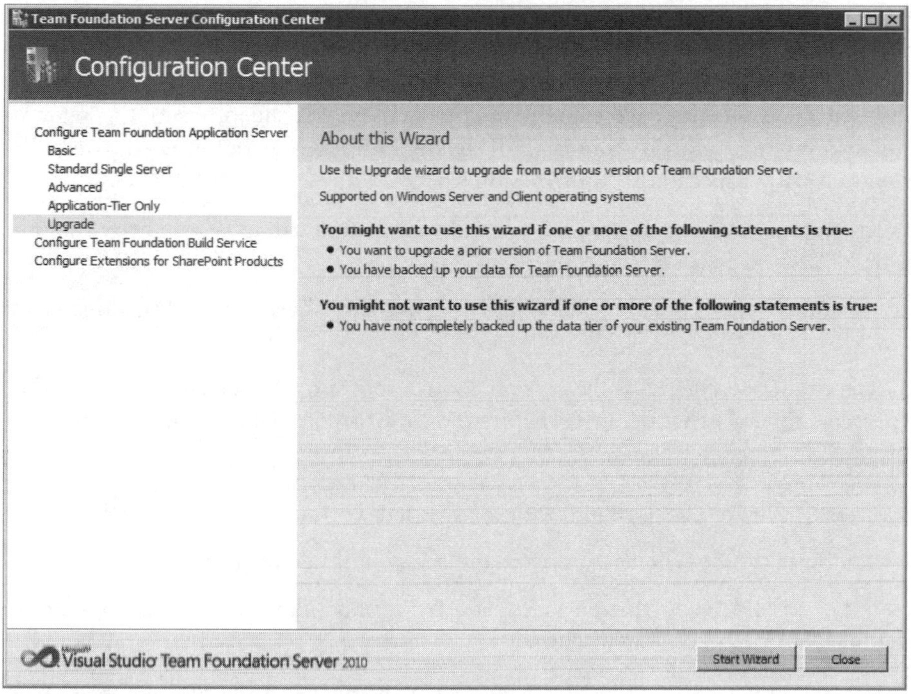

FIGURE 23-1: Upgrade wizard option

If you will be including multiple application tier servers that are behind a network load balancer, you must run the Upgrade wizard only once for the first application tier server. Then you can use the Application Tier wizard for each additional application tier server.

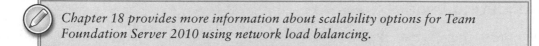

Chapter 18 provides more information about scalability options for Team Foundation Server 2010 using network load balancing.

Follow each of the upgrade wizard pages at this point and enter the information requested. The latest version of the *Installation Guide* has step-by-step directions and information about each option displayed within the upgrade wizard.

Before the upgrade process begins, all of the options and information that you input will be validated to ensure that there are no issues. If you see any errors listed, you must resolve them before continuing. For several errors that may occur, you are able to restart the check without leaving the wizard.

Once you are ready, you can begin the upgrade process. This will kick off several upgrade jobs that will run through the upgrade steps that are necessary for each subsystem of Team Foundation Server. It will show you the progress of each set of upgrade jobs for the default team project collection.

Verification of Upgrade

After all of the upgrade jobs have completed for the new default team project collection, a confirmation will be displayed. If there were any issues, you can restart the job using the Team Foundation Server Administration utility. But if all of the upgrade steps were followed, you will more than likely end up with a successful confirmation.

➤ Check to ensure that any existing version control workspaces still exist and are configured the same as before the upgrade.

➤ Open the version control repository and check to make sure shelvesets and pending changes for your workspace still exist.

➤ Check the maximum changeset in the version control repository and ensure that it is the latest expected changeset that occurred before the cut-off time and the full backup.

➤ Open and create work items.

➤ Run work item queries to check that all of the expected work items are returned.

➤ View existing builds and queue new builds with legacy build definitions.

➤ Navigate and open SQL Reporting Services reports. (It may take several hours before the new warehouse has been populated with data.)

➤ Ensure that you can navigate to the SharePoint team portal sites and that the `Documents` node shows all document libraries from the associated team portal sites.

Additionally, to ensure that the entire environment is healthy, you can run the Best Practices Analyzer for Team Foundation Server 2010 (as introduced in Chapter 17) that is available in the latest version of the Team Foundation Server 2010 Power Tools. This will run a full set of rules to check the entire environment to make sure everything is working as expected. You can also start monitoring the environment using the techniques you learned in Chapter 21.

Consolidating Legacy Servers

If your enterprise has several legacy Team Foundation Server environments, you may want to take this time to consolidate to one instance using multiple team project collections. You can actually perform full-fidelity upgrades by using the Team Foundation Server configuration utility, but unfortunately you can only use the UI for the first legacy database.

For each additional legacy set of databases, you can use the following command-line option to import and upgrade those databases as a new team project collection in the same Team Foundation Server 2010 instance:

```
TFSConfig.exe import /sqlinstance:SQLServerWithLegacyDatabases
        /collectionName:ImportedCollection /confirmed
```

For more information about the steps necessary for consolidating multiple legacy Team Foundation Server environments, Matt Mitrik has a blog post that includes more information about this scenario, as well as the relevant links to the documentation for how to perform the steps. See http://blogs.msdn.com/ b/mitrik/archive/2010/01/29/upgrade-vs-migration-server- consolidation-during-upgrade.aspx.

UPGRADING LEGACY TEAM PROJECTS

Now that you have a working Team Foundation Server 2010 environment based on the upgraded legacy version of the databases, you will notice that the legacy team projects will be working exactly the way they did in the earlier versions of Team Foundation Server. This means that several of the new features introduced in Team Foundation Server 2010 will not be available for end users. The following sections examine each of these features, and provide options for enabling them for existing team projects.

Alternatively, you can start using the new features by creating new team projects that use the latest version of the process templates included with Team Foundation Server 2010, and then perform a version control move operation into the new team project.

However, existing build definitions and work item tracking don't have standard tools available for moving to the new team project. For work item tracking, you could potentially use the Team Foundation Server Integration Platform tools, but, again, this would be a low-fidelity data transfer as previously discussed.

Allen Clark keeps an updated blog post that further summarizes the different components of a team project that need to be updated to use the new features at http://blogs.msdn.com/b/allclark/archive/2010/12/08/enababling-new- application-lifecycle-management-features-for-visual-studio-2010-in- upgraded-team-projects.aspx.

Enabling Branch Visualization

Heuristics are performed during the upgrade wizard to analyze version control folders that should be first-class branches. However, the process is not 100 percent accurate. You should attempt to look through the existing team projects and the branches that exist in each of them to ensure that everything is correct. You may find that you will need to re-parent branches, or convert existing folders to branch objects.

Chapter 9 provides more information about branch visualization in the Team Foundation Server version control repository.

Enabling Test Case Management

If you were to open Microsoft Test Manager to start creating and managing test plans for any of the legacy team projects, you would notice that they do not have the necessary components to enable test case management. There are several steps for ensuring that these legacy team projects have the necessary components.

For example, you will need to add the Test Case and Shared Steps work item types, as well as add the appropriate work item categories and work item link types that Microsoft Test Manager is wanting to use.

> *Each of the steps that are required for enabling the test case management features in a legacy team project is detailed in the MSDN article at* `http://msdn` `.microsoft.com/en-us/library/ff452591.aspx`.

Upgrading Work Item Type Definitions

You might have immediately noticed that the work item types are exactly the same in the upgraded legacy team projects as those that existed under your old Team Foundation Server version. This is by design, since it allows teams to continue working with their existing development process without forcing all users to move to a new process. If you want to take advantage of the new features that are included in the latest version of the process templates, you must make all of the changes manually.

The best way to do this is to download both the legacy process template from the server, as well as the latest version of the process template, and then compare each of the work item type definitions in your favorite comparison tool. Your goal is to "morph" the existing team project's work item type definitions from the old version to the new versions.

For some of the process templates (such as the MSF Agile process templates), you will notice that there are work item types that no longer exist, and new ones that are now included. For example, the MSF Agile v4.2 process template included a work item type named "Scenario," whereas the MSF Agile v5.0 process template includes a work item type called "User Story." You may decide that the appropriate process template upgrade step in this case would be to rename the Scenario work item type to use the new name. You can accomplish this by running the following command:

```
witadmin.exe renamewitd /collection:http://tfs:8080/tfs/DefaultCollection
    /p:LegacyTeamProject /n:"Scenario" /new:"User Story"
```

After renaming the work item type, you can then continue comparing the old work item type definition with the work item type definition of the new type. You may find yourself needing to create new fields, and even changing the names of some fields.

For example, there have been several fields that have changed names since the legacy versions of Team Foundation Server, as shown in Table 23-1. However, all of the team projects will use the old names instead of the new ones. You will find issues when comparing the process templates, though, if you do not change each of the fields to use the new names.

TABLE 23-1: Changed Core Field Names

REFERENCE NAME	OLD FRIENDLY NAME	NEW FRIENDLY NAME
System.AreaID	AreaID	Area ID
System.IterationID	IterationID	Iteration ID
System.HyperLinkCount	HyperLinkCount	HyperLink Count
System.ExternalLinkCount	ExternalLinkCount	External Link Count
System.AttachedFileCount	AttachedFileCount	Attached File Count

You might use the following command to update the name of one of the fields mentioned previously in the entire team project collection.

```
witadmin.exe changefield /collection:http://tfs:8080/tfs/DefaultCollection
    /n:System.AttachedFileCount /name:"Attached File Count"
```

You may notice that some fields have changed their type as well. For example, if you were using the MSF CMMI v4.2 process template, you would notice that the Bug work item type had a plain text field named "Steps to Reproduce." To support the new rich bug functionality in Microsoft Test Manager, however, the new process templates (including MSF Agile v5.0) have a new HTML field with a different name of Repro Steps. In this particular case, you should follow these steps:

1. Add the new field to the work item type definition.

2. Import the new work item type definition with the new defined field.

3. Copy the contents for all work items of that type from the old field to the new field (for example, using the integration in Microsoft Office Excel).

4. Remove the old field from the work item type definition and replace any entries in the form layout with the newly defined field.

5. Import the work item type definition with the old field removed.

> *Chapter 12 provides more information about how to edit process templates and work item type definitions.*

Automated Builds

Build definitions that existed before the upgrade process continue to exist after the environment has been upgraded. However, instead of using the new default build process template that is based on Windows Workflow Foundation 4.0, you will notice that the legacy build definitions use the UpgradeTemplate.xaml build process template.

The UpgradeTemplate.xaml build process template is a simple build process template that calls the legacy TFSBuild.proj MSBuild file that was defined and used in earlier versions of Team Foundation Server. This will allow you to continue using the legacy builds on the new server. You will want to ensure that each of your legacy build definitions continue to work successfully.

However, the UpgradeTemplate.xaml does not add any new features in Team Foundation Server 2010 that are included in the default build process template. For example, test impact analysis, source code indexing for Source server, and publishing symbols to Symbol server are just a few of the features that are only included in the default build process template.

You will want to convert your existing builds to using a build process template based on Windows Workflow Foundation 4.0 when you get the opportunity. If you did not make any customizations to the legacy build project files, you will find it simple to start using the new default build process template. However, if your project included lots of customization (including the use of custom MSBuild tasks), you must spend more effort defining a custom build process and converting the MSBuild tasks to custom build workflow activities.

> *Chapter 16 includes more information about how to customize the build process and create custom build workflow activities.*

Deploying New Reports

The data warehouse schema for Team Foundation Server 2010 has been updated and no longer works with the reports that were included in earlier versions. Thankfully, you can deploy a new set of reports using the new process templates (assuming you have performed all of the "morphing" steps to get your team project up to the latest process template version) by using a tool available from the latest version of Team Foundation Server Power Tools. It is available from the command line by using the following command:

```
tfpt.exe addprojectreports /collection:http://tfs:8080/tfs/
    DefaultCollection /teamproject:LegacyTeamProject /
    processtemplate:"MSF for Agile Software Development v5.0" /force
```

This command will download the specified process template and deploy all of the reports that are included in the process template appropriately to the reporting site associated with the specified team project. The /force option allows you to overwrite what already exists if there is a report with the same name. You can modify the reports, upload the updated process template, and repeat this process as necessary.

Deploying New SharePoint Team Portal Site

Team portal sites that exist in legacy team projects do not take advantage of all of the SharePoint dashboard features as described in Chapter 13. This is one of the toughest options, since there is no way to convert an existing site and enable the dashboards on a portal site template.

In this case, the best option would be to archive the document library content from the legacy team portal site, create a new team portal site using the latest process template, and then add the archived document library content. There may be other types of features that were used that may not be able to be migrated over successfully. You will have to weigh the options appropriately.

The latest version of the Team Foundation Server 2010 Power Tools also includes a command-line tool for creating a new team portal site and associating it with a team project. The following example command could be used to perform this step:

```
tfpt.exe addprojectportal /collection:http://tfs:8080/tfs/
    DefaultCollection /teamproject:LegacyTeamProject /
    processtemplate:"MSF for Agile Software Development v5.0"
```

You can specify additional options if you want the team portal site to be created in a different location from the default location specified for the team project collection.

SUMMARY

As you learned in this chapter, using the upgrade wizard that is available will allow you to move all of your data from a legacy version of Team Foundation Server to Team Foundation Server 2010 using a high-fidelity upgrade method. In this chapter, you learned about the two types of upgrades — an in-place upgrade and a hardware migrated-based upgrade.

Additionally, you learned about the preparation steps that are necessary for a successful upgrade, including taking care of any prerequisite software. Finally, you learned about the features that are not available on legacy team projects until they are enabled in Team Foundation Server 2010.

Chapter 24 introduces the issues that come up whenever you have geographically separated teams that need to use the Team Foundation Server environment. The chapter explores the different options available to resolve those issues, and provides methods for ensuring a smoothly operating worldwide environment for all of the geographically separated teams.

24

Working with Geographically Distributed Teams

WHAT'S IN THIS CHAPTER?

➤ Understanding the difficulties of a distributed development environment

➤ Getting to know Team Foundation Server Proxy

➤ Learning techniques for working with remote teams

➤ Dealing with build servers in a distributed environment

➤ Getting to know Team Foundation Server Integration Tools

➤ Understanding how to be effective when the server is not available

The development of software by distributed teams is a growing trend. People are working in a global economy with greater competition and choice. There are many reasons you may be working with a distributed team, including the following:

➤ Your company has grown and expanded, and has several field offices.

➤ Your company contracts out portions of development to third parties.

➤ A merger has occurred, and two companies must work interactively over great distances.

Even if you don't work in a distributed team, you may work in an environment whereby your server infrastructure is located at a different physical location. Following are a couple of examples:

➤ Your IT infrastructure is outsourced to another company.

➤ Your development team is located in a different city from the main office to take advantage of skilled workers in that area.

➤ You have a mobile workforce that moves between offices and has no main office.

When you work with Team Foundation Server 2010 in this environment, there are a number of challenges that you will face, and considerations that you must account for. This chapter explores those challenges, and explores ways that you can overcome them.

IDENTIFYING THE CHALLENGES

There are a number of challenges involved when working with geographically distributed teams. This chapter walks you through the challenges most relevant to your Team Foundation Server environment.

Latency Over the Wide Area Network (WAN)

Perhaps the biggest technical challenge that distributed teams will face is the network connection that separates them and the server. Network connectivity can be affected by many different factors. However, the biggest factor is latency.

Latency is the time that it takes for packets of data to travel between two points. Think of when you connect a garden hose to a tap and then turn it on. There is a delay between when you turn on the tap and when water starts pouring out the other end. This delay is called latency. Latency in a networking context can be "one-way" latency or "round-trip" latency. *Round-trip latency* is the time it takes data to travel from the client to the server and back again. It is usually measured by running the `ping` command against a server.

On a local area network (LAN), typical round-trip latency is less than 5 milliseconds. Between two computers within the same continent, typical round-trip latency is less than 100 milliseconds.

What's important to realize is that regardless of the speed of your Internet connection, your latency can never beat the speed of light. The speed of light in fiber-optic cable is roughly 35 percent slower than in a vacuum. As an example, the shortest distance between Sydney, Australia, and Seattle, Washington, is about 8,000 miles, or 12,000 kilometers. Therefore, the absolute minimum one-way latency is 60 milliseconds, and the round-trip latency is 120 milliseconds. In reality, though, the cables don't run directly between two points, and the latency is higher because of this and intermediate network equipment.

Another aspect of latency is that it isn't always symmetric. Latency could be greater in one direction compared to the other. This can be seen when using a one-way satellite Internet connection. The upstream data is sent using a landline, and the downstream data is received via a satellite dish. Because the data must travel from the Internet to a base station, to the satellite, and then back down to the receiving dish, typical round-trip latency is 300 milliseconds.

Microsoft recommends that a server running Team Foundation Server should have a reliable network connection with a minimum bandwidth of 1 Mbps and a latency maximum of 350 milliseconds.

Sources of Network Traffic

Within the components of a Team Foundation Server environment, there are many different sources of network traffic. Table 24-1 details the contribution of each component, which will vary in each environment. In most environments, version control and work item tracking are typically the biggest contributors. Depending on your configuration, virtual machine deployments from Lab Management can be a large contributor.

TABLE 24-1: Network Traffic Associated with Each Component

COMPONENT	TRAFFIC
Version control	Source files and operations
Work item tracking	Work items, operations, metadata cache, and attachments
Web access	Web pages, images, scripts, style sheets, attachments, and source files
Reporting	Reports, database queries, and Analysis Services queries
SharePoint products (including dashboards)	Web pages, documents, work items, and reports
Team Foundation Build	Build logs and build outputs
Lab Management	Commands, System Center Virtual Machine Manager (SCVMM) traffic, lab environments, and templates

Version Control

Version control in a Team Foundation Server environment will almost always be the largest contributor to network traffic. There are two sources of traffic:

➤ User commands

➤ File content downloads

Whenever a client performs a `Get`, the server will send the entire content of any file that has changed to the client. The more clients you have, the more traffic there is. The amount of traffic is also proportional to the number, frequency and size of files that change in the repository.

Work Item Tracking

There are three main sources of traffic for work item tracking:

➤ User commands (queries, opens, saves, and bulk updates)

➤ Metadata cache downloads

➤ Attachment downloads and uploads

The biggest contributor of these three is usually the metadata cache.

Every team project has a set of metadata that includes work item rules, global lists, form layouts, and other project settings.

Whenever a client communicates with the server to perform a work item related query, it tells the server what version of the metadata it is using. The server then sends back all the metadata that it doesn't know about yet, along with the data the client was actually asking for. This is called a *metadata refresh*. There are two types of metadata refreshes: *incremental* and *full*.

In Team Foundation Server 2008, certain administrative operations such as deleting a field caused the metadata cache to be invalidated. All clients would then download the full metadata cache the next time they performed a query.

In Team Foundation Server 2010, almost all operations that invalidate the cache will use an incremental update. This means that not only the load on the server (in the form of memory pressure and metadata requests) is greatly reduced, but the overall network traffic to the client is also reduced.

> *To measure the work item tracking metadata cache size, on any client computer, locate the* `C:\Users\<user>\AppData\Local\Microsoft\Team Foundation\3.0\Cache` *folder. Right-click a subdirectory that has a* `GUID` *as the name, select Properties, and read the size in the Properties dialog box. Remember that the metadata cache is likely to be compressed when it travels over the network, so you might have to use a network traffic sniffer like NetMon to see the actual network transfer size, rather than looking at the folder size.*

PROBLEMS WITH METADATA CACHE REFRESHES AT MICROSOFT

Because of the level of customization by various teams at Microsoft, there were a lot of unique fields, rules, and work items on the internal servers. In an effort to clean up some of the fields and consolidate them, the project administrators started to delete the unused fields.

This field deletion caused the metadata cache to be invalidated, and forced all clients to perform a full metadata cache refresh. The combination of a large metadata cache and a large number of clients effectively took the server offline by consuming all the memory available, and all available connections, while the clients refreshed their caches.

As a brute-force work-around before metadata filtering was available, the team renamed the stored procedure that invalidated the cache to prevent the problem from happening during business hours. Then, if there was a need to delete the fields and invalidate the cache, the team would rename it back and run the command on a weekend. The cache refreshes would then be staggered as people arrived at work on Monday and connected to the server.

Visual Studio 2010 clients perform an incremental update if a field is deleted on the server, so this is no longer a problem.

SOLUTIONS

There are a number of different ways to overcome the challenges of working with geographically distributed teams. Each of these solutions can be used by itself, or combined with others to fit your needs.

Central Server with Remote Proxy Servers

The Team Foundation Server Proxy is a server that is capable of caching downloads of files from version control, and it is discussed later in this chapter.

This is the recommended and simplest environment to configure and maintain. It is the best choice when your users are working from branch offices that can host remote proxy servers.

However, the drawback is that if your users are evenly spread around the world, then there is no central place to locate the server, and latency will be a problem for everybody.

Multiple Distributed Servers

If your distributed teams are working on different products that can be developed in isolation of each other, then running multiple servers may be an option.

This has the benefits of allowing everyone to work with a local server on their projects. The drawback, of course, is that there are now multiple servers to maintain, along with codebases in different repositories.

The remote team could host their own Team Foundation Server and maintain a dedicated team project collection. Then, when it comes time to hand off the product to the in-house maintenance team, the collection can be detached from the remote server, backed up, and then attached to the local server.

> *For more information on this procedure, see the "Move a Team Project Collection" page on MSDN at* `http://msdn.microsoft.com/en-us/library/dd936138.aspx`.

Mirroring

If your development cannot be partitioned between the different remote sites, then one option is to use the Team Foundation Server Integration Tools to mirror source code and work items between the different servers. This may sound like the silver bullet that can solve all of your problems, but it's not without a cost. Every mirror that you set up has an overhead associated with it. When people are depending upon the mirror, its operation and maintenance must be taken just as seriously as running the Team Foundation Servers themselves.

This topic will be looked at in more detail later in this chapter.

Remote Desktops

In some environments, it's not acceptable to have intellectual property stored on remote machines that are outside the IT department's control. This is especially true in highly regulated environments like governmental, defense, and financial industries.

One solution for these environments is to maintain a central Team Foundation Server along with Remote Desktop Services (RDS) or other Virtual Desktop Infrastructure (VDI) for clients. Essentially, a remote user will connect to a virtual desktop that is on the same network as the central server. The only traffic that must travel across the network is the keyboard and mouse input, and the video output. However, depending on your usage of Team Foundation Server, this may require more bandwidth than not using remote desktops.

Internet-Connected "Extranet" Server

Virtual Private Networks (VPNs) and other remote access technologies can become a bottleneck compared to accessing servers directly over the Internet. If you have teams that are clustered at remote sites, the site will often have a dedicated VPN that has less overall overhead and usually a better network connection. However, if you have mobile workers spread around the world, they will often be able to get a better Internet connection from their local ISP than connecting to the corporate network.

By exposing your server directly on the Internet, you allow people to connect directly to it without having the overhead of encapsulating their traffic in a VPN tunnel.

If you decide to connect your Team Foundation Server to the Internet, you should consider enabling and requiring the HTTP over SSL (HTTPS) protocol to encrypt the traffic to and from the server.

Mirroring to an Internet-Connected Server

As an example of combining different solutions, you can combine mirroring with an Internet-connected server. This allows you to synchronize a subset of your internal projects with a server that people on the Internet can connect to.

Metadata Filtering

As mentioned earlier in this chapter, the metadata cache has the potential to become a huge source of network traffic. When metadata filtering is enabled, the server will send the minimum amount of metadata required for the project that you are connecting to. This can reduce the network traffic if people generally only connect to one team project.

The downside is that the metadata cache is invalidated each time you connect to a new server. This can especially be a hindrance if people connect to more than one project on the server. In this case, the server will be sending some of the same metadata each time they connect. It would be more efficient to download the full metadata for all projects just once.

 More information on how metadata filtering works and how to enable it can be found on Martin Woodward's blog at `http://tinyurl.com/MetadataFiltering`.

BUILD SERVERS

When you work in a geographically distributed team, the availability of nightly builds to your testers can be an important decision point. There are a few different options available, and each of them has different benefits and trade-offs.

Local Build Server

This is the most common scenario for small to midsized teams, where the build server is on a server in the same location as the Team Foundation Server itself. In this scenario, the speed of the build isn't affected by the speed of the WAN.

The downside of this approach is that it will take time and use WAN bandwidth for remote teams to get the build outputs. Additionally, unless you use some other caching technology, or set up a script to copy build outputs to remote sites, then everyone at the remote sites will be transferring the same files over the WAN multiple times. This is slow, and can be expensive if you are charged for WAN traffic.

Remote Build Server

In this scenario, you would situate build servers at your remote locations. Combining this with a Team Foundation Server Proxy at each remote site, you get a good solution. The build servers have access to a local cache as facilitated by the proxy server, and the developers have access to local build outputs.

TEAM FOUNDATION SERVER PROXY

The Team Foundation Server Proxy is a server that is capable of caching downloads of files from version control. Even if you don't have a geographically distributed team, there are features that will be useful to all teams that use version control.

How the Team Foundation Server Proxy Works

The Team Foundation Server Proxy server is purely used for source control access. It is not utilized for work item tracking or any other functions in Team Foundation Server. Typically, the proxy server is used at remote offices to improve the performance of version control downloads. However, it can (and should) be a part of any reasonably busy Team Foundation Server installation.

> *For more detailed information on how the Team Foundation Server Proxy works, refer to* http://tinyurl.com/HowTFSProxyWorks.

Compatibility

Both the 2008 and 2010 proxy servers can act as proxies for Team Foundation Server 2008 and 2010. Both versions can proxy for multiple servers and collections. When a 2010 proxy server is configured and given access to a Team Foundation Server 2010 server, it automatically proxies requests for all team project collections on that server. This is useful when you add new collections to a server, because you don't need to do anything special to set up the proxy to be available for those collections.

Configuring Proxies

A proxy server doesn't necessarily have to be registered with the Team Foundation Server to be used. The only requirement is that the service account that the proxy server runs as must have the "View collection-level information" permission for each project collection.

The easiest way to set this up is to add the proxy service account to the built-in server-level group:

```
[TEAM FOUNDATION]\Team Foundation Proxy Service Accounts
```

Each project collection has its own group that the server-level group is a member of:

```
[DefaultCollection]\Project Collection Proxy Service Accounts
```

If you are setting up a proxy server for use by all users at a particular remote location, you'll want to do these three things:

1. Run the proxy as the built-in `Network Service` account, so that you don't have to update the service account password every time it changes.

2. Add the proxy service account to the server-level group on each server that you want it to proxy for.

3. Register the proxy server with the server, and set it as the default for the Active Directory site that it is located in.

> *To register a proxy server, substitute your own site and server names when you use the following command from any client with appropriate permissions:*
>
> ```
> tf proxy /collection:http://servername:8080/tfs/DefaultCollection
>         /add http://proxyserver:8081/VersionControlProxy
>         /site:HEAD-OFFICE /default:site
> ```

Proxy Cleanup Settings

A proxy server will perform best when it has a copy of the files that people most often request. In reality, that's easier said than done, since it's difficult to predict which version of which files people are going to want before they actually request them. To deal with this, the proxy will keep a copy in its cache of every version of every file that is requested. Without any cleanup, the cache directory will eventually fill to capacity.

The proxy has a built-in cleanup job that is designed to delete older files and make space available for more recently requested files.

You can express the cache limit in many ways, including as a percentage of disk space. For example, the proxy cache with the following configuration can only take up 75 percent of your hard drive space.

```
<PercentageBasedPolicy>75</PercentageBasedPolicy>
```

You can also express your cache limit as a fixed number of megabytes, as shown here:

```
<FixedSizeBasedPolicy>1000</FixedSizeBasedPolicy>
```

The cleanup will trigger when the available space on the cache drive exceeds the threshold.

> *For more information on these cache settings and how to change them see "How to: Change Cache Settings for Team Foundation Server Proxy" at* http://msdn .microsoft.com/en-us/library/ms400763.aspx.

Automatically Detecting the Proxy Settings

In Team Foundation Server 2010, there is a new feature that allows a proxy server to be registered with the collection. This means that users don't have to know which proxy server they should be using. In addition to the `tf proxy /configure` command, the Visual Studio IDE will automatically query and set a default proxy server if one is registered on the server. This is achieved through the `GetBestProxies` method in the version control object model.

Active Directory Sites

The physical structure of a Windows network is defined in Active Directory as a site. A site contains one or more subnet objects. Typically, a remote office will have its own subnet, and will be defined as a separate site.

Team Foundation Server leverages this infrastructure and allows you to define a default proxy server for each site in Active Directory. As an example, the Team Foundation Server product team is split between Raleigh, North Carolina, and Redmond, Washington. The corporate network has the Raleigh office configured as a separate site to the Redmond office. When a developer travels from one office to the other, and connects to the office network, the Visual Studio client automatically detects the new site and reconfigures itself to use the default proxy for that site.

Setting a Proxy

The version control proxy settings are a per-user and per-machine setting. To force your client to configure the default proxy for the site, you can run the following commands:

```
tf.exe proxy /configure
tf.exe proxy /enabled:true
```

You can query registry keys to see if you have a proxy configured by running the following commands:

```
reg.exe query HKEY_CURRENT_USER\Software\Microsoft\VisualStudio\10.0\
    TeamFoundation\SourceControl\Proxy /v Enabled
reg.exe query HKEY_CURRENT_USER\Software\Microsoft\VisualStudio\10.0\
    TeamFoundation\SourceControl\Proxy /v Url
```

You can also set registry keys to enable a proxy server without using `tf.exe` by running the following commands:

```
reg.exe add HKEY_CURRENT_USER\Software\Microsoft\VisualStudio\10.0\
    TeamFoundation\SourceControl\Proxy /v Enabled /d True /f
reg.exe reg add HKEY_CURRENT_USER\Software\Microsoft\VisualStudio\10.0\
    TeamFoundation\SourceControl\Proxy
    /v Url /d http://proxyserver:8081 /f
```

Although it's not documented or officially supported, you can also set the `TFSPROXY` environment variable, and any client that uses the version control object model will use the proxy.

```
set TFSPROXY=http://proxyserver:8081
```

Seeding Proxies

As was mentioned earlier in this chapter, the proxy server will only cache a copy of a file if someone requests it. Because of this, you may want to implement a process that will seed the proxy with the most commonly used files in an off-peak period, or after a period of high churn.

As an example, for the Team Foundation Server product team at Microsoft, the main servers are located in Washington on the West Coast. The other half of the team is in North Carolina on the East Coast. The nightly build checks in some of the build outputs to source control. These binary files can be quite large, and the bandwidth at the remote site is often strained during the day.

The team implemented a scheduled task at the remote site that requests the latest versions from the main server after the build has completed. Since the proxy server doesn't have these versions, it then downloads them and caches a copy. This means that the first person who needs those files the following day doesn't have to wait for the lengthy download, and that person gets sent the cached copy from the proxy server.

Using scheduled tasks is one approach to this problem. Another approach is to set up a build server at the remote site. The first part of a build is generally to create a workspace and get the latest version of the source code. If this build is set up to run nightly, or build every check-in (in other words, a Continuous Integration build), then it will keep the contents of the proxy fresh for other users of that code.

Personal Proxies

A personal proxy server is useful if you do not have a remote office with a proxy server near you. By setting up your own personal proxy server, you will only have to download a file's contents once.

One of the changes in the Team Foundation Server 2010 license agreement is that each MSDN subscription provides a license to deploy one instance of Team Foundation Server 2010 into production on one device. Since Team Foundation Server Proxy is just a different configuration of the product, this means that each user with an MSDN subscription could run a personal proxy server.

> *For the full details, see the "Visual Studio 2010 Licensing" whitepaper at* `http://go.microsoft.com/?linkid=9721784` *and your applicable licensing agreements.*

MIRRORING WITH THE TEAM FOUNDATION SERVER INTEGRATION TOOLS

In the past, there was a download available on CodePlex called the "TFS Migration Synchronization Toolkit." The intention of the toolkit was to allow people to build custom tools that enabled migration and synchronization with other version control and work-tracking systems. The original release of the toolkit received a lot of negative feedback, and not many people were able to successfully use it.

In 2008, the product team made a decision to invest in an effort to address the feedback from the previous version and build a solid platform that enabled synchronization with other systems. The result of this effort is the Team Foundation Server Integration Tools, which was released in the Visual Studio Gallery at `http://tinyurl.com/TFSIntTools`. The Integration Tools are fully supported by Microsoft Support, and are the same tools that Microsoft uses internally to keep data synchronized between different Team Foundation Server instances.

The platform uses an adapter architecture, and it ships with a Software Development Kit (SDK) that allows others to implement the interfaces and leverage all the capabilities of the platform.

The first adapters that were written were the work item tracking and version control adapters for Team Foundation Server 2008 and 2010. The selfish reason the product group invested in the platform was because they had a desire to start using early builds of Team Foundation Server 2010 for day-to-day usage. The problem with this was that the server code was not yet stable enough to risk upgrading the division's main server. This prompted the team to set up a second server and run a two-way synchronization of work items and source code between them.

This not only allowed the team to be confident in the quality of Team Foundation Server 2010 before shipping it, but it also allowed the Integration Tools team to test drive their solution to drive features and improvements into the product. The end result is a proven and versatile tool for migration and synchronization of other systems with Team Foundation Server.

Capabilities

In the first release, the built-in Team Foundation Server 2008 and 2010 adapters had the following capabilities:

- ➤ *Synchronization* — This included unidirectional or bidirectional synchronization.
- ➤ *Version control* — This included the migration of all files and folders, and support for preserving changeset contents. The following changetypes are currently supported: add, edit, rename, delete, branch, merge, and type.

➤ *Work item tracking* — This included the migration of all work item revisions, fields, attachments, areas and iterations, and links (including links to changesets).

➤ *Context synchronization* — The tool can synchronize work item types, group memberships, and global lists.

Field Maps, Value Maps, and User Maps

When synchronizing two different systems, you are almost guaranteed that the configuration will be different between the two endpoints. This is where mappings are useful. As an example, you might have a `Priority` field with values 1, 2, and 3 on one side, and values A, B, and C on the other. By defining a *field map* and associating it with a *value map*, the tool can seamlessly translate values back and forth when updates occur.

Another powerful capability is *user maps*. As an example, this is useful when you are synchronizing Team Foundation Server (which uses Active Directory for authentication) with a system that uses its own store of built-in usernames. The user mapping functionality allows you to map one system to the other.

Intelligent Conflict Resolution

In any type of synchronization, there will always be problems that you can't anticipate and automatically handle. Following are some examples:

➤ Someone changes the same field on both sides at the same time (an "edit/edit conflict").

➤ One endpoint encounters an error and the update can't be saved.

➤ Permissions are insufficient for making an update.

➤ An attachment from one side is larger than the limit on the other side.

➤ A field can't be renamed because the new name already exists.

In all of these cases, the tool will raise a conflict that requires manual intervention. Depending on the type of conflict, the tool may stop processing more changes, or if the changes don't depend on each other, it will continue processing others.

The conflict-resolution process allows you to resolve conflicts and give the resolution a "scope." For example, you can say, "Whenever an edit/edit conflict occurs, always choose the changes from the left endpoint." Over time, the system is given rules, and the number of new conflicts to resolve is reduced.

Health Monitoring

When you install the Team Foundation Server Integration Tools, there are two reports that get copied to your machine. To make use of these reports, you can follow the included instructions on how to set up the data sources and upload the reports. Once they are running, they will show you two things:

➤ Latency

➤ Conflicts

If people depend on synchronization for their day-to-day work, then you will want to make the reports available to users. You can also set up a data-driven subscription to e-mail you the report when latency exceeds a specific threshold. For example, at Microsoft, each of the synchronizations has a data-driven subscription that checks every 30 minutes to see if any endpoint is more than 30 minutes out of date. When one of them is, then it e-mails that report to the synchronization owner to alert him or her of the situation.

Following are the three most common reasons that an endpoint will be out of date:

➤ Someone has made a bulk update to hundreds of work items, and the mirror is catching up the backlog.

➤ In version control, a conflict will block the processing of future changes, since it's not valid to skip mirroring a changeset and continue on.

➤ The mirror is not running for some reason. This can happen if the service stops, the machine running the service loses connectivity, or the password changes.

Each of these conditions can be detected by a subscription to the latency report and the conflicts report.

Examples

Team Foundation Server Integration Tools include a number of templates to get started, but the following are some of the most common uses.

Version Control Two-Way Synchronization to a Second Server

Take a look at the following snippet from a version control session configuration:

```
<FilterPair>
  <FilterItem MigrationSourceUniqueId="1f87ff05-2e09-49c8-9e9b-0ac6db9dd595"
              FilterString="$/Project1/Main"
              MergeScope="$/Project1/Main" />
  <FilterItem MigrationSourceUniqueId="8c85d8eb-f3b3-4f05-b8dc-c0ab823f1a44"
              FilterString="$/Project1/Main"
              MergeScope="$/Project1/Main" />
</FilterPair>
```

In this scenario, you configure a left and right migration source, and provide two version control paths that you want to keep synchronized. It is possible to provide multiple paths, as well as different paths. The tool will translate the paths between the two endpoints.

You should always choose the smallest mapping possible, since the more changes that must be processed, the more likely it is to fall behind and get out of sync. If people are working on the same code in the two different locations, it's often a good idea to mirror into a branch of the code. That way, you can control when and how the changes from the remote server get merged into the main branch on the other side.

Work Item Synchronization to a Different Process Template

An outsourced development team may use a different process template than the in-house development team. This will cause a mismatch in the fields and values used to describe bugs, tasks, and other work items. Both organizations may have very valid reasons for using their own templates, and that's fine.

To accommodate this mismatch, the Team Foundation Server Integration Tools can be configured to map the different types to their closest equivalents.

The following snippet from a session configuration file shows how a field can be mapped using a value map:

```
<WITSessionCustomSetting >
  <Settings />
  <WorkItemTypes>
    <WorkItemType LeftWorkItemTypeName="Bug"
                  RightWorkItemTypeName="Defect"
                  fieldMap="BugToDefectFieldMap" />
  </WorkItemTypes>
  <FieldMaps>
    <FieldMap name="BugToDefectFieldMap">
      <MappedFields>
        <MappedField MapFromSide="Left"
                     LeftName="*"
                     RightName="*" />
        <MappedField MapFromSide="Left"
                     LeftName="Microsoft.VSTS.Common.Priority"
                     RightName="Company.Priority"
                     valueMap="PriorityValueMap" />
      </MappedFields>
    </FieldMap>
  </FieldMaps>
  <ValueMaps>
    <ValueMap name="PriorityValueMap">
      <Value LeftValue="1" RightValue="A" />
      <Value LeftValue="2" RightValue="B" />
      <Value LeftValue="3" RightValue="C" />
    </ValueMap>
  </ValueMaps>
</WITSessionCustomSetting>
```

WORKING OFFLINE

In a geographically distributed team, there may be scenarios where you need to work offline. There may be connectivity problems between your client and the server, or the server could just be offline for maintenance. In any case, there are things you can do to stay productive while you are working offline.

Version Control

If your solution file is bound to Team Foundation Server source control, both Visual Studio 2008 and 2010 will attempt to connect to the server when you attempt to open the solution. If the server is unavailable for some reason, the solution will be opened in "offline mode." This allows you to continue working on your code while you are disconnected from the server.

A solution will remain offline until it is explicitly taken online. Once the server is available again, you can click the Go Online button in Solution Explorer and the connection with the server will be attempted again. Alternatively, you can open the solution and, when the server is available, you will be prompted to go online.

When you go online again, Visual Studio will scan your workspace for writable files, and then check out the files and pend the changes that you made while you were working offline. If you don't do this, and you perform a "Get Latest," there is a chance you may overwrite your offline work, since the server doesn't know which changes you made while you were offline.

If you are planning to use this functionality, there are very specific instructions you must follow:

➤ When in offline mode, remove the read-only flag on the files you want to edit. You will need to do this from within Windows Explorer, not within Visual Studio. When you try to save a file that you haven't yet checked out, the file will be read-only, and Visual Studio will prompt you to see if you want to overwrite the file. This will unset the read-only flag and overwrite the contents.

➤ Don't rename files while offline. Team Foundation Server will not know the difference between a renamed file and a new file.

➤ When you are ready to connect to the server again, before doing anything else, run the online tool and check in the pending changes that it generates. That way, there will be no confusion between the new online work you will be doing and your offline work. If you don't do this, and you perform a "Get Latest," there is a chance you may overwrite your offline work, since the server doesn't know which changes you made.

Forcing Offline

If the connection to the server is slow or unreliable, it may be desirable to mark the Team Foundation Server as offline and disable auto reconnect on startup, so that you don't have to wait for it to time out. To do this, you need to have the Team Foundation Server Power Tools installed. Once you have them installed, you can follow these steps:

1. Open a Visual Studio 2010 command prompt.

2. Type the following:

   ```
   tfpt.exe connections
   ```

3. Once the TFS Connections dialog is displayed, as shown in Figure 24-1, select your server, expand the node, and select the collection.

4. Click Edit.

5. Deselect the "Automatically reconnect to last server on startup" check box.

6. Select the Server Is Offline check box.

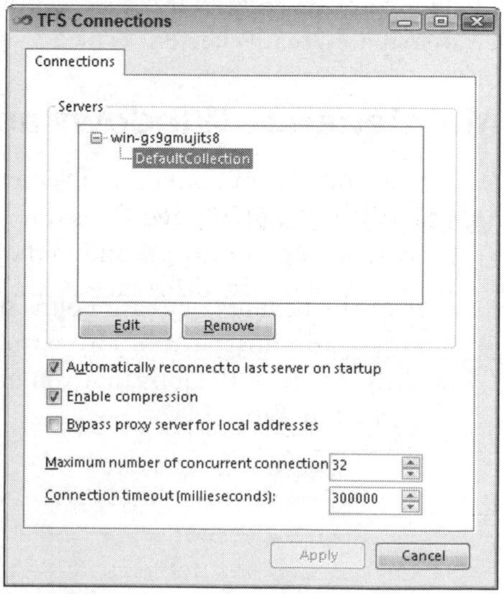

FIGURE 24-1: TFS Connections dialog

7. Click OK.

8. Close the dialog.

Now, when you open your solution, it will be marked offline until you click the Go Online button and connect to Team Foundation Server.

Work Items

The intended way to work offline with work items is to use the Microsoft Office Excel and Microsoft Office Project integration that is installed with the Team Explorer client.

With this integration, work items can be exported into a worksheet and saved to your machine for working offline. When you are ready to connect to the server again, the changes can be published back to the server.

There is a limitation while working offline that prevents you from creating links to work items and creating attachments.

> *For more information, see the "Work Offline and Reconnect to Team Foundation Server" article on MSDN at* `http://msdn.microsoft.com/en-us/library/ms244374.aspx`.

OTHER CONSIDERATIONS

There are several other considerations that can make the experience of working with geographically distributed teams better.

Maintenance Windows and Time Zones

The default Team Foundation Server installation will schedule optimization and cleanup jobs to start at 3 a.m. UTC time. This time means that these jobs run in the evening in North America, early morning in Europe, and in the middle of the day in Asia.

One of the benefits of Team Foundation Server is that you typically don't need the expertise of a database administrator or any extra SQL maintenance plans (beyond backups) to keep it reasonably healthy. Some of the jobs that you might want to assess the impact of and change the schedule of are described in Table 24-2.

TABLE 24-2: Built-in Server and Collection-Level Jobs

JOB NAME	DESCRIPTION	FREQUENCY
Optimize Databases (server-level job)	This job operates on the relational warehouse database. It reorganizes fragmented indexes and updates table statistics.	Daily
Full Analysis Database Sync	This job triggers a full process of the Analysis Services Online Analytical Processing (OLAP) cube.	Daily
Incremental Analysis Database Sync	This job triggers an incremental process of the Analysis Services OLAP cube.	Every 2 hours
Job History Cleanup Job	This job removes the internal job history log records that are older than 31 days.	Daily
Team Foundation Server Activity Logging Administration	This job removes command history older than 14 days.	Daily
Optimize Databases (collection-level job)	This job operates on the version control tables. It reorganizes and rebuilds fragmented indexes and updates table statistics.	
Version Control Administration	This job removes content in the database that has been previously destroyed. Additionally, it removes content that gets staged to a temporary table as part of a large check-in.	Daily
Work Item Tracking Administration	This job operates on the Work Item Tracking tables. It reorganizes fragmented indexes and updates table statistics. It also deletes work items and attachments that are no longer used by the system. It will also delete orphaned attachments, since saving a work item and uploading an attachment are two separate transactions, and one can succeed without the other.	Daily

Online Index Operations with SQL Server Enterprise

When the `Optimize Databases` job is running for each collection, it may cause blocking and slow performance for some version control commands. If you have users around the world, and you have large indexes, there may be no ideal time for this job to run. In this case, you may want to consider upgrading SQL Server to an edition that supports online index operations.

Team Foundation Server 2010 includes a restricted-use license for SQL Server 2008 Standard Edition. If you license the Enterprise or Data Center edition separately for your server, then Team Foundation Server will automatically make use of the online index operations that are available in these editions.

Distributed Application Tiers

In Team Foundation Server 2008, it was possible to install Team System Web Access on a separate server than your main application tier. In Team Foundation Server 2010, this is no longer possible, since Web Access is now integrated into the server itself.

In the 2010 version, it is not supported or recommended to have application tiers distributed away from your data tier servers. They should be on the same server (for a single-server installation), or in the same data center (for a multiple-server installation).

For version control operations, the architecture of the system is such that the application tier will request all the data that the user specified, and then discard the results that it doesn't need, or that the user doesn't have access to. This is because permission evaluation is done on the application tier.

These are just some of the reasons why Team Foundation Server 2010 does not support having application tiers distributed away from data tiers.

SQL Mirroring

SQL mirroring involves synchronizing the data on one server with a copy of that data on another server. The limitation of mirroring is that it only allows one server (the principal) to be active at a time. The mirrored server cannot be used until the mirror is failed over, and the application tiers are configured to use the new principal server.

Because of this limitation, mirroring is only useful in a disaster-recovery or high-availability situation, rather than a geographically distributed team situation.

SUMMARY

This chapter explored what it means to work with a geographically distributed team using Team Foundation Server 2010. You learned about some challenges, and then explored some of the solutions to overcome those challenges. Team Foundation Server Proxy was looked at in detail, and the potential of mirroring between servers with the Team Foundation Server Integration Tools was discussed. Finally, strategies for working offline while disconnected from the server were covered.

Chapter 25 describes extensibility best practices, as well as all the different ways that Team Foundation Server can be extended through custom plug-ins and tools.

Extending Team Foundation Server

➤ Getting started with the client object model

➤ Exploring the server object model

➤ Building server plug-ins

➤ Exploring other extension options

From the very start, Team Foundation Server was built to be extended. Microsoft acknowledged that it would never be able to build all the different features and functionality that customers would want. The philosophy was that Microsoft's own features should be built upon the same API that customers and partners can use to build additional features.

This proved to be a very wise design choice, and has led to a thriving ecosystem of products and extensions. Following are some examples of this ecosystem:

➤ Microsoft partners have built products that provide rich integration with products such as Outlook and Word.

➤ Competing and complementary Application Lifecycle Management (ALM) products have been built to integrate with Team Foundation Server.

➤ Consultants have leveraged the APIs to fill gaps to meet their client's very specific requirements.

➤ The community has built and shared useful tools and utilities for performing common tasks.

➤ The Visual Studio ALM Ranger community builds tools and solutions that address common adoption blockers and pain points.

➤ Microsoft itself builds the Team Foundation Server Power Tools to address gaps within the product outside of the normal release cycle.

Perhaps the two most successful examples of the extensibility model (and people leveraging it) are the products formerly known as TeamPlain and Teamprise:

➤ *TeamPlain* was a product built on the client object model to provide web browser-based access to Team Foundation Server. When it was first released, it was a "must-have" extension for organizations adopting Team Foundation Server. It allowed non-technical users to access the server and participate in the software development lifecycle.

➤ *Teamprise* was a fully featured, cross-platform client implemented in native Java. It allowed Mac, Linux, and Java users to access Team Foundation Server from their native environments.

Ultimately, both of these products and their development teams were acquired by Microsoft, and the products now ship as part of Team Foundation Server 2010. TeamPlain is now incorporated as *Team Web Access*, and Teamprise is available as *Team Explorer Everywhere*.

Extensibility Points

When people talk about Team Foundation Server extensibility, they are likely referring to building something that leverages the *client object model*. The client object model assemblies are installed with Visual Studio Team Explorer. It is the main API used by products, tools, and utilities that interact with Team Foundation Server.

All of the client object model interaction with the server is performed through web services. Although it is possible to invoke the web services directly, they are not documented, and, therefore, not supported for use. Microsoft reserves the right to change the web service interfaces in any future release, and only maintains backward compatibility via the client object model.

On the application tier, the web services then interact with services provided by the *server object model*. The server object model then accesses the internal SQL tables and stored procedures. Figure 25-1 shows how these different components interact.

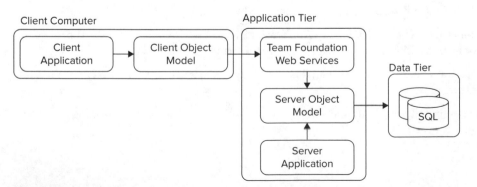

FIGURE 25-1: Team Foundation Server extensibility architecture

Additionally, the server provides other extensibility points, such as the following:

➤ Simple Object Access Protocol (SOAP) event subscription notifications

➤ In-process server events

➤ Request filters

➤ Server jobs

The functionality provided within Team Explorer and Excel clients can be also extended. As you can see, just about everything Microsoft ships as part of Team Foundation Server can be extended and built upon to suit your own needs and requirements.

CLIENT OBJECT MODEL

The client object model is the most commonly used way to programmatically interact with Team Foundation Server. It is the same API that Team Explorer and all client-side applications use to access the server.

> *This chapter only briefly covers the client object model. For more detailed instructions and plenty of examples on how to use the client object model, you should refer to the following sources: Team Foundation Server 2010 SDK at* http://code.msdn.microsoft.com/TfsSdk; *"Client Object Model" at* http://msdn.microsoft.com/en-us/library/bb130146.aspx#clientobjectmodel; *"Introducing the TfsCollection, TfsConfigurationServer, and TfsTeamProject Collection Classes" at* http://go.microsoft.com/fwlink/?LinkId=195542.

Connecting to the Server

Depending on what you want to do, to get connected to the server, you must use one of the following classes defined in the `Microsoft.TeamFoundation.Client.dll` assembly:

➤ `TfsConnection`

➤ `TfsConfigurationServer`

➤ `TfsTeamProjectCollection`

```
using System;
using Microsoft.TeamFoundation.Client;
using Microsoft.TeamFoundation.VersionControl.Client;

namespace ClientObjectModelSample
{
    class Program
```

```
    {
        static void Main(string[] args)
        {
            TfsTeamProjectCollection tfs =
                TfsTeamProjectCollectionFactory.GetTeamProjectCollection(
                new Uri("http://localhost:8080/tfs/DefaultCollection"),
                new UICredentialsProvider());

            VersionControlServer vcs = tfs.GetService<VersionControlServer>();
            int latestChangesetId = vcs.GetLatestChangesetId();
        }
    }
}
```

For this example to work, you will need to add a reference to both `Microsoft.TeamFoundation .Client.dll` and `Microsoft.TeamFoundation.VersionControl.Client.dll` in the references section of your project.

In this example, you create a connection to the collection using the collection URL. Then, you get the `VersionControlServer` service using `GetService<T>`. You then use it to retrieve the ID of the most recent changeset on the collection. It's that simple!

> *It's not strictly necessary, but it's a good habit to use the overloaded methods that accept an `ICredentialsProvider` as a parameter. By passing a new `UICredentialsProvider` object for this parameter, the application will prompt for alternate credentials if the current identity is not valid. This also allows the user to enter credentials from a different domain.*

TEAM FOUNDATION SERVER IMPERSONATION

Team Foundation Server Impersonation is a new feature in 2010. It allows a privileged user to execute commands as if the execution had been done by another user.

Impersonation was possible in Team Foundation Server 2008. However, it required knowing the impersonated user's username and password.

For more information, see "Introducing TFS Impersonation" at http://tinyurl .com/TFSImpersonation.

For another example, see "Using TFS Impersonation with the Version Control Client APIs" at http://tinyurl.com/TFSImpersonationVC.

Team Project Selection Dialog

Although you can enumerate the collections and team projects using the client object model, you can also leverage the `TeamProjectPicker` dialog. This is the same dialog that Team Explorer uses.

It is pre-populated with servers that the user has previously connected to.

The following snippet shows how to create a `TeamProjectPicker` that allows the user to select a server, collection, and multiple projects:

```
using (TeamProjectPicker tpp = new
    TeamProjectPicker(TeamProjectPickerMode.MultiProject,
    false))
{
    DialogResult result = tpp.ShowDialog();
    if (result == DialogResult.OK)
    {
        // tpp.SelectedTeamProjectCollection.Uri
        foreach(ProjectInfo projectInfo in tpp.SelectedProjects)
        {
            // projectInfo.Name
        }
    }
}
```

> *For more information, see "Using the TeamProjectPicker API in TFS 2010" at* http://tinyurl.com/TeamProjectPicker.

Handling Multiple API Versions

If you are building an extension using the client object model, you may want to ensure that it works against different server versions. There is no single, definitive way to do this. You can infer the server version by looking at the features and services provided by the server.

The following PowerShell script retrieves the `VersionControlServer.SupportedFeatures` property that can be used to tell you what the server version is:

```
# Get-ServerVersionUsingServerFeatures.ps1
#
# VersionControlServer.SupportedFeatures is an indicator of
# what server version you are talking to
#
# 7      Team Foundation Server 2008 RTM
# 31     Team Foundation Server 2008 SP1
# 895    Team Foundation Server 2010 RTM
# 1919   Team Foundation Server 2010 SP1
#

# Halt on errors
$ErrorActionPreference = "Stop"

$Uri = $args[0]

if ([String]::IsNullOrEmpty($Uri))
```

```
    {
        $Uri = "http://localhost:8080/tfs"
    }

    [void][System.Reflection.Assembly]::LoadWithPartialName
        ("Microsoft.TeamFoundation, Version=10.0.0.0")
    [void][System.Reflection.Assembly]::LoadWithPartialName
        ("Microsoft.TeamFoundation.Client, Version=10.0.0.0")
    [void][System.Reflection.Assembly]::LoadWithPartialName
        ("Microsoft.TeamFoundation.Common, Version=10.0.0.0")
    [void][System.Reflection.Assembly]::LoadWithPartialName
        ("Microsoft.TeamFoundation.VersionControl.Client, Version=10.0.0.0")
    [void][System.Reflection.Assembly]::LoadWithPartialName
        ("Microsoft.TeamFoundation.VersionControl.Common, Version=10.0.0.0")

    $Tpc = New-Object Microsoft.TeamFoundation.Client.TfsTeamProjectCollection
        - ArgumentList $Uri
    $vcs = $Tpc.GetService([Microsoft.TeamFoundation.VersionControl.Client.
        VersionControlServer])

    $vcs.SupportedFeatures
```

Using the integer that is returned, you can determine the server version using this list:

➤ 7 — Team Foundation Server 2008 RTM

➤ 31 — Team Foundation Server 2008 SP1

➤ 895 — Team Foundation Server 2010 RTM

➤ 1919 — Team Foundation Server 2010 SP1

> *An alternate way to get the server version using the Team Foundation Server 2008 client object model is discussed in "Determining the TFS Server Version Using Client APIs" at* http://tinyurl.com/TFSVersionClientAPI.

Displaying the Work Item Form

It is possible to populate and display the work item form to the user from within your own application. You must add a reference to the Microsoft.TeamFoundation.WorkItemTracking .Controls.dll assembly and use the WorkItemFormControl class. This assembly is available in C:\Program Files (x86)\Microsoft Visual Studio 10.0\Common7\IDE\PrivateAssemblies.

The following example shows how to use the WorkItemStore service, get a WorkItem object programmatically, and display the work item using the WorkItemFormControl class:

```
using System;
using System.Windows.Forms;
using Microsoft.TeamFoundation.Client;
```

```csharp
using Microsoft.TeamFoundation.WorkItemTracking.Client;
using Microsoft.TeamFoundation.WorkItemTracking.Controls;

namespace WorkItemFormSample
{
    class Program
    {
        static void Main(string[] args)
        {
            TfsTeamProjectCollection tfs =
                TfsTeamProjectCollectionFactory.GetTeamProjectCollection
        (new Uri("http://localhost:8080/tfs/DefaultCollection"),
      new UICredentialsProvider());
            tfs.Authenticate();

            WorkItemStore wis = tfs.GetService<WorkItemStore>();
            WorkItem workItem = wis.GetWorkItem(1); // First work item

            WorkItemFormControl formControl = new WorkItemFormControl();
            formControl.Item = workItem;
            formControl.ReadOnly = false;
            formControl.Dock = DockStyle.Fill;

            Form form = new Form();
            form.Text = String.Format("Work item {0}", workItem.Id);
            form.Size = formControl.Size;
            form.Controls.Add(formControl);
            form.ShowDialog();
        }
    }
}
```

If you want the user to be able to save the changes, you can add a button that calls the `Save()` method on the `formControl.Item` property.

You can also use the `IsDirty` property to track changes to the work item. Then, you can use `Fields[index].IsValid` to validate the field values before submitting them.

> Most of the user interface that you see in Team Explorer is integrated into Visual Studio and cannot be extended. The `WorkItemFormControl` class is an exception. For example, you cannot host the Pending Changes view in your own application.

Distributing the Client Object Model

Once you have built an application, you will probably want to make it available for others to use. Your application will have a dependency on the client object model assemblies that you are not allowed to redistribute with your application.

The general recommendation is that any client that requires the object model should have Visual Studio Team Explorer installed already.

> *There is an installer on the Team Foundation Server media for the client object model. It is chained into the installers for Team Explorer and Team Foundation Build. This package is not supported for standalone installation, since it has not been tested for patching scenarios.*

An alternative to installing Visual Studio Team Explorer (which also installs the Visual Studio Shell) is to use the Team Foundation Server installer to install the Team Foundation Build components. Since Team Foundation Build is a fairly lightweight install that has the client object model chained in, it can be a nice alternative. To use it, just run the server installer and skip the server configuration.

SOAP EVENT SUBSCRIPTIONS

All versions of Team Foundation Server include SOAP event subscriptions. You can subscribe to work item changes, check-ins, and other events. In the subscription definition, you specify the event type to subscribe to, and the SOAP endpoint that should be called. When an event is triggered, Team Foundation Server calls the `Notify` web method on your endpoint, and that code is executed.

A great example for the use of SOAP subscriptions came from the Team Foundation Server 2005 release. The product lacked Continuous Integration build functionality. The community responded by building a service that subscribed to the `CheckinEvent`. Then, when someone checked in a file to a particular path, the service would start a build on that path.

In Team Foundation Server 2010, SOAP event subscriptions are largely unchanged. However, there are two important things that should be considered:

➤ There can be a delay of up to 2 minutes for event delivery. SOAP event subscriptions are delivered using a job agent job. The default schedule of this job is to run every 2 minutes.

➤ The protocol version changed from SOAP 1.1 to SOAP 1.2. This means the `content-type` of the request is now `text/xml` instead of `application/soap+xml`. If you're using Windows Communication Foundation (WCF), you must change your bindings from `BasicHttpBinding` to `WSHttpBinding`.

There are two limitations of SOAP event subscriptions that you will want to consider before using them:

➤ SOAP event subscriptions only allow you to react after the fact. You cannot prevent an event from further execution. Team Foundation Server requests the endpoint asynchronously after the event has happened. This means that they are not very well-suited to "enforcement" activities. They can only send an alert or run further code to change the item back to its previous values.

➤ Delivery of SOAP event subscriptions is not guaranteed. If your endpoint is unavailable, or it has a problem processing the event, that event can be missed. If missed events are a problem for you, you will need to periodically run a task that reconciles missed events.

> *For more information, see "Does TFS guarantee event subscription delivery?" at* http://tinyurl.com/TFSGuaranteedEvents.

Available Event Types

To retrieve a list of all the SOAP events that are available for subscription, you can use the `IRegistration` service with the following PowerShell script:

```
# Halt on errors
$ErrorActionPreference = "Stop"

$Uri = $args[0]

if ([String]::IsNullOrEmpty($Uri))
{
    $Uri = "http://localhost:8080/tfs"
}

[void][System.Reflection.Assembly]::LoadWithPartialName
    ("Microsoft.TeamFoundation, Version=10.0.0.0")

$Tpc = New-Object Microsoft.TeamFoundation.Client.TfsTeamProjectCollection
    - ArgumentList $Uri
$reg = $Tpc.GetService([Microsoft.TeamFoundation.Server.IRegistration])

$reg.GetRegistrationEntries($null) | fl Type, EventTypes
```

This script calls the `GetRegistrationEntries` method and outputs the results. Table 25-1 lists the event types that are available in Team Foundation Server 2010 Service Pack 1.

TABLE 25-1: Available SOAP Event Types

COMPONENT	EVENT TYPE
Build	BuildCompletionEvent
	BuildCompletionEvent2
	BuildStatusChangedEvent
	BuildCompletionEvent

continues

TABLE 25-1 *(continued)*

COMPONENT	EVENT TYPE
	BuildCompletionEvent2
	BuildDefinitionUpgradeCompletionEvent
	BuildResourceChangedEvent
	BuildStatusChangeEvent
Version Control	CheckinEvent
	ShelvesetEvent
	BranchMovedEvent
	DataChangedEvent
	NodeCreatedEvent
	NodePropertiesChangedEvent
	NodeRenamedEvent
	NodesDeletedEvent
	ProjectCreatedEvent
	ProjectDeletedEvent
Work Item Tracking	WorkItemChangedEvent
	WITAdapterSchemaConflictEvent

> `WITAdapterSchemaConflictEvent` *is a notable new event available in Team Foundation Server 2010 Service Pack 1. It is triggered when the work item tracking warehouse adapter first detects a schema conflict, whenever the schema conflict reason changes, and, finally, when the schema conflict is resolved. Using this event, you can subscribe for e-mail alerts, or use a SOAP event subscription to try to automatically resolve warehouse schema conflicts.*

Building an Endpoint

The easiest way to host an endpoint is to build a Windows Service and use WCF with `WSHttpBinding` bindings. Alternatively, you can deploy it as a web site in IIS.

> *For more information on creating a SOAP event subscription handler, see Ewald Hofman's blog post, "How to use WCF to subscribe to the TFS 2010 Event Service," at* `http://tinyurl.com/TFSEventSubWCF`.

Adding the Subscription

Once you have a subscription handler, you must add the subscription to Team Foundation Server. The usual way of doing this is by running the `BisSubscribe.exe` tool from `C:\Program Files\ Microsoft Team Foundation Server 2010\Tools\` on any of your application tier servers. You can also copy this program to your local machine if you don't want to log on to the server for adding new subscriptions.

The Team Foundation Server Power Tools include an Alerts Explorer add-in that is much easier to use than `BisSubscribe.exe`. To add an event subscription using Alerts Explorer, perform the following steps:

1. Download and install the Team Foundation Server Power Tools.
2. Open Visual Studio.
3. Connect to your server using Team Explorer.
4. Right-click the topmost node in Team Explorer. This should be your current server and collection.
5. Select Alerts Explorer from the context menu.
6. Select New Alert.

The default settings for Alerts Explorer allow you to configure e-mail alert subscriptions. However, you can change the subscription type to SOAP and enter your endpoint URL. Once you have configured the subscription, be sure to save it before closing the dialog.

> *Project Collection Administrator permissions are required to add a SOAP subscription.*

Listing All Event Subscriptions

If you are a project collection administrator, you may want to see what subscriptions are configured for your collection for all users. This is not possible through `BisSubscribe.exe` or Alerts Explorer.

You can do this by using the following PowerShell script that calls the `GetAllEventSubscriptions` method on the `IEventService` service:

```
# Get all event subscriptions
#
# Halt on errors
$ErrorActionPreference = "Stop"
```

```
$Uri = $args[0]

if ([String]::IsNullOrEmpty($Uri))
{
    $Uri = "http://localhost:8080/tfs/"
}

[void][System.Reflection.Assembly]::LoadWithPartialName
    ("Microsoft.TeamFoundation, Version=10.0.0.0")
[void][System.Reflection.Assembly]::LoadWithPartialName
    ("Microsoft.TeamFoundation.Client, Version=10.0.0.0")

$Tpc = New-Object Microsoft.TeamFoundation.Client.TfsTeamProjectCollection
    - ArgumentList $Uri
$event = $Tpc.GetService([Microsoft.TeamFoundation.Framework.Client.IEventService])

$event.GetAllEventSubscriptions() | fl ID,EventType,ConditionString
```

If there are subscriptions that you'd like to remove, you can use `BisSubscribe.exe /unsubscribe`, or the following PowerShell line after running the previous script:

```
# Unsubscribe an event
$event.UnsubscribeEvent(<id here>)
```

SERVER OBJECT MODEL

With all the architectural changes in Team Foundation Server 2010 to support multiple collections, the server object model is now more accessible.

> *For more information on the server object model, see "Extending Team Foundation" on MSDN at* `http://msdn.microsoft.com/en-us/library/bb130146.aspx#serverobjectmodel`.

Server Extensibility Interfaces

Although many of the interfaces in the server object model are marked `public`, some are more suitable for customization and extending than others. Table 25-2 describes the interfaces and their suitability according to the following guide:

➤ *Suitable* — Intended for third-party extensions. Used by Team Foundation Server internally for extensibility.

➤ *Limited* — Some extension is expected by tool providers, though in a limited fashion.

➤ *Not Suitable* — Dangerous or not really intended for third-party extensions.

TABLE 25-2: Server Extensibility Interfaces and Their Suitability

INTERFACE	DESCRIPTION	SUITABILITY
ISubscriber	This is the in-process event system that is described later in this chapter.	Suitable
ITeamFoundation RequestFilter	This is intended to allow the extension to inspect and manage all incoming requests. It is described later in this chapter.	Suitable
ISecurityChanged EventHandler	This is really just a notification that is useful for reacting to security changes. The most common use would be to write an auditor of security changes to tie in to your needs. However, you would normally use an ISubscriber, since all security changes are published through events.	Limited
ITeamFoundationHost StateValidator	This is used to prevent a collection from being started. If a customer wants to implement custom online/offline semantics, this would allow it.	Limited
ICatalogResource TypeRuleSet	If you are going to extend the catalog with custom objects, and you want to implement some rules to enforce that your catalog objects conform to a specific set of rules, this is the interface you would implement. This is not a real high-profile interface, and there should not be many extensions in this area.	Limited
IStepPerformer	This is the servicing engine's API. *Servicing* is a method for performing a set of actions within the job agent scripted through an XML document. This is very similar to a workflow. You can add behaviors to a servicing job by writing IStepPerformers.	Limited
IServicingStepGroup ExecutionHandler	These are hooks in the servicing engine that allow you to alter the set of steps that are executed, or change the state of the execution engine before and after a step group.	Limited
ISecurityNamespace Extension	This allows you to override behaviors within an existing security namespace. This one is particularly dangerous. If you wanted to implement custom security rules for a given dataset, this will allow you to do it.	Not Suitable

continues

TABLE 25-2 *(continued)*

INTERFACE	DESCRIPTION	SUITABILITY
ILinkingConsumer, ILinkingProvider	The linking interfaces are used to extend the artifact system. This system is not currently used extensively throughout the server, and isn't a great place for third-parties to add extensions.	Not Suitable
ISubscriptionPersistence	This is used when eventing subscriptions are read and written. This allows subscriptions to be stored in a canonical form, and then expanded at evaluation time. There is very little value here for third parties.	Not Suitable
ITeamFoundationSystem HostStateValidator	This interface is internal and not intended for public use. See ITeamFoundationHostStateValidator.	Not Suitable
IIdentityProvider	This interface is to support other Identity types. Team Foundation Server 2010 has two identity types built in: WindowsIdentity and TeamFoundationIdentity. This interface should allow the overall support of other Identity types like ASP.NET Membership, Live ID, custom, and so on. However, some services (like Work Item Tracking) only support the built-in types. This may be available in a future release for extensions.	Not Suitable

> *Extending many of these interfaces can have negative effects on the performance and stability of your servers. The server will also disable any plug-ins that throw exceptions. If you don't want your plug-in disabled, you can catch* System .Exception *and log it so that you can diagnose failure conditions.*

Server Plug-Ins

Team Foundation Server 2010 introduces a concept of *server plug-ins*. These plug-ins are relatively straightforward to write, and very easy to deploy. Since they are deployed on the server, they don't require any client-side changes to be effective. These attributes make them a great candidate for extending and controlling Team Foundation Server.

There are two interfaces that are suitable for extending:

➤ `ISubscriber` — Real-time, in-process event subscriptions.

➤ `ITeamFoundationRequestFilter` — Inspect all requests.

To use these interfaces, you must add a reference to the `Microsoft.TeamFoundation.Framework` `.Server.dll` assembly from the `\Application Tier\Web Services\bin` directory of your application tier. You will also need a reference to the assemblies that contain the events that you want to subscribe to.

> *If you have multiple application tiers, your server plug-ins and job extensions must be deployed to all of them. If the plug-in is not available on a particular application tier, then requests to that application tier will not trigger the plug-in.*

ISubscriber: In-Process Eventing

This is the most common place for third parties to use extensions. Team Foundation Server 2010 fires events to all `ISubscribers` that sign up for events. Almost all major events on the server publish events.

There are two different types of events that you can subscribe to:

➤ `DecisionPoint` — You can prevent something from happening.

➤ `Notification` — You receive an event as soon as something happened.

In most (but not all) cases, a `DecisionPoint` and a `Notification` event will be fired, as shown in Table 25-3. This means that you must check the `NotificationType` in your event handler; otherwise, your code may run twice when you were only expecting it to run once.

TABLE 25-3: Available Notification Events

COMPONENT	SERVER OBJECT MODEL ASSEMBLY	EVENT	NOTIFICATION TYPE
Version Control	`Microsoft` `.TeamFoundation` `.VersionControl` `.Server.dll`		
		`CheckinNotification`	Decision, Notification
		`PendChanges` `Notification`	Decision, Notification
		`UndoPendingChanges` `Notification`	Decision, Notification

continues

TABLE 25-3 *(continued)*

COMPONENT	SERVER OBJECT MODEL ASSEMBLY	EVENT	NOTIFICATION TYPE
		Shelveset Notification	Decision, Notification
		Workspace Notification	Decision, Notification
		LabelNotification	Notification
		CodeChurnComplete dNotification	Notification
Build	Microsoft .TeamFoundation .Build.Server.dll		
		BuildCompletion NotificationEvent	Notification
		BuildQualityChanged NotificationEvent	Notification
Work Item Tracking	Microsoft .TeamFoundation .WorkItemTracking .Server .DataAccessLayer .dll		
		WorkItemChangedEvent	Notification
		WorkItemMetadata ChangedNotification	Notification (minimal)
		WorkItemsDestroyed Notification	Notification (minimal)
Test Management	Microosft .TeamFoundation .TestManagement .Server.dll		
		TestSuiteChanged Notification	Notification
		TestRunChanged Notification	Notification

COMPONENT	SERVER OBJECT MODEL ASSEMBLY	EVENT	NOTIFICATION TYPE
		TestPlanChanged Notification	Notification
		TestCaseResult ChangedNotification	Notification
		TestPointChanged Notification	Notification
		TestRunCoverage UpdatedNotification	Notification
		BuildCoverage UpdatedNotification	Notification
		TestConfiguration ChangedNotification	Notification
Framework	Microsoft .TeamFoundation .Server.dll		
		StructureChanged Notification	Notification
		AuthorizationChanged Notification	Notification
Framework	Microsoft .TeamFoundation .Framework .Server.dll		
		IdentityChanged Notification	Notification
		SecurityChanged Notification	Decision, Notification
		SendEmail Notification	Decision
		HostReadyEvent	Notification

For the *ISubscriber Interface definition, see* http://msdn.microsoft.com/en-us/ library/microsoft.teamfoundation.framework.server.isubscriber.aspx.

Decision Points

`DecisionPoint` events are triggered before the action is committed, and can be used to prevent the action from occurring. Most actions do not allow you to change the values, just accept or deny the request.

> These are handled on the request processing thread and, therefore, they should be lightweight and execute quickly. Otherwise, you will impact any caller that triggers that event.

For a `DecisionPoint` notification, your `ProcessEvent` call will be called before the change occurs. If you deny the request, you can set a message that will be shown to the user. The change will be aborted, and the processing will not continue.

The following code sample shows a simple `ISubscriber` plug-in that subscribes to the `CheckinNotification` event and `DecisionPoint` notification type:

```
using System;
using Microsoft.TeamFoundation.Common;
using Microsoft.TeamFoundation.Framework.Server;
using Microsoft.TeamFoundation.VersionControl.Server;

namespace DecisionPointSubscriber
{
    /// <summary>
    /// This plugin will reject any checkins that have comments
    /// containing the word 'foobar'
    /// </summary>
    public class DecisionPointSubscriber : ISubscriber
    {
        public string Name
        {
            get { return "Sample DecisionPoint Subscriber"; }
        }

        public SubscriberPriority Priority
        {
            get { return SubscriberPriority.Low; }
        }

        public Type[] SubscribedTypes()
        {
            return new Type[] {
                typeof(CheckinNotification)
            };
        }
```

```
    public EventNotificationStatus ProcessEvent(TeamFoundationRequestContext
requestContext, NotificationType notificationType,
object notificationEventArgs, out int statusCode,
out string statusMessage, out ExceptionPropertyCollection
properties)
    {
        statusCode = 0;
        properties = null;
        statusMessage = string.Empty;

        if (notificationType == NotificationType.DecisionPoint)
        {
            try
            {
                if (notificationEventArgs is CheckinNotification)
                {
                    CheckinNotification notification =
                        notificationEventArgs as CheckinNotification;

                    // Logic goes here
                    if (notification.Comment.Contains("foobar"))
                    {
                        statusMessage = "Sorry, your checkin was rejected.
                            The word 'foobar' cannot be used in
                            checkin comments";
                        return EventNotificationStatus.ActionDenied;
                    }
                }
            }
            catch (Exception exception)
            {
                // Our plugin cannot throw any exception or it will
                // get disabled by TFS. Log it and eat it.
                TeamFoundationApplication.LogException("DecisionPoint
                    plugin encountered the following error
                    while processing events", exception);
            }
        }
        return EventNotificationStatus.ActionPermitted;
    }
  }
}
```

Inside the `ProcessEvent` method, the plug-in checks if the check-in comment contains the string `"foobar"`. If it does, a custom error message is set, and the return value is `ActionDenied`. Figure 25-2 shows an example of what the user would see from Visual Studio in this scenario.

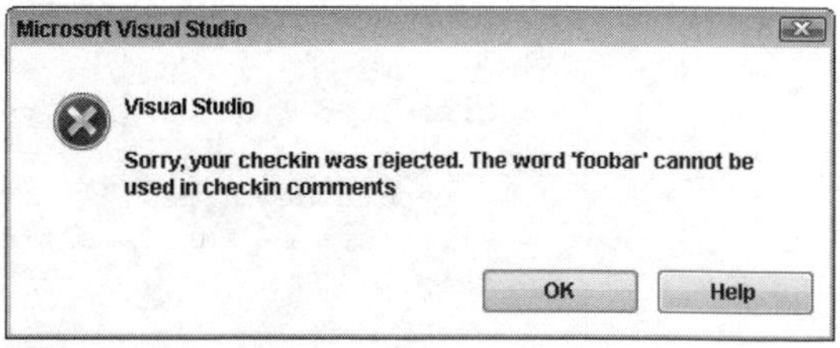

FIGURE 25-2: Example of a check-in denied using a DecisionPoint plug-in

Following are the other possible return values:

➤ `ActionDenied` — Action denied; do not notify other subscribers.

➤ `ActionPermitted` — Action permitted; continue with subscriber notification.

➤ `ActionApproved` — Similar to `ActionPermitted`, but do not notify other subscribers.

Notifications

For a `Notification` event, no return values are expected, and the publication serves as a notification of the occurrence of an event.

`Notification` events are performed asynchronously, and, therefore, do not have an impact on the caller. You should still take care to not consume too many resources here.

The following code sample shows a simple `ISubscriber` plug-in that subscribes to the `LabelNotification` event:

```
using System;
using System.Text;
using Microsoft.TeamFoundation.Common;
using Microsoft.TeamFoundation.Framework.Server;
using Microsoft.TeamFoundation.VersionControl.Server;

namespace NotificationSubscriber
{
    /// <summary>
    /// This request filter will log an event to the Application
    /// event log whenever TFS labels are changed
    /// </summary>
    public class NotificationSubscriber : ISubscriber
    {
        public string Name
        {
            get { return "Sample Notification Subscriber"; }
        }

        public SubscriberPriority Priority
        {
            get { return SubscriberPriority.Low; }
        }

        public Type[] SubscribedTypes()
        {
            return new Type[] {
                typeof(LabelNotification)
            };
        }

        public EventNotificationStatus ProcessEvent(TeamFoundationRequestContext
        requestContext, NotificationType notificationType,
        object notificationEventArgs, out int statusCode,
        out string statusMessage, out ExceptionPropertyCollection properties)
```

```
        {
            statusCode = 0;
            properties = null;
            statusMessage = string.Empty;

            if (notificationType == NotificationType.Notification)
            {
                try
                {
                    if (notificationEventArgs is LabelNotification)
                    {
                        LabelNotification notification = notificationEventArgs
                            as LabelNotification;

                        StringBuilder sb = new StringBuilder();
                        sb.AppendLine(string.Format("Labels changed by {0}",
                            notification.UserName));

                        foreach (LabelResult label in notification.AffectedLabels)
                        {
                            sb.AppendLine(string.Format("{0}: {1}@{2}",
                                label.Status, label.Label, label.Scope));
                        }

                        TeamFoundationApplication.Log(sb.ToString(), 0,
                            System.Diagnostics.EventLogEntryType.Information);
                    }
                }
                catch (Exception exception)
                {
                    // Our plugin cannot throw any exception or it will get
                    // disabled by TFS. Log it and eat it.
                    TeamFoundationApplication.LogException("Notification plugin
                        encountered the following error while
                        processing events", exception);
                }
            }
            return EventNotificationStatus.ActionPermitted;
        }
    }
}
```

Inside the `ProcessEvent` method, the plug-in extracts the user who changed the label, along with the label details. It then uses `TeamFoundationApplication.Log` to send the details to the Application event log.

```
Log Name:      Application
Source:        TFS Services
Date:          1/1/2011 12:00:00 AM
Event ID:      0
Task Category: None
Level:         Information
Keywords:      Classic
User:          N/A
Computer:      WIN-GS9GMUJITS8
```

```
Description:

Labels changed by WIN-GS9GMUJITS8\Administrator
Created: MyLabel@$/TestAgile

Application Domain: /LM/W3SVC/8080/ROOT/tfs-2-129366296712694768
```

Rather than writing to the event log, this plug-in could be easily modified to send an e-mail notification, or call another web service with the label change details.

ITeamFoundationRequestFilter: Inspecting Requests

This interface is intended to allow the plug-in to inspect and manage all incoming requests. Team Foundation Server 2010 includes two built-in request filters:

➤ `ResourceGovernorFilter` — Every method in Team Foundation Server is assigned a cost. As a request filter, the resource governor controls the number of requests that can run concurrently, and queues additional requests until there are available resources.

➤ `UserAgentCheckingFilter` — If you try to connect to Team Foundation Server 2010 with a Visual Studio 2008 client, you will receive an error saying that the client is not compatible without a patch. The check of the client's user agent and the rejection of the request are performed by this request filter.

> *For the ITeamFoundationRequestFilter Interface definition, see* `http://msdn .microsoft.com/en-us/library/gg244644.aspx`.

Since request filters don't rely on any particular events being implemented in the server, they are a way to inspect any and all server requests. Table 25-4 describes each of the methods in `ITeamFoundationRequestFilter` and when they are called in the request pipeline.

TABLE 25-4: ITeamFoundationRequestFilter Interface Methods

METHOD	DESCRIPTION
BeginRequest	BeginRequest is called after the server has determined which site or host the request is targeting, and verified that it is processing requests. A call to BeginRequest is not guaranteed for all requests. An ITeamFoundationRequestFilter can throw a RequestFilterException in BeginRequest to cause the request to be completed early, and an error message to be returned to the caller.
RequestReady	RequestReady is called once the request has completed authentication, and is about to begin execution. At this point, the requestContext .UserContext property will contain the authenticated user information. An ITeamFoundationRequestFilter can throw a RequestFilterException in RequestReady to cause the request to be completed early, and an error message to be returned to the caller.

METHOD	DESCRIPTION
EnterMethod	EnterMethod is called once the method being executed on this request is declared. At the time EnterMethod is called, the basic method information will be available. This includes method name, type, and the list of input parameters. This information will be available in requestContext.Method. An ITeamFoundationRequestFilter can throw a RequestFilterException in EnterMethod to cause the request to be completed early, and an error message to be returned to the caller.
LeaveMethod	LeaveMethod is called once the method is complete. Once EnterMethod is called, LeaveMethod should always be called as well. Exceptions are ignored, since the request is now complete.
EndRequest	EndRequest is called once the request is complete. All requests with a BeginRequest will have a matching EndRequest call. Exceptions are ignored, since the request is now complete.

The following code sample shows a simple ITeamFoundationRequestFilter plug-in that only implements EnterMethod:

```
using System;
using System.Diagnostics;
using System.Text;
using System.Text.RegularExpressions;
using Microsoft.TeamFoundation.Framework.Common;
using Microsoft.TeamFoundation.Framework.Server;

namespace RequestFilter
{
    /// <summary>
    /// This request filter will log an event to the Application event log
    /// whenever TFS group memberships are changed
    /// </summary>
    public class RequestFilter : ITeamFoundationRequestFilter
    {
        public void EnterMethod(TeamFoundationRequestContext requestContext)
        {
            switch (requestContext.Method.Name)
            {
                case "AddMemberToApplicationGroup":
                case "RemoveMemberFromApplicationGroup":
                    try
                    {
                        StringBuilder sb = new StringBuilder();
                        sb.AppendLine(string.Format("TFS group memberships have
                            been changed by {0}",
                            requestContext.AuthenticatedUserName));
                        sb.AppendLine(string.Format("{0}",
                            requestContext.Method.Name));
```

```csharp
            Regex regex = new Regex(@"^^IdentityDescriptor
                \(IdentityType: (?<IdentityType>[\w\.]+);
                Identifier: (?<Identifier>[S\d\-]+)\)?",
                RegexOptions.Compiled);
        foreach (string parameterKey in
            requestContext.Method.Parameters.AllKeys)
        {
            string parameterValue =
                requestContext.Method.Parameters
                [parameterKey];

            if (regex.IsMatch(parameterValue))
            {
                // If the parameter is an identity descriptor,
                // resolve the SID to a display name using IMS
                string identityType =
                    regex.Match(parameterValue).Groups
                    ["IdentityType"].Value;
                string identifier =
                    regex.Match(parameterValue).Groups
                    ["Identifier"].Value;
                IdentityDescriptor identityDescriptor = new
                    IdentityDescriptor(identityType,
                        identifier);
                TeamFoundationIdentityService ims =
                    requestContext.GetService
                    <TeamFoundationIdentityService>();
                TeamFoundationIdentity identity =
                    ims.ReadIdentity(requestContext,
                    identityDescriptor, MembershipQuery.None,
                    ReadIdentityOptions.None);

                sb.AppendLine(string.Format("{0}: {1}",
                    parameterKey, identity.DisplayName));
            }
            else
            {
                // Log other parameters, if any
                sb.AppendLine(string.Format("{0}: {1}",
                    parameterKey, parameterValue));
            }
        }

    TeamFoundationApplication.Log(sb.ToString(), 0,
        EventLogEntryType.Information);
}
catch (Exception exception)
{
    // Our plugin cannot throw any exception or it will get
    // disabled by TFS. Log it and eat it.
    TeamFoundationApplication.LogException("DecisionPoint
        plugin encountered the following error while
        processing events", exception);
}
```

```
                    break;
            }
        }

        public void BeginRequest(TeamFoundationRequestContext requestContext)
        {
        }

        public void EndRequest(TeamFoundationRequestContext requestContext)
        {
        }

        public void LeaveMethod(TeamFoundationRequestContext requestContext)
        {
        }

        public void RequestReady(TeamFoundationRequestContext requestContext)
        {
        }
    }
}
```

In this example, if the method name matches AddMemberToApplicationGroup
or RemoveMemberFromApplicationGroup, the plug-in logs a message. It uses the
IdentityManagementService from the server object model to resolve the SID from the method
parameters to a display name. It then logs a message to the Application event log, indicating that the
application group memberships have been modified.

Job Extensions

All jobs in Team Foundation Server are plug-ins that implement the
ITeamFoundationJobExtension interface. This is an example of the product using its own
extensibility interfaces.

> For the ITeamFoundationJobExtension *interface definition, see* http://msdn
> .microsoft.com/en-us/library/microsoft.teamfoundation.framework
> .server.iteamfoundationjobextension.aspx.

In addition to how they are invoked, the main difference between ISubscriber plug-ins and job
extensions is the deployment of them:

➤   Jobs are deployed by copying the assembly into the \Application Tier\TFSJobAgent\
    PlugIns directory, rather than the Web Services\bin\PlugIns directory.

➤   If a job plug-in is already loaded, and the job agent is currently running, then you must stop
    the job agent before you can replace the plug-in assembly. This releases the file handle.

➤   Along with having the assembly deployed, a job must be either scheduled to run, or
    manually queued using the job service API.

The following code sample shows a simple ITeamFoundationJobExtension plug-in that implements the Run method:

```
using System;
using System.Diagnostics;
using Microsoft.TeamFoundation.Framework.Server;
using Microsoft.TeamFoundation.VersionControl.Server;

namespace JobExtension
{
    /// <summary>
    /// This job will log an event to the Application event log with the
    /// current number of workspaces that have not been accessed in 30 days
    /// </summary>
    public class JobExtension : ITeamFoundationJobExtension
    {
        public TeamFoundationJobExecutionResult
            Run(TeamFoundationRequestContext requestContext,
            TeamFoundationJobDefinition jobDefinition, DateTime queueTime,
            out string resultMessage)
        {
            resultMessage = null;
            int warningDays = 30;
            int oldWorkspaces = 0;

            try
            {
                // Get all workspaces in the collection
                foreach (Workspace workspace in
                    requestContext.GetService
                    <TeamFoundationVersionControlService>
                    ().QueryWorkspaces(requestContext, null, null, 0))
                {
                    if (workspace.LastAccessDate <= DateTime.Now.Subtract(new
                        TimeSpan(warningDays, 0, 0, 0)))
                    {
                        oldWorkspaces++;
                    }
                }

                TeamFoundationApplication.Log(string.Format("There are {0}
                    workspaces that have not been accessed in the last {0}
                    days", oldWorkspaces, warningDays), 0,
                    EventLogEntryType.Information);
                return TeamFoundationJobExecutionResult.Succeeded;
            }
            catch (RequestCanceledException)
            {
                resultMessage = null;
                return TeamFoundationJobExecutionResult.Stopped;
            }
            catch (Exception exception)
            {
                resultMessage = exception.ToString();
```

```
                          return TeamFoundationJobExecutionResult.Failed;
                    }
                }
            }
        }
```

When this job is executed, it uses `TeamFoundationVersionControlService` from the server object model to enumerate all workspaces in the collection. It then checks if the workspace has been accessed in the last 30 days. If it has not been accessed, a counter is incremented.

Finally, the job logs a message to the Application event log, indicating how many workspaces are stale and have not been accessed in the last month.

Job Deployment

The most difficult part of custom job extensions is deployment. It's easy enough to define a single job for a single collection. However, if you want to have your job defined and scheduled for all new collections, there's not an easy way to do that.

> *The built-in jobs are scheduled using servicing steps that are part of the built-in project collection creation scripts. Unfortunately, these servicing steps are replaced with each patch of Team Foundation Server. So, if you customized them, they would get overwritten the next time you upgraded. A creative solution would be to build an* `ISubscriber Notification` *plug-in that subscribes to the* `HostReadyEvent`. *Each time the server starts, it could check if the job is scheduled for all project collections, and schedule it if it isn't.*

The following PowerShell script demonstrates how to use `ITeamFoundationJobService` from the client object model to define and schedule a job for a single collection:

```
# Install-JobExtension.ps1
# Usage: Install-JobExtension <TfsCollectionUri>
# Example: Install-JobExtension http://yourserver:8080/tfs/yourcollection
#
# Before running this, you will need to copy the assembly containing the
# class that implements ITeamFoundationJobExtension to the following directory
# on all Application Tier servers:
# C:\Program Files\Microsoft Team Foundation Server 2010\Application
# Tier\TFSJobAgent\plugins
#
# This will use the TFS client object model to register and schedule the job
# By default the job will be scheduled to run at 5 AM daily.

# Halt on errors
$ErrorActionPreference = "Stop"

$Uri = $args[0]

if ([String]::IsNullOrEmpty($Uri))
```

```
{
    $Uri = "http://localhost:8080/tfs"
}

# Define your own well-known GUIDs for your job
$JobDefinitionGuid = New-Object System.Guid -ArgumentList
    "8E0CC8CD-C345-4A94-8152-8AE02c2560CD"

[void][System.Reflection.Assembly]::LoadWithPartialName
    ("Microsoft.TeamFoundation, Version=10.0.0.0")
[void][System.Reflection.Assembly]::LoadWithPartialName
    ("Microsoft.TeamFoundation.Common, Version=10.0.0.0")
[void][System.Reflection.Assembly]::LoadWithPartialName
    ("Microsoft.TeamFoundation.Client, Version=10.0.0.0")

# Get the job service for the collection.
$Tpc = New-Object Microsoft.TeamFoundation.Client.TfsTeamProjectCollection -
    ArgumentList $Uri
$JobService = $Tpc.GetService([Microsoft.TeamFoundation.
    Framework.Client.ITeamFoundationJobService])

# Define the job agent job
$JobDefinition = New-Object Microsoft.TeamFoundation.
    Framework.Client.TeamFoundationJobDefinition                `
                                    -ArgumentList $JobDefinitionGuid,      `
                                                  "Sample Job Extension",  `
                                                  "JobExtension.JobExtension", `
                                                  $null

# Schedule the job to run at 5 AM every day, starting tomorrow.
$TomorrowFiveAM = [DateTime]::Today.AddDays(1).AddHours(5).ToUniversalTime()
$JobSchedule = New-Object Microsoft.TeamFoundation.
    Framework.Client.TeamFoundationJobSchedule `
                                    -ArgumentList $TomorrowFiveAM, 86400

$JobDefinition.Schedule.Add($JobSchedule)

# Save the job definition to the collection's job service.
$JobService.UpdateJob($JobDefinition)
```

This script connects to the specified collection, or the default collection if none is specified. It then creates a `TeamFoundationJobDefinition` object for the job extension. It then creates a `TeamFoundationJobSchedule` for the job that schedules it to be run every 24 hours (86400 seconds) starting at 5 a.m. tomorrow, UTC time.

Once the job and its schedule are defined, it is saved to the server using `ITeamFoundation JobService.UpdateJob()`.

To invoke the job manually, and to see if your job extension works, you can run the following PowerShell command:

```
# Run the job now manually
$jobService.QueueJobNow($JobDefinition, $false)
```

VISUAL STUDIO EXTENSIBILITY

You can extend Visual Studio by using macros, add-ins, `VSPackages`, and Managed Extensibility Framework (MEF) extensions. You can build macros and add-ins in Visual Studio without installing the Visual Studio Software Development Kit (SDK).

By leveraging Visual Studio extensibility, it's also possible to automate and extend some of the Team Explorer windows, dialogs, and events. Figure 25-3 shows a sample add-in that interacts with Source Control Explorer. Be warned, however, that not all of the dialogs are extensible. For example, it's not possible to add another channel to the Pending Changes view without getting deep into reflection.

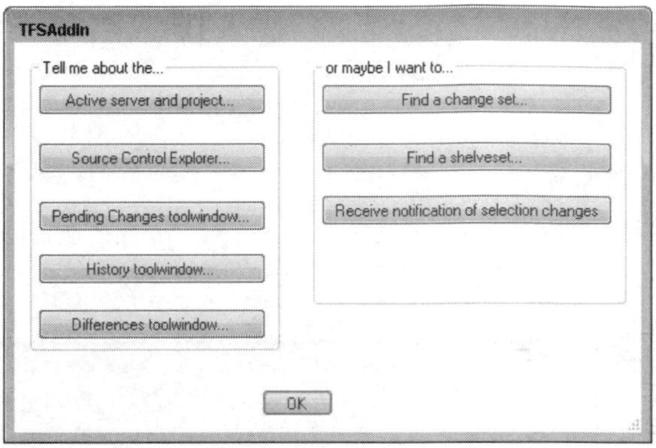

FIGURE 25-3: A sample Visual Studio add in that extends the Source Control Explorer

> *For an example of extending Source Control Explorer, see* `http://tinyurl .com/TFSExtendingSCE`. *For an example of extending the work item tracking context menu, see* `http://tinyurl.com/TFSExtendingWITMenu`. *For general information on Visual Studio extensibility, see "Customizing, Automating, and Extending the Development Environment" at* `http://msdn.microsoft.com/ en-us/library/ae3cxw0w.aspx`.

EXCEL AGILE WORKBOOKS

The MSF Agile process template in Team Foundation Server 2010 contains the Product Planning and Iteration Backlog Excel workbooks.

Manually Binding the Iteration Backlog

If you didn't have SharePoint configured at the time you created your team project, the planning workbooks won't be uploaded to the project portal. Additionally, if you created your team project with a different process template, you won't have the workbooks available.

The good news is that the workbooks are nothing more than just workbooks. You can manually set the document properties, define your own work item query, and rebind them to work with any team project.

You will need the Team Project GUID (as shown in Figure 25-4), which you can obtain from Team Explorer by selecting the team project and viewing the Properties Window. (The shortcut key is F4.)

Once you have the Team Project GUID, you can modify the document properties of the Excel worksheet to bind it, as shown in Figure 25-5.

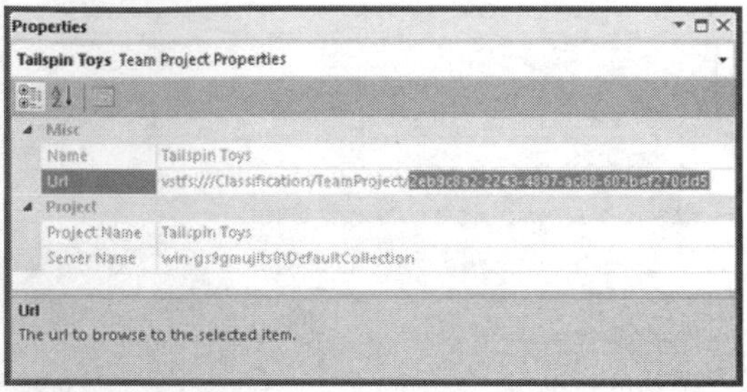

FIGURE 25-4: Visual Studio Properties Window showing the Team Project GUID

FIGURE 25-5: Document properties dialog in Excel showing the binding information

> For detailed steps on how to download and bind the Iteration Backlog workbook, see "Downloading Unbound Agile Workbooks" at `http://tinyurl.com/UnboundWorkbooks`.

Code Behind

One of the design goals of the agile planning workbooks was to not make them impossible for customers to change. The code to generate the PivotTable for the burndown and team capacity charts is all available in the worksheet as Visual Basic for Applications (VBA) code.

To access the code, open the planning workbook and press Alt+F11. You should see the module code listing, as shown in Figure 25-6.

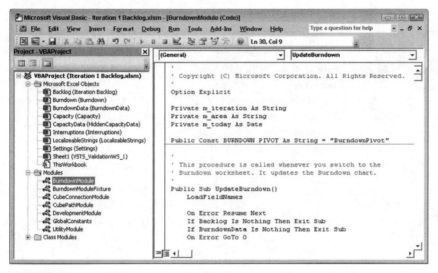

FIGURE 25-6: VBA code behind of Iteration Planning workbook

OTHER RESOURCES

Team Foundation Server is very extensible, and, accordingly, there are a number of solutions and resources available to assist you. These resources can have useful samples for getting started. The partners can also be engaged to build custom solutions for your needs.

Table 25-5 shows a breakdown of some available resources.

TABLE 25-5: Available Resources

RESOURCE	DESCRIPTION	NOTES
Visual Studio ALM Rangers	Visual Studio ALM Rangers deliver out-of-band solutions for missing features or for guidance. Periodically, they take nominations for new projects, vote for them, develop them, and then release them on CodePlex.	For more information, refer to the Visual Studio ALM Ranger page on MSDN at `http://msdn.microsoft.com/en-us/vstudio/ee358786.aspx`.
Visual Studio Industry Partners (VSIP)	The VSIP program provides technical resources, business insight, and extensive co-marketing to partners who sell products that integrate with and extend Visual Studio.	To learn about existing VSIP partners, see `http://www.microsoft.com/visualstudio/en-us/partner-directory-industry`.

continues

TABLE 25-6 *(continued)*

RESOURCE	DESCRIPTION	NOTES
Microsoft Partner Program: ALM Competency	The Application Lifecycle Management (ALM) Competency in the Microsoft Partner Program enables partners to demonstrate their expertise in providing training and consultation for, or deploying Microsoft Visual Studio tools.	To find partners who have achieved the ALM Competency, see Microsoft Pinpoint at `http://pinpoint.microsoft.com/en-US/companies/search?fs=120`.
		For more information on obtaining the ALM Competency, see `http://www.mstoolspartners.com/Anonymous/IC.aspx`.
CodePlex	CodePlex is Microsoft's Open Source project hosting web site. You can download and use many projects on CodePlex that extend Team Foundation Server. You can also use CodePlex to share your own extensions with the world.	For Open Source projects that extend Team Foundation Server, see `http://www.codeplex.com/site/search?query=tfs`.
Visual Studio Gallery	The Visual Studio Gallery provides quick access to tools, controls, and templates to help you get the most out of Visual Studio.	For a list of Visual Studio tools and extensions, see `http://tinyurl.com/VSGalleryTFS`.
MSDN Code Gallery	MSDN Code Gallery is a site where you may download and share applications, code snippets, and other resources with the developer community.	For a list of code snippets, see `http://tinyurl.com/MSDNGalleryTFS`.

SUMMARY

This chapter started with an overview of the high-level architecture of the extensibility available within Team Foundation Server. You learned how to get started with the client object model, as well as some useful tips for working with it. SOAP event subscriptions were then discussed, along with the available event types that can be subscribed to.

The server object model was examined, and examples of server plug-ins were provided. This included plug-ins that send real-time notifications, and plug-ins that can change the flow of a command.

This chapter briefly covered the extensibility available in Visual Studio and the agile planning workbooks.

Finally, other resources were discussed that can help you leverage the extensibility available in Team Foundation Server.

INDEX

INDEX

N

TfsConfigurationServer, 619
TfsConnection, 619
tfs.domain.local, 35
TFSJobAgent.exe, 503
TFSLAB, 33
TFSLabConfig.exe Permissions, 532
TfsRedirect.aspx, 320
TFSSecurity.exe, 531
TFSSERVICE, 33
TFSServiceControl, 502
TFSServiceControl.exe, 502
TfsTeamProjectCollection, 619
TfsVersion, 410–417, 422, 428–429
TfsVersionControl, 301
Tfs_Warehouse, 160, 306, 437, 509, 529
TfsWarehouseDataReader, 306
TfsWorkItemTracking, 301
tf:Test, 320
third parties
    code reviews, 171–172
    integration, 79
    migration, 177, 186–187
    process templates, 243, 252
    source code, 220–223
    UI, 221
    version control, 137–140
    work items, 263–264
ThoughtWorks, 334
Throw, 398
time zones, 614–615
Timeline Tracking, 207, 214, 215
Timely Migration, 186
timeout settings, 481
timestamps, 149–150
tip version, 177
Tools, 502, 508
TortoiseSVN, 152
Track Changeset, 206, 210, 214–216
transaction log backups, 489, 490
Transact-SQL (TSQL), 302
transitions, 242
    CMMI, 248
    rules, 273–274
    work items, 272–274

transparency, 12
Tree link type, 278
tree queries, 256
Trend Report, 311
trial edition, 7, 38
triggers, 167–168, 335–336, 353–357, 363
.trn, 493
trusts, 513
TryCatch, 398
try-catch-finally, 398
TSFServiceControl.exe, 458
TSQL. *See* Transact-SQL
TWA. *See* Team Web Access
Type, 165

U

UI. *See* user interface
UICredentialsProvider, 620
unique keys, 304
unit tests, 218, 572
UNIX, 72–73, 136, 326
UnlockOther, 110
unquiesce, 458
unset permissions, 529–530
unshelving, 116
Unspecified form layout, 275
updates
    installation, 40–41
    process templates, 284–286
Update Account Password dialog, 442
UpdateBuilderNumber, 401
Updates, 458
UpdateSiteArchive, 127
updateUserName, 99
upgrades, 19, 585–597
    branches, 593
    build definitions, 595–596
    legacy versions, 592–593
    migration and, 176–177
        hardware, 586
    planning, 588
    process templates, 252
    SharePoint, 589–590

Visual SourceSafe (VSS), 147–150
  working copy, 85
  working folder mapping, 85, 100–104
  workspace, 98–100, 125
`Version Control`, 268
`Version Control Administration`, 615
Version Control Path, 422
`VersionControlServer`, 620
`VersionControlServer.SupportedFeatures`, 621
`VersionControl.xml`, 268
`VersionNumberRegularExpression`, 427
versionspecs, 105
`VersionString`, 427
video recordings, 569
View History, 205–206, 210
view project-level information
  permission, 523
`ViewBuildResources`, 521
views
  history, 122
  Pending Changes view, 119–122, 131–133
  queries, 302–304
  work item query, 525–526
`VIEW_TEST_CONTROLLERS`, 521
`VIEW_TEST_RESULTS`, 521, 522
Virtual Directory, 440
virtual environment, 563, 578
  Lab Management, 582
virtual hard disk (VHD), 16, 574
virtual lab management, 15
virtual machine (VM), 29, 35, 563
  build agent, 342
  Lab Management, 577
  libraries, 563
  patching, 584
  RAM, 578
  SCVMM, 577
  templates, 563
    Lab Management, 577
    patching, 584
  WAN, 580
Virtual Private Networks (VPNs), 604
`virtualDirectory`, 56, 57

virtualization, 28–29
  backups, 491
  build, 342
  high-availability, 484
  tests, 561–562
visibility, 393–394
Visual Basic for Applications (VBA), 646
Visual SourceSafe (VSS), 19, 70, 88–89, 96
  AD, 178
  bindings, 178
  check-out, 86, 150
  concurrent editing, 150
  Converter, 179–184
  history, 148–149
  keyword expansion, 149
  labels, 148–149
  migration, 178–184
  pinning, 148
  repository, 180–183
  scalability, 148
  sharing, 148
  timestamps, 149–150
  version control, 147–150
Visual SourceSafe Converter
  `Analyze`, 180–183
  check-out, 182
  data integrity, 182
  history, 183
  `Migrate`, 184
  pinning, 183
  sharing, 183
  user mapping, 181–182
Visual Studio, 7–8
  Add Team Foundation Server dialog, 70
  ASP.NET web Applications, 351
  branches, 208
  Build Explorer, 365–368
  check-in policies, 113
  check-out, 106
  debugging, 325
  versus Eclipse, 134–135
  e-mail alerts, 365
  extensibility, 645
  `HintPath`, 221, 223